Foreword

by Professor Arthur J Willcocks, B.Com. Ph.D., F.I.S.W. F.A.C.Ch.O.
lately Professor of Social Administration University of Nottingham.

When the National Health Service was being designed, those at the Ministry of Health faced the task of setting out a structure for a wide range of services never before brought into one Service. A lot of time and effort was devoted to the development of a structure to run the to-be-nationalized hospitals. There were questions of number of tiers, size of units and much else. Additionally there was the task of doing something about the general practitioner services previously organized by Local Insurance Committees. If the government of the day thought of putting them under hospital control, or in local government, the British Medical Association soon made it abundantly and vociferously clear that they were not prepared to accept either of those solutions. In the end the government had to give in and resurrected the Local Insurance Committee system under a new name, the Local Executive Councils, with few changes of principle.

This left those services traditionally run by local authorities, ranging from hospitals to home helps. Aneurin Bevan decided that the nationalizing of hospitals had to involve the change of ownership of local authority hospitals, much to the chagrin of Labour Ministers like Herbert Morrison who had helped to build up the impressive local authority hospital service in London. Even if the Minister of Health had wanted to remove all the other health services from local government he did not do so, fearing the further wrath of those in Parliament who saw a proper and continuing role for local government in health. Hence he left a lot of services with them - and added a few more, possibly as a compensation for the loss of hospitals. The resultant array of services lacked a clear unity and it was a long time before they were called other than local authority health services.

As the authors of this book show, changes in policy and emphasis gradually put the local authority contribution on a different footing. Today these services, now long gone from local government, are generally called the community health services. But this title poses questions for the future as current policy debates demonstrate.

Those who follow the history of health service provision in this country will know how much has been published on hospitals and on general practitioners' services and how little has appeared on the community health services. This book fills this gap, in detailed, interesting and provocative style and will, I hope, come to be required reading for all those with an interest in the way health care services are provided in this country.

Preface

Community health services have always played an important part in the provision of health care. Indeed, in all societies they pre-date the emergence of institutionally based services and, in many respects, can be regarded as the more natural form of health care. Yet in the developed world they have been overshadowed, for most of the twentieth century, by curative, hospital services. Since the 1970s, however, there has been a revival of interest in community health services, of which, arguably, the Declaration of Alma-Ata is the most eloquent expression. This has been due, in part, to demographic and epidemiological trends and to changes in the socio-political environment, all of which have highlighted the need for, and importance of, well developed community based services within a comprehensive health care system.

Our interest in the community health services has grown out of our experience of teaching on a variety of health-related courses, for many years, and the consequent need to find suitable sources of information for students. An increasing number of our students are either working in community settings or may well do so in the future. Although there is a reasonable amount of literature on community based health care services, much of it concerns individual services and the role of specific professional groups, and, in recent years, there has been a tendency to concentrate on the clinical, as opposed to the social policy and managerial aspects of their provision. In other words, since the publication of Julia Parker's book on the health and welfare services in 1965 there has been a significant gap in the literature, with respect to the community health services as a whole. Moreover, virtually all of the general works on health care concentrate on the hospital and family practitioner services and pay relatively little, if any, attention to the community health services. Thus, in writing this book, our initial aim was to bring together material from a wide variety of sources and, in so doing, to provide the reader with a comprehensive analysis of these services in a single volume.

However, during the course of our researches it became clear that in order to do justice to the subject matter more than one volume was required. This was due, in part, to the fact that we wanted to demonstrate the breadth and variety of the community health services by including material on less familiar areas, for example speech therapy, orthoptics and community dietetics, as well as better known services, such as district nursing, school health and cervical screening. Since we did not wish to sacrifice this comprehensive coverage, we decided, with the publishers agreement, to concentrate, in this volume, on the growth and development of the community health services (primarily within England) from their origins in the nineteenth century to the present day and to postpone a detailed consideration of contemporary issues, which will be the subject of a companion volume. Nevertheless, we have tried to avoid a narrow, ethnocentric approach and have paid particular attention to their role within the wider health care system and their relationships with other services.

We hope, therefore, that this book will both inform and stimulate those with an interest in community health.

The Growth and Development of the

Community Health Services

are to be returned
st date be

Roger Ottewill and Ann Wall

Business Education Publishers Limited

0907679293

Published in Great Britain by Business Education Publishers Limited
Leighton House 10 Grange Crescent Stockton Road Sunderland
Tyne and Wear SR2 7BN

Telephone 091 567 4963

ISBN 0 907679 29 3

First published in 1990

Reprinted 1991

Printed in Great Britain by Athenaeum Press Limited
Unit 3 Mill Lane Industrial Estate Newcastle upon Tyne NE4 6TD
Telephone 091 273 7737

Acknowledgements

In preparing a book of this kind we have naturally incurred many debts. A very large number of people provided us, either directly or indirectly, with help. Unfortunately, however, like most writers we can name only a few. Our special thanks go to Eileen O'Keefe at the Polytechnic of North London and to Arthur Willcocks at the University of Nottingham for reading the whole of the text and for providing constructive criticism and considerable support and encouragement.

We are also indebted to the staff of the Community Unit, Rotherham Health Authority, to which one of us was seconded, on a part-time basis, during the preparation of the book. Everyone was extremely helpful and gave generously of their time and their contributions have undoubtedly added much to the book. We are specially grateful to Andrew Cash (General Manager) for helping to arrange the secondment; to Jeannette Rigby (Director of Nursing Services) for allowing unfettered access to her bookshelves, which proved to be a cornucopia, and for inspiring us with her commitment to community nursing and to Marian Ahmed (Nursing Officer - Midwifery), Ann Ashby (District Occupational Therapist), Sue Clifton (District Physiotherapist), Deanna Collins (District Chiropodist), Helen Crockett (Assistant Director of Nursing Services - Community), John Glasby (Assistant General Manager - Community), Steve Hawkins (District Health Promotion Officer), Dr Ian Ralph (District Medical Officer), Nigel Thomas (District Dental Officer), Jill Ward (District Dietitian), Julie Ward (Community Orthoptist), Mona Wareing (District Speech Therapist) and Pam Wood (AIDS Co-ordinator) for discussing issues relating to their areas of expertise and/or commenting on sections of the text. Various kinds of help were also received from many other sources and we are very sorry that it has not been possible to identify them all by name.

We, of course, accept full responsibility for the book as a whole and for the way in which we have interpreted the material provided by others. However, we hope that our views are not too idiosyncratic and that they reflect the feelings and opinions of those who are at the sharp end of the community health services.

We should also like to thank Paul, Peter, Caroline, Moira and Flora at Business Education Publishers for the parts which they have played in the production of this book.

Last, but by no means least, we apologise to our long-suffering spouses, Val and Toby, and to our children, who have borne the brunt of our preoccupation with the community health services for the past two years.

Roger Ottewill and Ann Wall *Sheffield City Polytechnic March 1990*

Postscript

The white paper Caring for People was published after we had finished the manuscript. Since its proposals followed closely the recommendations of the Griffiths Report on community care we considered it unnecessary to make any textual changes to take account of its publication.

List of Abbreviations

AHA	area health authority
AMC	Association of Municipal Corporations
AMT	area management team
ATO	area team of officers
BMA	British Medical Association
CCA	County Councils Association
CGC	Committee on Gynaecological Cytology
CHSs	community health services
CHC	community health council
CPN	community psychiatric nurse
DHA	district health authority
DHSS	Department of Health and Social Security
DMT	district management team
DNO	district nursing officer
FPC	family practitioner committee
FPSs	family practitioner services
GP	general medical practitioner
HSs	hospital services
LHSs	local health services
MOH	medical officer of health
NHS	National Health Service
NHSCR	National Health Service Central Register
OPCS	Office of Population Censuses and Surveys
RHA	regional health authority
RTO	regional team of officers
SI	statutory instrument
SR&O	statutory rules and orders
WHO	World Health Organisation
WTE	whole time equivalent
1907 Act	Education (Administrative Provisions) Act 1907
1946 Act	National Health Service Act 1946
1973 Act	National Health Service Reorganisation Act 1973
1977 Act	National Health Service Act 1977
1945 Reg	The School Health Service and Handicapped Pupils Regulations 1945

Contents

Figures

Tables

Statistical data relate to England only unless otherwise stated

Chapter 1

Introduction

What do the following health care services have in common: chiropody, health visiting, family planning clinics and school health? Faced with a question of this kind, anyone unfamiliar with the way in which the National Health Service (NHS) is organised is likely to reply: "very little"!

Since there are few, if any, obvious links between these services such a reply is understandable. Nevertheless, they do have something in common. For a variety of reasons, chiropody, health visiting, family planning clinics, school health, along with various other services including, district nursing, community midwifery, vaccination and immunisation, health education, home nursing aids, speech therapy, and the community dental service are usually grouped together, for management purposes, under the collective title of 'community health services' (CHSs).

This diverse group of services constitutes one of the three arms of the NHS, the other two being: family practitioner services (FPSs), which comprise pharmaceutical services and general medical, dental and ophthalmic services; and hospital services (HSs). Traditionally the CHSs have attracted far less attention than either the FPSs or HSs. This is mainly because they tend to have a lower profile than other health care services and, as Figure 1.1 illustrates, their share of the total NHS budget is much smaller than that of either the FPSs or HSs.

Nevertheless, although expenditure on the CHSs represents a relatively small proportion of total NHS expenditure (i.e. approximately 7.5%), the CHSs have contributed, in many ways, to the well-being of some of the most vulnerable groups in society, in particular children and the elderly, as well as the population at large. Furthermore, their contribution is likely to increase in the future for a number of reasons. First, demographic and epidemiological trends have resulted in a dramatic increase in the number of elderly and chronically sick people. Curative hospital based treatment can make no more than a minor impact on the health and well-being of patients of this kind. Second, the prevailing economic and political climate fosters a concern with economy and 'value for money'. Caring for patients in the community as opposed to hospital is believed to be cheaper.[1] Third, in the last three decades, again partly due to reasons of economy, there has been a growing interest in a more positive approach to health, which stresses prevention as opposed to cure. This approach relies on active and effective CHSs. Throughout the 1970s and 1980s issues of this kind have been highlighted by a wide variety of official publications, such as the DHSS *Priorities* documents (1976 and 1977), *Care in Action* (1981), and *Promoting Better Health* (1987). [2]

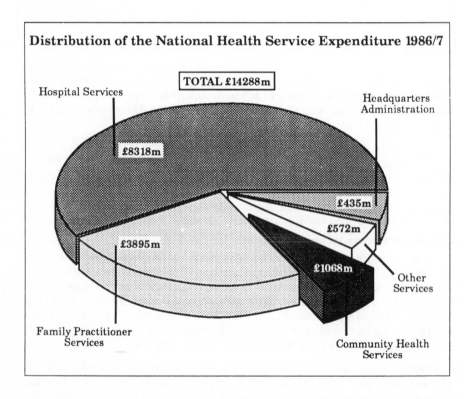

Distribution of the National Health Service Expenditure 1986/7

TOTAL £14288m

Hospital Services — £8318m

Headquarters Administration — £435m

£572m

Family Practitioner Services — £3895m

£1068m

Other Services

Community Health Services

Figure 1.1

Source: Based on data from House of Commons Paper No. 606 Session 1987/88, *Summarised Accounts of Health Authorities* (etc) for the year ended 31 March 1987.

Increasing interest in community based health care services is reflected in the availabilty of a growing number of specialised texts on particular aspects of the CHSs and related topics.[3] These, however, generally concentrate on specific clinical issues. By contrast, the purpose of this book is more comprehensive. It aims to provide the reader with an insight into the way in which the CHSs have evolved from their foundations in the 19th Century to the late 1980s. Particular attention is given to their range and scope; their management arrangements and some of the major issues to which they give rise.

What are the Community Health Services ?

In the absence of a formal, statutory definition of the CHSs, one clearly needs to look elsewhere for an appropriate response to the above question. In doing so, an ostensive definition, that is one which simply lists the services that are normally considered part of the CHSs (see above for an example), serves as a useful starting point. Many attempts to provide descriptive definitions of the CHSs go little or no further. Thus, in a government green paper, entitled *Primary Health Care: An Agenda for Discussion* (1986), CHSs are defined as 'those front line... services provided outside hospital... by community nurses, midwives, health visitors and other professions allied to medicine...',[4] which include chiropody, speech therapy, physiotherapy and dietetics. Similarly, Ham defines them as 'those services provided directly by health authorities who took over responsibility for them from local authorities at the time of health service reorganisation. They include family planning clinics, vaccination and immunisation, health education, clinics for mothers and children and fluoridation'.[5] In an article published in the *Hospital and Health Services Review* in 1976 CHSs are described as services 'most of which were provided before reorganisation by local authorities ... (and) are now organised at District level under the oversight of the District Community Physician and the District Nursing Officer.'[6]

Despite their limitations, definitions of this kind do have some value. First, they draw attention to the fact that CHSs are delivered in a community as opposed to a hospital setting. Community settings include the home, the school, the clinic and the health centre. Second, by making reference to specific CHSs they illustrate the variety of services which comprise this arm of the NHS. Third, they indicate that many of the CHSs originated in the local government sector. Finally, they may give some indication of the management arrangements for the CHSs.

Nevertheless, these definitions are, of course, inadequate conceptually and fail to convey the essential attributes of the CHSs. It is difficult, however, to move beyond a descriptive definition since on the face of it community based health care services are so diverse. Moreover, the use of the word community to indicate a shared characteristic creates more problems than it solves. One reason for this is the fact that its use is now so widespread in the fields of health care and social policy more generally that it is as likely to generate confusion as to shed light. Although in some cases its meaning is clear, since the word is being used simply to differen-tiate services provided outside institutions from those provided within,[7] this is not always the case.[8]

A major source of confusion, in this respect, is the relationship between the CHSs and community care. The expression community care, despite its popularity, is itself ambiguous. As Hunter and Judge point out, 'community care is variously defined as care outside hospitals, care outside institutions, and care outside the state.'[9] Nevertheless, in spite of this ambiguity, it is clear that community care has a different focus from that of CHSs. It is concerned with the provision of social support for the so-called priority groups, the: elderly, mentally ill, mentally handi-capped and physically handicapped. It involves the delivery of both professional and informal care to enable such people to lead normal lives and remain inde-pendent for as long as possible.[10] Since good health is clearly a prerequisite for independence, CHSs make an important contribution to the achievement of the objectives of community care.

However, the two are not synonymous. Many of the tasks performed by those engaged in the delivery of CHSs do not contribute directly to community care. For example, much of the work of school doctors, school nurses and health visitors is not confined to the priority groups. Equally, a great deal of community care does not depend for its success on the CHSs, but instead relies upon effective social services (such as home helps, meals on wheels, social work and day care) and the contribution of informal carers (such as relatives, neighbours and volunteers). Consequently, CHSs and community care can be said to overlap but each retains its distinctive character and objectives (see Figure 1.2).

The problems associated with determining a conceptually rigorous definition of CHSs are compounded because community is an emotive word, connoting positive images of belonging, fraternity and warmth. The word has, therefore, been used in some instances to persuade both carers and clients that a particular policy change will generate a more informal, friendly and participative climate for the delivery of care and that consequently the quality of that care will be improved. Thus, with respect to both CHSs and community care the use of the word com-munity can be misleading and should be treated with caution.

Despite these difficulties, in order to make progress in understanding the nature and objectives of CHSs a more analytical approach is required. An example of such an approach, which is commended by McNaught in an article entitled, 'Where are the Community Health Services Going?',[11] is that of the Korner Steering Group on Health Services Information. In the introduction to their fifth report, Korner and her colleagues make the following comments about the CHSs:

> In structuring information about community health services we have drawn an important distinction between services to the community, and services in the community.

Services to the community are services of prevention or intervention which are provided as a matter of public policy rather than individual demands for treatment or care ... Patient care in the community is the treatment or care outside hospitals of patients with identified physical or mental illness or disability (emphasis added).'[12]

Significantly, the distinction between services **to** the community and services **in** the community illustrates the different connotations of the word community, to which attention has already been drawn.

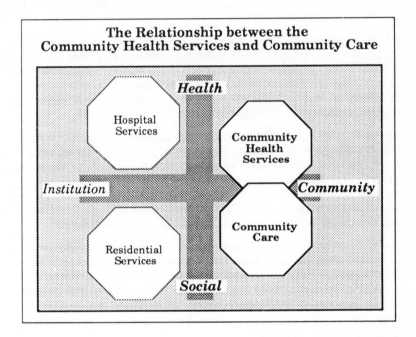

The Relationship between the Community Health Services and Community Care

Health
Hospital Services
Community Health Services
Institution
Community
Community Care
Residential Services
Social

Figure 1.2

The report goes on to suggest that services **to** the community should be divided into six types of programme. Three of these ' ... are delivered within a structured framework to a defined target population in order to prevent or identify a specific disease or condition' (i.e. immunisation, screening and contact tracing). Two other programmes, surveillance and health promotion and education, are delivered to individuals or client groups, such as neo-nates (newly born); pre-school and school children, and are '...directed towards [either] the identification of a range of possible disorders or health problems which can be treated, or their adverse consequences reduced more effectively by earlier, rather than later, intervention [e.g. cervical cancer, hypertension] [or] towards particular functions [e.g. parent-hood], conditions [e.g. obesity], or aspects of behaviour [e.g. drug abuse]'. The last of the programmes is professional advice and support, which comprises all the activities of community health professionals, such as health visitors, school nurses and health education officers that cannot be specifically attributed to any of the other programmes. It includes post-natal care by health visitors, counselling in cases of child abuse and support for those aged 75 or over.

With regard to services in the community, the Korner Report differentiates between general patient care services (i.e. district nursing); mental illness patient care services; mental handicap patient care services and other nursing services (e.g. those provided by continuing care nurses).

The Korner approach certainly goes some way towards bringing out a number of the key features of the CHSs in particular the emphasis on prevention and the fact that whilst some CHSs are directed at everyone living in a particular locality others are targeted at those members of the community who require specialised care and attention. It also highlights many of the principal client groups of the CHSs, such as pre-school children and the mentally handicapped.

Nevertheless, for McNaught the Korner approach does not go far enough. He is particularly unhappy that it does not take account of '... elements which the term 'community' has come to represent both in popular usage and in discussions of social policy'.[13] The elements with which McNaught is mainly concerned are those of citizen participation and control and voluntary provision. In his view those responsible for the management of CHSs should be seeking to maximise public involvement in the delivery and development of CHSs. For McNaught:

> *The community health services have a multiple role, including health surveill-ance, health education, the provision of domiciliary support and direct clinic services to ensure that levels of public health are maintained and improved. They are distinguishable from hospital services by their **lower technological base**, the fact that they are aimed at the population at large, and because their success is more dependent upon a more **active dialogue with the citizen and consumer** (emphasis added).*[14]

McNaught's definition has much to commend it, not least because it represents one of the few attempts to take an analytical and critical view of the CHSs. In so doing, however, the morally neutral definition which seeks simply to describe existing services has given way to a prescriptive approach. In other words, such definitions state what CHSs ought to be and include value judgements about their importance within a health care system and the rightness of the particular approach and emphasis which the providers of such services typically adopt. McNaught, for example, in the definition given, is not simply describing CHSs but is advocating 'active dialogue with the citizen and consumer' and supporting the validity of health services with a 'lower technological base'. These prescriptive statements also provide a set of criteria against which actual services can be judged.

In order to understand further the nature of CHSs it is necessary to examine their place within the health care system; their functions and their objectives.

The Place of the Community Health Services within the Health Care System

CHSs form part of a complex network of formal and informal sources of help and support, which are available to meet health care needs. This network is often conceptualised in terms of a number of different levels of health care. These are: self-care; primary care; secondary care and tertiary care. Self-care is largely self-explanatory. People look after themselves and, if necessary (and possible), receive help and support from family or friends and make use of medication and/or appliances bought over the counter. However, there are clearly many situations in which self-care fails to meet the need and help has to be sought from the services available at the primary level of health care. Thus, for most patients, the primary level represents their first point of contact with the formal health care services. It is also the level to which most patients return after receiving treatment at the secondary and/or tertiary levels. As Brearley and his colleagues comment:

> *The features of health care at this primary level are: that it is the point of entry for individuals to the health care services, involving functions of assessment and of mobilisation and co-ordination of further medical services; and that it provides personal, continuing and long-term care for individuals and families in a local community.*[15]

Secondary care involves the provision of those general specialist services which are available in most acute hospitals and tertiary care includes the super-specialist services, such as neuro-surgery, available in only a few select hospitals.

In terms of this model of the health care process CHSs are located at the primary level. However, for a variety of reasons, which will be considered later, the provision of primary care services is not the exclusive preserve of CHSs staff, but is a responsibility shared with family practitioners (i.e. doctors, dentists, chemists and opticians).

FPSs are organisationally separate from the CHSs and the practitioners who provide them are self-employed, independent contractors. Moreover, unlike CHSs, FPSs have not been 'cash limited' but have had an open ended budget.[16] Thus, they are in a more privileged position than the CHSs, a fact forcibly corroborated by the faster rate of growth of expenditure on the FPSs. This is shown in Table 1.1, which is based on data from the *Summarised Accounts of Health Authorities.*

TABLE 1.1 *Distribution of NHS Revenue Budget 1981/82 to 1986/87*

	1	2	3	4	5	6
Year	HQ Admin %	Other Services %	Hospital Services %	FPSs %	CHSs %	Col 4 less Col 5 %
1981/82	3.7	3.8	61.5	24.4	6.6	17.8
1982/83	3.4	3.5	60.5	25.9	6.7	19.2
1983/84	3.3	3.8	60.1 ·	26.1	6.7	19.4
1984/85	3.3	3.8	59.2	26.8	6.9	19.9
1985/86	3.0	3.9	58.9	27.0	7.2	19.8
1986/87	3.0	4.0	58.2	27.3	7.5	19.8

Sources: Based on data from House of Commons Paper No. 232 Session 1982/83, *Summarised Accounts of Health Authorities* (etc) for the year ended 31 March 1982; Paper No. 399 83/84, ... year ended 31 March 1983; Paper No. 331 84/85, ... year ended 31 March 1984; Paper No. 411 85/86, ... year ended 31 March 1985; Paper No. 20 87/88,... year ended 31 March 1986; and Paper No. 606 87/88, ... year ended 31 March 1987.

As the data in Table 1.1 show, between 1981/82 and 1986/87 the CHSs' share of the total NHS revenue budget increased by only 0.9% (i.e. from 6.6% to 7.5%) compared with a 2.0% increase in the FPSs' share. Consequently the gap between the CHSs and the FPSs, in terms of their spending, widened from 17.8% of total NHS expenditure in 1981/82 to 19.8% in 1986/87 (see column 6). Therefore, CHSs have tended to be overshadowed by FPSs, and primary health care is often treated as being synonymous with the care provided by family practitioners.

Nevertheless, despite the important, and politically sensitive, differences between CHSs and FPSs, it is generally felt that primary health care can be delivered only in an integrated and cost-effective manner if there is a degree of collaboration between CHSs staff and family practitioners. This need for collaboration is exemplified in the concept of the primary health care team, which has been widely advocated since the late 1960s. For example, the DHSS Annual Report for 1974 stated:

> *The aim is to create primary health care teams in which general medical practitioners, home nurses, health visitors and, in some cases social workers and dentists, work together as an inter-disciplinary team, thus facilitating co-ordination and mutual support in the planning and delivery of care.*[17]

The concept of the primary health care team is often coupled with that of the health centre since appropriate accommodation is considered to be an important prerequisite for the successful development of team working across the CHSs-FPSs divide. Although the existence of a health centre is not a necessary condition for team working it can be said to represent the physical expression of the primary health care team concept. Consequently health centres, where they exist, are extremely important locations for the delivery of both CHSs and FPSs. Because of their importance for the development of CHSs both primary health care teams and health centres will be examined in more detail in later chapters.

Although many commentators would argue that neither the concept of the primary care team nor that of the health centre has lived up to expectations, they remain important ideals as far as the realisation of a more cohesive approach to the delivery of primary health care services is concerned. They also demonstrate the need to take account of the links with FPSs when seeking to produce a more analytical definition of the CHSs.

In addition to their role within primary care, CHSs also have an important contribution to make to the management of the boundaries between the various levels of health care. The boundary between self-care and primary care, for example, has been managed in most parts of the NHS in what might be described as a 'laissez-faire' or reactive manner. In other words individuals have had to decide for themselves whether their condition warrants crossing the boundary from self-care to primary care and, when they have done so, health professionals have reacted to the problems presented to them. In contrast some of the CHSs, such as the school health service, health education, and vaccination and immunisation, have been far more proactive. Instead of prospective patients having to take the initiative in seeking treatment, the first move has come from the health profession-als. In this respect CHSs staff are playing an important role in some of the initiatives in prevention and screening, such as the establishment of call and recall systems for cervical cancer and mammography. Furthermore, health promotion initiatives play an important part in encouraging people to take care of themselves in ways which will reduce the need for them to cross the boundary from self-care to primary care.

CHSs are also a route by which patients enter and leave the secondary level of health care. Professionals within the community are 'gatekeepers', determining who should be referred to the specialist services available in hospital. For example, school doctors can, in certain circumstances, refer pupils to hospital consultants. When patients are discharged from hospital the CHSs make a very significant contribution to their after-care. This is becoming increasingly important as short-stay hospital patients are discharged more rapidly, with the development of 'hos-pital at home' schemes, and, long-term patients, in particular the mentally ill, mentally handicapped and the elderly, are moved out of institutions into the community. The effective management of the boundary between the primary and secondary levels of health care can therefore be regarded as an important aspect of the work of CHSs staff.

The Functions of the Community Health Services

It is clear from the foregoing analysis that health care is an extremely broad concept and subsumes a wide variety of related but distinct functions. These are identified in Figure 1.3, which also illustrates the essentially circular nature of health care.

Each of the functions shown in Figure 1.3 will be considered below. Before doing so, however, it is important to note that not every patient necessarily passes through all the stages of this process, but there is, nevertheless, a logical progression from one stage to the next. Moreover, the circular view of the health care process highlights the continuous nature of health care.

The functions identified in Figure 1.3 correspond in an imperfect way to the

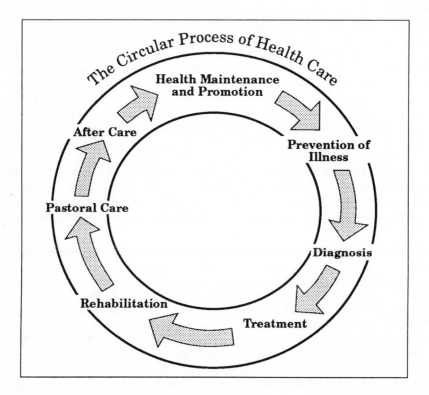

Figure 1.3

levels of health care introduced earlier. Thus, the principal functions at the primary level are health maintenance and promotion, illness prevention (including monitoring and referral), rehabilitation, pastoral care and after-care. and at the secondary and tertiary levels, diagnosis and treatment. Whilst neither the circular view of health care nor its links with the levels of health care are perfect bases for analysis, they do provide a useful framework within which to examine the functions of the CHSs.

Since CHSs staff are involved, to a greater or lesser extent, with the full range of health care functions, the CHSs could be viewed as a microcosmic health service located within the community. This, however, does not bring out the distinctive contribution which CHSs make to health care. A brief examination of their role with respect to each of the functions identified above will reveal that the efforts of those who provide them are not evenly spread. Their particular emphasis and expertise can be said to lie in those activities associated with the primary level of health care.

Health Maintenance and Health Promotion

The function of maintaining and promoting health is qualitatively different from that of preventing specific illnesses. It is founded on a positive definition of health such as that offered by the World Health Organisation (WHO): 'A state of complete physical, mental and social well-being and not merely the absence of disease or infirmity'.[18] Such an approach emphasises the subjective nature of 'feeling well' and the ability of the individual to participate in social and economic life, such as parenthood and work, rather than the objectively ascertainable absence of clinical abnormality.

Concern to maintain and promote good health therefore leads both policymakers and carers inexorably away from the narrow confines of the clinical arena into the wider environment. Experience suggests, and research confirms, that health is affected by a wide variety of interrelated factors, including family background, social class, diet, social relationships, aspects of the physical environment (e.g. housing conditions, exposure to pollution), income level, employment status and, if working, occupation.

The links between factors of this kind and the health of individuals has received renewed attention during the 1980s. This has been due mainly to the publicity given to the Black Report, which appeared in 1980, and the Health Education Council's Report entitled, *The Health Divide: inequalities in health in the 1980s* (1987).[19] Both these reports suggested that there is a close relationship between unemployment, poverty and deprivation on the one hand, and ill-health on the other, and that social class differences in health have been getting wider and are now larger than at any time this century. The point is made by Wilkinson, a research fellow at the Centre for Medical Research at Sussex University, that although life expectancy has been rising generally, those born into professional families can now expect to live at least seven or eight years longer than those in the unskilled manual classes. [20,21]

For Professor Peter Townsend, one of the authors of the Black Report, and others concerned about these differences, the health of those who are deprived can only be improved and subsequently maintained if: 'The Government (is prepared) to look outside the DHSS and address the wider issues of bad working, housing and environmental conditions and low income leading to a low standard of diet, heating and clothing.[22] Similarly, in 1979 the WHO Regional Committee for Europe emphasised that the basic prerequisites for health can be identified and achieved and that lifestyles significantly influence health.[23]

This all embracing view of health is also reflected in the view expressed by Pritchard that:

Keeping healthy is so much a part of the fabric of living, and is seen so differently by different individuals, that it defies description.[24]

As a result, the action which CHSs staff need to take to maintain health is challenging and complex and involves them in looking beyond their immediate responsibilities to other services and agencies. Specialists in community medicine, health visitors and health education officers, in particular, have an important contribution to make '... by their understanding of the process (ie whereby behaviour patterns and environmental factors affect the physical and mental health of individuals), by their example, and by education.'[25] They can also play a significant role in raising public consciousness regarding health maintenance issues, such as inequalities in health and the adverse consequences of certain food additives and dietary practices, with a view to altering individual behaviour and public policy in these areas, and through liaison and joint action with other health care professionals. Their role in this respect has been strengthened during the late 1980s by growing interest in a 'healthy public policy' which makes healthy choices the easier ones and by a renewed concern for public health.[26]

Illness Prevention

Clearly there is a degree of overlap between this function and that of health maintenance and promotion. Illness prevention, however, is a far more precise function and one where health professionals have much more clearly defined roles to play. These include taking action to prevent illness occuring (e.g. vaccination and immunisation) and the surveillance procedures, referred to earlier, which are designed to identify abnormalities and disorders as early as possible (e.g. chromosome counts to detect Downs Syndrome; audiological testing and vision assessment of children), so that, whenever necessary, referrals can be made either to services available elsewhere in the primary sector or to the appropriate specialist at the secondary level of health care.

Despite the relatively recent origin of many of these techniques, the prevention of illness has long been a key function of the CHSs. For example, the principle of making formal arrangements for the vaccination of young children dates from the mid-19th Century and under the provisions of Section 28 of the National Health Service Act 1946, local health authorities (i.e. the bodies responsible for the administration of CHSs from the establishment of the NHS in 1948 to the 1974 reorganisation) could ' ...make arrangements for the prevention of illness)' with the Minister's approval and had to make such arrangements if directed to do so by the

Minister. It seems probable that the illness prevention function will acquire even greater significance as more sophisticated screening techniques become available.

Diagnosis and Treatment

By comparison with health maintenance and promotion and illness prevention, diagnosis and treatment are far less significant functions of the CHSs. Although there is an element of diagnosis in many of the CHSs, if treatment is required it is likely to be provided by a general practitioner (GP) or a specialist. A good example of this is the school medical service where the role of the school medical officer is primarily to decide which children, on the basis of a preliminary diagnosis, need to be referred elsewhere for treatment.

However a number of CHSs, such as chiropody, the community dental service and family planning, explicitly incorporate treatment as well as diagnosis, and various kinds of routine treatments are provided for patients by district nurses, community midwives and other groups of health care professionals working in the community and it is therefore appropriate to include treatment, as well as diagnosis, as one of the functions of the CHSs. Nevertheless, this is not a major concern nor is it one that is likely to expand in the future.

Rehabilitation and After-Care

In the Mair Report (1973) rehabilitation was defined as the: '..restoration of patients to their fullest physical, mental and social capabilities, within the limits of a disability'.[27] Similarly, Pritchard takes the view that: 'Getting better is not just having the illness cured... (it) implies a return to normal physical and social function; and this is more an attitude of mind than a physical science' and he adds: 'Whereas rehabilitation as a hospital specialty is concerned mainly with physical function, in primary care the patient must be seen as a whole in his social context, with particular emphasis on motivation'.[28] Moreover, many of the groups concerned with the welfare of the disabled now specifically refer to the need for handicapping social conditions to be removed.

Health care professionals working in the community, such as community nurses, speech therapists and physiotherapists, make a far greater contribution to the rehabilitation and after-care of patients - in its broadest sense - than those based in hospitals. Furthermore, CHSs staff have more extensive and varied responsibilities in respect of the rehabilitation and after-care of patients than GPs. This, of course, is a function which requires careful management of the boundary between the secondary and primary levels of health care if it is to be performed in an effective and efficient manner.

Pastoral Care

For Pritchard, '...pastoral care consists of the sum of individual care, like the shepherd's care for his sheep'.[29] Thus, like rehabilitation, pastoral care involves responding to a patient's total needs and not just those which relate to his/her physical well-being. It also focusses on the individual as a person rather than as a patient and generally incorporates a significant element of counselling. Although there has always been a pastoral element in the role of certain groups of CHSs staff, such as health visitors and school nurses, this function is growing in importance as health care professionals based in the community become increasingly involved in the care of the terminally ill and the drug abuser, and in meeting the distinctive needs of the ethnic minority communities. Clearly, however, this is a function which CHSs staff share with other professionals within the NHS (e.g. clinical psychologists, GPs) and the world outside (e.g. teachers, social workers, the clergy).

In performing these different functions CHSs staff can be said to make a valuable contribution towards the well-being of individual patients and the community at large. Moreover with their particular expertise in the areas of health maintenance and promotion, illness prevention, after-care and pastoral care, the CHSs can be said to impart a particular ethos to the NHS which is in stark contrast to that imparted by hospital and specialist services. It is in the interests of all concerned with health care that this ethos is not lost and that CHSs command a share of NHS resources, which more adequately reflects their contribution.

The Objectives of the Community Health Services

In making their particular contribution to the health care of the population at large, it has been argued (e.g. by Pritchard and Morrell)[30] that those responsible for the management and delivery of the CHSs should seek to realise certain generalised objectives. These are: accessibility; acceptability; identification and meeting of needs; 'value for money'; and adaptability.

From the point of view of the CHSs, these objectives give rise to a number of interesting and important questions, and each deserves separate consideration.

Accessibility

In this context accessibility means the erosion and, wherever possible, the removal of barriers, which make it difficult and, sometimes impossible, for prospective clients to obtain the CHSs they need. Barriers of particular significance are those relating to situations where:

- the demand for certain services exceeds their supply (e.g. chiropody);
- distances between the homes of those needing services and their point of delivery (e.g. health centres) are too great to walk and transport facilities are inadequate;
- the timing of clinics is unsuitable for people working full-time;
- the design of premises does not take account of the needs of the physically disabled;

- differences between those needing particular services and the professional staff responsible for providing them, in terms of their education, cultural and ethnic background, social status and even language, give rise to communication problems; and

- psychological factors prevent people from seeking the help they need (e.g. fear, embarrassment).

Many of those responsible for the management and delivery of CHSs now recognise the need to ensure that services are as accessible as possible and are taking steps to realise this objective. This involves paying particular attention to the manner in which services in short supply are allocated; the siting of clinics and health centres and, where appropriate, the provision of transport; the communication skills of 'front line' staff and ways of overcoming or, at least, reducing the psychological and cultural barriers which inhibit many from seeking the help they need. [31]

Acceptability

The acceptability of CHSs is related to their acessibility, in that inaccessible services are clearly not acceptable to those wishing to use them. However, acceptability implies more than this. It means that once access is ensured the service does then meet all the needs of the client, even those which the service provider may see as peripheral. Dowling, for example, in her book on preventive health care in pregnancy and early childhood, stresses the importance of comfortable seats, the availability of refreshments and the provision of toys at ante-natal clinics. If services are not acceptable to their clients, they will not be used to the full and consequently, they will be neither effective nor efficient. In the words of Dowling: 'Great imagination is needed if we are to mould our precious resources into new and more appropriate shapes for the health of families'. [32]

The degree to which services are acceptable to clients can be judged, in part, by the extent to which they are used. However, this method of evaluation has two shortcomings. First, it fails to reveal the reasons why some potential clients do not make use of the service. Second, it does not attempt to examine the level of satisfaction amongst users. A generally low level of satisfaction may result in clients not continuing to use a service. It is therefore necessary to develop mechanisms for obtaining their views on the quality and nature of the services provided. Although various mechanisms are available (e.g. consumer surveys, analysis of complaints), there are factors, such as cost, bias and the raising of false expectations, which limit their value and usefulness. Nevertheless, despite these problems, acceptability is generally felt to be a laudable objective and one that should be vigorously pursued.

Furthermore, some commentators and practitioners go further and argue that not only should clients be canvassed for their views at periodic intervals, but also they should be directly involved in determining the type and level of services provided and the locations for service delivery. McNaught, for example, feels that because CHSs are more dependent for their success than other health care services on 'an active dialogue with the citizen and consumer', and make a significant 'contribution to the care of vulnerable groups', those responsible for their management should encourage 'consumer participation ... as well as more sensitive, people oriented approaches to service delivery.'[33]

Although there are a number of schemes designed to facilitate patient participation in the planning and delivery of primary care services, these are essentially experimental[34] and it remains to be seen how far the principle of patient participation can be applied to the management of individual CHSs and health centres.

Identification and Meeting of Needs

The point has already been made that the traditional approach to the provision of health care services at the primary level is predominantly reactive as opposed to proactive. This means, in effect, that health care professionals simply respond, or react, to the symptoms or 'demands' presented to them by their patients rather than taking the initiative. As a result a great deal of disease goes undetected and untreated. Morrell argues that 'greater efforts (should be made) to uncover the 'iceberg' of treatable disease',[35] and in order to overcome the bias towards reaction in primary health care even more attention should be given to planning services on a regular and comprehensive basis.

This involves the systematic identification and measurement of health care needs, in particular those which have not given rise to demands from members of the public (i.e. they form part of the 'iceberg' of disease); setting quantifiable objectives in relation to these needs (e.g. to increase the take-up rate for the immunisation of children against whooping cough by 10 percent, over two years; to screen every woman over the age of 21 for cervical cancer, at three yearly intervals); regular monitoring of progress towards the realisation of these objectives and the investigation of cases where these objectives have not been met. Although considerable progress has been made in this respect and, as suggested earlier, CHSs have been at the forefront of these developments, a great deal remains to be done. Moreover, there are considerable resource implications of seeking to meet unexpressed need, as well as responding to demands from the public for treatment.[36]

'Value for Money'

Despite the fact that far less is spent on CHSs than either FPSs or HSs (see Figure 1.1 and Table 1.1), and that CHSs are perceived as a relatively low cost form of health care, there is still a need to ensure that their resources (i.e. money, staff and materials) are used in an efficient and cost-effective manner. To pursue this objective, which has a high priority throughout the NHS,[37] it is necessary to look for ways of increasing efficiency. This involves:

- investigating, and taking action in, situations where resources are being wasted or used in an extravagant manner;

- ensuring that services which are provided by family practitioners as well as CHSs staff (e.g. family planning; vaccination and immunisation) are planned in such a way that resources are not left lying idle; and

- weighing up the relative costs and benefits of alternative methods of achieving given service objectives (e.g. reducing the incidence of heart disease).

However, even if action of this kind is taken, it will not overcome the fundamental problem that, as Pritchard points out, 'To implement all the desirable objectives of primary health care now would use far more resources than could possibly be afforded by society.'[38] Consequently, difficult choices have to be made between competing demands for the available resources (e.g. between using funds to finance a health education campaign or to employ some additional district nurses). This often involves a great deal of bargaining between those responsible for each of the CHSs concerned. Because of the subjective nature of many of the decisions which have to be made in respect of the allocation of scarce resources, complete agreement on the most equitable distribution of what is available is most unlikely.

From the point of view of those responsible for the management of the resources allocated to CHSs, another crucial issue is the resource implications of decisions taken elsewhere, particularly in the hospital sector, which result in additional demands being placed on services like district nursing (e.g. the development of 'hospital at home' schemes). Although decisions of this kind may well be cost- effective in terms of health care spending as a whole, they do imply the need for a shift of resources from hospital based services to the CHSs.

Adaptability

In their discussion of 'lay conceptions of health', Brearley and his colleagues argue that these conceptions vary not only between different groups in society, but also 'undergo changes (as) do patterns of health behaviour'.[39] These changes result from a variety of factors, which include increasing public awareness of health care matters; rising public expectations regarding health and the availability of facilities to respond to demands (e.g. for regular screening); the fact that 'many personal problems are becoming reclassified as health problems' [40] (e.g. alcoholism, child abuse); and the emergence of new diseases (e.g. AIDS).

Consequently, those with responsibility for the provision of health care services need to be flexible and adaptable in their approach if they are to respond adequately to changes in the nature of the problems presented to them. Effective performance of their health maintenance and illness prevention functions depends, to some extent, on their ability to anticipate and detect changes in 'lay conceptions of health' and changes in behaviour patterns which affect the health of individuals or the community at large.

Having examined the place of CHSs within the health care system; their functions and their objectives, it is now possible to offer a working definition which will provide a framework both for examining their evolution and for evaluating the contribution which they make to contemporary health care. CHSs are that diverse group of personal health services provided in the community which have a strong proactive orientation in the identification and meeting of need with respect, in particular, to: the promotion of health; the prevention of ill-health and the care of vulnerable groups.

The adequacy of these services clearly depends, to some extent, on effective management. Thus, the concluding section of this introductory chapter is devoted to a brief review of the distinctive challenges, which confront those responsible for the management of the CHSs.

Managing the Community Health Services

Not surprisingly, a number of the challenges, to which CHSs managers are having to respond, are the same as those faced by managers elsewhere in the NHS. Examples include the demands for a more consumer-orientated and business-like approach to service delivery and for greater sophistication in the assessment of performance. However, there are many other challenges which make the role of CHSs staff somewhat different from that of their colleagues, especially those with responsibility for the management of HSs, since 'In hospital the patient receives total care, for he is housed, fed and constantly under staff surveillance whereas in the community care is partial and intermittent.'[41]

First, unlike the situation in hospitals where it is necessary to organise 'a wide variety of services on a single site under close management supervision' in the community there is a 'need to provide particular services where and when they are needed throughout [a] district under much less supervision.'[42] This means that, by comparison with their hospital based colleagues, it is far more difficult for CHSs managers to build up close working relationships with service providers.

Second, as McNaught suggests: 'Because of their geographic spread and lack of corporate identity the manager of CHSs has to adopt a more visible and direct style of management and has to consciously work at developing an identity for the community unit.'[43]

Third, because of the emphasis on health surveillance and screening within the CHSs (e.g. in respect of child health and cervical cancer call and recall) a considerable amount of attention needs to be given to the establishment and maintenance of comprehensive and accurate record systems. Clearly this kind of health care activity can be fully effective only if suitable records are kept of everyone covered by the screening programme. This means that managers must be prepared to give a great deal of thought and attention to, and to allocate sufficient resources for, the development of reliable record systems, many of which are being computerised.

Fourth, it is more difficult for CHSs managers to identify where the power lies amongst the service providers and therefore who to cultivate in order to get things done in an expeditious manner. In hospitals, power generally lies with a group of consultants, but in the community the situation is less clear-cut. The most likely locus of power is general practice. If this is the case then, in view of the independent contractor status of GPs, it clearly presents CHSs managers with a major problem of determining how best to enlist their support.

Finally, it has proved more difficult for CHSs managers to establish and maintain constructive relations with their opposite numbers elsewhere in the NHS and in relevant organisations outside the formal structure of the NHS, such as local authorities and voluntary organisations. One reason for this is the feeling, on the part of CHSs staff, that since their budget is smaller than that for HSs and FPSs, they are very much the 'poor relation' or, at best, the 'junior partner'. Another reason is the fear on the part of other managers that a higher profile for the CHSs, arising from community care and other initiatives from the centre, might have adverse consequences for their budgets. As Levitt and Wall indicate with respect to HSs:

> *Although national policy envisages a shift of emphasis from hospital services to the community health services, this cannot easily be achieved with the limitations on available resources, since it would entail allowing hospital services to deteriorate so that the community services could benefit.*[44]

Not surprisingly, hospital managers would regard such a move as unacceptable and would do everything in their power to resist a major shift in the balance of resources.

Clearly, if CHSs are to be more effectively integrated with other health care services, considerable efforts will be needed to combat the fears and suspicions which inhibit the establishment and maintenance of sound relationships. Arguably, however, the difficulties in this respect have been exacerbated by the proposals contained in the white paper, *Working for Patients.*[45]

In considering these challenges it is important to note that they arise not only from the intrinsic nature of the CHSs but also, in part, from decisions taken and compromises reached at various stages in their historical development. Thus, the CHSs managers of today are, to a great extent, constrained and influenced by the actions of their predecessors.

It is for this reason that a historical perspective has been adopted in this book as the medium for examining: the nature and organisation of the CHSs, both collectively and individually; their role within the NHS and possible developments in the future.

Footnotes

1.   Various reports, most notably that of the Audit Commission, for Local Authorities in England and Wales, *Making a Reality of Community Care* (1986), have, in fact, questioned the claim that community care is cheaper than hospital care.

2.   DHSS, *Priorities for Health and Personal Social Services in England, A Consultative Document* (London: HMSO, 1976); DHSS, *Priorities in the health and social services. The Way Forward, further discussion of the Government's national strategy based on the consultative document Priorities for Health and Personal Social Services in England* (London: HMSO, 1977); DHSS, *Care in Action. A Handbook of Policies and Priorities for the Health and Personal Social Services in England* (London: HMSO, 1981) and DHSS, *Promoting Better Health. The Government's Programme for Improving Primary Health Care*, Cmd 249 (London: HMSO, 1987).

3.   See, for example:-
   * M. Jepson, *Community Child Health* (London: Hodder and Stoughton, 1983);
   * R. Acheson and S. Hagard, *Health, Society and Medicine: An Introduction to Community Medicine*, 3rd Edition (London: Blackwell Scientific Publications, 1984);
   * G. Baker, J. Bevan, L. McDonnell and B. Wall, *Community Nursing. Research and Recent Developments* (London: Croom Helm, 1987);
   * D. Challis and B. Davies, *Case Management in Community Care* (Aldershot: Gower, 1987); and
   * A. Gibson (ed.), *Physiotherapy in the Community* (Cambridge: Woodhead- Faulkner, 1988).

4.   DHSS, *Primary Health Care : An Agenda for Discussion*, Cmnd 9771 (London: HMSO, 1986), p. 1.

5.   C. Ham, *Health Policy in Britain*, 2nd Edition (London: Macmillan, 1985), p. 55.

6.   'Community Health Services', *Hospital and Health Services Review*, May 1976, pp. 184-5.

7.   The expression *community nursing* for example, refers to those services provided by health visitors, district nurses and midwives who work in the community as opposed to the hospital. Similarly *community physiotherapy, community dietetics*, and *community occupational therapy* are community based services which have their institutional counterparts.

8.   For example, three expressions in which the word community has different connotations are *community health councils, community hospitals* and *community action*. Community health councils are not, as is sometimes supposed, responsible for the administration of the CHSs. They are the agencies, set up in 1974, to represent the interests of the consumers of all health care services, including the CHSs (see Chapter 8). Community hospitals are small hospitals, mainly for elderly and maternity patients, in which GPs play an important role. They are not necessarily part of the CHSs. In the *Dictionary of Social Welfare* (London: Routledge and Kegan Paul, 1982), N. and R. Timms give examples of wide and rather more narrow definitions of community action. A wide definition would be one which included 'almost any movement by any minority groups using any methods to achieve change ...'(Community Work Group, p.40).' Whereas 'a definition of less wide scope would see community action as collective action on the part of the poor or those socially deprived in some way to overcome from a neighbourhood base some part of their general powerlessness."

9.   D. Hunter and K. Judge, *Griffiths and Community Care : Meeting the Challenge* (London: King's Fund, 1988).

10.   The official rationale for community care is well summarised in the following quotation from, *The Health Service in England : Annual Report 1984* (London: HMSO, 1985), para. 4.6:

   In relation ... to the care of old people and people with mental illness or handicap, there is a move towards community care (emphasis added) and away from reliance on the large and often remote institutions in which traditional services were concentrated. This reflects the desire of most people for the more normal life and ordinary networks of relationships which can more readily be provided when people are supported, according to their individual needs, in their own homes or in small units in their own local community.

11. A. McNaught, 'Where are the Community Health Services Going ?', *Hospital and Health Services Review,* January 1983, pp. 14-16.

12. Steering Group on Health Services Information [Chair: E. Korner] fifth report to the Secretary of State, *Community Services* (London: HMSO, 1984). See also P. Windsor, *Introducing Korner : A critical guide to the work and recommendations of the Steering Group on Health Services Information* (London: British Journal of Health Care Computing Books, 1986).

13. A. McNaught, op. cit., p. 15.

14. Ibid., p. 16.

15. P. Brearley, J. Gibbons, A. Miles, E. Topliss, and G. Woods, *The Social Context of Health Care* (London: Basil Blackwell and Martin Robertson, 1978), p. 66.

16. This is changing with:-

    * the introduction, in April 1990, of cash limited budgets for the ancillary staff and cost rent schemes, which are designed to encourage GPs to take action (i.e. employing support staff and improving their surgery premises) that will enable them to provide a better quality of service; and

    * the proposals in the white paper, *Working for Patients:The Health Service in the 1990s,* Cmd 555, which was published in January 1989, for indicative prescribing budgets for GPs.

17. DHSS, *Annual Report 1974*, Cmnd 6150 (London: HMSO, 1975), para. 4.1.

18. World Health Organisation, *Constitution: Basic Documents*, 15th Edition (Geneva: WHO, 1961).

19. DHSS, *Inequalities in Health*, [Black Report] (London: HMSO, 1980) and M. Whitehead, *The Health Divide : Inequalities in health in the 1980s* (London: Health Education Council, 1987).

20. R. Wilkinson, 'Does poverty equal poor health?', *The Times*, 2 April 1987.

21. Official recognition has been given to the link between deprivation and ill-health with the incorporation of the Jarman 8 index (see Chapter 9, footnote 168) into the Resource Allocation Working Party's formula, used by the Department of Health as the basis for distributing funds to regional health authorities. See Chapter 5 for further details of the Resource Allocation Working Party's formula.

22. Reported in *The Times,* 18th September 1986. Professor Townsend was commenting on a report by Bristol University (commissioned by Northern Regional Health Authority), which showed that there was a consistent correlation between poor health and social inequality. These findings backed up those of the Black Committee, of which Professor Townsend was a member.

23. Subsequently, in 1984, the WHO Regional Committee for Europe approved 38 targets designed to secure the realisation of the underlying objective of 'health for all' by the year 2000. These include:

    2. By the year 2000, people should have the basic opportunity to develop and use their health potential to live socially and economically fulfilling lives.

    5. By the year 2000, their should be no indigenous measles, poliomyelitis, neo-natal tetanus, congenital rubella, diphtheria, congenital syphilis of indigenous malaria in the region.

    7. By the year 2000, infant mortality in the region should be less than 20 per 1,000 live births.

16. By 1995, in all member states, there should be significant increases in positive health behaviour, such as balanced nutrition, non-smoking, appropriate physical activity and good stress management.

18. By 1990, member states should have multisectoral policies that effectively protect the human environment from health hazards, ensure community awareness and involvement and support international efforts to curb such hazards affecting more than one country.

For full details, see WHO Document, EUR/RC34/7.

24. P. Pritchard, *Manual of Primary Health Care: Its Nature and Organisation*, 2nd Edition (Oxford: Oxford University Press, 1981).

25. Ibid., p. 9.

26. See, for example:
* *Public Health in England : The Report of the Committee of Inquiry into the Future Development of the Public Health Function,* [Chair: Sir D. Acheson], Cm 289 (London: HMSO, 1988), in which public health is defined as 'the science and art of preventing disease, prolonging life and promoting health through organised efforts of society' (para. 1.3);
* *Healthy Public Policy : a role for the HEA* [i.e. Health Education Authority] (London: King's Fund Institute, 1987);
* *The nation's health, a strategy for the 1990s* (London: King's Fund Publishing Office, 1988); and
* J. Ashton and H. Seymour, *The New Public Health* (Milton Keynes: Open University Press, 1988)

27. Scottish Home and Health Department, Report of a Subcommittee of the Standing Medical Advisory Committee, Scottish Health Services Council, *Medical Rehabilitation :The Pattern for the Future,* [Mair Report] (Edinburgh: HMSO, 1972).

28. P. Pritchard, op. cit., p. 10.

29. Ibid., p. 11.

30. P. Pritchard, op. cit., and W. Marson, D. Morrell, C. Watkins and L. Zander, 'Measuring the quality of general practice', *Journal of the Royal College of General Practitioners,* No. 23, 1973, pp. 23-31.

31. For instance, S. Dowling, *Health for a change : The provision of preventive health care in pregnancy and early childhood* (London: Child Poverty Action Group in association with the National Extension College, 1983), gives many examples of good practice in these areas. She discusses, amongst other things, out-of-hours preventive health visitor and midwifery services and the practice of taking services into the workplace and shopping centres.

32. Ibid., p. 172.

33. A. McNaught, op. cit., p. 16.

34. In Chapter 8 of A Manual of Primary Health Care, op. cit., Pritchard provides details of a number of patient participation groups, which were set up for GP practices, including his own, in the early 1970s. Each practice was working from a relatively new health centre and recognised the need to involve patients in the provision of services and 'for a dialogue between the patients who receive a service and the professionals (including CHS staff) who provide it'. Groups of this kind, of which there are still very few, have served has a source of information on which to base plans for services and of feedback on facilities and a forum for suggestions and complaints and for health education.

35. W. Marson et. al., op. cit., p. 27.

36. For some further examples of objectives and targets see footnote 23.

37. During the 1980s there have been a variety of initiatives designed to secure greater 'value for money' in respect of the resources allocated to heath care. These include:
* cost improvement programmes, where health authorities have been expected to make savings on their running costs of between 0.5% and 1.0% of their budgets by providing services more economically;
* special studies, known as 'Rayner Scrutinies' , of particular areas of NHS spending, such as catering, transport and accommodation, with a view to identifying potential savings; and
* competitive tendering, which involves testing of existing costs of various services provided by directly employed NHS staff (i.e. domestic, catering and laundry services) against the amounts charged by outside contractors to provide the service.

See Chapter 6 for further details of these initiatives.

38. P. Pritchard, op. cit., p. 21.

39. P. Brearley et. al., op. cit., p. 25.

40.. Ibid., p. 25.

41. N. Chaplin (edited for the Institute of Health Service Administrators), *Health Care in the United Kingdom : Its organisation and management* (London: Kluwer Medical, 1982), p. 209.

42. Ibid.

43. A. McNaught, op. cit., p. 16.

44. R. Levitt and A. Wall, *The Reorganised National Health Service,* 3rd Edition (London: Croom Helm, 1984), p. 55.

45. *Working for Patients: The Health Service in the 1990s,* op. cit.

Chapter 2

The Development of the Community Health Services to 1948

Although the CHSs are today an integral part of the NHS, many of these services owe their origins to initiatives taken by private individuals and public authorities long before the NHS was formally established on 5th July 1948. The first district nursing service, for example, was started in Liverpool at the end of the 1850s by William Rathbone, a local philanthropist who also financed the service in its early days; whilst the legislative foundations of the school health service can be found in Section 13 of the Education (Administrative Provisions) Act 1907. As a result of these and similar initiatives many of the present day CHSs existed in an embryonic, if not a fully developed, form by the end of the First World War. Consequently, for the CHSs, the inter-war years was a period of growth and consolidation, as public authorities and voluntary bodies built on the foundations which had been laid prior to 1918. This meant that in 1948 the NHS inherited a reasonably well established group of CHSs.

Thus, in this chapter it is intended to examine the nature and origins of the community based services which the NHS inherited in 1948 and some of the important developments during their formative years. In pursing this aim it is, of course, necessary to make some reference to what was happening in other spheres of health care provision.

Origins

In the Victorian era the initiatives from which a number of the major CHSs evolved were to some extent overshadowed by what was happening in the field of environmental health, general medical services and public hospital services. Nevertheless they did play an important part in preparing the ground for some significant developments in the early years of the 20th Century, particularly in respect of measures to meet the health care needs of mothers and young children and school children.

A key figure in facilitating the development of community based health care services was, in many areas, the medical officer of health (MOH). Although initially concerned, almost exclusively, with environmental health, from the late 19th Century onwards, he became increasingly involved with developments in the field of personal health services. The first MOH was appointed by the Liverpool Corporation under the provisions of the Liverpool Sanitary Act 1846. As the following extract indicates, this piece of legislation contained, for the post of MOH, what would now be termed a job description.

It shall be lawful for the ... Council to appoint ... a legally qualified medical practitioner, of skill and experience, to inspect and report periodically on the sanitary condition of said borough, to ascertain the existence of diseases, more especially epidemics increasing the rates of mortality, and to point out the existence of any nuisances or other local causes which are likely to originate and maintain such diseases and injuriously affect the health of the inhabitants of the said borough, and to take cognisance of the fact of the existence of any contagious disease, and to point out the most efficacious modes for checking or preventing the spread of such diseases, and also to point out the most efficient means for the ventilation of churches, chapels, schools, registered lodging houses, and other public edifices within the said borough, and to perform any other duties of like nature which may be required of him; and such person shall be called the 'Medical Officer of Health for the Borough of Liverpool'.[1]

The Borough of Liverpool's example in obtaining local act powers to appoint a MOH was quickly followed by the City of London Corporation, which promoted similar legislation in 1847. In the following year the Public Health Act gave boroughs generally the right to appoint MOsH if they wished to do so. Most provincial boroughs, however, delayed making such an appointment for many years, since there was opposition to such a move from local businessmen and other ratepayers mainly on grounds of cost. Thus, Leeds Corporation did not appoint its first MOH until 1866, Manchester Corporation until 1868, Birmingham Corporation until 1872 and Newcastle Corporation until 1873.

Nevertheless, by the 1870s the value of having an officer of this kind, to promote the cause of preventive medicine, was so widely recognised that the Public Health Acts of 1872 and 1875 prescribed the appointment of full-time or part-time MOsH in all parts of the country. In the words of Ham, 'these officers (became) significant figures, both in the fight against infectious diseases, and in the campaign for better health. It was mainly as a result of their activities at the local level that more concerted action was pursued'.[2]

Almost inevitably this concern for the health of the population at large led to MOsH extending their sphere of responsibility into aspects of personal health care. As a result, from the late 19th and early 20th Centuries until 1974, when the post of MOH disappeared, those engaged in work of this kind can be said to have personified the complementary nature of environmental and community based personal health care services. 'Much of the credit for the local establishment of such Public Health services as sanitation, the control of epidemics, the care of mother and child (and) the treatment of tuberculosis and venereal diseases ... rests with Medical Officers of Health. They were the practical exponents of Preventive Medicine through whose agency discoveries made by science were used for the benefit of the health of the people'.[3]

However, MOsH were not alone in promoting the cause of better health and representing the health care interests of local communities. A variety of initiatives were taken, at national as well as local level, by other individuals and agencies who felt the need to respond positively to the health care problems associated with the appalling conditions in which the majority of the population lived; to make effective use of advances in medical knowledge and to create a more favourable climate of opinion for publically provided and financed health care services. From the point of view of the future development of community based health care services, the most significant of the initiatives taken during the Victorian and Edwardian eras were those relating to: the vaccination of children; district nursing and health visiting; midwifery and maternity and child welfare; and school health. Each of these is now considered in more detail.

Vaccination

As Lambert points out, 'vaccination ... constitutes the first continuous public health activity undertaken by the state'. Furthermore, because of 'its national, free and compulsory character' from 1853 until the end of the century, it can justifiably be called 'a Victorian National Health Service'.[4] It was also a community based service and can therefore be regarded as the very first of the CHSs.

Following Edward Jenner's discovery of vaccination as a way of protecting people against smallpox in 1798, pressure from private vaccinating bodies and the Royal College of Physicians led to the government setting up, in 1808, a National Vaccine Establishment to provide free vaccination at its London stations and to distribute vaccine-lymph to other vaccinators. This development, which was supported from public funds, was the first of many steps which the government was to take in respect of vaccination.

Because of public indifference and opposition to vaccination the results of this initiative were negligible, smallpox mortality remained high and reached epidemic proportions between 1837 and 1840. Consequently Parliament passed legislation in 1840, which introduced the principle of free vaccination on demand. In order to put this principle into practice, the poor law authorities had to be used because they were the only national administrative network available to the government. Furthermore, the poor law medical officer, who was to become 'a sort of general practitioner for the poor at large',[5] was the only widely available person with the necessary skills to carry out vaccinations. In this way a medical service was developed, through the poor law machinery, for anyone who wished to make use of it. Furthermore, vaccination by a poor law medical officer did not 'pauperise' the recipient.

However, because parents could choose whether or not to have their children vaccinated the ratio of vaccinations to births fluctuated from year to year and there were considerable variations between different parts of the country. As a result, various bodies, like the Epidemiological Society, began pointing out the inadequacies of the system and calling for compulsory infant vaccination, local prosecuting officers and central inspection. Parliament responded in 1853 by legislating for an element of compulsion.

Although the principle of nationwide, free and compulsory vaccination was legitimised by Parliament in 1853, the principle was not 'consummated' until 1871. The main reasons for this were the deficiencies in the system for registering births; the fact that poor law guardians could not prosecute defaulters and the lack of adequate supervision by the Poor Law Board at national level. As a result, for the next 18 years the figure for public vaccinations as a percentage of births was, for most years, only between 60% and 70%.

Nevertheless, during this period, developments at national level gradually improved the quality and quantity of vaccination and paved the way for the rigorous application of the principle of compulsion after 1871. These included the appointment in 1855 of John Simon, the MOH for the City of London, as the first Medical Officer to the government, and the establishment by the Medical Department of the Privy Council of a national education system for vaccinators in the late 1850s. In addition, a smallpox epidemic, which reached its climax in 1871, demonstrated the need for adequate protection and a select committee confirmed the principle of compulsion and lent its support to various reforms that Simon had been advocating for a number of years. Most of these reforms were embodied in the Vaccination Act 1871.

The principal elements of the post-1871 vaccination arrangements, as prescribed by this act, are outlined below:

• At local level, every board of guardians was required to appoint a vaccination officer, to supervise the vaccination procedure, to prosecute defaulters, and to enter into contracts with sufficient numbers of appropriately qualified medical practitioners to carry out the vaccinations.

• At national level the whole system was tightly controlled by the Medical Department of the Local Government Board, which had been formed in 1871 by merging the Poor Law Board and the Medical Department of the Privy

Council. By means of inspections and the control of contracts and appointments the Department was able to ensure that the principle of compulsory vaccination was applied effectively.

Not surprisingly, during the next few years vaccination rates increased dramatically, with rates of over 90% being achieved. These are considerably higher than some contemporary vaccination rates (see Chapter 7). However, for a variety of reasons, the strictness of this regime did not last for long. One reason for this was the gradual waning of endemic smallpox. Another was the increasing strength of the anti-compulsion lobby led by the Anti-Compulsory Vaccination League. Lastly, 'the development of a local health organisation equipped to detect and immediately to suppress rare outbreaks rendered the national preventive system less crucially important.'[6]

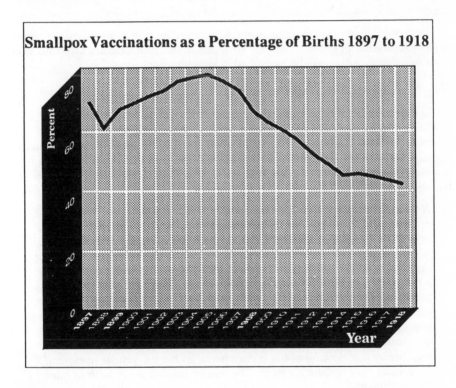

Figure 2.1

Source: Ministry of Health, *Report of the Chief Medical Officer for 1919/20*, Cmd 978.

Thus, the compulsory nature of the system was gradually eroded. An act of 1898 relaxed and modified compulsion by introducing the principle of 'conscientious objection' to vaccination. If parents could satisfy two justices or a stipendiary magistrate that they believed that vaccination would be prejudicial to their child's health then they could avoid having their child vaccinated. A further act in 1907 made a declaration by the parents before one justice or a commissioner for oaths sufficient for exemption from vaccination. The effect of this legislation on the vaccination rates is illustrated by Figure 2.1.

Although there was an unexpected increase in the percentage of children vaccinated for a few years after the legislation of 1898 came into force, from 1905 to 1918 the trend was downwards. Nevertheless, the incidence of smallpox also fell during this period. From 1906 onwards the amount of severe smallpox (i.e. variola major) was very small, with the outbreaks which did occur being 'mainly due to imported cases which had escaped through the net of the port sanitary authorities.'[7]

Interestingly, many of the ethical and administrative questions raised in respect of the vaccination of children against smallpox in the 19th Century are echoed in current debates, which will be examined in later chapters.

District Nursing and Health Visiting

As has already been mentioned the person, who did more than anyone else to establish district or home nursing as a public service, was the Liverpool philanthropist, William Rathbone. The inspiration for district nursing came from his genuine concern for the poor of Liverpool and the care and attention given by a privately employed nurse to his first wife, who died prematurely in 1858. As Rathbone himself wrote:

Having felt deeply grateful for the comfort which a good nurse had been to my wife, and thinking what intense misery must be felt in the houses of the poor from the want of such care, it occurred to me to engage Mrs. Robinson, her nurse, to go into one of the poorest districts of Liverpool and try, in nursing the poor, to relieve suffering and to teach them the rules of health and comfort. I furnished her with the medical comforts necessary, but after a month's experience she came to me crying and saying that she could not bear any longer the misery she saw. I asked her to continue the work to the end of her engagement with me (which was three months), and at the end of that time, she came back saying that the amount of misery she could relieve was so satisfactory that nothing would induce her to go back to private nursing, if I were willing to continue the work. The results induced me to wish to extend the experiment. [8]

During the next few years the extension of this experiment led to the development of a system of district nursing for the whole of Liverpool.

To underpin such a system William Rathbone and his supporters first had to secure an adequate supply of trained nurses to attend the poor in their own homes. This was done by establishing, in 1862, the Liverpool Training School and Home for Nurses. The School was attached to the Royal Infirmary, where the nurses received their training.

The next step was to divide Liverpool into 18 districts (hence the term 'district nursing'), based on groups of parishes, for organisational purposes. Lastly, lady superintendents, recruited from the wealthy Liverpool families, were appointed ooovervsee or, in modern terminology, to manage the delivery of the service in each district. The role of the superintendent included visiting those in receipt of the service to ensure that everything was in order.

Such rapid progress was made that by 1864 an effective service was operating in every one of the districts. Furthermore, the success of this innovation in Liverpool encouraged the formation of district nursing associations in other towns and cities. For example, an association was set up in Manchester in 1864, Derby in 1865 and Leicester in 1867. In 1868, with the founding of the East London Nursing Association, district nursing reached London. Six years later, in 1874, the Metropolitan and National Nursing Society was founded to promote the cause of district nursing on a more extensive basis. The concept of district nursing was also spread by some of the nurses, who had trained in Liverpool, starting schemes elsewhere, such as Oxford and Belfast.

Another important development during the 1870s was the recognition by Florence Nightingale, who lent her support to the development of domiciliary as well as hospital nursing services, and by others that district nurses needed expertise and qualities over and above those required by hospital nurses, since they had to work without the support of senior hospital staff. In recognition of this, arrangements were made for district nurses to receive additional training. For example, from 1879 'the practice was started of sending (nurses trained in Liverpool) back to the Royal Infirmary for three months' so that they could work 'in the medical, surgical and obstetric wards (thereby) refreshing their knowledge and learning more up-to-date methods and so returning with renewed energy to their district work'.[9]

As the century progressed the value of district nursing became more and more apparent and in 1889 the high standing which the service had acquired was symbolised by the founding, under royal charter, of the Queen Victoria Jubilee Institute for Nurses. This was followed, in 1898, by the founding of the Liverpool Queen Victoria Nursing Association, to continue and expand the provision of nursing support for the sick, aged and infirm in their own homes.

The dominant contribution made by voluntary bodies to the provision and development of district nursing continued well into the 20th Century, with a major role being played by the Queen Victoria Jubilee Institute for Nurses and local district nursing associations.

At the same time as William Rathbone was laying the foundations of the district nursing service, the female section of the Manchester and Salford Reform Association was doing the same in respect of health visiting. The Association had been founded in 1852 'to give information that the poor could use with advantage and to aid the infirm and enfeebled.'[10] More specifically, the female section (the Ladies Reform Association) had as its object the dissemination of health knowledge and 'the elevation of the people physically, morally and religiously'. However, after a number of years of distributing pamphlets to no avail, the Association decided in 1862 to employ 'a respectable working woman' to carry out day-to-day visits among the poor. The purpose of these visits was to teach mothers how to look after their children and the importance of cleanliness and to help those who were unwell.

According to Hale, there are two reasons why this initiative can be regarded as the foundation of the health visiting movement. The first is 'that it succeeded and expanded'. Between 1862 and 1890 the number of visitors employed by the Association rose to 14. Furthermore, in 1890, 6 of these 'were transferred to the Manchester Public Health Department to become the earliest health visitors employed by a local authority'. A second reason is that 'from the start it was visualised that the health visitor was to be a health teacher and social counsellor rather than a nurse.'[11] In other words the primary role of health visiting was that of preventive health care.

That there should be a clear distinction between health visiting, on the one hand, and nursing, on the other, was very much the view of Florence Nightingale, who stated emphatically in 1891 that: 'It seems hardly necessary to contrast sick nursing with this (ie health visiting) ... The needs of home health bringing require different but not lower qualifications, and are more varied ... She (ie the health visitor) must create a new work and a new profession for women.'[12] However, although health visiting has developed as a separate profession, it has retained close links with nursing and today anyone who wishes to become a health visitor must first obtain a nursing qualification.

Despite the fact that the foundations of health visiting were laid at the same time as those of district nursing it took considerably longer for the concept of health visiting to spread and it was not until the 1890s that health visitors or 'health missioners', as they were often called, were appointed in other parts of the country. After Manchester, the next area in which health visitors were appointed appears to have been Buckinghamshire. In 1892, Buckinghamshire County Council appointed three women to undertake, for the first time, health visiting in rural areas. These were women who had successfully completed a health visiting training course, which the North Buckinghamshire Technical Education Committee had started in response to pressure from the redoubtable Florence Nightingale. Gradually other local authorities followed the lead of Manchester and Buckinghamshire as they came to recognise the important part which health visitors could play in helping them to meet their increasing responsibilities in respect of the care of mothers and young children. As Hale comments: 'By the turn of the century it was being realised that a health visiting service had great possibilities in helping to reduce infant mortality and morbidity'.[13]

However, it was also recognised that if such a service was to realise its full potential then health visitors needed to be adequately trained. Unfortunately, the special training course for health visitors in North Buckinghamshire did not survive and it was a number of years before further initiatives were taken in this respect. Consequently, although fifty areas of Britain had a health visiting service or something similar by 1905, most of those providing the service had had no professional training. Of those who had been trained, some had medical qualifications and others were qualified female sanitary inspectors.

During the next few years, however, a number of steps were taken in order to meet what was clearly a pressing need. For example:-

• By 1907 Bedford College for Women and Battersea Polytechnic were both offering courses to prepare women for the profession of health visiting, a 2 year course for educated women without relevant qualifications and a six month course for those with a nursing qualification.

• In 1908 the Royal Sanitary Institute introduced its own examinations for those who wished to become qualified health visitors.

• The Health Visitors' (London) Order, made by the Local Government Board in 1909, required that those appointed to health visiting posts in the London area should possess one of the following qualifications: (i) a medical degree; (ii) full nurse training; (iii) the Certificate of the Central Midwives Board (see below); (iv) some nurse training and the Health Visitors' Certificate of a body approved by the Board; and (v) previous experience as a health visitor in the service of a local authority.

• In 1916 the Chief Medical Officer at the Local Government Board recommended that everyone engaged in health visiting should have at least two of the following qualifications: (i) nurse training; (ii) a sanitary inspector's certificate; and (iii) the certificate of the Central Midwives Board.

Thus, by 1918 a majority of the 3000 health visitors had had some form of professional training. Many of these developments, however, reflected a medical approach to health visiting and the training of health visitors, as opposed to a more educative or sociological approach.

Midwifery and Maternity and Child Welfare

Although improvements in environmental conditions and a gradual rise in the standard of living during the second half of the 19th Century had the effect of reducing the death rate from 22.7 per thousand population in the 1850s to 17.7 in the 1890s and the tuberculosis death rate from 3.6 to 1.9; the infant mortality rate remained relatively unchanged as the information in Table 2.1 indicates.

TABLE 2.1 *Infant Mortality Rates 1850 to 1900 (England and Wales)*

Year	Rate*	Year	Rate	Year	Rate
1850	145	1867	153	1884	147
1851	154	1868	155	1885	138
1852	158	1869	156	1886	149
1853	160	1870	160	1887	145
1854	157	1871	158	1888	136
1855	154	1872	150	1889	144
1856	144	1873	149	1890	151
1857	156	1874	151	1891	149
1858	158	1875	158	1892	148
1859	153	1876	146	1893	159
1860	148	1877	136	1894	137
1861	153	1878	152	1895	161
1862	142	1879	135	1896	148
1863	149	1880	153	1897	156
1864	153	1881	130	1898	160
1865	160	1882	141	1899	163
1866	160	1883	137	1900	154

* Children dying before their first birthday per 1000 live births.

Source: A. Macfarlane and M. Mugford, *Birth Counts: Statistics of pregnancy and childbirth. Tables* (London: HMSO, 1984), Table A3.1.

In addition, maternal mortality rates were at unacceptable levels and the number of still births showed no signs of falling.

It was the desire to tackle the problems and needs illustrated by these statistics that lay behind a number of initiatives taken in the late 19th Century and the early years of the 20th Century, at both local and national level, to improve the ante-natal, confinement and post-natal care available for women and the care given to newly born children.

The first of these initiatives was in respect of the practice of midwifery. During the 19th Century any woman, regardless of whether she was trained or had adequate knowledge, could engage in midwifery as a means of earning a living. This meant that most midwives were untrained and, to make matters worse, some of them were also dirty, dishonest and intemperate.

Consequently, in 1902, as a result of pressure from Sir Francis Champneys, a leading physician, the Midwives Institute and various other interested parties over a period of 20 years, Parliament was eventually persuaded of the need to legislate. The result was the Midwives Act 1902.

The principal objectives of this piece of legislation were 'to secure the better training of Midwives and to regulate their practice'. In order to realise these objectives the act:

- introduced the principle of certification, which meant that after certain time limits, [14] no one could use the name or title of midwife or practice midwifery unless they were appropriately certified under the act and their name was on a roll of midwives;

- placed upon the Lord President of the (Privy) Council responsibility for the establishment and supervision of a Central Midwives Board which was to have a wide variety of duties and powers including those of framing rules to regulate the conditions of admission to the roll of midwives, the course of training which anyone wishing to become a midwife should undergo, the conduct of examinations, the admission to the roll of women already in practice as midwives when the act was passed and the conditions under which midwives could be suspended from practice; publishing annually the role of midwives; and appointing examiners; and

- made county and county borough councils responsible for the local supervision of midwives in their area (i.e. they were designated local supervising authorities in respect of the Midwives Act), which entailed investigating charges of malpractice, negligence or misconduct and, where appropriate reporting this to the Central Midwives Board; suspending midwives from practice if this were necessary to prevent the spread of infection and reporting the death of any midwife and changes of name and address to the Board.

Clearly the provisions of the Midwives Act 1902 had far-reaching implications. However, there is some debate as to their precise significance. For example, according to Frazer, the provisions of this act 'elevated the hitherto despised occupation of midwife to the status and dignity of a profession.'[15] Whereas Versluysen argues that ' ... female midwives found their subordinate status confirmed by the 1902 Midwife Act which put a majority of medical men on the council responsible for the training and registration of midwives, thereby making clear that neither skilled women nor mothers could regard birth as their own concern any more.'[16] Whichever position one adopts it is clear that the act was an important turning point in the development of midwifery.[17]

A second initiative, in the sphere of maternity and child welfare, was to do with the procedure for notifying births. In order to ensure that newly born children receive the health care they need it is obviously necessary to have an effective system for notifying the relevant authorities of their birth. Such a system was not established until the first decade of the 20th Century.

Although it had been a statutory requirement, under the provisions of the Births and Deaths Registration Act 1874, to register a live birth before the infant was six weeks old, surprisingly there was no formal procedure for passing on this information to the MOH. However, even if there had been, it would not have been an entirely satisfactory arrangement because of the potentially long delay between birth and registration - a critical period for monitoring a child's health.

Nevertheless, in the absence of any other record of births, during the 1890s a number of enlightened local authorities reached an agreement with the registrar of births, deaths and marriages, whereby they paid him a fee in return for which he supplied them with a weekly list of registered births. With this information the local authority was able to arrange for the mother and child to be seen by a health visitor.

After the Midwives Act 1902 came into force, the London County Council went further and, in its capacity as a local supervising authority, it arranged for midwives to provide the MOsH of the metropolitan boroughs with information about the births in their borough. However, it was the County Borough of Huddersfield, under the leadership of its distinguished MOH, Dr S. G. Moore, which took the ultimate step in 1906 of obtaining local act powers to ensure that all births were notified promptly to the public health department.

In fact the promotion of the Huddersfield Corporation Act 1906 marked the culmination of Dr Moore's efforts to reduce infant mortality in the borough. Having made an intensive study of the problem he was convinced that the solution lay in ensuring that all mothers were visited in their homes by experts as soon after giving birth as possible. The object of the visit was to provide the nursing mother with help and support and to monitor the health and development of the child. On this basis Dr Moore drew up a scheme which the council adopted in 1905. The main elements of the scheme were as follows:

- the appointment of two assistant medical officers to act as full time, paid health visitors;

- the use of 80 volunteer health visitors, who belonged to the Huddersfield Public Health Union;

- the payment of one shilling to midwives and registrars for each notification of birth received within 24 hours of a child being born; and

- the visiting of each home as soon after the birth as possible.

Although this was an extremely progressive maternity and child welfare scheme for the first decade of the 20th Century, it was felt that it needed to be underpinned by a more accurate and precise method for obtaining details of births and as a result the decision to obtain local act powers for this purpose was taken in 1906.

One year later the government followed the example set by Huddersfield Corporation and introduced general legislation in respect of the compulsory notification of births. The Notification of Births Act 1907, however, was permissive rather than mandatory, which meant that local authorities (in this case borough, urban district, rural district and county councils) could choose whether or not to adopt its provisions. The most important of these are set out below:

In the case of every child born in an area in which the Act is adopted it shall be the duty of the father of the child, if he is actually residing in the house where the birth takes place at the time of its occurrence, and of any person in attendance upon the mother at the time of, or within six hours after, the birth, to give notice in writing of the birth to the medical officer of health of the district in which the child is born... [sec 1(1)]

Any person who fails to give notice of a birth ... shall be liable on summary conviction to a penalty not exceeding twenty shillings... [sec 1(3)]

It shall be the duty of any local authority by whom this Act is adopted... to bring (its) provisions to the attention of all medical practitioners and mid-wives practising in their area. [sec 2(3)]

Although a large number of authorities adopted the Notification of Births Act 1907, it was not long before its provisions were extended to those areas where they were not already in force. This was one of the major objectives of the Notification of Births (Extension) Act 1915, which also made it clear that local authorities could make arrangements for, and spend money on, 'the care of expectant mothers, nursing mothers, and young children.'

Since the 1890s local authorities and voluntary organisations had been developing a variety of services for mothers and young children, in addition to those provided in the home. The most important of these were:

- the establishment of milk depots or stations, from which mothers could obtain cows milk, suitable for feeding babies, at reasonable prices;

- the setting up of centres, often known as 'schools for mothers', where mothers could go to obtain advice on the feeding and general care of their children, one of the first being that started by Dr Sykes, the MOH of St Pancras, in 1907; and

- the opening of infant welfare centres, to which mothers could bring their newly born children for health surveillance and treatment purposes.

By 1918, despite the disruption of the First World War, statistics produced by the Chief Medical Officer at the Local Government Board indicate that there were in operation 700 centres for maternity and infant welfare work, which had been established by local authorities, and 578 centres, which had been established by voluntary societies. There were also nearly 3000 health visitors and district nurses and 7000 midwives working, on a full-time or part-time basis, for local authorities or voluntary bodies in the fields of maternity and child welfare.[18]

As mentioned earlier, during the first two decades of the 20th Century, initiatives were also taken in respect of the training of health visitors, which helped to advance the cause of maternity and child welfare and improve the quality of services available to mothers and young children. The most significant and satisfying result of these initiatives was the fall in the rate of infant mortality between 1900 and 1918. This is illustrated in Figure 2.2.

Whilst other factors, such as improvements in the standard of living, also played a part in lowering the rate of infant mortality there can be no doubt, that as pointed out in the Ministry of Health's *First Annual Report for 1919/20*: 'maternity and child welfare work ... materially contributed to its reduction.'[19]

Similarly, in his *Report for 1919/20*, the Chief Medical Officer referred to the progress made in the sphere of maternity and child welfare and its contribution to the decline in the infant mortality rate in the following terms:

> *It is one of the two or three most significant triumphs of preventive medicine in the present century. It is far reaching, first because of the lives saved, secondly because of the invalidity escaped by the surviving children, and thirdly because it is a movement springing in large degree from the people themselves and resulting in a new social conscience in respect of the physical well-being of mothers and children. These are immense and permanent gains to a nation.*[20]

During this period there were also significant improvements in the rate of maternal mortality. Between 1891 and 1895 there were 5.49 deaths from pregnancy and childbearing per 1000 live births. By 1918 the rate had fallen to 3.66.

Despite these important achievements of the maternity and child welfare service during its formative years, it is important to remember that the service did not emerge 'at some particular point in time as a fully organised scheme', instead 'it was allowed by the Local Government Board to develop in a somewhat haphazard manner in accordance with the standards of public spirit and enlightenment displayed by individual local authorities.'[21] In this respect, at least, maternity and child welfare can be contrasted with the school health service, which was established during the same period.

School Medical Services

Although a number of progressive school boards, such as those in London and Bradford, had begun to take an interest in the health and well-being of their pupils during the 1890s and had demonstrated their interest and concern by appointing school medical officers,[22] at that time the only statutory provisions relating to the medical condition of school children were those of the Elementary Education (Blind and Deaf) Children Act 1893 and the Elementary Education (Defective and Epileptic) Children Act 1899. These required every school board to provide for the education of blind, deaf, defective and epileptic children in special schools.

The situation was changed, however, by the Boer War (1899-1902), which set in motion a chain of events that led inexorably to the establishment of a comprehensive school health service. Because of the very poor standards of health and fitness of volunteers for the army, 48% of whom had to be rejected on physical grounds alone, the government set up an Interdepartmental Committee on Physical Deterioration. In its report, which was published in 1904, the committee reinforced the concern that was being expressed by school medical officers (who were being

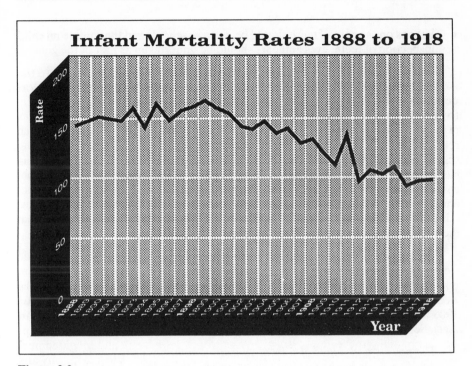

Figure 2.2

Source: A. Macfarlane and M. Mugford, *Birth Counts: Statistics of pregnancy and childbirth. Tables* (London: HMSO, 1984), Table A3.1

employed by an increasing number of education authorities) regarding the extent of the ill-health, malnutrition and disability amongst schoolchildren in their area. The members of the committee therefore recommended, amongst other things, that:

- every local education authority (under the provisions of the Education Act 1902, school boards had been abolished and their responsibilities transferred to county, county borough and non-county borough and urban district councils above a certain size, which became known as local education authorities) should have a statutory duty to provide for the systematic medical inspection of children in their schools;

- instruction about the effects of alcohol on physical efficiency should be given in schools;

- local education authorities should be required to provide meals for school children; and

- lessons on the care of teeth should be given in schools and the routine medical inspection of teeth, eyes and ears should be undertaken as part of the general programme of inspection.

Following the publication of this report, the government appointed an Inter-departmental Committee on the Medical Inspection and the Feeding of Children, to find out what was being done by local education authorities and voluntary bodies in respect of medical inspection and the provision of meals. This committee, which reported in 1905, found that 85 local education authorities were now employing school medical officers and the medical inspection of school children was being carried out in 48 areas. In addition, in some parts of the country voluntary school canteen committees were organising the provision of meals for elementary school children who would otherwise have been unable to take full advantage of their education due to a lack of food. The members of the committee felt, however, that these local initiatives needed to be buttressed by legislation.

The reports of these interdepartmental committees, together with the landslide victory of the Liberal Party in the general election of 1906, resulted in Parliament passing two very important pieces of legislation, both designed to improve the well-being of school children. The first was the Education (Provision of Meals) Act 1906 and the second the Education (Administrative Provisions) Act 1907 (1907 Act). Section 13 of the 1907 Act stated that:

The powers and duties of a local education authority... shall include... the duty to provide for the medical inspection of children immediately before, or at the time of, or as soon as possible after, their admission to public elementary school, and on such other occasions as the Board of Education direct and the power to make such arrangements as may be sanctioned by the Board of Education for attending to the health and physical condition of the children educated in public elementary schools.

In exercising its responsibilities under this section of the 1907 Act a local education authority could 'encourage and assist the establishment or continuance of voluntary agencies, and associate with itself representatives of voluntary associations.' Thus, the contribution which the voluntary sector could make to this particular personal health service was given statutory recognition.

In commenting on the circumstances which gave rise to this significant expansion of the state's role in health care matters, Hay makes the point that, although medical inspection of school children owed something to the climate of opinion created by the Boer War and backbench political pressure, the person most responsible for its introduction was Sir Robert Morant, the Permanent Secretary at the Board of Education, who ensured that it was 'hidden among the clauses of the Education (Administrative Provisions) Act 1907'. According to Hay, Morant was primarily motivated by the concept of 'national efficiency' and his desire to 'use medical inspection as a means of revealing the mass of preventable disease, which would result in the acceptance of medical treatment' [23]

Although the provisions of the legislation of 1907 were far from being comprehensive in that they related only to children in elementary schools and did not make local education authorities explicitly responsible for the medical treatment of elementary school children, they are still regarded by many commentators as an extremely important step along the road that led to the Welfare State.[24] Furthermore, because they applied to every local education authority it was necessary to set up within the Board of Education a Medical Branch, under a Chief Medical Officer, to ensure that there was compliance with the wishes of Parliament in respect of the medical inspection of elementary school children.

At local level much of the responsibility for applying the provisions of the 1907 Act fell on the shoulders of school medical officers. In many areas this post was held by the MOH, an arrangement favoured by the Board of Education as the following extract from the *Chief Medical Officer's Report for 1908/09* makes clear.

There are distinct advantages in the School Medical Officer being also the Medical Officer of Health. The duties of the two offices naturally overlap or may do so. The inspection of children for the spread of infectious diseases, and the sanitary inspection of the premises are examples of this. The union of the two offices tends to prevent duplication of work

In organising a system of medical inspection for elementary school children in their areas, school medical officers were expected to adhere to a code of regulations which was drawn up by the Board of Education and covered such matters as the timing, conduct and scope of inspections. However, for various reasons many school medical officers and their authorities felt the need to go further than their formal obligations under the code and the act. For example, by 1912 arrangements existed for carrying out medical inspections on children in at least one eighth of the secondary schools run by local education authorities. More significally, it was increasingly recognised that treatment facilities of various kinds were required if the service was to be fully effective.

Although local education authorities were not debarred from setting up facilities for treating pupils, under the provisions of Section 13 of the 1907 Act they had to obtain the Board of Education's approval before doing so.[25] Whilst such approval was usually given it had been falsely assumed when the 1907 Act was passed that parents would be responsible for taking appropriate action in respect of any health problems detected during a school medical inspection. In reality, however, many parents failed to exercise this responsibility, either through ignorance or because they could not afford the cost of the treatment needed. Consequently, as Frazer comments, many school medical officers were constantly finding at follow-up inspections that children had had 'no treatment for their defects, in spite of advice to consult private doctors, district medical officers or voluntary agencies.' [26]

In the circumstances it is hardly surprising that many progressive school medical officers and their authorities decided to take action of various kinds in respect of the provision of treatment. This included:

- the employment of school nurses to ensure that, as far as possible, children who needed treatment obtained it (this involved visiting parents and persuading them of the need to have their children treated or making the necessary arrangements themselves) and to treat minor ailments, such as scratches and bruises;

- the systematic provision of spectacles, since defective eyesight was a serious problem in many areas;

- the setting up of facilities for treating ringworm;

- the making of contributions to local hospitals for the provision of specialised treatment (e.g. tonsillectomy); and

- the establishment of school clinics for certain diseases, such as those of the skin, ears and eyes.

A number of education authorities also established school dental clinics. The first was set up in Cambridge in 1907 [27] and by 1909 the Board of Education had sanctioned the provision of dental services by 55 local education authorities. Since the Board of Education was keen to encourage developments in the field of dental health, in his *Report for 1912,* the Board's Chief Medical Officer provided local education authorities with advice as to what he considered constituted 'a satisfactory dental scheme'. As the following quotation from the report indicates, in devising their schemes, authorities were advised to give high priority to the preservation of teeth and preventive dentistry:

> *The treatment should be conservative in character and accordingly the bulk of treatment work should be by filling other than by extraction. Conservative dentistry includes also preventive measures, such as extraction work as contributes to the preservation of the dentition as a whole and any mechanical devices necessary to regulate the teeth.*

In many respects this was very enlightened advice and it was to stand the test of time. Furthermore, as early as the 1910s school dentists in some parts of the country were demonstrating their awareness of the importance of dental health education by giving talks on the subject to mothers, teachers, school inspectors and school nurses. [28]

One important issue associated with the provision of treatment was that of finance. Upon whom should the cost of providing treatment fall? Under the provisions of the Local Education Authorities (Medical Treatment) Act 1909, local education authorities were required to take whatever action was necessary to recover the cost of any treatment provided from the parent of the child concerned, unless they were satisfied that the parent was 'unable by reason of circumstances other than his own default to pay the amount.'

Clearly many parents were unable to pay and, in order to ensure that this did not deter local education authorities from providing treatment, the Board of Education introduced, in 1912, a system of grant aid towards their expenditure on the provision of various kinds of medical treatment (e.g. in respect of common skin diseases, defective eyesight or hearing and conditions of the mouth, nose and throat) and undertakings ancillary to medical treatment. Such an initiative from the centre undoubtedly played an important part in legitimising the involvement of local education authorities in medical treatment as well as inspection, with the number of clinics increasing from 50 in 1910 to 350 in 1914.

As a result of vigorous action at both national and local level considerable progress was made in the first few years of the school medical service and by 1914 it had become a well established component of the system of elementary education in this country. However, as Frazer indicates, during the First World War 'it was found impossible to continue fully the routine inspection of school children owing to the absence of many of the medical staffs of local education authorities on service in the armed forces. Until the end of the war, therefore, the School Medical Service was forced by stern necessity to accept a reduction in the standards which had been set for it, and it was not until 1919 that the rate of development attained in the pre-war years could be regained.'[29]

Nevertheless, despite this setback, in its emphasis on health maintenance and promotion, illness prevention and the monitoring of a large and well defined client group and on the importance of school doctors and school nurses working as a team, the school medical service exhibited, right from its foundation, many of the characteristics associated with the CHSs of today.

As the foregoing discussion has indicated, during the 19th Century and the early years of the 20th Century the foundations of the present day CHSs were laid, through a combination of individual and collective enterprise at both national and local level. At the same time, various other developments were taking place in respect of the provision of personal health care services.

The most important of these were:

•   the growth of hospital based services provided by poor law authorities, voluntary organisations and local authorities;

•   the National Insurance Act 1911, which introduced a system of national insurance, administered at national level by Insurance Commissioners, with various benefits for the insured when they were unemployed or ill, including access to free health care from GPs;

- the provision, by local authorities, of hospital and other facilities for the mentally ill and mentally handicapped in performance of their duties under various statutes;

- legislation relating to the notification of infectious diseases, which greatly helped local authorities with public health responsibilities to combat the spread of diseases of this kind; and

- the Venereal Diseases Act 1917, which substantially extended the role of local authorities in respect of the treatment of venereal disease and the educative and preventive aspects of dealing effectively with sexually transmitted diseases.

Nevertheless, despite these developments and pressure from various sources, including a minority of members of the Royal Commission on the Poor Laws and the Relief of Public Distress (1909), the services and facilities available by the end of the First World War did not constitute a comprehensive health care system. Services varied considerably between different parts of the country, as did the extent to which the agencies involved collaborated with each other. Furthermore, it was to be another thirty years before a comprehensive health care system, which formally linked the CHSs with the HSs and those provided by GPs.

Consolidation and Expansion: 1918 to 1948

For the CHSs the thirty years between the end of the First World War and the establishment of the NHS was a period of steady growth and expansion, as the advances made prior to 1918 were consolidated, rather than one of major new initiatives. It was also a period during which various proposals were put forward for the future direction and organisation of health care provision, including the CHSs, from which the NHS eventually emerged. Thus, in this section, consideration needs to be given not only to the growth and development of the CHSs, but also to the way in which they were affected by changes in the organisation of health care provision as a whole. Although most of the expansion and consolidation of the CHSs during this period was due to the efforts of authorities and voluntary organisations at the local level, inevitably these were influenced, to some extent, by developments at national level.

The Creation of the Ministry of Health

One of the most important of these developments was the establishment of the Ministry of Health in 1919. According to Fraser, the First World War, through its exposure of the poor physical condition of a very large number of those wishing to join the armed forces (some surveys suggest that as many as two in every three recruits were unfit for military service), strengthened the hand of health reformers led by Christopher Addison (Minister of Reconstruction 1917-1919; Minister of Health 1919-1921). His principal objective 'had always been the creation of a Ministry for health which would unify the various health services operating under so many different agencies.'[30] Thus, almost immediately the War was over, legislation was introduced to bring this about.

Under the provisions of the Ministry of Health Act 1919, certain powers and duties residing in other departments and organisations were grouped under the new Minister. These included:

- all the functions previously exercised by the Local Government Board, which included environmental health and housing as well as maternity and child welfare; and

- the powers and duties of the Insurance Commissioners, appointed in 1911 to administer the National Insurance Act; of the Board of Education in respect of the medical inspection and treatment of school children; of the Privy Council and Lord President of the Council under the Midwives Acts of 1902 and 1918; and of the Home Office in connection with infant life protection.

Significantly, however, the powers and duties of the Board of Education with regard to the medical inspection and treatment of school children were not formally transferred to the Ministry of Health. Instead the Ministry of Health Act 1919 prescribed that the Board would continue to exercise these powers and duties on behalf of the Minister of Health and with his authority, 'under such conditions as he may think fit'. To some extent this weakness was overcome by appointing the same person, Sir George Newman, as Chief Medical Officer to the Board of Education and to the Ministry of Health.

For those with responsibility for the provision of the CHSs at the local level the principal significance of these developments at the centre was the fact that they could now expect a more positive approach to, and greater co-ordination of, the making and implementation of policies designed to promote the expansion of community based health care services. To some extent this was reflected in the strengthening of the legislative framework for the school medical and maternity and child welfare services, which took place during the inter-war years.

Services for Children

The Education Acts of 1918 and 1921 dealt with the two limitations of the pre-war legislation by:

- extending the duty of local education authorities, in respect of medical inspection, to include children and young persons attending secondary as well as elementary schools; and

- imposing on local education authorities a duty to provide medical treatment (including dental treatment) for elementary school children and giving them the power to do so for secondary school children.

Although they could choose whether or not to provide medical treatment for secondary school children most local education authorities did respond positively to this need. Furthermore, many authorities also set up facilities for the dental inspection and treatment of school children, even though this was not specifically referred to in the legislation.

As the data in Table 2.2 indicate, between 1923 and the mid-1940s (when the provisions of the Education Act 1921 were superseded by those of the Education Act 1944), whilst the increase in the number of inspections was relatively modest, there was a very large increase in the number of minor ailments (e.g. cuts, septic sores, skin disorders) and dental 'defects' treated. Thus, during this period the expansion of the school medical service was mainly in the amount of treatment provided. Many local education authorities set up clinics to provide treatment of a specialised nature that was not within the scope of the GP and was too costly for most parents to obtain from a hospital specialist (e.g. ear, nose and throat, orthopaedic and eye clinics).

They also developed facilities for the treatment and, where necessary, the education (e.g. special classes and schools) of:

• visually handicapped children;

• children with defective hearing, who had been of particular concern to school medical officers since 1907;

• children with speech and language disorders, especially stammering, which marked the beginnings of the speech therapy service;

• educationally subnormal children;

• delicate and physically handicapped children; and

• maladjusted children (e.g. in 1932 Birmingham became the first local education authority to set up a child guidance clinic and Leicester a special school for maladjusted children).

With regard to dental treatment, the number of local education authorities providing facilities increased from 169 in 1918 to 312 (out of 316) in 1932. Furthermore, between 1918 and 1938 there was an increase in the number of dental clinics from 350 to 1700 and of whole time equivalent (WTE) school dentists from 150 to 780. Increasing attention was also given to dental health education, with the main approach being that of 'mass propaganda'. [31] Nevertheless, despite these developments, Webster regards the dental service of the inter-war period as being 'the one area of undisguised and conspicuous failure in the School Medical Service.' [32]

Not surprisingly, the net cost of providing the school medical service doubled between 1923 and 1938. Since prices were falling for much of this period the increase was even greater in terms of real resources (e.g. staff, equipment).

However, as Figure 2.3 indicates, the cost of the school medical service did not rise as fast as that of the maternity and child welfare services. There were two main reasons for the substantial increase in spending on the maternity and child welfare

TABLE 2.2 *School Medical Services : Selected Statistics 1923 to 1946 (England and Wales)*

Year	Children Inspected '000s	Inspec- tions[a] '000s	←——————— Treatment ———————→				Costs[c] £'000s
			Minor Ailments '000s	Visual Defects '000s	Adenoids Tonsils[b] '000s	Dental Defects '000s	
1923	1755	4001	622	178	48	618	1238
1924	1698	3953	641	187	49	654	1221
1925	1798	4211	712	202	61	768	1297
1926	1822	4317	733	206	68	853	1427
1927	1824	4406	818	218	81	936	1501
1928	1913	4713	845	231	92	1043	1612
1929	1832	4546	849	239	98	1106	1701
1930	1771	4637	923	262	110	1253	1815
1931	1759	4797	889	267	110	1253	1815
1932	1846	5054	937	264	96	1401	2079
1933	1855	5088	937	274	78	1383	2084
1934	1795	5034	937	275	73	1432	2093
1935	1729	4986	978	270	74	1474	2167
1936	1727	5209	1049	275	81	1537	2276
1937	1700	5295	1064	270	85	1545	2408
1938	1677	5423	1121	285	89	1635	2546
1939	n.a.	n.a.	n.a.	n.a.	n.a.	n.a.	n.a.
1940	1595	4517	986	238	75	1431	2982e
1941	1599	4434	1189	241	72	1420	3199e
1942	1619	4665	1238	248	90	1414	3417
1943	1335	4203	1304	248	97	1310	3635e
1944	1297	4022	1269	242	89	1239	3853e
1945	1322	3590	1124	233	86	1093	4071e
1946	1634	4281	1237	287	108	1452	4289

Key

n.a. = figures not available
e = estimate

Notes

a. Routine medical inspections, re-inspections and special inspections.

b. Operative treatment of adenoids and enlarged tonsils (1923 to 1938); 'defects' of ear, nose and throat (1940 to 1946).

c. Net expenditure (i.e. total expenditure less income from fees and charges).

Sources: Board of Trade, *Statistical Abstract for the United Kingdom* and Central Statistical Office, *Annual Abstract of Statistics*, various editions.

services. Firstly, as a result of changes in the legislation relating to these services, local authorities acquired additional powers and responsibilities and secondly, many authorities made extensive use of these powers as they sought to extend the range, and improve the quality, of the health care facilities available for pregnant women, mothers and infants in their area.

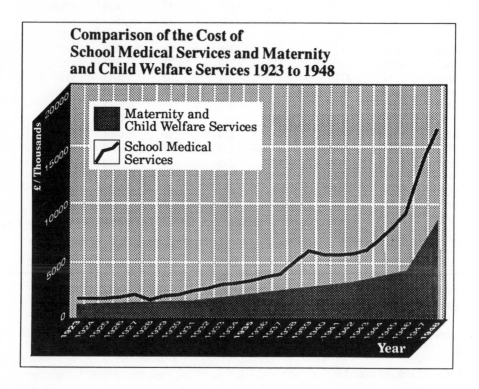

Figure 2.3

Sources: Board of Trade, *Statistical Abstract for the United Kingdom* and Central Statistical Office, *Annual Abstract of Statistics*, various editions.

The most significant changes in the legislative framework governing the maternity and child welfare services are summarised below.

Under the provisions of the Midwives Act 1918 local supervising authorities were given the power to make grants towards the training of midwives. They were also required to pay a fee to GPs who were called to the assistance of midwives in circumstances prescribed by the Central Midwives Board.

The powers of local authorities in respect of maternity and child welfare services were formalised by the Maternity and Child Welfare Act 1918. Section 1 stated that: 'Any local authority within the meaning of the Notification of Births Act 1907 (see above), may make such arrangements as may be sanctioned by the Local Government Board, for attending to the health of expectant mothers and nursing mothers, and of children who have not attained the age of five years and are not being educated in schools recognised by the Board of Education'. Furthermore, every local authority which took advantage of these powers was required to establish a maternity and child welfare committee, of which at least two members had to be women. This ensured that the service was given due recognition within the administrative structure of the local authority. To encourage local authorities to exercise these powers the Local Government Board introduced grants of up to 50% of approved expenditure.

The Midwives and Maternity Homes Act 1926 made local supervising authorities responsible for the registration of anyone providing a maternity home and also gave them the power to inspect homes should they wish to do so. This was a significant development since the principle of registration and inspection of privately provided health care facilities of this kind still continues to operate.

Amongst the many provisions of the Local Government Act 1929, which will be considered in a little more detail later in the chapter, were three of particular relevance for the maternity and child welfare service. First, responsibility for the functions relating to vaccination was transferred from the poor law authorities to the county and county borough councils. Second, county and county borough councils were required to rationalise the maternity and child welfare facilities in their areas which had been provided previously by both the poor law authorities, under the Poor Law Acts, and local authorities, under the Maternity and Child Welfare Act 1918 and earlier legislation. Last, the specific grant towards the cost of providing for maternity and child welfare, which had been introduced in 1918, was merged with other specific grants to form a block grant. Thus, from 1930 local authorities no longer received financial aid from central government which was specifically earmarked for their activities in the sphere of maternity and child welfare.

Despite improvements in the quality of maternity services during the 1920s and 1930s these had very little effect on the rate of maternal mortality, which actually increased after 1918 and showed little sign of falling significantly until the Second World War.[33] This caused a great deal of official concern, with the result that during the inter-war period the problem was investigated on a number of occasions.[34] The most important outcome of these investigations was the Midwives Act 1936. The principal objective of this piece of legislation was to secure the organisation, in every part of the country, of an adequate salaried midwifery service. Up to this time midwives had either been self- employed or employees of voluntary organisations. Under the provisions of the act local supervising authorities were made responsible for securing an adequate service by either employing their own midwives or entering into arrangements with such bodies as district nursing associations for this purpose. This led to the establishment in most urban areas of a municipal midwifery service, whilst rural authorities tended to make financial arrangements with voluntary organisations to secure the provision of an adequate service for their area.

Lastly, the Public Health Act 1936 consolidated all the earlier legislation relating to the notification of births and maternity and child welfare services (excluding midwifery). It also introduced the designation 'welfare authority' for those councils engaged in the provision of services of this kind and made it a mandatory requirement that they appoint a maternity and child welfare committee. Furthermore, all matters relating to the administration of their maternity and child welfare services had to be referred to this committee. Welfare authorities were the county borough councils and in the counties either the county council or county district council, with district councils being officially designated minor welfare authorities.[35]

By the late 1930s many local authorities had used their powers to build up an extensive range of community based services for expectant and nursing mothers and pre-school children. These included:

- ante-natal services, of which the most important were clinic facilities (by 1938 over 60% of expectant mothers were attending ante-natal clinics provided by local authorities or voluntary organisations); domiciliary visits by health visitors, home nurses and GPs; treatment for minor ailments; dental treatment and the provision of extra nourishment for necessitous mothers to supplement the National Milk Scheme;[36]

- post-natal services, because of the key role played by the midwife for the first 14 days after the birth of a child these were much smaller in scale than ante-natal services, nevertheless in certain areas post-natal clinic facilities were available (in 1938, however, only about 12% of nursing mothers attended clinics of this kind); domestic help was provided during the lying-in period and advice on birth control was available to women for whom a further pregnancy was inadvisable on medical grounds; and

- infant welfare services, such as health visiting, clinics for monitoring the child's development and vaccination against smallpox (however, as Figure 2.4 illustrates, the take-up rate for smallpox vaccination never rose above 50% between 1918 and 1946) and immunisation against diphtheria, which, in contrast with smallpox vaccination, grew in importance so that by the mid-1940s between 60 and 65% of children were being immunised.

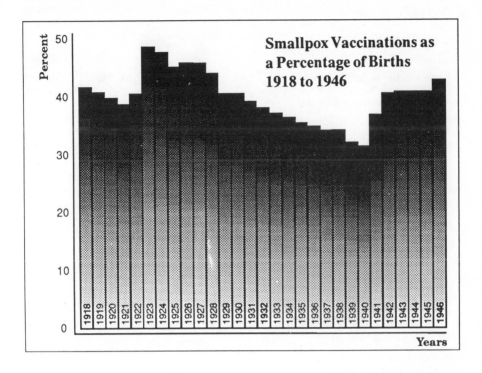

Figure 2.4

Source: Ministry of Health, *Annual Reports*, various years.

The growth of the maternity and child welfare services during the 1930s is illustrated by the statistical data in Table 2.3. Considerable satisfaction was derived from the fact that the increased availability of services was accompanied by a continuing fall in the rate of infant mortality (see Figure 2.5) and improvements in the health of children generally.

Unfortunately, however, despite the investigations referred to earlier and continuing efforts to improve the quality of services for expectant mothers, progress in reducing the rate of maternal mortality proved more difficult to secure and for much of the inter-war period the rate fluctuated between 3.50 and 4.50 deaths from pregnancy and childbearing per 1000 live births.[37]

TABLE 2.3 *Maternity and Child Welfare Services : Scale of Provision 1931 and 1938 (England and Wales)*

	1931	1938	1931-1938 Change
Total number of notified births	625404	641829	+16425
Ante-Natal Clinics			
Clinics provided and maintained by:			
* local authorities;	1055	1676	+621
* voluntary organisations.	198	288	+90
Total number of women who attended these clinics	204472	384865	+180393
as % of total notified births.	32.7%	60.0%	+27.3%
Total number of attendances.	728897	1579623	+850726
Infant Welfare Centres			
Centres provided and maintained by:			
* local authorities;	2192	2752	+560
* voluntary organisations.	841	833	-8
Total number of children under one year of age who attended these centres for the first time	338928	411750	+72822
as % of total notified births	54.2%	64.2%	+10.0%
Total number of attendances of children under 5.	7173782	10458332	+3284550
Health Visiting			
Officers employed for health visiting by:			
* local authorities;	2689	3672	+983
* voluntary organisations.	2532	2306	-226
Visits paid by health visitors:-			
* to expectant mothers			
first visits	170809	200811	+30002
total visits	460763	577434	+116671
* to children under 1 year of age			
first visits	624408	603938	-20470
total visits	3286566	3301656	+15090
*to children between the ages of 1 and 5	4061388	4815398	+754010

Source: Ministry of Health, *Annual Reports for 1933/34 and 1938/39*, Cmd 4664 and 6089.

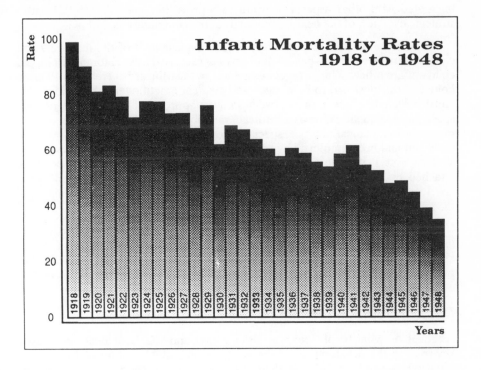

Figure 2.5

Source: A. Macfarlane and M. Mugford, *Birth Counts: Statistics of pregnancy and childbirth.*
Tables (London: HMSO, 1984), Table A3.1.

Moreover, as Wilson points out, the legislation (with the exception of that
relating to midwifery) remained discretionary until the establishment of the NHS
and there was considerable variation in the extent to which local authorities used
the powers at their disposal 'partly because of varying needs and partly because
some ... (were) more energetic than others in their use of them.'[38] The energy which
local authorities expended on the development of their maternity and child welfare
services depended greatly on the interest of the MOsH and their vigour in pushing
for improvements. They were the chief advisory and executive officer of the local
authority for maternity and child welfare purposes, but were responsible for the
management of a wide variety of other personal and environmental health care
services. This meant, of course, that they had relatively little time to devote
specifically to maternity and child welfare, unless they gave it a higher priority than
other aspects of their health care responsibilities. However, one advantage of this

situation was that maternity and child welfare services could be more closely integrated with other aspects of heath care provision, since the MOsH had a strategic overview of the health care needs of the community as a whole.

In most authorities responsibility for the management of the maternity and child welfare services on a day-to-day basis was exercised by a senior maternity and child welfare officer. Under regulations made by the Ministry of Health in 1930 the holder of this post had to be a registered medical practitioner, who, prior to 1st April 1930, held office in that capacity with the approval of the Minister, or who, subsequent to qualification as a medical practitioner, had had at least three year's experience in medical practice, special experience in midwifery and child welfare work and had been employed by a local authority under the Maternity and Child Welfare Act 1918. These requirements reflected the considerable importance attached by the Ministry of Health to the quality of the staff engaged in the development of services for expectant and nursing mothers and young children at the grass roots level.

Throughout the inter-war period the Ministry of Health took a detailed interest in many aspects of the maternity and child welfare service and took action of various kinds to encourage and compel local authorities to improve the facilities they provided. It is therefore surprising that the legislation which governed the provision of this service remained permissive until 1948.

District Nursing and Health Visiting

Although the Ministry of Health, at national level, and MOsH, at local level, played key roles in the development of the maternity and child welfare and midwifery services between 1918 and 1948, their responsibilities in respect of another import-ant CHS remained extremely limited. This was district nursing. As the following extract from the 1944 white paper, setting out the wartime Coalition government's plans for a comprehensive health service makes clear, even as late as the mid-1940s district nursing was still, to a significant extent, a responsibility of the voluntary sector.

> *Home nursing forms a most important branch of the health services, and one which is almost entirely the concern of voluntary organisations. Local auth-orities have limited powers to employ nurses for nursing at home patients suffering from infectious diseases, or expectant or nursing mothers or children under five suffering from various conditions, but they have no general power to provide a home nursing service and the number of nurses employed directly by them is very small... The home nursing service is for the most part provided through district nursing associations, the majority of which are affiliated directly or through the appropriate County Nursing Association to the Queen's Institute of District Nursing and are under the supervision of the Institute.*[39]

Thus, during the formative years of district nursing the principal role was played by the Queen's Institute of District Nursing, as the Queen Victoria Jubilee Institute for Nurses was renamed in 1925, rather than by MOsH and their colleagues and the Ministry of Health.

In contrast, the centre did play an important part in the development of health visiting. For example, according to Hale 'health visiting was formally established as a profession in 1919',[40] when the Ministry of Health and the Board of Education jointly promulgated an official scheme for the training of health visitors. This scheme prescribed three entry routes to the profession: (a) a one year, post-basic training course for qualified nurses; (b) a different one year training course for graduates and (c) a two year training course (later extended to two and a half years, with the first six months being spent in a hospital) for those who were neither nurses nor graduates. The training was normally provided by institutions attached to universities and included social science and domestic subjects.

Initially training in midwifery was not included in the courses for those who wished to become health visitors. In 1925, however, the Ministry of Health introduced the requirement that in future all health visitors had to have some training in midwifery. As a result the one year course was divided into two parts, six months being devoted to training in midwifery and the remaining six months to the other aspects of health visiting. Although this development reflected the increasingly important role that the health visitor was playing in the field of maternity and child welfare, it weakened 'the social and preventive training of the health visitor'[41] and posed a threat to the continued independence of the newly established profession.

Despite the inclusion of midwifery and other changes in the pattern of health visitor training during the 1920s and 1930s, health visiting maintained its separate identity and enhanced its status during this period. Its position was also strengthened by the fact that under regulations made by the Ministry of Health in 1928, from 1930 local authorities could appoint only fully qualified health visitors to their full time posts. Thus, by 1948 very few health visitors were unqualified. Furthermore, the value of the contribution made by health visitors to the maternity and child welfare and school medical services and the need for a profession which focussed on the preventive aspects of health care were fully recognised.

Health Education

An important development in the sphere of preventive health care was the establishment of the Central Council for Health Education in 1927, the initiative for which came from the Society of Medical Officers of Health. The aims of the Council, which was funded by local authorities and voluntary bodies, were:

(a) to promote and encourage education and research in the science and art of healthy living and to promote the principles of hygiene and encourage the teaching thereof and
(b) to assist and co-ordinate the work of all statutory bodies in carrying out their powers and duties under the Public Health Acts and other statutes relating to the promotion or safeguarding of Public Health or the prevention

or cure of disease in so far as such work comprises health education and propaganda.

One of the early achievements of the Council was to secure statutory recognition of the importance of health education in the Public Health Act 1936. Under the provisions of Section 149 local authorities were given the power, subject to any conditions or restrictions the Minister of Health might have wished to impose, to 'arrange for the publication within their area of information on questions relating to health or disease, and for the delivery of pictures and the display of pictures or cinematograph films in which such questions (were) dealt with.'

As an editorial in a 1953 edition of the *Health Education Journal* pointed out the late 1920s and 1930s was an era of propaganda with health education being mainly promoted by means of 'mass publicity on all fronts.'[42] Methods used included exhibitions; displays; carnivals and health weeks, during which films were shown, leaflets were distributed and talks were given by eminent members of the medical profession, and their success or failure was measured by the numbers attending.

Both the initiatives in the field of health education and the development of health visiting as a profession demonstrate that interest in preventive, as opposed to curative, approaches to health care is by no means a new phenomenon.

The Dawson Report

The need for adequate preventive and other community based health care services was also recognised in much of the discussion and debate, which took place between 1918 and 1948, on the question of how best to secure an adequate system of health care provision for the population as a whole and in the changes made to the administrative arrangements for health care in 1929.

One of the most important contributions to this debate was that of the Consultative Council on Medical and Allied Services, which published a blueprint for a comprehensive health service as early as May 1920. The Council, consisting of fifteen medical and five non-medical members under the chairmanship of the future Lord Dawson of Penn, was established by the Minister of Health in 1919. Almost immediately the Minister invited the Council:

> *To consider and make recommendations as to the scheme or schemes requisite for the systematised provision of such forms of medical and allied services as should, in (its) opinion ... be available for the inhabitants of a given area.*

As Pater indicates, what the Council produced in its interim report (a final report was never published) was 'nothing less than the outline of a national health service'. Furthermore, in setting out their recommendations the members of the Council 'laid down the main principles and raised the main issues which governed the pattern of discussion for nearly thirty years.'[43]

The principles on which the Council's Report (generally known as the Dawson Report) was based reflected a very enlightened attitude towards health care on the part of its authors. They considered that:

- the existing organisation of medicine was insufficient because it failed 'to bring the advantages of medical knowledge adequately within reach of the people' and that 'the general availability of medical services (could) only be effected by new and extended organisation, distributed according to the needs of the community';

- with increasing knowledge, measures for dealing with health and disease were becoming more complex and therefore required the 'combined efforts' (i.e. a team approach) of a variety of professionals based in the same institution;

- 'preventive and curative medicine cannot be separated ... and in any scheme of medical services (should) be brought together in close co- ordination'; and

- 'any scheme of services must be available for all classes of the community', although not necessarily free of charge.

In suggesting how these principles should be put into practice the members of the Council drew a distinction between domiciliary services on the one hand and institutional services on the other and between health care services for the individual and those for the community at large.

Domiciliary services constituted the 'periphery' of the Council's scheme, the remainder of which was mainly institutional in character and based on the concept of the health centre. In the report a health centre was defined as: 'an institution wherein are brought together various medical services, preventive and curative so as to form one organisation'.

Although domiciliary services were those health care services, preventive and curative, which revolved around the home (i.e. those of the doctor, dentist, pharmacist, nurse, midwife and health visitor), in the interests of efficiency it was proposed that for a given district they should 'be based on a Primary Health Centre ... equipped for services of curative and preventive medicine to be conducted by the general practitioners of that district, in conjunction with an efficient nursing service and with the aid of visiting consultants and specialists'.

It was also recommended that within primary health centres there should be accommodation for communal services such as pre-natal care, child welfare, medical inspection and treatment of school children and physical culture (i.e. health education) and in the larger centres, dental surgeries, an ambulance station and residential accommodation for district nurses and community midwives and a doctor's common room. In proposing the establishment of primary health centres and a more integrated approach to the delivery of what are now known as primary health care services (i.e. CHSs and FPSs), the authors of the Dawson Report were very much ahead of their time. Apart from one or two experiments in the inter-war years and the 1950s, it was not until the 1960s that ideas of this kind were actually put into practice on a large scale. Nonetheless it is interesting to note that as early as 1920 the need for greater co-ordination between CHSs and other health care services was clearly recognised.

The authors of the Dawson Report went on to suggest that 'a group of primary health centres should in turn be based on a secondary health centre', from which specialist health care services could be obtained. Thus, secondary health centres were similar in conception to that of the present day district general hospital.

The two remaining components of the scheme were 'supplementary services' (i.e. those regarded as needing separate institutions, such as tuberculosis sanitoria, convalescent homes and mental hospitals) and teaching hospitals (i.e. hospitals with a medical school attached). On the subject of medical education the report stressed the need for teaching to be provided in communal services (i.e. preventive medicine) as well as the theory and practice of curative medicine.[44]

If the recommendations of the Dawson Report had been implemented in the 1920s it is probable that the CHSs would not have developed as a separate and distinctive part of the heath care system. It is more likely that those working in the CHSs would have established close links with GPs and would have become part of a fully integrated primary health care service. However, for a variety of reasons, including that of the cost involved in developing a comprehensive health care system, no action was taken on the report's recommendations.

The Local Government Act 1929

Despite the government's failure to act on the recommendations of the Dawson Report some changes were made to the administrative arrangements for the provision of health care services during the inter-war years. These were intended to remedy two defects in the way existing services were administered. First, it was widely believed that the poor law authorities were no longer appropriate agencies for the administration of health care services. This was a view which had been formally expressed, as early as 1909, by some members of the Royal Commission on the Poor Laws and the Relief of Public Distress. Second, the health care system was fragmented, with the boards of guardians (i.e. poor law authorities) providing a similar range of health care services (e.g. for mothers and children, those suffering from tuberculosis, the blind, the mentally handicapped) to those provided by local authorities exercising powers conferred on them by various pieces of legislation. The intention, therefore, was to secure a more co-ordinated approach to the delivery of both primary and secondary health care services.

Thus, on the 1st April 1930, under the provisions of the Local Government Act 1929, the health care functions of the poor law authorities (as well as their responsibility for the administration of poor relief) were transferred to county and county borough councils. In order to promote the rationalisation of health care facilities counties and county boroughs were required to submit to the Minister of Health, within six months of the commencement of the act, 'a scheme ... of the administrative arrangements (they) proposed to (make) for discharging' their newly acquired functions. In preparing these schemes councils were statutorily obliged to take into account their powers to provide assistance (which included 'maintenance and treatment at hospitals and other places'), under the Maternity and Child Welfare Act 1918, Education Act 1921, and certain other statutes, as well as the provision of assistance by way of poor relief.

Frazer argues that, 'one of the most important effects of the Local Government Act (1929) was the union, under the Medical Officer of Health, of preventive and curative medicine.'[45] The case for combining responsibility for preventive and curative health care services, which had been acknowledged by the authors of the Dawson Report, was also supported by Sir George Newman, the Chief Medical Officer at the Ministry of Health, as the following extract from his Annual Report for 1928 makes clear.

> *The administration and fulfilment of the work transferred from the poor law authorities must now be absorbed into, and assimilated with, the communal system of preventive medicine. The antithesis between curative and preventive medicine which has been publically suggested recently is an entirely false antithesis. It is false administratively as it is false from the point of view of the science and art of Medicine itself. Such a division of Medicine can only be based on a misunderstanding of the position.*[46]

Nevertheless, despite the changes in the administrative arrangements for health, brought about by the Local Government Act 1929 and the support, at a high level, for a more integrated approach to the provision of health care, many services and facilities, in particular those provided by GPs and the voluntary hospitals, remained outside the scope of local government. Consequently, health care provision was still an extremely haphazard affair with the quantity and quality of resources, facilities and services varying considerably from area to area and with planning and co-ordination being conspicuous by their absence. Furthermore, the union of preventive and curative medicine which had been secured, at least in part, by the legislation of 1929 survived only until 1948.

The Establishment of the NHS

In August 1930, whilst the MOsH were coming to terms with their increased responsibilities, the British Medical Association (BMA) first published its proposals 'for a general medical service for the nation'. They were republished in a slightly revised form in November 1938.[47] These proposals envisaged an expanded and comprehensive general medical service, to which everyone would have access. In order to enlarge the scope of their work it was proposed that GPs should take over responsibility for most of the maternity and child welfare services and for the treatment, but not the inspection, of school children, as well as a number of other health care activities. Almost certainly, the implementation of these proposals would have prevented the CHSs from evolving into a separate and distinctive component of the health care system. Instead, they would have been subsumed within an extended general practitioner service. Whether the CHSs would have flourished and developed under an arrangement of this kind is a matter for conjecture.

Although the BMA's proposals for reforming the health care system, together with the Sankey Commission's Report on the Voluntary Hospitals set up by the British Hospitals Association (1937), and the survey of British health services (Political and Economic Planning 1937), had demonstrated that 'the time for change was only too obviously over-ripe,'[48] it wasn't until the Second World War that the government began to respond, in a positive manner, to the need for a comprehensive health care system.

During the war there were a number a very important developments which paved the way for the establishment of the NHS in 1948. Firstly, through participation in the Emergency Medical Service, which was set up to cope with military and civilian casualties and to provide a degree of co-ordination between the municipal health services and the voluntary sector, senior members of the medical profession saw at first hand the very poor state of many municipal hospitals and the smaller voluntary hospitals. They also became aware of the considerable regional inequalities in health care provision.

Secondly, the publication of the Beveridge Report on Social Insurance and Allied Services in 1942, which was based on the assumption that a 'comprehensive national health service' would be set up after the War was over, raised public expectations to such an extent that the Coalition government felt that it had to make an appropriate gesture. Thus, in February 1943 the government announced its acceptance of the assumptions of the Beveridge Report, including a comprehensive health service.

Thirdly, after extensive discussions with the interests involved the government published a white paper, entitled *A National Health Service*, in February 1944. Rather than being a statement of the government's legislative intentions the white paper was designed to continue and to broaden the debate. According to the white paper the objective of a 'national health service' was to ensure that everyone, regardless of their means, had access to the best and most up-to- date medical and allied services available. It was argued that maximum use should be made of existing facilities, which met the required standards, and experience, adapting and adding to them wherever necessary. In addition, it was assumed that the local organisation of the service would be based on the county and county borough councils, with joint authorities being set up by them to run the hospital based services.

As far as the CHSs were concerned, the white paper acknowledged that:

Apart from the hospital and consultant and family doctor services, the comprehensive health service (had to) include arrangements for home nursing and midwifery and health visiting and the various kinds of local clinic and

similar services which (had) either been provided in the past under special statutory powers or (would) have to be established in the future.
Furthermore, the authorities responsible for managing these services would be expected to ensure that they were not 'provided as entirely separate entities, but rather as parts of the one new general duty to secure a whole provision of health' and that all the various activities involved were 'properly related to each other, to the personal or family doctor service and to the hospitals and consultants, and that they (were) arranged in the right way and in the right places to meet the area's needs'. It was also anticipated that when these services were 'arranged and regarded as parts of the one planned service of the wider area, there (would) be room for experiment and innovation in the way they (were) provided.'[49] Thus, at this stage, it was assumed that the CHSs would lose their separate identity and would become part of a fully integrated health care system. Integration, however, proved to be a chimera because in the subsequent debate and negotiations with the major interested parties both the wartime Coalition government and, more importantly, the post-war Labour government and its Minister of Health, Aneurin Bevan, were forced to make a number of compromises.

Of particular significance was the compromise reached in respect of the administrative arrangements for the NHS. In order to secure the support of the leaders of the medical profession it was necessary, amongst other things, to take account of their outright opposition to local authority control of the hospitals and their desire to maintain the independence of GPs. Consequently, completely new bodies, regional hospital boards, hospital management committees and boards of governors, were set up to run all the hospitals (i.e. municipal as well as voluntary) and executive councils, to administer the contracts of GPs together with those of dentists, pharmacists and opticians (i.e. family practitioners). To some extent these arrangements reflected the dominance which the curative approach to health care had secured over the preventive approach during the 20th Century.

Nevertheless, although local authorities were the least successful of the main protagonists in the struggle over the structure of the NHS and some would argue that on democratic grounds they should have been given administrative responsibility for the NHS as a whole, they did not lose out entirely. Because of the experience and expertise they had acquired in running health care services prior to the establishment of the NHS; the vigour with which they argued their case and the fact that they had the support of a leading member of the Labour cabinet, Herbert Morrison, they were given a role to play, albeit a limited one, in the administration of the NHS. Certain types of local authority, designated local health authorities, were given the task of developing community based health care services (excluding those provided by family practitioners). Moreover, under the provisions of the Education Act 1944, local education authorities retained their responsibility for the administration of the school medical service, which was renamed the school health service under this legislation.

In the words of Ham, the administrative structure which emerged from the negotiations between the government and the parties, with a particular interest in the way the NHS was to be administered, was 'a representation of of what was possible rather than what might have been desirable.'[50] Thus, instead of a unitary structure, which would have facilitated the development of a more integrated approach to the delivery of health care services, the NHS acquired what is generally referred as a tripartite structure; the three parts being:

i) the hospital authorities (i.e. regional hospital boards, hospital management committees and boards of governors);

ii) executive councils; and

iii) local health authorities.

Not surprisingly, this arrangement, which was to last until 1974, deepened the cleavages that existed between the HSs, the FPSs and the CHSs or local health services (LHSs), as they were known during the tripartite era, and made integration an unlikely prospect. Furthermore, it can be argued that 'tripartism' contributed more than anything else to the development of a separate identity for the CHSs since it meant that, for 25 years, they evolved in relative isolation, and in a somewhat different context, from other health care services. The nature of this context and the way it affected the development of the CHSs during the tripartite era are examined in the next two chapters.

Footnotes

1.   See D. Fraser, *The Evolution of the British Welfare State* (London: Macmillan, 1973) for a fuller discussion of the Liverpool Sanitary Act 1846 and the conditions which gave rise to the need for legislation of this kind, especially Chapter 3 and the supporting documents.

2.   C. Ham, *Health Policy in Britain*, 2nd Edition (London: Macmillan, 1985) p. 9.

3.   W. Frazer, *A History of English Public Health 1834- 1939* (London: Bailliere, Tindall and Cox, 1950), p. 124.

4.   R. Lambert, 'A Victorian National Health Service: State Vaccination 1855-71', *The Historical Journal,* 1962, Vol. V, No. 1, p. 1.

5.   D. Fraser, op. cit., p. 85.

6.   R. Lambert, op. cit., p. 14.

7.   W. Frazer, op. cit., p. 370.

8.   Quotation from William Rathbone's Memoir. Extracts reproduced in G. Hardy, *William Rathbone and the Early History of District Nursing* (Ormskirk: G.W.and A. Hesketh, 1981).

9.   Ibid., p. 9.

10.   For further discussion of the constitution of the Manchester and Salford Reform Association and its activities see R. Hale, 'The History of Health Visiting' in R. Hale, M. Loveland and G. Owen, *The Principles and Practice of Health Visiting* (Oxford: Pergamon Press, 1968).

11.   Ibid., pp. 8-9.

12. Extract from letters of Florence Nightingale on health visiting in rural districts.

13. R. Hale, op. cit., p. 10.

14. These were 1st April 1905, in respect of the use of the term 'midwife', and 1st April 1910, in respect of attending women in childbirth, except under the direction of a qualified medical practitioner.

15. W. Frazer, op. cit., p. 250.

16. M.C. Versuylen, 'Midwives, medical men and 'poor women labouring of child': lying-in hospitals in eighteenth century London', in H. Roberts (ed.), *Women, Health and Reproduction* (London: Routledge and Kegan Paul, 1981), p. 43.

17. For further information on the provisions of the Midwives Act 1902, see G.F. McCleary, *The Maternity and Child Welfare Movement* (London: J.S. King and Son Ltd, 1935), especially Chapter X.

18. Local Government Board, *Report of the Medical Officer 1917/18*, Cd 9169. See G.F. McCleary, *The Early History of the Infant Welfare Movement* (London: J.S. King Ltd, 1933) for a more detailed account of the development of services and facilities for infants and expectant and nursing mothers during this period.

19. Ministry of Health, *First Annual Report 1919/20*, Cmd 923, p. 44.

20. Ministry of Health, *Report of Chief Medical Officer for 1919/20*, Cmd 978, p. 44. It is interesting to note that similar sentiments were expressed 60 years later in the Declaration of Alma-Ata (see Chapter 9).

21. W. Frazer, op. cit., p. 323.

22. The London School Board appointed a school medical officer in 1890 and the Bradford Board in 1893.

23. J. Hay, *The Origins of the Liberal Welfare Reforms 1906-1914* (London: Macmillan, 1975), p. 44.

24. B. Gilbert, for example, argues in *The Evolution of National Insurance in Britain* (London: Michael Joseph, 1966) that the 1907 Act, together with the Education (Provision of Meals) Act 1906, 'marked the beginning of the construction of the welfare state', p. 102.

25. The Board of Education made it clear in Circular 596 (1908) that '.. only those children shall be treated in a school clinic for whose treatment adequate provision cannot otherwise be made, whether by the parents or by voluntary associations or institutions, such as hospitals, or through the agency of the Poor Law' and that the Board would only sanction the establishment of clinics on this basis. The first such clinic was opened in Bradford in 1908.

26. W. Frazer, op. cit., p. 327.

27. The Cambridge dental clinic (or Institute) was funded initially by a private benefactor. However, with the passing of the 1907 Act, the local education authority decided to take over financial responsibility for it and in March 1909 appointed the first full time school dentist.

28. For more details of dental health education in the 1900s and 1910s see E. Towner, *History of Dental Health Education*, Health Education Authority Occasional Paper No.5, 1987?, Chapter 3.

29. W. Frazer, op. cit., p. 401.

30. D. Fraser, op. cit., p. 166.

31. E. Towner, op. cit., Chapter 4.

32. C. Webster, 'The health of the school child during the depression' in N. Parry and D. McNair (eds.), *The Fitness of the Nation- Physical and Health Education in the Nineteeth and Twentieth*

Centuries, Proceedings of 1982 Annual Conference of the History of Education Society of Great Britain (Leicester: History of Education Society, 1983), pp. 70-85.

33.   The rate of maternal mortality (i.e. deaths from pregnancy and childbearing per 1000 live births between the end of the First and Second World Wars was as follows: 1918 3.55; 1919 4.12; 1920 4.12; 1921 3.71; 1922 3.58; 1923 3.60; 1924 3.70; 1925 3.86; 1926 3.87; 1927 3.83; 1928 4.15; 1929 4.07; 1930 4.16; 1931 3.93; 1932 4.01; 1933 4.32; 1934 4.39; 1935 3.41 (change in the basis of calculation); 1936 3.19; 1937 2.79; 1938 2.70; 1939 2.57; 1940 2.24; 1941 2.26; 1942 2.02; 1943 1.84; 1944 1.53; 1945 1.47. Source: A.Macfarlane and M.Mugford, *Birth Counts: Statistics of pregnancy and childbirth. Tables* (London: HMSO, 1984), Table A10.1.

34.   Investigations into the problem of maternal mortality were initially undertaken by a team led by Dr Janet Campbell (Senior Medical Officer at the Ministry of Health during the 1920s). Reports covering every aspect of the problem were published in 1924 and 1927. These prompted the Minister of Health, Neville Chamberlain, to appoint, in 1929, a departmental committee of inquiry, chaired by Sir George Newman (Chief Medical Officer at the Ministry of Health), 'to advise upon the application to maternal mortality and morbidity of the medical and surgical knowledge available'. An interim report was published in 1930 and a final report in 1932. Finally, an investigation supervised by Dr Hugh Macewen (Senior Medical Officer at the Ministry of Health during the 1930s) was carried out between 1934 and 1937.

35.   Minor welfare authorities were the county district councils, which had adopted the provisions of the Notification of Births Act 1907 and (Extension) Act 1915 in their area, and were thereby entitled, under Section 1 of the Maternity and Child Welfare Act 1918, to make arrangements for attending to the health of expectant and nursing mothers and of pre-school children.

36.   The National Milk Scheme provided for the supply of one pint of milk a day to expectant mothers during the last months of pregnancy, at 2d per pint or free of charge to those with low incomes.

37.   See footnote 33.

38.   N. Wilson, *Municipal Health Services* (London: George Allen and Unwin, 1946), p. 26.

39.   Ministry of Health and Department of Health for Scotland, *A National Health Service*, Cmd 6502 (London: HMSO, 1944), p. 10.

40.   R. Hale, op. cit., p. 12.

41.   Ibid.

42.   Editorial, *Health Education Journal*, No 11, 1953, pp. 1-6.

43.   J.E. Pater, *The Making of the National Health Service* (London: King Edward's Hospital Fund for London, 1981), p. 7.

44.   See Ministry of Health; Consultative Council on Medical and Allied Services, *Interim report on the future provision of medical and allied services*, [Dawson Report], Cmd 693 (London: HMSO, 1920) for further details.

45.   W. Frazer, op. cit., p. 389.

46.   Ministry of Health, *Report of the Chief Medical Officer for 1928*, p. 95.

47.   *The British Medical Association's Proposals for a General Medical Service for the Nation.* A BMA pamphlet, 1938.

48.   J.E. Pater, op. cit., p. 20.

49.   A National Health Service, op. cit., p. 38.

50.   C. Ham, op. cit., p. 17.

Chapter 3

The Tripartite Era: Administrative Arrangements

Perhaps the most striking feature of the 'tripartite' structure was its relative longevity. Despite the fact that it was the product of compromise and was a far from ideal arrangement for the management of what was intended to be, in the words of Section 1 of the National Health Service Act 1946 (1946 Act): 'a comprehensive health service designed to secure improvement in the physical and mental health of the people of England and Wales and the prevention, diagnosis and treatment of illness', it survived for longer than anyone might reasonably have anticipated. A number of commentators argue that this was because, 'on the whole the NHS adapted itself successfully' to changes in the nature of society and the state of medical knowledge which took place during the 1950s and 1960s. Furthermore, in their view, 'much of the credit for the adaptability must go to the merits of the original structure, combined with the fact that the detailed arrangements were laid down by regulations, which could be amended to meet changing circumstances.' [1]

Nevertheless, as Figure 3.1 illustrates, the tripartite structure institutionalised the split, within the primary health care sector, between local (or community) health services on the one hand and FPSs on the other, and between primary and secondary health care services, and in so doing it seriously impeded the development of a truly integrated NHS.

For the CHSs the tripartite arrangement meant that, to some extent, there was little change from the pre-NHS system of administration, with local authorities continuning to exercise responsibility for maternity and child welfare clinics, midwifery, health visiting and vaccination and immunisation, as well as environmental health services. In addition, as Ham comments, the key local official

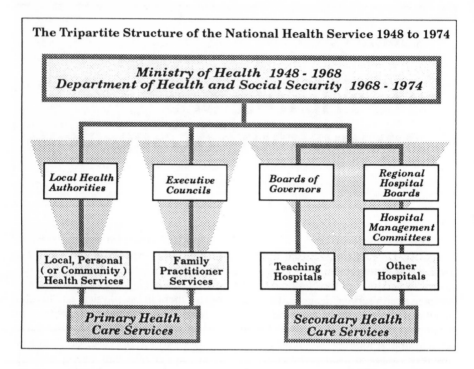

The Tripartite Structure of the National Health Service 1948 to 1974

Ministry of Health 1948 - 1968
Department of Health and Social Security 1968 - 1974

| Local Health Authorities | Executive Councils | Boards of Governors | Regional Hospital Boards |

Hospital Management Committees

| Local, Personal (or Community) Health Services | Family Practitioner Services | Teaching Hospitals | Other Hospitals |

Primary Health Care Services   *Secondary Health Care Services*

(England and Wales)

Figure 3.1

Notes

a. Initially there were, in England and Wales:

146 local health authorities;

138 executive councils;

14 regional hospital boards; 36 boards of governors and 376 hospital management committees.

As a result of changes in the structure of local government and in the pattern of executive councils and hospital authorities during the tripartite era, at 31st March 1974 (i.e. just prior to the reorganisation of the NHS) there were:

175 local health authorities;

132 executive councils;

15 regional hospital boards; 35 boards of governors and 291 hospital management committees.

A complete list of local health authorities can be found in Appendix I.

b.   For the most part executive council areas were identical with those of local health authorities.[2] As Webster points out, the principle of coterminosity (i.e. shared boundaries) was initially adopted because officials took the view that: 'if and when the time came to link the (executive council) to some other administrative body, that body should clearly be the local health authority: and it would be folly meantime to set up yet another area pattern differing from that of the local health authorities'.[3]

c.   During the tripartite era the status of the school health service, which is not included in this diagram, was that of a supplementary education service and it was administered by local education authorities[4] under the provisions of the Education Act 1944. In other words it was not formally part of the NHS.

d.   The 1946 Act also established the Central Health Services Council made up of members drawn from the major health professions and a variety of other sources and charged with the duty of advising 'the Minister upon such general matters relating to the services provided under (the) Act or any services provided by local health authorities in their capacity as such authorities as the Council (thought) fit and upon any question referred to (it) by him relating to these services.'[5]

e.   The Ministry of Health was abolished in November 1968 and its functions, together with those of the Ministry of Social Security and National Assistance Board, were transferred to the newly established Department of Health and Social Security (DHSS), headed by a Secretary of State. The holder of this post has been known officially as the Secretary of State for Social Services.

f.   Responsibility for the health service in Wales was transferred from the DHSS to the Welsh Office on the 1st April 1969.

remained the MOH and the services were still funded by a mix of central government grants and local rates.[6] However, although there were some similarities between the pre- and post-1948 administrative arrangements for the CHSs there were also a number of important differences. These arose, in the main, from the provisions of the 1946 Act, which extended, as well as consolidated, the role of local government in respect of the CHSs and paved the way for their continued growth and development during the tripartite era.

The 1946 Act also contained a more comprehensive and detailed set of prescriptions for the provision of CHSs than any other piece of legislation either before or since. The whole of Part III was devoted to 'health services provided by local health authorities' and there were further references to local health authorities and LHSs elsewhere in the act. It is interesting to note, however, that, as Webster indicates, in the first version of the bill the bulk of the local authority services were dealt with 'in Part II under hospitals, leaving only residual clinic services to be listed in Part IV, following the more substantial·general medical services (i.e. those provided by GPs) in Part III.' The promotion of LHSs to Part III, in the 1946 version, 'created a logical order, beginning with nationalised hospital services, continuing with municipalised services around the nucleus of health centres, and ending with Part IV private contractor arrangements.'[7]

Included within the 1946 Act were provisions relating to:

● local health authorities (Section 19 and the Fourth Schedule);

● proposals for the provision of services by local health authorities (Section 20);

- health centres (Sections 21 and 46);
- care of mothers and young children (Section 22);
- midwifery (Section 23);
- health visiting (Section 24);
- home nursing (Section 25);
- vaccination and immunisation (Section 26);
- ambulance services (Section 27);
- prevention of illness, and the care and after-care of persons suffering from illness or mental defectiveness (Section 28);
- domestic help (Section 29);
- grants to, and accounts of, local health authorities (Sections 53 and 55);
- default powers of the Minister of Health (Section 57); and
- the use of premises and equipment of local health authorities by other authorities and supply of goods by local health authorities (Sections 63 and 64).

Thus, the 1946 Act was very much a landmark in the history of the CHSs and some of its provisions, together with those of the Education Act 1944, had far reaching implications for the kind of administrative and financial framework within which the services developed between 1948 and 1974. Consequently it is necessary to examine these provisions in some detail and to consider the ways in which they were applied, and affected by legislative and other developments, during the tripartite era. A similar approach is adopted in Chapter 4 in respect of the provisions of this legislation which relate to specific services.

In this chapter consideration is also given to the relationship between local health authorities and the centre (i.e. the Ministry of Health/DHSS); between local education authorities and the centre (i.e. Ministry of Education/Department of Education and Science),[8] in respect of the school health service, and between local health authorities and other parts of the NHS. To complete the picture, the last part of this chapter is devoted to an examination of the lengthy debate that preceded the 1974 reorganisation of the NHS. This debate was of particular significance for the CHSs since its outcome had a profound effect on the way in which they were to be managed after 1974.

Whilst considering topics of this kind it is important to remember that they have a contemporary as well as an historical significance. Many of the issues and problems which arose during the tripartite era, and in some cases even earlier, still preoccupy those who are currently responsible for managing the CHSs. As a result it will be necessary to return to some of them in later chapters.

Local Health Authorities

As has already been mentioned, from 1948 to 1974 responsibility for the adminis-tration of CHSs, at the local level, rested primarily with local health authorities. These were defined by Section 19 of the 1946 Act as the councils of the (adminis-trative) counties and county boroughs. At that time the administrative counties, including London, and the county boroughs were the most important local auth-orities, in terms of their status and range of functions,[9] and in most cases they already had a considerable amount of expertise in running health care services.

However, it meant that many county district councils (i.e. non-county borough, urban and rural district councils), which also had some experience in this field (i.e. the minor welfare authorities), lost their health care responsibilities to the admin-istrative counties. As the Ministry of Health's *Annual Report for the year ended 31st March 1949* points out: 'On the appointed day (i.e. 5th July 1948) the county authorities in England and Wales took over responsibility for domiciliary mid-wifery, health visiting, domestic help, clinics and other arrangements for the care of mothers and young children previously provided, in the case of midwifery, by 43 authorities with delegate powers, and in the case of other services, by 261 welfare authorities.' Nevertheless, according to the Ministry, 'despite the size of the task... the authorities succeeded in effecting a smooth changeover.'[10]

Where it appeared 'to the Minister to be expedient in the interests of the efficiency of any services provided by local health authorities' he could, under the provisions of Section 19, constitute joint boards of these authorities to discharge their heath care responsibilities. The main reason for this provision was that, as the information in Table 3.1 indicates, some local health authorities had very small populations (i.e. under 75,000) and it was anticipated that, notwithstanding their previous experience in this field, they would find it difficult, on their own, to carry out their health care functions in an effective and efficient manner. As it happened no use was ever made of this provision, probably because of opposition and resistance to the principle of joint bodies from the authorities themselves.

Consequently it is rather ironic that only ten years later the Local Government Act 1958, by providing for a wide measure of delegation of the health care functions of county councils to certain of their district councils, paved the way for the involvement of relatively small administrative units in the running of LHSs. Dele-gation could be claimed by non-county borough or urban district councils with a population of at least 60,000 and by other county districts, if the Minister agreed that special circumstances made this desirable. The main purpose of delegation was to ensure that decisions regarding the organisation and delivery of personal health services were taken as close to the clients as possible. In other words it was designed to make the LHSs more accessible to those who used them and more responsive to local wishes.

TABLE 3.1 *Local Health Authorities : Numbers and Size 1951*

Population	County Boroughs		Administrative Counties*	
	number	%	number	%
less than 75,000	19	23	11	17
75,000 to 99,999	15	18	3	5
100,000 to 249,999	35	42	13	21
250,000 to 499,999	9	11	20	32
500,000 to 999,999	4	5	9	14
1,000,000 and above	1	1	7	11
Total	83	100	63	100

Population	Total	
	number	%
less than 75,000	30	21
75,000 to 99,999	18	12
100,000 to 249,999	48	33
250,000 to 499,999	29	20
500,000 to 999,999	13	9
1,000,000 and above	8	5
Total	146	100

*Including the Isles of Scilly

For further details see Appendix I.

Source: *Census Reports 1951.*

The delegation arrangements were set out in schemes made by the county district councils concerned, after consultation with the county council, and approved by the Minister. Schemes prescribed the conditions under which the county districts were to exercise their functions on behalf of the county council and the procedures for the submission of spending proposals by county district councils to the county council for its approval or otherwise and the reimbursement of approved expenditure by the county council. County district councils that wished to take advantage of these delegation provisions had to ensure that their schemes were made within one year of the passing of the Local Government Act 1958, otherwise they had to wait for 10 years. In fact, at that time, 29 county districts[11] made schemes and, in this way, were able to play an important role in the provision and development of LHSs. However, even where delegation schemes were in operation the county council formally remained the local health authority and retained ultimate responsibility for the services.

When local government was reorganised in the Greater London area in 1965 responsibility for LHSs was transferred from the top tier county authorities (i.e. the London and Middlesex County Councils, which were abolished and the Surrey, Kent, Essex and Hertfordshire County Councils, which lost part of the territory to the new county of Greater London) to the second tier London boroughs. Again this symbolised the desire to have personal services of this kind administered as close to their clients as possible.

As a result of this reorganisation and a number of other smaller scale changes in the pattern of local authorities there was a net increase of 29 in the number of local health authorities during the 1960s. Details of the numbers and populations of local health authorities in 1971 are provided in Table 3.2.

TABLE 3.2 *Local Health Authorities : Numbers and Size 1971*

Population	County Boroughs		Administrative Counties [a,b]	
	number	%	number	%
less than 75,000	16	19	9	15
75,000 to 99,999	18	32	1	2
100,000 to 249,999	34	41	11	19
250,000 to 499,999	11	13	19	32
500,000 to 999,999	3	4	12	20
1,000,000 and above	1	1	7	12
Total	83	100	59	100
Population	London Boroughs [c]		Total [d]	
	number	%	number	%
less than 75,000	1	3	26	15
75,000 to 99,999	0	0	19	11
100,000 to 249,999	22	67	67	38
250,000 to 499,999	10	30	40	23
500,000 to 999,999	0	0	15	8
1,000,000 and above	0	0	8	5
Total	33	100	175	100

Notes

a. Including the Isles of Scilly.

b. Not including the Greater London Council, which was responsible for the administration of the ambulance service in greater London.

c. Including the City of London Corporation.

d. Excluding the delegatee authorities.

For further details see Appendix I.

Source: *Census Reports 1971.*

Part III of the 1946 Act imposed the following duties on local health authorities:

- the provision of health centres;
- the making of arrangements for the care of expectant and nursing mothers and of children under 5 who were not attending school;
- the securing of the services of an adequate number of midwives in their area;

- the provision of a comprehensive health visiting service;
- the provision of a comprehensive home nursing service;
- the making of arrangements for the vaccination and immunisation of children by either their own staff or GPs; and
- the provision of an ambulance service for their area.

Local health authorities were also empowered to make arrangements for the purposes of preventing illness; for the care and after-care of persons suffering from illness or mental defectiveness and for the provision of domestic help to households who were in special need of it. The provision of a family planning service for their area was added to this list of duties and powers by the National Health Service (Family Planning) Act 1967.

However, despite the undoubted importance of these services in terms of the contribution that they made to the health and well-being of various groups within the community, they were by no means the most extensive and expensive of the services provided by administrative counties, county boroughs and, after 1965, London boroughs. The LHSs accounted for less than 5% of the budgets of these authorities. Consequently, there was always a danger that they could be overshadowed by one or more of the other services for which the authorities were responsible. The range and variety of the other service responsibilities of these authorities is illustrated by the information in Table 3.3.

Of the services listed in Table 3.3, LHSs had most in common with the welfare services, which were provided under the National Assistance Act 1948. This was because there was a considerable overlap between the clients of the two groups of services, with the elderly and the handicapped, in particular, receiving a considerable amount of support from both of them.

Under the provisions of this act local welfare authorities had a duty to provide:

- residential accommodation for persons who because of age, infirmity or any other circumstances were in need of care and attention which would not otherwise be available to them, and temporary accommodation for persons who were in urgent need of it through circumstances which could not have been foreseen (i.e. for the homeless) or in such circumstances as the authority in any particular case determined; and
- welfare services for certain physically handicapped persons the blind, deaf or dumb; others who were substantially and permanently handicapped by illness, injury or congenital deformity, or such other disability as might be prescribed by the Minister, and the mentally disabled.

TABLE 3.3 *The Major Service Responsibilities of Administrative Counties, County Boroughs and London Boroughs in the Late 1960s*

Services	Administrative Counties [a]	County Boroughs [a]	London Boroughs
* Education (inc. the School Health Service)	/	/	/[b]
* Libraries	/	/	/
* Welfare	/	/	/
* Child Care	/	/	/
* Police	/[c]	/[c]	
* Fire	/	/	
* Sewerage and Sewage Disposal		/	/[d]
* Refuse Collection and Disposal		/	/[d]
* Highways, Lighting and Parking	/	/	/[d]
* Parks and Open Spaces		/	/[d]
* Town and Country Planning	/	/	/[d]
* Housing	/	/[d]	

Notes

a. Administrative counties and county boroughs were abolished in 1974, when the structure of local government, outside Greater London, was reorganised at the same time as the structure of the NHS.

b. Only the 20 outer London boroughs were local education authorities. In inner London, education was the responsibility of the Inner London Education Authority.

c. During the 1960s many of the administrative counties and county boroughs were combined to form joint police authorities/forces.

d. These responsibilities were shared with the Greater London Council.

Services included the giving of instruction to persons, either in their own homes or elsewhere, in ways of overcoming some of the effects of their disabilities; the provision of work in workshops and homes and the provision of recreational facilities.

Because of their overlap LHSs and local welfare services were both the responsibility, at national level, of the Ministry of Health/DHSS and, at local level, a number of local health/welfare authorities designed their committee and departmental structures in ways that facilitated the development of a more integrated approach towards their administration. In addition, the delegation schemes introduced by the Local Government Act 1958 (see above) could also include a number of welfare services.

The Health Committee

With regard to the internal structure of local health authorities, under the provisions of the Fourth Schedule of the 1946 Act every local health authority had 'to establish a health committee' and, except in matters of urgency, the authority had to act through it as far as its heath care functions were concerned. This was designed to ensure that health care matters received the specialist attention they deserved. In addition, since non-council members could be co-opted onto the health committee, provided they did not constitute a majority, it was possible to secure, by this means, the services of experts in different aspects of personal health care.

In meeting their obligation to establish a health committee some local authorities took the opportunity, with the Minister's approval, to foster closer links between their health and welfare services by opting for a joint committee. By the mid-1960s approximately one quarter of the local health authorities had either established a joint health and welfare committee or made their health committee responsible for local welfare as well as LHSs (see Appendix I for details).

The principal functions of the members of health (and welfare) committees, as far as the personal health services were concerned, were to:

- discuss and make decisions concerning various aspects of service provision, in the light of advice, guidance and recommendations from the MOH and his colleagues (e.g. staffing levels; the development of new premises; making of grants to voluntary organisations);

- consider and approve reports from officers, of which the most important was the MOH's annual report on the health of the county or borough, and subcommittees (see below);

- receive and consider communications of relevance to personal health services from external sources, at the national level (Ministry of Health circulars; official reports), and at the local level (e.g. letters from voluntary organisations; reports from the executive council; petitions);

- monitor the day-to-day administration and delivery of services by the staff of the health department (e.g. by reviewing statistical data; by making inspection visits to premises and meeting staff and clients);

- appoint and nominate members of other bodies (e.g. hospital management committees; executive councils; regional federations of the Queen's Institute of District Nursing; community relations councils); and

- assess the implications of developments elsewhere within the authority for the LHSs.

In most local health authorities it was the chairman[12] of the health committee, who played the key role in the affairs of the committee and, together with the MOH, in promoting and protecting the interests of those with responsibility for the delivery of services on a day-to-day basis and their clients. Of particular importance, in this respect, was his effectiveness in the budgetary negotiations since the share of resources allocated to the LHSs depended, to an extent, on the political acumen of the chairman.

In those local health authorities where party politics played an important part in the conduct of affairs (i.e. some of the administrative counties; most of the county boroughs and all of the London boroughs) it was common practice for the committee chairman to be a leading member of the majority party and for the party political balance on the committee to reflect that of the whole council. However, during the 1950s and 1960s, even in authorities of this kind committees still operated, to a significant extent, on the basis of bipartisanship.

As well as the main committee local health authorities often established subcommittees to deal with specialised aspects of service provision, such as mental health, the welfare of disabled persons, family planning and the appointment of staff. Furthermore, the Minister of Health, in Circular 118/47, recommended that, where appropriate, administrative counties should set up area subcommittees of the health committee to provide for a more 'localist' input into the administration of LHSs.

In addition, Section 22 of the 1946 Act, which dealt with the care of mothers and young children, gave recognition to the fact that in implementing the Education Act 1944 a number of county authorities had introduced schemes of divisional administration for their education services, including the school medical service. Consequently, if there was to be close relations between the pre-school child health service and the school health service in these counties it was necessary to have corresponding schemes of divisional administration for their child welfare services. To this end Section 22 stated that:

> *Regulations may provide, in the case of areas where under Part III of the First Schedule of the Education Act 1944, schemes of divisional administration relating to the functions of local education authorities with respect to school health services are in force, for the making, variation and revocation of corresponding schemes of divisional administration relating to the functions of local health authorities... with respect to the care of children who have not attained the age of five years and are not attending primary schools maintained by a local education authority ...*

According to the Ministry of Health's *Annual Report for the Year ended 31st March 1949*, 37 out of the 63 counties (i.e. 59%) had 'adopted some measure of decentralisation,'[13] thereby facilitating the involvement of local people in the running of services. However, information from *The Municipal Year Book* indicates that by 1973 the percentage of counties with some form of area or divisional administration for their LHSs had fallen to about 36%.[14] Thus, there appears to have been some loss of interest in decentralisation during the tripartite era. Nevertheless, as far as CHSs are concerned, decentralisation is still on the 'administrative agenda' and it is therefore considered in greater depth in Chapters 8 and 10.

The Medical Officer of Health

Between 1948 and 1974 the chief officer with responsibility for the administration of local health and related services remained the MOH. The continuing importance of this post was reflected in the fact that under the provisions of the Local Government Act 1933 every local authority was required to appoint a MOH and, in the case of administrative counties, London boroughs and approximately half of the county boroughs, the holders of this office could only be dismissed with the approval of the Minister of Health.[15] Furthermore, regulations prescribed that only duly qualified medical practitioners could be appointed as MOsH and in the case of county boroughs with populations of over 50,000 the holder of the office also had to have an appropriate post-graduate qualification (i.e. a diploma in public health or state medicine).

Figures produced by the BMA for the Mallaby Committee on the Staffing of Local Government, which reported in 1967, show that local health authorities employed, either as MOsH and their assistants or as medical officers engaged on clinical duties (e.g. at child welfare clinics), only 3.7% of the total number of medical practitioners. Recruitment, however, was a problem because there was, at that time, a national shortage of medical practitioners and local health authorities were in competition with the other two parts of the NHS for their services. The situation was also exacerbated by the fact that the remuneration and conditions of service of medical practitioners employed by local authorities were generally less favourable than those of their colleagues working elsewhere in the NHS[16] and there was a great deal of uncertainty regarding the future of public health.

The MOsH of the local health authorities were invariably the chief officer of the health department although this was not, in fact, a statutory requirement. In this position they were responsible for the management of not only personal health, but also environmental health services as they had been since the 19th Century. By the 1950s and 1960s the environmental health responsibilities of MOsH included:

- the control of infectious diseases;

- food safety and hygiene;

- port health;

- public health aspects of planning and services like housing;

- the implementation of legislation relating to clean air;

- control of the diseases of animals in so far as they affected human health; and

- enforcement duties relating to environmental conditions at places of work.

Thus, MOsH had an extremely varied portfolio of responsibilities and were in a position to secure a degree of integration between the environmental and personal health care services.

In addition, by the mid-1960s about one third of the local health authorities had either established a joint health and welfare department headed by the MOH or appointed the MOH head of both their health and welfare departments. Both of these arrangements reflected the authority's acknowledgement of the interdependence between the local health and welfare services to which reference has already been made.

As well as their health and, in certain cases, welfare responsibilities, in all but two of the local education authorities the MOH was also the principal school medical officer. Like the post of MOH, that of principal school medical officer was a statutory appointment. Under the provisions of The Handicapped Pupils and School Health Service Regulations 1945 (1945 Regulations) every local education authority was required to appoint a school medical officer to 'be responsible to the authority for the efficient discharge of their functions in relation to the health and well-being of pupils who (were) within the scope of the school health service.'[17]

The main justification for effectively combining the posts of MOH and school medical officer was that such an arrangement provided a means of integrating the LHSs and school health services. As pointed out in Chapter 2, this practice had been commended by the central government as early as 1909.

Until the reorganisation of local government in the Greater London area in 1965, the same local authority was responsible for both the local health and education services so the arrangement did not present any particular problems. However, in 1965 the administrative link between education and health in inner London was broken with the creation of the Inner London Education Authority. Consequently, to ensure that this did not adversely affect the school health service, the 13 new local health authorities in inner London (i.e. the 12 inner London boroughs and the City of London Corporation) were required to make schemes jointly with the Inner London Education Authority for the co-ordination of school and other health services, by the joint use of professional staff, premises and equipment, and by consultation on the qualifications, conditions of service and appointment of relevant professional staff. Such a requirement was a clear demonstration of the value of close co-operation between the school health services and LHSs.

During the tripartite era one major development reduced the range of responsibilities of the MOH. This was the implementation of the recommendations of the Seebohm Committee on Local Authority and Allied Personal Social Services. The Seebohm Committee was set up in 1965 with the following terms of reference: 'to review the organisation and responsibilities of the local authority personal social services in England and Wales, and to consider what changes are desirable to secure an effective family service.'

The committee reported in 1968 and amongst its recommendations, which were put into effect by the Local Authority Social Services Act 1970, was the concept of the social services department. Under the provisions of this act every social service authority was required to establish a social services department headed by a director of social services. The services, which became the responsibility of the new department, included:

- family case work and social work with the sick and the mentally disordered;

- day centres, clubs, adult training centres and workshops for the mentally disordered;

- the day care of children under 5, day nurseries and childminding;

- the care of unsupported mothers, including residential care;

- residential accommodation for those who could not live at home but did not require continuing medical supervision; and

- home helps.

All of these had previously been the concern, either wholly or in part, of the MOH. In the words of Ham: 'the main effect of the Seebohm reforms was to divorce those local authority health services deemed to involve mainly medical skills ... from those services deemed to involve mainly social work skills.'[18]

The Relationships of Medical Officers of Health

The principal relationships of MOsH, from which their major roles and duties can be derived, are illustrated in Figure 3.2 and discussed below.

Underpinning the **relationship with members** was the statutory requirement that MOsH were to inform themselves 'as far as practicable respecting all matters affecting or likely to affect the public health (in their area) ... and be prepared to advise (their authority) on any such matter).' Nevertheless, despite the general nature of this prescription, in their dealings with council members MOsH normally had most contact with the chairman of the health or joint health and welfare committee. Indeed, in a local authority setting, the relationship between chief officers and their committee chairmen was, and still is, one of the most crucial as far as the making and implementation of policy are concerned. This is because the chief officer and chairman are the principal representatives of what are generally regarded as the two main ingredients of effective public policies, namely professional expertise and political acceptability.

However, as one of the research volumes of the Maud Report on the Management of Local Government (1967), points out 'personal enquiries and written comments... revealed considerable differences in the scope and quality of officer-member relationships, as between authorities and even within the same authority.'[19] This observation applied as much to relations between MOsH and chairmen of health committees as to those between other chief officers and their committee chairmen.

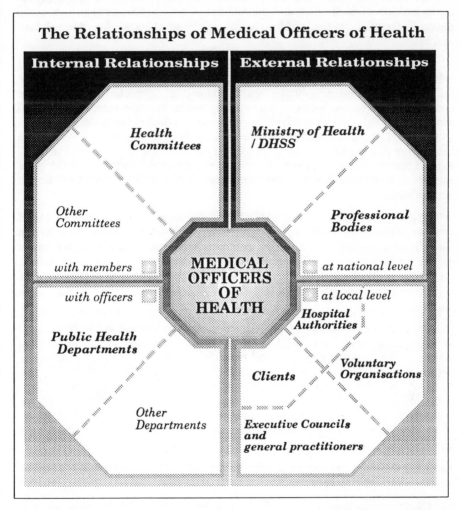

The Relationships of Medical Officers of Health

Internal Relationships | **External Relationships**

Health Committees

Ministry of Health / DHSS

Other Committees

Professional Bodies

with members

MEDICAL OFFICERS OF HEALTH

at national level

with officers

at local level

Hospital Authorities

Public Health Departments

Voluntary Organisations

Clients

Other Departments

Executive Councils and general practitioners

(England and Wales)

Figure 3.2

Factors affecting the nature of the relationship between the MOH and the chairman of the health committee included the traditions and culture of the authority concerned (e.g. the degree of party politicisation; the extent to which councillors participated in the making and implementation of policy; the degree of contact between councillors and staff, other than chief officers); the personalities of the holders of each office and the amount of time which the chairman could devote to the affairs of the health committee and his/her knowledge of health care matters.

At one extreme there were some authorities where there was 'a continuous relationship of trust.'[20] In this kind of relationship the MOH briefed the chairman fully before each meeting of the health committee, supported him during the meeting and consulted with him when taking action after the meeting; discussed aspects of health care policy and, in some cases, administrative detail with the chairman on a regular basis between meetings and collaborated with the chairman in ensuring that health care matters received the attention they deserved at meetings (of the whole council; chief officers and party groups). However, at the other extreme there were authorities where contacts between the MOH and the chairman were minimal.

Similarly the extent to which MOsH had contact with other councillors varied from authority to authority. In most cases, however, it was usually limited to liaison with the chairman of the education committee, in respect of the school health service, and with other committee chairmen on issues with health care implications; the provision of information on health care matters to enable members to fulfil their constituency role and the organisation of visits to premises run by the health department.

Turning to **relationships with officers** in an Appendix to the Report of the Working Party on Medical Administrators (1972), the point is made that 'as chief officer of the health department and principal medical officer to the education authority' the MOH was responsible 'for the planning and control of considerable resources in terms of skilled manpower and money' and had become 'increasingly involved in management functions relating to the assessment of objectives, the evaluation of services, and the determination of priorities.'[21] The principal groups of staff for whom the MOH had managerial responsibility during the tripartite era are shown in Table 3.4.

TABLE 3.4 *Groups of Staff for Whom Medical Officers of Health had Managerial Responsibility 1948 to 1974*

* Full-time and part-time medical officers, who were primarily concerned with maternity and child welfare; the mental health service; the prevention of illness and the care and after-care of those suffering from illness.

* Public health inspectors, who were principally involved with environmental health matters.

* Health visitors.

* Home nurses.

* Domiciliary midwives.
* Ambulance officers, drivers and attendants.
* Chiropodists (from the late 1950s and early 1960s).
* Domiciliary occupational therapists (from the 1950s).[a,b]
* Domestic helps.[a]
* Psychiatric social workers and mental health service support staff.[a]
* Nursery matrons and nursery nurses.[a]
* Administrative assistants and clerical officers.

Notes

a. With the implementation of the Seebohm recommendations (see above), managerial responsibility for these groups of staff was transferred from the MOH to the director of social services.

b. In the case of occupational therapy, the profession expressed considerable concern at the prospect of occupational therapists no longer being under direct medical control. However, despite these protestations, most occupational therapists employed by local authorities were transferred to the new personal social services departments. As Thomas comments, these organisational changes, together with the provisions of the Chronically Sick and Disabled Persons Act 1970 (which greatly extended the duties of local authorities in respect of the substantially and permanently handicapped) actually heralded 'a new era in (community) occupational therapy',[22] by giving community occupational therapists more scope to apply their skills.

However, as these groups of staff grew in size and became more professionalised so the MOH's managerial role gradually changed. Although, in organisational terms the staff of the health department remained subordinate and accountable to him he became far less involved in their supervision on a day-to-day basis and relied more and more on managers drawn from each of the staff groups concerned.

In the case of the three community nursing professions (i.e. health visiting; home nursing and domiciliary midwifery), many authorities initially appointed a superintendent health visitor, superintendent or principal nursing officer and a non-medical supervisor of midwives for this purpose. However, as Levitt and Wall point out, with the growth and expansion of local authority nursing services during the tripartite era, this pattern began to change and by the second half of the 1960s a relatively large number of local health authorities had appointed a chief nursing officer to organise and direct the work of all their nursing staff. [23]

Thus, the Mallaby Committee on the Staffing of Local Government (1967) was able to report that 'there was a great deal of support ... for the organisation of the nursing services of a local health authority under a principal nursing officer directly responsible to the medical officer of health.'[24] Indeed the Royal College of Nursing went even further and recommended that these services should be put into a separate unit, a nursing division, under the direction of a principal nursing officer with principal officer status and only responsible to the MOH in his/her capacity as head of the personal health services as a whole.

Consequently, it was hardly surprisingly that the principal recommendation of the Mayston Working Party on Management Structure in the Local Authority Nursing Services, which was set up in 1968 and reported in 1969, was that 'all local health authorities (which had) not already done so should appoint a chief nursing officer to co-ordinate the health visiting, home nursing and domiciliary midwifery services in their area and to provide a single channel of communication on policy matters through the medical officer of health to the health committee.'[25] Mayston and her colleagues took the view that the traditional fragmentation of the local authority nursing services was detrimental to their efficiency and effectiveness and that the appointment of a chief nursing officer would enhance their contribution to the provision of health care within the community. They also felt that 'it was a waste of medical skills for any medical officer personally to undertake direct responsibility for organising and administering these services.'[26] The report of the Mayston Working Party was commended to local health authorities by the Secretary of State in 1970 and during the next few years nearly every local health authority reorganised their nursing services management structure in accordance with the working party's recommendations.

Apart from managerial responsibilities within their own departments, MOsH also had dealings with staff from other departments, in particular chief officers and other senior staff of the authority. For example, in performing their duties in respect of the school health service they inevitably came into frequent contact with the chief education officer; the senior medical officer, to whom the day-to-day management of the service had been delegated, and the principal school dental officer, who was responsible, through the MOH, for the 'efficient conduct of such of the work of the School Health Service as relate(d) to the dental inspection and dental treatment of pupils.'[27] In many authorities, MOsH and their medical colleagues also assisted housing officers with the selection of tenants for council houses, in cases where the medical condition of the applicants (e.g. heart disease, arthritis) was one of the factors put forward in support of their claim for rehousing.

Primarily because of their professional backgrounds and responsibilities MOsH were key figures in the communication network linking local health authorities **with the Ministry of Health/DHSS HQ** in London, especially where the transmission of information and advice on technical matters was concerned. For MOsH the most important part of the Ministry of Health/DHSS was the Medical Department headed by the Chief Medical Officer.

As indicated in Chapter 2, the Chief Medical Officer had played an important part in the early development of the CHSs. Furthermore, ever since the establishment of the school medical service the holder of this post had been also the Chief Medical Officer to the Board/Ministry of Education. In order to ensure that there was a continuing link between the maternity and child welfare and school health services at the highest level this practice was to continue right up to the reorganisation of the NHS in 1974. Of course, this arrangement reflected that at local level whereby most MOsH also held the post of principal school medical officer (see above).

One of the most important tasks of the Chief Medical Officer was to prepare and publish an annual report on the state of the public health and a biennial report on the health of the school child.[28] Both of these reports provided MOsH with extremely valuable information about epidemiological and related trends at national level against which they could compare the situation in their area and the performance of their authority.

The Medical Department of the Ministry of Health/DHSS was staffed by medical officers with particular expertise in fields such as epidemiology; maternity and child welfare; mental health and the care of the elderly and MOsH were able to use this resource whenever they needed to do so. In addition, MOsH could invite medical officers from the Ministry/DHSS to visit their authority when there was a serious problem, such as an epidemic. This, however, was a relatively rare occurrence and no attempt was made to organise visits of this kind on a regular basis. Professional contact between local MOsH and their colleagues in Whitehall was, in many respects, the most important element of the relationship between local health authorities and the centre, which will be considered in more detail later in the chapter.

Another important relationship at national level was with their professional body, the Society of Medical Officers of Health. Like other professions in local government and elsewhere, MOsH had established a body to enable them to speak with a collective, and therefore more authoritative and powerful, voice on those matters with which they were particularly concerned. Thus, on numerous occasions during the 1950s and 1960s the Society of Medical Officers of Health provided both written and oral evidence to the various committees, which were set up to investigate and report on aspects of community health care. In addition, the Chairman of the Council of the Society of Medical Officers of Health was an ex-officio member of the Central Health Services Council thereby giving formal recognition to the Society's role as a significant source of advice on health care matters in general and community health care matters in particular.

At **local level,** throughout the tripartite era the MOH retained 'his traditional responsibility for supervising and maintaining the health of his community'. Thus his major role continued to be an outward looking one in the sense that he had a duty to inform himself about all matters affecting the health of his area and to ascertain, report and advise upon all conditions that were likely to affect the health of the community. In the words of Fraser Brockington:

The MOH (was) the voice of health in terms of the mass of people in his area. In his many contacts with professional colleagues, with committee members, with fellow officers in other services, with teachers and with the public, he (could) put forward the epidemiological point of view; and speak frankly and without restraint upon all matters affecting the health of the people.

As Brockington states, the epidemiogical point of view or approach stresses 'the importance of protecting and promoting the health of the whole community, and of preventing disease, in contrast to the more limited objective of curing the sick.'[29]

With the development of scientific and technical disciplines in various spheres of environmental health prior to 1948 the MOH had been able to give greater priority to the application of the epidemiogical approach to the medical aspects of health care. Furthermore, following the establishment of the NHS and the transfer of responsibility for HSs to the newly established regional hospital boards and hospital management committees the MOH was able to concentrate on preventive medicine, community based care and, most importantly, on meeting the medical and related needs of vulnerable groups. According to Brockington the following groups were of particular concern to the MOH:

• the mother and young child,

• the school child,

• the handicapped child,

• the deprived child,

• the adolescent and adult in industry,

• the mentally ill and mentally subnormal, and

• the aged.

In responding to the needs of these groups MOsH had to ensure the adequacy of directly provided services and maintain a constructive relationship with those voluntary organisations which were also contributing to their well-being.

Another aspect of the MOH's role as the 'voice of health' at the local level was the preparation of an annual report on the health of the community. This was a statutory requirement[30] and the report served as the local equivalent of the Chief Medical Officer to the Ministry of Health/DHSS's annual report on the state of the public health. In this report the MOH was expected to provide an overview of the health care needs of the community; to indicate the extent to which these needs were being met by existing services and to highlight local health care issues and problems of general professional concern.

Lastly, in seeking to promote and protect the health of the community as a whole, MOsH had a key role to play in bridging the gaps between the different types of health care provision.[31] This meant, for example, attempting to ensure that patients discharged from hospital had access to any after-care facilities that they might have required and fostering closer links between GPs, on the one hand, and health visitors and home nurses, on the other. However, this integrative role became more difficult after 1948 because, as Brotherston points out, the clinical relationship which MOsH had previously enjoyed with other doctors in their area through their involvement with hospital and other clinical services became attenuated.[32]

Thus, during the tripartite era the MOH was very much the central figure in respect of not only the clinical aspects of the CHSs, but also their planning, organisation and management and their integration with other health care services. In order to exercise these responsibilities in an effective manner and to respond positively to the challenges arising from changes in the political, administrative and epidemiological environments MOsH needed to be both flexible and politically astute, as well as competent professionals in their own sphere of expertise (i.e. public health). Furthermore, to ensure that the CHSs received an adequate share of financial and other resources, they needed to collaborate closely with the chairmen of their health committees.

Initially, however, there were problems of motivation and morale. Webster, for example, argues that with the establishment of the NHS and the transfer of responsibility for hospital services to the newly constituted hospital authorities, the health departments of local authorities were 'reduced to a dispirited rump' and lost 'their sense of purpose.' Moreover, in evidence presented to the Guillebaud Committee (see below) in 1954, the Society of Medical Officers of Health acknowledged that 'the Local Health Authority Service had suffered so much in status and prestige under the NHS that their medical staff had greatly degenerated both in quantity and quality.'[33] As a result some MOsH, at least, failed to exploit to the full the opportunities to which the relationships, outlined above, gave rise. Nevertheless, this somewhat negative view requires modification in the light of the overall performance of MOsH during the tripartite era, with regard to resource acquisition and service development.

The Financial Framework

The growth of revenue spending (i.e. salaries and wages; running costs and debt charges) on LHSs between 1948 and 1974 is shown in Figure 3.3.

It should be noted that the large reduction in spending between 1970/71 and 1971/72 was due entirely to the effect of the Seebohm reorganisation. This resulted in spending on domestic help, mental health and other services being transferred from the budget for LHSs to that of the newly constituted budget for personal social services. If this transfer had not taken place then it is probable that by 1973/74 spending on the LHSs would have exceeded £300m.

In cash terms spending on the LHSs increased by more than 500% between 1949/50 and 1970/71. However, although spending increased each year there were some significant fluctuations in the rate of increase. For example, between 1952/53 and 1953/54 spending increased only by 0.3%, whereas between 1969/70 and 1970/71 it increased by 18.7%. In general the rate of increase during the 1960s was faster than it had been during the 1950s, due to changes in attitude towards public expenditure at both national and local level.

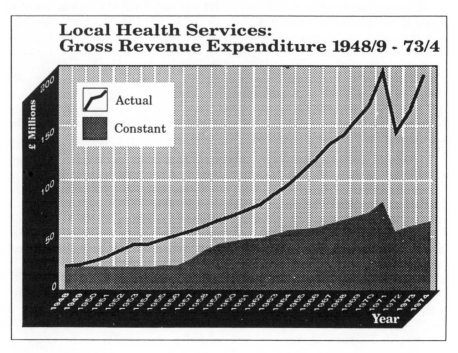

**Local Health Services:
Gross Revenue Expenditure 1948/9 - 73/4**

(England and Wales)

Figure 3.3

Note

For further details of the data on which this figure is based see Sections A, and C of Appendix II.

Sources: (a) Ministry of Health; (b) Ministry of Local Government and Planning; (c) Ministry of Housing and Local Government; (d) Ministry of Housing and Local Government and Welsh Office and (e) Department of the Environment and Welsh Office, *Local Government Financial Statistics England and Wales for (a) 1948/49; (b) 1949/50; (c) 1950/51 to 1964/65; (d) 1965/66 to 1967/68 and (e) 1968/69 to 1973/74.*

After making allowance for the effect of inflation the increase in spending between 1949/50 and 1970/71 was 170%. Thus, there was a significant expansion in respect of the real resources, such as staff and equipment, devoted to LHSs. Again, however, the figures for particular years show some significant fluctuations and in 1951/52 and 1953/54 spending, in real terms, on LHSs actually fell. [34]

In terms of the total amount of local authority revenue expenditure, approximately 3.5% was allocated to the provision of LHSs (until 1971/72) compared with 38% to education; 15% housing; 7% public health; 6% police and 2% welfare services.

Although the revenue expenditure on LHSs was primarily financed out of rate income and government grants, local health authorities were able, with the approval of the Minister, to recover such charges 'as the authority consider(ed) reasonable' in respect of certain items and services. These were:

* articles provided as part of the care given to expectant and nursing mothers and pre-school children (Section 22[2] of the 1946 Act);

* services connected with the prevention of illness, care and after-care (Section 28[2] 1946 Act);

* domestic help (Section 29[2] 1946 Act); and

* contraceptive substances and appliances (Section 1[2] of the National Health Service (Family Planning) Act 1967).

In every case where charges were recovered the local health authority was required to have 'regard to the means of those persons' on whom they were levied. Between 5% and 10% of the income needed to finance the provision of LHSs was derived from clients as opposed to national and local taxpayers.

Under the provisions of Section 53 of the 1946 Act every local health authority received a specific grant 'in respect of the expenditure, estimated in a prescribed manner, incurred by the authority in carrying out their functions as a local health authority'. The rate of grant was determined by the Minister but the legislation prescribed that it had to be between three-eighths and three-quarters of the total expenditure. Whilst these provisions were in force the rate of grant was 50%.

During the 1950s this kind of grant was criticised on the grounds that it was 'an indiscriminate incentive to further expenditure and also carried with it an aggravating amount of central checking and control of detail.'[35] As a result the LHSs and other specific grants were abolished by the Local Government Act 1958 and replaced by a general grant. Thus, from 1959/60 to 1973/74 almost none of the central government financial aid to local government was specifically earmarked for the LHSs.[36] However, the formulae for distributing financial aid of this kind (i.e. the general grant from 1959/60 to 1966/67 and the needs element of the rate support grant from 1967/68 to 1973/74) included a number of variables, such as the number of children under 5 years of age and the number of persons over 65 years of age, to take account of the fact that these client groups made above average demands on local health and related services.

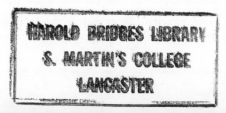

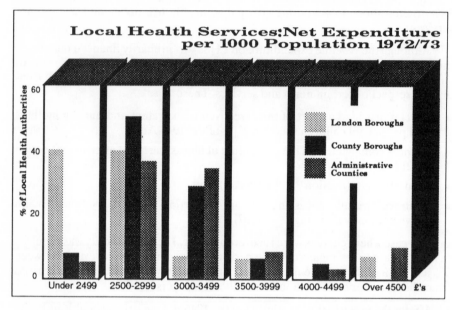

(England and Wales)

Figure 3.4

Source: The Chartered Institute of Public Finance and Accountancy and the Society of County Treasurers, *Local Health and Social Services Statistics 1972/73,* Nov 1974, pp. 85-97.

Interestingly revenue spending on LHSs increased more rapidly after the change in the grant arrangements than it had done before. For example, for the five years up to and including 1958/59 the average annual increase in spending at constant prices was 3.7% whereas for the five years from 1959/60 to 1963/64 it was over 7.0%. This was just the opposite of what might have been expected given that specific grants were claimed to be an 'indiscriminate incentive to further expenditure'.

One other important point concerning the total amount spent on the LHSs is that it increased more rapidly than spending on other health care services. Consequently between 1949/50 and 1970/71 LHSs' revenue expenditure increased as a percentage of total NHS revenue expenditure from 8.5% to 11.8%.[37]

With regard to the amounts spent by individual authorities on LHSs the pattern was one of considerable diversity as the information in Figure 3.4 indicates. The differences in the amount spent by individual authorities on a per capita basis reflects, in part, variations in the demographic composition of areas andtherefore the level of need for services and in part the party political composition of the authority concerned. There is evidence to suggest that Labour controlled authorities tended to spend more on LHSs than those controlled by the Conservative Party. For example, Sharpe and Newton in their analysis of the policy outputs of, and expenditure variations between, county boroughs and county councils in England and Wales, showed that in 1972/73 the pattern of per capita spending on the LHSs was as follows:

- authorities where the Conservative Party was in a monopoly or dominant position: county boroughs £2.88; administrative counties £3.27;

- authorities with a multi-party or two-party system: county boroughs £2.94; administrative counties £3.43; and

- authorities where the Labour Party was in a monopoly or dominant position: county boroughs £3.01; administrative counties £3.87.[38]

In view of the nature of local democracy such variations were to be expected. Surprisingly, however, a study by Noyce, Snaith and Trickey of the distribution of expenditure on health care services by the three main branches of the NHS shows that there was a greater disparity in the spending of hospital authorities than in that of local health authorities.[39] It is therefore reasonable to assume that between different parts of the country there was greater variation in the quantity and quality of hospital based services than in the quantity and quality of LHSs. Thus, during the tripartite era, efforts to secure a more equitable distribution of health care services in geographical terms (i.e. 'territorial justice'), were frustrated more by the actions of the hospital authorities, which tended to preserve the status quo, than by those of the more innovative local health authorities.

Levels of capital expenditure on new buildings, vehicles and other assets required for LHSs purposes are shown in Figure 3.5. Spending on capital projects (e.g. maternity and child welfare clinics, health centres, ambulance stations) was mainly financed by borrowing, the amount of which was strictly controlled by central government. Before a local authority could borrow money it had to submit details of the scheme (e.g. type, location, size, indication of need, effect on revenue expenditure in a full year, estimated cost), for which the loan was required, to the Ministry of Health where it was subject to detailed scrutiny. If approved then the Ministry would issue a loan sanction which served as a formal authorisation for the authority to proceed with the scheme. Thus, the total amount of capital spending was determined, to a significant extent, by the centre and the government's view of the economic situation, with spending being increased in deflationary periods and reduced in inflationary periods, hence the considerable fluctuations in capital spending illustrated by Figure 3.5.

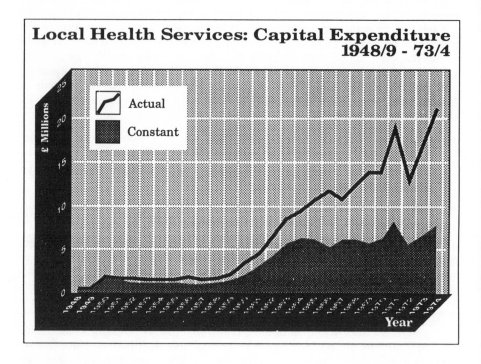

Figure 3.5   *(England and Wales)*

Note

For further details of the data on which this figure is based see Section C of Appendix II.

Sources: (a) Ministry of Health; (b) Ministry of Local Government and Planning; (c) Ministry of Housing and Local Government; (d) Ministry of Housing and Local Government and Welsh Office and (e) Department of the Environment and Welsh Office, *Local Government Financial Statistics England and Wales for (a) 1948/49; (b) 1949/50; (c) 1950/51 to 1964/65; (d) 1965/66 to 1967/68 and (e) 1968/69 to 1973/74.*

During the 1950s, in particular, the controls on local health authority capital expenditure were extremely tight and, as Webster indicates, despite the fact that authorities were keen to respond to public pressure for better clinic facilities, improvements of this kind were 'severely limited'.[40]

The growth of revenue spending on the school health service for the period 1948/49 to 1973/74 is shown in Figure 3.6

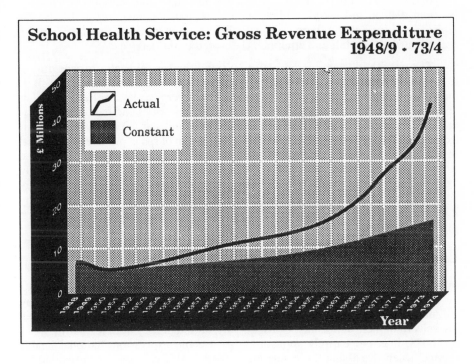

**School Health Service: Gross Revenue Expenditure
1948/9 - 73/4**

Actual

Constant

£ Millions

Year

(England and Wales)

Figure 3.6

For further details of the data on which this figure is based see Section C of Appendix II.

Sources: Central Statistical Office, *Annual Abstract of Statistics,* various editions (for years 1948/49 to 1964/65); Ministry of Education/Department of Education and Science, *Statistics of Education,* (for years 1965/66 to 1971/72) and Department of Environment and Welsh Office, *Local Government Financial Statistics England and Wales,* (for years 1972/73 and 1973/74).

During the tripartite era expenditure on the school health service formed part of the education committee's budget as opposed to that of the health committee. Nevertheless, this still meant that, like the other CHSs, the service was primarily financed out of income from rates and grants. Furthermore, until 1959/60 when it was absorbed into the general grant local education authorities received a specific grant towards the costs of the school health service. Since the service was essentially free, income from fees and charges covered only a very small proportion (under

2%) of the total cost of the service. Although spending on the school health service between 1949/50 and 1970/71 did not increase as much as spending on LHSs (see Appendix II for details) there was, nevertheless, an increase of about 25% in the real resources (i.e. staff and equipment) devoted to the service.

The growth in spending on both LHSs and the school health service during the tripartite era was, in part, a manifestation of the belief at national, as well as local, level that the CHSs needed to expand if they were to play an effective part in complementing the services provided by hospital authorities and family practitioners. This was particularly the case in the 1960s and early 1970s when Britain experienced what has been described as a 'revolution of rising public expectations' in respect of the provision of publically provided goods and services. In response to this change in public expectations, which was due, in part, to the increasingly extravagant promises made by politicians, the centre used its influence to encourage local health authorities and other public bodies to spend more and thereby improve the quantity and quality of the services, which they were responsible for providing.

Local Health Authorities and the Centre

In spite of the fact that there was less variation in the spending of local health authorities than hospital authorities, application of the principle of local autonomy still meant that during the tripartite era LHSs were characterised more by their diversity than their uniformity. Consequently, although they were formally part of the NHS, it is not entirely appropriate to use the expression 'national health service' when discussing the community based health care services provided by local health authorities. There were, in effect, 146/175 local health services as opposed to a single national health service.

This was mainly because on many aspects of LHSs central government was prepared to respect the principle of local autonomy. However, as has been mentioned, this did not prevent it from taking an interest in the administration and development of LHSs and interacting in various ways with local health authorities. Consequently, within the HQ of the Ministry of Health/DHSS there were administrative and professional staff (e.g. medical, nursing, dental) with specific responsibility for aspects of the LHSs or for matters (e.g. finance, personnel), which affected every branch of the NHS. There were also 11 regional offices and a Welsh Board of Health, with their own nursing, welfare and administrative staff.

Reference has already been made to a number of the ways in which the centre contributed to the development of the LHSs, such as the provision of grant aid, both general and specific; the making of regulations and the issuing of circulars and to the important role played by MOsH in linking the Ministry of Health/DHSS with local health authorities. However, some important aspects of the relationship between local health authorities and the centre remain to be considered.

When the NHS was set up local health authorities were required under the provisions of Section 20 of the 1946 Act to submit to the Minister, within a specified time period, 'proposals for carrying out their duties under' Sections 21 to 28. This was mainly to ensure that they adopted a positive approach to the exercise of their old and new health care responsibilities.

Copies of their proposals also had to be sent to every voluntary organisation engaged in the provision of services covered by the proposals, the executive council, the regional hospital board and county district councils, so that if they wished to do so they could make recommendations 'for modifying the proposals'. Circulars 66/47 and 118/47 provided local health authorities with guidance on the preparation of proposals for all services except health centres, on which no immediate action could be taken because of building difficulties and the need to give further consideration to their role.

Having received proposals from local health authorities and any recommendations for amending them from the bodies entitled to receive copies the Minister was required to approve them, with or without modification. Local health authorities were then obliged to adhere to what had been approved in performing their duties and developing their services. They were, however, entitled to submit new proposals 'at any time'. Furthermore, they had to draw up new proposals for all or some of their services if directed to do so by the Minister. In either case they had to go through the same procedure as that laid down for the initial proposals. By this means local health authorities and/or the Minister were able to take account of, and respond to, demographic and other changes which affected the demand for, and supply of, community based health care services.

Similarly, under the provisions of the 1945 Regulations, local education authorities had to submit to the Minister of Education, as soon after 1st April 1945 as possible, 'a statement in approved form of the arrangements they propose(d) to make for discharging their functions in carrying out the school health service.'[41] They were also required to present to the Minister 'in respect of each calendar year a report by their school medical officer on the health and well-being of pupils in his care and of the work of himself and his staff in relation thereto, including a report by the senior dental officer, together with such statistical and other information as the Minister (required).[42] Significantly, when the 1945 Regulations were substantially amended in 1953 the provisions relating to the submission of an annual report were retained.[43]

In 1953 and 1958, as part of the ongoing monitoring arrangements for the LHSs, local health authorities were asked to carry out 5 and 10 year reviews of their progress to date and summaries of their review findings were published in the annual reports of the Ministry of Health for those years. However, these tended to be backward rather than forward looking exercises. Furthermore, as Griffith observes, in his major study of the relations between central departments and local authorities (1966), there were in the 1950s 'few standards of performance by which local (health) authorities could be judged or could judge themselves.'[44] This meant that the Ministry of Health was unable to apply one of the principal methods by which central departments sought to control the activities of local authorities, namely the imposition of standards of performance. Indeed 'it was not even possible for the Department to seek to raise all local health and welfare authorities to the level of the best. For the standards of the best were unknown.'[45]

The first attempt to deal with this problem on a systematic basis was made in the early 1960s. It followed the publication of *A Hospital Plan for England and Wales* in 1962, which was based on the assumption 'that the first concern of the health and welfare services (would) continue to be to forestall illness and disability by preventive measures', that care would continue to be provided at home and in the community for patients who did not need to be hospitalised, and that the development of HSs would be 'complementary to the expected development of services for prevention and for care in the community.'[46]

During 1962 all local health authorities were required, not only to review their existing position with regard to service provision, but also to prepare 10 year plans for the long-term development of their health and welfare services. The results of this exercise were published in 1963 in the form of a white paper, entitled *Health and Welfare: The Development of Community Care*, which also included details of the plans of every local health authority for the period to 1971/72 in respect of health and welfare premises (e.g. numbers of maternity and child welfare clinics, places in training centres for the mentally subnormal, places in homes for the elderly); domiciliary services (i.e. numbers of health visitors, home helps, midwives and social workers); and their capital building programmes.[47]

A major feature of this white paper was that it marked a change in emphasis from the provision of services to the meeting of needs of particular client groups. This was reflected in the fact that, as Watkin states, much of 'the text was organised in chapters based on the needs of four broad groups of people: mothers and young children; the elderly; the mentally disordered; and the physically handicapped.'[48]

Later in 1963 local health authorities were requested to draw up revised plans to 1974 on a somewhat more extended scale and a summary of these plans was published in 1964.[49] In July 1965 the Minister of Health called for a second revision on a comparable basis with the first, covering the decade 1966-1976, with annual forecasts up to 1971 and a single forecast for the period from 1971 to 1976. These revised plans were published in 1966[50] and they, together with the white paper of 1963, provide a reasonably detailed picture of the scale of LHSs in the 1960s and what were perceived by local health authorities as priorities.

However, despite the fact that forward planning provided an opportunity for each local health authority 'to perform the essential task of reviewing its past performance, its present needs and its future expectations',[51] they were not required to carry out any further revisions to their plans. This was mainly because, by the late 1960s, enthusiasm for long-term planning had tended to wane and politicians and others had become preoccupied with the issue of reorganisation.

The centre could also take action in cases of default. Under the provisions of Section 57 of the 1946 Act, if in the view of the Minister an authority had failed to discharge its functions under the act he could by order declare the authority to be in default. An order of this kind would have directed the authority to carry out its obligations and if it had still defaulted the order could have been enforced through court action. This would have involved the issue of a prerogative order known as *mandamus* (i.e. 'we command'). As an alternative the Minister could have transferred the LHS functions of the authority to himself and have recovered the cost of discharging them from the defaulting authority.

In practice, although local health authorities differed in the priority they gave to their LHSs they all appear to have been reasonably conscientious in exercising their responsibilities under the 1946 Act and there are no recorded cases of the default powers ever having been used. Thus, in the words of Griffith, 'the importance of default powers (lay) not so much in their exercise as in their existence and in the threat of their use.'[52]

Despite the existence of these default powers and the interest taken by the Ministry of Health in service development during the planning exercises of the 1960s and in other ways the expression used by Griffith to summarise the attitude of the Ministry of Health towards local health and welfare authorities is 'laissez-faire'. However, he defines 'laissez-faire' in this context not as 'a negative attitude of indifference', but as 'a positive philosophy of as little interference as possible within the necessary fulfilment of departmental duties.'[53] Griffith justified his position on the grounds that the Ministry of Health seemed 'in three ways to be doing less than some parts of other departments: namely in the collation, analysis and dissemination of the experience of local authorities; in research; and in insisting that local authorities follow(ed) departmental policies.'[54]

According to Griffith the attitude of the Ministry of Health can be explained by reference to the fact that Ministers and civil servants respected the professionalism of MOsH and that there was within the Ministry a 'greater traditional respect for local authorities as independent entities in their own right' arising from 'its long period of office as the principal local government Department.'[55] Moreover, many members of the medical staff of the Ministry had previously worked for local health authorities.

This can be contrasted with the principle of inspection by the centre which was applied to the school health service. Because there had been a long tradition in the education service of using a nationally appointed inspectorate to act as an intermediary between the Board/Ministry of Education and local education authorities and to carry out inspections of, and produce reports on, educational establishments, not surprisingly, the school health service was subject to a similar regime. Thus, the 1945 Regulations, referred to earlier, contained the following provision

> The premises used for the school health service shall be open to inspection by an Inspector and the authority shall afford an Inspector all the facilities he requires for informing himself as to their arrangements.

Similarly the School Health Service and Handicapped Pupils Regulations 1953 stated that:

> The Authority's arrangements for their School Health Service and the premises used for that Service shall be open to inspection by any person approved for that purpose by the Minister.[56]

Problems arose, however, because for most of the tripartite era the Ministry of Education lacked a corps of adequately qualified inspectors of sufficient size to carry out a systematic and comprehensive programme of visits.[57]

One final point, Griffith also draws attention to the distinction made in the 1946 Act between the Minister of Health's relationship to the local health authorities and his relationship to the hospital authorities. It can be argued that the most appropriate term for describing the first of these relationships is 'partnership' and the second 'agency'. Due, in part, to these differences the centre was unable to secure a truly integrated approach to the delivery of health care services during the tripartite era and consequently relations between local health authorities and the other bodies responsible for the administration of health care services failed to develop in the way that was originally intended.

Local Health Authorities, Hospital Authorities and Executive Councils

Clearly, for the tripartite structure of the NHS to work effectively it was essential for local health authorities to collaborate on a regular and ongoing basis with executive councils and hospital authorities and for the centre to use its influence and powers to facilitate this collaboration. Initially the centre anticipated that 'by interlocking membership ..., by liaison committees at different levels and by day-to-day co-operation' the activities of the three parts of the NHS would be 'continuously co-ordinated to provide ... a single service to the community.'[58] Furthermore, it was hoped that the proposed health centres would act as a catalyst for close relations between those engaged in the delivery of LHSs and their colleagues in other parts of the NHS.

However, as Parker comments, this was an unduly optimistic assessment of the situation and it was not shared by the local health authorities, which were still extremely upset at their loss of health care functions to the newly constituted hospital authorities.[59] Moreover, the loss was all the more traumatic because 'it represented a sudden and unexpected reversal of policies since the beginning of the century,'[60] which had enlarged significantly the health care role of local authorities (see Chapter 2).

In 1951 the Association of Municipal Corporations (AMC), which represented some of the major local health authorities, referred to the split between the hospital based services and those provided by local authorities as 'that fatal dichotomy which is the bane of the whole service'. The AMC was also critical of the inflexible financial arrangements for secondary health care services. It was argued that since hospital authorities derived nearly all their funds from central government, as opposed to having an independent power of taxation like local authorities, there was a greater degree of Treasury control over health care spending than would otherwise have been the case. Furthermore, since they were appointed bodies, hospital authorities were not directly accountable to the public for their spending decisions, which again resulted in the need for control from the centre. Not surprisingly, the AMC suggested that the best way of overcoming this problem was to return hospitals to the control of democratically elected local authorities.

In the circumstances such a stance was both predictable and understandable. However, it was clearly not calculated to endear local health authorities to hospital authorities, which was unfortunate since, in the view of Webster and others, following their 'obvious demotion' they 'depended for their rehabilitation on co-operation from other branches of the NHS.'[61]

Thus, despite the official optimism regarding the mechanisms for collaboration and the achievement of a fully integrated health care service, the omens were not particularly good. Consequently, in 1950 the Central Health Services Council set up a committee to consider the existing state of co-operation and how it might be encouraged. The committee's report, which was published in 1952, first distinguished between the various devices for co-operation that were already in use. These were interlocking membership of the different types of health authority (e.g. local health authorities appointed some of the members of executive councils and a number of hospital management committee members were also councillors); the exchange of papers between the different bodies; Ministerial circulars and memoranda; informal co-operation and meetings between officers and standing joint committees for specific subjects and for general purposes. Although the committee did not suggest any innovatory methods of co-operation it did recommend the establishment of local joint health consultative committees for convenient groupings of local health authorities, executive councils and hospital management committees. These would 'discuss local arrangements of mutual concern... receive information of major developments contemplated by member authorities and... suggest, if thought necessary, modifications... to the responsible executive authority.'[62]

However, one of the members of the Central Health Services Council's committee, with a background in hospital management, produced a supplementary memorandum in which he expressed his opposition to the majority recommendations in the following terms: 'I have come to the conclusion that such a mass creation of additional committees would on balance do more harm than good' and made some perceptive remarks on what he considered to be the essential prerequisites for effective collaboration. These were an appreciation of the 'human element'; a recognition of the need for co-operation on the part of those involved, which had to be based on education, and the use of persuasion and example rather than compulsion. Furthermore, if individuals were to work together for a particular purpose then they had to have a 'clear conception of what that purpose (was) and all of them (had to) have the same conception.'[63] Unfortunately many attempts at collaboration, not only in the 1950s but also in more recent times, have foundered because too much attention has been given to structures and too little to behavioural factors of this kind.

The reactions of local health authorities to the majority recommendations of the Central Health Services Council's *Report on Co-operation between Hospital, Local Authority and General Practitioner Services* were entirely negative and their representative bodies, the AMC and the County Councils Association (CCA), expressed, in no uncertain terms, their opposition to the possible imposition of a uniform system of regional advisory committees, arguing that the means of co-operation should be devised at local level to suit local circumstances.

The reluctance of local authorities to accept a standardised solution to the problem of co-ordination was due mainly to their desire to limit the interference of central government in local affairs and to keep hospital authorities and executive councils at arms length. There was a feeling on the part of many local health authorities that a too formalised system of co-operation might lead to hospital authorities and executive councils encroaching into their areas of responsibility. On the other hand local health authorities tended to support proposals which would have increased their influence in other parts of the NHS, such as the recommendation of the Guillebaud Report that MOsH should be appointed, on an honorary basis, to the medical staff of hospitals in their area.

The difficulties involved in devising and establishing mutually acceptable devices for collaboration were also exacerbated by the absence of precise guidelines specifying the exact nature and extent of the responsibilities of the bodies concerned. This was a particularly serious problem in respect of after-care. Since there was no precise definition of the point at which a patient ceased to be the responsibility of the hospital management committee and became the responsibility of the local health authority, there were many arguments over which authority should accept responsibility for the after-care of particular patients.

A similar problem arose during the early days of the NHS over the allocation of responsibility for patients who needed hospital treatment but were unable to obtain it immediately because of a shortage of beds. In 1949 the Minister of Health stated that they had to receive treatment in their own homes and that 'such persons, not being in fact hospital patients, (were) outside the scope of the hospital service' and there was no question of the hospital service being responsible for the nursing of persons who were not hospital patients. According to the Minister this was clearly a local health authority duty under Section 25 of the 1946 Act.[64] Not surprisingly, local authorities, recognising the additional burden that this would place on their budgets, were unhappy with the Minister's view. Matters were made worse by the fact that he would not agree to the CCA's proposal that regional hospital boards should reimburse local health authorities the cost of any provision they were obliged to make as a result of a failure by the hospital authorities to fulfil their statutory obligations. However, despite their unhappiness with the situation, there was, in practice, relatively little that they could do about it.

Poor relations between local health authorities and hospital authorities also had adverse consequences for the tuberculosis service. In 1948 responsibility for the main parts of the service (i.e. hospitals, sanitoria, village settlements, dispensaries and mobile X-ray units) was transferred to the newly constituted regional hospital boards, leaving local health authorities with a number of residual functions (see Chapter 4). This meant that, as Webster argues, 'continuing development of an integrated tuberculosis service was to some extent dependent on the Tuberculosis Standing Advisory Committee at the centre, and liaison arrangements between regional boards and local (health) authorities at the periphery.' Unfortunately, however, neither of these arrangements worked very effectively. 'After an initial burst of activity the Standing Advisory Committee became a dead letter ... (and) most regional boards pressed ahead with their own services with very little reference to the local (health) authorities.'[65]

Furthermore, during the 1950s very little progress was made in securing effective co-ordination between the services provided by local health authorities and those provided by GPs. In notes prepared for the Central Health Services Council's Committee on General Practice, in 1951, the Ministry of Health acknowledged that one of the most serious deficiencies of the newly established NHS was the 'lack of liaison between the services provided by Executive Councils (sic) and those provided by Local Health Authorities' and that 'unhappily anything in the nature of a team is still difficult to seek.'[66]

Similarly, four years later, the Ministry admitted that it had not made much progress in securing support for the recently formulated concept of the domiciliary team (i.e. the precursor of the primary health care team). Although the centre had been doing all it could 'to build up the idea of the domiciliary team under the the clinical leadership of the general practitioner' it was finding it extremely difficult 'to attract the interest of general practitioners, who... (were) reluctant to make use of the Health Visitors and the other domiciliary services provided by Local Health Authorities.'[67]

Throughout the 1950s and early 1960s, disputes over various issues were used by local health authorities and their representative bodies to keep the shortcomings of the tripartite structure in the public eye and to demonstrate that under these arrangements it was not possible to secure a truly integrated approach to the provision of health care services. Although some progress was made towards the development of a more collaborative relationship between local health authorities and the other other parts of the NHS, particularly in East Anglia and the West Riding of Yorkshire, in general the attitude of local authorities was one of antipathy, if not hostility, regarding the tripartite arrangements and the various attempts to make them work more effectively. As Parker suggests, this was almost certainly due to the fact that the tripartite structure represented 'a permanent reminder (to local authorities) of the diminution of their own powers.'[68] Ironically, however, the failure to make the structure work effectively resulted in the powers of local authorities being diminished even further when the NHS and local government were reorganised in 1974.

Prelude to Reorganisation

The debate which led ultimately to the reorganisation of the NHS in 1974 and the transfer of responsibility for CHSs from local health authorities to the newly constituted regional health authorities (RHAs) and area health authorities (AHAs) was a notable feature of the tripartite era. Within a few years of the establishment of the NHS attention was being drawn to some of the disadvantages of the tripartite structure. For example, Sir John Maude, one of the members of the Guillebaud Committee set up by the Ministry of Health in 1953 to inquire into the costs of the NHS,[69] expressed the view that the principal 'weakness of the NHS (was) its division into three parts operated by three sets of bodies having no organic connection with each other (and that) their separate funding from central and local government underlined the weakness.'[70] In order to overcome this weakness Maude favoured reorganising local government in such a way that it would have adequate financial, organisational and political resources to exercise responsibility for the administration, at local level, of the NHS as a whole.

Although Maude's diagnosis of, and remedies for, the weakness of the NHS were not shared by any of his colleagues on the Guillebaud Committee, his view that the disadvantages of the tripartite structure more than outweighed any advantages, gained gradual acceptance during the late 1950s and the early 1960s. However, the process which was to lead inexorably to the creation of a unified structure in 1974 did not formally begin until November 1967 when Kenneth Robinson, the Minister of Health in the Labour government (led by Harold Wilson), announced that there was to be a review of the administrative structure of the medical and related services for which he was responsible. The results of this review were published in July 1968, in what was to become known as the 'First Green Paper'.

The 'First Green Paper'

The review, initiated by Kenneth Robinson, was prompted not only by increasing concern regarding the effectiveness of the tripartite structure, but also by the fact that two other enquiries, the results of which were likely to have implications for the NHS, were being undertaken at that time. One of these was the enquiry into local authority and allied personal social services, chaired by Frederick Seebohm (see above). The other was being carried out by the Royal Commission on Local Government in England, under the chairmanship of Sir John Maud (later Lord Redcliffe-Maud). Maud and his colleagues had begun their enquiry in 1966.

Although technically a discussion document the 'First Green Paper' (entitled *National Health Service: The Administrative Structure of Medical and Related Services in England and Wales*) made it clear that the Labour government accepted the view that the time had come to replace the tripartite structure and that 'there should be single (health) authority in each area and that these area authorities should replace and undertake the functions of the Executive Councils, Regional Hospital Boards, Boards of Governors and Hospital Management Committees, and... **should be responsible for some important functions... in the hands of... local authorities** (emphasis added).'[71] Such an approach to the reorganisation of the NHS had, in fact, been advocated a few years earlier by the Medical Services Review Committee, under the chairmanship of Sir Arthur Porritt and composed of representatives of the Royal Colleges of Physicians, Surgeons, Obstetricians and Gynaecologists; the Society of Medical Officers of Health, the College of General Practitioners and the BMA. The report of the committee, which was published in 1962, stated unequivocally that 'the full advantages of the preventive and personal health services and their effective integration with the family doctor and hospital services (could) only be achieved by transferring both services and staff to Area Health Boards.'[72]

The 'First Green Paper' anticipated that there would be between 40 and 50 area boards, with an average population of 1.25 million. The question of whether or not these area boards should be an integral part of a reorganised system of local government was left open. However, there was little doubt that the Labour government favoured the establishment of entirely separate health authorities, which would be directly accountable to the Minister.

In outlining the arguments in favour of making the area (health) boards responsible for CHSs, as well as HSs and FPSs, the green paper identified six aspects of health care where it was felt that such an arrangement would be of particular importance in facilitating a more co-ordinated and comprehensive approach to service delivery. These aspects were:

- **home nursing and health visiting** and other services for the prevention of illness, care and after-care, which increasingly needed to be 'provided alongside and in close association with general medical care by the family doctor';

- **maternity care,** for which there was 'an urgent need to organise comprehensive services which (took) into account the high proportion of hospital confinements and the possibilities of earlier discharge from hospital' and the close connections between the domiciliary midwifery services and the GP and the hospital maternity and specialist services;

- **the child health service,** which the report of the Sheldon Subcommittee (see Chapter 4) recommended should be 'part of a family health service provided by family doctors working in groups from purpose built family health centres';

- **care of the long-term sick,** including disabled persons requiring medical and nursing support, and of the elderly and the mentally disordered, for whom the development of a comprehensive service, with contributions from GPs and hospital and community health staff, was a top priority;

- programmes of **vaccination and immunisation, family planning clinics and health education,** which needed to be closely integrated with other services; and

- the **ambulance service.**[73]

In addition, it was argued that MOsH would 'be able, as officers of the area authority, to extend their role as community physicians-specialists in community medicine.'[74] According to the green paper their duties would include the epidemiological evaluation of the standards of health in each area; the prevention of communicable disease and aspects of environmental hygiene.

It was recognised, however, that if responsibility for the CHSs and some of the environmental health services was transferred from local government to newly constituted health authorities there would still be 'a continuing need for close collaboration between' these services and other local services for which local authorities remained responsible, in particular those concerned with public health and social care. Furthermore, although the school health service was not specifically mentioned in the green paper, there would be a similar need for collaboration between local education authorities and the NHS whatever administrative arrangements were made for the service.

The response of the members of the Royal Commission on Local Government to the green paper proposals was to suggest in their report, which was published in 1969, that the unitary authorities they were recommending would be well suited for administering the NHS as well as other public services. In their view such an arrangement would have the additional advantages of facilitating the co-ordination of health care services with the services provided by the social services departments recommended by Seebohm and of securing greater democratic control over the administration of the NHS at local level. [75]

The members of the Maud Commission also sought to deal with the two principal concerns of those who opposed local authority control of the NHS, namely the inadequacy of existing sources of local authority income for financing such a large and complex service and the threat to clinical autonomy if local politicians played a part in the running of the NHS. They suggested that the financial problem could be overcome by giving local authorities additional sources of income and argued that local authority control would not mean that doctors and nurses were so closely supervised by elected members that their traditional autonomy would be placed in jeopardy.

Needless to say the position of the Royal Commission on these issues was fully supported by the local authority associations, in general, and the CCA and AMC, in particular. They argued that the transfer of responsibility for the administration of the CHSs from local government to separately constituted AHAs would not only weaken the existing links between CHSs and other 'community' services, such as housing and environmental health, but also would affect adversely the motivation of the staff concerned. According to the associations, community health staff felt a loyalty to their existing employers and they would see the transfer of administrative responsibility for the CHSs to another set of agencies, mainly run by those who had previously worked for hospital management committees, as a takeover. Consequently morale would fall and patient care would suffer.

The 'Second Green Paper'

Despite the representations of the CCA and AMC, in the 'Second Green Paper' on the NHS, which was published in February 1970 and entitled *The Future Structure of the National Health Service,* it was made clear that the Wilson government did not support the views of the Royal Commission on this matter. In the foreword to the 'Second Green Paper' the Secretary of State for Social Services, Richard Crossman, who had replaced Kenneth Robinson as the Minister responsible for the NHS in 1968, indicated that the Labour government had reached three firm decisions regarding the health services. Firstly, it had been decided that the NHS would not be administered by local authorities but by AHAs directly responsible to the Secretary of State and 'closely associated with local authorities'. Secondly, a decision had been made on the administrative boundary which it was necessary to draw between the NHS, on the one hand, and the public health and personal social services which were to remain the responsibility of local authorities, on the other. Thirdly, the number and areas of the new health authorities had to match those of the new local authorities in order to facilitate collaboration between them.[76] It had been decided also that in each area the FPSs would be administered by a special statutory committee of the AHA, but that they would continue to be separately financed by the Exchequer.

According to the green paper there were two main reasons why the Labour government could not accept the suggestion of the Royal Commission for consideration to be given 'to the possibility of unifying responsibility for the National Health Service within the new system of local government'. Firstly, they deferred to the view of the medical and other professions that only a service administered by special bodies on which the professions were represented could 'provide a proper assurance of clinical freedom'. Secondly, they felt that the independent financial resources available to the local authorities were 'not sufficient to enable them to take over responsibility for the whole health service.'[77] Thus, by this stage it was clear that whatever hopes local authority interests might have had in this respect there was little chance of them acquiring responsibility for the administration of a unified health service and that, given the desire of the policy-makers to integrate CHSs with HSs and FPSs, their role in the field of health care was to be reduced even further.

As well as dealing with matters of principle and various aspects of the structure of the proposed new AHAs, which were now expected to number between 80 and 90, the 'Second Green Paper' also contained a definitive statement of the responsibilities of these authorities. Apart from the existing hospital and specialist services and FPSs they were to be responsible for the administration of:

• the ambulance service;

• epidemiological work (i.e. the general surveillance of the health of the community);

• family planning;

• health centres;

• health visiting;

• home nursing and midwifery;

• maternity and child health care;

• prevention of illness, care and after-care, through medical, nursing and allied services (including chiropody, health education other than its place in the school curriculum and screening);

• residential accommodation for those needing continuing medical supervision and not ready to live in the community;

• vaccination and immunisation; and, significantly,

• the school health service.

The inclusion of the school health service in this list reflected the Labour government's belief that by transferring responsibility for the service from local education authorities to the proposed AHAs it would be possible 'to secure continuity in the medical and dental care (of children) from birth through their school days ...; and a closer association between what (was) provided as part of the school health service and what (was) provided for (children and their families) by general practitioners, other community health workers and hospitals.'[78] Furthermore, it was felt that the transfer would avoid the risk of duplication and that there would be opportunities for improving the efficiency in the use of medical, dental and nursing staff.

Although these proposals represented a significant reduction in the powers and duties of local authorities, they were to retain responsibility for those personal services which were going to be transferred from their health departments to the social services departments advocated by Seebohm, and for a variety of public health services. In addition, health education was to be a concurrent responsibility of both local and health authorities.

Not surprisingly this did not satisfy either the AMC or the CCA and both expressed opposition to the green paper's proposals. The AMC argued that the Labour government's reasons did not justify separating the administration of the health services from that of closely related local authority services and that, with appointed rather than democratically elected health authorities, there would be an absence of real local public accountability. Similarly the CCA was particularly critical of the Wilson government's view that in order to secure 'effective central control' the Secretary of State for Social Services had to have a full range of powers and, if necessary, the power of direction in respect of the standards of service provision. The CCA regarded this proposal as undemocratic, inconsistent with the Labour government's professed intention to reverse the trend towards centralisation and tragicallly short-sighted for the health services. Unfortunately for the interests of local government, little account was taken of these views.

The Consultative Document

It was Richard Crossman's intention to follow up the 'Second Green Paper' with the publication of a white paper during the summer of 1970 and the preparation of the necessary legislation in 1971. However, with the defeat of the Labour government by the Conservatives, led by Edward Health, in the general election of June 1970, he was unable to proceed with these plans. Following the general election it was not immediately clear what the attitude of the new Conservative Secretary of State, Sir Keith Joseph, would be towards the reorganisation of the NHS. The situation was clarified to some extent on 5th November 1970 when, in answer to a parliamentary question from Dr Gerard Vaughan, he made the following statement.

> The government intend to unify the administration of the National Health Service. Legislation will bring the change into effect at the same time as alterations are made in the structure of local government (i.e. 1st April 1974).

> The National Health Service will be administered by health authorities **outside local government** working closely with local authorities responsible for the personal social services and the public health services (emphasis added).

This, however, did not stop the CCA and AMC from continuing to lobby the Conservative government in the hope that they could still persuade Ministers to reconsider their position on the proposed transfer.

Six months later, in May 1971, the Secretary of State issued a consultative document.[79] Since it was intended to reorganise the NHS at the same time as local government there was only a limited amount of time available for consultation and consequently the document was distributed only to interested parties with a request to submit their views and comments within two months.

Although the consultative document modified and supplemented many of the 'Second Green Paper's' proposals regarding the structures for the reorganised NHS, it accepted most of the principles on which its proposals were based including the unification of administrative responsibility for CHSs and HSs; coterminosity of health authority and local authority boundaries and the co-ordination of health and personal social services, which were to remain the responsibility of local government. To these principles the consultative document added that of 'effective management'.

Like the 'Second Green Paper' the consultative document proposed the establishment of between 80 or 90 AHAs, with the same boundaries as the local authorities responsible for the administration of personal social services. It was recommended that these should be the operational authorities 'with responsibility for planning, organising and administering comprehensive health services to meet the needs of their areas ... (and) for the management of the integrated health services in the various parts of its area ('districts') served by separate district general hospitals and the **community health services** associated with them (emphasis added).'[80] Furthermore, although AHAs were to be responsible for co-ordinating FPSs with CHSs and HSs, and for providing support services and health centres, they would be required to delegate to a special statutory committee, namely a family practitioner committee (FPC), the functions of regulating FPSs and reimbursing claims for fees and allowances from practitioners.

In addition it was proposed that between the AHAs and the DHSS there should be RHAs with responsibility for planning the development of health care services in their region; allocating resources to AHAs and co-ordinating the activities and monitoring the performance of AHAs.

Another important innovation mentioned in the consultative document was the proposal that AHAs should be required to set up a body to represent the interests of consumers, to be called community health councils (CHCs), for each of their constituent districts. According to the Document this would 'ensure that in making plans and operating services, area authorities (would) take full account of the public they serve(d).'[81]

An issue which the consultative document reopened was that of the future administrative arrangements for the school health service. Although the previous Labour government had come to the conclusion that responsibility for the administration of the school health service should be transferred from local education authorities to the proposed AHAs, the new Secretary of State still wanted the subject to receive 'special consideration'. This was due, in part, to lobbying by the local authority associations with an interest in the education service. Following a meeting between these associations and representatives of the Department of Education and Science in January 1971, they had produced a paper in which they expressed regret at the Conservative government's decision to unify the administration of the health services outside local government. They were also sceptical about the likely benefits of transferring responsibility for the school health service from local education authorities to the NHS, as proposed in the 'Second Green Paper'. Lastly, they argued that a study should be undertaken of the likely effect of the reorganisation on the school health service and the various professional, administrative and financial factors involved. However, although such a study was carried out (see below), ultimately it was decided to adhere to the Labour government's proposal and transfer responsibility for the administration of the school health service from local government to the NHS.

The consultative document also indicated that the Secretary of State intended to take two further initiatives in preparation for the reorganisation of the NHS. One of these was to be the appointment of a study group to consider and make recommendations for 'the detailed management arrangements, at both member and officer level, in the area headquarters, in the districts and in the individual hospitals and other institutions.'[82]

The other was the establishment of a working party with the following terms of reference:

In the context of the proposed reorganisation of local government and the National Health Service to consider the need for **collaboration and co-ordination** *including any factors likely to impede or prevent them between the local authorities and the health authorities, both from the point of view of those receiving services and the public generally, and in order to ensure the most effective and efficient use of staff buildings and other resources and to make recommendations to the Government on these matters* (emphasis added).

Both the Management Study Group and the Collaboration Working Party were set up during the Summer of 1971.

The study group consisted of a number of civil servants from the DHSS, an MOH, a senior nurse, administrators from various parts of the NHS and a business manager. It was assisted in its research and deliberations by a firm of management consultants, McKinsey and Co, which had carried out a large number of commissions for public sector organisations during the late 1960s when managerialism had come into vogue as far as the public sector was concerned, and by the Health Services Organisation Research Unit of Brunel University under Professor Jacques. One of the techniques practised by the Unit was 'social analysis', which involved 'the clarification of role structures through discussion with those who participated in them.'[83]

In pursuing its objectives the study group worked under the general direction of a steering committee. This was a much larger body and it was made up of representatives of many of the political and professional interests that were likely to be affected by changes to the way in which the NHS was managed (e.g. civil servants, doctors, health care administrators). However, although those involved with the Management Study Group were formally required 'to take account of the present arrangements for the administration of the individual parts of the NHS and the current developments in the organisation of the work of the medical, nursing and other relevant professions',[84] it would appear that, given the likely significance of the results of the study for the future management of the CHSs, the interests of local health authorities and the professional staff working in the CHSs were not as well represented on the steering committee and study group as they might have been.

In contrast, local government interests were well represented on the Collabor- ation Working Party. This was a large body made up of 18 representatives of local government (including 5 MOsH; 3 directors of social services and a chief nursing officer); 18 civil servants and 11 representatives of the NHS. Because of the multifaceted nature of the issue of collaboration most of the detailed work was carried out by a number of subcommittees and specialist groups. Subcommittees were set up to examine the implications of collaboration for the personal social services; the school health service; the environmental health service; financial relationships between the NHS and local government and the situation in greater London, with its distinctive pattern of local authorities. Specialist groups were established to consider ancillary services; building and engineering; supplies and management services and statistics.

Whilst the Management Study Group and the Collaboration Working Party were carrying out their investigations and deciding on their recommendations, the Heath government took further steps towards meeting its 1st April 1974 deadline for the reorganisation of the NHS.

The White Paper

A white paper, *National Health Service Reorganisation: England*, was published in August 1972. This began with a clear and unambiguous statement of the Conser- vative government's belief in the principle of unification and a reiteration of the weaknesses inherent in the tripartite structure.

> *The National Health Service should be a single service. Its separate parts are intended to complement one another and not to function as self-sufficient entities. In practice, however, the fragmented administration we now have throws barriers in the way of efforts to organise a proper balance of services hospital and* **community** *throughout the country. The administrative unifi- cation of these services will make a firmer reality of the concept of a single service* (emphasis added).[85]

It went on to identify the services, including the school health service, that would be brought together under unified NHS administration and those that would remain the responsibility of local authorities (e.g. environmental health services) and other bodies, such as the Health Education Council and the Department of Employment (i.e. occupational health services) and outlined the functions of the DHSS; AHAs (including FPCs) and RHAs in the reorganised NHS and the steps that would need to be taken in order to implement the reorganisation proposals by 1st April 1974.

With regard to the school health service the white paper made it clear that, although it had been decided to make it part of the NHS, it accepted many of the initial points made by the Collaboration Working Party's Subcommittee on the School Health Service. Moreover, those responsible for providing services for schoolchildren would still need to work closely not only with the hospital service and personal health services for families but also with the education service. Furthermore, since local education authorities were to remain responsible for the assessment and education of children requiring special facilities due to a handicap or disability it was confirmed that the NHS would make available to local education authorities the advice and the medical, dental, nursing and allied services that they would need to exercise these responsibilities in an effective manner. They would also provide them with similar help in respect of health education and school hygiene.

In giving health authorities responsibility for the school health service it was also hoped to secure a greater degree of integration between the health care services for pre-school children and those for school children. The Conservative government's commitment to a more closely integrated and therefore more effective child health service had been demonstrated with an announcement from the Secretary of State, a couple of months prior to the publication of the white paper, that he was initiating, together with the Secretary of State for Education and Science and the Secretary of State for Wales, a review of the child health services. Although it was not until the middle of 1973 that a committee, under the chairmanship of Professor Court, was set up for this purpose, the Secretary of State's announcement clearly reflected his desire to improve the quality of the child health services; his belief that 'the reorganisation of the National Health Service and the transfer of the School Health Service provided an unrivalled opportunity to achieve this improvement'[86] and his wish to see a truly integrated child health service embracing both the existing pre-school and school health services. Because the Court Committee did not complete its review until 1976, its recommendations and the reactions to them are considered in Chapter 6.

Also of significance for the future of the CHSs were the comments of a white paper on the role of specialists in community medicine. These were to be the successors to the MOsH in the reorganised NHS and the identification of their likely responsibilities at each level of authority within a unified structure had been undertaken by a Working Party on Medical Administrators, chaired by Dr R Hunter. The working party's report, which was published in 1972, drew attention to the important contributions that specialists in community medicine would be able to make to the development of an integrated approach to the provision of health care and related services. It was suggested that they would be primarily concerned with assessing the need for health services; evaluating the effectiveness of existing services; planning the best use of health resources; developing preventive health services; fostering links between CHSs, HSs and FPSs on the one hand and local authority personal social, environmental and education services on the other and providing local authorities with the help that they would need for the administration of services which contributed to the health and well-being of their community.[87]

Although the deliberations of the Management Study Group and the Collaboration Working Party were by no means complete in mid-1972 enough was known of what they were likely to recommend for the white paper to indicate the Heath government's broad agreement with their general approach.

The 'Grey Book'

The Management Study Group completed its work during the second half of 1972 and at the end of the year published its final report, *Management Arrangements for the Reorganised NHS,* popularly known as the 'Grey Book'.[88] This was a particularly influential document and the acceptance and application of many of its recommendations resulted in the CHSs being subject, after 1974, to a somewhat different style of management from that which had prevailed during the tripartite era.

The members of the study group and its steering committee took as their starting point the following principles from the consultative document:

* that there should be a 'fully integrated health service' in which every aspect of health care would be provided, as far as possible, locally and in accordance with the needs of people; and

* 'that throughout the new administrative structure there should be a clear definition and allocation of responsibilities; that there should be maximum delegation downwards, matched by accountability upwards; and that a sound management structure should be created at all levels'.

To these were added two further principles:

* that the clinical autonomy of doctors and other clinicians responsible for the diagnosis and treatment of patients should be fully preserved; and

* that to provide for the exercise of professional discretion in their work professional staff should be 'managed by members of their own profession'.

In applying these principles to the proposed organisational framework for the reorganised NHS the study group members made various recommendations about the way in which health care services, including CHSs, should be managed after the 1st April 1974. The most significant of these recommendations are summarised below.

Responsibility for the day-to-day management of operational activities should be decentralised by AHAs to their districts, which were defined as 'geographic unit(s) within which it (was) possible to satisfy the greater part of the population's health care needs' and as 'a population served by **community health services** supported by the specialist services of a district general hospital (emphasis added).'[89] It was anticipated that most districts would have a population of between 200,000 and 300,000.

At district, area and regional level multidisciplinary management teams should be formed to plan and co-ordinate the provision of health care services. Teams should comprise the heads of the major hierarchically organised disciplines or professions, such as finance and nursing; a specialist in community medicine and, at district level, two elected medical representatives, one consultant and one GP, to act as a link with the non-hierarchically organised medical and dental professions. In reaching decisions on the issues before them such teams should operate on the basis of general agreement or consensus.

District management teams (DMTs) should establish a number of multidisciplinary health care planning teams 'to concentrate on planning services to meet particular groups of needs'. Planning teams could be set up on either a permanent basis to plan for certain groups of needs which required 'a high level of interaction between hospital and community care', such as those of the elderly, children and the mentally ill, or on an ad hoc basis to carry out special projects (e.g. a review of primary care services or the introduction of day surgery). The composition of these teams should reflect the nature of their terms of reference but it was anticipated that there would have to be 'representation of general practitioners, consultants, hospital and community nurses, health visitors, relevant paramedical staff and representatives of local authority services, particularly social services' and that they would have to be supported by the district community physician and an administrator.[90]

Health care management should be patient centred and therefore there should be active participation by clinicians, through membership not only of management teams and health care planning teams, but also through the establishment of professional advisory machinery at district, area and regional level. Lastly, a systematic and comprehensive planning system should be developed to provide for a more rational approach to the allocation of resources, the setting of standards and the monitoring and review of performance.

Significantly, in view of what was to happen ten years later (see Chapter 6), the authors of the 'Grey Book' explicitly rejected the idea of organising the management of health care on the basis of a single staff hierarchy headed by a chief executive or general manager. This was because they regarded health care as being too complex and too dependent on teamwork to justify such an approach.[91] In their opinion the needs of patients were more likely to be met effectively by a collaborative and consensus approach than by one in which there was an element of authoritarianism. How CHSs were affected by the application of the concept of consensus management and the other recommendations of the study group following the reorganisation of the NHS in 1974 are considered in Chapter 5.

Despite its importance the 'Grey Book' was not without its limitations. One of these was the omission of any detailed analysis of the kind of management structure and processes that would be required at the sub-district level in the reorganised NHS. Although the consultative document had stated that the study group would consider management arrangements 'in individual hospitals and other institutions' and the 'Grey Book' itself referred to the importance of developing a 'patient centred' approach to management, in practice those concerned appear to have devoted little attention to the problems and issues of management at the 'sharp end' of the NHS. Apart from the inclusion of a role specification for a sector administrator, who was to 'co-ordinate the various administrative support services in the hospitals, health centres and clinics in his sector with each other, and ensure that they combine(d) effectively with doctors, nurses, paramedical and social services staff working in the sector',[92] most of the other material in the 'Grey Book' related to managerial roles and activities at district level and above. Thus, it was left to individual health authorities to determine, with relatively little guidance, their management structures for the sectors, into which it was recognised districts would need to be divided, and the distribution of responsibility for the administration of health care institutions and the CHSs between the sectors. Because of the shortage of time most authorities were unable to do this until after 1st April 1974.

The Reports of the Collaboration Working Party

Unlike the Management Study Group, the Collaboration Working Party did not finally complete its work until 1974. However, all its key recommendations that had implications for the reorganisation legislation were known in time for them to be included in the 1972 white paper. These were that the legislation should:

● require the authorities concerned to collaborate;

● make it obligatory for them to set up joint consultative committees, composed of members from each authority and responsible for the health and social care needs of each area and the planning of services to meet these needs; and

● give them the fullest possible powers to provide each other with goods and services.[93]

The School Health Service Subcommittee of the Collaboration Working Party, which published its first report in July 1972, also made two recommendations regarding the reorganisation legislation. Firstly, because the school health service was of such importance specific reference should be made to the duties of health authorities in respect of this service (i.e. in terms analogous to the relevant provisions of the Education Act 1944). Secondly, 'to assist in (the) carrying out (of those) functions of the (local education authority) which require(d) the involvement of health related services' the NHS should be statutorily obliged 'to provide staff, services and equipment and should make available to local authorities suitably experienced registered medical practitioners'; local education authorities should be statutorily required 'to provide appropriate accommodation and reasonable facilities within their premises for the operation of these services by the NHS; and that, in these arrangements,' local education authorities and the NHS would be expected to co-operate with one another in the interest of securing and advancing the health of school children.[94]

The Legislative Stage

Most of the proposals in the white paper, including those relating to collaboration between the NHS and local government and the school health service, were incorporated in the NHS Reorganisation Bill. This was published in November 1972. Clause 10 of the bill stated unequivocally that: 'In exercising their respective functions Health Authorities and local authorities should collaborate with one another in order to secure and advance the health and welfare of the people of England and Wales.' Whilst Clause 3 spelt out the Secretary of State's duties in respect of the medical and dental inspection and treatment of pupils attending schools maintained by local education authorities.[95]

During its passage through Parliament the bill was subject to a number of minor amendments but none of these directly affected the principle of collaboration or the future administrative arrangements for the CHSs.[96] Significantly, however, a number of MPs, from both sides of the House, expressed their reservations regarding the substantially reduced role that local authorities would play in the administration of health care services if the provisions of the bill were implemented. Two Conservatives who argued the case for local government, during the debate on the second reading of the bill, were Arthur Jones and Enoch Powell.

After referring to the 'proud tradition' of 'local democracy in the United Kingdom' and the fact that 'many of the great social advances of the nineteeth and twentieth centuries had their origin in local government', Arthur Jones went on to argue that the proposals in the bill represented 'an undesirable erosion of local democratic control over essential services' and that what was 'needed in the Health Service (was) increased sensitivity and responsiveness to local communities'.[97]

Similarly, Enoch Powell argued that, in rejecting a localist solution to the problem of how to apply the related concepts of democratic representation and financial accountability to the arrangements for the administration of health care, the Heath government had been obliged to adopt the only logical alternative, namely 'that of nationalising the community health services'. According to Mr Powell the bill marked the culmination of 'the process of the nationalisation of health care in this country which (had) commenced with the National Health Service Act 1946.' He feared, however, that in adopting a centralist solution the losses would probably exceed the gains.

Arguably, in what Mr Powell had to say about one of the most significant of these losses one can find a fitting epitaph to commemorate the formal ending of local government responsibility for the CHSs.

In the first place, we have lost the only sources of independent initiative and decision which existed outside the Central Government in the whole range of health services. After drawing up the first hospital plan (as Minister of Health in the Macmillan government), I well remember, when, in 1962, I moved on to attempt a similar plan for community health services (see above), how astonished and delighted I was to find that there was not one Minister of Health but 145 Ministers of Health : one Minister of Health and at that time 144 local health authorities. I realised that there were potentially 144 separate and independent sources of initiative, experiment, variation and adaptation to local conditions. I saw how rich were the sources of experience available to the health service under such a system compared with those that were still possible in the monolithic structure of the nationalised hospital service.

From now on there will only be one sort of policy and initiative in the community health services as in the rest of the National Health Service. There will be sources of information and opinion but this is something quite different from an authority which, having formed a view, can act upon it and be responsible for the consequences. That will have disappeared.

With it will go the independent status of local officials. I do not know whether this is not just as important as the independence of local authorities. There one had men equal to any in the National civil service who enjoyed independence and an independent responsibility which nothing can replace. They had an immediacy of contact with the people of their area. Every hon Member, in assisting his constituents with their problems, has hitherto had reason to bless the existence of independent local authority officials of high calibre with whom he could deal directly and between whom and himself there could be completely unrestricted exchange of opinion and advice.[98]

Unfortunately, despite the reservations of Arthur Jones, Enoch Powell and others, the main principles of the bill were approved by relatively large majorities and the bill eventually received the royal assent on 5th July 1973. This legitimised the formal transfer of responsibility for the administration of the CHSs from local health authorities to RHAs and AHAs, on 1st April 1974.

The Demise of the Local Health Authorities

The late 1960s and early 1970s was, in many ways, a particularly difficult period for the members and officers of local health authorities. At first they had to cope with the uncertainty over the Conservative government's intentions regarding the future administrative arrangements for the LHSs. Then, once it became clear that responsibility for the administration of the LHSs was to be transferred from local government to newly constituted health authorities, they had to come to terms with the fact that, in the case of members, they would be losing responsibility for a significant group of services, and, in the case of officers, with a change of employer. Furthermore, there was considerable concern over the fact that reorganisation would result in the break up of some major local health departments, such as those of the West Riding of Yorkshire and Lancashire, and the allocation of their staffs to a number of successor authorities (for details see Appendix IV). Consequently, as the local authority associations had predicted, morale suffered.

Anticipating the adverse effect that low morale might have on service delivery the Secretary of State for Social Services wrote personally to the mayors and chairmen of local health authorities on 1st April 1971 'reminding them of the importance of continuing effort by all concerned, including central and local government, to ensure that standards of local health services and the morale and interests of staff (were) maintained and strengthened.'

This letter was followed up, in February 1972, with a circular.[99] Although the circular was mainly concerned with the issue of good practice in the community nursing services, it also made reference to a number of very important matters affecting the LHSs as a whole. First, it drew attention to the Secretary of State's conviction that the LHSs needed 'to be absorbed into the reorganised NHS in a strong and viable form' and his confidence that local health authorities shared this conviction, 'despite the competing demand on them for the expansion of other services in the immediate future.'[100] As the circular pointed out, the concern of the Secretary of State for the LHSs reflected the growing importance which he attached 'to measures for the prevention of ill-health and the trend towards maximum treatment, care and after-care of patients outside hospital.'[101] Second, the circular made it clear that not only were additional funds being made available to support the development of community based heath care services in the period leading up to the transfer of responsibility for the administration of the CHSs from local government to AHAs, but when the LHSs were transferred loan charges and other financial liabilities would be transferred with them. Thus, the financial burden of capital schemes carried out prior to reorganisation (e.g. the building of a health centre) would not be carried by local authorities after 1st April 1974. Third, the circular announced the setting up of an NHS Staff Commission 'to aid the smooth transfer of staff from existing to the new employing authorities ...; to ensure that full account (was) taken of the interests of staff who (would) be called upon to move'[102] and to keep under review the recruitment of staff by the new health authorities. Finally, the circular expressed the Secretary of State's confidence that he 'could look to local health authorities and their staffs to make every effort to maintain and develop the local health services' whilst these services remained under their control and suggested three ways in which local health authorities could particularly help during the transitional period. Two of these related specifically to community nursing and are discussed elsewhere (see Chapter 4). The third suggestion was for local health authorities to undertake 'studies designed to identify existing and likely future need for health care in the community and to assess the service implications of such need.'[103]

In addition to the letter and circular the Secretary of State and his ministerial colleagues held a series of regional conferences in late 1971 and early 1972 for members and senior officers of local health authorities. These were designed to boost morale by giving those with direct responsibility for the administration of the LHSs an opportunity to communicate directly with Ministers and to provide a forum within which Ministers could exhort those at the 'sharp end' to maintain and strengthen services in the period leading up to the transfer of responsibility on 1st April 1974.

Clearly it is not possible to measure precisely the effect of these exhortations on the members and officers of local health authorities. However, there is evidence to suggest that in general they did respond positively. For example, the average annual increase in revenue spending on the LHSs, in real terms, for the three years 1971/72; 1972/73; 1973/74 was 7.9% compared with an average annual increase for the three years 1968/69; 1969/70; 1970/71 of 6.4% and the rate at which new health centres were being built and opened actually accelerated during the three years leading up to reorganisation (see Chapter 4). Thus, there is little doubt that the LHSs were in fact transferred from local health authorities to the newly constituted AHAs, on 1st April 1974, in a 'strong and viable form'.

Before examining the impact of this transfer of responsibility on the management and development of the CHSs it is necessary to consider how the individual services fared throughout the tripartite era. This is the theme of Chapter 4.

Footnotes

1.   N.Chaplin (edited for The Institute of Health Service Administrators), *Health Care in the United Kingdom: its organisation and management* (London: Kluwer Medical, 1982), p. 16.

2.   In a number of cases, however, local health authority areas were combined to form executive council areas. Full details can be found in Appendix I.

3.   Evidence of the Ministry of Health to the Guillebaud Committee (see footnote 69), quoted in C. Webster, *The Health Services since the War : Volume 1 Problems of Health Care The National Health Service before 1957* (London: HMSO, 1988), p. 348.

4.   There were 146 local education authorities in 1948. These were exactly the same authorities as those responsible for LHSs. However, due to changes in the structure of local government during the tripartite era, especially in Greater London, by 1974 the number of local education authorities had risen to 163.

5.   Initially the Council consisted of a Chairman, Vice-Chairman, plus 15 medical practitioners, 5 persons with experience in hospital management, 5 persons with experience in local government, 3 dental practitioners, 2 persons with experience of the mental health service, 2 registered nurses, 1 certified midwife, 2 registered pharmacists and a number of ex-officio members (e.g. President of Royal College of Physicians of London; Chairman of the Council of the BMA; President of the General Medical Council). Most of the detailed work of the Council was done through a number of standing advisory committees and various ad hoc committees and subcommittees. Nine standing advisory committees were set up in 1948. These were:

Medical Standing Advisory Committee;

Dental Standing Advisory Committee;

Pharmaceutical Standing Advisory Committee;

Ophthalmic Standing Advisory Committee;

Nursing Standing Advisory Committee;

Maternity and Midwifery Standing Advisory Committee;

Mental Health Standing Advisory Committee;

Tuberculosis Standing Advisory Committee;

Cancer and Radiotherapy Standing Advisory Committee.

All but the last two of these committees operated throughout the tripartite period. The Council was also required to report annually to Parliament on its activities and those of its committees.

6.   C. Ham, *Health Policy in Britain*, 2nd Edition (London: Macmillan, 1985), p. 17.

7.   C. Webster, op. cit., pp. 95-96.

8.   The Board of Education had been reconstituted as the Ministry of Education in August 1944. Twenty years later, in April 1964, the Ministry of Education was abolished and its functions, together with those of the Office of the Minister of Science and certain residual research functions of the Lord President of the Council, were transferred to the newly established Department of Education and Science.

9.   Administrative counties were the top tier authorities in those parts of the country where a two or three tier system of local government was in operation (i.e. London; suburban areas; medium sized and small towns and rural areas). Under this system service responsibilities were shared between the administrative county, which was responsible for most of the major services (see Table 3.3 for details) and the county districts (i.e. non-county boroughs, urban districts and rural districts). County boroughs were outside the multi-tier system of local government and in their areas, which tended to be the largest towns and cities, they were responsible for all local authority services. Consequently they were known as 'all purpose' authorities.

10.   Ministry of Health, *Annual Report for the year ending 31st March 1949*, Cmd 7910, p. 254.

11.   Initially 72 authorities applied for consent to make delegation schemes, but for various reasons only 29 eventually had their schemes approved. These were Basildon Urban District; Bedford Borough; Cambridge Borough; Cheltenham Borough; Chesterfield Borough; Colchester Borough; Crosby Borough; Easington Rural District; Gillingham Borough; Gosport Borough; Havant and Waterloo Urban District; Hove Borough; Huyton-with-Roby Urban District; Keighley Borough; Luton Borough; Middleton Borough; Newcastle-under-Lyme Borough; Nuneaton Borough; Oldbury Borough; Poole Borough; Rhondda Borough; Scunthorpe Borough; Solihull Borough; Stockton-on-Tees Borough; Stretford Borough; Sutton Coldfield Borough; Swindon Borough; Woking Urban District; and Worthing Borough. In 1965 delegation schemes were approved for Epsom and Ewell Borough; Esher Urban District; and Peterborough Borough and in 1967 for Aldridge-Brownhills Urban District.

12.   Since the term 'chairman' was in commmon currency during the tripartite era it has been used in this chapter, despite its sexist connotations. Similarly the masculine pronoun has sometimes been used when referring to the chairman of the health committee even though some of the occupants of this post were women.

13.   Ministry of Health, op. cit., p. 254.

14.   In 1973 administrative counties with a divisional or area organisation for their LHSs included Cheshire, Dorset, Glamorgan, Lancashire, Northumberland and the East and West Ridings of Yorkshire. Not surprisingly, it tended to be the largest counties in terms of area which had some

form of decentralisation. There were, however, some exceptions (e.g. Devon, Somerset, Lincolnshire [Parts of Lindsey]).

15. The medical officers of the county boroughs covered by these provisions were those where the county council had contributed to the salary of the MOH before the district concerned acquired county borough status.

16. See Ministry of Housing and Local Government, *Staffing of Local Government*, [Mallaby Report] (London: HMSO, 1967), paras. 103-113. According to evidence which the BMA submitted to the Mallaby Committee only about 3% of the medical officers employed in the public health service commanded salaries at consultant level.

17. Statutory Rules and Orders (SR&O) No. 1076 1945, *The Handicapped Pupils and School Health Service Regulations 1945*, Reg. 43. The term 'principal school medical officer' was formally introduced by Statutory Instrument (SI) No. 1156 1953, *The School Health Service and Handicapped Pupils Regulations 1953*.

18. C. Ham, op. cit., p. 23.

19. Ministry of Housing and Local Government, *Management of Local Government*, [Maud Report] (London: HMSO, 1967), para. 138.

20. Ibid., para. 138.

21. DHSS, *Report of the Working Party on Medical Administrators*, [Chair: Dr R. Hunter] (London: HMSO, 1972), p. 61.

22. C. Thomas, 'BJOT: Occupational Therapy in the Community', *British Journal of Occupational Therapy, October 1987, 50(10), p. 353.*

23. R. Levitt and A. Wall, *The Reorganised National Health Service*, 3rd Edition (London: Croom Helm, 1984), 'by... 1968, forty-two county councils, thirty-four county boroughs and seventeen London borough councils had appointed a Chief Nursing Officer to organise and direct the work of their community nursing services', p. 195.

24. Staffing of Local Government, op. cit., para. 132.

25. DHSS, Scottish Home and Health Departments and Welsh Office, *Report of the Working Party on Management Structures in the Local Authority Nursing Services*, [Chair: E.L. Mayston], 1967, see paras. 137 and 151-158.

26. Ibid., para. 156.

27. SI No. 1156 1953, op. cit., Reg. 6.

28. The annual reports of the Chief Medical Officer on the state of the public health for the years up to and including 1961 were issued as command papers (i.e. a form of parliamentary paper) and from 1949 were formally part of the annual report of the Ministry of Health. Subsequent reports have been published as non-parliamentary papers by HMSO. The biennial reports on the health of the school child were always published as non-parliamentary papers. The last in this series, which was essentially a review of the school health service from its inception in 1908 to 1974, was published in 1975.

29. C. Fraser Brockington, *The Health of the Community: Principles of Public Health for Practitioners and Students*, 3rd Edition (London: Churchill, 1965), p. 92.

30. In the words of SI No. 962 1959, *The Public Health Officers Regulations, 1959*, 'A medical officer of health of a county (similar provisions applied to the MOsH of district councils) (was required) ... as soon as practicable after the 31st of December in each year make an annual report (emphasis added) to the county council for the year ending on that date on the sanitary circumstances, the sanitary administration and the vital statistics of the county, containing in addition to any matters upon which he (might) consider it desirable to report, such information as (might) from time to time be required by the Minister (of Health).'

31.   C. Fraser Brockington, op. cit., p. 93.

32.   J. Brotherston, 'Change and the National Health Service' in A. Gatherer and M. Warren (eds.), *Management and the Health Services* (Oxford: Pergamon, 1971) p. 21. Integration was also hindered, according to C. Webster, op. cit., by the 'survival of deep-rooted animosity between Medical Officers of Health and other members of the (medical) profession', p. 345.

33.   Quoted in C. Webster, op. cit., p. 374. In a similar vein Webster speaks of 'a sense of impending doom' hanging over local health authorities 'from the outset of the NHS' and 'the weak political position' of local authority health departments.

34.   See Section C of Appendix II for further details.

35.   Ministry of Housing and Local Government, *Local Government Finance (England and Wales)*, Cmd 209 (London: HMSO, 1957), p. 3.

36.   For example, in 1970/71 the Conservative government introduced a specific grant as part of the Urban Programme, to encourage local health authorities to develop family planning services in areas of special social need. By 1973/74 approximately 5.0% of the income needed to finance the family planning services of local health authorities was being derived from specific grants of this kind.

37.   Further details of the distribution of gross revenue spending on health care services in 1949/50 and 1970/71 are provided below:

	1949/50		1970/71	
	£m	%	£m	%
Hospital services	205.4	54.5	997.2	59.4
Family practitioner services	139.5	37.0	483.3	28.8
Local health services	**32.1**	**8.5**	**198.1**	**11.8**
Total	377.0	100.0	1678.6	100.0

The equivalent figures for 1973/74 (i.e. after the Seebohm reorganisation) are:

	1973/4	
	£m	%
Hospital services	1551.2	65.0
Family practitioner services	643.1	26.9
Local health services	192.0	8.1
Total	2386.3	100.0

Figures for spending on HSs and FPSs have been taken from House of Commons Paper 158 Session 1950/51; HC 280 Session 1971/72 and HC 400 Session 1974/75.

38.   L. Sharpe and K. Newton, *Does Politics Matter? The determinants of public policy* (Oxford: Oxford University Press, 1984), Table 9.9, p. 195.

39.   J. Noyce, A. Snaith and A. Trickey, 'Regional Variations in the Allocation of Financial Resources to the Community Health Services', *The Lancet*, 30 March 1974, pp. 554-7.

40.   For a more detailed account of the capital spending of local health authorities between 1948 and the second half of the 1950s, see C. Webster, op. cit., pp. 220-222.

41.   SR&O No 1076 1945, op. cit., Reg. 45.

42.   Ibid., reg. 55.

43.   SI No 1156 1953, op. cit., Reg. 13.

44. J. Griffith, *Central Departments and Local Authorities* (London: Allen and Unwin, 1966), p. 466.

45. Ibid., pp. 466-7.

46. Ministry of Health, *A Hospital Plan for England and Wales*, Cmd 1604 (London: HMSO, 1962), para. 31.

47. Ministry of Health, *Health and Welfare : The Development of Community Care*, Cmnd 1973 (London: HMSO, 1963).

48. B. Watkin, *Documents on Health and Social Services, 1834 to the present day* (London: Methuen, 1975), p. 158.

49. Ministry of *Health, Health and Welfare. The Development of Community Care (Cmnd 1973). Revision to 1973/74 of Plans for the Health and Welfare Services of the Local Authorities of England and Wales* (London: HMSO, 1964).

50. Ministry of *Health, Health and Welfare. The Development of Community Care. Revision to 1975/76 of Plans for the Health and Welfare Services of the Local Authorities of England and Wales*, Cmnd 3022 (London: HMSO, 1966).

51. Ibid., p. 1.

52. J. Griffith, op. cit., p. 58.

53. Ibid., p. 515.

54. Ibid., p. 515-6.

55. Ibid., p. 518.

56. SR&O No 1076 1945, op. cit., Reg. 48 and SI No 1156 1953, op. cit., Reg. 8(1).

57. For example, in 1963 it was disclosed by Dr Peter Henderson (Principal Medical Officer of the Ministry of Education) whilst giving evidence to Subcommittee C of the House of Commons Estimates Committee during their investigation of the dental services. that only one member of his staff was a qualified dentist and he was expected to give advice to the Ministry on dental matters as well as inspect school dental services throughout England and Wales! See House of Commons Paper No. 40 Session 1962/63 for further details.

58. Ministry of Health, *Annual Report for the year ending 31st March 1949*, op. cit., p.242.

59. J. Parker, *Local Health and Welfare Services* (London: Allen and Unwin, 1965), pp. 77-88.

60. C. Webster, op. cit., p. 373.

61. Ibid., p. 374.

62. Central Health Services Council, *Report on Co- operation between Hospital, Local Authority and General Practitioner Services* [Chair: F. Messer] (London: HMSO, 1952), para. 66.

63. Ibid., para. 66.

64. Letter from Ministry of Health dated 26th February 1949 and quoted in the County Councils Association Gazette Supplement 1949 p. 98.

65. C. Webster, op. cit., p. 322.

66. Ibid., p. 375.

67. Ibid., p. 375.

68. J. Parker, op. cit., p. 82.

69. The precise terms of reference of the Guillebaud Commmittee were: 'To review the present and prospective cost of the National Health Service; to suggest means whether by modification of organisation or otherwise, of ensuring the most effective control and efficient use of such

Exchequer funds as may be made available; to advise how, in view of the burdens on the Exchequer, a rising charge upon it can be avoided while providing for the maintenance of an adequate service; and to make recommendations'.

70. *Report of the Committee of Enquiry into the Cost of the National Health Service,* [Chair: C.W.Guillebaud], Cmd 9663, (London: HMSO, 1956), p. 276..

71. Ministry of Health, *The Administrative Structure of Medical and Related Services in England and Wales* (London: HMSO, 1968), para. 20.

72. Medical Services Review Committee, *A Review of Medical Services in Great Britain* (London: Social Assay, 1962).

73. The Administrative Structure of Medical and Related Services in England and Wales, op. cit., paras. 25-30.

74. Ibid., para. 32.

75. Royal Commission on Local Government in England 1966-1969, [Chair Lord Redcliffe-Maud], *Report,* Cmnd 4040 (London : HMSO, 1969), paras. 359-367.

76. DHSS, *The Future Structure of the National Health Service* (London: HMSO, 1970).

77. Ibid., para. 19.

78 Ibid., para. 32.

79 DHSS, *National Health Service Reorganisation : Consultative Document* (London: DHSS, 1971).

80 Ibid., para. 7.

81 Ibid., para. 20.

82 Ibid., para. 7.

83. R.G. Brown, *Reorganising the National Health Service : A Case Study of Administrative Change* (Oxford: Blackwell, 1979), p. 47.

84. DHSS, *Management Arrangements for the Reorganised National Health Service* (London: HMSO, 1972), p. 7.

85 *National Health Service Reorganisation : England,* Cmnd 5055 (London: HMSO, 1972), para. 1.

86. DHSS, Committee on Child Health Services, [Chair: Professor S. Court], Cmnd 6684) *Fit for the Future* (London: HMSO, 1976), p. iv.

87. Report of the Working Party on Medical Administrators, op. cit.

88. Management Arrangements for the Reorganised National Health Service, op. cit.

89. National Health Service Reorganisation : England, op. cit., Appendix III, para. 13 and Management Arrangements for The Reorganised National Health Service, op. cit., para. 1.15.

90. Ibid., para. 2.46 to 2.52.

91. Ibid., para. 1.24.

92 Ibid., pp. 151-152.

93. For full details of these and the other recommendations of the Collaboration Working Party see DHSS, *Reports from the Working Party on Collaboration between the NHS and Local Government on its Activities: (a) to the End of 1972* (London: HMSO, 1973); (b) *from January to July 1973* (London: HMSO, 1973) and (c) *from July 1973 to April 1974* (London: HMSO, 1974).

94. Ibid., (a) para. 6.20

95.   Clause 3 also stated that it was to be the duty of local education authorities to make available to the Secretary of State the accommodation he needed to carry out his responsibilities in respect of the provision of medical and dental services for pupils. Similarly clause 11 required the Secretary of State to make available to local authorities, insofar at it was 'reasonably necessary and practicable', services and other facilities to enable them 'to discharge their functions relating to social services, education and public health'.

96.   The most contentious issue at this time was that of charging for family planning appliances etc. This is discussed more fully in Chapter 4.

97.   Hansard (Commons), Vol. 853, 26th March 1973, col. 1021.

98.   Ibid., 27th March 1973, col. 1125.

99.   DHSS, Circular 13/72, *Aids to Improved Efficiency in the Local Health Services. Deployment of Nursing Teams.*

100.   Ibid., para. 3.

101.   Ibid., para. 3.

102.   Ibid., para. 4.

103.   Ibid., para. 5.

Chapter 4

The Tripartite Era: Service Developments

In spite of the weaknesses inherent in the tripartite structure significant progress was made between 1948 and 1974 in respect of the development of individual services. Furthermore, from the mid-1960s, there was a rapid expansion in the number of health centres and, in many areas, they came to play a key role in the delivery of primary care. Having considered, in Chapter 3, the administrative and financial framework within which this progress was made, attention is now focussed on the development of health centres and of the individual services.

Health Centres

As pointed out in Chapter 2, the case for (primary) health centres was first made by Dawson and his colleagues at the beginning of the 1920s. However, the first and only piece of legislation to make specific reference to health centres was the 1946 Act. Thus, it took just over 25 years for the concept of the health centre to gain statutory recognition.

Under the provisions of Section 21 of the 1946 Act every local health authority was required 'to provide, equip and maintain, to the satisfaction of the Minister, premises' to be known as 'health centres' at which facilities were to be made available for all or some of the following purposes:

- the provision of general medical services;
- the provision of general dental services;
- the provision of pharmaceutical services;
- the provision or organisation of LHSs;
- the provision of out-patient services; and

- the exercise of powers conferred on local health authorities in respect of 'the publication of information on questions relating to health or disease, and for the delivery of lectures and the display of pictures or films in which such questions are dealt with' (i.e. health education).

It was therefore anticipated that health centres would serve as the focal point for the delivery of a wide variety of health care services and thereby contribute to the development of closer relations between those engaged in the provision of LHSs, on the one hand, and family practitioners and some hospital staff on the other. Moreover, according to Aneurin Bevan, health centres were 'an innovation' to which the Labour government attached 'very great importance' and would help to counterbalance the fissiparous tendencies inherent in the tripartite structure.[1]

However, for reasons which have already been mentioned, health centres were specifically excluded from the initial proposals which local health authorities were required to make in respect of their responsibilities under the 1946 Act (see Chapter 3). Thus, apart from formally approving as health centres 10 dispensaries and other establishments, which were already in operation prior to 1948 (5 in England and 5 in Wales) and incorporated facilities for either general medical, or general dental or pharmaceutical services, little else was done until the early 1950s and even then progress was extremely slow.

The first of the centres established, at Faringdon in Berkshire, was opened in March 1951. However, this was an adaptation of existing buildings and only cost £400. The first purpose-built health centre, costing £16,122, was opened in Bristol in September 1952. For the remainder of the decade[2] and during the first half of the 1960s the number of centres opened in any one year never exceeded 3 and it was not until the late 1960s that large scale development took place. Table 4.1 shows the number of health centres opened in England during the tripartite era.

Of the 28 health centres opened between 1948 and the mid-1960s the vast majority were located on new housing estates or in rural areas. With the benefit of hindsight, this is hardly surprising given the fact that they were expensive to build and therefore had to be justified more in terms of the efficient use of resources rather than simply ideology.

Apart from resource constraints the slow development of health centres can also be explained by reference to the somewhat negative attitude of many GPs towards the concept. Although they recognised some of the benefits to be gained from group working many felt that health centres would undermine their independent contractor status and that it would be more expensive, in terms of the costof accommodation, to practice from health centres than either privatively rented or owner occupied premises.

On the question of health centre development a majority of those who gave evidence to the Guillebaud Committee took the view that health centres had to remain for some time in an 'experimental phase and that meantime other experiments ought to be carried out to discover how far group practice working in close association with maternity and child welfare and school clinics might be able to provide at least some of the welfare and school clinics might be able to provide at least some of the benefits of a health centre at a much lower cost.[3]

TABLE 4.1 *Health Centres : Numbers Opened 1950 to 1973*

Year	No Opened[a]	Cumulative Total	Cumulative[b] Total
1950	0	0	5
1951	1	1	6
1952	3	4	9
1953	0	4	9
1954	1	5	10
1955	2	7	12
1956	1	8	13
1957	0	8	13
1958	2	10	15
1959	0	10	15
1960	3	13	18
1961	1	14	19
1962	2	16	21
1963	1	17	22
1964	3	20	25
1965	1	21	26
1966	7	28	33
1967	12	40	45
1968	36	76	81
1969	50	126	131
1970	61	187	191
1971	83	270	274
1972	91	361	365
1973	103	464	468

Notes

a.   As at 31st December

b.   This includes the premises which were already in operation in 1948 and were formally approved as health centres because they incorporated facilities for one or more of the FPSs as well as a variety of LHSs.

Source: Ministry of Health and DHSS, *Annual Reports,* various years.

Not surprisingly, therefore, health centres hardly figured at all in the first version of local health authority plans for the development of their health and welfare services from 1962-63 to 1971-72. According to the Ministry of Health the circumstances which justified their provision did not arise very frequently, namely that there had to be a local need for new premises 'coinciding with a keen desire on the part of both the local health authority and general practitioners to develop this particular form of co-operation.'[4] Clearly this keen desire was conspicuous by its absence in the early 1960s.

However, by the mid-1960s, when local health authorities revised their plans for a second time, the Ministry was able to report 'an upsurge in interest in health centres.'[5] Their plans now showed that they proposed to open 284 health centres by 1976. In fact, as the data in Table 4.1 indicate, this was a substantial underestimate since 468 health centres were actually opened by 1974.

Although the Ministry welcomed these developments it did not attempt to force the pace. This is somewhat surprising given the fact that the Labour Party, which could be regarded as more sympathetic to the concept of health centres, had been in office since 1964.

In a circular on health centres, which the Ministry issued in 1967,[6] there was no suggestion that local health authorities and family practitioners were obliged to opt for health centres when deciding how best to secure the provision of more integrated primary care services. Instead, the circular simply stressed the importance of early consultations between all the parties concerned. It also provided guidance on a number of technical aspects of health centre development, such as the financial regime governing the use of centres by GPs and other family practitioners. Since family practitioners based in heath centres retained their independent contractor status, they were required to pay a sum of money to the local health authority, which included a rental element and a contribution towards the running costs of the centre.

As Beales points out, the upsurge of interest in health centres on the part of GPs during the second half of the 1960s was due to a variety of factors. First, GPs were concerned about their 'declining status vis-a-vis the hospital consultant,'[7] especially with regard to the physical condition of the premises from which they were often practising, and the adverse effect of these conditions on their patients. In the words of Beales:

There must have been patients who looked upon a visit to their doctor in much the same way as their ancestors had contemplated admission to hospital. Sat upon mouldy furniture beside damp walls, listening to the clank of the water pipes, and watching the insects race each other across the rotten floorboards; crowded into a tiny room with so many other coughing and sneezing and poorly looking people, trying to remember who was there when he arrived and who had come after; not knowing how long it would be before his turn to see the doctor came, the patient must have wondered whether he was more likely to get better as a result of the visit or to contract something far worse.[8]

Thus, some doctors at least began to see health centres as less of a threat to their independence and more as a way of securing premises of a much higher standard than they had been used to. In this way they hoped to make themselves seem less like 'one of the consultant's poorer relations' and to improve the quality of the service they were able to offer to patients.

Second, as a result of slum clearance programmes many GPs in inner city areas lost their existing premises through compulsory purchase and could not afford to practice from anywhere other than a health centre. Moreover, due to rapidly increasing property prices elsewhere GPs were sometimes encountering difficulties in finding suitable surgery accommodation at a price they could afford. Thus, 'towards the end of the decade the increasing cost of land and building persuaded many doctors, particularly younger doctors, to revise their attitude towards health centres provided by the local authority.'[9]

Third, under the so called 'Doctors' Charter' of 1966, which was designed to improve the quality of general medical services by significantly changing the way GPs were remunerated, GPs were able to claim reimbursement of rent if they chose to lease rather than own their surgery premises. Furthermore, this provision of the 'Doctors' Charter' covered rental payments to local health authorities for the use of health centres as well as to private landlords.

Last, some of the more enlightened GPs were being attracted to the concept of the primary care team,[10] which had been advocated by the Gillie Committee in 1963,[11] and recognised that if it was to be put into practice there was a need for premises which would accommodate a much larger number and wider variety of health care professionals than the traditional surgery. Furthermore, as the report of the Harvard Davies Subcommittee on Group Practices (1971) pointed out, the increasing popularity of health centres amongst GPs was due not only to the advantages that they saw for their patients but also to the high costs 'of providing their own modern group practice premises designed to accommodate the health team.'[12]

Consequently the number of GPs practising from health centres increased from approximately 240 in 1966 to just over 2500 in 1973. This meant that within the space of seven years the percentage of GPs practising from health centres rose from 1.5% to nearly 12.0%. However, this rate of increase did not match the increase in the number of health centres and as a result the average number of GPs practising from a health centre fell from 9, in 1966, to 5.4 in 1973. Of the 468 health centres operating at 31st December 1973 all but 4 provided general medical services. However, general dental services were only available at 39 centres and pharmaceutical services at 5.

Unfortunately, similar data on the range and volume of LHSs provided at health centres are not available. However, some idea of the type and scale of provision can be obtained from material collected by Edwards for his study of health centres in Devon,[13] which was one of the first local health authorities to develop an extensive network of health centres (see Appendix III). Of the 21 health centres opened by the late 1960s all provided clinics for child health, ante-natal care, school health, chiropody and speech therapy; ophthalmology services were available in 12; dental services in 6; family planning services in 12 and occupational therapy in 1. In addition, approximately half of the centres served as a base for home helps and social workers and retirement clinics were held in 4.

Although these data relate only to health centres in one part of the country, it can be safely assumed that elsewhere they were being developed as a base for the delivery of an equally varied range of LHSs. Furthermore,increasingly their potential as a setting for the development of primary care teams was being recognised.

However, with the reorganisation of the NHS in 1974 responsibility for the building and administration of health centres and therefore for realising their full potential was transferred from local health authorities to the newly created RHAs and AHAs.

Individual Services

The services to which particular attention will be given are:

- care of mothers and young children;
- midwifery;
- health visiting;
- home nursing;
- vaccination and immunisation;
- care and after-care of persons suffering from illness, including community based mental health services;
- family planning; and
- school health service, including the school dental service.

With the exception of family planning and school health, detailed provisions for all of these services were contained in Part III of the 1946 Act. The ambulance service and the provision of domestic help, to which reference was also made in Part III of the Act, are not considered in detail since neither is currently classified as a CHS.

Care of Mothers and Young Children

It was pointed out in Chapter 3 that, as far as the care of expectant and nursing mothers and young children was concerned, one of the most important consequences of the 1946 Act was the fact that 261 county districts lost their power to provide services of this kind. This clearly reduced the status of many medical officers and, according to Webster, 'created friction between the two levels of authority (i.e.county and district)'![14]

The 1946 Act also made two other important changes to the law relating to the care of mothers and young children by local authorities. First, in contrast with earlier legislation which had only given local authorities permissive powers to attend to the needs of mothers and young children, Section 22 imposed on local health authorities the duty of 'making arrangements for the care... of expectant and nursing mothers and of children who (had) not attained the age of five and (were) not attending primary schools maintained by a local education authority'. This primarily involved continuing and, where necessary, expanding the provision of ante-natal and post-natal clinics and infant welfare centres, which were already well established in most areas by 1948. As Webster comments, since maternity and child welfare centres 'were the only major institutional expression left' with local health authorities (prior to the rapid expansion in the development of health centres), 'they took on a special symbolic importance (and) it was a particular point of principle to furnish new housing estates with ... (centres) at the same rate as schools.'[15]

Second, for the first time specific reference was made to the dental, as well as the general, care of mothers and young children. This responsibility presented local health authorities with far more problems since it proved impossible to recruit an adequate number of staff and indeed some of the existing dental staff resigned to take up general practice. Consequently the priority dental services, as they were known, did not develop to the extent that originally had been intended.

Local health authorities were also given the discretionary power to make, with the approval of the Minister, contributions to voluntary organisations engaged in the care of mothers and young children. In practice, however, this power was only of marginal significance since relatively few ante-natal clinics (2.5% in 1950); post-natal clinics (2.6% in 1950) and infant welfare centres (7.0% in 1950) were run by voluntary organisations. The vast majority were directly provided and controlled by local health authorities, a responsibility which they exercised throughout the tripartite era.

Information relating to the number of women who attended ante-natal clinics provided by local authorities and voluntary organisations between 1949 and 1973 is provided in Figure 4.1. Although there were some fluctuations in the level of usage the underlying trend was downward, especially between 1960 and 1970. This was also reflected in the number of sessions held at clinics of this kind which fell from approximately 115,000 in 1949 to approximately 80,000 in 1973. This steady decline in attendance at local authority ante-natal clinics was more than could be accounted for by variations in the birth rate and according to Webster could be regarded as a sign of their obsolescence.[16] Part of the explanation for this was an increase in the percentage of confinements taking place in hospital, from under 60% in 1948 to nearly 95% in 1973, accompanied by an expansion in the ante-natal care provided at hospital clinics and a greater involvement by GPs in the care of expectant mothers. Alongside this decline, however, must be set the increasing significance of mothercraft and relaxation classes run by local health authorities, with between 135,000 and 145,000 women per annum attending classes of this kind during the 1960s and early 1970s.

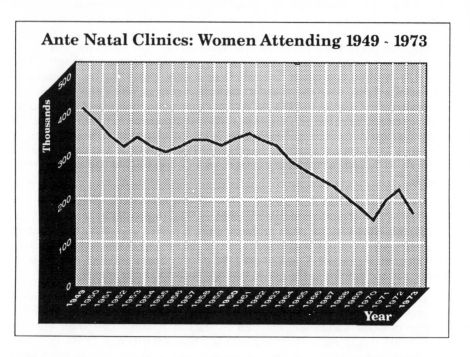

(England and Wales)

Figure 4.1

Sources: Ministry of Health and DHSS, *Annual Reports,* various years; DHSS, *Digest of Health Statistics* and *Health and Personal Social Services Statistics for England,* various editions, and Welsh Office, *Health and Personal Social Services Statistics for Wales, various editions.*

Local authority/voluntary organisation post-natal clinics, which had never been provided on any thing like the same scale as ante-natal clinics, also declined in importance during the tripartite era. Furthermore, their importance declined at an even faster rate than that of ante-natal clinics. In 1949 67,000 women had attended post-natal clinics run by local health authorities and voluntary organisations, but by 1973 the number had fallen to 27,000.

In contrast with both ante-natal and post-natal clinics the trend in the numbers attending, and in the number of sessions held at, child welfare centres/clinics (or child health centres/clinics as they became known) run by local health authorities and, to a limited extent, voluntary organisations was upward, once allowance is made for fluctuations in the birthrate. This is illustrated by Figure 4.2.

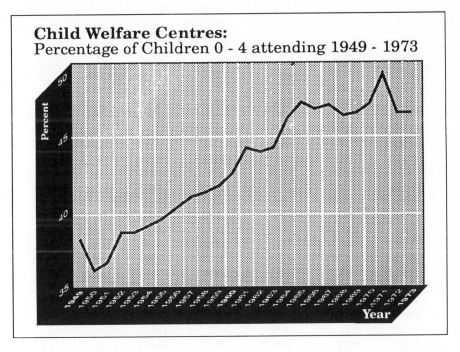

Child Welfare Centres:
Percentage of Children 0 - 4 attending 1949 - 1973

(England and Wales)

Figure 4.2

Source: Ministry of Health, *Annual Reports,* various years; DHSS, *Digest of Health Statistics* and *Health and Personal Social Services Statistics for England,* various editions, and Welsh Office, *Health and Personal Social Services Statistics for Wales*, various editions.

It is significant, however, that much greater use was made of these centres by mothers when their children were under one year of age than when they were older.

Some additional statistical data on centres for pre-school children are provided in Table 4.2.

TABLE 4.2 *Child Welfare Centres : Scale of Provision 1949 to 1973*[a]

Year	Centres[b]	Sessions[c]	Children attending	Children aged 0-4 attending	% of Children 0-4
		'000s	'000s	'000s	
1949	4731	n.a.	1405	3701	38.0
1950	4910	256	1856	3725	36.4
1951	5030	262	1369	3719	36.8
1952	5119	266	1360	3505	38.8
1953	5363	271	1314	3385	38.8
1954	5494	276	1304	3326	39.2
1955	5575	283	1296	3283	39.5
1956	5676	286	1326	3291	40.3
1957	5745	290	1372	3328	41.2
1958	5817	293	1392	3383	41.1
1959	5875	300	1433	3452	41.5
1960	n.a.	291	1500	3546	42.3
1961	n.a.	308	1618	3665	44.1
1962	n.a.	314	1648	3783	43.6
1963	n.a.	329	1710	3899	43.9
1964	6411*	333	1857	4010	46.3
1965	n.a.	343	1948	4113	47.4
1966	n.a.	348	1950	4167	46.8
1967	n.a.	352	1960	4174	47.0
1968	n.a.	348e	1932	4156	46.5
1969	n.a.	348e	1911	4108	46.5
1970	n.a.	351e	1880	4008	46.9
1971	6608*	359e	1917	3920	48.9
1972	6722*	360e	1783	3825	46.6
1973	6506*	369e	1740	3733	46.6

Key

* Maternity and child welfare centres. The number of premises used solely for child health purposes is not known.

n.a. = data not available.
e = estimated figure.

Notes

a.   Figures for England and Wales.

b.   Premises included purpose built centres (approximately 20% of centres were purpose built by the late 1960s); rented accommodation, such as church halls; mobile centres; GP surgeries and in the later years health centres.

c.   Sessions were conducted by medical officers, assisted by health visitors; GPs employed on a sessional basis; health visitors on their own and occasionally by hospital doctors.

Source: Ministry of Health, *Annual Reports*, various years; DHSS, *Digest of Health Statistics* and *Health and Personal Social Services Statistics for England*, various editions; Welsh Office, *Health and Personal Social Services Statistics for Wales*, various editions; Central Statistical Office, *Annual Abstract of Statistics*, various years, and DHSS, Committee on Child Health Services, [Chair: Professor S.Court], *Fit for the Future*, Volume 2.

The greater usage of child welfare centres was almost certainly due to the increasing effectiveness of health visitors in persuading mothers to have their children regularly screened so that any 'defects' could be detected as early as possible and to the fact that they were the principal distribution points for welfare foods, which included National Dried Milk, concentrated orange juice, cod liver oil and vitamin tablets. Until 1954 the Ministry of Food was formally responsible for the administration of the welfare foods scheme. However, with the end of food rationing and the closure of food offices in June of that year, local health authorities took over full responsibility (including funding) for the distribution of welfare foods, other than liquid milk.

At many centres, as well as obtaining welfare foods, parents could purchase goods such as proprietary brands of milk for babies, nutrients, infants' foods, vitamin supplements, milk products, toothbrushes and other items, mainly for young children, at prices lower than retail. Usually the selling price was cost plus a handling expenses charge. In a few areas certain items (e.g. proprietary brands of milk for babies) were supplied free to families considered to be in financial need. Much of the sales work was undertaken by volunteers. It is important to note that this service was provided primarily as a convenience to parents and not as a means of generating income.

The functions and staffing of child welfare centres were investigated in the 1960s by a subcommittee of the Central Health Services Council's Standing Medical Advisory Committee, under the chairmanship of Sir Wilfred Sheldon. After receiving evidence from a wide variety of sources the members of the subcommittee were left in 'no doubt about the continuing need for a preventive service to safeguard the health of children.'[17] In their report, which was published in 1967, they also specified what they considered to be the principal functions of a child health service. These were:

- routine medical examinations of children presumed to be healthy;
- advice on infant nutrition and hygiene;
- early detection of physical, mental and emotional 'defects';
- counselling of parents;
- health education;
- recording the heights and weights of children in order to monitor their physical development;
- immunisation and vaccination; and

• the distribution of welfare and proprietary foods.

The members of the subcommittee also expressed the view that the organisation of the child health service called for a highly trained administrator with a medical training and that the service should remain the administrative responsibility of the MOH. However, they also noted the increasing interest in the health, growth and development of children shown by GPs and paediatricians and recommended that service provision should eventually become the responsibility of general practice. At the time this radical proposal proved to be unacceptable. Local health authorities felt that in order to fulfil their statutory duties and to administer the child health service in an effective and efficient manner they still needed to employ their own medical staff. Moreover, they were instinctively opposed to any proposals which threatened to diminish their powers.

Alongside the provision of ante-natal and post-natal clinics and infant welfare centres many local health authorities also contributed to the health and well-being of mothers and young children by running day nurseries for pre-school children. These were intended primarily for children with special health or social needs, such as a physical handicap or the fact that their mother was the breadwinner. During the 1950s and 1960s, however, there was a gradual reduction in the number of places provided in local authority day nurseries.

In addition, local health authorities had a duty under the Nurseries and Child-Minders Regulation Act 1948 to keep a register of persons, who in their own home and for reward minded three or more children under five years of age, and of premises where pre-school children were looked after. They also had the power to impose specified requirements as a condition of registration and to inspect premises. As the number of places in local authority day nurseries fell (e.g. from 26109 in 1956 to 21169 in 1967), the number of registered private nurseries and child minders rapidly increased. For example, in 1956 there were 464 registered private nurseries providing places for 12018 children and 881 childminders, who were able to look after 6964 children. By 1967, however, the number of nurseries had increased to 9382 (109141 places) and child minders to 5039 (42696 children).

Lastly, a few local health authorities provided pre-natal and post-natal accommodation for unmarried mothers and their children and some social workers and health visitors employed by local health authorities were involved with the provision of help and support for unmarried mothers.

Thus, in the years preceding the Seebohm reorganisation, local health department responsibilities in respect of the care of mothers and young children extended well beyond their physical well-being. Consequently, there was the potential, at least, to develop a broadly based service for mothers and young children. Realisation of this potential, however, was undermined by the transfer of responsibility for the day care of children under 5 and family case work from the health departments of local authorities to the newly created social service departments as part of the Seebohm reorganisation in the early 1970s and, more significantly, by the reorganisations of local government and the NHS in 1974, which led to RHAs and AHAs taking over responsibility for the health care of mothers and young children, and, in the case of AHAs for the distribution of welfare food.[18]

Midwifery

Under the provisions of Section 23 of the 1946 Act local health authorities were designated the local supervising authority for the purposes of the Midwives Acts of 1902 to 1936. This meant that, as mentioned in Chapter 3, 43 minor welfare authorities lost their delegated powers in respect of the supervision of midwives.

The 1946 Act also placed on local health authorities the duty of ensuring that 'the number of certified midwives... available... in (their) area... for attendance on women in their homes as midwives, or as maternity nurses during childbirth and from time to time thereafter during a period not less than the lying-in period, (was) adequate for the needs of the area'. In fulfilling this obligation local health authorities could **either** make arrangements with boards of governors of teaching hospitals/hospital management committees or voluntary organisations; **or** employ sufficient midwives themselves.

According to the Ministry of Health's *Annual Report for the year ended 31st March 1949* an overwhelming majority of local health authorities in England (i.e. 93 out of 129) opted to fulfil their statutory obligation by directly employing midwives. Of the remainder 9 made arrangements with voluntary organisations and 27 used the services of both directly employed midwives and those employed by voluntary organisations. Significantly, however, a relatively large percentage of midwives (i.e. over 50%) were employed only on a part-time basis and spent the remainder of the time as either health visitors, home nurses or school nurses. This pattern of staffing continued throughout the tripartite era. For example, in 1968 only 3406 out of 7014 domiciliary midwives (i.e. 48%) were employed on a whole-time basis, the remainder being part-timers.

The role of the local health authority as the local supervising authority for the midwives practising in their area was redefined by the Midwives Act 1951. Under the provisions of this legislation every local supervising authority was required to:

- exercise general supervision over all certified midwives practising within their area;

- investigate any charge of malpractice, negligence or misconduct on the part of a certified midwife and, if a prima facie case was established, to report it to the Central Midwives Board;

- suspend a certified midwife from practice if it appeared necessary to do so in order to prevent the spread of infection;

- report immediately to the Central Midwives Board the name of any certified midwife practising who had been convicted of an offence;

- keep the Central Midwives Board informed on an annual basis of all certified midwives who had notified the authority of their intention to practise within their area;

- report immediately to the Central Midwives Board the death of a certified midwife or a change in the name or address of a certified midwife; and

- provide or arrange for the provision of any necessary courses of instruction for certified midwives.

The statutory duties of local health authorities, in respect of midwifery, were further extended by the provisions of the Health Services and Public Health Act 1968. These required local health authorities not only to secure the services of an adequate number of midwives but also to ensure that midwives were 'enabled to render all services reasonably necessary for the proper care of the women upon whom' they attended. In addition, local health authorities were able to make provision for midwives to attend women in their area 'elsewhere than in their homes or in hospitals' (e.g. in health centres or clinics). These provisions reflected some of the changes which had been occurring in the nature of the domiciliary midwifery service.

Firstly, the increase in the percentage of hospital confinements, to which reference has already been made, meant that the need for the traditional services of domiciliary midwives (i.e. to attend home deliveries) had gradually declined. As the data in Figure 4.3 indicate this decline was much sharper after 1960 than before.

The steeper decline after 1960 can be explained by reference to the recommendations of the Cranbrook Committee on Maternity Services, which were published in 1959.[19] This committee had been established because the Minister of Health felt that 'he needed advice from a carefully balanced expert group, in view of the divergent opinions expressed on maternity services within the medical profession.'[20] In their report Cranbrook and his colleagues recommended that there should be greater supervision of expectant and nursing mothers by specialist obstetricians and that at least 70% of deliveries should take place in hospital. This recommendation was very much in line with the dominant view within the medical profession. However, the Cranbrook Committee supported the retention of a separate domiciliary midwifery service and local authority ante-natal clinics, but recommended that medical officers employed by local authorities,who staffed these clinics, should gradually be replaced by general practitioner obstetricians.[21]

Following the publication of the Cranbrook Report effective steps were taken to increase the proportion of hospital confinements. Not surprisingly, this not only contributed to the decline in the number of domiciliary confinements but also resulted in a significant change in the relative staffing positions of the community and hospital midwifery services (see Figure 4.4).

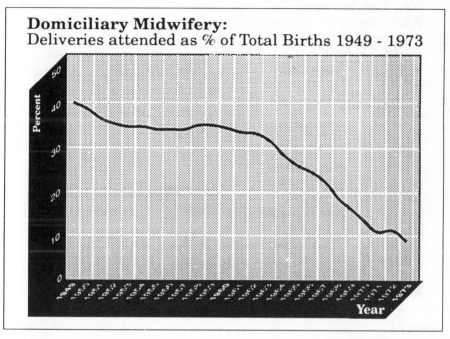

Domiciliary Midwifery:
Deliveries attended as % of Total Births 1949 - 1973

(England and Wales)

Figure 4.3

Sources: Ministry of Health, *Annual Reports,* various years, and DHSS, *Digest of Health Statistics* and *Health and Personal Social Services Statistics for England,* various editions, and Welsh Office, *Health and Personal Social Services Statistics for Wales,* various editions.

Secondly, in order to implement the Cranbrook recommendations it was necessary to increase throughput in respect of maternity beds and consequently there was a significant rise in the number of early discharge cases (i.e. where mothers are discharged from hospital within a few days of giving birth), from 148,494 in 1959 to 485,559 in 1973. During the 1960s the Ministry of Health provided local health authorities, hospital authorities and executive councils with advice on how to plan early discharge schemes, which clearly involved a considerable amount of inter-agency co-operation if they were to operate effectively, and this helped to increase their popularity. From the point of view of domiciliary midwives the main significance of early discharge schemes was the fact that they helped to maintain the demand for their services since they were required to attend the mother and child after their return home from hospital. This is illustrated by Figure 4.5.

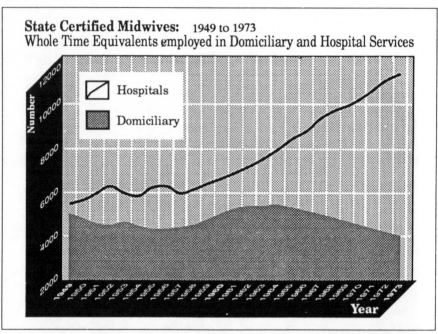

State Certified Midwives: 1949 to 1973
Whole Time Equivalents employed in Domiciliary and Hospital Services

Figure 4.4   *(England and Wales)*

Sources: Based on data from Ministry of Health, *Annual Reports*, various years, and DHSS, *Digest of Health Statistics*, various editions, and *Health and Personal Social Services Statistics for England* and Welsh Office, *Health and Personal Social Services Statistics for Wales,* various editions. However, since the published information is incomplete, particularly in respect of the conversion of part-time staff numbers into whole-time staff equivalents for the 1950s, it has been necessary to estimate certain figures.

Lastly, because of the changes in their working pattern, domiciliary midwives had more time to devote to complementary activities such as running ante-natal advice sessions and taking relaxation classes.

However, although the domiciliary midwifery services had been able to adapt to changing circumstances, there was a need for a review of the service and a realistic assessment of its likely role in the future. Consequently, in the late 1960s the Standing Maternity and Midwifery Advisory Committee of the Central Health Services Council appointed a subcommittee, under the chairmanship of John Peel, 'to consider the future of the local health authority domiciliary midwifery service, and the question of bed needs for maternity patients, and to make recommendations'.[22] One of the main recommendations of the subcommittee (1970) was a call for the amalgamation of the domiciliary midwifery service with the hospital

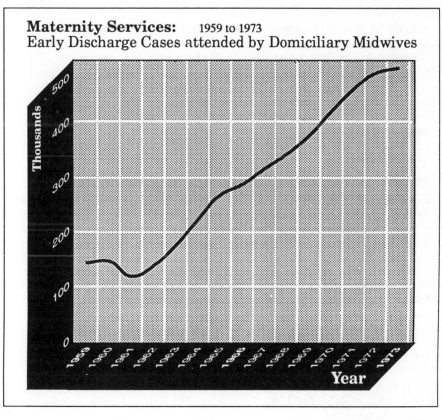

Maternity Services: 1959 to 1973
Early Discharge Cases attended by Domiciliary Midwives

(England and Wales)

Figure 4.5

Sources: DHSS, *Digest of Health Statistics,* various editions, and *Health and Personal Social Services Statistics for England,* various editions, and Welsh Office, *Health and Personal Social Services Statistics for Wales*, various editions.

midwifery service. Although not formally required to do so, a number of local health authorities took immediate steps to implement this recommendation. Furthermore, it seemed likely that this approach would be adopted in all parts of the country following the reorganisation of the NHS in 1974 and the transfer of responsibility for the employment of domiciliary midwives from local health authorities to AHAs, which would also be responsible for employing hospital midwives.

Thus, by the early 1970s there were clear signs that the era of a separate and distinctive domiciliary midwifery service was drawing to a close.

At the same time the implementation of the recommendations of the Mayston Working Party (see Chapter 3) meant that the management of domiciliary midwives was becoming more closely integrated with that of the other two groups of nurses who were based in the community, namely home nurses and health visitors, and it seemed likely that this trend would continue after 1974. Finally, under the provisions of the National Health Service Reorganisation Act 1973, the statutory responsibilities of the local supervising authority were transferred from local health authorities to RHAs.

Health Visiting

Although health visiting was reasonably well established by 1948, both as a profession and as a publically provided service, it was the 1946 Act which placed on local authorities a statutory obligation to provide a service of this kind. Section 24 imposed on local health authorities the duty of making 'provision in their area for the visiting of persons in their homes by ... 'health visitors', for the purpose of giving advice as to the care of young children, persons suffering from illness and advice as to the care of young children, persons suffering from illness and expectant or nursing mothers, and as to the measures necessary to prevent the spread of infection'. In spelling out the nature of these provisions in more detail, departmental circulars made it clear that the term 'illness' included mental illness and any injury or disability requiring medical or dental treatment or nursing. It was also acknowledged that the provisions of Section 24 of the 1946 Act represented a significant extension of the functions, which had been traditionally assigned to the health visitor, and that in future the health visitor was to 'be concerned with the health of the household as a whole', rather than that of just expectant and nursing mothers and pre-school children.

In exercising these extended responsibilities health visitors were expected to take what steps were necessary to preserve health and to prevent the spread of infectious diseases, both notifiable (e.g. smallpox, cholera, diphtheria) and non-notifiable (e.g. influenza, mumps, venereal diseases). This could involve explaining the notification procedure for infectious diseases to the heads of households and other interested parties; contact tracing and assisting the staff of clinics for sexually transmitted diseases in persuading patients to continue attending until their course of treatment was completed.

Mention also needs to be made of the fact that in certain parts of the country health visitors played an important part in establishing and developing home or domestic help services, for expectant and nursing mothers and certain other groups, and day care facilities for pre-school children.

Local health authorities were able to discharge their duty under Section 24 of the 1946 Act either by employing health visitors themselves or by making arrangements with voluntary organisations. In fact, by the end of 1948, local health authorities directly employed over 99% of the whole-time health visitors (i.e 1976 out of 1993) and approximately 93% of the part-time health visitors (i.e. 3467 out of 3720).

To supplement the provisions of the 1946 Act and to safeguard and improve the standards of health visiting the Ministry of Health made new regulations in respect of the qualifications of health visitors. Whilst maintaining the qualifications prescribed by earlier regulations, the new regulations introduced two important changes: 'firstly they applied those qualifications to officers employed part time as well as officers employed whole time on health visiting, and secondly they applied those qualifications to health visitors employed by voluntary organisations', which were providing a health visiting service on behalf of a local authority.

Under the provisions of The National Health Service (Qualification of Health Visitors and Tuberculosis Visitors) Regulations 1948 local health authorities and voluntary organisations could employ as a health visitor only a woman (!) who:

- had been qualified prior to 5th July 1948 to hold the appointment of health visitor; or

- had obtained the health visitors' certificate of the Royal Sanitary Institute under conditions approved by the Minister; or

- had obtained the health visitors' certificate issued by the Royal Sanitary Institute of Scotland;

and as a tuberculosis visitor a woman (!) who

- was qualified as a health visitor; or

- had been qualified prior to 5th July 1948 to hold the appointment of tuberculosis visitor; or

- was a qualified nurse who had had at least three months experience at a sanitorium or hospital for the treatment of tuberculosis or at a tuberculosis dispensary.[23]

It was hoped that more highly qualified health visitors would be able to cope more effectively with the additional demands that would arise as their role expanded.

However, although there was an undoubted commitment at the national level to a broader concept of health visiting,'in the first four or five years of the Health Service the health visitor service remained little more than an extension of the maternity services. In 1949 ... ninety per cent of (the) ten million visits (made by health visitors) were to advise on the care of infants, and for some years the percentage of visits to mothers with infants remained in the upper eighties. Many areas were unable to provide the wider aspects of the service envisaged in the Act simply because of the shortage of staff.'[24]

Both the shortage of health visitors and the need to clarify their changing role within the NHS prompted the Ministers of Health and Education (the Minister of Education was involved with this initiative because many health visitors also acted as school nurses) and the Secretary of State for Scotland to set up, in 1953, a working party, under the chairmanship of Sir William Jameson, to advise on the proper field of work, and the recruitment and training of health visitors.

In their report, which was published in 1956, the members of the Jameson Working Party, argued that the role of the health visitor could and should be much wider than that envisaged in the 1946 Act. They expressed the view that the health visitor should share in the work of a variety of family health and welfare teams that might not have a complete membership without her. As a member of these teams the contribution of the health visitor would be to act as: 'the common point of reference and a source of standard information, a common adviser on health teaching, a common factor in family welfare. In the ordinary course of her work she could be, in a real sense, a general purpose family visitor.'[25] This represented a departure from the traditional view of the health visitor and in order put it into practice the working party underlined the need for recognition to be given to the profession of health visitor; financial assistance for health visitor training; regular staff meetings; refresher courses; a new grade of group adviser to support newly qualified health visitors and, most importantly, far greater co-operation and colla-boration between health vistors and hospital staff, social workers and GPs. Jameson and his colleagues also recommended that, on average, there should be one health visitor to every 4,300 persons.

The recommendations of the Jameson Working Party were accepted by the Ministers of Health and Education and in 1959 they were commended to local health and education authorities. At national level the most significant result of these recommendations was the establishment, in 1962, of the Council for the Training of Health Visitors, with a duty to promote the training of health visitors by securing suitable facilities and courses, by seeking to attract recruits; by con-ducting or making arrangements for the conduct of examinations and by carrying out, either directly or through the provision of support for other bodies, research relevant to this training.[26]

The Council, which took over certain functions that had been performed by the Royal Sanitary Institute since 1925, was set up jointly with the Central Council for the Education and Training of Social Workers by the Health Visiting and Social Work (Training) Act 1962. Initially the two Councils had a common chairman since it was felt that there were considerable similiarities between the two professions. This arrangement, however, was ended in 1970 following the Wilson government's acceptance of the recommendations of the Seebohm Committee and the desire to reassert the separate identities of the social work and health visiting professions.

Thus, under the provisions of Section 11 of the Local Authority Social Services Act 1970, the Council for the Training of Health Visitors was renamed and reconstituted as the Council for the Education and Training of Health Visitors. The role and membership of the Council, however, remained unchanged. A majority of the members of the Council were appointed by the Minister of Health and his Scottish counterpart (with a number of these being appointed jointly with the Secretary of State for Education and Science) and the remainder by the local authority associations. As Levitt and Wall indicate, the members represented a variety of interests, including health visiting, nurse education, medicine, and education.[27]

One of the first initiatives taken by the reconstituted Council was the formulation and publication of a revised definition of the functions of the health visitor. According to which the health visitor was now responsible for:

- the prevention of mental, physical and emotional ill-health and its consequences;

- early detection of ill-health and the surveillance of high risk groups;

- recognition and identification of need and mobilisation of resources where necessary;

- health teaching; and

- provision of care, including support during periods of stress and advice and guidance in cases of illness as well as in the care and management of children.

These functions were intended to reflect changes which had taken place in the 1950s and 1960s, yet in describing the results of a sample survey in the mid-1970s, the Health Visitors' Association referred to them as a 'desirable theoretical aim.'[28]

Despite these developments, the shortage of health visitors remained a serious problem and in this respect, at least, health visiting was in a similar position to other female dominated professions. As the data in Figure 4.6 demonstrate, although there was some growth in the total number of health visitors between 1949 and 1973 this was due entirely to increases in the number engaged part-time on health visiting duties. Most 'part-time' health visitors were, in fact, holders of joint health visitor-school nurse posts and therefore spent the remainder of their time on school nursing duties.

Indeed, the number of whole-time health vistors fell significantly from 1655 in 1949 to a low point of 923 in 1959. Furthermore, during the mid-1960s the Ministry of Health became so concerned about the age profile of health visitors, with over 2000 aged between 50 and 60, that it formally requested local health authorities to support the Council for the Training of Health Visitors by sponsoring suitable candidates for training as instructors and by providing facilities for field work training.

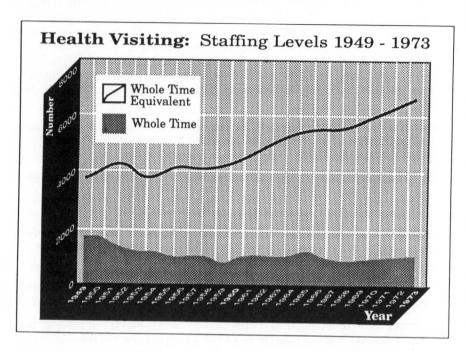

(England and Wales)

Figure 4.6

Sources: Ministry of Health, *Annual Reports,* various years; DHSS, *Digest of Health Statistics* and *Health and Personal Social Services Statistics for England,* various editions, and Welsh Office, *Health and Personal Social Services Statistics for Wales,* various editions.

Another initiative designed to increase the number of health visitors was taken in the early 1970s. This involved the erosion of the traditionally 'sexist' nature of the profession by changing the regulations to allow men to become qualified health visitors.

As well as the general shortage of health visitors there was also a problem regarding their geographical distribution. The information collected as part of the planning exercises in the 1960s revealed that some local authorities were well below and others were well above the average ratio of health visitors, in WTEs, per 1000 population. The complete picture for 1965 is presented in Figure 4.7.

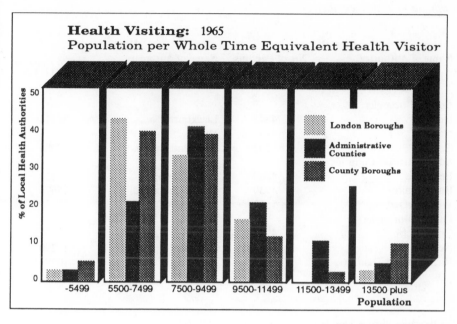

Health Visiting: 1965
Population per Whole Time Equivalent Health Visitor

London Boroughs

Administrative Counties

County Boroughs

% of Local Health Authorities

-5499 5500-7499 7500-9499 9500-11499 11500-13499 13500 plus
Population

(England and Wales)

Figure 4.7

Source: Based on data from Ministry of Health, *Health and Welfare. The Development of Community Care. Revision to 1975-76 of Plans for the Health and Welfare Services of the Local Authorities of England and Wales,* Cmnd 3022 (London: HMSO, 1966).

The authorities with the lowest and highest ratios are identified in Table 4.3. As the information in this table indicates even those authorities with the best ratios had not reached the target recommended by the Jameson Working Party (i.e. 1 health visitor to every 4,300 persons).

Furthermore, the forecasts for the end of 1975 indicated that there would still be significant differences between local health authorities in respect of their health visitor staffing levels and that many authorities would still be below the Jameson target.[29] In 1972 the DHSS indicated its concern by drawing the attention of local health authorities to the ratio recommended by Jameson and his colleagues and pointing out that although subsequent experience had confirmed this ratio 'as reasonable for some areas, a ratio of one health visitor to 3000 population might be desirable in others eg those with a highly developed system of attachments to general practice (see below) or with a high immigrant population.'[30] With regard

TABLE 4.3 *Health Visiting : Ratios of Whole-Time Equivalent Health Visitor to Population 31st December 1965*

	Lowest		Highest	
Name of Authority	No. of Persons per WTE HV		Name of Authority	No. of Persons per WTE HV
County Boroughs				
Dewsbury	4847		Blackburn	36811
Newport	4935		Halifax	19018
Cardiff	5203		Southend on Sea	18086
Administrative Counties				
Berkshire	4869		Lincs (Holland)	20131
Radnorshire	4930		Buckinghamshire	15676
Westmorland	5533		Derbyshire	13650
London Boroughs				
Greenwich	4931		Enfield	14937
Newham	5654		Bromley	11290
Richmond on Thames	5805		Redbridge	10781

Note

For the ratios of every local health authority see Appendix III.

Source: Ministry of Health, *Health and Welfare. The Developmemt of Community Care. Revision to 1975-76 of the Plans for the Health and Welfare Services of the Local Authorities of England and Wales*, Cmnd 3022 (London: HMSO, 1966).

to this latter point it was recognised that due to cultural and language differences members of ethnic minority groups were likely to require more time from the health visitor.

Despite the recruitment problems experienced during the tripartite era progress was made in expanding the range of cases dealt with by health visitors and in bringing about closer links with GPs, both of which had been advocated by the Jameson Working Party. As the statistics in Table 4.4 indicate, there was a gradual increase in the percentage of visits made to the elderly, the mentally disordered and persons discharged from non-psychiatric hospitals and a gradual decline in the percentage of visits made to mothers and young children, as well as to tuberculosis households. It is also of significance that between 1955 and 1973 the number of WTE specialist tuberculosis visitors employed by local health authorities fell from 562 to 216. To some extent these developments reflected changes in the age structure of the population and the incidence of tuberculosis.[31]

TABLE 4.4 *Health Visiting : Pattern of Visits 1951 to 1973 (England and Wales)*

Year	Mothers and Children 0-4	TB House holds	Elderly	Mentally Handicapped	Other
	%	%	%	%	%
1951	88.5	<———————— 11.5 ————————>			
1952	87.4	<———————— 12.6 ————————>			
1953	88.4	2.1	<———— 9.5 ————————>		
1954	87.3	2.1	<———— 10.6 ————————>		
1955	85.8	2.1	<———— 12.1 ————————>		
1956	87.0	2.2	<———— 10.8 ————————>		
1957	86.9	1.9	<———— 11.2 ————————>		
1958	86.8	1.7	<———— 11.5 ————————>		
1959	86.2	1.6	<———— 12.2 ————————>		
1960	86.2	1.5	<———— 12.3 ————————>		
1961	85.5	1.3	<———— 13.2 ————————>		
1962	85.6	1.2	<———— 13.2 ————————>		
1963	85.0	1.2	5.8	0.5	7.5
1964	84.4	1.2	6.0	0.5	7.9
1965	83.8	1.0	6.3	0.5	8.4
1966	83.0	1.0	6.9	0.4	8.5
1967	82.4	0.9	7.5	0.5	8.6
1968	80.7	0.9	7.9	0.5	10.0
1969	79.9	0.8	8.4	0.6	10.3
1970	78.9	0.7	9.0	0.6	10.8
1971	76.4	0.6	10.0	0.7	12.3
1972	75.0e	0.5e	11.0e	0.7e	12.8e
1973	73.5e	0.4e	12.0e	0.8e	13.3e

Key

e = estimated figure.

Sources: Based on data from Ministry of Health, *Annual Reports,* various years; DHSS, *Digest of Health Statistics* and *Health and Personal Social Services Statistics for England,* various editions, and Welsh Office *Health and Personal Social Services Statistics for Wales, various editions.*

Thus, by the early 1970s most health visitors had a more varied portfolio of cases than those who had been practising as health visitors in the late 1940s. In addition, under the provisions of the Health Services and Public Health Act 1968, health visitors were enabled to practice in locations other than a client's home. This meant that from the late 1960s onwards health visitors were officially able to arrange individual and group sessions in schools, clinics and health centres and to play a greater role in health education activities generally.

As far as links with GPs were concerned the most significant development was the growth of what are still known as 'attachment schemes'. This is essentially an arrangement whereby each health visitor works only or mainly with the patients of a defined group of GPs.

Prior to the introduction of 'attachment schemes' health visitors were organised in such a way that they covered a defined geographical area. This arrangement, known as 'zoning', is still in use in certain parts of the country. However, because of the pattern of general practice, 'zoning' usually results in health visitors serving the patients of many different GPs. Consequently, in order to overcome the drawbacks inherent in this arrangement and to establish closer links between health visitors and GPs, from the mid-1950s MOsH gradually moved towards a system of 'attaching' health visitors (and home nurses) to specific GP practices. According to Hicks the first MOH to negotiate an 'attachment scheme' was J.F.Warin, the Medical Officer of Health and Principal School Medical Officer of the City of Oxford. Warin had been a member of the Jameson Working Party and firmly believed that 'the future of health visitors lay in working in the closest possible relation with general practitioners.'[32] As a result, by March 1965 he had secured the 'attachment' of all community nursing staff in Oxford to GP practices.

Warin's belief in 'attachment schemes' was shared by the members of the Gillie Committee, which reported in 1963 (see above). By the early 1970s over 70% of health visitors in England and Wales were 'attached' to GP practices.[33] However, because there were far fewer health visitors than GPs, most health visitors were 'attached' to more than one GP.

The relatively rapid expansion of 'attachment schemes' was due not only to the efforts of Warin and the Gillie Committee but also to encouragement from the centre. In Circular 13-69 the DHSS drew the attention of local health authorities to, and commended the conclusions of, a report from the Department's Social Science Research Unit on the staff implications of 'attachment'. The report took a favourable view of 'attachment schemes' and local health authorities were therefore asked to give serious consideration, in consultation with executive councils, local medical committees and interested GPs, to the introduction or extension of schemes of 'attachment' or associations with general practice and to inform the Secretary of State, by the end of the year, of the arrangements in their area.

Despite the undoubted popularity of 'attachment schemes' a number of areas retained 'zoning' and the debate surrounding the relative merits of these two arrangements for organising the work of health visitors has continued right up to the present day (see Chapter 9 for details of some of the arguments). Thus, the transfer of responsibility for the employment of health visitors and the management of the health visiting service from local health authorities to AHAs in 1974 did not result in the application of a completely standardised approach to the way in which the service was organised at the 'grass roots' level. It did mean, however, that in future health visitors would be employed by the same authority as all other branches of the nursing profession.

Home Nursing

As well as imposing on local health authorities the duty of providing a comprehensive health visiting service, the 1946 Act (Section 25) also required them 'to make provision in their area , whether by making arrangements with voluntary organisations for the employment by those organisations of nurses or by themselves employing nurses, for securing the attendance of nurses on persons who require nursing in their own homes'. Since local authorities had only discretionary power to provide a home nursing service for certain categories of patient under earlier legislation (e.g. those suffering from infectious diseases; children) this represented a significant extension of their role in the field of home nursing. Furthermore, although local health authorities could discharge their duty under the 1946 Act by contracting with voluntary district nursing associations, which had traditionally been at the forefront of developments in this field, a majority (i.e. 75 out of 146) opted for the alternative, namely the direct employment of home nurses.

As Figure 4.8 illustrates, during the 1950s many of the authorities which had initially contracted with a voluntary district nursing association changed to direct employment, with the result that the role of the voluntary sector in service provision contracted still further. At national level, however, the Queen's Institute of District Nursing continued to make a significant contribution to the service through the provision of training courses and the awarding of certificates of competence; the sponsorship of research programmes designed 'to obtain information from which to determine the future role and education of the district nurse and the relationship of district nursing to other community services'; the publication of educational and other material and pressure group activity.

The 1950s also saw some other significant developments in the field of home nursing. Firstly, the 1950s marked the beginning of a shift towards the involvement of home nurses in the care of the elderly. In 1953 the first year for which appropriate statistics are available 44% of the visits made by home nurses were to patients aged 65 or over. By 1959 this had increased to 61%. This was also reflected in the fact that the average number of visits received by each patient nursed increased from 20 in 1949 to 24 in 1959 and that visits tended to be of longer duration. The main reason for this gradual change in the workload of home nurses was the recognition that 'regular care from the district nurse' enabled many elderly 'to stay in their own homes rather than have to accept institutional care.'[34]

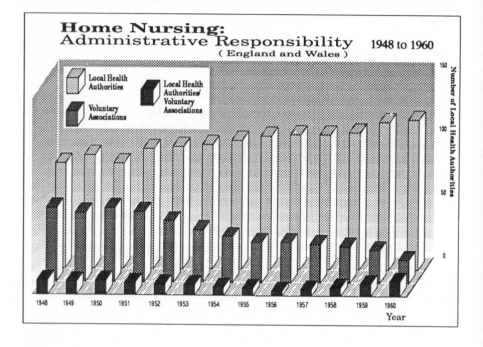

Figure 4.8

Source: Ministry of Health, *Annual Reports*, various years.

Secondly, attempts were made to expand the home nursing workforce. These were reasonably successful as the data in Table 4.5 indicate.

Furthermore, the increase in the number of home nurses more than kept pace with the rise in the numbers of elderly in the population. For example, the ratio of home nurses to elderly persons (i.e. those over 65) improved from 1 WTE home nurse to 816 elderly persons in 1949 to 1 WTE home nurse to 758 elderly persons in 1959.

Thirdly, the foundations of what was to become community psychiatric nursing were laid during the 1950s. In 1954 a 'nursing after-care' scheme for psychiatric patients was established at Warlingham Park Hospital, Surrey. Under the scheme two nurses were seconded to work with patients after they had been discharged from hospital. This involved visiting them at home, ensuring that they were taking medication, making an assessment of their mental state, and discussing their programme of treatment with relatives. Three years later a similar scheme was set up in Devon.[35] Although these initiatives came from hospital authorities, as opposed to local health authorities, they are worthy of mention because community psychiatric nursing was later to become a significant component of the total nursing support available to patients in their own homes (see Chapters 7 and 9).

TABLE 4.5 *Home Nursing : Staffing Levels 1949 to 1959*[a,b]

Year	Part-time	Whole-time	Total No	WTE
1949	4865(2316)[c]	3460	8325	5776
1950	4948(2326e)	3450	8398	5776e
1951	4979(2290e)	3721	8700	6011e
1952	5021(2259e)	3863	8884	6122e
1953	5241(2306e)	4280	9521	6586e
1954	5233(2250e)	4409	9642	6659e
1955	5200(2148e)	4684	9884	6868e
1956	5315(2179e)	4789	10104	6968e
1957	5243(2097e)	4933	10176	7030e
1958	5195(2026e)	4994	10189	7020e
1959	5171(1960)	5127	10298	7087

Key

e = estimated figure.

Notes

a. Figures for England and Wales.

b. Employees of both local health authorities and voluntary organisations.

c. The figures in brackets are the WTEs of part-time staff.

Source: Ministry of Health, *Annual Reports*, various years.

Lastly, from the mid-1950s a number of local health authorities began to attach' their home nurses, as well as their health visitors, to GP practices. Again these 'attachment schemes' were designed to facilitate liaison and collaboration between GPs and community nursing staff.

Although comparable statistical data are not always available, there is sufficient evidence to confirm that these developments continued during the 1960s and early 1970s. Thus, the percentage of elderly patients nursed at home continued to increase; the home nursing workforce continued to grow, apart from a slight fall in the early 1960s (see Figure 4.9), and, according to a survey carried out by the Royal College of Nursing, by 1966 42 hospitals were employing over 200 community psychiatric nurses (CPNs) (although only 26 of these were working full-time in a community setting).[36] Furthermore, by 1972 68.1% of home nurses were 'attached' to GP practices.

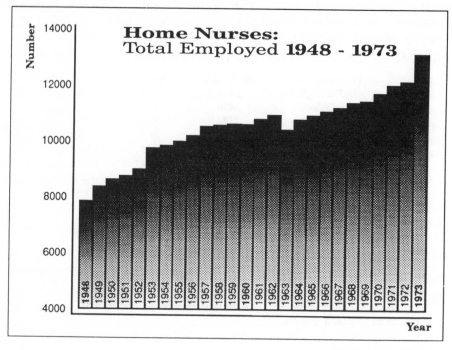

(England and Wales)

Figure 4.9

Sources: Ministry of Health, *Annual Reports*, various years; DHSS, *Digest of Health Statistics* and *Health and Personal Social Statistics for England,* various editions, and Welsh Office, *Health and Personal Social Services Statistics for Wales*, various editions.

However, like health visitors, the way that home nurses were distributed geographically appeared to be somewhat inequitable. For example, some local health authorities employed more than three times as many home nurses, per 1000 population, than other authorities. Further details of the distribution of home nurses are provided in Figure 4.10 (see page 154).

Significantly, as the information in Table 4.6 indicates, some of the lowest ratios were to be found in the least heavily populated parts of England and Wales (i.e. where access to institutionally based health care facilities was difficult for people who did not have their own transport) and in retirement areas. Some of the highest ratios were to be found in the conurbations.

TABLE 4.6 *Home Nursing : Ratios of Whole-Time Equivalent Home Nurse to Population 31st December 1965*

	Lowest		Highest	
Name of Authority	No of Persons per WTE HN	Name of Authority		No of persons per WTE HN
County Boroughs				
Eastbourne	3231	Salford		12355
Worcester	3412	Walsall		10024
Brighton	3458	Portsmouth		9403
Administrative Counties				
Cardiganshire	1778	Huntingdon and Peterborough		9465
Radnorshire	2532	Cheshire		8443
Westmorland	2837	Staffordshire		8315
London Boroughs				
Greenwich	4292	Harrow		9113
Lewisham	4455	Havering		8944
Richmond on Thames	4767	Hillingdon		8630

Note

For the ratios of every local health authority see Appendix III.

Source: Ministry of Health, *Health and Welfare. The Development of Community Care. Revision to 1975-76 of the Plans for the Health and Welfare Services of the Local Authorities of England and Wales*, Cmnd 3022 (London: HMSO, 1966).

To a limited extent the variations in the provision of home nursing (and, as indicated earlier, health visiting) can be explained by reference to the differences between the demographic and physical characteristics of the areas concerned. It is probable, however, that political factors were also at work. Whilst not a major issue at this time, inequality in health and health care were to become of greater concern in the late 1970s.

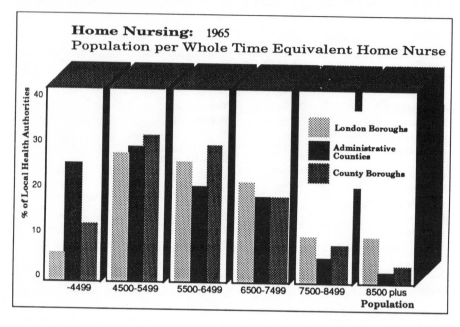

(England and Wales)

Figure 4.10

Source: Based on data from Ministry of Health, *Health and Welfare. The Development of Community Care. Revision to 1975-76 of the Plans for the Health and Welfare Services of the Local Authorities of England and Wales*, Cmnd 3022 (London: HMSO, 1966).

In commenting on the situation revealed by local health authority plans for home nursing the Ministry drew attention to 'the growing numbers of elderly, and the growing proportion of their time which home nurses (had) to devote to the needs of the elderly' and suggested that those authorities whose planned ratios were low should consider whether 'their assessment should be revised.'[37] More precise guidance on this subject was provided a few years later. In 1972 the DHSS indicated that, in the light of a sample survey it had conducted, an average of one home nurse to 4,000 persons was a suitable ratio for some areas, whilst in others with extensive 'attachment schemes' or with a high proportion of elderly and/or disabled people a ratio of one home nurse to 2,500 persons was probably more appropriate.[38] In practice, however, very few local health authorities reached these targets. One reason for this was a general shortage of qualified nurses, which has continued to be a problem for managers right up to the present day (see Chapters 7 and 9).

During the mid-1960s various aspects of the district nursing service were studied as part of the Queen's Institute of District Nursing research effort, to which reference has already been made. These included:

- the background, deployment, work and opinions of district nurses;
- the GPs knowledge and use of the district nursing service, their opinion of the service and the nature of their communications with district nurses;
- liaison between the district nursing service and other health and welfare services provided by local health authorities and voluntary organisations; and
- the administration of the district nursing service.

The main findings (published in 1966) were that:

- district nurses spent surprisingly little time in contact with patients and a very high proportion of their time on travelling and clerical work;
- much of the work carried out by district nurses did not require their professional skills, which they were rarely able to use;
- district nurses frequently lacked comprehensive information about their patients' condition and the nature of their treatment;
- district nurses had very little contact with GPs, hospitals and other CHSs staff;
- most GPs were unfamiliar with the qualifications of district nurses and the help they could provide their patients;
- although a majority of GPs were completely satisfied with the care given to their patients by district nurses over half felt that the role and functions of the district nursing service could be broadened;
- nearly 50% of GPs had difficulty in making contact with district nurses; and
- very few superintendent nursing officers had had any administrative training.[39]

Although there have been changes in the district nursing service since the mid-1960s, a number of these findings have a depressingly familiar ring about them.

On a more positive note, by the late 1960s the members of the Mayston Working Party were able to summarise the expanding role and functions of the home nursing service in the following terms:-

The home nurse's principal function is to provide skilled nursing care under the clinical direction of the general practitioner, not only in the home but also for example in health centres (The provisions of the Health Services and Public Health Act 1968, which enabled community based nursing staff to work in locations other than a patient's home, applied to home nurses as well as health visitors). *She is concerned with rehabilitation and elementary home physiotherapy, and the interpretation to the patients and their families of medical diagnosis and advice on recommended treatment. The home nurse is also increasingly working within schemes of attachment to general practice and her continuous observation of the physical and mental condition of patients and their families is invaluable to the general practitioner. The pattern of the home nursing service is changing to meet the demands placed upon it. Care of the elderly and chronic sick is a major function.*[40]

Nevertheless, despite the progress that was being made in the development of the service, the members of the working party felt that this was at risk for two main reasons. First, in many areas local health authorities had begun to experience 'considerable difficulty in coping with demand'[41] and second it was feared that recruitment might well suffer, at least in the short-term, as a result of the implementation of the recommendations of the Salmon Committee in respect of management structures for the hospital nursing service[42] and the probable transfer of responsibility for the home nursing service from local health authorities to the proposed new AHAs.

Naturally Mayston and her colleagues hoped that their proposals for revamping the management structure for community nursing services and the appointment of chief nursing officers by local health authorities (see Chapter 3) would help to safeguard the position of the home nursing service during the period of uncertainty which lay ahead. In the event the transition from local health authority to AHA control passed off relatively smoothly and some of the fears of the Mayston Working Party proved to be unfounded.

Another important event at this time was the publication, in October 1972, of the report of the Committee on Nursing chaired by Lord Briggs. The committee had been appointed in March 1970 'to review the role of the nurse and the midwife in the hospital **and the community** and the education and training for that role, so that the best use is made of available manpower to meet present needs and the needs of an **integrated health service** (emphasis added).'[43] On the basis of their findings the members of the committee recommended that:

- there should be a single central body responsible for the professional standards, education and discipline of nurses and midwives in Great Britain (i.e. it should replace the existing registration bodies, including the General Nursing Council, Central Midwives Board and Council for the Education and Training of Health Visitors);

- the education and training of nurses and midwives should be revamped;

- efforts should be made to increase male recruitment and more mature entrants, including those with A levels and undergraduates and graduates should be attracted to the profession;

- the conditions of work for nurses should be made less stressful;

- improved liaison between hospital and community services should be vigorously pursued;

- there should be a continuing distinction of function and qualification between nurses engaged in home nursing and those engaged in health visiting;
- nursing and midwifery management hierarchies should be grafted onto existing structures and there should be opportunities for nurses and midwives from all levels to reach the top of these hierarchies; and
- there should be strong nursing and midwifery teams at AHA level with executive functions.

Although the recommendations relating to the regulation of the education and training of nurses and midwives were not implemented until the late 1970s and early 1980s (see Chapter 7), those which dealt with the administration and management of nurses and midwives and relations between nursing services in hospitals and the community were reflected in the advice given by the DHSS to health authorities on the preparation and development of substantive schemes of management for the nursing and midwifery services in the reorganised NHS. Thus, whilst accepting the need for interim management arrangements to provide for the continuity of the service and to ensure as little disruption to staff as possible, the DHSS stressed the importance of health authorities taking advantage of the opportunities presented by the reorganisation for securing greater integration between nursing and midwifery and between hospital and community nursing in their new management structures.

Vaccination and Immunisation

Section 26 of the 1946 Act affected the law relating to vaccination and immunisation in a number of different ways. First, it repealed the Vaccination Acts of 1867 to 1907 and thereby removed from the statute book the principle of compulsion in respect of smallpox vaccination for infants, which had been introduced in 1871 (see Chapter 2). Since compulsion had not been applied strictly for many years this was simply a legitimisation of the existing state of affairs. Nevertheless, the repeal did have a certain symbolic significance.

Second, the 1946 Act imposed on local health authorities the duty of making 'arrangements with medical practitioners for the vaccination of persons in the area of the authority against smallpox, and the immunisation of such persons against diphtheria'. Thus, for the first time specific reference was made in legislative provisions relating to vaccination and immunisation to a disease other than smallpox.

Third, under the provisions of Section 26 local health authorities could, with the approval of the Minister, and if directed by the Minister had to 'make similar arrangements for vaccination and immunisation against any other disease'. Initially, the only disease for which a number of local health authorities used this power was pertussis (whooping cough), although it was not officially classified as an immunisable disease until 1957. However, with advances in medical knowledge and procedures it was not long before immunisation was being made available in respect of other diseases, such as tetanus, which was classified as an immunisable disease in 1955, and poliomyelitis. A vaccine for polio was introduced in 1956 and its availability quickly spread. On the other hand progress in introducing BCG vaccination against tuberculosis, which first became available in the late 1940s, was relatively slow. As Webster points out, it needed the first notification, in 1956, of the successful outcome of an investigation by the Medical Research Council into the vaccination of school children to breathe 'new life' into what he describes as a 'lethargic vaccination campaign.'[44]

Fourth, the 1946 Act required local health authorities, when making arrangements for vaccination and immunisation, to give 'every medical practitioner providing general medical services in their area' the opportunity to participate. This provision reflected the desire of GPs to be involved with this aspect of prevention. Nevertheless, the principle of GP participation in the vaccination and immunisation of children has created a number of administrative problems.

Last, the 1946 Act placed on the Minister a responsibililty for supplying, free of charge, to local health authorities and GPs, the vaccines, sera and other preparations they needed to provide this service. Thus, it was accepted that vaccination and immunisation should be a free service.

At this time, the principal concerns of both central government and local health authorities were the historically low take-up rates for smallpox vaccination (i.e. in 1948 the rate was approximately 27% and it fell to as low as 23.8% in 1950) and the fact that many parents were not having their children immunised against diphtheria (i.e. over 40% of children). Consequently, considerable attention was given to the production of publicity material designed to increase vaccination and immunisation rates. However, as the author of an Office of Health Economics booklet on the LHSs suggests: 'In the early 1950s, most people were left unmoved by the Ministry's publicity campaign for diphtheria and smallpox protection' and consequently it was increasingly felt that 'personal representations by the general practitioner or health visitor were ... the most effective way of getting' parents to take the appropriate action.[45]

Nevertheless, although the persuasive powers of health care professionals had some effect, vaccination and immunisation rates in the 1950s remained below 50%. Ironically, it generally required 'a dramatic manifestation of (a) disease', such as an outbreak of diphtheria in 1958 and the death from poliomyelitis of a popular footballer in 1959, to make parents appreciate the need to have their children vaccinated and/or immunised.

By 1962 all local health authorities were providing protection against smallpox, diphtheria, poliomyelitis, whooping cough, tetanus and tuberculosis. In July of that year they were requested in a circular from the Ministry to make and put into effect a comprehensive plan for reaching and maintaining as high a level of vaccination and immunisation as possible. The circular suggested that vaccination and immunisation programmes should cover all six diseases and should ensure that maximum protection was given from early infancy to adolescence. In addition, local health authorities should provide for immunisation to be given in the manner and order that would:

• afford the greatest measure of immunity against each disease when the risk of exposure to infection was at its greatest;

• involve the least risk of harmful reactions and complications; and

• reduce to the minimum the number of separate innoculations and therefore of visits to GPs or clinics.

This circular also advised local health authorities to vaccinate children against smallpox during their second year rather than at 4 or 5 months old as previously recommended.

In response to the ever increasing range of questions surrounding this issue and the need for more extensive advice on this subject the Central and Scottish Health Services Councils decided in 1962 to replace their Joint Committee on Poliomyelitis Vaccine with a new joint body having wider terms of reference. The title of this new body was the Joint Committee on Vaccination and Immunisation and its principal role was 'to advise the Health Ministers on all the medical aspects of vaccination and immunisation'.

Some of the key recommendations made by the Joint Committee and accepted by the Labour and Conservative governments, between 1962 and 1974, are summarised below:

• the offer of measles vaccination to all children between one and fifteen years old who had not had the disease or been vaccinated against it fifteen years old who had not had the disease or been vaccinated against it (1967);

• the introduction of a single schedule of immunisation (1968);

• the offer of vaccination against rubella (german measles) to all girls aged between eleven and fourteen (1970); and

• the ending of vaccination against smallpox as a routine procedure in early childhood (1971).

Generally speaking, as the data in Table 4.7 indicate, the higher profile afforded vaccination and immunisation and more vigorous and concerted action in this field by local health authorities during the 1960s and early 1970s greatly improved take-up rates. Needless to say it was hoped that the high take-up rates would be sustained and, if possible, improved still further when AHAs assumed responsibility for the provision and promotion of vaccination and immunisation on 1st April 1974. Furthermore, during the course of the reorganisation the shadow AHAs were required to ensure that there was 'no hiatus in the provision of vaccination and immunisation services.'[46]

TABLE 4.7 *Vaccination and Immunisation : Numbers Vaccinated and Take-Up Rates 1960 to 1973*[a]

Year	Smallpox Number[b] '000s	%[c]	Diphtheria Number[d] '000s	%[e]	Whooping Cough Number[d] '000s	%[e]
1960	384.2	47	755.3	39	626.4	n.a.
1961	422.6	48	875.0	68	690.1	72
1962	1807.5[f]	70[f]	652.9	67	578.5	66
1963	203.9[g]	17[g]	700.0	65	619.2	64
1964	344.7	32	764.5	69	679.4	72
1965	393.9	33	767.7	71	697.6	70
1966	480.4	38	772.2	73	693.8	72
1967	463.5	39	794.8	75	711.3	74
1968	456.4	38	707.9	78	629.2	76
1969	389.2	31	516.6	67	457.4	66
1970	n.a.	n.a.	680.5	80e	620.4	78e
1971	n.a.	n.a.	715.2	80e	642.6	78e
1972	n.a.	n.a.	691.6	80e	632.5	78e
1973	n.a.	n.a.	637.7	80e	579.3	78e

Year	Poliomyelitis Number[d] '000s	%[e]	Tetanus Number[d] '000s	%[e]	TB BCG Number[h] '000s	Measles Number[b] '000s
1960	777.2	n.a.	n.a.	n.a.	455.0	n.a.
1961	1237.4	n.a.	n.a.	n.a.	449.0	n.a.
1962	852.8	66	n.a.	n.a.	435.5	n.a.
1963	891.6	71	n.a.	n.a.	412.0	n.a.
1964	855.2	71	n.a.	n.a.	410.4	n.a.
1965	921.4	65	848.9	n.a.	382.1	n.a.
1966	866.8	68	836.5	72	425.5	n.a.
1967	827.9	71	849.3	75	431.1	n.a.
1968	728.8	78	753.5	78	453.5	719.2
1969	552.6	65	557.8	67	465.6	398.1
1970	695.4	79e	722.5	81e	458.1	623.4
1971	711.7	81e	750.9	81e	517.8	537.8
1972	697.4	80e	725.0	81e	511.0	513.2
1973	639.9	80e	672.2	81e	529.6	472.4

Key

n.a. = data not available.
e = estimated figure.

Notes

a.   Figures for England and Wales.

b.   Number vaccinated under age 16.

c.   Number vaccinated under age 2 as a percentage of live births during previous year.

d.   Number under age 16 who completed a primary course of injections.

e.   Percentage of children born in preceding calendar year who were vaccinated by the end of the year stated.

f.   Exceptionally high rate connected with an outbreak of smallpox.

g.   Very low rate due to change in recommended age for vaccination from first to second year of life.

h.   Number of people vaccinated under the school children and students scheme.

Sources: DHSS *Digest of Health Statistics* and *Health and Personal Social Services Statistics for England*, various editions, and Welsh Office, *Health and Personal Social Services Statistics for Wales*, various editions.

Care and After-Care

Under the provisions of Section 28 of the 1946 Act local health authorities could, and if directed to do so by the Minister had to, make arrangements for the prevention of illness, for the care of persons suffering from illness or mental defectiveness and for their after-care. However, they were explicitly prohibited from making payments of money to such persons as part of their provision of care and after-care.

The main purpose of Section 28 was 'to provide a latitude for (local health authorities) to expand their stipulated services and introduce a wider range of non specified services (thereby) allowing the local health services to develop their logical position as the mainstay of preventive medicine and care in the community.'[47]

Initially the Minister used his power of direction in respect of the making of arrangements for the prevention of tuberculosis and for the care and after-care of those suffering from tuberculosis. In many areas local health authorities used existing tuberculosis care committees for this purpose. Their function was 'to help in meeting the special problems of the tuberculous household, and so to facilitate treatment by relieving anxiety, to safeguard the restored patient against relapse, and to preserve the health of the family which (was) exposed to special risk.'[48]

Whilst medical treatment for tuberculosis was the responsibility of GPs and the hospital authorities, most local health authorities provided out of door shelters and made arrangements to segregate tuberculosis sufferers, to aid convalescence and, where necessary, to board out children. In addition, as mentioned earlier, health visitors and, in some areas, specialist tuberculosis visitors provided domiciliary care and support for sufferers and their families. As the information in Table 4.4 indicates there was a significant decline in the need for services of this kind between 1948 and 1974.

Other services provided under Section 28 of the 1946 Act included the loan of home nursing equipment and apparatus (e.g. bed pans, walking frames, back rests, wheelchairs), which became of increasing importance as more and more people were nursed in their own homes rather than hospitals; the supply and delivery of incontinence pads and related items and the collection and disposal of soiled pads;[49] facilities for a holiday home type of accommodation and for convalescence; from the early 1960s, the employment of domiciliary occupational therapists to assist with the rehabilitation and social adjustment of the handicapped and those suffering from tuberculosis;[50] the provision of a night attendance service for persons who were seriously ill; a mobile meals service; a laundry service (by 1962 48 local health authorities were providing a laundry service for the housebound) and, from 1959, a **chiropody service**.

During the 1950s local health authorities and their representative bodies, together with the BMA, the Executive Councils Association and voluntary organisations, especially those working with the elderly, had campaigned vigorously for a publically provided chiropody service. They argued that voluntary organisations were no longer able to meet the demand for chiropody treatment and that such a service would alleviate a great deal of pain and suffering amongst the elderly and would, in the long run, produce economies by reducing the number of people having to be taken into residential accommodation. However, despite the vigour of the campaign, the Minister took the view that, although he was keen to sanction chiropody services, while resources were so scarce priority had to be given to mental health services, old people's homes and hospital building. This remained the position until 1959, when approval for local health authorities to provide a chiropody service was finally given.

Once they had received the necessary approval most local health authorities wasted no time in putting forward their proposals for ministerial approval and, indeed, by 1968 a publically provided chiropody service was available in every part of the country. Initially most schemes provided for a service run by voluntary organisations to supplement that operated directly by the local heath authority. However, by the late 1960s these were very much in the minority. As recommended by the Minister local health authorities generally gave priority to the physically handicapped, expectant mothers and the elderly. Some statistical data relating to the staff and clients of the local health authoritiy chiropody services are provided in Table 4.8.

TABLE 4.8 *Chiropody Service : Staff and Clients 1966 to 1973*[a]

		Staff[b] Whole Time Equivalent Total			Clients Total	Over 65[c]		Treatment
Year	Number		LHA	VO	'000s	'000s	%	'000s
1966	3014	723	602	121	n.a.	n.a.	n.a.	n.a.
1967	3325	829	701	128	827	779	94.2	3705
1968	3401	897	756	141	857	807	94.2	3902
1969	3441	948	803	145	891	846	94.9	4072
1970	3473	1006	850	156	926	887	95.8	4256
1971	3559	1147	972	175	992	950	95.8	4446
1972	3526	1224	1070	154	1060	1012	95.5	4678
1973	3474	1241	1090	151	1111	1066	95.9	4905

Key

LHA = local health authority.
VO = voluntary organisation.
n.a. = data not available.

Notes

a. Figures for England and Wales.

b. As at 30th September.

c. Other client groups were the physically handicapped or otherwise disabled under 65 (2% approx) and expectant mothers (0.1% approx).

d. Treatment was provided in clinics (51% approx); patients' homes (24% approx); chiropodists' surgeries (17% approx) and old peoples homes (8% approx).

Sources: DHSS, *Health and Personal Social Services Statistics for England*, various editions, and Welsh Office *Health and Personal Social Services Statistics for Wales* various editions.

The data in Table 4.8 illustrate both the expansion of the service in terms of personnel and clients between 1966 and 1973 and the position of the elderly as the dominant client group of the service.

With the reorganisation of the NHS in 1974 the chiropody service provided by the health departments of local authorities was merged with that provided by their education departments (as part of the school health service) and their personal social service departments and with that provided by hospital authorities.

In addition to the services already mentioned were those for the **mentally disordered**, which were the most costly provided under the provisions of Section 28 of the 1946 Act, especially after 1959. During the 1950s approximately 55% of the net revenue expenditure on prevention, care and after-care went on services for the mentally disordered, whereas in the 1960s it was nearer 75%.

Although considerable progress was made, during the 1950s, in the development of community based services for the mentally ill and disordered, they remained relatively limited in scope until the provisions of Section 28, in respect of the mentally disordered, were clarified and extended by Section 6 of the Mental Health Act 1959. This incorporated the recommendations of the Royal Commission on the Law Relating to Mental Illness and Mental Deficiency (1954 to 1957).

Under this legislation, local health authorities were empowered to make arrangements for the prevention of mental disorder and the care and after-care of the mentally ill and subnormal, which could include the following:

- the provision, equipping and maintenance of residential accommodation;

- the provision of centres and other facilities for training, occupational or social purposes and the equipping and maintenance of such centres;

- the employment of mental welfare officers to provide specialist support for the mentally ill and subnormal and their families and to carry out domiciliary visits;

- the guardianship function; and

- supplementary services for the benefit of the mentally ill or subnormal.

Significantly, in July 1960 a direction from the Ministry of Health made it a duty of local health authorities to provide these services. Thus, between 1960 and 1971 (when they were transferred to the newly created social services departments) services for the mentally ill and handicapped were one of the fastest growing areas of responsibility for the staff of local health departments.

In the words of Griffith, 'the shift of emphasis, reflected in the report of the Royal Commission (on the Law Relating to Mental Illness and Mental Deficiency) and in the action and legislation which followed it, was from institutional to community care and clearly required the expansion of all forms of domiciliary and home visiting services, residential homes and hostels, training and occupation centres... day hospitals and social clubs.'[51] Consequently, it can be argued that these developments in the sphere of community based mental health services played an important part in creating a climate of opinion which was favourable to the 'care in the community' initiatives of the post-1974 period. Some of these initiatives and their significance for the CHSs are discussed in Chapter 7.

As well as the provision of services to specific client groups, the more enlightened local health authorities used their powers under Section 28 to engage in a limited range of **health education activities**. In so doing they were acknowledging implicitly that, due to epidemiological changes, more attention needed to be given to education and prevention. By the late 1940s, cancer and heart disease had become as important a cause of death as the great epidemic diseases (e.g. typhoid, cholera and tuberculosis) had been in the past. Indeed, 'tobacco smoking was destroying life on a scale greater than the infectious diseases that had inspired the sanitarian movement of Victorian times'.[52] It was also recognised by some that the most effective way of tackling these newer 'giants of disease'[53] was by means of preventive rather than curative measures. Initially, however, those seeking to realise the potential of health education and preventive medicine, at both national and local level, were severely constrained by inadequate resources, opposition from vested interests, and a lack of suitable techniques.

Although the Ministry of Health was able to make considerable use of the mass media for health education purposes in the early days of the NHS, 'as the war-time sense of national unity dispersed the media proprietors were prepared to give less time to these projects, and concurrently a normal peace time state of suspicion as to the motives of government propaganda revived among the populace. Partly for these reasons, and partly due to the lack of specialist knowledge of propaganda techniques, health education campaigns ... often had a rather forlorn appearance.'[54] Subjects covered in the health education campaigns of the 1950s included mass X-ray; diphtheria and poliomyelitis protection; venereal disease and home accidents. Owing to a lack of resources and expertise the efforts of local health authorities in the field of health education were generally designed to supplement larger scale initiatives taken at national level.

During the 1950s a contribution continued to be made by the Central Council for Health Education. The Council, which had been established in 1927 (see Chapter 2), was reconstituted in 1950 and was controlled by a council of management consisting of representatives of local authorities and medical, dental, nursing and educational interests. Meetings of the council were also attended by observers from the Ministry of Health and other central government departments to facilitate collaboration in health education initiatives. Most of the income of the Central Council was derived from the voluntary contributions of local health authorities, which were able to obtain a limited amount of advice from this source on the methods and techniques of health education and materials for their own campaigns.[55]

Notwithstanding the efforts of the Central Council and local health authorities, in 1956 the BMA criticised the Ministry of Health's performance in the field of health education and called for a health education budget. Two years later the Chief Medical Officer to the Ministry of Health commented in his *Annual Report* that one of the most important contributions which the Ministry could make was 'the development and expansion of health education on a firmer and sounder basis than hitherto.'[56]

Moreover, in his definitive study of the NHS between 1948 and 1957, Webster is also critical of the failure of the health service in its early years to take seriously its responsibility for preventive medicine and health education. 'Major preventive issues such as class, occupational, or regional differentials in health, family planning, nutritional habits, fluoridation of water, cigarette smoking, alocohol abuse, mental health or cancer education ... were either neglected, or provoked such fears of public controversy that concerted action was precluded.'[57] In the case of cigarette smoking, for example, even though the first paper by Richard Doll and A. Bradford Hill explicitly linking smoking with lung cancer was published in 1951, opposition from the Treasury concerned about the tax revenue derived from the duty on tobacco and a number of other factors, prevented any serious attempt to tackle the problem of smoking until the mid-1960s. Indeed, during the 1950s, there was a significant increase in the amount of cigarette smoking. Thus, those who had initially expected that the NHS would 'give priority to a positive conception of health'[58] were disappointed.

It was largely in response to these concerns, and to the 'suspicion that preventive medicine had greater potential than was allowed in the health services at that time',[59] that the Central and Scottish Health Services Councils set up a committee in 1960, under the chairmanship of Lord Cohen of Birkenhead, to determine the nature and scope of health education and to assess its future role. The report of the Cohen Committee, which was published in 1964, recommended that many more subjects should be covered by health education campaigns and that more field studies should be undertaken to evaluate the effectiveness of different methods and the results they achieved. It also proposed the setting up of new strong health education boards for England and Wales, with responsibility for organising 'blanket' campaigns on key topics and securing support from commercial and voluntary interests as well as assisting local authorities. In the report it was estimated that if implemented these proposals would raise expenditure on health education by about £0.5 million per year, a ten fold increase on what was actually being spent!

The Cohen Committee's recommendations were well received and in 1966 the Labour government announced its acceptance of the main conclusion of the committee namely that increased effort was needed in health education and that the first priority was a new and stronger central organisation. This resulted in the creation of the Health Education Council in 1967, chaired by Baroness Serota. To ensure that the Council had some independence from the government it had the status of a company limited by guarantee.

During the late 1960s and early 1970s the Council was involved in a number of important health education initiatives regarding smoking and health, family planning and sexually transmitted diseases. By 1974 the Council had developed a wide variety of functions, the most important of which are outlined below:

• To advise on priorities for health education on the basis of the best information and evidence available.

• To devise and carry out national campaigns, and local or regional campaigns in co-operation with local authorities.

• To produce information and publicity material in support of national and local campaigns and of such other activities as the Council may undertake; and to make such material available to local authorities and voluntary and other appropriate bodies.

• To undertake or sponsor research and surveys designed to ensure the availability of reliable and up-to-date information and statistics on which to base the campaigns and other activities of the Council.

• To seek advice and to review relevant medical, epidemiological, sociological, psychological and other information available and, as necessary, to undertake or sponsor research and surveys designed to obtain such information, to assist the Council in its determination of priorities and in the measurement of the effectiveness of the results of its national and experimental campaigns.

• To act as the national centre of expertise and knowledge in all aspects of health education, so that advice is available at all times to (those) engaged in health education; and, with the agreement of the National Health Service and local authorities, educational and voluntary bodies, to co-ordinate health education activities where appropriate.

• To encourage and promote training in health education work; and to provide other bodies with advice and guidance on the organisation and content of courses of training, together with such practical help as may seem appropriate and within the resources of the Council.

• To co-operate with local education authorities, educational establishments and the Schools' Council in the development of health education in schools, colleges and polytechnics.

• To maintain contact with national voluntary bodies engaged in particular aspects of health education work; and to give aid and advice to such bodies as appropriate and to the extent that the resources of the Council permit.

• To publish material of interest and value to those engaged in health education.[60]

At local level, however, authorities varied considerably in their level of commitment to health education. Some were extremely active, whilst others adopted an essentially 'laissez-faire' stance. Initiatives taken by the more enterprising authorities included the appointment of specialist health education officers, with the number of such appointments increasing from 28 in 1964 to 91 in 1970,[61] the setting up of anti-smoking clinics and monitoring their success rate and the establishment of a community nutrition service headed by a community dietitian.

Despite the importance of developments in the sphere of health education at national and, to some extent, local level, it can be argued that the most significant development of the tripartite era, from a preventive point of view, was the introduction of a **screening service for cervical cancer**. Professional and public interest in the routine screening for cancer of the cervix of all women at risk emerged in the early 1960s. Initially, due to a shortage of facilities and of trained laboratory staff for the testing of smears, progress was relatively slow. However, by 1965 the Ministry was able to report that '66 local health authorities had (had) proposals approved under section 28 of the National Health Service Act 1946 to collect smears for examination by hospitals and 26 local health authorities'[62] were either awaiting approval or making enquiries. Furthermore, hospital boards, local authorities and local medical committees were co-operating in plans to expand the service.

In 1966 the Ministry gave general approval to all local health authorities wishing to make arrangements for the collection and testing of smears and announced its intention to make screening available to all women at risk, starting with those aged 35 and over. As Figure 4.11 indicates between 1966 and 1973 there was a steady increase in the number of tests carried out for cervical cancer, with smears being taken by GPs and in hospital and Family Planning Association clinics as well as clinics run directly by local health authorities.

In 1972 arrangements for recalling women aged 35 and over at 5-yearly intervals were introduced. Under these arrangements local health authorities were made responsible for the issue of invitations (from information supplied by the National Health Service Central Register[63] and verified by the executive councils) to women to be retested either by their GPs or at local health authority clinics, and to follow up with reminders wherever necessary. Thus, by the early 1970s the principle of cervical cytology screening was reasonably well established and its value generally accepted. However, for a variety of reasons, which will be examined in later chapters, the development and operation of an effective call and recall system for this purpose proved to be far more difficult than originally anticipated.

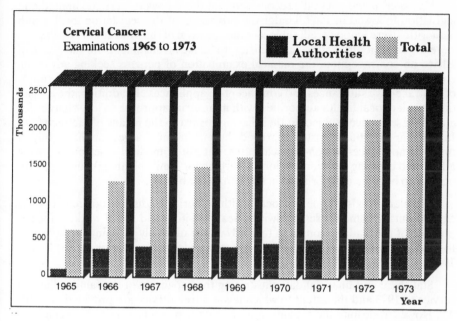

Figure 4.11 *(England and Wales)*

Sources: DHSS, *Digest of Health Statistics* and *Health and Personal Social Services Statistics for England*, various editions, and Welsh Office, *Health and Personal Social Services Statistics for Wales*, various editions.

Family Planning

Until the passing of the National Health Service (Family Planning) Act 1967 the role of local health authorities in the field of family planning was extremely limited. In the main, it consisted of the provision, either directly, or more usually, through the Family Planning Association and similar bodies, of a certain amount of contraceptive advice and treatment to women whose health might be impaired by pregnancy. The power to operate this limited service was derived from the provisions of Section 28 of the 1946 Act.

An indication that the Wilson government wished to expand the publically provided family planning service came in 1966 with the issue of a circular, which emphasised that an adequate family planning service was an essential part of the family welfare service. The circular also suggested ways in which family planning facilities could be developed through co-operation between local health authorities and voluntary organisations and encouraged local health authorities to use their existing powers to the full.[64]

However, it was generally recognised that these powers were too limited and legislation followed in 1967. Under the provisions of this legislation local health authorities were empowered, subject to the approval of the Minister of Health, and were required, if directed by the Minister, to 'make arrangements for the giving of advice on contraception, the medical examination of persons seeking advice on contraception for the purpose of determining what advice to give and the supply of contraceptive substances and contraceptive appliances'. In addition, the legislation enabled local health authorities, with ministerial approval, to levy charges for any of these services subject to their having regard to the means of the recipient. In Circular 5/67 the Minister approved the making of charges for the supply of drugs or appliances in non-medical cases, but not in medical cases or for giving advice and carrying out examinations. Charging for family planning drugs/appliances was to become a major issue in the 1970s (see below).

Circular 5/67 also requested local health authorities to use the domiciliary visits carried out by home nurses, midwives, health visitors and social workers for the purpose of persuading women to take advantage of family planning facilities and to send in reports on action taken or proposed under the legislation by 31st March 1968.

Statistical and financial data illustrating the expansion of the family planning service to 1973 and the extent to which it was a free service are provided in Table 4.9. However, despite the expansion of the family planning service between 1970 and 1973, in some parts of the country it remained underdeveloped. Consequently, it was hoped by many that the transfer of responsibility for this service from local health authorities to AHAs in 1974 would be the first step towards the development of a comprehensive family planning service within the NHS.

Furthermore, various bodies took the view that in the interests of preventing unwanted pregnancies it should be an entirely free service once it became the responsibility of AHAs. Surprisingly, this was the position taken by the House of Lords and as a result it came into conflict with the Conservative government during the passage of the NHS Reorganisation Bill through Parliament. Initially, the Conservative government had intended that after 1974 only certain categories of client should receive free contraceptives. Other categories would either have to pay the price of a prescription or meet the full cost. Since this was not acceptable to the Lords, a compromise proposal was put forward. Under this proposal contraceptives were to be issued on prescription, with the standard charges and exemptions being applied.

TABLE 4.9 *Family Planning Services : Scale of Provision 1970 to 1973*[a,b]

	No of Authorities[c]			
	1970	**1971**	**1972**	**1973**
Body Providing Service				
LHA only	10	13	21	32
LHA and FPA or other agency	37	47	50	59
FPA or other agency only	125	114	103	83
No service	3	1	1	1
Total	175	175	175	175
Type of Provision				
Medical cases				
Service provided	166	174	172	172
Advice given free	162	170	172	172
Supplies given free	158	169	170	171
Non-Medical but needy cases				
Services provided	158	162	160	163
Advice given free	152	162	160	163
Supplies given free	143	150	147	150
Other non-medical cases				
Service provided	134	132	144	149
Advice given free	98	107	126	144
Supplies given free	27	32	26	64
Service for the unmarried	139	148	159	156
Domiciliary service[d]	55	63	98	124
Cost of Provision (£'000s)	**1969/70**	**1970/71**	**1971/72**	**1972/73**
Gross Cost	582	935	1716	3598
less net income[e]	49	78	228	532
Net Cost	533	857	1488	3066

Key LHA = local health authority FPA = Family Planning Association.

Notes

a.   Figures for England and Wales.

b.   Unfortunately, comparable data for 1974 are not available. Furthermore, for this period, there is no published information on the number of people in receipt of family planning services.

c.   As at 31st March.

d.   In some cases the service only covered part of the authority's area.

e.   Income from specific government grants; sales and fees and charges.

Sources: DHSS *Health and Personal Social Services Statistics for England,* various editions; Welsh Office *Health and Personal Social Services Statistics for Wales,* various editions, and Department of the Environment and Welsh Office *Local Government Financial Statistics England and Wales,* various editions.

Again this was rejected by the Lords, who remained firmly committed to the principle of free contraceptives for all. Furthermore, their commitment was such that they tried on three occasions to amend the NHS Reorganisation Bill in such a way that after 1974 the NHS family planning service would be completely free. However, on each occasion the amendment was rejected by the Commons. The impasse ended in July 1973 when the Lords backed down and reluctantly agreed to accept the wishes of the Commons on this matter.

However, this was not the end of the affair. Shortly after the Labour Party's surprise victory in February 1974, Barbara Castle, Secretary of State for Social Services in the new Labour government announced that from 1st April 1974 contraceptives prescribed and dispensed at NHS family planning clinics would be free of any charge. Thus, on this issue, at least, the electorate played a part in determining the final outcome.

School Health Service

It might reasonably have been expected that with the establishment of the NHS in 1948 there was no longer a need for a separate and distinctive school health service. However, as Dr Yellowlees, the last Chief Medical Officer at the Department of Education and Science, has pointed out the school health service was not incorporated into the NHS in the 1940s 'because it was considered that the welfare of school children was so important that a dual system, however illogical, was justified.'[65] Furthermore, it was likely that any attempt to remove the school health service from their sphere of control would have been resisted by the Ministry of Education and the representative bodies of local education authorities. Thus, the status of the school health service, namely that of a supplementary education service, remained unchanged throughout the tripartite era.

Nevertheless, although the school health service was not formally part of the NHS between 1948 and 1974, it was one of the most important CHSs and, in the words of Webster, 'it enjoyed a phase of buoyant growth.'[66] During this period its primary function continued to be the promotion of the health and well-being of school children through a system of routine medical inspections followed up, whenever necessary, with treatment. This was enshrined in Section 48 of the Education Act 1944 which stated that:

- 'It shall be the duty of every local education authority to provide for the **medical inspection** ... of pupils ... at any (maintained school or county college) ...'

- 'It shall be the duty of every local education authority to make such arrangements for securing the provision of free **medical treatment** for pupils in attendance at any school or county college maintained by them as are necessary for securing that comprehensive facilities for free medical treatment are available to them under this Act or otherwise ...'

• 'It shall be the duty of every local education authority to make arrangements for encouraging and assisting pupils to take advantage of such facilities ...(emphasis added)'

These duties were spelt out in more detail in the 1945 Regulations.

Under these regulations local education authorities were required to make arrangements for:

• following up pupils who were found on inspection to need supervision or treatment;

• referring to consultants pupils in respect of whom further advice was needed;

• encouraging pupils to obtain any treatment that they required;

• assisting pupils to obtain any treatment other than domiciliary treatment;

• providing pupils with treatment, other than domiciliary, which was not otherwise available;

• ensuring the cleanliness of pupils; and

• securing the hygienic condition of educational establishments maintained by the authority.[67]

These arrangements also had to include adequate provision for the medical and dental inspection of handicapped pupils who were receiving special educational treatment and of pupils who were attending institutions for the further education and training of disabled persons and for their supervision and treatment. The examination and treatment of handicapped pupils had to be carried out 'by a medical practitioner possessing special experience of the particular disability' from which they were suffering.[68] Furthermore, local education authorities had to ensure that 'their school health service (was) in harmony with ... other services in their area relating to health and education'.[69]

Despite a number of references to dental inspection and treatment in the 1945 Regulations some doubt arose over their legality and, specifically, whether local education authorities had the power to provide free dental inspection and treatment, since dental services had not been explicitly referred to in the Education Act 1944. Consequently, specific provision for dental services was made in the Education (Miscellaneous Provisions) Act 1953. Under the provisions of Section 4 every local education authority had '...to make such arrangements as (were) necessary for securing that there (were) available for pupils for whom primary, secondary or further education (was) provided by them... comprehensive facilities for free dental treatment provided either... by persons employed or engaged by, and at the expense of, the authority ... (or) under arrangements made by a Regional Hospital Board or the Board of Governors of a teaching hospital ... '

In meeting their obligations under the Education Acts of 1944 and 1953 most local education authorities took advantage of the considerable degree of overlap between the school health and dental services and some of the other CHSs and, where possible, sought to achieve economies of scale and a more integrated approach to service delivery by combining administrative responsibilities.

As mentioned in the previous chapter, in all but two cases, local education authorities appointed the MOH to the post of principal school medical officer. Similarly in many areas the school dental service and the priority or maternity and child health dental service (see above) were administered by the same dental officers. Likewise, in most local health authorities, the head of the authority's nursing service was also responsible for the management of the school nursing service. Thus, after 1948, the integration of the school with the maternity and child welfare nursing services became the norm in most parts of the country.

One of the most significant trends in the school health service during the 1950s and 1960s was a move away from the routine medical inspection of every child at regular intervals to a more selective system. This was facilitated by amendments made in 1953 and 1959 to the provisions of the 1945 Regulations, which dealt with the conduct of school medical inspections.

Under the 1945 Regulations every child had to be inspected:

• as soon after admission to a maintained school as possible;

• during the last year of attendance at a maintained primary school;

• during the last year of attendance at a maintained secondary school; and

• 'on such other occasions as the Minister (might) from time to time direct' or a local education authority might determine with the Ministers approval.

The School Health Service and Handicapped Pupils Regulations 1953, which superseded those of 1945, were less specific and merely stated that the arrangements made by local education authorities for the medical inspection of pupils attending maintained schools had to ensure: 'a general medical inspection of every pupil on not less than three occasions at appropriate intervals during the period of... compulsory school age and other medical inspections of any pupil on such occasions as (might) be necessary or desirable.'[70] Finally, when the regulations were amended yet again, in 1959, all reference to the occasions on which medical inspections had to be carried out and their frequency was dropped, thereby increasing the autonomy of local education authorities in respect of this aspect of the school health service.

The net result of this increased autonomy was a significant reduction in the number of routine inspections during the 1960s and early 1970s, as the data in Table 4.10 indicate.

TABLE 4.10 *School Health Service : Medical Inspections 1948 to 1973*[a]

Year	School Population[b]	Routine Inspections[c]	Special Inspections and Re-inspections[d]	Defects Treated or Under Treatment[e]
	'000s	'000s	'000s	'000s
1948	5302	1799	2883	2047
1949	5486	1825	2688	1936
1950	5633	1876	2582	2042
1951	5771	1889	2531	2049
1952	5932	1989	2491	2010
1953	6197	2068	2389	1979
1954	6372	2140	2354	1960
1955	6510	2132	2215	1869
1956	6643	2150	2140	1640
1957	6777	2114	2034	1553
1958	6840	2080	1453	1566
1959	6901	2139	1745	1636
1960	6924	2112	1752	1645
1961	6962	2056	1660	1479
1962	6965	2110	1621	1383
1963	6925	2010	1591	1369
1964	7034	1972	1538	1352
1965	7092	1887	1478	1149
1966	7182	1892	1392	1125
1967	7328	1870	1354	1153
1868	7532	1803	1291	1123
1969	7753	1797	1216	1078
1970	7960	1786	1179	1052
1971	8167	1746	1245	1020
1972	8366	1632	1177	1042
1973	8514	1537	1143	1033

Notes

a. Figures for England and Wales.

b. Number of pupils on registers of maintained and assisted primary and secondary schools (excluding nursery and special schools) in January.

c. Routine inspections were carried out at age 4 or 5 (i.e. school entry) and at various other ages depending upon the regulations in force and/or the policy of the local education authority.

d. The term 'special inspection' was generally used in respect of examinations of children who had been referred to a medical officer by a school nurse, teacher or parent. 'Re-inspections' were usually follow-up examinations of children who had been found to have, or were suspected of having, health care problems.

e. See Table 4.11 for further details.

Source: Central Statistical Office, *Annual Abstract of Statistics,* various editions.

Nevertheless, despite this trend, school medical inspection remained, in the words of Kershaw, 'the backbone of the service', and its purpose the detection of 'defects at the earliest possible stage, with a view to their being treated while treatment (was) most likely to be effective.'[71]

The importance attached to medical inspection was also reflected in the fact that under the provisions of Section 48(2) of the Education Act 1944:

Any (authorised) officer of a local education authority ... (could) require the parent of any pupil in attendance at any ... school to submit the pupil for medical inspection in accordance with arrangements made by the authority, and (could) require any pupil in attendance at a county college or other educational establishment maintained by the authority to submit to such medical inspection; and any person who fail(ed) without reasonable excuse to comply with any such requirement (was to) be liable on summary convic-tion to a fine not exceeding five pounds.

In addition, the regulations required local education authorities to give parents, so far as was reasonable and practicable, the opportunity of attending medical inspec-tions. Most authorities were extremely conscientious in exercising this responsi-bility and not only invited but also encouraged parents to attend.

Throughout the tripartite era it was generally agreed that every child should be inspected on starting school. This was because, only a minority of children were being screened during the third and fourth years of their lives and it is during this period that some 'defects' start to develop and important latent 'defects' begin to appear. The case for a 'leaver' inspection was also generally accepted on the grounds that if a 'defect' were to be found and it required treatment it was best to have this carried out whilst the child was still at school. It might also have revealed a 'defect' that could affect a child's choice of employment.

However, there was no general agreement about the most appropriate pattern of inspections at other stages in a child's school career. Consequently, as local education authorities gained more freedom with regard to the frequency and timing of inspections a variety of patterns emerged. In some areas all children had a single intermediate inspection at 10 or 11, whilst in others only children giving cause for concern were inspected.

Factors influencing the inspection policies of local education authorities in-cluded the availability of staff; the views of the principal school medical officer and the number and incidence of 'defects' in their area. Although the total number of 'defects' treated or under treatment fell significantly between 1948 and 1973 (see Table 4.10), the proportion of 'defects' to school populations varied significantly from area to area.

These variations were highlighted by the Chief Medical Officer at the Ministry of Education in his *Report on the Health of the School Child 1956-57*. Analysis of returns from local education authorities showed that in some areas (e.g. Cornwall,

Wiltshire, Bootle, Lincoln) there was a consistently high incidence of all kinds of 'defect' and in other areas (e.g. Devon, Northamptonshire, Bristol, Wakefield) a consistently low incidence. According to the Chief Medical Officer this could have been due to heredity, environment, problems of recording or observer decisions. However, since there was little evidence to suggest that heredity or environment had played a part in causing these variations it was assumed that differences in the methods used to record 'defects' were a far more significant factor.[72] It can therefore be concluded that since there was no uniform procedure for the conduct of inspections and the recording of findings the data would have provided an unsound basis for generalising about variations in the health of the schoolchild.

Further details of the various kinds of 'defect' detected and treated by the school health service and the numbers of pupils involved are provided in Table 4.11. Interestingly, despite the overall reduction in the numbers receiving treatment there were two fields, namely child guidance and speech therapy, where there was a significant increase. To some extent this reflected the changing emphasis of the service, with more attention being given to the meeting of needs where treatment was not readily available elsewhere and less to those health care problems which could be dealt with elsewhere (i.e. by GPs or in hospitals).

During the 1950s it became the usual practice for local education authorities to arrange for as much medical treatment as possible to be provided through the NHS rather than the school health service since this was seen to be a more effective way of using scarce resources. In most areas, however, local education authorities still found it necessary to continue providing specialist clinics. These were staffed either on a sessional basis, with doctors and other health care professionals employed by regional hospital boards and hospital management committees, or by medical officers and other staff employed by the local health authority. Table 4.12 gives an idea of the range of specialist clinics in 1970 and the scale of provision of clinics of this kind.

TABLE 4.11 School Health Service : 'Defects' Treated or Under Treatment 1948 to 1973[a]

Year	Defective Vision or Squint	Defects of Ear, Nose & Throat	Orthopaedic & Postural 'Defects'	Child Guidance Treatment	Speech Therapy	Minor Ailments[b]	Total
1948	363	143	145e	18	18	1360	2047
1949	367	110	143e	21	25	1270	1936
1950	457	199	141	22	24	1199	2042
1951	491	218	140	25	28	1147	2049
1952	516	215	136	27	34	1088	2016
1953	533	211	130	28	40	1037	1979
1954	540	204	137	30	45	1004	1960
1955	552	178	126	31	48	934	1869
1956	556	173	119	31	46	615	1540
1957	560	146	121	32	49	645	1553
1958	553	164	128	35	52	634	1566
1959	560	159	129	36	56	605	1545
1960	560	149	121	40	58	604	1532
1961	539	134	119	46	59	582	1479
1962	518	126	109	44	62	524	1383
1963	526	128	105	49	61	500	1369
1964	533	128	105	46	58	482	1352
1965	502	125	94	54	62	312	1149
1966	491	117	89	57	65	306	1125
1967	487	117	85	62	68	334	1153
1968	469	110	79	64	81	320	1123
1969	434	104	79	66	82	313	1078
1970	435	102	71	69	88	287	1052
1971	406	99	70	69	94	282	1020
1972	408	95	69	75	104	291	1042
1973	389	90	79	79	109	287	1033

Key

e = estimated figure.

Notes

a.   Figures for England and Wales.

b.   These were 'defects' or diseases (e.g. cuts, septic spots, scabies, minor eye 'defects') which could be effectively treated in a school clinic by simple treatment and careful nursing.

Source: Central Statistical Office, *Annual Abstract of Statistics,* various editions.

TABLE 4.12 *School Health Service: Clinics 1970*

Examination and/or Treatment	Number of Premises Available as at 31 December 1970
Minor ailment	1580
Asthma	63
Audiology	395
Audiometry	792
Child guidance	670 approx
Chiropody	305
Ear, nose and throat	214
Enuretic	236
Ophthalmic	955
Orthoptic	121
Orthopaedic	281
Paediatric	52
Physiotherapy and remedial exercises	427
Speech therapy	1605
School medical officer's special examination	1402
Others	589

Source: School Health Subcommittee of the Working Party on Collaboration, *Report.*

Thus, the staff of the school health service came to devote more of their time to screening those aspects which were likely to have implications for educational progress and development and to discussing the problems they detected with parents. Inevitably, this meant paying particular attention to the needs of handicapped pupils.

The 1945 Regulations identified the following categories of handicapped pupil as being in need of special educational treatment and, by implication, of special attention from the school health service:

- blind pupils;

- partially sighted pupils;

- deaf pupils;

- partially deaf pupils;

- delicate pupils (i.e. 'pupils who by reason of impaired physical condition (could not), without risk to their health, be educated under the normal regime of an ordinary school');

- diabetic pupils;

- educationally subnormal pupils (i.e. 'pupils who, as a result of limited ability or other conditions resulting in educational retardation' required some form of special education);

- epileptic pupils;

- maladjusted pupils (i.e. those showing evidence of 'emotional instability or psychological disturbance');

- physically handicapped pupils; and

- pupils suffering from speech 'defect'.[73]

Many of the children in these categories, some of whom were in special schools and the remainder in ordinary maintained schools, received a great deal of help and support from the staff of the school health service.

With regard to staffing, those with responsibility for the management of the school health service were confronted, for most of the tripartite era, with serious recruitment problems. Although there was an increase in the numbers employed in the service (see Table 4.13) and a growing diversity of staff employed during this period, demand tended to outstrip supply. This, of course, also played a part in encouraging the move towards greater selectivity and specialisation.

The duties of school medical officers included:

- the assessment of, and guidance about, the special education needs of handicapped children from the age of 2;

- medical supervision of children in nursery schools;

- the conduct of routine and special inspections and re-inspections of pupils;

- the examination of children as part of the process of ascertainment for special education;

- the review of handicapped children in special and ordinary schools and discussion of their progess with teachers and other health care professionals;

- health education;

- liaison with GPs and hospital consultants in respect of pupils referred to them for further investigation and-or treatment;

- the investigation and control of outbreaks of infection in schools;

- the giving of advice on hygiene and safety precautions, in consultation with public health inspectors, and medical advice, where requested, in respect of the provision of school meals;

- the carrying out of special surveys; and

- the giving of advice about the health and physical capacity for teaching of teachers and students.

TABLE 4.13 *School Health Service : Staffing Levels 1948 to 1973*[a]

Year	Medical Officers[b] WTE	School Nurses[c] WTE	Nursing Auxiliaries WTE	Speech Therapists WTE
1948	832	2366	195	n.a.
1949	861	2516	217	n.a.
1950	907	2464	215	183
1951	893	2516	218	220
1952	898	2519	229	246
1953	899	2551	236	275
1954	932	2565	232	295
1955	946	2548	244	302
1956	971	2570	221	313
1957	978	2581	226	335
1958	941	2589	244	349
1959	948	2667	242	376
1960	959	2637	242	370
1961	954	2660	255	392
1962	972	2667	260	385
1963	955	2607	276	n.a.
1964	983	2666	300	379
1965	1037	2835	318	374
1966	949	2929	317	n.a.
1967	931	2873	285	434
1968	1035	3020	280	n.a.
1969	981	3335	231	471
1970	1058	3313	355	504
1971	1078	3644	353	557
1972	1063	3371	366	617
1973	1225	3420	365	658

Other staff groups included:

	1953 WTE	1957 WTE	1963 WTE	1967 WTE	1973 WTE
Physiotherapists	111	134	135	162	250
Audiometricians	n.a.	n.a.	52	82	125
Chiropodists	6	11	20	24	57
Orthoptists	19	24	22	19	28
Ophthalmic specialists	n.a.	n.a.	51	56	66
Psychiatrists	52	66	111	130	172
Educational psychologists	133	163	300	376	682
Psychiatric social workers	108	124	155	186	n.a.

Key

n.a. = figures not available.

Notes

a.   As at 31st December.

b.   Includes the following four categories of medical officer:

   * those working solely for the school health service (approx 15% WTE);

   * those working part-time for the school health service and the rest of the time on local health authority work (e.g. child health clinic sessions) (approx 70% WTE);

   * those working part-time for the school health service and the rest of the time as GPs (under 10% WTE); and

   * those working part-time for the school health service and for the rest of the time on other medical work (under 10% WTE).

c.   Includes nurses with a health visiting qualification (approx 50%) and those without (approx 50%).

Source: Ministry of Education, *On the Health of the School Child*, various editions.

The organisation of the duties of school medical officers varied from authority to authority. In some authorities medical officers were expected to carry out most or all of the duties listed above, whilst in others there was a degree of specialisation, especially in respect of work with handicapped pupils. Usually the more senior medical officers spent most of their time on administration, planning, committee work, special education duties and, if necessary, giving advice to their colleagues in the field.

As the data in Table 4.13 indicate school medical officers were supported by a large number of nursing staff. In an attempt to improve the quality of the school nursing service; to secure continuity in the care and supervision of children; to facilitate the interchange of staff and to link the school health and child welfare services the 1945 Regulations required every nurse employed by a local education authority 'for the purposes of the school health service (to) possess the qualifications prescribed for a health visitor by the Local Government (Qualifications of Medical Officer and Health Visitors) Regulation, 1930 or by any Regulations amending those Regulations.' This requirement could be dispensed with, however, in the case of any nurse employed on school health nursing duties prior to 1st April 1945 and 'any nurse employed solely in a school clinic, or on duties of a specialist character, or on full-time duties in boarding special schools' or where failure to comply was 'due to (the) unavoidable lack of qualified nurses owing to difficulties arising out of war conditions.'[74] No significant changes were made to these provisions when the regulations were amended in 1953 and 1959. Thus, throughout the tripartite era, local education authorities were, to some extent, constrained as who they could employ on school nursing duties.

In order to cope with this situation most local authorities had staffing structures for their school nursing service which incorporated two categories of post. These were joint health visitor/school nurse posts filled by nurses with a health visitor qualification, who spent some of their time on health visiting duties and the remainder on school nursing duties, and assistant to health visitor posts filled by nurses without a health visiting qualification, who spent all of their time on school nursing duties. A minority of authorities had an entirely separate school nursing service staffed, in the main, by nurses without a health visiting qualification. However, whatever arrangements were in operation, the tasks of nurses employed on school nursing duties were fairly standard. They included:

- persuading parents who were reluctant to attend medical inspections to do so;

- assisting medical officers at routine and special inspections and re-inspections (e.g. by ensuring that everything was in order before the inspection started; weighing and measuring pupils);

- following up cases where a 'defect' had been detected to make sure that appropriate action was taken (e.g. attendance at a school health service clinic; consultation with a GP or hospital consultant);

- routine hearing and vision testing of pupils;

- providing treatment at minor ailment sessions, under the general supervision of a medical officer;

- carrying out cleanliness inspections (Between 1948 and 1973 school nurses and other authorised persons carried out, on average, 13 million cleanliness inspections per annum. Each year approximately 275,000 pupils were found to be infested with vermin e.g. head lice, ringworm.);

- making home visits, to dicuss health care matters with parents;

- liaising between the school health administrative staff and teachers to minimise the disruption to class work caused by medical inspections; and

- taking health education classes on a variety of subjects, such as hygiene, exercise, menstruation and other aspects of growing up, smoking and, from the late 1960s, drug abuse.

In some areas school nurses also played a part, along with their medical colleagues and teachers, in the identification of pupils with psychological and emotional disorders and their referral for treatment at child guidance clinics run by local education authorities.

Authorities derived their powers to provide a **child guidance service** from Sections 34 and 48(3) of the Education Act 1944[75] and the 1945 Regulations, which identified maladjusted children as one of the groups requiring special attention. As indicated earlier child guidance was, in fact, one of the growth areas within the school health service, during the 1950s and 1960s (see Table 4.11). This was due to variety of factors including a growing awareness of the psycho-social aspects of health, changing family patterns and increasing pressures at school.

The value of teamwork in assessing the psychiatric, social and educational factors responsible for a child's difficulties and maladjustment was recognised from the early days of child guidance work. Thus, from the 1940s child guidance clinics were usually staffed by a child psychiatrist (a medically qualified person with special training or experience in child psychiatry); an educational psychologist (a qualified teacher with an honours degree in psychology and special clinical training) and a psychiatric social worker (a qualified and experienced social worker with special training in mental health). In 1955 the Underwood Committee on Maladjusted Children recommended that a basic child guidance team should consist of one consultant child psychiatrist (seconded, if necessary, from the hospital service); two educational psychologists and three psychiatric social workers. In the view of Underwood and his colleagues the appropriate school population for a team of this kind was approximately 45,000. Five years later the Royal Medico-Psychological Society suggested that the school population target for a basic child guidance team should be reduced to 35,000 and in 1968 the members of the Summerfield Committee on Psychologists in the Education Service argued that one educational psychologist could deal adequately only with the needs which arose for services in a school population of 10,000. Needless to say, despite the substantial increases in the numbers of staff engaged on child guidance work (see Table 4.13), none of these targets was reached by 1974.

Furthermore, in his *Report on the Health of the School Child 1971-72* the Chief Medical Officer at the Department of Education and Science drew attention to the fact that between 1955 and 1972 there had been only a marginal increase in the productivity of the child guidance service. During this period the number of clinics had increased from 211 to 498 whilst the average number of pupils treated per clinic had risen only from 147 to 150.

Other causes for concern, in the early 1970s, included:

• the unsatisfactory nature of the division of responsibility between the child guidance service run by local education authorities and the child psychiatric service provided by the hospital authorities and the fact that the staff of child guidance clinics were rarely involved in the work of the child psychiatric service and vice versa;

• the limited involvement of school medical officers and nurses with maladjusted children once they had been referred to the child guidance and/or child psychiatric service;

• the increasing demand for child guidance and the extent to which the rate of emotional and psychological disturbance among schoolchildren varied between areas; and

• the lack of hard data for measuring the effectiveness of the child guidance service, with some experts actually suggesting that the improvement rate of children attending a child guidance clinic was no higher than that of children with similar psychological disturbances who were not attending a clinic.[76]

In addition, the members of the School Health Service Subcommittee of the Collaboration Working Party (see Chapter 3) had received evidence which implied that, notwithstanding the impending reorganisations of the NHS and local government, each of the specialties which contributed to the child guidance service would in future be wedded to their professional bases to an even greater extent than had previously been the case. Thus, child psychiatry would be based increasingly on the psychiatric departments of district general hospitals; social work on the personal social services departments of local authorities and educational psychology on the education departments of local authorities. As a result it would be even more difficult to secure the 'close co-ordination and co-operation' between the three specialties which the subcommittee regarded as an essential prerequisite for an effective service.[77]

Nevertheless, this did not prevent the Chief Medical Officer at the Department of Education and Science from expressing the hope that as health increasingly became the 'focus for the development of community health services and include(d) facilities for child guidance' the members of the primary health care team would become much more involved with the treatment of behavioural disorders in children. In his view it was also important for 'doctors and nurses doing child welfare and school health work and paediatricians ..., (to) be in close touch with child psychiatrists, educational psychologists and social workers'.[78]

During the tripartite era the number and variety of **paramedical staff** employed by local education authorities, on either a full-time or part-time basis, significantly increased as part of the trend towards the provision of a more specialised range of services.[79] Of these speech therapists were, for most of the tripartite era, by far the largest group (see Table 4.13) and particular attention needs to be given to their role. This is because the speech therapy service run by local education authorities was to become the principal component of the area speech therapy services, which were established after 1974.

Although a small number of education authorities had arranged for members of their teaching staff to hold classes for stammerers and to give speech training to children with cleft palates prior to 1944, it was not until the late 1940s and the 1950s that speech therapy became a well established component of school health. The impetus for this came from two sources. First, speech 'defect' was identified as one of the educational categories of handicap in the regulations issued in 1945 and revised in 1959 (see above). Second, the founding of the College of Speech Therapists in 1945 led to the adoption of a common syllabus for the training and examination of those wishing to practise speech therapy.

Conditions treated by speech therapists included stammering, lisping speech and lalling speech (i.e. a persistence of baby speech). They also became involved increasingly in the treatment of children with language disorders and those whose defective speech was due to neurological or other anatomical impairment. To treat conditions of this kind in an effective manner speech therapists generally had to collaborate closely with consultants, psychologists, audiologists and teachers.

Because of the growing importance of speech therapy and the difficulty of recruiting an adequate number of speech therapists, the Secretaries of State for Education and Science, for the Social Services, for Scotland and Wales decided, in 1969, to set up a committee to investigate the nature and availability of the speech therapy services provided by local education authorities and in hospitals. The terms of reference of this committee, which was chaired by Professor Randolph Quirk, were:

To consider the need for and the role of speech therapy in the field of education and of medicine, the assessment and treatment of those suffering from speech and language disorders and the training appropriate for those specially concerned in this work and to make recommendations.

Although the committee reported in 1972, because the recommendations of Quirk and his colleagues were of greater significance for the post-1974 period than the tripartite era, they are considered in Chapters 5 and 7.

Alongside speech therapists various other groups of paramedical staff made their contribution to the health and well-being of school children. Physiotherapists were employed mainly in special schools for the physically handicapped, where their expertise was applied not only in treating pupils but also in the classroom and in giving other members of staff advice about the best methods for feeding and handling children with physical handicaps. In addition, some authorities employed physiotherapists to visit ordinary, as well as special, schools for the purpose of providing treatment and giving advice and to hold clinic sessions in health centres and other premises.

Although most of the routine hearing tests were performed by school nurses, in some cases this task was the responsibility of audiometricians. Their role was to carry out tests which would enable them to identify children who needed to be referred to an audiology clinic for more sophisticated examination and testing by an audiologist.

In some parts of the country, but by no means all, chiropodists were employed by local education authorities to provide treatment for children who had been referred to them by medical officers and others. They also gave advice on the prevention of minor foot deformities or ailments. However, it was very rare for chiropodists to undertake the routine inspection of childrens' feet.

Alongside the school medical and associated paramedical services was the **school dental service**. The principal aim of this service was to ensure that, as far as was practicable, children left school without having lost any of their permanent teeth, free from dental disease and irregularity, and trained in the care of their teeth.

Statistical data illustrating the scale of provision of the school dental service during the tripartite era are provided in Table 4.14. On the basis of this data it is possible to make a number of important points about the development of the school dental service between 1948 and 1973.

First, following the establishment of the NHS the demand from the public for free dental treatment was so great that during the period 1947 to 1950 the equivalent of over 200 full-time dental officers left the school dental service for the general dental service. However, as the data in Table 4.14 indicate, this situation did not last for very long and by the early 1950s recruitment to the service had improved. Furthermore, after 1962 the service expanded fairly rapidly in terms of the numbers of dental officers and support staff employed in school dental clinics. Nevertheless, recruitment continued to be a problem for the managers of the service.[80] This was partly due to the fact that income levels were higher in the general dental service than in the school dental service.

The two most significant categories of support staff, in terms of the assistance they could provide dental officers, were dental auxiliaries and dental hygienists. Dental auxiliaries were first appointed to the school dental service in 1962. This followed the establishment, in 1960, of an experimental two year training course for dental auxiliaries at New Cross Hospital. Under the provisions of The Dental Auxiliaries Regulations 1960, dental auxiliaries were able to fill teeth or extract milk teeth, but were prohibited from fitting, inserting and fixing dentures. Furthermore, they could give treatment only after a dental officer had examined a patient and indicated that such treatment was necessary. The main functions of oral or dental hygienists were to instruct parents and their children, both individually and collectively, in the care of the teeth and mouth; to carry out scaling and polishing and to apply fluoride solution to the teeth as a prophylactic. By enabling dental officers to concentrate on the provision of more complex treatment dental auxiliaries and oral-dental hygienists played an important part in helping managers to expand the service.

Second, between 1951 and 1973 the number of pupils inspected each year more than doubled. Under the provisions of the 1945 Regulations every child had to be inspected by a dental officer as soon as possible after being admitted to a maintained school for the first time and on such other occasions as the Minister directed.

TABLE 4.14 *School Dental Service : Staff and Clients 1948 to 1973*[a]

Year	← Staff[b] →			← Clients →				
	Dental Officers	Dental Attend-ants	Dental Auxiliaries	Pupils Inspected	Requiring Treatment		Pupils Treated	
	WTE	WTE	WTE	'000s	'000s	%[c]	'000s	%[d]
1948	880	944	/	3503	2125	60.7	1628	76.6
1949	732	863	/	2807	1761	62.7	1422	80.7
1950	717	794	/	2487	1593	64.1	1293	81.2
1951	712	797	/	2446	1729	70.7	1249	72.2
1952	850	927	/	2788	1897	68.0	1382	72.9
1953	945	1010	/	3194	2192	68.6	1494	68.2
1954	979	1052	/	3391	2343	69.1	1532	65.4
1955	1008	1091	/	3489	2419	69.3	1488	61.5
1956	1024	1101	/	3524	2429	68.9	1424	58.6
1957	1014	1105	/	3434	2324	67.7	1350	58.0
1958	1032	1140	/	3570	2403	67.3	1343	55.9
1959	1016	1119	/	3595	2381	66.2	1301	54.6
1960	1030	1157	/	3722	2420	65.0	1254	51.8
1961	1069	1201	/	3777	2394	63.4	1227	51.2
1962	1072	1316	41	3997	2492	62.3	1252	50.2
1963	1215	1346	72	4041	2506	62.0	1286	51.3
1964	1243	1434	94	4327	2594	59.9	1310	50.5
1965	1330	1594	124	4047	2367	58.5	1260	53.2
1966	1335	1647	144	4140	2363	57.1	1279	54.1
1967	1364	1638	156	4271	2417	56.6	1287	53.2
1968	1417	1682	172	4354	2431	55.8	1294	53.2
1969	1422	1767	178	4447	2497	56.2	1312	52.5
1970	1462	1815e	182	4578	2557	55.9	1314	51.4
1971	1421	1766e	165	4771	2667	55.9	1385	51.9
1972	1450	1800e	189	4962	2719	54.8	1431	52.6
1973	1592	1969	217	5107	2742	53.7	1443	52.6

As at 31st December 1973 the staff of the school dental service also included 104 WTE dental technicians; 19 WTE dental health education personnel and 15 WTE dental hygienists.

Key

e = estimated figure.

Notes

a.   Figures for England and Wales.

b.   As at 31st December.

c.   Pupils requiring treatment as a percentage of pupils inspected.

d.   Pupils treated as a percentage of pupils requiring treatment.

Source: Central Statistical Office, *Annual Abstract of Statistics*, various editions.

Similar provisions were incorporated in the 1953 version, but, as in the case of medical inspections, when the regulations were amended for a second time in 1959 all reference to the frequency and timimg of dental inspections was dropped. Unlike medical inspections, however, the number of dental inspections steadily increased throughout the tripartite era and many local education authorities sought to ensure that their pupils were inspected annually. Nevertheless, despite the importance of regular inspection, dental officers spent only about 6% of their time on this particular activity.

Third, the percentage of those inspected who were found to need treatment fell from about 70% in the early 1950s to just over 50% in the early 1970s. This was due to a variety of factors including the greater attention paid by children and their parents to the care of teeth; the reduction in sugar consumption after 1958, when it reached its peak; and the increasing used made of the general dental services for check ups and treatment.

Improvements in the dental health of schoolchildren during the 1960s and early 1970s were also detected by a series of five-yearly surveys, sponsored by the Ministry/Department. The surveys were carried out in seven areas; Manchester, Middlesex, Northumberland, Nottingham, Somerset, West Riding of Yorkshire and East Sussex; and they focussed on the dental health of five and twelve year olds. The key results are summarised in Figure 4.12. These show that the peak of dental disease for five year olds was reached in 1958 and for 12 year olds in 1963. However, improvements in dental health were more rapid in the case of 5 year olds than in the case of 12 year olds.

Last, although the number of pupils treated by the service remained fairly constant at between one and a quarter and one and a half million, for most of the tripartite era, in percentage terms this represented a reduction of the service's role in the provision of treatment. However, from the information in Table 4.14 it is clear that most of this reduction occurred during the 1950s and from 1959 the figure for pupils treated as a percentage of pupils found to require treatment remained within the range 50 to 55%. Nearly 90% of a dental officer's time was spent on providing treatment, the vast majority of which was designed to conserve teeth. Furthermore, circulars issued by the Ministries of Education and Health in 1955[81] made it clear that orthodontic treatment was recognised as an element in a satisfactory school dental scheme.

As well as carrying out inspections and providing treatment, school dental officers were also responsible for initiating and supervising the implementation of dental health education programmes, by dental auxiliaries, and where they were employed, by dental hygienists. A number of commentators suggest dental health education underwent some significant changes during the tripartite era. For example, Towner argues that 1956 marked the beginning of 'the modern phase of dental health education', because the first attempt in Britain 'to evaluate and to

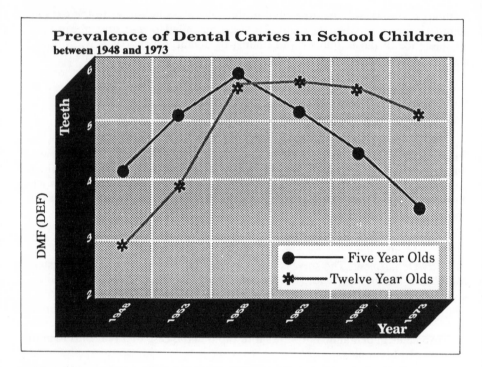

Figure 4.12

Key

Average number of D(ecayed), M(issing) and F(illed) teeth per child examined. [D(ecayed), E(xtracted) and F(illed) teeth, in the case of 5 year olds.]

Source: Department of Education and Science, *The School Health Service 1908-1974*, (London: HMSO, 1975).

quantify the effects of a (health education) programme' was made in that year and from then onwards 'accountability became far more important.'[82] She also draws attention to three main themes which began to emerge in dental health education from the early to mid-1960s. These were:

- recognition of 'the need for more epidemiological data from which target groups could be delineated and attitudes to dental health determined';[83]

- a questioning of 'the value and effectiveness of popular dental health messages';[84] and

- more detailed investigation(s) of the materials and methods employed in dental health education.[85]

Although these themes applied to dental health education in general, given that children were a key target group for a majority of dental health education programmes they had a particular significance for the school dental service and for the activities of dental officers and their colleagues in this sphere.

The expansion of the service which took place during the 1960s and early 1970s was due, in part, to the greater availability of financial resources and, in part, to a fairly critical report on the service from the House of Commons Estimates Committee (1963). Although the members of the subcommittee, which undertook the investigation on which the report was based, were concerned with dental services as a whole, they devoted a considerable amount of attention to the school dental service and received evidence on the operation of the service from a wide variety of sources. They reached the conclusion that the productivity of the service was falling, on the grounds that in 1952 the number of children treated per dental officer had been approximately 1900 compared with only 1200 in 1962.[86] In their view, the declining productivity of the service was due to poor management at local level and inadequate supervision of local education authorities by the Ministry of Education. To remedy the situation they recommended closer supervision of the service from the centre and more effective management of the service by principal school dental officers. In response to these recommendations the Ministry of Education increased its complement of staff with dental qualifications from 1 to 3 and established two posts (i.e. chief and senior dental officer) jointly with the DHSS.

In his *Report on the Health of the School Child 1971-72* the Chief Medical Officer at the Department of Education and Science was able to comment favourably on the way in which the expanded corps of departmental dental advisers had been able to assist authorities 'in their quest for higher standards'. Routine visits had been followed up with 'written communication of both commendation and criticism', which had left 'no doubts in the mind of the recipients of the Department's continued interest and willingness to be of assistance.' Moreover, 'the interchange of views between officers in the field and Departmental Officers (had) been of advantage to both and an important factor in the improving standards within advantage to both and an important factor in the improving standards within the service.'[87]

Undoubtedly **the school health service as a whole** made a significant contribution to the health and well-being of school children between 1948 and 1974. Furthermore, as pointed out by the Health Visitors' Association in the early 1970s, since 10% of children in primary schools were not registered with a GP and 14% of children were starting school with some health 'defect', it continued to have an important role to play. Nevertheless, the service was not without its critics. They argued, with some justification, that most of the doctors and nurses working for local education authorities lacked the training and qualifications needed to provide a high quality service and in many areas the nature and organisation of the service and 'its concentration on regular medical examination'[88] had restricted its ability to adapt to the changing needs of schoolchildren and their parents and teachers.

Partly in response to these criticisms and partly because by the early 1970s, 'the illogicality of a separate and independent school health service (had) become more obvious', the decision was taken, after a lengthy debate, to incorporate the service in the reorganised NHS (see Chapter 3). It was hoped that by doing so the school health service would become more closely integrated with other health care services for children.

By 1974 then, most of the **CHSs** were far larger, in terms of their spending and staffing levels and numbers of clients served, than they had been in 1948. Furthermore, as a result of the development of new services such as chiropody, family planning and speech therapy, the range of CHSs was broader and more diverse. Thus, despite the feeling, in certain quarters, that there was in the decision to transfer administrative responsibility for these services from local health authorities to the newly constituted RHAs and AHAs an implicit criticism of the performance of some, if not all, local health authorities, the CHSs had, in general, fared extremely well under local authority control.

It is also the case that although the CHSs had been administered separately from other health care services this had not prevented them from making significant contributions to the improvements in the health and well-being of members of the public which had taken place between 1948 and 1974. Attention was drawn to some of these improvements by Abel-Smith in a short account of the first 30 years of the NHS, which was published in 1978, to mark the NHS's thirtieth anniversary. As he observed:

Taken as a whole, the population was receiving (in 1974) a vastly better service than when the National Health Service started a quarter of a century earlier. For example, the risk of a mother dying in child birth was, by 1974 one-eigth of that in 1948. Deaths from diphtheria, polio, whooping cough and measles fell from 1468 in 1948 to 33 in 1974. Nearly 22000 people died from tuberculosis in 1948 and only about 1200 in 1974.[89]

Similarly, the infant mortality rate (i.e. deaths of children under one year old in England and Wales had fallen from 33.93 (per 1000 related live births) in 1948 to 16.3 in 1974 and the neo-natal mortality rate (i.e. deaths of children under 4 weeks old) from 19.7 to 11.0.

Some of this progress was due to advances in medical knowledge and to developments in the hospital sector and other spheres of public service provision, such as housing and environmental health. However, the part played by the members and staff of local health and education authorities should not be underestimated.

Clearly it is not possible to quantify every aspect of their contribution to the improvements in the well-being of the population at large and of of particular groups, especially children and the elderly. However, from the evidence presented in this chapter, it is clear that without the dedication and commitment of those at the front line the quality of life for those in receipt of CHSs would have been very much the poorer. Whether these improvements would be sustained under a unified structure remained to be seen.

Towards an Integrated Approach to Service Delivery?

It is not without significance that during the tripartite era, despite an increasing awareness on the part of service providers and others of the unifying features of the CHSs and the consequent need for a more integrated approach to service delivery, each service retained its separate identity. This was due to a variety of factors, including the distinctive origins and long established traditions of many of the services; the discriminatory and prescriptive nature of the legislation which had governed their provision and the tendency for most service providers to identify with a specific service rather than the services collectively. Nevertheless, as has been indicated elsewhere, some attempts were made to secure an element of integration in the delivery of services. For example, there were the joint health visitor-school nurse posts established by a large number of authorities and the arrangements whereby clinical medical officers undertook both school health and maternity and child welfare duties.

Moreover, by the late 1960s and early 1970s, expectations in this respect were being raised by the rapid development of health centres and the emergence of the related concepts of 'attachment' (on which an increasing amount of research was being undertaken)[90] and the primary health care team. Increasingly, health centres and primary care teams were being seen as a way of eroding some of the traditional divisions between not only the individual CHSs but also CHSs and the FPSs and of securing more extensive and effective collaboration and integration in the delivery of services.

During this period a number of high powered conferences and seminars were held on the theme of the primary health care team. For example, in 1967 the Health Visitors' Association, the National Association of State Enrolled Nurses, the Queen's Institute of District Nursing, the Royal College of General Practitioners, the Royal College of Midwives, the Royal College of Nursing and the Society of Medical Officers of Health, jointly sponsored a two day conference at the Wolfson Institute on the theme: 'Family Health Care - The Team'. Similarly in 1972 and 1973 the Council for Education and Training of Health Visitors organised multidiscipli-nary seminars at which different aspects of team working within primary care were discussed.

Thus, by the time that responsibility for the CHSs came to be transferred from local health and education authorities to the newly constituted AHAs and RHAs, it was assumed by many that the next phase in the growth and development of the CHSs would be characterised by increasing integration in the delivery of care. However, for reasons which are examined in the next three chapters, this did not turn out to be the case.

Footnotes

1.   Quoted in C. Webster, *The Health Services since the War : Volume I Problems of Health Care The National Health Service before 1957* (London: HMSO, 1988), p. 97.

2.   See ibid., pp. 380-388 for further details of those health centres which were opened in the 1950s

3.   *Report of the Committee of Enquiry into the Cost of the National Health Service*[Chair: C.W Guillebaud], Cmnd 9663, (London: HMSO, 1956).

4.   Ministry of Health, *Health and Welfare. The Development of Community Care*, Cmnd 1973 (London: HMSO, 1963), p. 11.

5.   Ministry of Health, *Health and Welfare. The Development of Community Care. Revision to 1975-76 of Plans for the Health and Welfare Services of the Local Authorities of England and Wales*, Cmnd 3022 (London: HMSO, 1966), p. 6.

6.   Ministry of Health, Circular 7-67.

7.   J. Gerald Beales, *Sick Health Centres and How to Make Them Better* (Tunbridge Wells: Pitman Medical, 1978), p. 18.

8.   Ibid., p. 16.

9.   B. Watkin, *Documents on Health and Social Services, 1834 to the present day* (London : Methuen, 1975), p. 260.

10.   During the late 1960s and early 1970s the concept of the primary care team was endorsed by many different bodies, including the BMA's Board of Science and Education.

11.   Ministry of Health, Central Health Services Council, Standing Medical Advisory Committee, *The Field Work of the Family Doctor,* [Gillie Report] (London: HMSO, 1963).

12.   DHSS, Welsh Office, Central Health Services Council, *The Organisation of Group Practice. A Report of a Subcommittee of the Standing Medical Advisory Committee,* [Harvard Davies Report] (London: HMSO, 1971), p. 7.

13.   J. Edwards, *A Survey of Health Centres in the South-West,* Health Service Reports, No. 2 (London: Update Publications, 1972).

14.   C. Webster, op. cit., p. 374.

15.   Ibid., p. 378.

16.   Ibid., p. 379.

17.   Ministry of Health, Central Health Services Council, Standing Medical Advisory Committee, *Child Welfare Centres,* [Sheldon Report] (London: HMSO, 1967), p. 35.

18.   At that time the following were classified as welfare foods : liquid milk, National Dried Milk and vitamin A, D and C tablets and drops. In certain circumstances expectant mothers and children under school age were entitled to free milk and vitamins. For further details, see DHSS, Circular HRC(74)6, *Operation and Development of Services. Welfare Food Service.*

19.   Ministry of Health, *Report of Maternity Services Committee,* [Cranbrook Report] (London: HMSO, 1959).

20.   C. Webster, op. cit., p. 245.

21.   Ibid., p. 380.

22.   Central Health Services Council, *Domiciliary Midwifery and Maternity Bed Needs,* [Peel Report] (London: HMSO, 1970).

23.   SI No. 1414, 1948.

24. *The Local Health Services,* (London: Office of Health Economics, 1965), p. 19.

25. *Report of a Working Party on the Field of Work, Training and Recruitment of Health Visitors,* [Jameson Report] (London: HMSO, 1956), para. 315.

26. See Section 2 of the Health Visiting and Social Work (Training) Act 1962 for a definitive statement of the functions of the Council.

27. The membership arrangements for the Council were set out in the First Schedule of the Health Visiting and Social Work (Training) Act 1962. Significantly in making a number of their appointments the Health Ministers were required, under the provisions of the act, to consult with associations representing health visitors, the BMA and the Society of Medical Officers of Health and the General Nursing Councils for England and Wales and for Scotland.

28. 'Health Visiting in the Seventies', *Health Visitor,* September 1975, Vol. 48, p. 324.

29. Health and Welfare. The Development of Community Care. Revision to 1975-76, op. cit., p. 12.

30. DHSS, Circular 13-72, *Aids to Improved Efficiency in the Local Health Services. Deployment of Nursing Teams,* para. 9.

31. Between the censuses of 1951 and 1971 the number of over 65s in the population increased from 4.8 million (1.6 million of whom were aged 75 and over) to 6.5 million (2.3 million over 75). At the same the number of tuberculosis notifications fell from 60,683 to 13,757.

32. D. Hicks, *Primary Health Care : A Review* (London: DHSS, 1976), p. 248.

33. DHSS, *Annual Report 1972,* Cmnd 5352, p. 23.

34. The Local Health Services, op. cit., p. 21.

35. S. Simmons and C. Brooker, *Community Psychiatric Nursing : A Social Perspective* (London: Heinemann Nursing, 1986), p. 43.

36. Ibid.

37. Health and Welfare. The Development of Community Care. Revision to 1975-76, op. cit., p. 13.

38. DHSS, Circular 13-72, op. cit., para. 10.

39. L. Hockey, *Feeling the Pulse. A Survey of District Nursing in Six Areas* (London: Queen's Institute of District Nursing, 1966).

40. DHSS, Scottish Home and Health Department, Welsh Office, *Report of the Working Party on Management Structures in the Local Authority Nursing Services,* [Mayston Report], 1969, para. 37.

41. Ibid. para. 202.

42. The Salmon Committee was set up by the Minister of Health and the Secretary of State for Scotland in July 1963 to enquire into 'the senior nursing staff structure in the hospital service (ward sister and above), the administrative functions of the respective grades and the methods of preparing staff to occupy them.' The report (May 1966) recommended the establishment of clearly defined management hierarchies for hospital nursing staff headed by a chief nursing officer.

43. Committee on Nursing, [Chair: Lord Briggs], *Report,* Cmnd 5115 (London: HMSO 1972).

44. C. Webster, op. cit., p. 323.

45. The Local Health Services, op. cit., p. 28.

46. DHSS, Circular HRC(74)17,*Arrangements for Vaccination and Immunisation against Infectious Diseases,* February 1974, para. 4.

47. The Local Health Services, op. cit., p. 29.

48.   Many tuberculosis care committees performed this function by distributing clothing, bedding and extra provisions to patients and operating schemes of financial aid to assist patients on home leave at Christmas time and the families of patients with low incomes.

49.   Home nurses and health visitors played an important part in the development and administration of incontinence services (e.g. providing information, assessing need).

50.   See C. Thomas, 'BJOT: Occupational Therapy in the Community', *The British Journal of Occupational Therapy*, October 1987, 50(10), pp. 351-354, for further details of the origins of community based occupational therapy services.

51.   J. Griffith, *Central Departments and Local Authorities* (London: Allen and Unwin, 1966), p. 448.

52.   C. Webster, op. cit., p. 236.

53.   Ibid.

54.   The Local Health Services, op. cit., p. 30.

55.   Some like Webster, however, argue that by the 1950s the Council had become 'moribund'.

56.   Ministry of Health, *On the State of the Public Health 1958*, Annual Report of the Chief Medical Officer, Cmnd 871, p. 137.

57.   C. Webster, op. cit., p. 377.

58.   Ibid., see pp. 233-237 for a detailed account of the debate surrounding the issue of smoking and health during the 1950s.

59.   Ibid., p. 378

60.   DHSS, Circular HRC(74)27, *Reorganisation of the National Health Service and Local Government : Operation and Development of Services. Health Education*, March 1974, Appendix.

61.   I. Sutherland, 'History and Background' in I. Sutherland (ed.), *Health Education, Perspectives and Choices* (London: George Allen and Unwin, 1979), pp. 1-19.

62.   Ministry of Health, *Annual Report for 1965*, Cmnd 3039, p. 52.

63.   The principal function of the National Health Service Central Register (Southport) is to maintain a basic record of everyone in England and Wales, who is registered for general medical services.

64.   Ministry of Health, Circular 5-66.

65.   Department of Education and Science, *The School Health Service 1908-1974* (London: HMSO, 1975), p. 1.

66.   C. Webster, op. cit., p. 373.

67.   SR&O No. 1026 1945, *The Handicapped Pupils and School Health Service Regulations 1945*, Reg. 50.

68.   Ibid., Regs. 45 and 46.

69.   Ibid., Reg. 54.

70.   SI No. 1156 1953, *The School Health Service and Handicapped Pupils Regulations 1953*, reg. 10(1).

71.   J.D. Kershaw, 'The School Health Services' in P.J. Cunningham (ed.), *The Principles of Health Visiting* (London: Faber and Faber, 1967) and SI No. 365 1959, *The Handicapped Pupils and Special Schools Regulations 1959*.

72.   Ministry of Education, *The Health of the School Child. Fifty years of the School Health Service*, Report of the Chief Medical Officer for the years 1956 and 1957 (London: HMSO, 1958), p. 93.

73. SR&O No. 1026 1945, op. cit., Reg. 3.

74. Ibid., Reg. 54.

75. Under Section 34 of the Education Act 1944 it became a duty of local education authorities to ascertain which children required special educational treatment and under the provisions of Section 48(3) they had to provide free medical treatment for pupils in maintained schools.

76 M. Shepherd, B. Oppenheim and S. Mitchell, *Childhood Behaviour and Mental Health* (London: University of London Press, 1971).

77. DHSS, *Report of the Working Party on Collaboration between the NHS and Local Government on its Activities to the End of 1972*, para. 6.45.

78. Department of Education and Science, *The Health of the School Child 1971-72*, Report of the Chief Medical Officer (London: HMSO, 1974), p. 19.

79. In 1966 The School Health Service Regulations were amended to provide that from 1st April 1966 persons practising one of the professions supplementary to medicine (i.e. chiropody, dietetics, medical laboratory work, occupational therapy, physiotherapy, radiography and remedial gymnastics) could only be employed in the school health service if they were registered with the Council for Professions Supplementary to Medicine.

80. The problem of recruitment was investigated by an interdepartmental committee under the chairmanship of Lord McNair. The terms of reference of this committee, which reported in 1956, were, 'to ascertain the reasons for the lack of candidates for training as dentists, and to indicate possible directions in which remedies might be sought.'

81. Ministry of Education, Circular 288, and Ministry of Health, Circular HM(55)67.

82. E. Towner, *History of Dental Health Education*, Health Education Authority Occasional Paper No.5, 1987?, p. 38. The study, carried out in St Albans, involved providing an experimental group of school children with tooth brushes and weekly lessons on dental health by their teachers for one term. The dental health knowledge and oral hygiene of the group was assessed at the beginning and end of the term and at the end of the following term. Comparisons were also made with a control group. Overall, the results were disappointing since the improvement in the dental behaviour and oral hygiene of the experimental group was only marginal. As a result, those conducting the experiment were forced to conclude that 'fundamental oral hygiene habits were difficult to alter'.

83. Ibid., p. 40.

84. Ibid., p. 41. An example of a popular dental health message was: '(1) Eat nourishing meals, with nothing sweet or sticky in between, (2) finish meals with raw fruit or vegetables and rinse the mouth with water, (3) brush the teeth and gums after eating, and especially after breakfast and before going to bed, (4) use a soft toothbrush, and an up-and-down motion and (5) visit the dentist regularly for advice' (British Dental Association 1961).

85. Ibid., p. 42.

86. It is not entirely clear what data were used as the basis for calculating these ratios. If the figures in Table 4.14 are used then the ratio for 1952 is 1 dental officer to 1600 children treated and for 1962, 1 dental officer to 1200 children treated.

87. The Health of the School Child 1971-72, op. cit., p. 51.

88. The School Health Service 1908-1974, op. cit., p. 1.

89. B. Abel-Smith, *National Health Service, the first thirty years* (London: HMSO, 1978), p. 30.

90. For details see P. Hawthorn, *The Nurse Working with the General Practitioner An Evaluation of Research and a Review of the Literature,* (London: DHSS, 1971).

Chapter 5

Managing the Community Health Services: 1974 to 1982

For those with responsibility for the administration and management of the CHSs the 1974 reorganisation of the NHS and local government represented both a threat and an opportunity. The threat arose from the potential domination of the CHSs by the hospital based services which were far larger (in terms of expenditure and staffing) and more prestigious. Despite the assurance given in the Conservative government's white paper of 1972, that there was 'no question' of the hospital based services 'swallowing up'[1] the CHSs, many people felt that this would in fact be the eventual outcome of transferring responsibility for the administration of the CHSs from local health authorities to the newly created RHAs and AHAs. Furthermore, given the disparity in the budgets of the two services it was feared that CHSs would receive less attention than previously and that their share of the total resources allocated to health care would fall. In the event neither of these more extreme predictions came to pass.

For the idealists the reorganisation offered a major opportunity for the development of a truly integrated approach to the provision of health care services based on the principles of mutual respect for the contributions made by community health and hospital staff and family practitioners to the well-being of patients. Again, however, as the following quotation from the report of the Royal Commission on the National Health Service (1979) makes clear, the 1974 reorganisation had far less impact than had been anticipated:

The reorganisation of the NHS was, of course, intended to integrate health services in the community with those in hospitals, but at working level, with which the patient is concerned, the effects will often not have been felt. The employer may be the same but health service workers in the community and in hospitals may still go their own way.[2]

Thus, by 1982 when the administrative structure of the NHS was again reorganised the CHSs still retained many of the functional characteristics which they had exhibited in 1974.

This lack of progress was due mainly to the fact that administrators and managers were so preoccupied with the problem of making the new structure work and, from the mid-1970s, of coping with the financial consequences of the economic depression, that they had little opportunity of considering how best to integrate the CHSs with the other health care services. Consequently, for a number of years, the CHSs 'marked time' and few initiatives were taken.

Nevertheless, despite an element of inertia, the 1974 reorganisation was an important turning point for the CHSs. It brought about major changes to the way in which they were financed and managed and to the organisational environment within which they were provided. These changes are now explored in more detail.

The Unified Structure

For the CHSs one of the most significant consequences of the 1974 reorganisation was the transfer of responsibility for their administration from democratically elected and relatively autonomous local authorities to RHAs and AHAs. With an appointed membership, these latter authorities formed part of a unified and hierarchical structure within which there was less scope for the exercise of autonomy. As indicated in Chapter 3 this structure was designed to overcome the weaknesses inherent in the tripartite arrangements and thereby secure a more integrated approach to the provision of health care services. It was also hoped that the new structure would lead to less disparity in the quantity and quality of health care services available in different parts of the country.

The services which were affected by the transfer of responsibility from local health authorities to AHAs included:

- community health services for mothers and pre-school children, including the priority dental service;

- school health (including the school dental service), apart from the exercise of various powers under the Education Act 1944, such as those relating to special educational provision for handicapped pupils, the cleanliness of pupils and certification of the fitness of pupils for employment, which remained the responsibility of local education authorities;

- vaccination and immunisation;

- home nursing;

- health visiting;

- domiciliary midwifery, both in respect of the employment and the regulation of midwives;

- family planning, including cervical cytology screening;

- health education, local authorities, however, retained their power to carry out health education activities under the provisions of Section 179 of the Public Health Act 1936 and to undertake health education within schools and colleges and in support of their responsibilities for environmental health, including the control of communicable diseases and food poisoning, personal social services and consumer protection;

- chiropody; and

- ambulance services.

In addition, AHAs took over the running of health centres and the registration of private nursing homes, with local personal social services authorities retaining responsibility for the registration of private nursing agencies.

The major components of the unified and hierarchical structure created by the architects of the 1974 reorganisation are shown in Figure 5.1. At national level the DHSS retained its responsibility for the overall direction and control of the NHS. This involved setting objectives, establishing priorities, making policies and monitoring the performance of health authorities. With the introduction of the NHS planning system in 1976, the policy-making and the monitoring roles of the DHSS were further strengthened. In the words of Ham, the planning system was designed 'to ensure greater compliance among health authorities with central government priorities.'[3] For the CHSs this meant much stricter monitoring and control from the centre than had been the case during the tripartite era and a more active role for the DHSS in respect of service development. It also implied that there would be far less toleration of variations in service provision between authorities.

The initial contribution of the DHSS to the process of planning and priority setting was the publication of a consultative document entitled *Priorities for Health and Personal Social Services* (1976 *Priorities* document).[4] This was described as a 'new departure', since it represented the DHSS's first attempt at establishing 'rational and systematic priorities throughout the health and personal social services' for a number of years ahead. In determining these priorities account was taken of:

- the resources likely to be available for health and local authorities' personal social services according to the *White Paper on Public Expenditure for the period 1975/76 to 1979/80;*

- the likely changes in demand for services from the principal client groups (e.g. the elderly, children);

- the areas of service provision in which past neglect had resulted in serious deficiencies (e.g. services for the mentally ill and mentally handicapped);

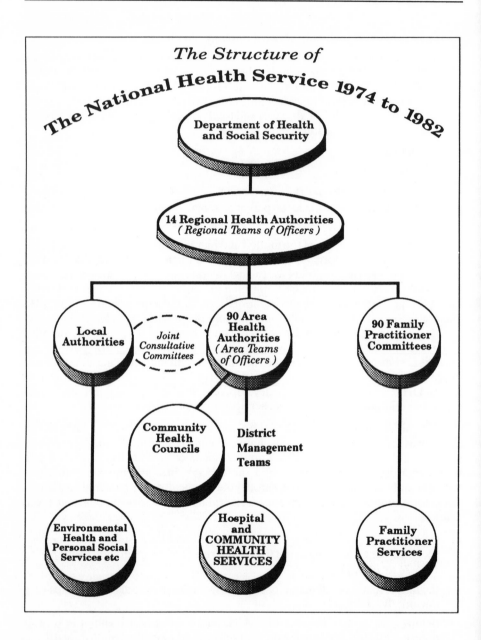

The Structure of The National Health Service 1974 to 1982

Department of Health and Social Security

14 Regional Health Authorities
(Regional Teams of Officers)

Local Authorities

Joint Consultative Committees

90 Area Health Authorities
(Area Teams of Officers)

90 Family Practitioner Committees

Community Health Councils

District Management Teams

Environmental Health and Personal Social Services etc

Hospital and COMMUNITY HEALTH SERVICES

Family Practitioner Services

Figure 5.1

Notes

a. To begin with there were 205 DMTs in England. By 31st March 1982 the number of DMTs had fallen to 199. This was due to the merging of districts in a number of multi-district areas. A complete list of AHAs can be found in Appendix IV.

b. As a general rule there was one CHC per health district. However, for geographical reasons, initially two of the districts were served by two CHCs, making a total of 207. Furthermore, when districts were merged it was the usual practice to retain the existing pattern of CHCs. Consequently, by 1982 the number of CHCs had fallen by only one to 206.

c. As indicated in Figure 3.1 there was also the Central Health Services Council, which continued to function until 1980 when it was wound up as an economy measure. However, four of the five Central Health Services Council's Standing Advisory Committees (i.e. Medical, Dental, Pharmaceutical, and Nursing and Midwifery) survived. Only the Standing Ophthalmic Advisory Committe was abolished. In 1981 the Joint Committee on Vaccination and Immunisation was granted the status of a standing advisory committee.

d. In addition there was a complex network of professional advisory committees at regional, area and district level. These were designed to ensure that health authorities and their officers made 'decisions in the full knowledge of expert opinion (and) ... at all levels the health professions exercise(d) an effective voice in the planning and operation of the NHS.'[5] The professions with their own advisory committees generally included medicine, nursing and midwifery, pharmacy, dentistry and ophthalmics.

- ways in which the available resources could be used to get their best return; and

- the contribution that could be made by joint planning by health and local authorities.

This exercise in the setting of priorities generated a considerable amount of discussion, and, in the light of comments from interested parties and the first plans of RHAs, a follow-up document was published by the DHSS in 1977. Entitled *Priorities for Health and Personal Social Services : The Way Forward* (1977 *Priorities* document),[6] it was far less specific than its predecessor about rates of increase in services and time scales. Nevertheless, like the earlier document, it emphasised the importance of establishing priorities and of ensuring that they were implemented.

These documents also stressed the 'importance of adjusting the balance of care to provide greater support in the community'and the consequent need for health authorities to develop their community based health care services and give greater priority to preventive medicine and health promotion. Similarly the DHSS planning guidelines, which were issued on an annual basis from 1978/79, encouraged health authorities to devote more resources to community care.[7] Surprisingly, these priorities were unaffected by the change of government in 1979, since on this issue there was no significant difference between the political parties. Indeed, the new Conservative government demonstrated its commitment to the development of community care in not only its planning guidelines but also the publication by the DHSS, in 1981, of *Care in Action : A Handbook of Policies and Priorities for the Health and Personal Social Services in England* and *Care in the Community: A Consultative Document on Moving Resources for Care in England.*[8] Both of these documents indicated that, amongst other things, health authorities should pay particular attention to the building up of those CHSs which contributed directly towards the prime objectives of preventing mental and physical ill-health and of providing care for people in their own homes, such as health visiting and district nursing. In the interest of achieving a more co-ordinated and cost-effective approach to the provision of community care, these documents also stressed the importance of collaboration between health authorities and other bodies (e.g. local authorities, voluntary organisations, the private sector). It was the second of the two documents, *Care in the Community,*which dealt in detail with some of the financial and staffing implications of caring for more people in the community as opposed to in hospital.

As well as making plans and setting priorities the DHSS was also responsible for acquiring and distributing funds for health care (see below); taking the lead in promoting policies designed to improve the health of the nation and to prevent ill-health, and encouraging experimentation and the evaluation and exchange of ideas on health care matters.

In anticipation of its enhanced role after 1974, the organisation and operation of the health and personal social services parts of the DHSS had been reviewed and modified during the early 1970s. In the revised structure of the DHSS there was a move away from service demarcations as a basis for allocating responsibilities to different parts of the organisation (i.e. separate sections for hospitals, FPSs, CHSs and local authority personal social services) towards more cross-service groupings, based on geographical divisions, since this was felt to be more in keeping with the principle of integration.

As Figure 5.1 indicates, immediately below the DHSS within the NHS hierarchy came the 14 RHAs. Although some of the participants in the debate which had preceded the reorganisation had argued that a regional tier was unnecessary, as the authors of *Health Care in the United Kingdom* point out, 'the 1973 Act hardened the regional concept and introduced regional health authorities as corporately accountable management bodies in a hierarchical position between the Secretary of State and area health authorities.'[9] For the CHSs the principal significance of the decision to retain and strengthen the regional tier was the fact that, whereas regional hospital boards had played no part in the provision of community services, RHAs were required to plan strategically and allocate current (or revenue) and capital resources to AHAs for community as well as hospital based services.

In accordance with the principles set out in the 'Grey Book' (see Chapter 3), the chair and members of each RHA, who were all appointed by the Secretary of State, received professional advice and support from two main sources: the professional advisory committees, and a regional team of officers (RTOs). The latter consisted of the regional administrator, the regional treasurer, the regional medical officer, the regional nursing officer and the regional works officer.

Each of the 14 regions was divided into a number of areas (see Table 5.1), which were, in general, coterminous with the local authorities responsible for the administration of personal social services (i.e. metropolitan districts; non-metropolitan counties and London boroughs), to facilitate collaboration.

TABLE 5.1 *NHS Regions, Areas, and Districts 1974*

Region	Pop (m)	No of Areas	No of Areas with: 1 2 3 4 5 6 Districts					
Northern	3.1	9	6	0	2	1	0	0
Yorkshire	3.5	7	1	4	0	2	0	0
Trent	4.5	8	3	1	3	1	0	0
East Anglia	1.7	3	0	2	1	0	0	0
N W Thames	3.5	7	1	3	1	2	0	0
N E Thames	3.8	6	0	3	2	0	1	0
S E Thames	3.7	5	1	1	1	1	0	1
S W Thames	3.0	5	2	0	2	0	0	1
Wessex	2.6	4	1	1	1	1	0	0
Oxford	2.1	4	1	3	0	0	0	0
South Western	2.9	5	1	2	0	2	0	0
West Midlands	5.1	11	7	0	2	1	1	0
Merseyside	2.5	5	1	3	0	0	1	0
North Western	4.1	11	9	0	1	0	0	1
Totals	46.1	90	34	23	16	11	3	3

Source: DHSS, Circular HRC(74)23, *Management Arrangements: Health Districts,* March 1974.

In the words of Levitt and Wall, AHAs were 'the embodiment of an 'integrated' service'. This was because they had no clear precedent in the pre-1974 tripartite structure and they had a 'dual responsibility for planning and providing services'. In other words 'they not only provided comprehensive health services including hospitals, community and domiciliary care but also studied the health needs of the area, and found out where provision fell below required standards.'[10] AHAs were therefore expected to plan and make policies for all health care services within their area; to allocate current and capital resources between districts and to monitor the performance of the DMTs, where they existed (see below).

In addition, it was intended that AHAs should play the key role in the joint planning of services with local authorities. Under the provisions of Section 10 of the National Health Service Reorganisation Act 1973 (1973 Act) health authorities and local authorities were required to 'co-operate with one another in order to secure and advance the health and welfare of the people of England and Wales' and for this purpose AHAs and their coterminous local authories had to set up joint consultative committees on which they were both represented. Inevitably collaboration and co-operation between the NHS and local government in the years following the 1974 reorganisation involved, amongst other things, consideration of how best to maintain and develop links between the CHSs and related local authority services, such as personal social services and education. In practice, however,relatively little was achieved for reasons which are discussed in Chapters 8 and 10.

AHAs were also responsible for the management of various services, including some of the major CHSs, such as the pre-school child health service, the school health service, community dental services and health education.

The members of AHAs were appointed partly by the RHA and partly by local authorities. Like their counterparts on the RHA they received advice and support from profesional advisory committees and a team of chief officers. The team comprised the area administrator, area treasurer, area nursing officer and area medical officer, who, together with the district community physician (see below), can be regarded as the nearest equivalent to the MOH within the reorganised structure of the NHS. In a minority of areas, which were not subdivided into districts, the team was formally designated the area management team (AMT), and its membership also included the chairman and vice-chairman of the area medical committee (who were usually a consultant and a GP). In the majority of areas, which were multi-district, (see Table 5.1) the team was formally designated the area team of officers (ATOs).

Most of the districts had a population of between 100,000 and 500,000. Although there was no statutory authority at this level the district was intended to serve as the basic unit for the planning, management and operation of most health care services, in order to keep 'operational control ... as close as possible to the point of direct patient care.'[11] In multi-district areas responsibility for the provision of a comprehensive range of health care services, on a day-to-day basis, rested with DMTs, which were made up of the district administrator, the district nursing officer (DNO), district community physician, district finance officer and two clinical representatives, one consultant and one GP. In single district areas the AMT performed this role.

The 'Grey Book' had anticipated that in an average district, with a population of about 250,000, the DMT or AMT would have probably been faced with the task of planning not only for the health care needs of the community at large but also for the specific needs of:

• 60,000 children, of whom 500 might have been physically handicapped and 200 mentally handicapped;

• 35,000 people over the age of 65, of whom 4,500 might have been physically handicapped, 800 in hospital, 800 in old people's homes and 100 living at home alone and requiring domiciliary care;

- possibly 7,000 severely physically handicapped people of all ages;
- possibly 700 mentally handicapped people of all ages, of whom 350 might have been in hospital;
- possibly 2,500 mentally ill people of all ages, in contact with hospitals, of whom 580 might have been in-patients; and
- possibly 19,000 people requiring acute medical and surgical care each year as in-patients and in many cases care at home following their hospitalisation.

In seeking to meet these needs the DMT would have had at its disposal approximately ten hospitals, including a district general hospital and a number of maternity and psychiatric hospitals and health centres plus the services of 3,500 to 4,000 staff, including 140 hospital doctors, 1,300 hospital nurses, and 140 community nurses. It was, of course, the hope of those responsible for the 1974 reorganisation that by bringing together within a single organisational unit responsibility for both hospital based services and staff and community based services and staff that the health care needs of each district would be met in a more integrated and therefore more effective and efficient manner.

Since most of the day-to-day management of services was carried out at district level, the number of operational units for the CHSs was slightly increased by the reorganisation. Before 1974 CHSs were managed, in England, by 158 local health authorities (if the 29 county districts with delegated powers are excluded) and after 1974 by 205 DMTs (AMTs in single district areas). This meant that the average population of the operational units was slightly smaller. Moreover, as Figure 5.2 illustrates there was less deviation from the average population.

Some guidance was provided by the DHSS, but it was mainly left to the AHAs and their DMTs to determine their sub-district structures. Most subdivided their districts into sectors. According to a circular the term 'sector' was one that could be conveniently used 'to describe substantial subdivisions of a District'. However, although AHAs were expected to ensure that the arrangements for different groups of staff at subdistrict level were such that they facilitated multidisciplinary working, sectors were not intended to be 'a multidisciplinary management tier separate from the District'. It was anticipated that most districts would be subdivided into two or three sectors and that sectors would be responsible for:

- a large hospital or group of hospitals; or
- hospitals and other institutions (such as health centres and clinics) and associated services in a geographical subdivision of a district; or
- non-hospital services for the whole (or a large part) of a district.[12]

In practice a variety of patterns emerged, some of which were geographically based, others functionally based and others a mixture of both. For the CHSs this meant that there were considerable differences in the way that they were incorporated into sub-district structures. As McNaught comments: 'The 1974 reorganisation produced tremendous variety in the organisation and management of community health services."[13] Consequently generalisations about the period between the 1974 and 1982 reorganisations need to be treated with caution.

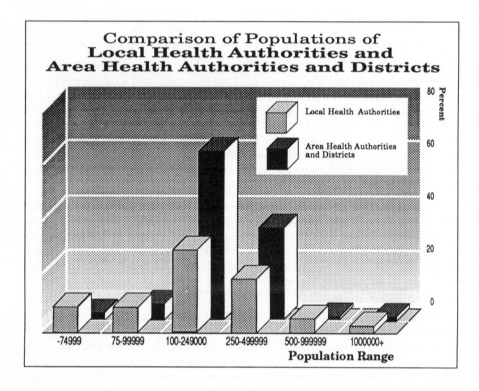

Comparison of Populations of
Local Health Authorities and
Area Health Authorities and Districts

Figure 5.2

Sources: *Census Reports* 1971 and DHSS, Circular HRC(74)23, *Management Arrangements: Health Districts,* March 1974.

In districts where the sectors were functionally based it was usual to have a sector with sole responsibility for the CHSs. Although this ensured that there was relatively little disruption in the provision of services it ran counter to the principles of the 1974 reorganisation, since CHSs staff were, to some extent, isolated from the staff with responsibility for other health care services and as a result there was less likelihood of an integrated approach to service delivery. The main alternative to what can be described as a 'separatist' solution to the problem of how best to incorporate the CHSs into sub-district structures was that of 'integration'. This generally involved giving each sector responsibility for both CHSs and HSs within a geographically defined part of the district. In theory such an arrangement was more likely to lead to an integrated approach to service development than that of 'separation'. However, it ran the risk of undermining the cohesion and links which had developed between the CHSs during the tripartite era.

One further alternative was that of the 'care group' sector. Under this arrangement sectors were made responsible for all the services required by a particular client group, such as the acutely ill, the elderly and the mentally handicapped and the CHSs were allocated accordingly. This had the great advantage of bringing together, within a single sector, staff with similar interests and of facilitating continuity of care. However, problems arose over the allocation of responsibility for those services, like community nursing and family planning, which were required by more than one client group.

Thus from the point of view of securing both greater integration of community and hospital based services and the continued cohesion and development of the CHSs none of these arrangements was entirely satisfactory.

In keeping with the principle of multidisciplinary working it was common practice for health care activities within the sector to be managed by a sector management team. In those sectors with responsibility for the delivery of the CHSs the team normally consisted of the sector administrator; a divisional nursing officer; a principal physician (child health); a principal physician (environmental health) or (social services) and, as a co-opted member, a GP representative. Their links with officers at higher levels within the NHS hierarchy are shown in Figure 5.3.

The sector administrator was expected to manage directly some of the staff providing administrative support services within the sector (e.g. general administrative staff) and co-ordinate the work of other groups of administrative and ancillary staff (e.g. personnel officers, finance officers, domestics), thereby ensuring that they met the needs of the sector. At the same time s/he was required to 'co-ordinate the interaction of the different managerial systems within his sector, seeking to promote an effective working relationship between professional and other staffs' (e.g. community nurses, community dentists). However, given the changes in management arrangements which were to occur ten years later with the introduction of general management, it was significant that the role specification for the sector administrator made it clear that it was *not* a duty 'to co-ordinate (the) activities of staff within another discipline.' [14] This remained the responsibility of the manager for that discipline or function. In other words the principle of functional self-management which had developed during the 1960s continued to operate, despite the recognition of the need for inter-disciplinary working.

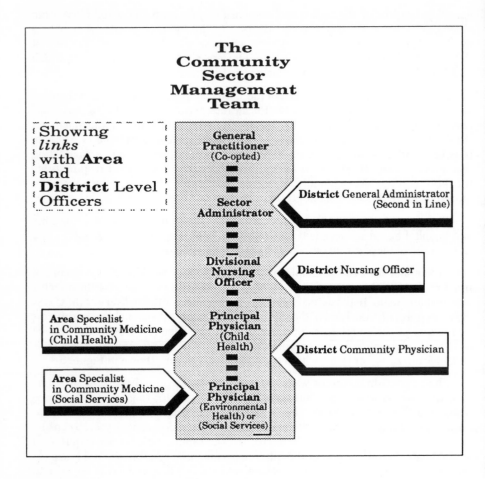

Figure 5.3

Other duties of the sector administrator included:

- the monitoring of services provided in the sector;
- participation in the planning process, through the provision of inputs in the form of statistical and other data and membership of the primary health care planning team;
- liaison with district functional departments, such as works and supplies; and
- control of appropriate budget heads.

Because of the close relationship between the CHSs and various local authority services and the emphasis on collaboration, sector administrators with responsibility for the CHSs were also expected to establish and/or maintain close links with appropriate local authority officers.

The Financial Framework

Another important change for the CHSs arising from the 1974 reorganisation was in their method of financing. No longer were the staff and running costs of the CHSs financed out of rate and grant income, but from the current (i.e. revenue) advances which the DHSS made to the RHAs and which they then distributed between their AHAs. After 1976/77 the DHSS used the formula produced by the Resource Allocation Working Party as the basis for determining each region's allocation of revenue resources. The underlying objective of the Resource Allocation Working Party formula was to secure 'through resource allocation, equal opportunity of access to health care for people at equal risk'. One element of the formula took account of the varying utilisation rates of the CHSs by different age groups in the population. To calculate these rates the Resource Allocation Working Party used data from the 1971/72 expenditure returns submitted by local health authorities to the DHSS. These showed that out of £30.50 spent on the CHSs per 1000 population, £15.32 (i.e. 50%) went on services for the 0 to 4 year olds; £7.36 (i.e. 24%) on services for the 5 to 14 year olds; £0.67 (i.e. 2%) on services for the 15 to 64 year olds and £7.15 (i.e. 24%) on services for those aged 65 or more.[15] The formula also used standardised mortality ratios as a proxy for need. However, many commentators have drawn attention to the fact that these failed to reflect variations in the rates of morbidity and disability between different parts of the country. This failure was of particular significance for the CHSs, because of the contribution which they make to the care of people who are chronically sick and disabled.

Many of the principles incorporated in the Resource Allocation Working Party formula were also applied in the distribution of revenue resources at sub-regional level. However, it is important to note that, although the need for CHSs is usually reflected in the resource allocation process, funds are not specifically earmarked for the CHSs. Consequently the amount they receive depends largely on the way in which health authorities decide to share their financial resources between the services for which they are responsible.

As has already been mentioned some commentators feared that this would lead to the CHSs not doing as well, in terms of their budgetary allocations, as the far more costly HSs. However, as the data in Table 5.2 indicate there was a modest increase in the share of the revenue resources allocated to the CHSs between 1974/75 and 1981/82. This was due, in part at least, to the 1976 and 1977 *Priorities* documents which indicated that CHSs should grow at a faster rate than acute and general hospital services (although more slowly than spending on the FPSs).[16]

TABLE 5.2 *NHS Revenue Resources Allocated to the Community Health Services 1974/75 to 1981/82*

	1	2	3	4	5	6
				←—CHSs Revenue Expenditure—→		
Year	NHS Revenue Expenditure	CHSs Revenue Expenditure	Column 2 as % of Column 1	on Patient Care	of which Nursing	on Administration & General
	£m	£m		£m	£m	£m
1974/75	3164.0	199.2	6.3	149.7	102.6	49.5
1975/76	4063.7	261.4	6.4	198.7	133.4	62.6
1976/77	4647.2	299.3	6.4	226.9	154.8	72.5
1977/78	5209.8	334.1	6.4	251.4	172.3	82.7
1978/79	5930.4	377.3	6.4	284.7	194.8	92.6
1979/80	7107.5	457.5	6.4	348.1	240.5	109.4
1980/81	9107.2	607.3	6.7	472.2	333.3	135.1
1981/82	10176.8	675.7	6.6	526.0	365.2	149.7

Source: House of Commons Papers, *Summarised Accounts of Health Authorities etc,* various years.

Of the revenue resources devoted to the CHSs by far the largest percentage was used to pay the salaries and related staff costs of the community nursing services (i.e. district nursing, health visiting, community midwifery and school nursing). The dominance of community nursing and school health service within the overall revenue budget for the CHSs is also illustrated by the data in Table 5.3.

Because Table 5.3 shows spending on each of the CHSs programmes at constant prices it is possible to determine which expanded the most and which the least, in real terms (i.e. staff and equipment), between 1976/77 and 1981/82. Thus, during this period there was a 35.8% real increase in spending on district nursing; 29.4% on prevention and 15.5% on health visiting and only a 1.3% increase on family planning; whilst chiropody experienced a decrease in real terms of 10.3% and other CHSs a decrease of 14.7%.

TABLE 5.3 *Programme Budget for the Community Health Services 1976/77 to 1981/82 (at 1981/82 prices)*

Year	HV £m	DN £m	CM £m	Pr £m	Ch £m	FP £m	SH £m	Other £m
1975/76	90.5	156.4	52.1	25.5	25.2	23.9	104.8	109.5
1976/77	90.1	169.0	50.5	28.8	22.4	23.8	101.1	99.3
1977/78	95.5	170.8	51.0	27.8	22.8	23.4	106.2	14.7
1978/79	96.7	179.2	47.6	29.2	23.5	24.2	109.6	108.7
1979/80	97.0	186.9	48.6	30.3	22.5	23.7	107.0	106.3
1980/81	98.8	203.8	52.9	31.0	22.1	23.6	109.4	104.2
1981/82	104.6	212.4	55.2	33.0	22.6	24.2	119.9	93.4

(Provisional)

Key
HV = health visiting
DN = district nursing
CM = community midwifery
Pr = prevention (i.e. vaccination and immunisation)
Ch = chiropody
FP = family planning
SH = schooi health service

Note

It is not possible to compare the figures in this Table with those in column 3 of Table 5.2 (except for 1981/82), since they are based on constant prices.

Source: House of Commons Paper No. 321 Session 1982/83, The Social Services Committee, *Public Expenditure on the Social Services,* Minutes of Evidence, DHSS.

With regard to capital spending the use of loans as the principal method of financing capital projects, such as the construction and improvement of premises and the purchase of plant and equipment, was replaced by allocations from the capital advances, which the DHSS made to RHAs. Although capital investment programmes for major schemes were prepared and executed at regional level, AHAs were responsible for the preparation of capital programmes for smaller schemes financed out of block allocations made to them by RHAs. Such allocations were subject to a variety of constraints on their use, which varied from region to region. In the main, however, the schemes delegated to area level were those involving modest extensions to existing premises, the refurbishment of equipment and the construction of specific types of premises, including health centres. The share of NHS capital resources allocated to CHSs is shown in Table 5.4.

Lastly, reference needs to be made to the joint financing arrangements, which were introduced in 1976/77 to stimulate the co-operation between health authorities and local authorities referred to earlier. Under these arrangements, every health authority received a small earmarked allocation of funds (i.e. between 0.5% and 1.5% of its total allocation) for the financing of schemes, jointly planned with local authorities. Schemes of this kind generally involve the provision of community based care for members of the priority groups (i.e. elderly, mentally ill, mentally

TABLE 5.4 *NHS Capital Resources Allocated to the Community Health Services 1974/75 to 1981/82*

Year	NHS Capital Expenditure £m	CHSs Capital Expenditure £m	CHSs as % of NHS Capital Expenditure
1974/75	267.5	13.7	5.1
1975/76	331.7	19.9	6.0
1976/77	334.5	22.9	6.8
1977/78	316.0	19.6	6.2
1978/79	367.0	18.4	5.0
1979/80	416.4	36.1	6.3
1980/81	563.2	84.9	6.2
1981/82	671.4	37.1	5.5

Source: House of Commons Papers, *Summarised Accounts of Health Authorities etc,* various years.

handicapped, physically handicapped). Since some of the CHSs make a contribution to the well-being of those within the priority groups they have benefitted, albeit marginally, from the availability of joint finance monies.[17]

Management Arrangements for Individual Services

Although the 1974 reorganisation did little, in the short-term, to bring about closer relations between the CHSs and the other health care services, it did result in some major changes to the way in which the CHSs were managed both individually and collectively. The relatively simple, cohesive and standardised arrangements which had existed during the tripartite era were replaced by arrangements which were far more complex, fragmented and varied. The point is made by the authors of *Health Care in the United Kingdom* that:

> The 1974 reorganisation was designed to integrate the health services but while it brought community and hospital services together it led to some disintegration within the community services themselves. Previously managerial responsibility for all these services had lain with a single individual - the medical officer of health - but they were now split up.[18]

The diffusion of managerial responsibility for the CHSs was due partly to the hierachical nature of the reorganised NHS, partly to the application of the principles of functional and team or consensus management and partly to the variety of arrangements that were made for the management of services at sub-district level.

The fragmentation inherent in the post-1974 arrangements for the management of the CHSs is illustrated by Table 5.5. This identifies the officers with managerial responsibility for those CHSs where detailed guidance on post-reorganisation management structures was provided by the DHSS.

TABLE 5.5 *Management Arrangements for the Community Health Services 1974 to 1982*

Service	Managerial Responsibility
Community Medicine	Shared between regional medical officers, area medical officers, district community physicians and community physicians at sector level.
Community Nursing (including Health Visiting and Midwifery)	Shared between nursing officers at regional area, district and divisional or sector level.
Child Health Services	Shared between area medical officers or specialists in community medicine (child health) at area level or the district community physicians and principal physicians (child health) at sector level.
Health Education	Area medical officers, assisted by area health education officers, and colleagues from other professions.
Chiropody	Usually an area or district head of service (i.e. area or district chiropodist), accountable to the area medical officer or district community physician.
Speech Therapy	Usually an area head of service (i.e. area speech therapist), accountable to the area medical officer.
Community Dental Service	Usually an area head of service (i.e. area dental officer) assisted by district dental officers.
Family Planning	At area level specialists in community medicine and at district level the DMTs

In the following sections the post-reorganisation management arrangements for each of the services identified in Table 5.5 are considered in more detail.

Community Medicine

Prior to the 1974 reorganisation considerable attention had been given to the role of community medicine in the unified NHS and to the roles of those medical staff who would be the successors to the MOsH (see Chapter 3). Of particular importance, in this respect, was the report of the Hunter Working Party (1972), which reviewed in detail the responsibilities of the future 'specialists in community medicine'. The principles advocated by Hunter and his colleagues were incorporated in both the 1972 white paper and the 'Grey Book' and in a circular which the DHSS issued to the new authorities in 1974.

This drew attention to the distinctive character of community medicine by referring to the following quotation from the report of the Royal Commission on Medical Education (1968).

Community medicine is the specialty concerned not with the treatment of individual patients but with broad questions of health and disease in... sections of the community and in the community at large.

In response to the recommendations of the Royal Commission and the Hunter Working Party, the Royal Colleges of Physicians in Great Britain jointly established a Faculty of Community Medicine in 1972, thereby enhancing the status of community medicine and ensuring that by 1974 it was 'recognised as a specialty in its own right.'[19]

With regard to the structure of community medicine in the reorganised NHS, the circular identified the principal posts at each level, namely those of regional medical officer, area medical officer, district community physician and specialists in community medicine. The generic term for these was to be that of 'community physician' and the post holders were to have the status of a hospital consultant.

The circular also outlined the principal roles of community physicians at each level of the NHS hierarchy. Thus, the regional medical officer was to act as:

- adviser to the authority, through membership of the RTOs and as the authority's senior community physician; and

- leader of a team of specialists in community medicine, with responsibility for the planning and monitoring of hospital and community based health care services; the medical aspects of health care information services and research and of capital building projects and personnel work for medical staff.

Similarly at area level the area medical officer was to perform the role of adviser to the authority and leader of a team of specialists in community medicine employed by the AHA. The responsibilities of members of this team were to include:

- the planning of health care services generally;

- the medical aspects of information services;

- the planning and organisation of health services for pre-school and school children (see below);
- making contributions to the development of services, including those for the mentally ill and mentally handicapped, the elderly, and the physically handicapped, the planning of which required close co-operation between the NHS and local authority social services departments;
- in certain areas, environmental health; and
- personnel work for medical staff.

In addition certain members of the team were to be responsible for co-ordinating the work of the clinical medical officers on the staff of area medical officers. These were the medical officers who had previously been employed by local authorities, often on a part time basis, to perform clinical duties at maternity and child welfare, school health, family planning and other clinics. Thus, although their work was organised by community physicians, staff of this kind did not practise community medicine and were therefore outside the formal management structure for community medicine.

The roles and responsibilities of the district community physician were described in the following terms:

The District Community Physician will be a member of the NHS District Management Team, and will share the joint responsibility of the team for the management of health services in the district. His particular role will involve the co-ordination of health care planning teams (eg for the elderly, the mentally ill, etc) at district level. He will share responsibility for formulating plans for operational health services, the implementation of various preventive services such as vaccination and immunisation, screening procedures and health education. He will assist the process of integration by advising his consultant colleagues in his capacity as a community physician, using his knowledge of the needs of the district and his expertise in the organisation of health care and the proper use of information on health and disease. In non-metropolitan county districts he will usually be the medical adviser on environmental health matters and proper officer for the control of notifiable disease and food poisoning.[20]

In addition, although not specifically mentioned in the circular, it was generally assumed that district community physicians would play a key role in co-ordinating the work of other specialists in community medicine employed at district and, in some cases, at sub-district level.

It was therefore intended that community medicine should have a high profile at every level in the reorganised NHS and that specialists in community medicine should make an important contribution to the future development of health care services in general (i.e. hospital as well as community based services). Furthermore, as the information in Table 5.5 indicates, it was also the intention of those responsible for the 1974 reorganisation that specialists in community medicine should play an important part in developing and co-ordinating many of the CHSs, not only through direct participation with those from other disciplines in service planning and management (e.g. child health; family planning) but also by being able to hold to account some of the area/district heads of service (e.g. health education, chiropody, speech therapy) for various aspects of their performance as managers. In many areas, however, the management arrangements proved to be so complex and unwieldy that the area medical officers/district community physicians could not make them work in the manner intended.

In addition, as Levitt and Wall indicate, 'the Medical Officer of Health (had been) a highly influential officer in local authorities whose work (had been) widely appreciated ... (and consequently) the holders of these posts did not find it altogether easy to adapt to the different management principles'[21] which applied after 1974. They had particular problems in adapting to the concepts of consensus and team management. Prior to reorganisation many had been able, as chief officers, to manage staff and services in a far more direct manner, and had either taken decisions on their own or else presented them to the health committee for approval, which was usually forthcoming. Thus, decision-making was a relatively speedy process. Now they were faced with a situation in which even fairly routine matters, such as clinic times at child health centres, had to be discussed with other members of a management team until a consensus was reached. This resulted in decision-making becoming a much more time consuming process, and in the expertise and status of community physicians being downgraded.

Many ex-MOsH also missed the political support which they had usually received from the chairman of the health committee. Not only were health authority members appointed rather than elected, but also none of them had a particular brief for either community medicine or the CHSs.

Similarly, in looking at the problems of community medicine in the reorganised NHS, the members of the Royal Commission on the National Health Service drew attention to the contrast between the pre-1974 and post-1974 situation facing community physicians. As they observed:

Whatever the deficiencies of the pre-reorganisation arrangements at least the role of medical officers of health and their departments ... were reasonably clear and accepted. Reorganisation broke traditions which had been built up over many years, and launched the holders of the new posts in the reorganised NHS on largely uncharted waters.[22]

In seeking to navigate these uncharted waters the holders of the new posts also had to contend with the marked hostility towards management and administration and towards managers and administrators on the part of many of their fellow doctors. To illustrate this point the members of the Royal Commission included the following comments from the British Hospital Doctors Federation in their report:

Furthermore, new posts have been created in some special specialties eg Area Pharmacist, Area Chiropodist, Area Nursing Officer - whose function is difficult to determine, let alone understand. Such people perform a purely administrative function which we regard as a waste of their training and skills which were acquired for the treatment of patients. The same applies to the large number of doctors in purely administrative posts and as Community Physicians.[23]

Ironically, however, community physicians were often unable to exercise their public health and administrative role to the full, not because of hostility from medical colleagues, but because, as the regional medical officers commented in their evidence to the Royal Commission, they were 'appointed without management support' and were therefore 'in the position of attempting professional practice with no tools of the trade'. To remedy this deficiency the Royal Commission recommended that 'community physicians should be given adequate supporting staff.'[24]

The Committee of Inquiry into the Future Development of the Public Health Function (1988), reached the following conclusions on the state of community medicine after the 1974 reorganisation:

In some parts of the country community physicians seized the opportunity which was presented to them in 1974 and created vigorous departments which continue to make important contributions to the planning and development of health services for the populations they serve. In other places, some simply failed to make the transition. The out-dated approach of community physicians, coupled with confused lines of accountability within multi-district areas ..., exacerbated by the paucity of resources available in some places, impeded the proper discharge of the public health function. The failure of some community physicians to meet the expectations required by the Hunter recommendations also contributed to the failure of the specialty to establish its professional standing.[25]

However, some community physicians argued that their failure to meet these expectations was due as much to the recommendations themselves as to anything else. In particular they felt that the change of title for their specialty from 'public health' to 'community medicine' had not been helpful. This was because many of their medical colleagues, especially at district level, argued that as community physicians they should only be concerned with community based health care services not those provided in hospitals. Unfortunately this had the effect of undermining the potential contribution which community physicians could have made to the development of a more integrated approach to the delivery of health care.

One final point, unlike their predecessors, community physicians played only a marginal role (if that) in the management and development of the community nursing services, which in many respects were the most important of the CHSs.

Thus, even if they had been able to overcome all the constraints outlined above they still lacked the authority they needed to secure the integration of community nursing with the other CHSs.

Community Nursing

With regard to nursing, the principal aims of the 1974 reorganisation were to integrate the community and the hospital nursing services and 'to improve contact and co-operation between nursing and other disciplines at all levels throughout the structure.'[26] A supplementary aim was to enable the nursing profession to make a significant contribution to the management of not only nursing services but also health care services as a whole. As a result the management arrangements for community nursing proved to be more complex than those for other CHSs.

At regional level, as has been mentioned already, the regional nursing officer was a member of the RTOs. In this capacity s/he provided nursing and midwifery advice to the members of the authority, to the RTOs and to individual chief officers and played 'a full role in the planning and achievement of (the RTOs') objectives and the formulation of its plans and policies.'[27] In most regions the regional nursing officer was supported by 3 regional nurses responsible for capital projects; professional education and development; and personnel and management services respectively. Although, at this level, nurse managers were primarily concerned with hospital based services, nonetheless their responsibilities formally extended to the CHSs as well.

Like her/his counterpart at regional level, the area nursing officer was a member of the ATOs and, as such, was responsible for providing nursing and midwifery advice to the members of the AHA, the ATOs and individual senior officers, and for contributing to the co-ordinating, planning and policy-making functions of the ATOs. In addition the area nursing officer played an important role in providing the AHA's 'matching' local authority with advice. The area nursing officer was also expected to monitor and coordinate the work of the DNOs and to manage nursing and midwifery staff based at area headquarters.

To assist the area nursing officer, AHAs usually appointed a number of second-in-line staff, known as area nurses. The spheres of work which the area nurses covered either singly or in combination were: minor capital projects, which often included health centres; the planning of both community and hospital based services; personnel; local authority liaison and, most significantly from the point of view of the CHSs, child health services, including the school health service. The role of the area nurse with the child health portfolio is considered in some detail in the next section.

For the organisation of nursing and midwifery services at district level and below, the 'Grey Book' suggested three alternative structures. In each case the structure was headed by the DNO, who, as a member of the DMT, participated in the planning of health care services for the district; played a part in achieving the

Alternative Nursing Structures within Districts

A

Hospital and Community Nursing Divisions

District Nursing Officer

| Education | Hospital A | Hospital B | Community |

B

Functional Divisions with a Community Care Division

District Nursing Officer

| Education | General | Midwifery | Psychiatry | Community |

Hospital Hospital   Hospital Community   Hospital Hospital   Community Community

C

Functional Divisions without a Community Care Division

District Nursing Officer

| Education | General Nursing | Midwifery | Psychiatry |

Hospital Community   Hospital Community   Hospital Hospital

Figure 5.4

Source: DHSS, *Management Arrangements for the Reorganised National Health Service* (London: HMSO, 1972), Exhibit XI.

team's objectives and co-ordinated nursing with other services. The DNO was also responsible for managing the nursing and midwifery services, both hospital and community, for the district as a whole; maintaining professional nursing and midwifery standards and providing advice to the DMT and individual officers. Under the DNO the service was to be organised on the basis of 'divisions' each headed by a divisional nursing office .The divisional structures recommended in the 'Grey Book', with the position of community nursing within them highlighted, are shown in Figure 5.4. (see page 221).

In deciding which of these alternatives to adopt AHAs and their DMTs were asked by the DHSS to ensure that:

- established and effective services could continue unhindered, whilst at the same time allowing for the likely future expansion of services;

- divisions, were of an adequate size, thereby avoiding the disadvantages of small divisions, to which the Mayston and Salmon Reports had both drawn attention;[28] and

- wherever practical 'hospital and community nursing services (were)... integrated on a functional basis at divisional level.'[29]

Although most health authorities followed these guidelines to the extent of adopting one of the alternative structures suggested by the authors of the 'Grey Book', with or without modifications, in a majority of districts the principle of integration was not applied and community nursing preserved its separate identity within the divisional structure. Furthermore, some authorities with a community nursing division did not have a community sector and vice versa. Clearly, in designing their divisional nursing structures and their management arrangements at sector level authorities should have ensured compatibility. Unfortunately, however, this did not always happen due to local political factors.

In every district each functional nursing division was headed by a divisional nursing officer, who was accountable to the DNO for managing the nursing services of the division, for giving professional nursing advice to other staff and for contributing to the planning of health care services for the district and the formulation and execution of district nursing policies. More specifically divisional nursing officers, including those with responsibility for community nursing divisions, were expected to:

- control and co-ordinate divisional nursing services and manage a budget for the division;

- assess the financial implications of the division's needs and plans in consultation with medical staff and other officers;

- advise the DNO on the progress of integration and the implications of service proposals for the division;

- participate in the formulation of district nursing policies and initiate, prepare and review divisional nursing policy in collaboration with other divisional nursing officers;

- prepare and ensure implementation of policies for the division on nurse deployment, whilst taking account of the views of medical and administrative staff, district policy on the standards and type of service being provided and the needs of nurse education and training;

- review overall work load and advise on the best use of available nursing skill and staff;

- report to the DNO whenever it was impossible to maintain adequate nursing services and advise on acceptable measures for modifying the nursing service;

- develop an efficient divisional communication system and links with other divisions, disciplines, departments, local authorities and other agencies;

- discuss and agree with the education division the plans for nurse education and training and the provision of clinical experience;

- promote and encourage research and studies related to the nursing service and nurse education, and, where appropriate, participate in other disciplines' studies and training;

- ensure the development of personnel services and in- service training needs and the provision of appropriate counselling and career advice for all the nursing staff of the division;

- advise and inform support services departments of the division's needs and inform the DNO of the effect on nursing services of proposed changes in the policies of these departments;

- investigate accidents and mishaps within agreed procedures and participate in the development and surveillance of corrective action;

- participate in the activities of, or provide skilled nursing staff for membership of, multidisciplinary and health care planning teams;

- establish and maintain links for the division with the professional advisory committees, the CHC and voluntary organisations; and

- 'act up' as required for the DNO and provide advice and information on divisional nursing matters for the DMT.

As has already been mentioned divisional nursing officers might also be members of sector management teams. However, complications clearly arose in those districts where nursing divisions did not correspond to sectors.

Child Health Services

One of the principal objectives of the 1974 reorganisation was the establishment of 'a comprehensive range of integrated health services for children.'[30] To this end the 1973 Act had brought together, under the AHAs, responsibility for the local authority health services for the pre-school child, for the medical and dental inspection and treatment of school children and for the services for children provided by general medical and dental practitioners and the hospital and specialist services.

In order to realise this objective it was also necessary for AHAs to liaise with their matching education authority, when organising and planning their services. This was because local education authorities retained certain responsibilities for the health and well-being of children attending their schools, especially in relation to the special educational provision for handicapped pupils.

Because of the multidisciplinary nature of the child health service it was recommended that at area headquarters three senior officers should share responsibility for its management. These were:

a specialist in community medicine;

a senior dental officer; and

the area nurse, with the child health portfolio.

In view of their significance, a precis of the role specifications prepared by the DHSS for each of these posts is provided below.

The specialist in community medicine with responsibility for child health services (including school health services), in conjunction with clinical colleagues, is responsible for the planning and organisation of integrated child health services including preventive care. This includes the provision of advice and information on child health to the area medical advisory committee and the joint consultative committee. S/he is also responsible for the mobilisation of resources for the medical inspection and treatment of school children; ensuring the availability of support services; providing welfare foods; establishing research programmes and advising on health education. With respect to local education authorities, s/he provides advice and information and undertakes executive responsibility for the health aspects of local education authority functions and advises and reports on child health services as required by the local authority. In addition s/he: attends local authority meetings; ensures the availability of staff for local education authorities with respect to their responsibility for handicapped pupils; gives advice, as necessary, to head teachers and organises services for the medical supervision of entrants to teacher training.

The senior dental officer with responsibility for child dental health (including school dental services), in conjunction with clinical colleagues, is responsible for planning and co-ordinating a comprehensive child dental health (including school dental health) service. This involves the identification of the dental needs children; the provision of services for the dental inspection and treatment of pre-school and school children; dental health education and preventive care and the arrangement of facilities for handicapped children. In addition s/he gives advice, as necessary to: local education authorities; the health care planning team; head teachers and the joint consultative committee. S/he provides information to the ATO/AMT and the area dental committee.

The area nurse (child health) is appointed in agreement with the local education authority. She is accountable to the area nursing officer for all child health, including school health, nursing matters in the area, is professionally responsible for all nursing staff employed in the field of school health, and collaborates with the senior doctor. She provides nursing advice on child health (including school health) matters to the area nursing officer and, usually through her, to the AHA and to other officers at area level. To the matching local authority she provides similar advice on child health, including health education in schools. She collaborates with the DNOs in the management of staff engaged in school health services and, as necessary, with the local education authority. She is responsible for nursing participation in making and monitoring policy on screening, assessment and prophylaxis measures within the child health services.

Health Education

Because health education was recognised as 'a fundamental component of the preventive health services ... (and) ... an activity in which all health workers should be involved'.[31] AHAs were strongly encouraged by the DHSS to make their medical officer responsible for the drawing up of health education programmes as part of the wider role in developing preventive health services. In exercising this responsibility it was recognised that the area medical officer would require advice from professional colleagues, including the area nursing officer, and assistance from an area health education officer and possibly one of his/her medical staff with a special interest in health education.

This was, in fact, the pattern which emerged in most areas, with the area medical officer undertaking the strategic planning and the area health education officer having executive responsibility for health education work. This included the provision of information, advice and materials for use by doctors, dentists, nurses, and other health care professionals; assistance with their in-service training in health education and, resources permitting, giving advice and help to local authorities and voluntary bodies.

Chiropody

In April 1974 AHAs were advised by the DHSS to organise their chiropody services 'primarily on a district basis' and to appoint district chiropodists to head the service. The district chiropodist was to be accountable to the district community physician and to 'be responsible for the running and organisation of chiropody services throughout the district whether provided in hospitals, health centres, clinics, old people's homes, in the patient's own home, in chiropodists' surgeries, schools or elsewhere.'[32] In addition, the district chiropodist was normally expected to undertake some clinical work.

It was also recommended that AHAs appoint an area chiropodist, on either a full-time basis or in combination with a district post, to assist in:

• the planning and development of chiropody services for the area as a whole:

• developing manpower policies, including recruitment, and in-service and post-basic training for qualified chiropodists, technicians and other aides;

• collaboration as necessary with social service and education departments of the local authority in the planning and provision of chiropody services eg within the school health service;

• monitoring and co-ordinating district chiropody services; and

• providing statistical returns on chiropody services.[33]

Area chiropodists were to be accountable to the area medical officer for the performance of these duties.

However, because there was a serious shortage of registered chiropodists many of the ideals lying behind these recommendations remained unrealised. Most AHAs opted for combined area/district posts and required the holders to carry out as much clinical work as possible. Consequently, the planning and management of the service tended to take second place to the exigencies of service delivery.

Speech Therapy

Prior to the 1974 reorganisation, speech therapy services had been provided as an integral part of the school health service and, to a much lesser extent, within hospitals. Local education authorities employed nearly three times as many speech therapists as hospital management committees. By 1972 local education authorities were employing approximately 430 full-time and 500 part-time speech therapists in the school health service. In contrast hospital management committees employed only about 140 full-time and 170 part-time speech therapists.

The disadvantages of having speech therapy divided in this way had been spelt out in the Quirk Report (1972). After reviewing the evidence, Quirk and his colleagues had come to the conclusion that the way ahead for the profession lay in the development of a unified management structure, which would facilitate closer relations and mutual help and support between speech therapists working solely with children in schools and those working mainly with adults in hospitals.

The views of the Quirk Committee were accepted by the DHSS and, predictably, AHAs were given the task of developing a unified speech therapy service. To this end it was recommended that they appoint an area speech therapist, accountable to the area medical officer and responsible for directing the service and for overall planning. More specifically, the area speech therapist was expected to:

• manage all speech therapy services within the area;

- advise the area medical officer of the long-term planning requirements for the area;
- liaise with the education service;
- consult with the ATOs about the allocation of financial resources and manpower;
- perform a number of personnel duties, including the recruitment and appointment of staff and taking 'responsibility for attracting married women back into the profession';[34]
- organise the clinical placement of students;
- advise other AHA officers on the accommodation needs of the speech therapy service in the area;
- ensure the adequacy and availability of in-service training;
- liaise with the statistician within the management services organisation in respect of the collection of area statistical information;
- liaise with speech therapy training establishments;
- disseminate information about speech therapy within the profession and to other professions;
- advise on the placement of patients requiring specialised treatment outside the area;
- co-ordinate locally organised research projects within the area;
- liaise with other area speech therapists within the region and with members of other professions; and
- ensure that all newly-qualified speech therapists had adequate clinical supervision.

Although a number of the very large AHAs delegated responsibility for the day-to-day running of their speech therapy service to their districts, due to the comparatively small scale of the service and a grave shortage of qualified speech therapists, speech therapy was generally organised on an area rather than a district basis.

Community Dental Service

Because dentistry had been represented in all three parts of the pre-1974 NHS, as well as the school health service, those responsible for preparing the 'Grey Book' paid particular attention to the post- reorganisation management structure for this service. They recommended that the AHA should be 'the central management point for dentistry' and that every AHA should appoint an area dental officer to exercise a variety of responsibilities, including those of the existing principal school dental officer. Thus the area dental officer was to be responsible for:

- advising the local authority on dental matters, especially in respect of the dental health of school children;

- 'planning and managing the school dental health services and the priority services for mothers and young children, in collaboration with the local authority and the medical officer responsible for school health, and managing the area's auxiliary dental staff ...' [35]

- advising the AHA, the FPC and the ATOs on 'all matters concerned with or having implications for dentistry';

- monitoring the effectiveness of the dental services in the area; and

- putting forward proposals and plans for improving the service to the AHA.

It was anticipated that in most areas the area dental officer would be a full-time administrator and that in very large areas s/he would need to be assisted by district dental officers, exercising some administrative responsibilities.

The 'Grey Book' also emphasised that, unlike the principal school dental officer during the tripartite era, the area dental officer would be directly accountable to the AHA and not to its medical officer. However, the area dental officer was not to be a member of the ATOs, although it was intended that s/he should receive all team papers and attend meetings when matters in which s/he had an interest were being discussed

In June 1975 the DHSS provided AHAs with guidance as to the procedure they should adopt when appointing district dental officers. However, as indicated above, it was made clear that AHAs were to establish district dental officer posts only where the area dental officer needed 'substantial administrative assistance.'[36] As far as community dentistry was concerned one of the first tasks of newly appointed area dental officers was to develop a fully integrated community dental service out of the formerly separate school and priority dental services.

Family Planning

In view of the fragmented nature of family planning and the fact that it was both a relatively new service and one requiring contributions from a variety of disciplines, the DHSS recommended that 'the main responsibility for the planning and management of family planning services (should) rest with the District Management Team.'[37] Furthermore, it was felt that within each district early action should be taken to establish a working group to advise the DMT on the family planning services and the most effective methods of integrating the community based services, developed by voluntary organisations, local health authorities and GPs, with those provided in the obstetrics, gynaecology and urology departments of hospitals. It was also recommended that the district community physician play a key role in the activities of this group and in the planning and organisation of services on a day-to-day basis. Consequently, it was proposed that at area headquarters one of the specialists in community medicine should be allocated (inter alia) responsibility for the co-ordination of family planning services in the area as whole and that s/he should work closely with the district community physicians and their clinical colleagues.

Other Services

In addition to the detailed guidance on the post-reorganisation management arrangements for community nursing, health education, family planning and other services, which had previously been the responsibility of local health authorities, the DHSS also made recommendations in respect of the organisation and management of various services, which had traditionally been provided mainly (although not exclusively) by hospital based staff, but were to become more community orientated following reorganisation. The most important of these services were **physiotherapy, occupational therapy** and **dietetics**.

Because consideration was still being given, at the time of the 1974 reorganisation, to the report of the McMillan Working Party (1973) on the future role of the remedial professions (i.e. physiotherapy and occupational therapy together with remedial gymnastics) in relation to other professions and the patient.[38] The DHSS provided AHAs with only interim guidance as to how they should organise the services provided by these professional groups. It was anticipated that this would remain valid for at least eighteen months. In the meantime decisions would be reached on the recommendations of the McMillan Working Party, the most far reaching of which were that ultimately 'all three professions should evolve to form one comprehensive profession'; both in hospital and in the community therapists should determine the nature and duration of treatment, with the doctors' role being restricted to diagnosis, objective setting and review; and 'members of the remedial professions should co-ordinate, organise and administer their own services.'[39]

The guidance, issued in late 1974, included the recommendation that the remedial services and linked therapies (i.e. industrial, art, drama and music therapy) should 'normally be organised on a district basis, either separately or partially grouped (eg combined physiotherapy - remedial gymnast departments) or in a comprehensive department of rehabilitation'[40] and that, in deciding on the most appropriate form of organisation for their districts, AHAs should take 'account of the needs of local authority social services and education departments and of any employment of members of the remedial professions by local authorities.'[41] Authorities were also encouraged to designate in each district a senior physiotherapist and a senior occupational therapist to be responsible for advising 'district community physicians on the organisation of their services for the district' and ensuring the maintenance of professional standards.[42] It was made clear, however, that district community physicians would still need medical advice on the clinical aspects of remedial services and rehabilitation so that the DMTs, of which they were members, would be 'in a position to formulate plans for the provision of a comprehensive rehabilitation service.'[43]

Although it was not intended that senior therapists should give up all their clinical duties to enable them to cope with their new responsibilities, it was anticipated that there would be some diminution of their clinical role. In exercising the advisory and professional responsibilities outlined above senior therapists were to be accountable to the district community physician, but they were to remain responsible to doctors in respect of their other duties.

Most, but by no means all, authorities followed this guidance and appointed senior therapists. However, there was little uniformity in the range and scope of their responsibilities. Not surprisingly, this led to a considerable amount of 'uncertainty, both within the remedial professions themselves and in the professions most in contact with them.'[44] Difficulties were being experienced also with regard to the recommendations of the McMillan Working Party, which were not proving acceptable to all the parties concerned, in particular the medical profession. Consequently, during the second half of the 1970s there was increasing pressure on the DHSS to declare its position on the proposals and produce the further guidance which it had promised in 1974. The DHSS eventually responded to this pressure by issuing a circular in October 1979 on the management, as opposed to the organisation, of the remedial professions.

Underlying the guidance contained in this circular was the DHSS's acceptance of the principle advocated by the McMillan Working Party that the remedial professions should be responsible for their own management. The DHSS took the view that self-management would in no way undermine the medical profession's central role in advising authorities and DMTs 'on general rehabilitation policies and on priorities for the development and deployment of rehabilitation services as a whole.'[45]

Thus, it was recommended that as soon as resources permitted, health authorities should 'appoint district therapists in the remedial professions to manage and plan the services of their professions within the district.'[46] According to the job description for the district therapist - manager, which was issued as an appendix to the circular, s/he was to have a link to the DMT by being made accountable either to the district community physician or to the sector administrator 'for the management and planning of services in the district and personnel matters relating to those services', and was to 'liaise with Consultants with a special interest in rehabilitation and other professional groups concerned in the planning, co-ordination and development of rehabilitation services in the district.'[47]

Although the circular made no specific reference to the management, planning and development of services outside hospitals (i.e. in the community), it can be argued that the phrase 'in the district' implied the full range of locations for the delivery of services (e.g. patients' homes, schools and health centres as well as hospitals). This was because the trend towards a more community orientated approach to the delivery of remedial services, referred to earlier, was reasonably well established by the late 1970s, with the result that managers were having to take increasing account of demands for the expansion of community based services in planning the deployment of their resources.

Like physiotherapy and occupational therapy, **dietetics** was seen as a district, rather than an area, based service. Thus, in 1974, DMTs were advised to 'consider at the earliest practicable moment the co-ordination of the dietetic service under a district dietitian'.[48] The district dietitian was to be responsible for:

- managing the dietetic services in the district;

- providing 'personally some of the hospital and/or community dietetic service';

- advising the DMT on the 'planning and staffing (of) the nutrition and dietetic services in the district';

- arranging, in consultation with appropriate colleagues (e.g. health education officers), 'nutrition and dietetic in-service training in hospitals and the community';

- participating 'in the training of student dietitians'; and

- giving advice on dietary matters to local authorities and other bodies.

In addition, in multi-district areas one of the district dietitians was made responsible for advising the authority. However, before giving advice, s/he was normally expected to consult with fellow district dietitians.

Although well-intentioned, the advice and guidance given by the DHSS to health authorities in respect of the post-reorganisation management arrangements proved to be divisive as far as the CHSs were concerned, despite the leading role that specialists in community medicine were expected to play in co-ordinating their future development. This was mainly because the advice and guidance from the DHSS related to individual services and there was little, if any, attempt to consider the management needs of the CHSs as a whole. Thus, in carrying out the wishes of the DHSS, health authorities unwittingly created management structures which accentuated the divisions between the CHSs and failed to give expression to the features which united them.

The situation was further complicated, especially in multi-district areas, by the complex tier-structure of the reorganised NHS and the allocation of responsibilities between the various levels at which services were being managed. Thus, the relatively simple and cohesive management structures for the CHSs which existed prior to 1974 in most parts of the country were superseded by arrangements that were more complex.

This complexity was not, of course, confined to the management arrangements for the CHSs. It was a feature of the reorganised NHS as a whole and was one of the reasons why, in some respects, the debate on the structure of the NHS and the management of health care was more intense after the 1974 reorganisation than before.

The Royal Commission on the National Health Service

Between 1974 and 1982 one of the most important manifestations of the growing concern over the post-1974 management arrangements for health care was the investigation by, and report of, the Royal Commission on the National Health Service, which was chaired by Sir Alec Merrison, the Vice Chancellor of Bristol University.

The Royal Commission was set up by the Secretary of State for Social Services, Barbara Castle, in May 1976, with the following terms of reference:

> *To consider in the interests both of the patients and of those who work in the National Health Service, the best use and management of the financial and manpower resources of the National Health Service.*[49]

The principal reason for the establishment of the Royal Commission was the fact that, despite the relatively long gestation period of the 1973 Act and the good intentions of the reformers, various factors had combined to create serious problems for those charged with responsibility, at both local and national level, for ensuring a smooth transition from the tripartite structure to one based on the principle of integration. These included a disinclination on the part of some staff to make the new system work; industrial disputes involving ambulancemen, some ancillary staff and hospital doctors and dentists; the controversy surrounding an attempt by the Secretary of State to restrict private practice facilities and, most significantly, the deteriorating economic situation which meant that the service was being 'denied ... the growth ... it had come to expect to help it meet the rising demands made upon it.'[50]

In carrying out their investigation into many different aspects of health care, including the CHSs, the 16 members of the Royal Commission received evidence from a wide variety of sources. Some of these sources, such as the Association of District Community Physicians, the Guild of Health Education Officers Ltd and the Health Visitors' Association, were closely connected with the delivery of CHSs. In addition six special research projects were comissioned. One of these (jointly with the National Consumer Council) was a survey of the problems encountered (in Stoke Newington and West Cumbria) by the parents of young children and the elderly in gaining access to primary care. However, the only CHS covered by this study was chiropody. Other projects were concerned with the way in which the reorganised NHS was operating; resource allocation and medical manpower.

The report of the Royal Commission contained many recommendations relating to individual services and, where relevant, these are touched on in Chapter 7. However, in terms of its influence on future public policy, the Royal Commission's most significant recommendation was one dealing with the overall structure of the NHS. Merrison and his colleagues took the view that below regional level there should be only one management level carrying 'operational responsibility for services and for effective collaboration with local government.'[51] This prepared the ground for the 1982 restructuring of the NHS which is considered in the next chapter.

Other recommendations concerning the structure and management and finance of the NHS, which could have had a profound influence on the future development of the CHSs, such as the abolition of FPCs and the taking over of their functions by health authorities, as a step towards the complete integration of the FPSs with the CHSs and HSs, and the commissioning of a study 'of the desirability and feasibility of common budgets for family practitioner' and other health care services, aroused such opposition from vested interests that they had very little, if any, influence.

Footnotes

1.   DHSS, *National Health Service Reorganisation : England*, Cmnd 5055 (London: HMSO, 1972), para. 9.

2.   Royal Commission on the National Health Service [Chair: Sir A. Merrison], *Report*, Cmnd 7615 (London: HMSO, 1979), para. 10.76.

3.   C. Ham, *Health Policy in Britain: The Politics and Organisation of the National Health Service*, 2nd Edition (London: Macmillan, 1985), p. 65.

4.   DHSS, *Priorities for Health and Personal Social Services in England. A Consultative Document* (London: HMSO, 1976)

5.   National Health Service Reorganisation : England, op. cit., para. 100.

6   DHSS, *Priorities in the Health and Personal Social Services. The Way Forward. Further Discussion of the Government's National Strategy Based on the Consultative Document Priorities for Health and Personal Social Services in England* (London: HMSO, 1977).

7.   For example, DHSS, Circular HC(78)12, *Health and Personal Social Services in England. NHSS Planning Guidelines*, March 1978.

8.   DHSS, *Care in Action. A Handbook of Policies and Priorities for the Health and Personal Social Services in England* (London: HMSO, 1981) and DHSS, *Care in the Community. A Consultative Document on Moving Resources for Care in England* (London: HMSO, 1981).

9.   N. Chaplin (edited for The Institute of Health Service Administrators), *Health Care in the United Kingdom* (London: Kluwer Medical, 1982), p. 86.

10.   R. Levitt and A. Wall, *The Reorganised National Health Service*, 3rd edition (London: Croom Helm, 1984), pp. 18- 21.

11.   DHSS, Circular HRC(74)29, *Management Arrangements : Consolidation of Interim Arrangements : Preparation of Substantive Schemes : Filling of Posts*, April 1974, para. 13(a).

12.   Ibid., para. 13(d).

13.   A. McNaught, 'Where are the Community Health Services Going?', *Hospital and Health Services Review*, January 1983, p. 14.

14.   DHSS, Circular HRC(74)30, *Management Arrangements : Administrative Management Structures and Preparation of Substantive Schemes*, para. 19.

15.   The following data taken from Table C21 of the report of the Resource Allocation Working Party, *Sharing Resources for Health in England* (London: HMSO, 1976), show the differences

between the crude (i.e. actual) populations for each of the English Regions and their populations weighted to reflect their need for CHSs as determined by the 1971/72 spending patterns of local health authorities.

Region	Crude Population '000s	Weighted Population '000s	Difference Actual '000s	Difference %
Northern	3126	3404	+278	+8.9
Yorkshire	3577	3825	+248	+6.9
Trent	4545	4631	+86	+1.9
East Anglia	1780	1638	-142	-8.0
NW Thames	3475	3086	-389	-11.2
NE Thames	3718	3518	-200	-5.5
SW Thames	3603	3459	-144	-4.0
SE Thames	2880	2696	-184	-6.4
Wessex	2645	2453	-192	-7.3
Oxford	2199	1980	-219	-10.0
South West	3149	3044	-105	-3.3
W Midlands	5178	5289	+111	+2.1
Mersey	2499	2839	+340	+13.6
North West	4078	4599	+581	+14.9

Thus, on the basis of these data the highest relative need for CHSs was in the North West Region and the lowest relative need in the North West Thames Region.

16. According to the 1976 *Priorities* document the average expenditure growth rates (per annum) for the period 1975/76 to 1979/80 were to be as follows:

* family practitioner services: 3.7%;

* services used mainly by the elderly (including home nursing): 3.2%;

* services for the mentally handicapped: 2.8%;

* services mainly for children and families with children (including health visiting, child health services): 2.2%;

* services for the mentally ill: 1.8%;

* acute and general hospital services: 1.2%;

* hospital maternity services: -1.8%.

17. For example, in some parts of the country joint finance monies were used to fund jointly managed home nursing aids schemes (i.e. by local personal social services authorities and AHAs) and to employ occupational therapists to work in special schools and elderly persons homes.

18. N. Chaplin (ed.), op. cit., p. 209.

19. DHSS, Circular HSC(IS)13, *Community Medicine in the Reorganised Health Service*, March 1974, para. 3.

20. Ibid., para. 14.

21. R. Levitt and A. Wall, op. cit., p. 180.

22. Royal Commission on the National Health Service, op. cit., para. 14.52.

23. Ibid., para. 14.53.

24. Ibid., para. 14.56.

25. *Public Health in England. The Report of the Committee of Inquiry into the Future Development of the Public Health Function* [Chair: Sir D. Acheson], Cm 289 (London: HMSO, 1988), paras. 2.6 and 2.7.

26. R. Levitt and A. Wall, op. cit., p. 197.

27. DHSS, Circular HRC(74)31, *Management Arrangements : Nursing and Midwifery Management Structures*, para. 5.

28. See Chapters 3 and 4 for earlier references to the Mayston Report on Management Structures in the Local Authority Nursing Services, which was published in 1970. The recommendations of the Mayston Report reflected, to a significant extent, those of the Salmon Committee on Senior Nursing Staff Structures in Hospitals, which had published its report four years earlier.

29. Circular HRC(74)31, op. cit., para. 13.

30. DHSS, Circular HRC(74)5, *Operation and Development of Child Health Services (Including School Health Services)*, January 1974, para. 1.

31. DHSS Circular, HRC(74)27, *Reorganisation of National Health Service and of Local Government : Operation and Development of Services : Health Education*, March 1974, paras. 4 and 6.

32. DHSS, Circular HRC(74)33, *Reorganisation of National Health Service and of Local Government : Operation and Development of Services : Chiropody*, April 1974, para. 6.

33. Ibid., para. 7.

34. DHSS, Circular HSC(IS)22, *Speech Therapy Services : Interim Guidance*, April 1974, Appendix.

35. Management Arrangements for the Reorganised National Health Service, op. cit., p. 78.

36. DHSS, Circular HSC(IS)168, *Appointment of District Dental Officers*, June 1975, para. 3.

37. DHSS, Circular HSC(IS)32, *Family Planning Services*, May 1974, para. 7.

38. The main reason for setting up the McMillan Working Party was the fact that the remedial professions had been very disappointed with the 1972 report of a subcommittee of the Standing Medical Advisory Committee on rehabilitation and, in the same year, a statement by the Committee on the Remedial Professions and felt they had been let down. Moreover, 'they saw no prospects of progress in the development of their professions or proper recognition of the skills and service they had to offer to the community.' More specific problems considered by the working party were the misuse and waste of professional skills; dissatisfaction with career and salary structure; shortage of trained therapists; inadequate support from clerical, secretarial and portering staff and overlapping responsibilities.

39. DHSS, *The Remedial Professions. A Report by a Working Party set up in March 1973 by the Secretary of State for Social Services*, [Chair: E. McMillan] (London: HMSO, 1973), paras. 19, 22, and 25. On the sensitive issue of relations between therapists and doctors the members of the working party made it clear that the principles outlined in their report were also applicable in cases where NHS therapists worked in the community (see para.23).

40. DHSS, Circular HSC(IS)101, *The Remedial Professions and Linked Therapies*, December 1974, para. 3.

41. Ibid., para. 13. Most members of the remedial professions working for local authorities (e.g. physiotherapists in the school health service) became employees of the newly constituted AHAs on 1st April 1974. However, local social services authorities could continue to employ and recruit occupational therapists for 'the purposes of social care and social rehabilitation.' See DHSS, DS 36/74, *The Remedial Professions and Linked Therapies; Transitional Arrangements.*

42.   Ibid., para. 4.

43.   Ibid., para. 10.

44.   DHSS, Circular HC(79)19, *Health Services Development: Management of the Remedial Professions in the NHS,* October 1979, para. 3.

45   Ibid., para. 1.

46.   Ibid., para. 7.

47.   Ibid., Appendix.

48   DHSS, Circular HSC(IS)56, *The Organisation of the Dietetic Service within the National Health Service,* July 1974, para. 2.

49.   Royal Commission on the National Health Service, op. cit., para. 1.1.

50.   Ibid., para. 1.4.

51.   Ibid., para. 20.46.

Chapter 6

Community Health Services and the Pursuit of Efficiency

During the first half of the 1980s the organisation and management of the CHSs were profoundly affected by a number of significant developments. The first was the 1982 restructuring exercise and the second was the Conservative government's acceptance and implementation of the recommendations of the NHS Management Inquiry, chaired by Roy Griffiths, which were published in 1983 (see below).

Although both these developments were designed to improve the organisation and strengthen the management of the NHS as a whole, it can be argued that their impact on the CHSs was, in some respects, greater than that on other health care services. By facilitating a return to the more integrated approach to running the CHSs associated with the tripartite era, both developments played a part in reversing the fragmentation which had been the legacy of the 1974 reorganisation. They also provided the CHSs with a clearer identity and sharper focus within the unified NHS. However, in the process they undermined still further the role of community physicians in the management of community based health care services and made the integration of CHSs and HSs even less likely.

The early 1980s also saw a wide variety of government sponsored initiatives designed to increase the efficiency of the NHS. As a result those responsible for managing the CHSs were increasingly preoccupied with their levels of performance and the utilisation of resources and the need to ensure that services were being delivered as cost-effectively as possible.

The 1982 Restructuring of the NHS

Two months before the publication of the report of the Royal Commission on the National Health Service (July 1979) there was a change of government. The Labour government, which had been responsible for the establishment of the

Royal Commission, under the chairmanship of Sir Alec Merrison, was defeated in May by the Conservatives led by Margaret Thatcher. Whilst in opposition the Conservative Party had given some attention to the NHS and had reached the conclusion 'that the structure and management arrangements of the Service introduced in 1974 (did) not provide the best framework for the effective delivery of care to patients.'[1] Thus, despite the the the fact that the 1974 reorganisation was the product of a Conservative government, Mrs Thatcher and her colleagues were very much in sympathy with the widespread criticism of the 1974 changes to which the Merrison Report drew attention. These were summed up as:

- too many tiers;

- too many administrators, in all disciplines;

- failure to take quick decisions; and

- money wasted.

However, whilst the Thatcher government was in broad agreement with the Royal Commission's diagnosis of the structural problems of the NHS it rejected two of the radical remedies discussed by Merrison and his colleagues. One of these was that RHAs should become accountable to Parliament for matters within their competence. This was rejected because it conflicted with the Secretary of State for Social Services' statutory accountability to Parliament for the activities of the NHS. The other remedy was the amalgamation of responsibility for health and personal social services under either local or health authorities. Both of these were rejected on the grounds that neither would command general support. Instead the Conservative government opted for a more incremental approach. Its draft proposals were outlined in a consultative paper entitled *Patients First,* which was published in December 1979.

Patients First

Underlying the proposals in *Patients First* was a desire on the part of Ministers to simplify and streamline the structure, policy-making processes and management of the NHS and to ensure that, in future, decisions were taken as close to the point of service delivery as possible. In other words they reflected 'a strong distaste for the managerialist and centralist attitudes which had marked the 1974 reorganisation'.[2]

Of particular significance were proposals to restructure the NHS by reducing the number of tiers and devolving responsibility downwards. This would involve replacing the 90 AHAs (but not the 90 FPCs) with a much larger number of district health authorities (DHAs); simplifying the professional advisory machinery; streamlining the planning system; reviewing the future of CHCs; and, most importantly, strengthening management at 'hospital and community services level'. It was made clear that 'there should be maximum delegation of authority to hospital and the **community services** (emphasis added) level' and at this level 'there should be an administrator and nurse of appropriate seniority to discharge an individual responsibility in conjunction with the medical staff.' Furthermore, there should be no additional tiers of management between the 'hospital and community services level and district headquarters.'[3]

Thus, one of the key principles underlying the 1982 restructuring exercise was that of 'localism'. In the words of Patrick Jenkin, the Secretary of State for Social Services in the newly elected Conservative government, the NHS had to be seen 'not as a single national organisation but as it (was) perceived by those who use(d) it and work(ed) in it at local level as a series of local services run by local management, responsive to local needs and with a strong involvement from the local community.'[4]

From the point of view of the CHSs this emphasis on 'localism' was welcome, since those responsible for the management and delivery of community based health care services could only put the needs of patients first if they were in a position to respond positively to the particular requirements and distinctive concerns of their communities. Similarly the Conservative government's declaration in *Patients First* that it would expect proposals for the restructuring of health authorities to take collaboration into account, indicated that it was aware of the need for close relations between CHSs staff and their local authority counterparts in the planning and delivery of complementary services.

With regard to the future of FPCs, *Patients First* made it clear that Ministers did not support the Royal Commission's view that they should be abolished and their functions transferred to health authorities and, in the short-term would be retaining the existing committees. As a result it had introduced legislation to enable, where appropriate, one FPC to cover the area of more than one DHA. In many respects this was a retrograde step in that it impeded the development of an integrated approach to the planning and delivery of primary health services.

As well as setting out the Conservative government's proposals for the restructuring of the NHS, *Patients First,* together with other policy statements, also gave notice of its intention to look critically at the way the NHS used its resources and to introduce measures for increasing efficiency. For example, in their introduction to *Patients First* the Secretaries of State for Social Services and for Wales emphasised that 'the efficient management of the Service ... (was) of (the) highest importance, not least (because) resources (were) tight' and that if the NHS was more economical in its use of resources more would be available for patient care.'[5]

Since the DHSS was anxious to ensure that the consultation process was completed as quickly as possible it allowed interested parties only four months to comment on the proposals in *Patients First.* Nevertheless, such was the interest, that even within this relatively short period of time, over 3500 comments were received by the DHSS from organisations and individuals. According to Ministers 'the broad thrust' of these comments 'support(ed) the aims set out'[6] in the consultative document. Perhaps a more objective view of reactions to *Patients First*, however, is one expressed in a King's Fund project paper. This suggests that they ranged 'from incredulity at its simplicity, compared with the complexities of the 1974 'Grey Book', to grudging respect for the consistency of format.'[7] After reviewing the comments, the Conservative government outlined its intentions in Circular HC (80)8 (July 1980).

Health Circular HC(80)8

The circular confirmed that:

- all the existing AHAs and health districts in England were to 'be replaced by one or more district health authorities, each served by one team of officers';
- each DHA was to 'be responsible for the planning, development and management of health services in its district within national and regional guidelines';
- DHAs would be expected to arrange their services into units of management and ensure that as much decision-making authority as possible was delegated to these units; and
- CHCs were to be retained.

It also clarified many important points of detail concerning the future structure of the NHS and the management arrangements for the delivery of hospital and community based health care services.

Firstly, it was made clear that RHAs were to be responsible for making recommendations to the Secretary of State about the pattern of DHAs in their region and that in exercising this responsibility they were to be guided by the need to establish DHAs 'for the smallest geographical areas within which it (was) possible to carry out the integrated planning, provision and development of **primary care and other community health services** (emphasis added), together with those services normally associated with a district general hospital, including those for the elderly, mentally ill and mentally handicapped.'[8] In addition health districts were, as far as possible, to comprise 'natural communities' and their boundaries, either singly or jointly, were to be coterminous with those of social services or education authorities.

However, despite this reference to coterminousity, in delimiting the boundaries of the restructured health districts, RHAs were expected to give precedence to the catchment areas of district general hospitals. Thus, it can be argued that the architects of the 1982 restructuring exercise gave a higher priority to the delivery of acute hospital services than to collaboration in respect of community based health care services and personal social services. Furthermore, as the members of the Harding Working Party pointed out, in their report entitled *The Primary Health Care Team* (1981), 'in many cases the catchment area of the major hospital was not necessarily the most effective management unit for community services.' They also took the view that if 'hospital consideration (were to) be paramount in determining management arrangements' it would result 'in management at senior nursing levels being even less sensitive to or experienced in aspects of primary health care.'[9]

In practice, however, relatively few changes were made to existing boundaries. This was because the Conservative government made it clear that, notwithstanding the identification of explicit criteria for delimiting the boundaries of the restructured health districts, 'new DHAs should follow the boundaries of existing districts or single district areas ... to minimise the disruption to health services ... unless there (were) powerful reasons to the contrary'.[10] Examples of powerful reasons included cases where DHAs would have been either too small or too large (i.e. with a population of over 500,000) to exercise their responsiblities for the integrated planning and provision of health care services in an effective manner and 'where changes in the organisation that would flow from a change of district boundaries ... would be such as to justify the disruption that would be caused.'[11] In carrying out their reviews RHAs were expected to consult a wide variety of bodies, such as existing authorities and their management teams, CHCs, universities, local authorities and any other body or individual which they considered should be consulted.

Secondly, the circular indicated that each DHA was to appoint a district management team with the same composition and functions as the superseded AMTs/DMTs. This meant that community medicine would continue to be represented on the DMT. In addition, the principle of consensus was to continue to apply as far as management decision-making was concerned. However, the circular drew attention to the fact that consensus did 'not mean seeking unanimity at all costs' and that consensus management should not be allowed to undermine or blur the individual responsibilities of managers. On the other hand it was also made clear that 'in a service as complex as the NHS and comprising so many different independent disciplines and functions' there had to be clear arrangements for administrative co-ordination, which were understood and accepted by all concerned, and that these were to be the responsibility of the district administrator. Thus, some attention was given to the need for a more co-ordinated approach to management, which would reduce the centrifugal tendencies inherent in the concept of functional management. However, the circular did not go as far as the recommendations of the NHS Management Inquiry, which were published three years later, and proposed the appointment of general managers. Indeed, in *Patients First* the government had explicitly rejected the proposition that each health authority should appoint a chief executive with responsibility for all the authority's staff. Thus, district administrators were to be responsible for providing members of the authority with an account of how its policies and priorities were being implemented and for ensuring that the officers responsible for carrying out the wishes of the authority were clearly identified but they were not to have 'any managerial authority over other chief officers'.[12]

Thirdly, the circular dealt with the organisation below district level. DHAs were required to 'arrange their services into units of management'. In doing so it was recommended that 'in the main authorities should establish units that (were) smaller than existing sectors and nursing divisions'. The circular also gave a number of examples of the types of unit which DHAs might establish. Amongst these was a unit with responsibility for 'the community services of the district'.[13]

For management purposes each unit was to have an administrator and a director of nursing services, directly accountable to the district administrator and district nursing officer respectively and, as indicated in *Patients First*, 'of appropriate seniority to discharge an individual responsibility in conjunction with a senior member of the medical staff.'[14] Furthermore, although not mentioned explicitly in the circular it was assumed by many that the principle of consensus management would also be applied at unit level. The government's intentions on this matter, however, were not entirely clear. Indeed, in the equivalent circular for Wales it was actually stated that there would 'be no formal consensus management at unit level.'[15] Nevertheless, most English units were in fact collectively managed by a unit management team comprising a unit administrator, a director of nursing services and one or more representatives of the medical profession. Furthermore, given the make up of the team, decisions usually had to be made on the basis of consensus. In addition to playing a part in the collective management of the unit, the unit administrator was expected, like his/her counterpart at district level, to take responsibility for the administrative co-ordination of functions and services within the unit.

The continuing interest in, and commitment to, team management, particularly at sub-district level, was reflected in the large number of articles on this subject which appeared in health care journals during the early 1980s. Many of these identified criteria for successful team working, such as the need for teams to be small enough to work effectively, be convened easily and make decisions rapidly - but also large enough to be representative and for effective relationships and working procedures within the team. The articles also gave examples of team management at unit level.[16] However, little attention appears to have been given to the distinctive problems of operating a team approach to the management of community based health care services. These were problems which arose, in the main, from the dispersed nature of the services and the fact that, because of their independent contractor status, it was more difficult to involve GPs in the process than hospital consultants.

Fourthly, in contrast with the 1974 reorganisation and in keeping with the principle of 'localism', DHAs were given far more freedom to determine their management arrangements. Apart from the references to the team posts at district level and the unit posts mentioned above it was left to DHAs 'to decide what appointments to make and determine arrangements for accountability.'[17] They were therefore faced with the task of deciding on the management arrangements for their district without the kind of detailed guidance that was provided at the time of the 1974 reorganisation.

Lastly, in order to secure the maximum delegation of authority to units of management, DHAs were to determine:

* which decisions currently taken at area or district level could be delegated to units, and

* which decisions originating within units but currently drawn up to district headquarters level as a result of the existence of functional management hierarchies, should in future be contained at unit level by limiting the functional chain.[18]

They were also expected to give priority to the early establishment of unit budgets and to ensure that 'wherever possible staff working within units in non-clinical support functions ... (e.g. domestic services) (were) accountable to the unit administrator rather than to district level managers.'[19]

It was intended that RHAs should take about six months over their boundary reviews (allowing 3 months for consultation) and submit their recommendations for the boundaries of the new DHAs to the Secretary of State by the end of February 1981. Once this had been done it was hoped to reach decisions on most recommendations within three months of receiving them and be in a position to secure the necessary parliamentary approval for bringing the new DHAs 'into formal existence on or before 1 April 1982.'[20]

Implementation

The Conservative government was anxious to implement the changes outlined in the circular with the minimum of upheaval. Moreover, it had powers under Section 1 of the Health Services Act 1980, to make certain changes to the structure of the NHS. Nevertheless, the restructuring exercise proved to be more time consuming and more disruptive than had originally been anticipated. As Levitt and Wall observe, 'the cost in human terms and hard cash was considerable.'[21]

The easiest part of the implementation process proved to be the regional reviews. Very few problems were encountered and, as indicated earlier, most regions adhered very closely to their exisiting area/district boundaries and sought to make as few changes to them as possible. However, from the point of view of the CHSs this was a mixed blessing. Whilst it avoided the upheavals of 1974 it meant that in many parts of the country DHA boundaries would not be coterminous with those of local personal social services authorities, thereby making collaboration even more difficult. There is, in fact, little evidence to indicate the extent to which the interests of CHSs were taken into account as part of the regional reviews, but it is likely that, in view of the emphasis given to district general hospitals and their catchment areas in the circular, precedence was given to the views of bodies representing the interests of hospitals.

In addition, the problems of securing closer links between CHSs and FPSs were exacerbated by the Thatcher government's failure either to abolish FPCs and transfer their functions to DHAs, as recommended by the Royal Commission, or to reorganise them in such a way that they had the same boundaries as DHAs. The situation was made even worse by a Commons statement from the Minister of Health in November 1981 to the effect that when legislative time permitted, FPCs would become separate employing authorities in their own right, thereby removing the remaining structural links between the bodies responsible for CHSs and HSs and those responsible for administering the FPSs.

Since the regional reviews were completed on time the Secretary of State was able to announce in July 1981 that 193 (later 192) DHAs would formally take over responsibility from the existing authorities on 1st April 1982. Much slower progress, however, was made in determining the management structures for the new authorities and their units. This was because many of the new authorities had to make a large number of fairly complex decisions concerning their management arrangements at both district and unit level. Furthermore, in making these decisions they had, as intended, a considerable amount of autonomy. Whilst this was not unwelcome it did mean that authorities took longer than might otherwise have been the case to devise structures that were best suited to the needs of their district. One of the most important tasks which faced the new DHAs was that of deciding on, and setting up, their unit structures. In carrying out this task they had to consider how many units they should establish and their size; the division of service responsibilities between units and managerial relationships within units and between units and district headquarters. They also had to absorb the advice they received from various quarters and to contend with pressure from interested parties.

In a King's Fund project paper published just before 1st April 1982 a number of criteria were identified for assessing unit structures. These were:

- Did the proposals leave as much flexibility as possible to adjust structures in the light of future learning?

- Did they fit in with the DHA's strategy, in the sense of facilitating as opposed to inhibiting future development (e.g. in respect of care in the community initiatives)?

- Did they seem workable for all the main professions and take account of the following organisational principles: institutional, geographic, client group and functional specialisation?

- Did they make sense in the local context and pass the tests of common sense and of minimum unnecessary disruption?

- Did they represent value for money compared with other possible solutions?[22]

In the event DHAs differed a great deal in the design of their unit structures and there was considerable variation in the sizes and responsibilities of individual units. Furthermore, within a few years many DHAs felt the need to reduce the number of units in their district and/or rearrange the responsibilities of units, which suggests that they did not get it right first time.

The case for having a community unit was articulated by a variety of bodies including the Royal College of Nursing, the BMA and the Acheson Study Group on Primary Health Care in Inner London. In their report, which was published in May 1981, the members of the study group argued for a community unit in the following terms:

In view of the severe problems confronting the community services in inner London and of the urgent need to develop these Services in order to cope with proposed reductions in the acute hospital sector we RECOMMEND that each DHA should give high priority to the establishment of a unit of management for the community services of the whole District. This will give the community services a **single and authoritative voice** (emphasis added) within each authority.[23]

A year later the Royal College of Nursing circulated a letter to regional chairmen and nursing officers complaining that, contrary to DHSS guidelines, districts were not providing 'for the organisation of community nursing within discrete management units'[24] and in July 1982 a motion was carried at a BMA conference supporting the view that the CHSs 'should be encompassed by a single community care unit in which the general practitioner should be represented as of right.' One of the speakers supporting the motion maintained that all community workers including district nurses, health visitors and CPNs should be directly accountable to a unit of this kind, whilst another argued that there needed to be 'clear and straightforward lines of accountability and responsibility' between community units and DHAs.[25] As McNaught points out,[26] a relatively large number of DHAs opted for a community services unit of this kind. Other types of unit included client based units (e.g. geriatric services units); geographically based units, with responsibility for both hospital and community services within a territorially defined part of the district and acute units.

In considering the extent to which unit structures reflected the priorities of DHAs (i.e. one of the King's Fund's criteria), Dixon makes the interesting point that the strongest units, using post gradings as an indicator of the relative strengths of units, were usually the acute hospital units whereas most DHAs were in fact committed to an expansion of their community based services and a contraction of their hospital based services.[27] Thus, on the basis of this analysis, it can be argued that community units failed to secure the status that the priority accorded to community care implied.

One further reason why the restructuring exercise took longer than expected was the fact that many staff at district and sub-district level had to compete for new posts and inevitably this was both disruptive and time consuming, as well as traumatic for those involved. Even as late as mid-1983 the journals were still full of advertisements for unit level jobs.

The structure which eventually emerged from the 1982 restructuring exercise is shown in Figure 6.1.

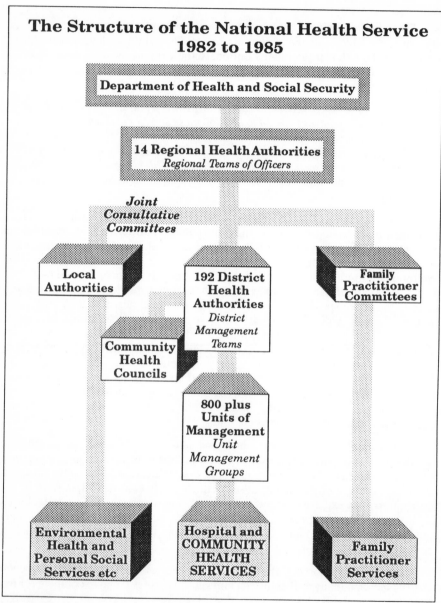

The Structure of the National Health Service 1982 to 1985

Department of Health and Social Security

14 Regional Health Authorities
Regional Teams of Officers

Joint Consultative Committees

Local Authorities

192 District Health Authorities
District Management Teams

Family Practitioner Committees

Community Health Councils

800 plus Units of Management
Unit Management Groups

Environmental Health and Personal Social Services etc

Hospital and COMMUNITY HEALTH SERVICES

Family Practitioner Services

Figure 6.1

Notes

a.   For details of the DHAs see Appendix V.

b.   The relationship between health districts and FPC areas was as follows:

A No of health districts per FPC area	B No of FPC areas	AxB Total no of health districts
1	40	40
2	20	40
3	17	51
4	7	28
5	4	20
6	1	6
7	1	7
Total	**90**	**192**

c.   Since FPCs retained the same boundaries as local personal social services authorities (i.e. metropolitan district councils; non- metropolitan county councils and London borough councils), note b also indicates the extent to which two or more DHAs had to collaborate with one local authority.

d.   This diagram does not include the special health authorities (see Figure 8.1) or the standing advisory committees (see Figure 5.1).

However, the 1982 structure was destined to be short lived and by 1986 it had been modified in two main ways. Firstly, in accordance with the government's declared intention (see above), FPCs eventually acquired their independent status on 1st April 1985. Secondly, the decision to implement the recommendations of the NHS Management Inquiry resulted in the establishment of a Health Services Supervisory Board and an NHS Management Board within the DHSS; the appointment of general managers at regional, district and unit levels and, in many districts, a reduction in the number of units of management.

The Community Unit

For the CHSs the most significant feature of the post-1982 structure of the NHS was the existence, in many health districts, of a unit of management and management team with district-wide responsibility for the provision of community based health care services and with a considerable amount of autonomy for the day-to-day running of these services. This meant that despite the fact that community units did not have the status of acute units (see above), for the first time since 1974, there was at least the potential for the development of a more integrated approach to the management and delivery of CHSs. In districts which did not have a single community unit, responsibility for the CHSs was generally shared between either two or more community units (e.g. Portsmouth and South East Hampshire Health Authority) or, more commonly, a number of geographically based units (e.g. Scarborough Health Authority).

Those DHAs which opted for a community unit did so mainly on the grounds that:

- it helped to raise the profile and strengthen the position of CHSs within the district;

- since CHSs were significantly different from HSs, in respect of their wider geographical spread, lower technological base and greater emphasis on health maintenance and illness prevention, the skills and attributes needed to manage them in an effective and efficient manner could be fully developed only in a unit specialising in this kind of health care provision;

- CHSs were likely to fare better in terms of the resources allocated to them and in other ways if they had a unit to promote and protect their interests in a single minded manner; and

- collaboration between those responsible for the planning and delivery of CHSs and of related services (e.g. FPSs; personal social services) was more likely to develop if there was a unit with which FPC staff, family practitioners and local authority employees could clearly identify.

DHAs which did not establish community units took the view that, since units of this kind tended to be smaller than average, opportunities for economies of scale in respect of administrative and related costs could not be fully realised. Furthermore, they would tend to encourage isolationalism on the part of their staff and thereby make the integration of CHSs and HSs and of CHSs and services for priority groups (e.g. mentally ill) that much more difficult to accomplish.

Although there were differences between community units in respect of the services for which they had some degree of managerial responsibility, the pattern of responsibilities found in most units is summarised in Table 6.1.

TABLE 6.1 *The Service Responsibilities of Community Units*

Full Responsibility	Shared Responsibility	Shared or Full Responsibility. [a]
Health centres and clinics.	Child health (with District Medical Officer).	Community Midwifery.
Welfare foods.	Family Planning (with District Medical Officer and Director of Nursing Services[Midwifery]).	Chiropody.
District nursing.		Speech Therapy.
Health visiting.		Health Education.
Home nursing aids.		Physiotherapy.
Incontinence service.		Occupational Therapy.
		Orthoptics.
		Dietetics.
		Dentistry. [b]

Notes

a.   See Table 6.2 for examples of different ways of allocating responsibility for these services.

b.   The district dental officer had direct access to the DHA in respect of matters coming within his/her own sphere of professional competence.

In addition to the responsibilities identified in Table 6.1, a number of units were also required to manage peripheral hospitals (e.g. cottage hospitals; relatively small long-stay hospitals; day hospitals) and district-wide services, such as laundry, transport, fire prevention and security.

Although DHAs initially retained responsibility for a number of CHSs at district level, in keeping with the spirit of 'localism' most looked for ways of securing maximum delegation downwards. Particular difficulties arose, however, with regard to those paramedical services with 'patterns of patient care which transcend(ed) units and institutions',[28] such as physiotherapy, occupational therapy and chiropody, and district-wide functions, such as personnel, works and finance. For community units this was a particularly important issue since a number of paramedical services (e.g. speech therapy) were mainly delivered in the community, whilst many of the services which had been available only in hospitals were gradually moving into the community (e.g. physiotherapy). Furthermore, many community unit managers felt that they needed some control over functions, like personnel, if they were to be in a position to exploit fully the potential of unit management in respect of the future development of the CHSs.

At the time a number of models for incorporating services and functions of this kind into the management structures of the newly constituted health authorities were suggested by Dixon and others. These are summarised in Table 6.2.

TABLE 6.2 *Models of Management for Paramedical Services and District-Wide Functions*

Centralised or Integrated Service Model

Basic Features

* District head of service/function (e.g. district chiropodist) managerially accountable to district manager (e.g. district medical officer) or authority.
* District head manages staff some of whom might be outposted to units.
* District head controls district-wide budget for service.

Relationship to Unit

District head responsible for ensuring that the unit receives adequate provision of the service/function and the necessary staff input.

Comments

* Favoured by many of the existing heads of paramedical services.
* Potential for achieving economies of scale.
* Optimum use of scarce resource.
* Uniformity of service across district.
* Unit management (i.e. unit administrator or unit management team - see below) unable to control service/function either managerially or financially.

Decentralised or Fragmented Service Model

Basic Features

* No district head of service/function.
* Unit heads of service/function (e.g. community physiotherapist; unit personnel officer) responsible for staff within unit.
* Unit budgets for service/function controlled by unit head or unit management.

Relationship to Unit

Full managerial accountability of service/function to unit management.

Comments

* Favoured by unit managers.
* Effective control of service/function at unit level.
* Management of service/function closer to points of service delivery (e.g. health centres) and other operational managers (e.g. director of nursing services).
* Greater flexibility within units and variety between units.
* Creates difficulties for service/function with very few staff (e.g. dietetics).

Unit Adviser Model

Basic Features

* No district head of service/function.
* The unit head (with the largest budget) co-ordinates the other unit heads of that service/function as and when required.

Relationship to Unit.

* Full managerial accountability to unit management.
* In performing his/her co-ordinating role, unit head remains accountable to unit management.

Comments

* Provides for inter-unit co-operation in respect of service/function.
* Retains control at unit level.

District Adviser Model

Basic Features

* District head of service/function accountable to district management (e.g. district occupational therapist).
* Unit heads of service/function accountable to unit management (e.g. community occupational therapist).
* District head monitors and co-ordinates unit heads and their budgets.

Relationship to Unit

Two levels of managerial accountability - district and unit.

Comments

* Provides for leadership role within service/function at district level.
* Source of professional advice for district management and the authority.
* Likely to give rise to a situation of dual accountability (i.e. unit heads professionally accountable to district head and managerially accountable to unit management).

Source: Modified version of Table 3 from M. Dixon, 'The organisation and structure of units' in I. Wickings (ed.), *Effective Unit Management* (London: King's Fund Publishing Office, 1983), p. 34.

It is clear from information collected by a research team at the Health Services Management Centre of Birmingham University, which undertook a detailed study of unit management between 1983 and 1985, that there were considerable variations between DHAs in the way in which they dealt with the question of what were the most appropriate arrangements for the management of district-wide services/functions. From the point of view of the CHSs, one of the most significant findings was that in a relatively large number of districts, heads of community services, such as speech therapy, chiropody and health education, remained accountable to the district medical officer. Furthermore, in some districts the medical officer also had responsibility for monitoring the budgets of these services.[29] Thus, the 1982 restructuring exercise did not completely destroy the links between community medicine and the CHSs.

Managing the Unit

In accordance with the principles outlined earlier in the chapter, responsibility for the management of the community unit was exercised by the unit management team (or group). The composition of the management team of a typical community unit and the relationships of its members to staff at district level and within the unit are shown in Figure 6.2.

Initially there was some debate as to the exact nature of the collective accountability of the team for the quality of the services under its control. Some commentators argued that the individual accountability of team members to their counterparts at district level was the key element in the relationship between unit and district and that collective accountability was a fiction. Dixon, for example, expressed the view that since the unit administrator and nurse were 'fully accountable to their respective managers at district level and the medical representatives (were) answerable to (their colleagues) ... in the final analysis it (was) these individual accountabilities that (would) guide and effect the decision making of members' of unit management teams.[30] In the event, however, despite the importance of the individual accountability of team members, mechanisms for securing a degree of collective accountabilty of unit management teams to DMTs did evolve in most districts. These included monthly reports and regular review meetings. The Birmingham Research Team found that, on average, unit management teams met their DMTs once every six months.[31]

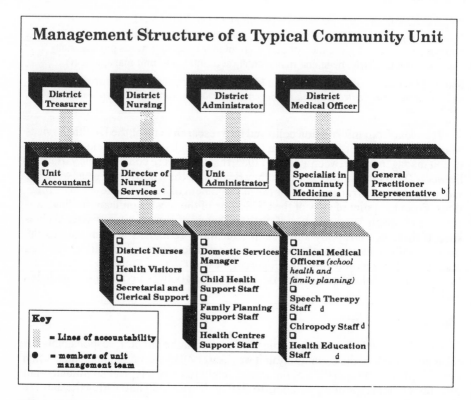

Figure 6.2

Notes

a.   In some community units a representative of the clinical medical officers, as opposed to a specialist in community medicine, occupied this position on the team.

b.   Some community units had more than one GP representative.

c.   In a number of districts the situation was complicated by the fact that there was not a complete match between unit administrator and director of nursing services posts. This meant that a community unit administrator might have to relate to more than one director of nursing services (e.g. where there were separate directors for district nursing; health visiting and maternity services).

d.   In some districts these staff were accountable either to the unit administrator or to a district head of service, who was in turn accountable either to the district medical officer or to the DMT.

Furthermore, in their study of community nursing, Baker and colleagues go as far as to argue that 'since the trio managing the unit were... collectively responsible to the district health authority for the functioning of the unit, this implied that the chief nursing officer of the district (could) no longer be regarded as the hierarchical superior of the unit's director of nursing services.'[32] Support for this view comes from the Birmingham University study which found that, although professional links between the director of nursing services and the DNO (as well as between the unit administrator and the district administrator) were maintained in most districts, they 'were sometimes tenuous' and attention was seldom given 'to performance related issues.'[33]

The principal functions of the unit management team were to agree budgets for the unit with the DMT; to consider policy issues relating to the planning of services, new developments, organisational changes, budgetary control and the monitoring of the unit's performance and to reach decisions on these issues within a framework of policies and priorities determined by the DHA; to assist in the co-ordination of the management of the unit and to ensure good communications throughout the unit. Matters considered by community unit management teams included:

- the upgrading of health centres and clinics;

- the allocation of accommodation at health centres and authority-owned clinics;

- the expansion, contraction and cessation of clinic sessions (e.g. for child health services; family planning);

- negotiating with district heads the increased provision of paramedical services in the community (e.g. dietetics; physiotherapy);

- the development of more sophisticated record and information systems (e.g. for child health surveillance programmes);

- the expansion of domiciliary services;

- the operation of virement (i.e. offsetting an overspending on one budget head against an underspending on another budget head);and

- the taking of health promotion initiatives (e.g. smoking and health).

Many unit management teams also established visiting panels to enable members to keep in touch with staff and service provision at the grass roots level. Panels of this kind served as an important two-way channel of communication between team members and the 'front line' staff of the unit (e.g. health centre receptionists; health visitors).

Not surprisingly, the research team referred to above, found considerable differences in the styles of management adopted by unit management teams and the quality of the relationships between team members. One significant finding was that in community units the working relationship between the director of nursing services and the unit administrator was often closer and more mutually supportive than in acute units. It was suggested that this might have been due to the fact that 'hospital unit officers tend(ed) to look more often to their district counterparts for support' than community unit officers, since district officers often knew far more about hospital than community services.[34]

As a result of the greater cohesion of team members and a tendency for DHAs to adopt a 'laissez-faire' approach to the CHSs, it was possible for community unit management teams to be more positive and creative in exercising their responsibilities than some, at least, of the management teams responsible for acute units. Thus, in the period between 1982 and the implementation of the Griffiths recommendations, important foundations were laid for a revival of the CHSs in many parts of the country.

As Figure 6.2 makes clear, in addition to their management team responsibilities, the director of nursing services and unit administrator were responsible, on an individual basis, for managing discrete groups of staff. **Directors of nursing services** of community units usually had responsibility for the management of district nurses; health visitors and school nurses. Details of the way that many districts organised their community nursing staff are provided in Figure 6.3.

Their duties included:

- the planning and management of community nursing services within available resources;

- the recruitment and selection of staff;

- the deployment of staff and the handling of issues arising from the operation of GP attachment schemes;

- the development and maintenance of an effective communication system throughout the community nursing service and with other agencies etc. (e.g. schools, GPs);

- giving assistance and advice to clinical nursing officers in respect of setting professional standards of care;

- monitoring the effectiveness of care patterns set by clinical nursing officers;

- ensuring the co-operation of clinical nursing officers with other health care professionals in the development of primary health care teams;

- staff induction and training, including liaison with educational institutions;

- giving advice to clinical nursing officers on problems encountered in carrying out their professional nursing duties and on grievance and disciplinary procedures and other aspects of the industrial relations and personnel function;

- the investigation of mishaps and complaints and the taking of appropriate preventive and corrective action; and

- ensuring the keeping of accurate records and the provision of statistical data as and when required.

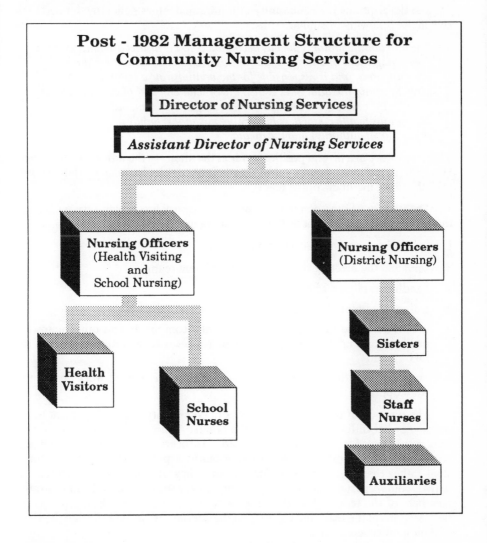

Figure 6.3

Underlying these duties was the vitally important leadership role which the director of nursing services was expected to play in respect of community nursing. Since nurses were, in quantitative terms, the dominant staff group within the community

unit, the director of nursing services was clearly a figure of considerable importance.

Job descriptions for **community unit administrators** generally defined their
role in the following or similar terms:

> *The unit administrator is directly accountable to the district administrator for
> the management of a range of administrative services and non-clinical sup-
> port functions, and is responsible for the administrative co-ordination of all
> services within the unit. S/he is also the official channel of communication
> between the unit and the DHA; district management team; outside bodies (eg
> community health council; voluntary organisations; family practitioner com-
> mittee; local authority) and the media.*[35]

Thus, they were in a pivotal position as far as the affairs of the unit were concerned.
However, as mentioned earlier, the unit administrator had no managerial authority
over the other members of the team.

The staff for whom a community unit administrator was usually responsible and
the way in which they might well have been organised is shown in Figure 6.4.

Unit administrators were also responsible for:

- servicing the meetings of the unit management team;

- handling relations with the media;

- acting as a point of contact between the unit and the CHC;

- undertaking the investigation of accidents, complaints and other untoward
  incidents and taking appropriate action (in accordance with the policy of the
  DHA); and

- ensuring that effective security, fire and health and safety at work procedures
  were operated in the unit.

The position of the **medical members** of community unit management teams
was somewhat different from that of the others. Although, in certain cases, they
were responsible for managing clinical medical officers and their support staff (e.g.
secretaries, clerical officers), they were primarily representatives of their professions rather than line managers. Furthermore, they were not usually accountable
to their counterpart on the DMT in the same way as the nursing and administrative
members of the team. Thus, their role was to provide the medical input to the
deliberations of the team and ensure that the decisions reached reflected the views
of their medical colleagues.

In assessing the extent to which management at unit level was strengthened
after 1982, the Birmingham Research Team (see above) concluded that, although
every DHA had met the formal requirements of the 1982 restructuring exercise by
appointing unit management teams, some authorities had been 'much more determined and successful than others in implementing the policy of devolution.'[36]

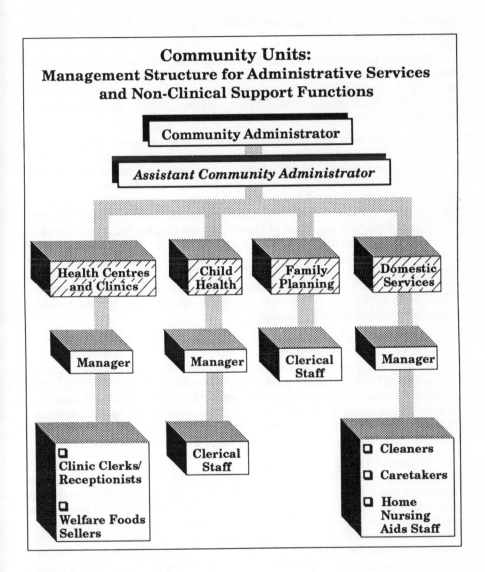

Figure 6.4

The Continuing Debate

Despite the upheaval caused by the 1982 restructuring exercise it did little to dampen down the debate surrounding the management of the NHS. If anything the debate was even more intense after 1982 than it had been before. This was due to a variety of factors.

First, the restructuring had created more uncertainty about the managerial relationships and lines of accountability than had been intended. As already mentioned particular problems arose in respect of the concept of collective accountability and the arrangements for managing those services and functions which straddled the boundary between two or more units.

Second, as Levitt and Wall point out, there was a growing 'impatience with consensus management which had been seen by many, particularly doctors, as an excuse to procrastinate.'[37] Other criticisms of consensus management were that it had resulted in fundamental issues and difficult decisions being avoided, fudged or delayed and in management becoming unduly passive and conciliatory. However, despite these criticisms, many important bodies, such as the Royal College of Nursing and the Confederation of Health Service Employees, retained a strong commitment to consensus management and argued that it was the only possible management style for the NHS, given its complexity and the wide variety of staff groups engaged in the provision of health care services. Moreover, it can be argued that if team working was to be implemented effectively at the service delivery level, through the application of concepts like that of the primary care team, then an example needed to be set by managers.

Third, because of the Conservative government's commitment to reducing the size of the public sector borrowing requirement, as part of its strategy for controlling inflation, the resources available to the NHS were being increasingly squeezed. As the data in Table 6.3 indicate, although the amount spent on health care services continued to rise, in real as well as cash terms, there was only a 4.7% increase in real terms between 1981/82 and 1986/87. When account is taken of advances in medical technology and the increasing number of over 75s, with their heavy demands on health care resources, this implied a contracting service.

Although the CHSs fared better in terms of resources than health care services in general (i.e. an 18.7% increase in real terms between 1981/82 and 1986/87 compared with 4.7% for health services generally), due mainly to the government's continuing commitment to the policy of community care, they were by no means immune from the growing financial problems of the NHS during this period. For example, managers of the CHSs, like their colleagues elsewhere in the NHS, were often faced with the need to hold back the growth of some services in order to finance the expansion of others. This can be illustrated by reference to the data in Table 6.4 (see page 260). Unlike the period from 1976/77 to 1981/82 (see Table 5.3), the services which grew fastest were those in the 'other' category (e.g. community physiotherapy, community psychiatric nursing, speech therapy, home nursing aids and services for the incontinent), whilst services like district nursing, prevention and school health did not expand as much as they might have done.

TABLE 6.3 NHS and Community Health Services : Revenue Expenditure 1981/82 to 1986/87

National Health Service

Year	1 Actual Expenditure £m	2 Inflation Rate for Service %	3 Expenditure at 1981/2 level Allowing for Inflation £m	4 Expenditure Increase over and above Inflation £m	5 % Increase over and above Inflation %
1981/82	10176.8	-	10176.8	-	-
1982/83	11078.5	7.4	10929.5	148.6	1.4
1983/84	11764.2	5.0	11475.9	287.9	2.5
1984/85	12586.3	5.9	12153.0	432.8	3.6
1985/86	13273.3	5.4	12809.3	463.5	3.6
1986/87	14288.5	6.5	13641.9	646.1	4.7

Community Health Services

Year	Actual Expenditure £m	Inflation Rate for Service %	Expenditure at 1981/2 level Allowing for Inflation £m	Expenditure Increase over and above Inflation £m	% Increase over and above Inflation %
1981/82	675.5	-	675.7	-	-
1892/83	739.5	6.5	719.6	19.9	2.8
1983/84	791.7	5.1	756.3	35.4	4.7
1984/85	868.9	5.8	800.2	68.7	8.6
1985/86	954.2	5.2	841.8	112.4	13.4
1986/87	1068.5	6.9	899.9	168.6	18.7

Key   Col 4 = column (1) minus column (2)   Col 5 = column (4) as % of column (3)

Sources: *Summarised Accounts of Health Authorities etc* (1981/82, House of Commons Paper No. 232, Session 1982/83; 1982/83, HC Paper No. 399, Session 1983/84; 1983/84 HC Paper No. 331, Session 1984/85; 1984/85 HC Paper No. 411 Session 1985/86; 1985/86 HC Paper No. 20 Session 1987/88; 1986/87 HC Paper No. 606 Session 1987/88). Inflation rate (column 2) taken from evidence submitted to the Social Services Committee during its investigation into the resourcing of the NHS. (See HC Paper No. 264-II Session 1987/88, p. 15.)

For those responsible for managing the CHSs the difficult financial situation was exacerbated by two other factors. First, the rapidly increasing number of elderly people, which put great pressure on services like district nursing and chiropody, ensured that there was a constant demand for more staff. Second, as hospitals sought to increase their throughput of patients (i.e. number of cases per available bed), by discharging them earlier, the CHSs, in particular district nursing, had to provide more and more care on a domiciliary basis. Not surprisingly, many CHSs managers argued that insufficent recognition was given to the 'knock on' effect of these developments in the acute sector when decisions were taken on the allocation of resources to CHSs and HSs.

TABLE 6.4 *Programme Budget for the Community Health Services 1981/82 to 1986/87 (at 1986/87 prices)*

Year	HV £m	DN £m	CM £m	Pr £m	Ch £m	FP £m	SH £m	Other £m
1981/82	140.2	282.0	73.2	42.6	30.6	31.7	161.4	124.2
1982/83	148.0	287.4	74.6	45.0	31.0	31.9	161.8	130.9
1983/84	150.8	288.8	74.9	45.8	31.3	33.8	162.9	139.4
1984/85	154.7	300.7	78.0	47.0	31.8	33.9	161.0	155.7
1985/86	159.2	312.8	81.1	48.4	32.6	34.0	166.0	171.8
1986/87	164.3	331.6	86.0	49.9	34.5	33.4	165.4	189.4
(Provisional)								

% Increase 17.2   17.6   17.5   17.1   12.7   5.4   2.5   52.5
81/2-86/7

Key
HV = health visiting
DN = district nursing
CM = community midwifery
Pr = prevention (i.e. vaccination and immunisation)
Ch = chiropody
FP = family planning
SH = school health service

Source: House of Commons Paper No. 548 Session 1987/88, Social Services Committee, *Public Expenditure on the Social Services,* Memorandum received from the DHSS containing replies to a written questionnaire from the Committee.

During the early 1980s the Conservative government also became increasingly concerned about what it perceived as the poor quality of management in the NHS and the failure of managers to control costs and secure value for money. As a result it felt the need to introduce a number of controversial measures designed to strengthen the effectiveness and efficiency of NHS managers. Some of the most significant of these initiatives and measures, which had both a short-term and a long-term impact on the CHSs, as well as other health care services, are summarised below.

Following the publication of a report from the Public Accounts Committee (see Chapter 8) on financial control and accountability in the NHS (during the 1981/82 session of Parliament), in which it was argued that there needed to be greater accountability to Parliament for the NHS, the Secretary of State introduced a new system of **accountability reviews**. This involved holding annual meetings between regional chairmen and RTOs and Ministers and senior civil servants from the DHSS, to review the performance of the RHA in the light of policies from the centre and regional plans and the extent to which resources were being used effectively and efficiently and to agree objectives for the year ahead. In turn, RHAs held similar review meetings with their DHAs. Significantly, a number of the issues initially raised at both regional and district reviews were of direct concern to CHSs staff. For example, an analysis by the DHSS of issues discussed at the first round of district reviews, referred to by Ham, shows that services for the elderly were a major issue in 123 reviews; collaboration with local authorities and joint planning in 46 and community services in 45.[38]

One of the most controversial initiatives taken by the government during the first half of the 1980s related to **competitive tendering**. In February 1983 it made clear its intention of promoting the greater use of commercial contractors in the provision of health care services. Later in the year the DHSS issued a circular instructing DHAs to test the cost- effectiveness of their domestic, laundry and catering services by putting them out to tender. Although these services were of only marginal concern to most CHSs managers, if the principle of competitive tendering were to be extended to other services it could have implications as far reaching for CHSs as for HSs.

From the financial year 1981/82 health authorities were required to make **efficiency savings** of 0.2% in the first year; 0.3% in the second and 0.5% in the third. As Ham observes these were 'savings the government expect(ed) health authorities to make while maintaining the same level of service provision.'[39] Inevitably, as an integral part of the NHS, CHSs were affected by this initiative and in most districts managers responsible for the CHSs were expected to identify areas in which savings could be made through increased efficiency. Often these involved making changes to working practices in clinics (e.g. family planning) with a view to reducing staff costs.

An initiative which did not immediately affect the CHSs, but was destined to have long-term consequences for them was the development of **performance indicators**. This involved the presentation of statistical data in ways that would facilitate its use by managers. According to Best, underlying the introduction of performance indicators was the belief that 'by quantifying various characteristics of NHS performance, the overall achievement level of an individual authority, unit or other functional sub-division of the service, (could) be cast in a comparative perspective.'[40] Thus managers would be able to identify variations in performance, investigate and take whatever managerial action they felt to be appropriate.

The first national package of performance indicators was developed by the DHSS, in collaboration with the Northern Regional Health Authority, and published in book form in 1983. In the same year the DHSS also announced that it was setting up a Joint Departmental/NHS Group on Performance Indicators to develop the concept, by extending their coverage and improving their quality. Detailed work was to be carried out by eight working groups covering: acute services; estate management; support services; services for the mentally ill; services for the mentally handicapped and (of particular significance for CHSs managers) children's services; services for the elderly and manpower.

In February 1980, the DHSS announced the setting up of the NHS/DHSS Steering Group on **Health Services Information** headed by Edith Korner, a former vice-chair of the South Western Regional Health Authority. The terms of reference of the group were:

- 'to agree, implement and keep under review principles and procedures to guide the future development of health services information systems';

- 'to identify and resolve health services information issues requiring a co-ordinated approach';

- 'to review existing health services information systems'; and

- 'to consider proposals for changes to, or developments in, health services information systems arising elsewhere and, if acceptable, to assess priorities for their development and implementation'.

The pressure for this initiative came from two sources. The first was the Three Chairmen's Review (1976), which had concluded that 'much information (was) demanded quite unnecessarily and ... that the Department and the Service should ... jointly embark upon (a) study based upon the simple question: 'Is what you are collecting of value; and who actually uses it?'[41] The second was the Merrison Commission, which had expressed the view that: 'The information available to assist decision makers in the NHS leaves much to be desired. Relevant information may not be available at all, or in the wrong form. Information that is produced is often too late to assist decisions or may be of dubious accuracy.'[42]

For the CHSs one important consequence of this initiative was the fact that, as mentioned in Chapter 1, Korner and her colleagues pursued a far more sophisticated approach to the analysis of the nature of community based health care services than had previously been attempted. Their fifth report (October 1984), was devoted entirely to the community services and was destined to have a considerable impact on the methods of 'data capture' and the processing and management of information within community units.

Another set of initiatives were the so-called **'Rayner scrutinies'**. Carried out under the direction of Sir Derek Rayner (Joint Managing Director of Marks and Spencer), the Prime Minister's special adviser on efficiency, each scrutiny focussed on a particular activity (e.g. transport, recruitment advertising) and was designed to establish whether it represented value for money.

Lastly, increasing attention was given to the role and status of **consumers** in relation to the planning and delivery of services. Many felt that the objective of a more effective and responsive NHS could be achieved only by convincing managers and health care professions of the need to take greater account of the views of clients, both individually and collectively. Consequently, various attempts were made to strengthen the 'voice of the consumer'. For example, in its first report the Maternity Services Advisory Committee (which had been established by the Conservative government in 1981 to advise on matters relating to maternity and neo-natal services) recommended the setting up of a maternity services liaison committee in every district, made up of hospital and community based health care professionals and lay persons, 'to keep under review the whole spectrum of maternity services.'[43] The DHSS also continued to give financial support to a wide variety of voluntary organisations, such as MIND, Age Concern and the Patients' Association, which played an important part in articulating the views of particular client groups on various aspects of service delivery.

In response to these developments a number of health authorities began to look more critically at their relations with clients and to undertake surveys to find out the views of consumers on such matters as the timing of clinics and conditions in health centres. Furthermore, as Scrivens indicates, CHCs, which had been threatened with abolition in the early 1980s, appeared to gain in popularity 'as reactions against the centralising forces apparent' in the DHSS grew.[44]

In a climate of this kind it was not really surprising that less than twelve months after the 1982 restructuring, the Secretary of State for Social Services, decided to appoint, in February 1983, a four man team led by Roy Griffiths (Deputy Chairman and Managing Director of J. Sainsbury) 'to give advice on the effective use and management of manpower and related resources in the National Health Service.'

The NHS Management Inquiry

Initially it was intended that Griffiths and his colleagues should not only carry out their investigation as speedily as possible, but also communicate their conclusions and recommendations to the Secretary of State in the form of a letter which would not be published. However, this somewhat secretive approach aroused considerable criticism and as a result the Secretary of State had a change of heart and published the letter in October 1983, two weeks after he had received it. The letter was in two parts. The first consisted of recommendations for management action and the second some general observations and the reasoning behind the recommendations.

'Because of ... (unspecified) work going on at the centre between (the) DHSS and the professions'[45] the members of the NHS Management Inquiry were advised by the Secretary of the State not to give detailed consideration to the CHSs and FPSs and to concentrate on the HSs. Consequently their letter contains relatively few explicit references to the CHSs. However, Griffiths and his colleagues did make clear that they recognised the important role played by CHSs staff in the delivery of health care and that, by implication, the principles which they espoused were as applicable to the CHSs as to the HSs. They also made the point that hospitals, FPSs and CHSs clearly interacted with and affected each other and that, more importantly, the patient did not observe 'such separate services'. In their view much more needed 'to be done to recognise this interaction, in everyday management, in policy making and planning, and in the allocation of resources.'[46] Furthermore, there was a clear need for issues of this kind to be brought within the 'coherent management process' they were proposing. Significantly, this is one aspect of the Griffiths recommendations which did not receive the attention it deserved.

Griffiths and his colleagues also referred to the CHSs in the context of their recommendations regarding patient involvement in the planning and delivery of services. In their view it was essential for managers to ascertain how well services 'were being delivered at local level by obtaining the experience and perceptions of patients and the community', which could be 'derived from CHCs and by other methods, including market research and from the experience of general practice and the **community health services** (emphasis added)'.[47] Unfortunately, it would appear that very little notice was taken of this particular recommendation.

The main conclusion of Griffiths and his colleagues was that the NHS lacked, at every level of decision-making, 'a clearly defined general management function.' This was defined as 'the responsibility drawn together in one person, at different levels of the organisation, for the planning, implementation and control of performance.'[48]

In order to remedy this and other deficiences they made a series of recommendations for management action at each level within the NHS. These included:

at national level (i.e. action by the Secretary of State)

- the setting up, within the DHSS, of a Health Services Supervisory Board, to determine the purpose, objectives and direction of the NHS; approve the overall budget and allocation of resources for the NHS; take strategic decisions and receive reports on performance and other forms of evaluation from within the NHS;

- the setting up, within the DHSS, of a small, multiprofessional and full- time NHS Management Board to plan the implementation of policies approved by the Supervisory Board; provide the NHS with managerial leadership; control performance and achieve consistency, drive and momentum over the long-term;

- the appointment of a personnel director to serve on the Management Board and develop the personnel function within the NHS;

at regional and district level (i.e. action by chairmen)

- the extension of the accountability review process (see above) right through to unit managers;

- the identification of a general manager, at authority level, regardless of discipline 'charged with the general management function and overall responsibility for management's performance in achieving the objectives set by the authority';

- the clarification of the roles of chief officers;

- reviewing and reducing, at every level, the need for functional management structures, and ensuring that, in future, the primary reporting relationship of functional managers (e.g. chief nursing officers) was to the general manager;

- the initiation of major cost improvement programmes for implementation by general managers;

at unit level (i.e. action by the district chairman)

- planning for all day-to-day decisions to be taken within the units of management;

- the closer involvement of clinicians in the management process;

- the clarification of the general management function and the identification of a general manager;

- ensuring that each unit had a total budget;

- arranging for district procedures to spell out the role of the Treasurer's department in providing management accountant support to unit general managers; rules for virement between and within unit budgets; 'authorisation limits and the flexible use of total budgets; and the financial relationship between Unit budgets and any district wide budgets for functional services on which they (might) call (e.g. physiotherapy; dietetics in the case of community units).'

It was also recommended that the NHS Management Board should ensure the development of a property function within the NHS and 'should undertake a general review of levels of decision taking in the NHS' and 'review all consultation arrangements' and should ensure a more consumer-orientated approach to the planning and delivery of health care services.

Despite the emphasis which the members of the NHS Management Inquiry placed on general management and consumerism they did not regard the more traditional concepts of functional and consensus management as completely redundant. In the notes accompanying their recommendations they made the point that although 'the primary reporting relationship of functional managers should be to the general manager (this) would not weaken the professional responsibilities of ... chief officers, especially in relation to decision taking on matters within their own spheres of responsibility.' For example, nurses would still lead the nursing function; personnel officers the personnel function and dentists the dental function.[49]

On consensus management they took the view that the appointment of general managers did not imply the end of the positive aspects of this approach to management. Indeed they saw general managers as being able to 'harness the best of the consensus management approach (ie the attempt to reach interdisciplinary agreement on points that cross professional boundaries)', whilst at the same time avoiding some of the problems it created (e.g. 'lowest common denominator decisions' and 'long delays in the management process').[50]

Significantly for the CHSs the members of the NHS Management Inquiry also stressed the need for the further development of unit management. In their view units of management provided 'the bedrock for the whole NHS management process' and were large enough 'in management terms to take all their own day to day management decisions.' Thus, the onus was on 'higher management to argue away from this position, if they (thought) that there (was a) clear and accepted justification for taking particular decisions at an identified higher level of management.'[51] The members also felt that the 1982 restructuring had not resulted in the devolution of real decision-making powers to unit level and that urgent action was needed if units were to fufill their potential (i.e. of the kind outlined above).

The initial reaction of the Conservative government to the recommendations of Griffiths and his colleagues was extremely favourable and in his statement to Parliament Norman Fowler, the Secretary of State for Social Services, made it clear that he and his colleagues accepted its 'general thrust'. At the same time he announced that he would be setting up, within his department, the Health Services Supervisory Board, that the Supervisory Board would establish the Management Board and that he would be consulting with health authorities, professional bodies and other interested parties on the Inquiry's recommendations. He also expressed the hope that, subject to the outcome of these consultations, authorities would be able to start implementing the general management function from April 1984.

Implementing the General Management Function

The consultation process began in November with the issue of a letter to health authority chairmen inviting comments. According to the Secretary of State the comments he received in response to his letter indicated 'that most authorities support(ed) the management aims and objectives recommended by the Inquiry Team.'[52]

Nevertheless, there were some voices of dissent and many of these were heard during an investigation into the recommendations of the NHS Management Inquiry by the House of Commons Select Committee on Social Services (see Chapter 8). This was carried out in early 1984 and amongst the bodies who submitted evidence, there were a number with a direct interest in the impact of the recommendations on the CHSs. One of these was the Health Visitors' Association.

In its written evidence the Association made two specific observations regarding the CHSs. Firstly, it wanted to know to what extent, if any, the recommendations of the NHS Management Inquiry were intended to apply to the community units, given the fact that Griffiths and his colleagues had been advised not to give detailed consideration to the CHSs. Secondly, in its opinion directors of community nursing services had inherited the general management functions, identified by the NHS Management Inquiry, from their predecessors - the divisional nursing officers (community) between 1974 and 1982 (see Chapter 5) and chief nursing officers of local health authorities before 1974. Since the community services were 'concerned almost exclusively with direct relationships between health visitors and nurses and their clients and patients, they (had) practically no dependence on support services and it (was) therefore inevitably the senior nurse manager who had responsibility for planning, implementation and control of performance.'[53] Predictably, such a view was anathema to non-nursing staff within the NHS and, in the event, very few nurses secured general manager posts.

In their report the members of the Social Services Committee expressed support for the general conclusions of the NHS Management Inquiry. They welcomed 'its emphasis on the need (recognised in the 1982 reorganisation) to devolve management to Unit level and below, its proposed extension of accountability reviews, its emphasis on the primacy of the patient and its search for more vigorous, efficient, effective, consistent and sensitive management.'[54] However, whilst accepting that the general critique of Griffiths and his colleagues commanded general assent, they were sceptical about the form of general management that was being proposed and urged Ministers to exercise caution in implementing the Management Inquiry's recommendations especially at unit level.

Notwithstanding the reservations of the Social Services Committee and other interested parties, the Thatcher government maintained its commitment both to the Management Inquiry's diagnosis of the problems of the NHS and to the proposed remedies. Thus, in a circular amplifying its response to the Inquiry, which was issued in June 1984, the DHSS confirmed that it accepted the need for a clearly defined general management function at every level within the NHS and that it was taking steps to bring this about.

The circular also set out the requirements for establishing a general management function and the arrangements for appointing general managers at regional, district and unit level. In doing so it was made clear that general managers were to carry personal responsibility, and be personally accountable to the authority, 'for the planning, implementation and control of the authority's or unit's performance.'[55]

Thus, as a minimum, the general manager's broad areas of responsibility were to include:

- direct accountability to the authority, or in the case of units to the district general manager, for the general management function within the undertaking;

- direct responsibility and accountability for the managerial performance within the authority or unit;

- leadership of the authority's management team, or unit equivalent, and accountability for the performance of the team as a whole in developing policies and possible courses of action and ensuring the provision of proper advice;

- ensuring that management and administrative practices enable the care of patients to be constantly to the fore.[56]

Clearly each of these broad areas of responsibility was as relevant to the CHSs as to the HSs and implied that the general managers of community units would be in a position to provide the managerial leadership and drive which the services had lacked since the demise of the MOH.

The circular also spelt out what general managers were expected to do. First, they had to ensure that the authority or unit was provided with the advice and information it needed to be able 'to formulate policies, decide priorities, set objectives and monitor progress' towards the realisation of these objectives. Thus, it was expected that general managers would need to give a considerable amount of attention to the development of the planning and information function within their authority or unit. In addition, they had to make sure that full weight was given to clinical priorities in the light of advice from nurses and doctors. Second, the circular drew attention to the need for general managers to ensure that timely decisions were reached and that objectives were achieved. Third, they had to provide leadership of the kind that would 'stimulate initiative, urgency and vitality in management'. Fourth, they were required to co-ordinate the activities, functions and staff of their authority or unit. Fifth, general managers were expected to ensure that responsibility for managing budgets and resources generally was delegated to the point where action could be taken effectively. Last and most importantly, it was made clear that general managers had to 'secure (the) effective motivation of staff.'

The timetable envisaged by the circular was an extremely tight one, since it was intended that the general management function should be established at every level by the end of 1985 at the latest. Furthermore, although not formally required to do so, many DHAs used this opportunity to review their unit structures. The net result of these reviews was a reduction in the number of units from approximately 850 to approximately 620. In the process many community units were merged with mental handicap, mental illness and geriatric units to form priority services units. Although this was a logical development it did mean that in many districts the CHSs would no longer be managed as a separate entity. Instead, for management purposes, they would form part of a broader grouping of institutional (e.g. psychiatric hostels/hospitals), as well as community, based services.

Having determined their unit structures, DHAs then had the task of recruiting and selecting their unit general managers. In doing so it is not entirely clear whether account was taken of the backgrounds of candidates in deciding whether they were more suited for one kind of unit than another. Griffiths and his colleagues took the view that 'in identifying a unit general manager ... the District Chairman should go for the best person for the job, regardless of discipline ... the main criterion for appointment (being) the ability to undertake the general management function at unit level and manage the total unit budget.'[57] With regard to the CHSs, however, it can be argued that their distinctive qualities are such that they can be managed effectively only by a general manager with a particular type of background (e.g. community medicine; community nursing). In fact, as the data in Figure 6.5 illustrate, in terms of their backgrounds, community unit general managers were not significantly different from general managers as a whole. Thus, it would appear that in selecting their community unit general managers most health authorities followed the advice of Griffiths and his colleagues and chose the best person for the job regardless of their professional background.

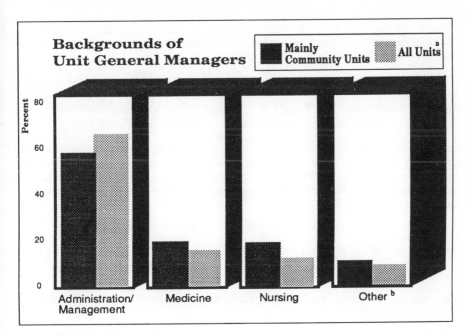

Figure 6.5

Notes

a.   All Units = All 687 units covered in the survey (including Wales, Scotland and special health authorities in England).

b.   Other:

	All Units	'Mainly Community' Units
*Finance	1.3%	1.1%
*Armed Forces	2.3%	4.8%
*Dentistry	1.6%	3.8%
*Therapy	0.3%	0.0%
*Miscellaneous	2.8%	1.6%
	8.3%	**11.3%**

Source: Information from a collaborative study of unit general managers carried out by The Institute of Health Services Management and The Health Service Journal. See *The Health Service Journal*, 2nd July 1987, Centre Eight.

Although most health authorities had their district and unit general managers in post by late 1985, very few, if any, had made much progress in implementing the general management function at sub-unit level. For the vast majority of unit general managers this was their top priority during the first few months of 1986.

In devising structures for their units general managers had to take account of a variety of factors. These included the existing management arrangements; the priorities for service development set out in the authority's strategic plan; the staff they inherited and the principles underlying the philosophy of general management.

In particular, community unit general managers had to find a way of:

- reconciling the desire of community nurses to retain their traditional autonomy and right to self-management with the need for a more integrated approach to service delivery;

- strengthening the involvement of the paramedical professions in the affairs of the unit;

- ensuring that all the professions providing services within the unit had a sufficient number of opportunities to contribute to the making of policies;

- applying the principles of general management to the running of health centres and other institutions and to the delivery of services within geographical subdivisions of the district;

- creating a corporate identity for a relatively disparate group of services and a sense of 'community' between a very varied group of staff; and

- facilitating closer relations with the other agencies engaged in the provision of primary care and related services (e.g. local authorities; FPCs; voluntary organisations) and with family practitioners.

In addition, community unit general managers, like their counterparts in other units, were faced with the major task of promoting a significant change in the organisational and managerial culture of the NHS. This involved a shift away from the traditional 'administrative maintenance' model of management to a more critical and proactive approach. It was generally recognised, however, that changing structures was far easier than changing values and behaviour.

Consequently, some would argue that in many health authorities general management is still no more than 'skin deep' and may never modify the organisational culture in the manner intended. Nevertheless, the debate surrounding the recommendations of the NHS Management Inquiry, the recruitment of general managers and the application of general management principles at sub-unit levels have played an important part in making managers, throughout the NHS, more aware of the need to increase managerial efficiency and effectiveness.

Other Initiatives

Many of the initiatives designed to improve the efficiency and effectiveness of NHS managers, which were outlined earlier in the chapter, and which predate Griffiths, were subject to further development during the mid-1980s.

Griffiths and his colleagues recommended an extension of the principle of **accountability reviews** to unit level. This was accepted by Ministers, and health authorities were encouraged to implement a formal system of unit reviews based on the arrangements operating at higher levels within the NHS. Some health authorities have not established a system of unit reviews, on the grounds that they are very costly in terms of staff time and that effective accountability at unit level can be secured by less formal means. However, where they have been introduced they have served to concentrate the minds of managers on key issues. Examples of issues highlighted and discussed at community unit review meetings include vaccination and immunisation rates; cervical cytology screening arrangements; health education initiatives in respect of heart disease; relations with GPs and the development of community based services for priority groups.

Although the Social Services Committee had expressed doubts, as early as 1982, as to the ability of health authorities to make **efficiency savings** on the scale intended by the Ministers without cutting services, every year since 1981/82 health service managers have been faced with the task of finding ways to save money through improved efficiency. Since 1984/85 this exercise has been known as the **cost improvement programme** and authorities have been set an annual target of one percent of their revenue budget. DHAs may use the savings from these programmes for whatever purpose they consider appropriate.

However, authorities have experienced increasing difficulty in meeting their cost improvement targets, many considering them little more than a euphemism for spending cuts. In many districts cost improvement programmes have tested the ingenuity of CHSs and other managers to the full. Moreover, in a report on value for money developments in the NHS (1986), the Comptroller and Auditor General, made it clear that RHAs should 'monitor closely and probe the validity of cost improvement programmes submitted by districts' and should expose 'any attempt ... to disguise cuts in services as genuine cost improvements'.[58]

The Joint Group on Performance Indicators, set up in 1983 (see above), reported to the Secretary of State in January 1985, and its recommendations form the basis of the current set of **performance indicators,** of which there are approximately 425. These indicators were first issued in July 1985, using 1983/84 data. Further issues were made in December 1985 and 1986, using 1984/85 and 1985/86 data respectively. In keeping with the moves towards greater technological sophistication in the handling of information, since 1985 the data on performance indicators have been distributed to health authorities on floppy diskettes for use with a BBC microcomputer.

Some examples of indicators of particular significance for CHSs staff are shown in Table 6.5.

TABLE 6.5 *Examples of Performance Indicators for Community Based Health Care Services*

Childrens' Services

C 19 Post Neonatal Mortality Rate
The annual no. of deaths of children aged from 28 days to 1 year per 1,000 live births in the DHA.

C 41 Child Clinic Attendance Rate
The annual no. of first attendances of children aged under 1 year at child health clinics per 1,000 live births to mothers resident in the DHA.

C 43 H.Visitor Contact Rate : 1-4yrs
The annual number of children aged 1-4 years who are seen for the first time by a health visitor during the year per 1,000 of the DHA's resident child population aged 1-4 years.

Services for the Elderly

E 2 District Nurse Contact Rate
The annual no. of patients aged 65+ years and over who have had contact with a district nurse at any place of treatment during the year as a % of the DHA's total resident population aged 65yrs+.

E 3 Chiropody Cost/1000 Pop 75+
The annual revenue expenditure by the DHA in chiropody services related to the DHA's resident population aged 75yrs and over (in '000s).

Manpower

M 69 Staff Cost/Resident - Speech Therapy
The total annual staff costs of all speech therapy staff in the DHA related to the DHA's resident population (per head).

MM25 Community H. Doctors (Child)/Resident Population
The no. of community health doctors (WTE) working in child health in the DHA related to the DHA's resident child pop (in '00,000s).
Source: DHSS, *Performance Indicators for the NHS. Guidance for Users,* 1986.

The indicators listed in Table 6.5 reflect not only their diversity but also their relative crudity. This was due mainly to the fact that existing data sources had to be used at this stage in their development. Since performance indicators are 'designed to inform judgements about how well NHS services are being provided',[59] it is important for them to take account of the outcomes and quality of services as well as the inputs. This has been recognised and as a result continuing efforts are being made by the Performance Indicator Group to find ways of improving the quality of indicators and thereby increasing their value to CHSs and other health care managers. In doing so the group has been able to take advantage of the additional information being generated as a result of the implementation of the recommendations of the Korner Steering Group and the moves towards the development of a comprehensive **information strategy** for the NHS as a whole (see below).

The implementation programme for the Korner recommendations was announced by the DHSS in April 1984.[60] For the CHSs the key date was the 1st April 1988, one year later than the deadline for most other services. By then DHAs and the units of management responsible for the CHSs were expected to have systems in place which would produce the required information on services to the community and patient care in the commmunity (emphasis added). Thus, between 1984 and 1988 many CHSs managers had to devote a considerable amount of attention to the implementation of the Korner recommendations, especially those set out in the fifth report. This involved the preparation, of detailed implementation plans, the key features of which had to be reflected in the annual programmes of DHAs; the appraisal of options for data capture, processing and storage, both manual and electronic; and, most importantly, the training of 'front line' and other staff, who would be directly affected by this exercise.

Whilst managers were carrying out these tasks further initiatives relating to information management were being taken at national level. For example, in November 1984, the NHS Computer Policy Committee set up the Community Health Information Project. The purpose of Phase 1 of the project was 'to undertake a general appraisal of the information needs of the CHSs with the objective of producing an outline functional specification, independent of (computer) hardware, identifying the immediate priority areas and producing plans for the development of this specification to (a more) detailed level.' The principal recommendation to come out of Phase 1 was that of a community health index (i.e. a register of everyone resident in a health district and therefore an actual or potential client of the CHSs). This was to be based on the population register maintained by FPCs (i.e. of those registered for general medical services), suitably enhanced to take account of clients receiving services from the DHA who were not on the FPC register. The project, however, was overtaken by other developments, the most important of which was the publication by the DHSS, in October 1986, of a national strategy document for the management of information by health authorities. Entitled *A National Strategic Framework for Information Management in the Hospital and* **Community Health Services** (emphasis added), this set out the parameters within which health authorities were to develop objectives in respect of their own information needs.

In his foreword to the document Mike Fairey, the Director of Planning and Information Technology on the NHS Management Board, drew attention to the fact that in 'an immense and complicated organisation like the NHS success (could) be planned, achieved and demonstrated' only if managers and service providers were provided 'with the right information, in the right form and at the right time.' He also went on to point out that 'information was a valuable and expensive resource and, like any other resource', needed to be carefully managed.[61] Thus, in the main body of the document, the key issues that health authorities had to resolve were identified and discussed. These were the issues of how to integrate information management with the 'business' of health care; develop better information systems; use information to find ways of increasing the productivity of existing staff and financial resources; and help managers and clinicians make the best use of the information at their disposal and thereby improve the quality of services.

From the point of view of CHSs managers, one of the most significant comments in the document related to the last of these issues, since it was argued that 'getting the best out of better information' depended, in part, on a 'greater shared understanding of the importance of the relationship between primary and secondary care provision'.[62] Therefore, it was essential to encourage the development of an understanding of this kind. Unfortunately, past experience suggests that it is likely to take a very long time to achieve this objective. Many in the CHSs still feel that decisions are taken by the managers of secondary care services without any consideration being given to their implications for the primary care sector.

The attention given to **'consumerism'** by the members of the NHS Management Inquiry greatly strengthened the position of those who believed that as part of any attempt to improve the quality of health care services it was necessary to take account of the views of service users. Despite the developments which had been taking place in this field, Griffiths and his colleagues argued that, although 'businessmen had a keen sense of how well they (were) looking after their customers ..., whether the NHS (was) meeting the needs of the patient, and the community, and (could) prove that it (was) doing so, (was) open to question.'[63] Thus, they saw one of the principal functions of general managers as being the development of mechanisms for monitoring patient and community opinion.

With regard to the future role of CHCs, the members of the NHS Management Inquiry were moved to comment that they had been 'impressed with the grass-roots work' of some councils and, as mentioned above, they saw them as one of the sources which managers could use when seeking the views of clients on aspects of service delivery at the local level. However, as Scrivens observes, 'though the idea of the councils has received considerable support, their work is constantly being eroded' with general managers moving, 'of their own volition, towards using market research techniques to inform their decision making.'[64]

Whatever, the future of CHCs there is little doubt that during the past few years there has been a significant increase in initiatives designed to obtain feedback from patients and to personalise existing services. Furthermore, many districts and units have included within their management structures posts with specific responsibility for quality assurance, performance review and consumer issues.

For the CHSs, developments of this kind and the higher profile being given to public participation have been of particular importance because of the contribution which they make to the health care needs of the population as a whole, as well as those of specific client groups. Action taken by community units either in response to initiatives at higher levels (such as Trent Regional Health Authority's campaign to personalise health care services) or of their own volition include:

- the production of booklets (in various languages) designed to make parents and teachers better informed about the school health service (e.g. Nottingham Health Authority);

- the conduct of surveys to discover the shortfalls in community services (e.g. Riverside Health Authority) and the views of clients on different aspects of service provision (e.g. facilities in health centres, the availability of chiropody clinics);

- the introduction of a 'patch' approach to the delivery of child health and other services, with one of the key elements being 'community participation and the involvement of service users'[65] (e.g. Newcastle Health Authority);

- the setting up of training programmes for 'front line' staff on how to deal with telephone enquiries, provide clients with information in a clear and unambiguous manner, relate to clients in a more friendly and supportive manner, keep cool under pressure, handle complaints and 'put the consumer first at all times and in all circumstances'[66] (e.g. South Birmingham Health Authority); and

- the establishment of staff workshops to help with the generation of ideas for improving communications (with patients and the public) and patient satisfaction with the services provided and to facilitate a more corporate approach to service delivery (e.g. Doncaster Health Authority)

It remains to be seen whether these initiatives result in fundamental changes to the way in which the CHSs are delivered. Undoubtedly improvements have been made. However, it can be argued that these are simply 'window dressing' and that any attempt to give clients real powers, in respect of the services they receive, would be resisted by the service providers and their professional bodies. Furthermore, in the present financial climate, it seems likely that the only proposals to which health authorities can respond positively are those which are relatively cheap to implement.

Whether or not the CHSs have become more efficient and effective as a result of these measures must remain an open question. What is clear, however, is that developments of this kind have played a significant part in setting the agenda for community unit general managers as well as their colleagues in other units.

The Beginning of a New Era?

There can be little doubt that by the mid-1980s the CHSs were on their way towards recovering the collective identity and status which they had lost between 1974 and 1982. This was due, in part at least, to the 1982 restructuring and the establishment, in most districts, of a unit with specific responsibility for the management of the CHSs and to the NHS Management Inquiry and subsequent appointment of community unit general managers. Thus, there was now at least the potential for a 'renaissance' of the CHSs under the leadership of community unit general managers, who can be regarded, in management if not professional terms, as the heirs to the MOsH. However, a number of problems still needed to be resolved.

First, it remained to be seen whether, in their dealings with the general managers of other units, community unit general managers would possess the 'political clout' to secure for the CHSs their rightful share of the available resources and the greater shared understanding of the relationship between primary and secondary health care services, referred to earlier. In contrast with the MOH, the general managers of community units did not usually have a clearly identifiable 'political' ally amongst the members of the health authority. In other words there was no equivalent of the chairman of the health committee, who had often provided the MOH with a considerable amount of support during the tripartite era.

Second, given the dominant role of GPs in the delivery of primary care services, community unit general managers needed their support, or at the very least, acquiescence, if they were to promote to the full, the interests of staff engaged in the provision of CHSs. Unfortunately, past experience suggests that a majority of GPs would be unlikely to accept any initiative which could be interpreted as undermining their own position within the field of primary care.

Third, there was the issue of relations between those with responsibility for managing the CHSs and the specialists in community medicine and of how to ensure an epidemiological input to the planning and delivery of CHSs. Although a few general managers had a background in community medicine, most did not (see Figure 6.5). Furthermore, in most districts, epidemiological data and expertise resided in the district medical officer's department, rather than the community unit. Thus, ways had to be found of establishing and maintaining a close relationship between the community unit and the staff of the district medical officer's department.

Attention was drawn to one aspect of this relationship by the Public Accounts Committee in its report on preventive medicine (1986). Quoting evidence from Dr Donald Acheson, the Chief Medical Officer at the DHSS, it reported that one of the reasons why there were significant variations in immunisation rates between health districts was the fact that since the abolition of the office of MOH in 1974 'there had been a blurring of the chain of accountability for the organisation and development of certain preventive measures in districts ... (However), although very concerned about this factor the DHSS were hoping to use the accountability review process through the regions and districts to produce better performance.'[67] In addition, the DHSS had asked every health authority to appoint someone to be personally responsible for immunisation performance. This solution was accepted by the Public Accounts Committee with the proviso that the DHSS should give consideration 'to the feasibility of designating personal responsibility locally for other preventive programmes besides immunisation, particularly screening for cervical cancer.'[68]

A more radical solution would have been to reintroduce the office of MOH and in so doing combine responsibility for community and preventive medicine with that for the management of the CHSs. Such an idea, however, was rejected even by the Acheson Committee of Inquiry into the Future Development of the Public Health Function (1988). In its view neither 'the re-introduction of the medical hierarchy into local authorities nor the creation of large departments managed by public health doctors in health authorities' was necessary. What it called for was 'simply the co-operation of teams of professionals to maximise resources available in order to achieve improvements in health.'[69]

Last, faced with the many conflicting pressures on their time, most community unit general managers were likely to find it extremely difficult, if not impossible, to devote sufficient energy to the task of securing for the CHSs a higher profile than the one they had had prior to 1982. Nevertheless, despite these problems, the prospects for the future development of the CHSs were far brighter than they had been for many years.

Footnotes

1. DHSS and Welsh Office, *Patients First : Consultation Paper on the Structure and Management of the National Health Service in England and Wales* (London: HMSO, 1979), p. 1.

2. The National Association of Health Authorities, *NHS Handbook*, 3rd edition (London: Macmillan Reference Books, 1987), p. 11.

3. *Patients First*, op. cit., para. 12.

4. Quoted in R. Klein, *The Politics of the National Health Service* (London: Longman, 1983), pp. 138-9.

5. Patients First, op. cit., p. 2.

6.   DHSS, Circular HC(80)8, *Health Service Development : Structure and Management*, July 1980, p. 1.

7.   King Edward's Hospital Fund for London, *Unit Management in Context*, K.F. Project Paper No. 31. (London: King's Fund Centre, 1982), p. 13.

8.   Circular HC(80)8, op. cit., para. 3.

9.   DHSS, *The Primary Health Care Team*, Report of the Joint Working Group of the Standing Medical Advisory Committee and the Standing Nursing and Midwifery Advisory Committee, [Chair: Dr W. Harding], (London: DHSS, 1981).

10. Circular HC(80)8, op. cit., para. 4.

11. Ibid., para. 4.

12. Ibid., para. 25.

13. Ibid., para. 28. Other examples given in the circular were :
* A large single hospital.
* Client care services (e.g. a mental illness hospital with psychiatric community services and possibly the psychiatric unit of a district general hospital).
* The maternity services of the district.
* An individual hospital, or group of hospitals, with community services (i.e. a 'geographical' unit).
* A group of smaller hospitals.

14. Ibid., para. 27.

15. Welsh Office, Circular WHC(81)8, *Health Service Development, Structure and Management*.

16. See, for example, A.J. Collin, 'Can Teams Manage? A discussion of some factors relevant to the concept of a team having a managerial role at unit level', *Hospital and Health Services Review*, June 1981, pp. 168-172, and F. Eskin, 'Team Development in the NHS', *Hospital and Health Services Review*, June 1981, pp. 172-174.

17. Circular HC(80)8, op. cit., para. 26.

18. Ibid., para. 29.

19. Ibid., para. 31.

20. Ibid., para. 9.

21. R. Levitt and A. Wall, *The Reorganised National Health Service*, 3rd Edition (London: Croom Helm, 1984), p. 27.

22. King Edward's Hospital Fund for London, op. cit., p. 7.

23. *Primary Health Care in Inner London*, Report of a study group commissioned by the London Health Planning Consortium [Chair: E.D. Acheson], May 1981, para. 8.11.

24. *Health and Social Services Journal*, 27th May 1982, p. 636.

25. *Health and Social Services Journal*, 15th July 1982, p. 842.

26. A. McNaught, 'Where are the Community Services Going?', *Hospital and Health Services Review*, January 1983, p. 15.

27. M. Dixon, 'The organisation and structure of units', in I. Wickings (ed.), *Effective Unit Management* (London: King's Fund Publishing Office, 1983), pp. 17-18.

28. J. Williams, E. Parry, W. Deeley, M. Atherton and N. Lauder, 'Paramedical Services: Low cost efficiency', *Health and Social Services Journal*, 10th April 1981, p. 418.

29. See J. Carruthers, J. Clark, W. Davey and D. Williams, 'Unit Structure': four articles (i) 'Piecing together the jigsaw'; (ii) 'Patterns of communication'; (iii) 'Creating a certain degree of tension' and (iv) 'All words and no performance', *Health and Social Services Journal,* (i) 30th May 1985, pp. 668 670; (ii) 13th June 1985, pp. 736-737; (iii) 27th June 1985, pp. 800-801 and (iv) 1st August 1985, pp. 956-957.

30. M. Dixon, op. cit., p. 27.

31. J. Carruthers et.al., op. cit., (ii) p. 736.

32. G. Baker, J.M. Bevan, L. McDonnell and B. Wall, *Community Nursing. Research and Recent Developments* (London: Croom Helm, 1987), p. 8.

33. J. Carruthers et. al., op. cit., (ii) p. 736.

34. Ibid., (i) p. 669.

35. Adapted from a job description produced by Rotherham Health Authority.

36. J. Carruthers et. al., op. cit., (i) p. 670.

37. R. Levitt and A. Wall, op. cit., p. 28.

38. C. Ham, *Health Policy in Britain,* 2nd Edition (London: Macmillan, 1985), p. 149.

39. Ibid., p. 48.

40. G. Best, 'Performance indicators: a precautionary tale for unit managers', in I. Wickings (ed.), op. cit., p. 62.

41. DHSS, *Regional Chairman's Enquiry into the Working of the DHSS in relation to Regional Health Authorities* [Three Chairman's Report], 1976. This enquiry was undertaken in 1975/76 at the instigation of the then Minister of Health, Dr David Owen. The three regional chairman, who carried out the enquiry were invited by the Minister to examine the functions of the DHSS and its relationship with RHAs and to consider whether or not any of the functions of the DHSS should be abolished or transferred to RHAs.

42. Royal Commission on the National Health Service [Chair: Sir A. Merrison], Report, Cmnd 7615 (London: HMSO, 1979), para. 21.56.

43. DHSS, *The Health Service in England. Annual Report 1984* (London: HMSO, 1984), para. 6.5.

44. E. Scrivens, 'Consumers, Accountability and Quality of Service', in R. Maxwell (ed.), *Reshaping the National Health Service* (Policy Journals: Oxford, 1988), p. 176.

45. *The NHS Management Inquiry* ['Griffiths Report'], General Observations, para. 33.

46. Ibid., para. 33.

47. Ibid., Recommendations for Action, para. 13.1.

48. Ibid., General Observations, para. 4.

49. Ibid., Accompanying Notes, no. 6.

50. Ibid., General Observations, para. 15.

51. Ibid., para. 18.

52. DHSS, Circular HC(84)13, *Health Services Management: Implementation of the NHS Management Inquiry,* June 1984.

53. House of Commons Paper No. 202 Session 1983/84, First Report from the Social Services Committee, *Griffiths NHS Management Inquiry Report. Together with the Proceedings of the Committee, the Minutes of Evidence and Appendices,* Memorandum by the Health Visitors' Association. Comments on the NHS Management Inquiry.

54.   Ibid., para. 4.

55.   Circular HC(84)13, op. cit., Annex C, para. 3.

56.   Ibid., para. 4.

57.   The NHS Management Inquiry, op. cit., General Observations, para. 21.

58.   HC Paper No. 212 Session 1985/86, National Audit Office, Report by the Comptroller and Auditor General, *Value for Money Developments in the National Health Service* (London: HMSO, 1986).

59.   Performance Indicator Group, *Performance Indicators for the NHS: Community Services*, Consultation Paper No. 6, June 1987.

60.   DHSS, Circular HC(84)10, *Health Services Development. Report of the Steering Group on Health Services Information: Implementation Programme.*

61.   DHSS, *A National Strategic Framework for Information Management in the Hospital and Community Health Services*, October 1986.

62.   Ibid., para. 7(iv).

63.   The NHS Management Inquiry, op. cit., General Observations, para. 2.

64.   E. Scrivens, op. cit., p. 177.

65.   D. Platt, 'Cultivating a child health patch', *The Health Service Journal*, 11th September 1986, p. 1198.

66.   See news item in *The Health Service Journal*, 31st July 1986, p. 1009.

67.   HC Paper No. 413 Session 1985/86, Forty-Fourth Report from the Committee of Public Accounts, *Preventive Medicine*, para. 11.

68.   Ibid., para. 25 (iv).

69.   *Public Health in England. The Report of the Committee of Inquiry into the Future Development of the Public Health Function*, [Chair: Sir D. Acheson], Cm 289 (London: HMSO, 1988), para. 4.47.

Chapter 7

Service Developments 1974 to 1986

By comparison with the 1946 Act, the National Health Service Reorganisation Act 1973, and the Consolidating Act which was passed in 1977 (1977 Act), are far less detailed and specific in their references to the CHSs, both collectively and individually. Although the 1973 and 1977 Acts contain some detailed provisions relating to the school health service and family planning (see below), other CHSs are subsumed in the sections dealing with services generally.

The provisions of Section 2 of the 1973 Act, which were incorporated, without alteration, in Section 3 of the 1977 Act, state that the Secretary of State has a duty to provide,to such extent as he considers necessary to meet all reasonable requirements:

- hospital accommodation;

- other accommodation for the purpose of any service provided under this Act;

- medical, dental, nursing and ambulance services;

- such other facilities for the care of expectant and nursing mothers and young children as he considers are appropriate as part of the health service;

- such facilities for the prevention of illnesss, the care of persons suffering from illness and the after care of persons who have suffered from illness as he considers are appropriate as part of the health service;

- such other services as are required for the diagnosis and treatment of illness.

However, despite the generalised nature of these provisions, it was made clear in a circular on the statutory framework of the NHS after the 1974 reorganisation, (September 1973) that:

- the 'other accommodation' referred to did include 'health centres and maternity and child health centres of the kind provided by local health authorities under the 1946 Act';

- 'medical, dental, nursing and ambulance services' were to be provided in not only hospitals and other accommodation but also 'patients' homes or any other place';

- the facilities referred to covered services supplementary to medical and dental services 'which local health authorities had previously provided under section 22(1) of the 1946 Act';

- the Secretary of State would continue to provide the same wide range of services and facilities for 'the prevention of illness, the care of persons suffering from illness and the after care of persons who have suffered from illness ..., as those previously provided by local health authorities.'[1]

In addition, under the provisions of Section 5 of the 1977 Act, the Secretary of State had a duty 'to provide for the medical and dental inspection at appropriate intervals of pupils in attendance at schools maintained by local education authorities and for the medical and dental treatment of such pupils; and to arrange, to such extent as he considers necessary to meet all reasonable requirements in England ... , for the giving of advice on contraception, the treatment of such persons and the supply of contraceptive substances and appliances.' The specific references to the school health and family planning services in both the 1973 and 1977 Acts reflect the fact that at that time there were fears that without statutory recognition of this kind they would not be given sufficent priority.

In the event legislative changes were of less significance in respect of health centres and individual services than other developments which took place between 1974 and 1986, including those referred to in Chapters 5 and 6.

Health Centres

As the data in Figure 7.1 indicate the rapid growth in the number of new health centres, which had begun in the mid-1960s, continued until the early 1980s.

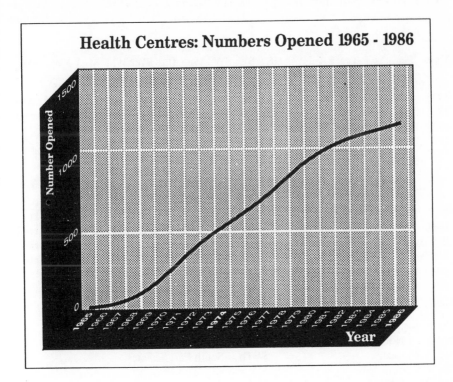

Figure 7.1

Source: DHSS, *Annual Report*, various years, and the Institute of Health Service Administrators, *Hospital and Health Services Yearbook*, various editions.

Between 1974 and 1982 responsibility for the planning and development of health centres was exercised primarily by AHAs. However, in performing this function they were expected to take account of general guidance issued by the DHSS and of regional policy. Both the 1976 and 1977 *Priorities* documents made it clear that the health centre programme would be maintained, but as the data in Table 7.1 indicate the pace of health centre development between 1974 and 1986 varied considerably from region to region.

TABLE 7.1 *Distribution of Health Centres by Region 1974 to 1986*

									Region						
Year	No	Yo	Tr	EA	NW Th	NE Th	SE Th	SW Th	We	Ox	SW	WM	Me	NW	TOT
1974	47	52	72	14	24	27	10	42	24	45	74	56	23	45	555
1975	50	62	83	15	30	31	12	46	29	50	80	64	27	60	639
1976	53	66	90	15	34	35	12	47	31	50	86	68	28	68	683
1977	58	73	97	25	36	36	15	49	34	53	94	74	38	79	761
1978	65	81	102	25	40	41	20	47	36	58	97	78	42	91	823
1979	72	94	113	30	41	44	24	48	37	59	99	84	43	98	886
1980	75	99	119	34	42	44	27	51	45	60	103	90	45	103	937
1981	82	105	131	41	47	49	29	53	47	62	106	96	47	109	1004
1982	86	110	145	47	47	56	37	52	48	63	107	107	52	121	1078
1983	88	114	146	48	50	60	37	53	54	63	110	113	56	128	1120
1984	90	114	151	48	53	63	38	54	58	63	111	115	57	130	1145
1985	90	116	153	49	55	63	50	55	59	63	111	116	56	135	1171
1986	92	123	153	50	56	66	50	55	59	63	110	119	57	136	1189
1987	92	123	153	50	55	66	49	55	58	61	110	119	59	137	1187

Key

No = Northern   NW = North West
NWTh = North West Thames   Tr = Trent
We = Wessex   SETh = South East Thames
Me = Merseyside   SW = South West
Yo = Yorkshire   EA = East Anglia
NETh = North East Thames   SWTh = South West Thames
Ox = Oxford   WM = West Midlands

For details of the distribution of health centres between areas and districts see Appendices IV and V.

Source: The Institute of Health Service Administrators/ The Institute of Health Services Management, *Hospital and Health Services Yearbook,* various editions.

This reflected differences between regions not only in respect of their relative need for premises of this kind but also in respect of their commitment to health centre development.

With regard to the planning of new health centres the DHSS again drew attention, in 1974, to the need for 'full and continuing consultation with all those who (had) agreed to provide services in the centre, on matters of siting, timing, operational policy, design costs and staffing'.[2] This, of course, included GPs and other family practitioners, as well as directly employed CHSs staff, such as district nurses and health visitors, who would be using the health centre as their base.

Since the 1974 reorganisation made no changes in the financial arrangements for GPs and other family practitioners using health centres, AHAs also had to undertake the sensitive task of negotiating details of the users agreements and levels of charges, with the practitioners concerned. To assist AHAs with this task the DHSS issued a model form of user agreement or licence in 1977. The accompanying circular recommended that service charges should be fully reviewed every three years and that there should be also a health centre committee, to represent the interests of all staff working at the centre.[3]

Two years later, in April 1979, the Labour government issued a detailed memorandum, which consolidated its guidance on health centre policy and demonstrated its continuing commitment to their development as one of the principal locations for the delivery of primary health care services and as a way of assisting and promoting 'the development of a team approach to primary health care'. According to this memorandum, the primary aim of health centres was 'to facilitate co-operation and teamwork between general practitioners, district nurses and health visitors by providing suitable accommodation, equipment and ancillary support in NHS premises'.[4] Such a view, of course, had been in vogue since the mid-1960s (see Chapter 4) and had been reiterated in a variety of official documents published in the intervening years. For example, the 1976 *Priorities* document referred to the 'important contribution' which health centres could make to the development of primary care teamwork and in a report on preventive medicine, published in 1977, the House of Commons Expenditure Committee called for more health centres to be built on the grounds that they were a far more suitable base for the development of primary health care teams than 'the traditional type of surgery'.[5]

With the change of government in May 1979, however, national policy towards health centres began to change. In its report the Royal Commission on the National Health Service drew attention to evidence from a survey which suggested that health centres were by no means 'universally popular' with either GPs or their patients. It was also pointed out that:

> *Doctors, nurses and the other professions who together provided care in the community (did) not necessarily require purpose-built premises to work together efficiently...(and that) working under the same roof (did not) guarantee good communication.*[6]

Nevertheless, despite these reservations, Merrison and his colleagues felt that the development of health centres or similar premises, in order to attract GPs to areas where sites were particularly expensive or difficult to obtain, such as London and other inner city areas, should be given priority.

The Conservative government's views on the future of health centres were outlined in a DHSS circular issued in May 1980. This stated that although health centres might 'have an important role to play in improving services especially in deprived areas such as inner cities ... previous guidance had placed too much emphasis on the building of health centres and may have led authorities and doctors to consider drawing unnecessarily on authorities' allocations of capital, and increasing unnecessarily the number of publically owned premises'.[7]

AHAs were therefore asked to review, with the help of their FPCs, every scheme for the building of a health centre that was planned or under consideration. In carrying out this review they were required to apply the following criteria:

- Was the scheme clearly supported by the doctors who would have a place at the health centre? If the answer was uncertain, the scheme had to be discontinued.

- Would the scheme make a marked improvement in the existing standards of primary health services, particularly where there were areas of population deprived of satisfactory services?

- Had the authority considered the possibilities open to doctors of improving premises or services by their own efforts assisted by improvement grants ... or by the General Practice Finance Corporation and the Department's Cost Rent Scheme?

- Were the facilities proposed a reasonable, rather than ideal, level of provision and of appropriate size to achieve the intended improvement of service both in terms of standard of provision and range of services taking account of both medical and nursing needs?[8]

The issue of this circular marked the first significant change in public policy towards premises for primary care services since 1946. In future priority was to be given to the development of GP owned medical centres, as opposed to health centres built and owned by public authorities. Thus, it can be regarded as a portent for the ultimate 'privatisation' of health centres. Predictably, the principal effect of the circular was a significant reduction in the health centre building programme, with only 36 centres being opened, on average, in each of the five years between 1981 and 1986, compared with an average of 65 for the period 1976 to 1981.

Individual Services

Between the unification of the NHS in 1974 and the implementation of the general management function at unit level in 1985 and 1986, the most significant of the CHSs, in terms of their cost and scale of provision, were:

- health visiting;

- district nursing;

- maternity and child health services (including midwifery; vaccination and immunisation and the school health service);

- health education;

- chiropody;

- family planning and cervical cancer screening;
- community dental service; and
- speech therapy.

Furthermore, for most of the services listed above this was a period of significant growth, due in part to the developing commitment to care in the community. It was also a period during which many of the issues that currently confront those responsible for the delivery of these services either emerged or became more salient.

Health Visiting

The trend towards a more varied caseload for health visitors (see Chapter 4) was unaffected by the 1974 reorganisation. This is illustrated by the data in Table 7.2.

Whilst the broadening of the health visitor's workload had long been a policy objective, the 1976 *Priorities* document made it clear that health visitors still had a vital part to play in the care and support of children and parents through their home visits.[9] However, as Baker and her colleagues indicate, between 1974 and 1986 a number of factors caused the health visiting profession to question further 'what (its) role ... should be and how (it) should fit into the (NHS) organisation.'[10]

First, the 1974 reorganisation separated health visitors, in organisational terms, from the staff of social services departments, to whom responsibility for various aspects of the welfare of children and families had been transferred in 1971. As a result, it was far more difficult to develop an integrated approach to family centred problems, such as non-accidental injury to children (to which the 1976 *Priorities* document had drawn particular attention); the care of handicapped children and financial and emotional crises caused by unemployment.

Second, health visitor 'attachment schemes' had raised questions for both health visitors and GPs regarding the exact nature of the relationship between their respective professions and the differing roles of health visitors and GPs. In the view of many health visitors, schemes of this kind were undermining their traditional autonomy. Furthermore, the emphasis of the health visitor on counselling and preventive work was somewhat at odds with the essentially curative approach of the GP and other attached nurses.

Third, although there was some acceptance of the view that health visitors had a role to play in meeting the needs of the elderly, it was 'not one that appealed universally to the profession.'[11] This was mainly because the elderly had such different needs from those of the health visitor's traditional client group (i.e. young children and their mothers). Significantly, however, as the data in Table 7.2 show, the over 65s as a percentage of the total number of clients of health visitors actually fell between 1974 and 1986.

TABLE 7.2 *Health Visiting : Staffing Levels and Distribution of Clients by Age 1972 to 1986*[a]

Year	Staff[b,c,d]	Persons Visited '000s	Age 0-4 '000s	Age 0-4 %	Age 5-64 '000s	Age 5-64 %	Age 65 '000s	Age 65 %
1972	6181	3978	2884	72.5	579	14.6	515	12.9
1973	6214	3810	2685	70.5	593	15.6	533	14.0
1974	6480	3807	2626	69.0	632	16.6	549	14.4
1975	6643	3539	2379	67.2	657	18.6	504	14.2
1976	7090	3576	2333	65.2	712	19.9	531	14.9
1977	7602	3546	2249	63.4	777	21.9	520	14.7
1978	7807	3597	2260	62.8	832	23.1	505	14.0
1979	8111	3734	2287	61.2	941	25.2	506	13.6
1980	8817	3817	2329	61.0	1007	26.4	481	12.6
1981	9117	3760	2285	60.8	1014	26.9	462	12.3
1982	9350	3812	2301	60.4	1053	27.6	458	12.0
1983	9550	3858	2315	60.0	1096	28.4	446	11.6
1984	9214	3987	2318	58.1	1217	30.5	452	11.3
1985	10147	4080	2331	57.1	1284	31.5	466	11.4
1986	10353	4129	2348	56.9	1347	32.6	434	10.5

Notes

a. The figures in this table are not directly comparable with those in Figure 4.6 because they relate only to England (i.e. not England and Wales) or with those in Table 4.5 because they relate to numbers of persons visited as opposed to numbers of visits.

b. As at 30th September.

c. Includes health visitor field work teachers; tuberculosis visitors, with a health visitor certificate; health visitor/district nurse/ midwives and bank health visitors. Health visitor students (784 in 1974 and 832 in 1986) and tuberculosis visitors, without a health visitor certificate (147 in 1974 and 48 in 1986) are excluded.

d. Due to changes in definition, the figures for the years prior to 1980 are not directly comparable with those for later years.

Source: DHSS, *Health and Personal Social Services Statistics for England*, various editions, supplemented with data directly supplied by the DHSS Statistics and Research Division.

Fourth, there was a decline in the number of births between 1970 and 1978 and 1980 and 1982 (see Figure 7.2), which substantially reduced the size of the health visitor's principal client group.

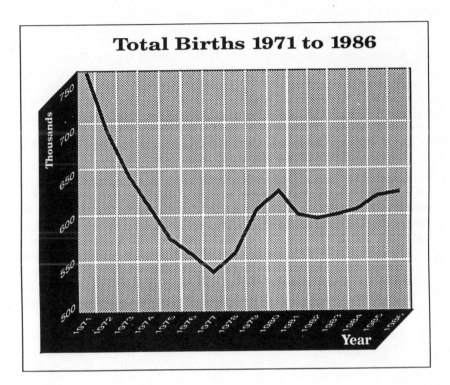

Figure 7.2

Notes

a. The data on which this figure is based are not directly comparable with those in Figure 4.3 since they relate only to England (not England and Wales).

b. Includes still births (1.1% of total births in 1974 and 0.5% in 1986).

Source: DHSS, *Health and Personal Social Services Statistics for England*, various editions.

Last, the reorganisation of 1974 and restructuring of 1982, resulted in health visitors in many areas/districts/divisions being managed by nurses who did not possess a health visiting qualification. Furthermore, in some parts of the country, those responsible for managing the health visiting service were not even sympathetic, let alone committed, to the health visitor's educative and preventive role in health care.

In addition to these factors, a number of health visitors were concerned about changes that were made in the late 1970s and early 1980s to the arrangements for their registration and regulation of their training and professional conduct. Under the provisions of the Nurses Act 1979, which were based on the recommendations of the Briggs Committee (see Chapter 4) the Council for the Education and Training of Health Visitors and a number of other bodies, such as the General Nursing Council for England and Wales and the Central Midwives Board,[12] were replaced, in 1983, by the United Kingdom Central Council for Nursing, Midwifery and Health Visiting.[13] This meant that health visiting was 'now seen as being firmly located within nursing.'[14] Whilst there were many within health visiting who were quite happy with this view of their profession there were those who feared that it might result in a dilution of their distinctive role.

For most of the period from 1974 to 1986 concerns of this kind were exacerbated by staff shortages. Although the number of WTE health visitors increased from 6480 in 1974 to 8111 in 1979 and, on a different basis of calculation, from 8817 in 1980 to 10147 in 1985 (see Table 7.2), this represented annual average increases of only 4.5% and 2.9% respectively, which compared unfavourably with the increase implied by the 1976 *Priorities* document. At that time the Labour government saw the 'expansion of the health visiting service, with its crucial role in protecting the health of the most vulnerable children and bringing to notice cases of neglect and ill-treatment ... (as) a key priority ... (and) propose(d) a 6 percent increase in expenditure (most of which would have been staff costs) on the service.'[15]

Furthermore, as the data in Figure 7.3 indicate, in 1976 very few authorities had achieved the target set by the DHSS in 1972 (see Chapter 4) of 1 health visitor per 4300 (or 3000 in areas with extensive 'attachment schemes' or high immigrant population) and although the situation had improved by 1986 over 50% of authorities still had not reached the target.[16] Significantly, however, the transfer of responsibility for the health visiting service from local health authorities to AHAs in 1974 lessened the disparity between areas in respect of the number of persons per health visitor.[17]

A major effect of the staffing situation and the factors mentioned above was a growing sense of unease, on the part of many health visitors, about the future of their profession. By the early 1980s both the Health Visitors' Association and the Royal College of Nursing were calling for the establishment of a committee to conduct an in-depth inquiry into the role and state of health visiting and, in so doing, update and place on a more scientific basis the findings and recommendations of the Jameson Working Party (see Chapter 4). As part of their campaign for a committee of inquiry the Health Visitors' Association published in 1981 an updated version of an earlier document entitled *Health Visiting in the Seventies* (1975).

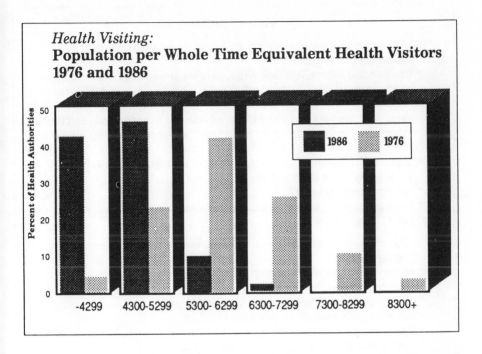

Health Visiting:
Population per Whole Time Equivalent Health Visitors
1976 and 1986

Figure 7.3

Source: DHSS and Child Poverty Action Group, *Reaching the Consumer in the Ante-Natal and Child Health Services* : Report of Conference 4 April 1978, pp. 47-53, and DHSS, *Performance Indicators for the NHS.*

Health Visiting in the 1980s (i.e. the updated version) drew attention to many of the problems outlined earlier, and dwelt at length on those relating to GP 'attachment schemes'. In view of these problems the authors argued that health visitors should give careful consideration to their priorities and reproduced the following recommendations, which had appeared in the earlier version, to help them do this.

Priorities in Health Visiting

1. Recommended selection of work for health visitors working within severe staff shortages.
* Urgent home visiting, ie to new births; to newly arrived families with small children; actual or suspected cases of non-accidental injury to children; in response
to requests from families; to handicapped children; to newly reported TB cases; to ante-natal mothers, especially primiparaes (i.e. women pregnant for the first time).
* Urgent referrals from other agencies (i.e. social workers, teachers, GPs etc), which are properly within the health visitor's province.
* Efficient record keeping.
* Involvement in the training of student health visitors.
* Child Health Clinics.

2. Recommended additional work for health visitors working under only average pressure.
* Routine visiting of all children up to school age.
* Visits to all ante-natal mothers.
* Supportive visits to families under temporary stress.
* Follow-up of immunisation failures.
* Paediatric developmental testing at home of non-clinic attenders.
* Health teaching to groups of adults and in schools.
* Further liaison with hospitals and professional colleagues.
* Involvement in the training of medical students, student nurses and social work students.

3. Recommended additions for health visitors who may, one day, have really small case loads.
* Routine visiting of all children up to school leaving age with time to attend to the needs of all members of the family.
* Support for families under stress from eg psychiatric problems, chronic illness, handicap.
* Counselling and health education at family planning and cytology sessions and other appropriate clinics.
* Visits to play groups and nurseries.
* Involvement in research projects.
* Regular visits to schools and hospital wards.[18]

Partly in response to the concern of the health visiting profession over its future role and organisation the Conservative government appointed, in June 1985, the Community Nursing Review Team, under the leadership of Julia Cumberlege (who was, at the time, chair of Brighton Health Authority). Its terms of reference were: 'To study the nursing services provided outside hospital by Health Authorities (including those provided by health visitors), and to report to the Secretary of State on how resources (could) be used more effectively, so as to improve the services available to client groups' (see Chapter 9).

Moreover, important initiatives were taken in various parts of the country. For example:

- in Huddersfield, Richmond and Plymouth there were experiments with 'crying baby' and other advisory services, operating on a 24 hour basis, with the aim of reducing the incidence of baby battering;

- notwithstanding the comments made earlier, which implied that the elderly were of declining significance as far as health visiting was concerned, in a number of areas (e.g. Reading and Suffolk) health visitors participated in the development of screening and surveillance programmes for the elderly and elsewhere (e.g. Kidderminster and Manchester) geriatric health visitor liaison officers were appointed to act as a link between hospitals and primary care agencies on behalf of elderly patients;

- in Sheffield and other districts health visitors played a key role in the intensive home visiting of infants where there was a high risk of 'cot death';

- in East London and elsewhere initiatives were taken in the provision of health care for 'travelling families' and these often involved the appointment or designation of a health visitor with specific responsibility for this group of clients;

- increasingly health visitors took the lead in establishing self-help groups (e.g. for isolated and depressed mothers; the carers of elderly relatives; hysterectomy patients and their families);

- as well as liaising between hospitals and the community in respect of the elderly, in a number of districts health visitors played a similar role for diabetics; orthopaedic and chest clinic patients; and mothers returning home with their newly born infants; and

- in some parts of the country, health visitors became more actively involved in the screening of adults through the establishment of 'well-woman', and from the mid-1980s, 'well-man' or 'well-person' clinics.

Clearly, many of these initiatives involved an element of specialisation on the part of the health visitors concerned. Thus, if initiatives of this kind represent the direction in which part, at least, of the health visiting profession is to go this will have implications for future training requirements and career development.

District Nursing

For district nurses the problems generated by the rapidly increasing demand for their services, which had been articulated by the Mayston Working Party (see Chapter 4), became even more acute during the 1970s and 1980s. This can be illustrated by reference to the data in Table 7.3.

TABLE 7.3 *District Nursing : Clients and Staff 1972 to 1986*[a]

Year	Persons Nursed '000s	0-4 '000s	Age 65+ '000s	% of Persons Nursed	Rate per 1000 Pop	Staff[b,c,d] WTEs No
1972	1841.4	144.4	833.9	45.3	92.8	9535
1973	2083.2	157.0	882.8	42.4	133.2	10220
1974	2142.8	143.3	929.2	43.4	143.7	10827
1975	2401.7	164.8	1008.0	42.0	153.6	11665
1976	2779.6	171.2	1129.6	40.6	169.9	12274
1977	2985.4	181.3	1191.0	39.9	176.9	12648
1978	3157.5	180.2	1256.5	39.8	184.1	13186
1979	3248.5	181.3	1313.9	40.4	190.2	13738
1980	3421.0	182.8	1417.7	41.4	202.6	13905
1981	3367.0	170.8	1441.0	42.8	202.1	14523
1982	3407.6	171.2	1489.1	43.6	210.8	14898
1983	3551.2	166.1	1559.9	43.9	220.9	15124
1984	3550.7	159.4	1587.8	44.7	225.7	15174
1985	3522.0	155.9	1611.4	45.8	224.3	15591
1986	3435.7	136.2	1584.3	46.1	217.2	15187

Notes

a   The figures in this table are not directly comparable with those in Table 4.6 and Figure 4.9 since they relate only to England (not England and Wales).

b.   As at 30th September.

c.   Includes district nurse practical work teachers, state registered nurses, senior state enrolled nurses and state enrolled nurses assisting district nurses, district nurse/midwives and bank district nurses. District nurse students are excluded.

d.   Due to changes in definition, figures for the years prior to 1980 are not compatible with those for later years.

Source: DHSS, *Health and Personal Social Services Statistics for England,* various editions, supplemented with data supplied directly by the DHSS Statistics and Research Division.

Although there was a 27% increase in the number of WTE district nurses between 1974 and 1979 (when the basis on which staffing statistics were collected was changed), because the demand for district nursing services rose at an even faster rate, the ratio of district nurses to persons nursed fell from 1:198 clients in 1974 to

1:236 clients in 1979. After 1980 there was a slight improvement in the situation with the number of district nurses increasing by 12% in the following 5 years and the ratio of district nurses to clients improving from 1:246 in 1980 to 1:226 in 1986. However, this made little difference to the pressures on the service, which continued to intensify. Furthermore, as the data in Figure 7.4 show, the staffing position in many areas was still much worse than the average and by 1986 some authorities had not reached the targets set by the DHSS in 1972 of 1 district nurse per 4000 persons or 1 district nurse per 2500 persons in areas with extensive 'attachment schemes' or with a high proportion of elderly and/or disabled people.

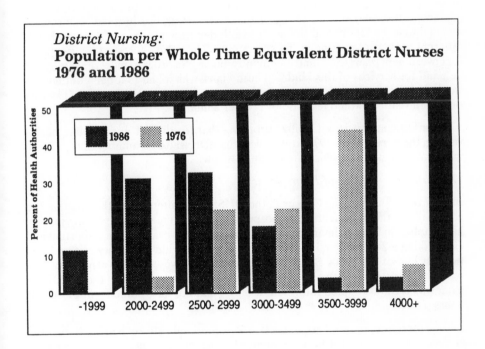

Figure 7.4

Note

a. 1976 area health authorities and 1976 district health authorities.

b. Figures for 1976 are estimates

Source: Based on DHSS, *Performance Indicators for the NHS*

Significantly, for England as a whole, between 1974 and 1986 the percentage of clients aged 65 and over remained fairly constant, even though the number of elderly per 1000 population who were nursed more than doubled (see Table 7.3). Thus, the increased demand for the district nursing service was not only due to the growth in the number of elderly. Various other factors, in particular earlier discharge from hospital and the development of 'hospital at home' schemes (see below), were also at work.

Notwithstanding these pressures on the service, Merrison and his colleagues took the view that there was 'considerable scope for expanding the role and responsibilities of ... district nurses (as well as health visitors) ... not just in the treatment room but in health surveillance for vulnerable groups and in screening procedures, health education and preventive programmes, and as a point of first contact, particularly for the young and elderly.'[19] With this in mind they recommended that the DHSS and the other health departments promote research into different aspects of nursing in the community. They also expressed their support for government plans to expand community nursing 'in order to meet the increasing demand for services of this kind.'[20] These plans, which had first been outlined in the 1976 *Priorities* document, envisaged that spending on district nursing (like that on health visiting) would increase by 6% per annum.

Consequently, it is not really surprising that for district nursing, like health visiting, the period from 1974 to 1986 was characterised by a number of significant initiatives, examples of which are outlined below.

The Introduction of Out-of-Hours Services

In 1977 the Chief Nursing Officer at the DHSS drew attention to the fact that the earlier discharge of patients from hospitals and the increasing use of day surgery had 'implications for primary health care, meaning for example the importance of establishing a 24 hour nursing service in order to provide continuity of care.'[21] By the first half of the 1980s Baker and her colleagues were able to report that the results of a postal survey which they had undertaken showed that of the 151 DHAs from which they obtained information only 2 did not have some form of out-of-hours service.

Furthermore, in some areas, such as Peterborough, efforts had been directed at developing 'hospital at home' schemes for patients who needed intensive care for a short period. Schemes of this kind were welcomed by the DHSS since they were generally regarded as a cheaper alternative to care in hospital and during the first half of the 1980s one such scheme was evaluated as part of the DHSS research programme.

Increasing Specialisation

During this period a considerable number of authorities established specialist nursing posts in one or more of the following fields: stoma care (i.e. attending to the physical and psychological needs of patients who are unable to excrete in the usual way due to surgery), coronary care, incontinence, orthopaedics, oncology, diabetes, mastectomy care, and stroke care. In addition, some authorities appointed nurse liaison officers to ensure a smooth transition of patients from hospital to the community and vice versa and thereby realise one of the principal objectives of the 1974 reorganisation, namely a closer relationship between the primary and secondary levels of health care.

Furthermore, as Simmons and Brooker argue, the 1970s were a 'watershed' for community psychiatric nursing. This was because:

- a large number of new community psychiatric services were established between 1970 and 1980 and by 1980 only 6 districts did not have a service;

- in the late 1970s there was a definite movement towards the 'attachment' of CPNs to general practices or health centres and clinics and the operation of an open referral system (i.e. the acceptance of referrals from any professional source and not just from psychiatrists and self-referrals from clients), which meant that they became more independent 'working in a relatively unsupported environment, responsible for the assessment and investigation of suspected mental health problems, aiming to establish and maintain a supportive role not just with the identified client but with their family and friends as well and, in some cases, becoming responsible for establishing a programme of treatment or rehabilitation'; and

- for the first time CPNs began to specialise, 'usually with a specific client group but sometimes with specialist functions, such as crisis intervention, within a multidisciplinary team.'[22]

Thus, within community nursing the concept of 'generalism' was very much in retreat in the years leading up to the publication of the Cumberlege Report.

Care of the Terminally Ill

Inspired by developments in the voluntary sector (e.g. hospice movement; care provided by Marie Curie and Macmillan nurses - see Chapter 8) the 1970s and early 1980s saw health authorities setting up a variety of schemes for the provision of care to those dying at home and their relatives. Many of these schemes included an advisory service, from which district nurses could obtain guidance on pain control, the unpleasant side effects of drugs, counselling the bereaved and related matters. It was generally found that the domiciliary services of the kind provided by district nurses enabled patients to remain at home for longer than might otherwise be the case.

Initiatives in Respect of the Elderly

Since the care of the elderly forms a substantial part of the district nurse's workload it is not surprising that considerable attention was given by district nurses to ways in which the needs of this priority group could be met in a more effective and sensitive manner. For example, in Cleveland a scheme of 'augmented home nursing' was developed as an alternative to hospital for elderly patients who were chronic invalids; in Norfolk a district nurse acted as trainer and organiser of a group of volunteer 'nurses' and in Birmingham district nurses participated in a sample survey of the medical and social needs of the elderly.[23]

During this period the status of district nursing was also enhanced by two important developments. First, as result of pressure from bodies representing the interests of district nurses, the United Kingdom Central Council for Nursing, Midwifery and Health Visiting (see Chapter 8) was required to set up a district nursing joint committee. Furthermore, this committee has to be consulted by the Central Council and the National Boards on all matters relating to their district nursing functions. Second, in the late 1970s and early 1980s action was taken to deal with the issue of the training and qualifications of district nurses. This had long been a cause for concern within the profession and it had contributed to the feeling that the district nursing function was not fully appreciated by those responsible for primary health care and the sense of inferiority that many district nurses felt when they compared themselves with health visitors. Whereas a qualified nurse could practise as a health visitor only if s/he had completed further training leading to the award of the health visitor's certificate, the same principle did not apply to district nursing. Although there was a nationally recognised qualification for district nurses (the national district nursing certificate)[24] and health authorities did all they could to encourage those nurses, who wished to work in the community, to obtain this qualification, it was not a mandatory requirement. In other words a state registered nurse did not have to undertake further training before being employed as a district nurse.

Eventually, after lengthy consultations involving the Chief Nursing Officer at the DHSS, the Panel of Assessors, which supervised the training and examinations for the national district nursing certificate, and the District Nursing Association, it was agreed to introduce the principle of mandatory training for district nurses in 1981.[25] It was hoped that this would boost the morale of district nurses and ensure that they received the training they needed to play a full part in the initiatives mentioned above and in determining the future direction of the community nursing services.

During the first half of the 1980s the importance attached by central government to these services was reflected in official publications[26] and in the decision to launch the independent review, led by Julia Cumberlege, of nursing services provided outside hospitals (see above).

Maternity and Child Health Services

As far as domiciliary midwifery was concerned, the influence of the Cranbrook Report of 1959, which had stressed the need for a higher percentage of deliveries to take place in hospitals, and the Peel Report of 1970, which had advocated a more integrated approach to maternity care (see Chapter 4), continued to be felt after

1974. First, as the data in Table 7.4 show, the number of home confinements continued to fall. This meant, of course, that the domiciliary midwives' traditional role (i.e. attending home deliveries) contracted still further. However, to offset this, the percentage of hospital confinements attended by domiciliary midwives remained fairly constant and the number of early discharge cases continued to rise, thereby increasing the need for midwives to carry out home visits to ensure that mother and child were progressing satisfactorily.

TABLE 7.4 *Domiciliary Midwifery : Service and Staffing Levels 1974 to 1986*

| | | ←——Deliveries Attended——→ | | Women Attended | |
Year	Total Births[a] No	Domiciliary Confinements No[d]	Hospital Confinements No	after Discharge from Hospital[b] No	Staff[c] No
1974	609894	25539	26698	426985	3625
1975	574818	18800e	23700e	447024	2955
1976	555722	14138	23494	446295	2825
1977	542040	10383	23513	452233	3041
1978	567380	9184	23390	503934	2790
1979	606127	9160	24202	546836	2984
1980	622894	8134	22039	586352	2773
1981	602102	6712	22213	571120	3406
1982	593442	5779	24140	573786	3504
1983	596667	5682	24164	569061	3713
1984	603998	5440	24629	578525	3858
1985	622727	4892	24441	603678	4041
1986	626946	5103	22305	607091	4127

Key

e = estimated figure.

Notes

a. Including still births.

b. Known formally as early discharge cases.

c. Excluding pupil midwives. State certified midwives 1974 to 1979; district midwives 1980 to 1986.

d. Women attended under NHS arrangements.

Source: DHSS, *Health and Personal Social Services Statistics for England,* various editions, supplemented with data supplied directly by the DHSS Statistics and Research Division.

Second, as mentioned in Chapter 5, after 1974 domiciliary midwifery was incorporated within the management structure for all branches of nursing within each health district. Thus, there was the potential, at least, for domiciliary midwives to establish closer relations with their hospital based colleagues as well as district nurses and health visitors.

Third, the number of women attending mothercraft and relaxation classes at community based clinics (see Figure 7.5), which were often taken by domiciliary midwives, continued to increase rapidly after 1974. Similarly, there were significant increases in the numbers of women attending community based ante-natal and post-natal clinics between 1974 and 1978, when figures ceased to be collected (i.e. from 178,981 to 277,422 and from 38,012 to 72,582 respectively). Since domiciliary midwives played an important part in the running of these clinics there was clearly an increasing demand for their services.

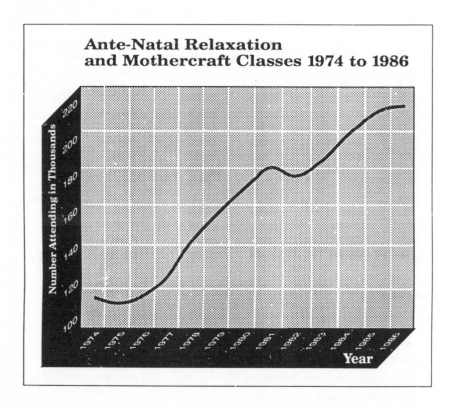

Figure 7.5

Source: DHSS, *Health and Personal Social Services Statistics for England,* various editions.

As a result of these developments there was a steady increase in the number of domiciliary midwives from the mid-1970s onwards (see Table 7.4) and a marked diversification of their workload. The increasingly varied nature of the roles and responsibilities of domiciliary midwives during this period is clearly illustrated by the following quotation from a letter issued by the Chief Nursing Officer at the DHSS in 1977.

Midwives are, in most areas, working within Midwifery Divisions, but there is an important role for them as a member of one or more primary health care teams in the provision of ante and post natal care, and health education. They may attend confinements of those mothers delivered in their own homes, and may deliver mothers in hospital. Those mothers discharged early from hospital come under their care until responsibility is transferred to the Health Visitor. Midwives in primary health care are professionally accountable for their own work. Midwives are becoming increasingly involved in family planning and genetic counselling.[27]

During the first half of the 1980s the Maternity Services Advisory Committee produced a series of reports on midwifery and other aspects of maternity care entitled *Maternity Care in Action*. Members favoured greater integration between hospital and community maternity services. They also argued (amongst other things) for the midwife to be recognised as a professional in her own right, capable of dealing with all aspects of normal pregnancy and birth and able to identify when a client needed to be referred for specialist care.[28] Some of the issues relating to the role and status of midwifery are examined further in Chapter 9.

With regard to health care services for pre-school and school children, it was pointed out in Chapter 3 that those responsible for the 1974 reorganisation, including Sir Keith Joseph the Secretary of State for Social Services, had been anxious to ensure that integration resulted in a significant improvement in the quality of these services. It was also mentioned that in pursuit of this objective, a committee, under the chairmanship of Professor S. Court, had been set up to investigate both the pre-school child and school health services. Its terms of reference were:

To review the provision made for the health services for children, up to and through school life, to study the use made of these services by children and their parents and to make recommendations.

The report of the Court Committee, entitled *Fit for the Future*, was published in December 1976.

Although the report acknowledged that improvements in the health of children during the twentieth century had been 'spectacular and heartening', the members of the committee also expressed their concern and 'profound anxiety about the... state of child health... about the shortcomings of the services and those working in them, and about the prospects for new generations if they (were) to grow up in the same deprived physical and emotional circumstances',[29] with which many children were having to contend. Court and his colleagues were particularly critical of the fact that, despite the longevity of the child health services in this country, there remained striking differences in the infant and childhood mortality rates between different parts of the country and different social classes. Furthermore, they felt moved to describe infant mortality in Britain as a 'holocaust', on the grounds that the rate of infant mortality was far higher than that of many other countries.

In their view many of the shortcomings of the child health services were the direct result of the way that responsibilities had been allocated during the tripartite era, which had helped 'to create the belief and practice that primary health care for children could be divided into separate components of prevention and care',[30] and of the lack of specialisation on the part of medical officers and other service providers.

As far as the pre-school child health services were concerned the Court Report drew particular attention to the following weaknesses in the existing arrangements. The 'attachment' of health visitors to GP practices in many parts of the country had led to the erosion of their territorial responsibilities and this had made 'the task of locating and offering help to mobile families and others who (made) ineffective use of health services'[31] far more difficult. Furthermore, although 'attachment' had strengthened the 'family' dimension of the health visitor's work by enabling her to work with children alongside their GP, it had created difficulties in respect of the continuity of care since mothers attending local health clinics could no longer be certain of seeing their practice health visitor.

In the years leading up to the 1974 reorganisation of the NHS 'less than half the child population under 5 years (was attending) local authority child health clinics'[32] and research indicated that among the non-attenders there was a disproportionate number from families in socio-economic classes IV and V. Research studies also showed that a majority of the non-attenders were not using their GP as an alternative to the local health authority clinic doctor. Furthermore, there was no evidence to suggest that the situation was improving. Consequently, the service was failing to meet the health care needs of an unacceptably large proportion of pre-school children.

Lastly, many parents appeared to 'be confused about the differences between the role of the clinic doctor which was primarily advisory and that of their GP which was essentially that of treatment'. It was also questionable as to 'how effective preventive and developmental surveillance (could) be when it (could not) be followed through with treatment'.[33]

With regard to the school health service Court and his colleagues were very critical of the fact that 'neither clinical medical officers nor general practitioners (were) required to have undergone any special training either in paediatrics or educational medicine'[34] before working with school children. They also criticised the lack of a close working relationship between the school health service and general practice.

As the report made clear:

Parents and teachers ...found themselves faced with a school health service which knew something of the child's health at school and had (some) skills in educational medicine - but could rarely provide treatment and had no first hand knowledge of the child's behaviour or development out of school; and a general practitioner service which could provide treatment but had no opportunity to study the child's behaviour in school and to discuss problems of health and adjustment with the teaching staff concerned and had no experience of educational medicine... (Unfortunately there was) still a striking lack of any national or local policy aimed at achieving rational, efficient co-operation between general practitioners and school doctors or resolution of the underlying dichotomy between promoting health and treating illness.[35]

Other weaknesses, to which the members of the Court Committee drew attention, were the fact that school health service staff worked largely in isolation from child health specialists in hospitals, who had been relatively slow to apply the increasing knowledge of developmental and educational medicine; the restricted ability of the service to meet the needs of school children due to the nature and organisation of, and concentration on, regular medical examinations; a failure to meet the needs of adolescents directly by advising parents and teachers rather than the teenagers themselves and the generally low profile given to health education in schools. Similarly on the issue of health education in schools, Merrison and his colleagues 'were not impressed by the account (they) received of existing arrangements... from the main authorities concerned' and recommended that 'they should examine seriously their efforts in this field.'[36]

Nevertheless, despite these shortcomings the Court Committee felt that the existing services provided a suitable foundation on which to build a new child health service. The new service, however, had to be designed in such a way that it would realise certain objectives, which were expressed in the following terms:

We want to see a child and family centred service, in which skilled help is readily available and accessible; which is integrated in as much as it sees the child as a whole, and as a continuously developing person. We want to see a service which ensures that these paediatric skills and knowledge are applied in the care of every child whatever his age or disability, and wherever he lives, and we want a service which is increasingly oriented to prevention.[37]

Thus, the Court Committee recommended changing the existing structural arrangements for the child health services to provide 'an integrated two-tier child health service based on comprehensive primary care linked with supporting consultant and hospital care'[38] and creating a number of new specialisms and associated groups of specialists, in various spheres of child health, namely general practitioner paediatricians, child health visitors, consultant community paediatricians and child health nurses.

Alongside these central recommendations were a large number of detailed proposals covering every aspect of child health. Because the report was so detailed and its recommendations so far reaching and, in certain respects, controversial, it took the Labour government well over 12 months to determine its position on the contents of the report and its response. Eventually, it was decided that the Secretary of State for Social Services, David Ennals, should use the opportunity provided by his invitation to give the 1978 Eleanor Rathbone Memorial Lecture to make public the government's reaction to the Court Report. Immediately following the lecture the DHSS issued a circular, which formally advised health authorities of the Labour government's conclusions on the recommendations of Court and his colleagues and requested them to review their services in the light of its decisions.

Both the Secretary of State's speech and the circular made it clear that he and his colleagues accepted the underlying philosophy of Court and that AHAs should use the statement of objectives in the report 'as a starting point for future plans for health services for children'.[39] The key factors which AHAs were required to take into account in their planning were:

The changing pattern of child health with chronic illness, handicap and psychiatric disorders assuming greater significance; the extent to which ill health among children (was) preventable, and the significance of social and geographical factors in determining survival and healthy development.[40]

Particular attention was also drawn to the fact that there had been no narrowing of social class differences in significant health indicators, such as peri-natal and infant mortality rates; dental caries were still widespread and accidents were the major cause of death in children over one year of age.

In addition, AHAs were to give due consideration to:

- the importance of the family dimension in all child health care and the need to develop a closer partnership between parents and professional staff;

- the inter-relationship between the health, education and social needs of children and their families;

- the need for integration within the child health service, in particular of preventive and therapeutic care and of hospital and community services; and

- the need to ensure in a time of financial constraint, that resources were deployed in a way that would secure value for money.[41]

More specifically it was the Labour government's intention that:

- specialist paediatric services should be increasingly extended into the community (possibly through the appointment of consultant community paediatricians);

- the number of health visitors should be increased and work with children and families, 'particularly those in the lower socio-economic groups', should be their top priority (see above);
- in future, all GPs should have adequate training in child health and play an increasing role in preventive work, especially in respect of pre-school children;
- the role of clinical medical officers should be reviewed;
- every effort should be made to tackle the long standing problem of the very low take-up of ante-natal and child health services by those most in need of them;
- in every district there should be a multidisciplinary handicap team consisting of representatives from the health, education and social services and having close links with voluntary organisations and parents' groups, to plan and monitor the delivery of services for handicapped children in a more integrated manner than had been the case in the past;
- further progress should be made towards the integration of child guidance work with the hospital based psychiatric services for children and adolescents; and
- the professional training of doctors, nurses and other health care providers, who worked with children should be strengthened in order to secure a uniformly high standard of service.

It was indicated that, following consultations with interested parties, a document on good practice in prevention in child health care would be made available.

Three months after issuing its circular on the Court Report, the DHSS took another initiative in the field of child health. In collaboration with the Child Poverty Action Group, it organised a conference of experts to consider ways and means by which the consumer in the ante-natal and child health services could be reached more effectively. The most significant outcome of the conference was the publication of a list of practical ideas and suggestions, from the participants, for making these services more accessible and the service providers more proactive in their approach. Amongst these ideas and suggestions were a number relating to:

- the siting of clinics, transport arrangements, timing of clinics, appointments and waiting time and facilities at clinics (e.g. 'mobile clinics could be useful in the country and also in some inner-city areas'; 'appointment times should be carefully spaced to avoid long waits');
- the manner in which clinic staff related to patients (e.g. 'staff should be sensitive to patients' feelings and treat them as intelligent equals');
- the special needs of ethnic minorities (e.g. 'literature must be provided in various languages');
- the role of health visitors (e.g. 'an informal approach is invaluable');

- the role of midwives (e.g. 'midwives could be used more extensively to make contact with vulnerable mothers and possibly be present at the first ante-natal clinic visit'); and

- communication and liaison between GPs, midwives and health visitors; the hospital and community and health and other services (e.g. 'all primary health care teams should have a social worker attached').[42]

However, despite the Labour government's commitment to raising the standards of, and increasing access to, the child health services and improving the training given to service providers and support from the Merrison Commission for the Court Committee's general approach,[43] neither felt able to support the Court Committee's recommendations in respect of the creation of new specialties in the field of child health. This was due, in part, to opposition from vested interests and, in part, to 'a fear that the creation of these special groups would integrate the services for children at too high a price in disintegrating the mainstream ... services',[44] especially at the primary care level where it was felt primacy should be given to the family as a whole. Thus, as Ham points out, public policies designed to meet the health care needs of children have tended to concentrate 'on extending existing services rather than developing new ones'.[45] Even prior to the publication of the Court Report, the DHSS had recommended, in the 1976 *Priorities* document, an expansion of the health visiting service and the consolidation of the school health service, with particular attention being given to the encouragement of 'closer and more continuous links between health service staff and teachers'.[46] Similarly, annual planning guidelines published in the late 1970s and documents, such as *Care in Action*, continued to stress the need for priority to be given to the further development of existing services for children. In the event the Conservative government (which came into office in 1979) decided not to publish guidance on good practice, as its predecessor had intended (see above). Nevertheless, following consultations with health authorities and interested professional organisations, in 1980 the DHSS issued a paper entitled *Prevention in the Child Health Services*. This outlined the main objectives and content of a preventive approach to child health care in the light of the government's decisions on the Court Report and suggested a basic programme of child health surveillance, covering such topics as the phasing of screening tests, vaccination and immunisation and health education and preparation for parenthood.[47]

Despite the favourable response to many of the recommendations of the Court Report, the good intentions of policy-makers at both local and national level and the devotion of more resources to child health, it is debateable how much progress was actually made in this field between 1977 and 1986.

First, although infant mortality rates continued to fall during the second half of the 1970s, following an intensive investigation into peri-natal and neo-natal mortality the Social Services Committee (see Chapter 8) published a highly critical report on the subject in 1980. This drew attention to the potential for improving the quality of care given to mothers and their children just prior to and just after confinement and the need for more resources to be made available for this purpose. Not surprisingly, the report was not favourably received by the Thatcher government.

Second, as the data in Table 7.5 indicate, the various initiatives taken by health authorities in the late 1970s to improve clinic attendance rates, such as making clinics more accessible, employing more health visitors to follow up non-attenders and taking clinic services to vulnerable groups, were only marginally successful.

TABLE 7.5 *Child Health Clinics 1974 to 1986*[a]

Year	Premises[b] No	Sessions[c] '000s	Total Attendances[d] '000s	Year of Birth %	1 Year Old %	2-5 Year Olds %
1974	6038	329.5	1669.3	97.4	77.6	20.2
1975	6159	331.8	1506.9	88.0	73.8	20.3
1976	6243	339.4	1500.8	90.1	77.0	21.1
1977	6255	338.9	1472.1	90.5	78.3	22.2
1978	6188	344.2	1470.3	83.6	80.7	23.1
1979	6244	350.1	1476.5	87.5	82.6	23.9
1980	6427	359.3	1533.6	89.1	81.1	25.0
1981	6500	360.4	1595.4	86.2	82.5	26.7
1982	6574	365.0	1724.7	86.5	81.8	27.4
1983	6650	366.4	1659.6	84.1	79.2	26.2
1984	6672	368.2	1697.7	82.9	79.6	26.0
1985	6584	367.5	1616.7	82.2	78.9	25.3
1986	6768	377.3	1602.7	81.4	77.0	25.1

Notes

a.   The figures in this table are not directly comparable with those in Table 4.3 since they relate only to England (not England and Wales).

b.   Premises include health centres (9.2% in 1974 and 16.3% in 1986); maternity and child welfare clinics, both purpose built and adapted (30.9% in 1974 and 24.0% in 1986); GP surgeries (9.3% in 1974 and 22.9% in 1986) and other premises occupied on a sessional basis, such as church halls and village halls (50.6% in 1974 and 36.8% in 1986).

c.   Conducted by either clinical medical officers (51.7% in 1974 and 53.4% in 1986); or GPs employed on a sessional basis (19.9% in 1974 and 10.2% in 1986); or hospital doctors (0.9% in 1974 and 0.7% in 1986) or health visitors on their own (27.4% in 1974 and 35.7% in 1986).

d.   0 to 5 year olds, first visits during calendar year (irrespective of whether child had attended in previous years).

Source: DHSS Statistics and Research Division.

Furthermore, since 1982, the situation has deteriorated with attendance rates falling across all the age groups.

Third, despite the expectations raised by the 1974 reorganisation and the Court Report, there were relatively few significant developments in the **school health service**. Staffing continued to be a problem (see Table 7.6), especially with regard to the recruitment of medical officers.

TABLE 7.6 *School Health Service : Staffing Levels 1974 to 1986*

			←	Nursing Staff		→
Year	Medical[a] Officers WTE	Senior Nursing Officers WTE	Health Visitors WTE	Registered Nurses WTE	Enrolled Nurses WTE	Miscellaneous WTE
1974	791	-	1993[b]	1837	172	231
1975	868	-	1050	1850	205	181
1976	923	103	968	1896	228	219
1977	923	101	876	1968	262	188
1978	938	98	866	2036	234	167
1979	929	112	898	2110	245	204
1980[c]	943	34	71	2190	225	170
1981	964	27	127	2404	205	228
1982	949	27	150	2434	225	272
1983	959	20	157	2445	218	233
1984	917	35	148	2443	219	251
1985	944	38	137	2493	189	248
1986	905	33	77	2482	182	215

Notes

a.   Excludes doctors in community medicine other than senior medical officers (community medicine) and staff holding occasional sessional appointments only.

b.   This figure contains duplication.

c.   Since 1980, owing to changes in the methods used to collect data on nursing and midwifery staffing levels, it has not been possible to apportion the total WTE of nursing staff working in both the school health and non-school health community services. Consequently, the figures for the years prior to 1980 are not comparable with those for later years.

Source: DHSS, *Health and Personal Social Services Statistics for England,* various editions.

Moreover, although there was a fairly large increase in the number of school nurses, to some extent this was offset by the sizeable reduction in the contribution made by health visitors to the school nursing service. The withdrawal of health visitors from school nursing was due partly to the fact that the regulations governing the qualifications of school nursing staff (see Chapter 4) lapsed in 1974 and partly to the growing demands being placed on health visiting staff from other sources (see above).

These developments resulted in increasing attention being given to the preparation and training of those school nurses who did not possess a health visiting qualification. Many in the nursing profession felt that the existing arrangements were inadequate and called for a more rigorous approach to the preparation and training of those nurses who wished to work in the school health service. For example, in a report on the future of the school nursing service (1982), the Society of Area Nurses (Child Health) recommended that 'the Council for Education and Training of Health Visitors approved school nurse training (which had been introduced in 1977) should become mandatory for school nurses other than health visitors' and that 'the title 'school nurse' should apply by statute to health visitors or nurses with Council ... approved school nurses training only.'[48] Furthermore, school nurses should receive regular in-course training. Although these recommendations were not implemented they did symbolise the nursing profession's desire to improve the quality of school nursing and enhance the status of school nurses. They also reflected the increasingly dominant role which nurses were coming to play within the school health service. According to Tyrell, by the early 1980s the school nurse had become 'the key person providing health (care) in schools ensuring the health of all children, helping them understand how to maintain a positive state of health, and communicating with parents and teachers' and that her responsibility towards children, especially those who confided in her, overrode her responsibility to the school doctor.[49]

Between 1974 and 1986 the principal functions of school nurses and doctors continued to be, in the words of the 1976 *Priorities* document, the provision of 'health surveillance for all children throughout the(ir) school years'; the promotion of greater 'awareness among teachers and parents of the effect that medical, surgical and neurodevelopmental disorders of childhood (might) have on a child's ability to learn' and health education. However, in line with central government policy, there was a shift in emphasis away from routine medical examination of children in particular age groups (see Table 7.7) to the fostering of closer and more continuous links between school health staff and teachers. It was anticipated that this would lead 'to better and more economical use of staff.'[50]

TABLE 7.7 *School Health Service : Clients and Service Levels 1974 to 1986*[a]

Year	School Popula- tion[b] '000s	Routine Inspections[c] '000s	%	Special Inspections & Re-inspec- tions[d] '000s	Pupils seen by nurses '000s	% Referred	Vermin Infestation Inspections '000s	No Infested '000s
1974	8750	1391	16.2	n.a.	n.a.	n.a.	n.a.	n.a.
1975	8638	1399	16.2	n.a.	n.a.	n.a.	n.a.	n.a.
1976	8714	1405	16.1	851	n.a.	n.a.	12392	172
1977	8740	1319	15.1	788	n.a.	n.a.	13964	154
1978	8666	1247	14.4	789	n.a.	n.a.	13905	138
1979	8562	1168	13.6	752	4027	4.9	14500	161
1980	8397	1125	13.4	727	4533	5.4	14573	180
1981	8185	1077	13.2	697	4579	5.5	14223	189
1982	7973	1010	12.7	660	4621	5.6	12795	170
1983	7752	962	12.4	624	4492	5.2	11682	173
1984	7574	917	12.1	589	4450	5.6	9402	132
1985	7433	868	11.7	579	4510	5.6	7288	106
1986	7312	847	11.6	564	4426	5.8	6090	95

Key

n.a. = data not available.

Notes

a. The figures in this table are not comparable with those in Table 4.11 because the method and coverage adopted by the DES, which was responsible for collecting school health service statistics up to the 1974 reorganisation of the NHS, was different from that adopted by the DHSS, which has been collecting the statistics since 1974. In addition, they relate only to England (not England and Wales).

b. Maintained nursery, primary, secondary and special schools.

c. Full medical examination.

d. A special inspection is one carried out at the special request of a parent, doctor, nurse, teacher or other person. A re-inspection is a follow-up to a routine medical inspection or special inspection.

Source: DHSS, *Health and Personal Social Services Statistics for England,* various editions; Central Statistical Office, *Annual Abstract of Statistics,* various editions, and Department of Education and Science, *Statistics of Education,* Volume 1 Schools, various editions, supplemented with data supplied directly by the DHSS Statistics and Research Division.

Interestingly, however, the number of premises used for most categories of school health service clinic continued to grow during the 1970s (see Table 7.8).

TABLE 7.8 *School Health Clinics 1976 and 1979*

Examination and/or Treatment	Number of Premises Available as at: 31st December 1976	31st December 1979
Minor ailment	1038	1394
Asthma	122	114
Audiology	430	482
Audiometry	988	1114
Chiropody	531	563
Ear, nose and throat	223	217
Enuretic	431	508
Obesity	293	296
Ophthalmic	762	705
Orthoptic	187	231
Orthopaedic	193	170
Paediatric	285	263
Physiotherapy and remedial exercises	511	797
Speech therapy	1802	2146
School medical officer's special examination	1470	1464
Other	516	527

Note

Equivalent data for the years after 1979 are not available.

Source: DHSS Form 20M Part A.

Last, very little progress was made in bringing about the integration of the pre-school child and school health services. Although, the Conservative government elected in 1979 was as keen as its predecessor to achieve this objective, it was made clear in *Care in Action* that this could be done only when 'resources permitted' but the necessary resources were not to be forthcoming.

Nevertheless, some progress was made in respect of certain aspects of the child health service between the publication of the Court Report and 1986. The two most important developments were those relating to the assessment of children with **special educational needs** and to the **vaccination and immunisation** programmes for children.

Under the provisions of the Education Act 1981, which came into force in 1983, local education authorities are required to identify and assess individually every child aged two or more, who has or is likely to have **special educational needs** and not simply categorise him/her by type of disability (i.e. the system which was in operation until 1983). This change of approach had been prompted by the recommendations of the Warnock Committee (1978), the most far reaching of which were the dropping of the distinction between special and remedial education; the abolition of the statutory categorisation of handicapped pupils and the introduction of a new system for assessing children in need of special educational provision.[51]

Thus, the main focus is now on the child as a whole, rather than just his/her disability, and in assessing needs account is taken not only of the nature and severity of the disability but also of his/her personal resources and attributes and the help given at home and at school. In the words of the relevant circular 'a child's special educational needs are ... related to his abilities as well as his disabilities, and to the nature of his interaction with his environment.'[52]

A key element of the assessment procedure is the written statement of special educational need, which local education authorities are required to prepare in respect of every child for whom special educational provision is (or is likely to be) required. In preparing this statement local education authorities must seek professional advice from a number of different sources. These include health authorities and their medical, nursing and paramedical staff, who have a duty to advise local education authorities, in writing, of factors which they think might result in a child experiencing difficulties with learning. Health authority staff must also discuss the health aspects of any statement of special educational needs with the child's parents, and must inform the parents of any voluntary organisations which might be able to provide them with help.

From the mid-1970s there were steady, if in many cases unspectacular, increases in the take-up rates for the **vaccination and immunisation** programmes for children, which had evolved during the tripartite era. Details of these programmes are provided in Table 7.9.

TABLE 7.9 *Vaccination and Immunisation Programmes for Children 1974 to 1986: Recommendations*[a]

Age	Vaccine	Timing	Comments
During first year of life.	*Diphtheria *Tetanus *Pertussis (whooping cough) *Poliomyelitis	1st dose,(3 months of age)[b] 2nd dose, preferably after an interval of 6-8 weeks (i.e. 4.5 to 5 months of age).3rd dose, preferably after an interval of 4-6 months (i.e. 8.5 to 11 months of age).	Parents could opt for Diphtheria; Tetanus; and Pertussis in a single injection or for any combination (e.g. Diphtheria and Tetanus). Poliomyelitis was an oral vaccine.
During second year of life.	Measles	After an interval of not less than 3 weeks following another live vaccine.	Available up to puberty.
At school entry or entry to nursery school.	*Diphtheria *Tetanus *Pertussis *Poliomyelitis	Preferably after an interval of at least 3 years following completion of basic course.	Reinforcing or 'booster' doses of triple vaccine or any combination and oral polio vaccine.
Between 11 and 13 years of age.	BCG (tuberculosis)	Interval of least 3 weeks between BCG and rubella vaccination.	For tuberculin negative children[c] (i.e. where skin test is negative).
Between 11 and 13 years of age. Girls only.	Rubella (German measles)	Interval of at least 3 weeks between BCG and rubella vaccination.	
On leaving school or before employment or entering further education).	*Tetanus *Poliomyelitis		

Notes

a.   From Joint Committee on Vaccination and Immunisation and endorsed by the Standing Medical Advisory Committee of the Central Health Services Council and the Chief Medical and Chief Nursing Officers at the DHSS.

b.   Prior to 1978 the favoured age for the first injection was 6 months.

c.   Given at birth to children from backgrounds with a high risk of contracting tuberculosis.

Source: Standing Medical Advisory Committee's booklet, *Immunisation Procedures,* issued with Chief Medical Officer's letter ML 3/72, and *Revised Schedule of Vaccination and Immunisation,* issued with Chief Medical Officer's letter CMO(78)15 and Chief Nursing Officer's letter CNO(78)12.

As noted in Chapter 4, responsibility for the administration of these programmes was transferred from local health authorities to AHAs on 1st April 1974. In exercising this responsibility AHAs were required to:

• make arrangements for the routine vaccination and immunisation of children;

• employ suitably qualified staff to perform the injections and provide accommodation in which vaccinations and immunisations could be carried out;

• ensure that GPs were able to participate in these programmes, if they wished to do so;

• obtain supplies of certain vaccines from the DHSS or the Public Health Laboratory Service or commercial sources and issue to GPs on request;

• provide education and publicity in this field for parents; and

• maintain records of vaccinations and make returns of the number of vaccinations performed on children under 16, which was particularly onerous because of the participation of GPs.

Implicit in these duties was the assumption that AHAs would seek to maximise take-up rates for vaccination and immunisation in their area. However, as the information in Table 7.10 shows, following the reorganisation of the NHS there was, in fact, a significant drop in take-up rates across all the programmes in the mid-1970s.

TABLE 7.10 *Vaccination and Immunisation Programmes for Children: Take-Up Rates 1974 to 1986*

Year	Diphtheria		Whooping Cough		Poliomyelitis		Tetanus	
	'000s[a]	%[b]	'000s[a]	%[b]	'000s[a]	%[b]	'000s[a]	%[b]
1974	521.4	80	430.2	77	528.5	79	549.8	80
1975	480.5	74	249.6	60	485.0	74	500.4	74
1976	487.8	75	240.6	38	495.6	75	510.2	75
1977	490.9	78	191.9	40	515.6	78	513.1	78
1978	506.0	78	199.4	31	518.8	78	524.4	78
1979	528.6	80	250.3	35	533.6	80	543.7	80
1980	545.9	81	285.6	41	549.7	81	560.2	81
1981	552.2	83	320.5	46	554.5	82	564.4	83
1982	558.1	84	384.8	53	562.8	84	572.7	84
1983	528.5	84	406.8	59	531.5	84	538.3	84
1984	532.1	84	391.7	65	534.0	84	540.2	84
1985	544.4	85	414.2	65	548.9	85	551.6	85
1986	563.6	85	475.9	67	569.1	85	573.1	85

Year	Measles		Tuberculosis[d]		Rubella	
			Skin Test	Vaccinated		
	'000s[c]	%	000s'	'000s	'000s[e]	%[f]
1974	346.6	53	554.4	478.4	237.3	n.a.
1975	308.8	47	601.4	519.1	246.8	n.a.
1976	323.7	47	649.3	564.4	278.1	68
1977	304.9	50	678.4	590.1	280.0	69
1978	302.1	48	660.3	576.6	294.9	74
1979	331.7	51	638.9	563.9	341.0	78
1980	351.6	53	694.8	617.9	319.5	84
1981	368.5	55	652.6	575.1	312.8	84
1982	390.7	58	627.7	547.1	324.4	83
1983	392.9	60	624.0	539.8	314.7	84
1984	435.6	63	591.9	507.9	312.3	86
1985	473.8	68	607.6	518.7	269.2	86
1986	502.9	71	573.9	486.7	269.6	87

Notes

a. Number of children under age 16 completing primary course.

b. Acceptance rate 2 years after end of year of birth (e.g. the 1979 figure represents the percentage of children born in 1977, who had been vaccinated by the end of 1979).

c Number aged under 16 who had been vaccinated.

d. Student scheme (from 1981 only students up to age 16 are included).

e.   Number of schoolgirls vaccinated.

f.   Acceptance rate, schoolgirls at age 13 (1976 and 1977) and 14 (1978 to 1986).

Source: DHSS, *Health and Personal Social Services Statistics for England*, various editions, supplemented with data directly supplied by the DHSS Statistics and Research Division.

This was due, in part, to the disruption arising from the transfer of responsibility for their administration from the local health authorities to the AHAs and the practical problems faced by AHAs in seeking to adhere to the DHSS's request that there should be 'no hiatus in the provision of vaccination and immunisation services in the course of reorganisation'.[53] Another factor, however, was the adverse publicity which was given during the first half of the 1970s to the possible link between whooping cough vaccine and brain damage. This caused the dramatic decline in the take-up rates for whooping cough vaccination, which, in turn, had a 'knock on' effect in respect of other vaccines. Inevitably, one unfortunate consequence of the low take-up rates for whooping cough vaccination were significant increases in the number of reported cases of the disease in 1978 and 1982 (see Figure 7.6).

Although the members of the Court Committee had relatively little to say about vaccination and immunisation, they were anxious to offset what they described as 'a disproportionate emotional reaction to the unfortunate, but rare, side-effects (of vaccination) in a tiny minority of children'[54] and to secure a reduction in the variations in take-up rates between different parts of the country and different socio-economic groups. They also recommended the adoption by AHAs of 'computer linked schemes for immunisation appointments and records, as a means of improving the level of immunisation among children'.[55] In fact, by the mid-1970s the DHSS had already developed a standard computer based immunisation system and following successful trials in 10 areas, the system was made available, free of charge, to all AHAs in May 1977.[56] During the early 1980s this system was modernised and extended to incorporate pre-school child health and school health modules.

Whilst developments of this kind did not automatically increase take-up rates they did help to increase the efficiency of the administrative procedures that were needed to support the delivery of the vaccination and immunisation programmes. Because parents had a choice of whether or not to have their child vaccinated and, if they decided in favour of vaccination, a choice of whether to have it carried out by a GP or health authority doctor, these procedures were inevitably more complicated than might otherwise have been the case. Furthermore, these elements of choice made it far more difficult for health authorities to maximise take-up rates. The DHSS's concern over take-up rates was reflected in the special campaigns which it launched in the 1980s in respect of rubella and measles and in its acceptance, in 1985, of a recommendation from the Joint Committee on Vaccination and Immunisation that 'each health authority should designate a particular person (or persons) to take on special responsibility for implementing improvements to immunisation programmes at local level.'[57]

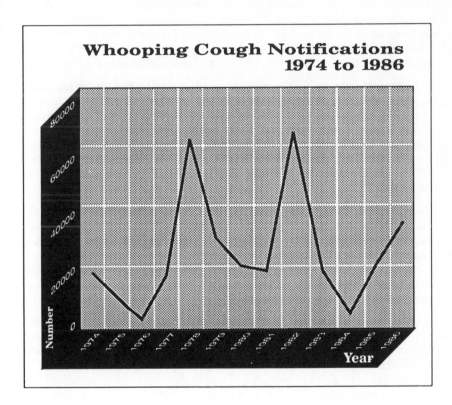

Figure 7.6

Source: DHSS, *Health and Personal Social Services Statistics for England,* various editions

Health Education

As the white paper *Prevention and Health* (1977) indicates, in 1974 AHAs inherited from local health authorities 'a patchwork of health education services, some well organised and equipped and others virtually non-existent'. Furthermore, 'health education staff, where they were in post, had been appointed from a wide variety of disciplines and it was not until NHS reorganisation that Health Education Officers were accorded a recognised status in their own right'.[58]

The architects of the 1974 reorganisation hoped that by enhancing the status of those engaged on health education work and by removing the organisational separation of health education from HSs and FPSs there would be many more opportunities for the development of preventive health care activities by the newly appointed area medical officers. However, although some progress was made in this respect all the evidence suggests that between 1974 and 1986 developments in the field of health education were somewhat patchy and that health education retained some of the characteristics which it had exhibited during the tripartite era.

For example, the 1976 *Priorities* document drew attention to the fact that 'in some areas existing health education work was very limited' and emphasised the need for the authorities concerned to take appropriate action.[59] Similarly, the Merrison Report pointed out that 'many health authorities (had) been slow to appoint area health education officers' and that by the late 1970s six areas in England had still not appointed any health education officers. According to the report the main reason for this lack of progress had 'been a shortage of able qualified staff'.[60]

Nevertheless, during this period the need for a more positive approach to health education work was recognised increasingly by the more enlightened AHAs and attempts were made to exploit some of the opportunities arising from the fact that health education departments were now closer, in an organisational sense, to hospital staff and family practitioners. Some AHAs also responded positively to the Merrison Commission's recommendation that 'health education should be emphasised in (their) forward planning.'[61]

Furthermore, at national level various initiatives were taken to give health education and preventive health care a higher profile. Firstly, in 1976 the DHSS published a booklet entitled *Prevention and Health: Everybody's Business*,[62] which was designed 'to promote discussion in the health, education and social services and encourage authorities to give greater emphasis to preventive activities both in planning and in the allocation of resources' and, as its title suggests, 'to bring home to everyone how much they (could) do to improve their own health and that of their family'.[63] Thus, its major purpose was not to recommend specific programmes of activity, but to stimulate greater public awareness of the contributions which preventive measures could make to tackling health problems and to indicate 'where and how, within existing resource constraints',[64] recent developments in the sphere of health education and related activities could be extended by individuals, voluntary organisations and public sector agencies at local and national level. The publication of this booklet was followed up with a number of others dealing with specific aspects of health education, such as diet, and the issue of a circular drawing attention, for the first time, to the need for health authorities to have an explicit policy on cigarette smoking in NHS premises.[65]

A second initiative came from the Expenditure Committee of the House of Commons. Between 1975 and 1977 its Social Services and Employment Sub committees jointly carried out a wide ranging investigation into many different aspects of health education and in the process took evidence from a wide variety of sources. This evidence, together with the Expenditure Committee's recommendations, was published in the 1977 report on preventive medicine (see above). Amongst other things, it was recommended that AHAs should make public the proportion of their budgets which they were prepared to devote to preventive services; the government should give increasing financial support to the Health Education Council; health education should begin as early in life as possible and teaching at home should be supplemented by more and better teaching at school and supported by more effective community services; and vigorous action should be taken to deal with health risks such as smoking, poor diet, alcohol abuse and lack of exercise and to improve dental health, family planning services and screening facilities. In the report attention was also drawn to the fact that since decisions affecting health (e.g. on such matters as transport planning; food pricing; housing and fluoridation of the water supply) were taken in departments other than the DHSS more effective co-ordination was required.[66]

The Labour government's response to the report of the Expenditure Committee was the white paper, *Prevention and Health*, referred to earlier. Dealing with each of the Expenditure Committee's recommendations in turn the government indicated that it accepted most of them either in whole or in part. It also emphasised the point that members of the public would benefit only if they were prepared to take appropriate action themselves and thereby contribute to the cause of prevention along with health care professionals.

Thirdly, between 1974 and 1986 the Labour and Conservative governments took steps to expand the work of the Health Education Council. For a number of years it was provided with resources, over and above its normal budget (e.g. an extra £1m in 1977/78 and 1978/79) to support the expansion of its training and campaigning activities. These included the provision of additional training courses to help deal with the shortage of qualified health education officers and campaigns,for many of which the Health Education Council made greater use of TV than had been the case in the past. Whilst welcoming developments of this kind, since they helped to counteract, at least marginally, the adverse consequences of commercial advertising which was promoting the excessive use of alcohol, tobacco and sweets, the Merrison Commission felt that the high cost of using TV should be reflected in the funding levels of the Health Education Council and recommended an increase for this purpose.[67]

Fourthly, a whole chapter of *Care in Action* was devoted to prevention and the need for every health authority to develop 'a local strategy of health promotion and preventive medicine'[68] covering such matters as smoking in public places; ante-natal and post-natal care; health surveillance of children; vaccination and immunisation; measures to reduce the incidence of heart disease and strokes; health education in schools; accidents on the road and in the home; fluoridation and the harmonisation of efforts by public, voluntary, community and commercial organisations 'to ensure that the community has a positive approach to health promotion and preventive medicine'.[69]

Lastly, during the first half of the 1980s the DHSS took various steps to deal with specific problems. These included:

- the provision of pump priming funds for experimental local services aimed at meeting the needs of problem drinkers;

- assisting with the establishment of a new voluntary organisation called Alcohol Concern;

- requesting the British Nutrition Foundation and the Health Education Council to produce practical dietary advice based on a report on diet and heart disease from a Panel of the Chief Medical Officer's Committee on Medical Aspects of Food Policy (1984); and

- funding the appointment of new member of staff at the National Children's Bureau to collate and disseminate good practice in dealing with the problem of solvent abuse.[70]

However, as the 1980s progressed all of these initiatives were overshadowed by the health education issues generated by the problem of AIDS.

Chiropody

The expansion of the chiropody service, both in terms of staffing levels and number of clients, which had taken place during the 1960s and 1970s, continued after 1974. As the data in Table 7.11 indicate, the numbers of staff and persons treated and the amount of treatment given all increased significantly between 1974 and 1986. However, due to the serious shortage of registered chiropodists (see Chapter 5), the demand for chiropody far outstripped supply during this period, with the result that most AHAs had to ration their service. This meant giving priority to those groups who had been entitled to the service before the reorganisation, namely the elderly, the handicapped, expectant mothers, school children and some categories of hospital patient. Of these groups the elderly were, and remained, by far the largest.

TABLE 7.11 *Chiropody Service : Clients and Treatment 1974 to 1986*[a]

	← Persons Treated →				←	Treatment				→
	Staff[b,c,d]		of whom 65+[e]		Rate per 1000				Location		
Year	Total WTE	Total '000s	'000s	%	pop	Total '000s	Clinics '000s	%	Domiciliary '000s	%	Other[f] '000s	%
1974	1207	1279	1235	96.6	191	4589	2314	50.4	1285	28.0	990	21.6
1975	1254	1182	1086	91.9	165	5113	2521	49.3	1325	25.9	1267	24.8
1976	1677	1248	1148	92.0	172	5352	2677	50.0	1345	25.1	1330	24.9
1977	1972	1324	1215	91.8	180	5434	2826	52.0	1307	24.1	1301	23.9
1978	1913	1393	1274	91.5	187	5398	2930	54.3	1267	23.5	1201	22.2
1979	1933	1426	1299	91.1	188	5311	2967	55.9	1210	22.8	1134	21.3
1980	2068	1469	1331	90.6	190	5525	3236	58.6	1176	21.3	1113	20.1
1981	2100	1522	1370	90.0	192	5646	3395	60.1	1167	20.7	1084	19.2
1982	2190	1592	1426	89.6	201	5819	3550	61.0	1194	20.5	1075	18.5
1983	2392	1631	1470	90.1	208	5903	3744	63.4	1152	19.5	1007	17.1
1984	2293	1708	1535	89.9	218	6109	3995	65.4	1159	19.0	955	15.6
1985	2366	1772	1594	89.9	222	6167	4142	67.2	1129	18.3	896	14.5
1986	2445	1835	1644	89.6	225	6399	4379	68.4	1103	17.2	917	14.3

Notes

a. The figures in this table are not directly comparable with those in Table 4.9 since they relate only to England (not England and Wales).

b. As at 30th September.

c. Employed by AHAs/DHAs (employees of voluntary bodies are excluded).

d. Figures include hospital as well as community chiropodists since it is not possible to distinguish between these two categories. Foot care assistants are not included.

e. The other client groups are: physically handicapped under age 65 (2.7% in 1986); expectant mothers (0.2% in 1986); school children (5.6% in 1986) and miscellaneous (1.9% in 1986).

f. Old peoples' homes (5.9% in 1986); chiropodists' surgeries (2.5% in 1986); school/school clinics (3.1% in 1986) and elsewhere (2.8% in 1986).

Source: DHSS, *Health and Personal Social Services Statistics for England*, various editions, supplemented with data supplied directly by the DHSS Statistics and Research Division.

Nevertheless, despite rationing the service in this way, in most parts of the country it remained 'generally inadequate even for the priority groups'.[71] In an effort to ease the situation the DHSS issued a circular in 1977, which suggested a number of measures that AHAs could take in order to improve their 'chiropody services within existing resource constraints'.[72] These included:

- examining the scope for more economical alternatives to domiciliary visits, which the DHSS felt were an 'unnecessarily high proportion of the total number of treatments' (e.g. transporting patients to chiropodists; using local centres and mobile clinics);

- employing foot care assistants to carry out simple tasks, such as the cutting of toenails, which did not require the application of a fully qualified chiropodist's skills and expertise, thereby enabling chiropodists to devote more of their time to those patients requiring more complex treatment;

- providing chiropodists with adequate support staff to relieve the burden of having to carry out clerical and administrative tasks, such as making appointments and reception duties, as well as perform their professional role; and

- transferring some forms of treatment from private practitioners to salaried staff.

Many AHAs responded positively to these suggestions. As the figures in Table 7.11 show, the percentage of treatment provided on a domiciliary basis fell from 28.0% in 1974 to 17.2% in 1986. In addition, a growing number of AHAs started to employ foot care assistants, which facilitated the introduction of a system of two chair clinics. This involved foot care assistants supporting registered chiropodists by preparing patients for treatment and carrying out a variety of simple tasks under their direction.

Furthermore, AHAs also cut back on the number of treatments paid for on an item of treatment basis (i.e. where the AHA paid a per capita fee to self- employed registered chiropodists for each patient treated). In 1974 nearly 40% of treatment was paid for on this basis, whilst the equivalent figure for 1986 was 6%.

However, as the DHSS planning guidelines for 1979/80 made clear, despite these measures the general situation remained difficult:

> *Demand for chiropodists ... continues to be at a rather higher rate than the overall rate of growth of NHS resources and this will remain true for a number of years if the cumulative shortages of past years are to be corrected. However, as regards chiropody there is unlikely to be an increase in the overall supply of newly qualified practitioners of more than a marginal kind before 1982 because of difficulties in expanding the number of training schools and the intakes of students to existing schools.*[73]

Moreover, as the Merrison Report pointed out, the NHS was 'competing for registered chiropodists with the attractions of independent private practice'.[74]

Family Planning and Cervical Cancer Screening

Unlike most of the other CHSs the foundations of a comprehensive, publically provided family planning service were still being laid when the NHS was reorganised in 1974. Considerable progress had been made between the passing of the

National Health Service (Family Planning Act) in 1967 and the transfer of responsibility for this service from local health authorities to AHAs in 1974. Additionally in March 1974 the newly elected Labour government had announced that from 1st April 1974 there would be no charge for family planning drugs and appliances supplied at NHS clinics. Nevertheless, much still remained to be done.

Following reorganisation the initial priorities for AHAs, and more especially their DMTs, were to:

- secure by September 1976 the transfer to their direct control of those services still being provided on an agency basis by the Family Planning Association and take responsibility for the employment of those Family Planning Association staff who wished to continue with this kind of work;

- extend clinic based services to those areas where family planning was still underdeveloped;

- develop domiciliary services;

- arrange for the training of staff in order to extend and improve the quality of services;

- ensure that services were available to the unmarried as well as the married;

- provide adequate publicity for the services; and

- expand the range and variety of services available to include not only the giving of advice on contraception and the supply of contraceptive substances and appliances, but also pregnancy testing, genetic counselling, psycho-sexual counselling, infertility counselling and vasectomies.

Most AHAs and their DMTs responded positively to the challenge of developing their family planning services. However, as the data in Table 7.12 show, the scale of provision remained relatively static throughout the period 1975-1986 in terms of both clients and attendances. This was very much in line with the assumptions made in the 1976 *Priorities* document.[75]

In considering the data in Table 7.12 it is important to note that during this period AHAs and their DMTs were not alone in providing community based family planning services. From 1st July 1975 any GP, if s/he wished to do so, could enter into a contract to provide contraceptive services. Like the health authority services these were free of charge, regardless of whether there was a medical need to avoid pregnancy. By January 1976 over 90% of GPs had contracted to provide contraceptive services. In addition, some of the voluntary organisations which had pioneered family planning continued to operate independently of the NHS, although a number of these, such as the Brook Advisory Centres, received financial support from health authorities.

Thus, health authorities have been in competition with other suppliers of community based family planning services, especially GPs, since the mid-1970s. In the

1976 *Priorities* document it was pointed out that the rates of growth of the health authority family planning service and the family planning activities of GPs were interdependent. It was therefore hoped that the family planning working groups, which every DMT was required to set up (see Chapter 5), would 'assist in the preparation of integrated plans for developing family planning in each locality'.[76]

TABLE 7.12 *Family Planning Services : Scale of Provision 1974 to 1986*

	←————— AHA/DMT Services —————→					GP Services[a]
	Community Clinics		Domiciliary			
Year	Patients[c] '000s	Attendances	Patients '000s	Visits '000s	Vasectomies[d] '000s	Patients[e] '000s
1974[b]	999.1	2408.8	13.6	50.1	10.9	not app
1975	1423.1	3591.4	20.7	65.6	16.6	1157.3
1976	1457.9	3605.2	19.1	66.8	16.9	1898.3
1977	1537.1	3665.1	18.2	69.2	16.9	2038.0
1978	1521.4	3490.0	16.5	64.6	17.5	1959.0
1979	1494.0	3306.5	16.3	60.9	15.7	1921.8
1980	1492.7	3269.4	17.1	60.0	14.0	2023.9
1981	1473.0	3150.8	15.9	59.4	13.8	2091.5
1982	1460.7	3099.3	16.8	60.3	12.7	2190.6
1983	1468.5	3105.6	16.9	56.9	13.8	2358.2
1984	1509.3	3202.9	14.7	52.2	14.7	2374.4
1985	1479.6	3105.5	14.3	51.6	13.3	2455.8
1986	1432.8	2989.0	13.5	45.4	13.8	2571.0

Notes

a.   From 1st July 1975 (see text).

b.   Period 1st April to 31st December only.

c.   Each patient counted at first visit during period.

d.   Vasectomies performed in community clinics only.

e.   Number of patients at end of year in respect of whom a fee is payable to the GP for the provision of contraceptive services.

Source: DHSS, *Health and Personal Social Services Statistics for England*, various editions, supplemented with data supplied directly by the DHSS Statistics and Research Division.

Another service closely linked with family planning was cervical cancer screening. A national recall system based on the National Health Service Central Register (NHSCR) at Southport had been established in 1971 (see Chapter 4). Under this system the priority groups for testing were women over 35 and those under 35 who had been pregnant on 3 or more occasions. Invitations for testing were issued initially by local health authorities and after 1974 by AHAs, every five years.

These arrangements continued to operate throughout the 1970s, with AHAs taking over responsibility for the issue of invitations from local health authorities in 1974. However, although the number of smears increased throughout the 1970s (see Table 7.13), it became increasingly evident that the system was not very effective, with some studies showing that under 20% of women in the priority groups were actually being tested.

TABLE 7.13 *Cervical Cancer : Examinations 1973 to 1986*

Year	No of Smears Examined[a] '000s	Positive Cases per 1000 Smears
1973	2226	4.3
1974	2352	4.6
1975	2375	4.7
1976[b]	2448	5.2
1977	2424	5.8
1978	2470	6.2
1979	2623	6.3
1980	2789	6.8
1981	2850	7.1
1982	2809	7.5
1983	3046	7.8
1984	3245	8.9
1985	3696	9.2
1986	3709	9.5

Notes

a. Figures for the years 1973 to 1980 inclusive are based on a 20% sample of negative smears taken during January and July.

b. Excludes figures from University of Liverpool.

Source: DHSS, *Health and Personal Social Services Statistics for England*, various editions.

In the early 1980s the system was reviewed by a working party set up by the Committee on Gynaecological Cytology (CGC). It concluded that the centralised recall scheme, which was manually operated, was ineffective and, in resource terms, inefficient. More specifically the scheme was criticised on the grounds that it was 'labour intensive, near its technical limits and isolated from other screening developments'. Furthermore, it did not and could not 'generate useful information about its own effectiveness'.[77] The working party also drew attention to the fact that, although in certain parts of the country there were relatively efficient local recall arrangements which relied on the NHSCR only for information about changes of address, in others there was no form of recall scheme.

The working party acknowledged that there was a great need for a recall scheme and expressed a preference for a fully computerised system operated by the NHSCR, with the staff at Southport not only keeping the records but also sending out the call and recall notifications. The CGC accepted the working party's criticisms of the existing call and recall arrangements and endorsed its preference for a new scheme. Furthermore, it took the view that if it was not possible to computerise the system it should be set up on a manual basis.

In its response to the CGC's recommendations, which were published in the form of a consultation paper in April 1981,[78] the Conservative government made it clear that, whilst acknowledging the weaknesses of the existing scheme, financial constraints and staff cuts at Southport ruled out both the setting up of a computer system solely for cervical cancer and the adoption of a manual system. It was also argued that, for similar reasons, the screening facility at Southport could not continue in its present form. Consequently, 'any recall system in the near future would (have) to take the form either of arrangements made by individual general practitioners for their own patients or local arrangements, by health authorities or FPCs with recourse to the NHSCR only to obtain a new address where a woman (had) moved out of the area in order to identify the new FPC and thus ensure that her general practitioner (was) kept fully informed of progress on smears.'[79]

After a relatively brief period of consultation the DHSS issued a circular in December 1981 in which it spelt out the arrangements for the rundown of the existing recall scheme based on the NHSCR and requested authorities to devise their own local schemes.[80] According to the DHSS comments received during the period of consultation reflected the existing variety of provision and supported the view that the current arrangements were unsatisfactory and urgently needed replacing with a more efficient system. However, there was apparently no consensus regarding the type of scheme which should be adopted. Thus, the DHSS took the view that health authorities should have a great deal of discretion in designing their schemes and confined itself to providing general guidance on what it considered to be the basic components and broad principles of a simple, manually operated, recall system.

The circular outlined these principles in the following terms:

Health Authorities in conjunction with Family Practitioner Committees, and in consultation with others concerned, are asked to institute local arrangements to replace the present recall system, where it relies wholly or partly on the Central Register, and for these arrangements to be ready by 1 April 1983. The aim should be to ensure that all women who have come forward for screening, and who would have been recalled in due course through the Central Register, are recalled for testing at the appropriate time...

The organisation and location of the provision will be a matter for local decision having regard to particular local circumstances. Given the variety of existing provision, and the need to ensure that there is no duplication of effort, authorities will need to work closely with all those likely to be involved in cervical screening. One object should be to ensure that new arrangements do not preclude the option of using any future FPC computer system.

The scale of provision will also be a matter for authorities, but although authorities will need to determine how a basic local service can best be provided within existing staffing and other resources, Ministers feel that complex arrangements are not essential to a satisfactory system and that the emphasis should be on reducing the financial and manpower implications to the lowest practical level.[81]

Despite the fact that by 1981 the need for an effective screening system for cervical cancer had been recognised for over 15 years and a considerable amount of experience had been gained in operating systems for this purpose, the likelihood of these new arrangements working satisfactorily was small. This was because the Conservative government's top priority appeared to be saving resources and many health authorities were, at this time, preoccupied with the restructuring exercise (see Chapter 6).

Inevitably, fewer smears were examined in 1982 than in 1981. Furthermore, although there was an 8.4% increase in the number of smears examined between 1982 and 1983 and a 6.5% increase between 1983 and 1984, there was still a great deal of concern about the efficacy of the arrangements, especially since they appeared to be having very little demonstrable impact on the number of deaths from cervical cancer.

This concern prompted the DHSS in 1984 to ask the CGC to consider all the available evidence on the desirable age and frequency of screening, with a view to providing health authorities with some further guidelines. Having considered the available evidence the CGC reached the conclusion that, since over 94% of deaths from cervical cancer occurred amongst women aged over 35, this was clearly the group at greatest risk and therefore the one on which a screening programme should concentrate. Furthermore, research indicated that the majority of women who developed cervical cancer had never been screened, which suggested that 'the population screening programme (had) failed to reduce mortality not because existing policy (was) wrong but because the policy (had) not been properly implemented'.[82]

In response to the CGC's findings the DHSS issued a further circular on screening for cervical cancer in July 1984. This reaffirmed existing policy with regard to the giving of priority to women aged over 35 and those who had been pregnant on three or more occasions and the delegation of responsibility to health authorities for the setting up and the operation, in collaboration with their FPC(s), of local recall arrangements. It also recommended ways in which the effectiveness of these arrangements could be improved. Suggestions included 'mounting targetted health education campaigns; looking at the delivery of the screening service to ensure that the women at greatest risk were encouraged to use it; using community nurses and Health Visitors to identify women at greatest risk'.[83]

Additionally, the circular stressed the need for health authorities to monitor the effectiveness of their cervical screening programme, in particular its coverage and the outcome of smear tests.The most significant advice, however, related to the screening of younger women (i.e. those under 35) and the need to restrict their access to screening facilities in the interests of using available resources more effectively. During its investigation the CGC had discovered that 55% of smear tests were being carried out on younger women and that the 20-24 age group was the most intensively screened, with some in this group being tested annually, even though it was the over 35s who were at greatest risk from cervical cancer. However, since the number of cervical cancer registrations was, in fact, increasing amongst younger women the CGC did not feel that they should be denied access to screening facilities, rather that there should be some rationalisation of the existing situation. It therefore recommended that all women who were or had been sexually active should be tested when they presented themselves for contraceptive advice or requested a first test and thereafter at five yearly intervals. In accepting this recommendation and commending it to health authorities the DHSS anticipated that it would have the effect of reducing the number of smears taken from younger women thereby releasing resources which could be devoted to the screening of older women.

This circular, however, did not conclude the long running saga of cervical cancer screening. Despite the guidance and exhortations which authorities had received from the centre it appears that, for various reasons, a number did not respond in the manner intended. Therefore,in April 1985, the DHSS felt it necessary to write to newly appointed district general managers with a request that their authorities 'urgently review the organisation and effectiveness of their screening programmes against (an) attached checklist'[84] and provide the department with the results of their review. This showed that, as at June 1985:

- 128 out of 192 DHAs had recall schemes;

- 13 DHAs were operating call as well as recall schemes; and

- 24 DHAs were to introduce call alongside their recall schemes during 1985, and 38 DHAs planned to do so in 1986.[85]

However, half these schemes were still operated on a manual basis and were therefore relatively inefficient. Consequently, in early 1986 the DHSS informed DHAs that computerised call and recall schemes had to be installed not later than March 1988.[86]

Thus, by 1986, a great deal of thought and attention had been given, both nationally and locally, to the resolution of issues arising from cervical cancer screening. Nevertheless, during the mid-1980s a number of incidents indicated that there was still considerable room for improvement in the way that screening arrangements were being operated in various parts of the country.[87]

Moreover, the considerable length of time it had taken to get this far, as well as the many and varied difficulties encountered by local and national policy-makers, had clearly demonstrated the magnitude of the task facing anyone charged with the responsibility for introducing an effective screening programme. Nevertheless, there was growing interest in screening and, during the late 1970s and early 1980s, the need for it was advocated in various reports. For example, in its report on preventive medicine the House of Commons Expenditure Committee recommended the introduction of a national breast screening programme and the Merrison Commission, although opposed to mass screening on the grounds that it was both impracticable and ineffective, recommended 'the expansion of proven screening programmes'[88] such as the screening of 'at risk' pregnant women for foetal abnormalities. A similar position was taken by the members of the Black Working Group on Inequalities in Health. Whilst rejecting most forms of screening because they felt that 'on balance, the cost ... and the possible production of anxiety (could) well outweigh any likely benefits even where there (was) a known higher incidence of disease in lower income groups,'[89] they did support ante-natal and hypertension screening.

One other significant development in the field of family planning and screening during the late 1970s and early 1980s, to which reference was made in the section on health visiting (see above), was the setting up by a number of AHAs of what have become known as 'well- woman' clinics. These are essentially sessions to which women can go for a general check up and for breast and cervical examinations and they have now become a firmly established feature of the CHSs.

Community Dental Service

The community dental service was formed in 1974 by amalgamating the formerly separate local education authority school dental service and the local health authority priority dental service for mothers and young children (see Chapter 5). Thus, the major client groups of this service were school children, pre-school children and expectant and nursing mothers. In addition, after 1978 AHAs had the discretionary power to provide facilities for the dental treatment of handicapped adults, but they could not do so until they had met their primary responsibilities to the other client groups.[90]

However, despite these developments the community dental service was still in many respects the school dental service 'writ large'. As the data in Table 7.14 indicate, between 1974 and 1986 over 95% of those inspected by the service were school children. Furthermore, from the mid-1970s there was a significant improvement in the coverage of the service as far as school children were concerned (i.e. from 54.7% of the school population to just over 70.0%).

TABLE 7.14 *Community Dental Service : Scale of Provision 1974 to 1986*

	←— All Clients —→			←——— of Whom School Children[b]———→				
Year[a]	In-spected '000s	Re-quired Treat-ment '000s	Treated '000s	Inspected '000s	Clients %	SP[c] %	Required Treatment '000s	Treated '000s
1974	4815	2503	1412	4684	97.3	54.7	2427	1325
1975	4847	2480	1395	4725	97.5	55.5	2416	1319
1976	4761	2406	1394	4649	97.6	53.4	2348	1322
1977	4992	2432	1344	4882	97.8	55.9	2375	1280
1978	5262	2432	1329	5152	97.9	59.5	2381	1267
1979	5310	2420	1279	5195	97.8	60.7	2367	1214
1980	5426	2387	1295	5299	97.7	63.1	2333	1224
1981	5387	2247	1273	5257	97.6	64.3	2191	1193
1982	5459	2218	1264	5305	97.2	66.5	2155	1173
1983	5494	2113	1224	5317	96.8	68.6	2045	1123
1984	5512	2032	1226	5312	96.4	70.5	1954	1108
1985	5491	1973	1213	5274	96.0	71.0	1891	1083
1986	5604	1966	1194	5333	95.2	n.a.	1869	1047

Key

e = estimate figure
n.a. = data not available

Notes

a.   1974 to 1985 figures are for calendar years. 1986 figures are for year ended 31st March 1987.

b..   The other client groups were expectant mothers and women who had borne a child within the previous 12 months (0.2% in 1975 and 0.3% in 1985); children under 5 (2.3% in 1975 and 2.8% in 1985) and handicapped adults, who did not become eligible for this service until 1978 (0.9% in 1985).

c.   Percentage of school population.

Source: DHSS, *Health and Personal Social Services Statistics for England*, various editions.

Interestingly, this improvement in service coverage was achieved with only a modest increase in the numbers employed in the service.

TABLE 7.15 *Community Dental Service : Staffing Levels 1974 to 1986*

Year	Total[a] WTE	Dental Officers Adminis- trative WTE	Clinical WTE	Medically Qualified Anaesthetists WTE	Dental Therapists WTE	Dental Hygienists WTE
1974	1569	145	1207	n.a.	202	15
1975	1633	138	1319	15	139	22
1976	1671	128	1300	16	197	30
1977	1724	124	1325	17	227	31
1978	1820	125	1360	20	271	44
1979	1788	120	1358	20	249	41
1980	1749	119	1334	15	242	39
1981	1778	117	1355	15	238	53
1982	1790	114	1365	17	238	56
1983	1780	117	1344	17	246	56
1984	1418[b]	134	1269	15	n.a.	n.a.
1985	1431[b]	143	1273	15	n.a.	n.a.
1986	1404[b]	141	1249	14	n.a.	n.a.

Key

n.a. = data not available

Notes

a.   Figures relate to staff in post at 30th September.

b.   Excluding dental therapists and dental hygienists.

Source: DHSS, *Health and Personal Social Services Statistics for England*, various editions.

As the data in Table 7.15 imply one of the problems facing those with responsibility for running the community dental service was that of recruitment. This was due in part to the fact that the community dental service had to compete for staff with the general dental service and hospital dental service, where the financial rewards were generally greater.

As to what constituted an appropriate staffing level for a community dental service, in a circular issued in 1975 the DHSS laid down staffing maxima for senior dental officers based on the size of the maintained school population.[91] With regard to other staff, however, the DHSS was not prepared to be so prescriptive. Thus, the DHSS planning guidelines for 1979/80 merely stated that:

> *No set norm can be expressed for Dental Officers because of the varying needs in the community, the impact of fluoridation and the amount of service provided by local general (dental) practitioners. As a working guide the target*

should be the level of staffing which enables authorities to discharge their statutory duties to provide an annual inspection for all school children plus any necessary subsequent 'treatment'.[92]

During this period questions were also raised about the necessity for a separate and distinctive community dental service. On this issue Merrison and his colleagues took the view that whilst there should be some rationalisation of dental services, a community dental service was needed since it had a number of distinctive functions to perform, especially as far as children were concerned. These included:

● the annual inspection of all children of school age and where possible pre-school children, and the collection of epidemiological data;

● the encouragement of those needing treatment to attend their family dentist;

● the identification of those who are not getting treatment;

● the capacity to offer a comprehensive service to those children who are not getting treatment in the general dental service; and

● the organisation of dental health education and preventive measures in school and community.[93]

It was felt that the existence of a salaried service alongside the general dental service, provided by independent contractors, offered a more flexible approach towards meeting the complex and varying needs for dental health care than a unitary service. The Royal Commission also recommended an increase in the staffing levels of the community dental service so that it could perform effectively all the functions mentioned above.

During the first half of the 1980s community dental staff were strongly encouraged to give a higher priority to the conduct of local dental health surveys and education programmes. In 1984, following the receipt of recommendations on dental health education from the Dental Strategy Review Group, the DHSS issued a health notice, which stressed the need for action at local level to complement nationally organised initiatives, and announced the setting aside of funds to help health authorities meet the cost of mounting local campaigns and undertaking surveys.[94]

Thus, by 1986 there appeared to be a sufficient number of distinctive roles for the community dental service to perform to ensure its survival, at least in the short-term.

Speech Therapy

Throughout the period 1974 to 1986 the principal function of the speech therapy service remained the treatment of children and adults with speech disorders. In 1976, the last year for which figures showing the split between community and hospital based speech therapists are available, approximately 70% of WTE speech therapists were employed in the community and many of these would have been treating children.

Because it had been investigated by the Quirk Committee in the early 1970s, speech therapy was not closely examined by Court and his colleagues as part of their review of health care services for children (see above). However, they did receive evidence which indicated concern over delays in the implementation of some of the Quirk recommendations. As a result they felt the need to endorse 'the recommendations (of the members of the Quirk Committee) for a large expansion in the number of speech therapists and a substantial force of aides'[95] and to indicate that they shared the concern of those who felt that insufficient priority was being given to their implementation. In fact, as the data in Figure 7.7 show, after 1977 there was a relatively steady increase in the number of WTE speech therapists.

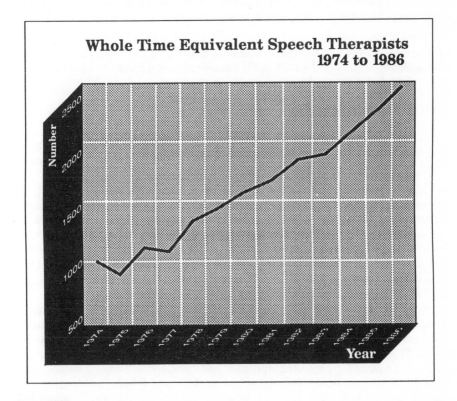

Figure 7.7

Source: DHSS, *Health and Personal Social Services Statistics for England*, various editions.

As well as supporting the call for more speech therapists the members of the Court Committee also stressed the need for closer links between the speech therapy and paediatric services. With the bringing together of responsibility for the formerly separate local health and local education authority speech therapy services in 1974 and the appointment of area speech therapists, the forging of links of this kind was felt to be far more likely. However, whilst advocating links, the Court Committee also drew attention to two potential dangers. One was the fear that, even though the Quirk Committee had attached great importance to the treatment of speech and language disorders in young children, staff might be deployed in such a way that the needs of children did not in fact receive the attention they deserved. The other related to the training of speech therapists. Court and his colleagues took the view that in the planning of the additional training for speech therapists, which had been advocated by the Quirk Committee, those responsible might not give sufficient emphasis to the wide range of communication disorders experienced by children. In the event both these fears proved to be groundless.

Thus, for all the services considered above, the period between the reorganisation of the NHS in 1974 and the implementation of the recommendations of the NHS Management Inquiry in the mid-1980s was one of mixed fortunes. Some advances were made, but many problems and uncertainties remained.

Other Developments

The period was also one in which there was increasing diversification of the CHSs. This trend can be attributed to a number of developments.

First, there was a significant expansion of community based **physiotherapy** services. As Partridge and Warren observe, by the mid-1970s 'a course of treatment in a hospital (was) no longer considered to be the only appropriate physiotherapy.'[96] Furthermore, during the first half of the 1970s a number of physiotherapists had commented on the need to develop physiotherapy services outside hospital in response to the increasing emphasis on care in the community. On the basis of their review of fourteen schemes for the provision of physiotherapy services in non-hospital settings Partridge and Warren reached the conclusion that there was a clear need for an expansion of physiotherapy services in the community. However, they also took the view that services should be developed gradually and 'new services should be monitored and established services reviewed.' Responsibility for the management of community based physiotherapy services was to be exercised by the DMT and district physiotherapist. Significantly, Partridge and Warren also stressed the need for physiotherapists to 'collaborate with doctors, nurses, occupational therapists, health visitors, social workers and others in the care of the patient, and ... with other professions and planners and non professional field workers of various services.'[97] In other words it was important for physiotherapists to be represented on the primary health care team.

Although figures are not available for the period after 1976, between 1974 and 1976 there was a steady increase in the percentage of WTE physiotherapists working in the community (i.e. from 7% in 1974 to 11% in 1976)[98] and all the evidence suggests that this trend continued into the 1980s. Thus, by 1986 it is probable that 40% or more of physiotherapy treatment was being provided in community settings, such as health centres and patients' homes.

Second, similar trends occurred in **occupational therapy**. However, the situation was complicated by the fact that occupational therapists were employed by local personal social services authorities as well as health authorities. The implementation of the Seebohm recommendations (1971) and the provisions of the Chronically Sick and Disabled Persons Act 1970 paved the way for a significant expansion of occupational therapy within the personal social services (see Chapter 3). With the unification of the health services in 1974 the few occupational therapists still employed in local authority health departments were automatically transferred to AHAs, along with the much larger number of occupational therapists previously employed in hospitals. However, occupational therapists working in personal social services departments only transferred to AHAs if 'they were employed wholly or mainly in providing occupational therapy services under medical supervision and treatment for persons who (were) receiving or (had) received medical treatment under the health service or they were working without supervision or being supervised by occupational therapists.'[99] This selective transfer was based on the principle that whilst some occupational therapists were providing help and support to patients under active medical supervision others were dealing primarily with clients needing social care and rehabilitation. Furthermore, there was a desire to ensure that occupational therapists did not become professionally isolated.

Consequently local authorities were able to continue recruiting and employing occupational therapists to meet the needs of client groups, such as the physically disabled, for whom they had a wide range of statutory responsibilities. By definition these occupational therapists were engaged primarily in the provision of community based services, such as 'assessment for aids to daily living, instruction in their use, assessment for home alterations; ... advice to disabled patients and their relatives on simple treatment procedures; ... assessment at day centres as part of a planned programme of activities for physically disabled and mentally ill people and at child assessment centres (and) occupational advice to the home bound'.[100]

In the case of occupational therapists employed by the NHS the policy was initially 'to concentrate scarce staff resources in hospital treatment and assessment facilities and to provide medical rehabilitation on an in- or out-patient basis.'[101] Thus, by 1976 (the last year for which figures are available) only 5% of WTE NHS occupational therapists were working in the community. Nevertheless, between the mid-1970s and mid-1980s, some progress was made by health authorities, in various parts of the country, towards the development of a more community orientated approach to the delivery of the services provided by occupational therapists.

As a result of the increasing emphasis on community care and a growing awareness of the valuable contribution which occupational therapists could make to the rehabilitation of patients in the community, there was considerable pressure on health authorities in the late 1970s and early 1980s to adopt a more outward looking approach to the organisation and provision of their occupational therapy services. Enlightened authorities responded to this pressure by arranging for occupational therapists to work in elderly persons' homes, special schools, day centres for the mentally and physically handicapped and as members of community mental handicap teams. Thus, by the mid-1980s it had become quite common to find NHS occupational therapists practising in a wide variety of community settings.

However, this inevitably raised questions about the nature of the relationship between NHS occupational therapists and those employed by local authorities and their respective roles and responsibilities. As early as December 1974 the DHSS had drawn attention to the overlap between the roles of the two and the fact that 'health service therapists (saw) their responsibility for their patients extending to their resettlement in the community, while local authority therapists (saw) their responsibility for clients continuing when they came under medical care.'[102] At the time health and local authorities were asked to deal with this issue by using the newly created machinery for collaboration to review jointly 'the needs for occupational therapy in their areas and to agree a co-ordinated policy on the employment of occupational therapists.'[103] Whilst this was not an unreasonable request, given the general shortage of occupational therapists and the desire to ensure that any wasteful duplication in the provision of occupational therapy services was minimised, it did reflect a somewhat optimistic view of the potential for cross-authority co-operation.

In the event relatively little progress was made and even after 1977, when joint finance monies became available for this purpose, collaboration between local and health authorities in the planning and delivery of their occupational therapy services often left much to be desired. Thus, in December 1985, 11 years after the original request, the DHSS felt moved to write again to health and local authorities on this subject. The official reason for doing so was 'to inform those who (were) in a position to influence practice of the need to look closely at the deployment of occupational therapists..., and at the extent of co-operation between NHS and personal social services in their use.'[104] Not unreasonably, the comment was made also that a 'failure to develop an overall occupational therapy philosophy and structure across the boundaries' between the NHS and local government in a particular area might well have been due to the inadequacy of the co-operation between the authorities concerned.[105]

By 1985 local authorities were employing about 900 WTE occupational therapists compared with approximately 3600 WTE occupational therapists employed by health authorities. The principal role of local authority occupational therapists was the provision of an aids and adaptation service for physically disabled people, many of whom were elderly. Most of the requests for this service came from health care professionals working in the primary sector or from the clients themselves. In addition, they provided a substantial advisory service to housing departments, especially in relation to major adaptations and the assessment of requests from disabled people for rehousing. Whilst these were important tasks, the DHSS argued that 'large personal case loads ... in the aids and adaptations service ... sometimes (made) the intervention rather superficial' and left occupational therapists with relatively little time to make 'a more strategic contribution' to the care of clients and the planning of services. It was therefore suggested that authorities should give careful consideration to the employment of support staff in areas such as aids and adaptations, so that the fully trained therapists could make a far larger contribution to the assessment, rehabilitation and support of the mentally ill, mentally handicapped and physically disabled, as part of the general move towards care in the community. In other words occupational therapists employed by local authorities should seek to become more like their NHS colleagues by devoting far more attention to the provision of a "remedial' service across the 3 broad areas of physical handicap, mental handicap and mental illness' and far less to aids and adaptations.[106]

The DHSS also put forward various suggestions for securing a more integrated and cohesive occupational therapy service. These were:

- agreement between the two authorities on their specific responsibilities for an overall service;

- closer liaison between OT (i.e. occupational therapy) principal officers in the two services;

- shared funding of posts;

- the provision of services for one authority by the other;

- the development of systems for the joint issue of aids;

- a co-ordinated approach to a broader community role for NHS OTs;

- increased involvement of FPCs and community health councils;

- co-operation between NHS/LA and Voluntary bodies that employ OTs to provide a service in a particular specialist area; and

- joint planning with the voluntary sector to integrate service provision.[107]

Examples of good practice in this field included 'co-operation between authorities in agreeing their occupational therapy needs and priorities' and the development of flexible management structures to facilitate the 'allocation of resources in relation to client needs', irrespective of the boundary between local government and the NHS. For the future, it was hoped that authorities would be able to provide further examples of good practice 'in the effective and efficient use' of occupational therapy staff, which could be used to promote similar developments elsewhere.[108]

Third, between 1974 and 1984, some health authorities and local personal social services authorities sought to come to terms with the fact that since the early 1970s both had been responsible for supplying **home nursing aids** to sick and disabled people. Indeed, under the provisions of the Chronically Sick and Disabled Persons Act 1970 local personal social services authorities had a statutory duty to provide handicapped people with such aids. As a result there were, in most areas, two storage and delivery systems for the supply of aids and appliances. Furthermore, because the DHSS had not provided any guidance as to how authorities should handle this situation, the division of responsibility between them was usually an arbitrary one and there was often a considerable amount of ambiguity and duplication in the arrangements at local level. Factors that were often taken into account in determining which authority should be responsible for supplying an aid to a particular client included which health care professional initially assessed the need for an aid; whether the need was deemed to be a temporary or permanent one and whether the aid was primarily to increase the client's independence or to assist the professional carer who was looking after him/her.

Since dual systems were usually unwieldy and inefficient to operate a number of the more enlightened health and local authorities took advantage of the availability of joint finance monies for collaborative ventures (after 1977) to establish and operate an integrated home nursing aids service in their area/district (e.g. Hastings; Durham; Wiltshire).[109] With a single, integrated service it was possible to secure economies of scale and to avoid disagreements over which authority was responsible for supplying an aid to a particular client. It was also far easier for the client to use an integrated service since s/he had only to deal with one delivery point. Nevertheless, despite its undoubted advantages over the dual arrangements, by 1984, only about 10% of the population was, in fact, covered by an integrated service.[110]

Closely related to the home nursing aids service was that provided for the **incontinent**. Again there was an element of duplication since both local and health authorities had the power to provide laundry services for those who were incontinent and had difficulty in doing their own washing and to supply incontinence pads.

Throughout this period both the home nursing aids and incontinence services were provided free of charge. However, the scale of provision depended upon the policies of the authorities concerned and, as a result, there were considerable differences between areas/districts in the quantity and quality of the services provided and in the publicity given to the availability of the service.[111]

Fourth, like physiotherapy and occupational therapy, **other paramedical services**, such as dietetics, audiology and orthoptics, became more community based between 1974 and 1984. In the case of dietetics, the DHSS had expressed the view, at the time of the 1974 reorganisation, that 'the involvement of the dietitian outside the hospital (would) develop' and that such a development would be facilitated by bringing together responsibility for the CHSs and HSs.[112] Thus, by the second half of the 1970s Islington and a number of other AHAs had established a community dietetic service, providing nutritional advice to health care professionals and the general public and help to patients in their own homes (e.g. stoma care cases),[113] and this approach spread to other areas and districts in the 1980s.

Fifth, during this period, the CHSs began to take more account of the special health care needs of those from the **ethnic minority** communities. Increasing awareness of these needs was due to a variety of factors. These included the comment of Merrison and his colleagues that 'the special needs of patients who (came) from ethnic minorities require(d) sensitive handling by the NHS';[114] pressure group activity by members of ethnic minority communities (e.g. the 'Sickle Cell Campaign') and a number of initiatives taken by the DHSS (e.g. from 1981 to 1983 a 'Stop Rickets Campaign' was undertaken in conjunction with the Save the Children Fund and local authorities; in 1984 an 'Asian Mother and Baby Campaign' was launched to encourage and help Asian mothers make better use of maternity services and ensure that NHS staff were aware of the particular needs of mothers from the Asian community).

At local level health authorities responded by:

- introducing sickle cell screening (primarily for members of the West Indian community);
- establishing family planning services and 'well-women' clinics, specifically for Asian women;
- providing vitamin tablets for those (mainly Asians) at risk from rickets;
- appointing specialist health workers to provide services to the more closed communities, such as the Chinese; and
- producing health education and related literature in languages other than English.

A number of commentators, however, criticised some of these initiatives for being 'racist' in their approach.[115]

Sixth, from the late 1970s more and more attention was drawn to the problems faced by those with responsibility for the provision of primary health care services in the **inner cities**. An important part in this process was played by the Acheson Study Group on Primary Health Care in Inner London, to which reference was made in the previous chapter. The report of the study group (1981) highlighted many of the deficiencies in these services, such as the fact that:

- there was a high turnover of CHSs staff, because district nurses, health visitors and others were faced with large case loads in difficult circumstances;
- it was far harder to develop a team approach to primary care, because a much higher proportion of GPs than elsewhere were elderly and/or worked single handed and practised in cramped or unsuitable premises;

- spending on community services represented a smaller proportion of the budget of health authorities than elsewhere; and

- the public image of primary care services was poor and this acted as a deterrent to their use.

However, despite their distinctive problems, Acheson and his colleagues concluded that the best way to improve the situation in inner city areas was to apply the approach being developed elsewhere. In other words they supported 'a system of primary care based on teams of professionals working closely together in the care of patients and towards the promotion of their health and well being.'[116] They also argued that the DHSS and health authorities should seek means, more effective than ministerial exhortation, of shifting resources from secondary to primary care in the inner cities to make up for the traditional underfunding of community based health care services in these areas. The Conservative government's response to the problems articulated by the Acheson Study Group was the allocation of an extra £9m to be spent over a five year period on projects designed to improve the quality of primary care services in inner city areas. Projects supported out of this allocation included the development of incontinence and home laundry services; care schemes for the terminally ill; the provision of training opportunities for health visitors and district nurses and health education initiatives.

Finally, in the 12 years following the 1974 reorganisation, a number of the more innovative health authorities began to make tentative responses to some other needs and problems which were gradually moving up the community health care agenda. These included alcohol counselling services; care for the terminally ill and action to cope with the escalating problem of drug abuse. By the mid-1980s CHSs staff were also becoming aware that they would have to address seriously the problem of AIDS.

As a result of developments of this kind, by the mid-1980s there were signs that the pattern of community based health services which the NHS had inherited in 1974 was, at last, beginning to change. This is a theme which will be explored further in Chapter 9.

Relationships between Services

Despite the advances which took place in the years following the 1974 reorganisation, little progress was made in establishing closer relations between CHSs staff and either family practitioners or hospital staff. Thus, by the mid-1980s it was clear that the expectations of the architects of the 1974 reorganisation with regard to integration had not been realised and it can be argued that divisions within the NHS were as deep as they had always been.

It had been anticipated that the principal mechanism for securing a more integrated approach to service delivery on the part of CHSs staff and family practitioners would be the primary health care team. However, there is a considerable amount of evidence to suggest that in many parts of the country teams existed only 'on paper' and that for a variety of reasons there was very little genuine co-operation between team members.

Although Merrison and his colleagues were encouraged by the way primary health care teams had developed, this somewhat sanguine view was not shared by others. For example, as mentioned earlier in the chapter, many health visitors had reservations about the efficacy of 'attachment schemes', which were felt to be the best way of promoting the close working relationships that were essential if there was to be a genuine team approach, on the grounds that too few GPs understood or even respected the contribution that health visiting could make to primary care. In addition, restrictions were sometimes being placed on the activities of the nursing members of primary care teams because their managers did not fully appreciate the nature and potential of teamwork.[117]

Indeed, the situation was causing so much concern that in 1980 the Standing Medical Advisory Committee and the Standing Nursing and Midwifery Committee felt the need to set up a joint working group 'to examine problems associated with the establishment and operation of primary health care teams and to recommend solutions'.[118] Whilst in no doubt about the importance and value of teamwork in primary care, in its report the working group painted a rather sombre picture of its practical application. It also referred to the growing disenchantment with 'attachment schemes' and to the fact that these arrangements were being reviewed by a large number of health authorities and that in certain cases, particularly in urban areas, authorities had reverted to 'zoning'.

On the question of relationships between hospital and community services the picture was little better. As the Chief Nursing Officer at the DHSS pointed out in a letter sent to regional, area and district nursing officers in 1977, 'one of the major aims of National Health Service Reorganisation was to facilitate the combined planning of primary health care and specialist hospital services' and in order to achieve this aim there was a 'need for more effective communications between the specialist and primary health care services.'[119] Similarly in commenting on the links between HSs and CHSs the Merrison Commission made the point that:

From the patient's point of view it is most important that these services should operate in an integrated and consistent way. The services should be provided so that the patient can move easily from being cared for in the community to hospital and as he improves, back to the community. This requires good communications between those who work in hospitals and those who work in the community, and some overlap between what might be considered the spheres of responsibility of staff who are hospital or community based.[120]

Unfortunately the members of the Merrison Commission found that in practice there was 'frequent criticism of communications across the hospital/community boundary'. Furthermore, although there were well established conventions as far as the medical profession was concerned for transferring responsibility for a patient between community based doctors and hospital based doctors, 'the development of such conventions between nursing staff (had) been slow.'[121] As mentioned above, a number of health authorities sought to secure effective communication between hospital based medical and nursing personnel and health care professionals based in the commmunity, on matters relating to the admission, treatment, discharge and after-care of patients, by appointing nurse or health visitor liaison officers. These authorities, however, tended to be the exception rather than the rule.

In their consideration of the community/hospital interface Merrison and his colleagues paid particular attention to the rehabilitation services and went as far as commissioning a paper from Mildred Blaxter of the Medical Research Council's Medical Sociology Unit in Aberdeen, on 'the principles and practice of rehabilitation'. What Blaxter had to say on this subject was of particular significance for CHSs staff, since rehabilitation is one of the principal functions of the CHSs. It is also an aspect of health care in which co-operation between CHSs staff, GPs and employees of various other agencies is an essential prerequisite for effective service delivery and therefore one in which the 1974 reorganisation, with its emphasis on integration and collaboration, should have led to significant improvements. Not surprisingly, however, Blaxter found that the situation had changed very little from that described in the Tunbridge Report of 1972. At that time:

> *A major complaint in all the evidence was the general failure of co-ordination and communication between the hospital, the general practitioner, the community services and the services of the Department of Employment, and the unnecessary delays in starting rehabilitative treatment which result from this.*[122]

According to Blaxter the failure to make progress was due mainly to factors which lay 'very deeply within professional practices' and to the continuing divisions between the responsibilities of health authorities and those of other agencies. In her view there would be significant improvements in the situation only if fundamental changes were made to the distribution of responsibilities for the rehabilitation of patients with serious disabilities. For example, it needed to be formally recognised that 'overall responsibility for long term chronic illness and disability for the patient living at home rest(ed) with the general practitioner', assisted by members of the primary care team, and that 'within the ... team, practical responsibility for advice and co-ordination (of services) should rest with the health visitor.'[123] Although Blaxter's analysis and recommendations were endorsed by the Merrison Commission this did not lead to any major advances in this sphere.

Thus, in many respects, the period from 1974 to 1986 can be regarded as one of unfulfilled potential as far as the development of closer relations between the CHSs and other health care services is concerned. Despite a plethora of publications and pronouncements extolling the need for, and virtues of a more integrated approach to service delivery, it can be argued that its realisation was as far away as it has ever been. Whether integration will continue to be a chimera in the future only time will tell. The omens, however, are not particularly good.

Footnotes

1. DHSS, Circular HRC(73)26, *Statutory Provisions : Framework of National Health Service after Reorganisation*, September 1973, para. 9.

2. DHSS, Circular HRC(74)21, *Health Centres*, March 1974, para. 10.

3. DHSS, Circular HC(77)8, *Health Services Management. Health Centres : Licence for Occupation of Premises by General Medical Practitioners*, April 1977.

4. DHSS, Circular HC(79)8, *Health Services Development. Primary Health Care : Health Centres and Other Premises*, April 1979. In a report on primary health care teams prepared by the BMA's Board of Science and Education and published in 1974, it was suggested that teams should consist of:

   * a permanent nucleus (i.e. GP, district nurse, community midwife, health visitor, social worker and medical secretary);
   * representatives of allied professions, as and when required (i.e. dentist, physiotherapist, radiographer, dietitian, pharmacist, occupational therapist and chiropodist); and
   * administrative staff and auxiliaries (i.e. practice administrator, typists/receptionists, driver, dental auxiliaries, home helps, voluntary services).

5. DHSS, *Priorities for Health and Personal Social Services in England. A Consultative Document* (London: HMSO, 1976), para. 3.10, and House of Commons Paper No. 169-(i) Session 1976/77, *Preventive Medicine*, Report together with minutes of evidence taken before the Social Services and Employment Subcommittees of the Expenditure Committee in sessions 1975/76 and 1976/77, paras. 99 and 114.

6. Royal Commission on the National Health Service [Chair: Sir A. Merrison], *Report*, Cmnd 7615 (London: HMSO, 1979), para. 7.50.

7. DHSS Circular HC(80)6, *Health Services Development Health Centre Policy*, May 1980, para. 1.

8. Ibid., para. 3.

9. Priorities for Health and Social Services in England, op. cit., paras. 9.8 and 9.25.

10. G. Baker, J.M. Beavan, L. McDonnell and B. Wall, *Community Nursing. Research and Recent Developments* (London: Croom Helm, 1987), p. 21.

11. Ibid.

12. Also replaced by the United Kingdom Central Council for Nursing, Midwifery and Health Visiting were The General Nursing Council for Scotland; The Central Midwives Board for Scotland; The Northern Ireland Council for Nurses and Midwives; The Joint Board for Clinical Nurses Studies; The Committee for Clinical Nursing Studies and The Panel of Assessors for District Nurse Training.

13. The members of the Central Council are appointed by (i) the four National Boards for Nursing, Midwifery and Health Visiting (i.e. for England, Wales, Scotland and Northern Ireland), which were also established in 1983, and (ii) the Secretary of State.

14. G. Baker et. al., op. cit., p. 42.

15. Priorities in the Health and Social Services in England, op. cit., para. 9.25.

16. See DHSS, Circular 13/72, *Aides to Improve Efficiency in the Local Health Services Deployment of Nursing Teams*, for details of these targets.

17.   For example, in the mid-1960s the ratio of health visitors to population ranged from 1 WTE health visitor to 4847 persons in Dewsbury to 1 WTE health visitor to 36811 persons in Blackburn (see Appendix III for full details). In 1976 the ratio ranged from 1 : 3290 in Buckinghamshire to 1 : 8543 in Barking/Havering (see Appendix IV for full details). These figures, however, need to be treated with caution.

18.   Health Visitors' Association, *Health Visiting in the 80s*, (London: Health Visitors' Association, 1981).

19.   Royal Commission on the National Health Service, op. cit., para. 7.26 and 7.27. Aspects of community nursing which the Royal Commission considered needed investigation included:

*the workload of district nursing and the respective demands of domiciliary care and treatment room work;

*the respective roles of the district nurse, treatment room nurse and the practice nurse, employed by the GP, vis-a-vis the GP; and

*the use of aides in community nursing.

20.   Ibid., para 7. 22.

21.   DHSS, Chief Nursing Officer Letter CNO(77)8, *Nursing in Primary Health Care*, 14th June 1977, para. 8.1.

22.   S. Simmons and C. Brooker, *Community Psychiatric Nursing: A social perspective*, (London: Heinemann Medical Books, 1986), pp. 45-46.

23.   For further details of schemes of this kind see Baker et.al., op. cit., pp. 146-149.

24.   This was introduced in 1968 when the Queens Institute of District Nursing ceased awarding its certificate.

25   Since 1981 anyone wishing to enter district nursing has had to undergo training leading to the award of the national certificate in district nursing. Furthermore, those district nurses who, in 1981, did not possess an appropriate qualification and wished to continue to practice were given five years within which to obtain the national certificate. District nurse training is open to any registered nurse with at least 2 years post-registration experience. It involves 6 months study at an educational establishment followed by 3 months supervised practice.

26.   See, for example, DHSS, *Care in Action. A Handbook of Policies and Priorities for the Health and Personal Social Services in England* (London: HMSO, 1981), and the Annual Reports on The Health Service in England which have been published for each year since 1984.

27.   DHSS, CNO(77)8, op. cit., Appendix para. 4.5.

28.   DHSS, Maternity Services Advisory Committee, *Maternity Care in Action. Part 1 : Antenatal Care : A Guide to Good Practice and a Plan for Action* (London: DHSS, 1982), Part 2 : *Care during Childbirth (Intrapartum Care)...* (London: DHSS, 1984), and Part 3 : *Care of the Mother and Baby (Postnatal and Neonatal Care)* ... (London: DHSS, 1985)

29.   DHSS, Committee on Child Health Services [Chair: Professor S. Court], *Fit for the Future*, Cmnd 6684 (London: HMSO, 1976), p. 4.

30.   Ibid., para. 4.2.

31.   Ibid., para. 4.22.

32.   Ibid., para. 4.23.

33.   Ibid., para. 4.27.

34.   Ibid., para. 4.30. Educational medicine is defined in the Court Report as 'the study and practice of child health and paediatrics in relation to the processes of learning. It requires an understanding of child development; the educational environment; the child's response to schooling;

the disorders which interfere with a child's capacity to learn, and the special needs of the handicapped. Its practitioners need to work ... with the teachers, psychologists and others ... involved ... to understand the influences of family and social environment' (para. 10.8).

35. Ibid., paras. 4.32 and 4.34.

36. Royal Commission on the National Health Service, op. cit., para. 5.15.

37. Fit for the Future, op.cit., para. 5.24.

38. Ibid., ch. 7.

39. DHSS, Circular HC(78)5, *Health Services Development: Court Report on Child Health Services*, January 1978, para. 2.

40. Ibid., para. 2.

41. Ibid., para. 2.

42. DHSS and Child Poverty Action Group, *Reaching the Consumer in the Ante Natal and Child Health Services*, Report of Conference held on 4th April 1978.

43. Royal Commission on the National Health Service, op. cit., para. 6.54. In the view of Merrison and his colleagues routine school health care was 'a logical extension of the responsibilities of the primary health care teams' and therefore a valuable contribution would be made to the health care of children if post-graduate medical education programmes enabled some GPs to obtain the training they needed to pursue their interest and develop their skills in paediatrics.

44. Circular HC(78)5, op. cit., Annex A.

45. C. Ham, *Health Policy in Britain*, 2nd Edition (London: Macmillan, 1985), p. 67.

46. Priorities for Health and Social Services in England. A Consultative Paper, op. cit., para. 9.10.

47. DHSS, *Prevention in the Child Health Services*, 1980.

48. The Society of Area Nurses (Child Health), *The Future of the School Nursing Service*, sec. 5.7.

49. S.Tyrrell, 'Community Child Health: A Big Step Forward', *The Lancet*, March 31st 1984, No. 8379, p. 726.

50. Priorities for Health and Personal Social Services in England, op. cit., para. 9.10.

51. The Warnock Committee was set up in 1974 with the following terms of reference:

'To review educational provision in England, Scotland and Wales for children and young people handicapped by disabilities of body and mind, taking account of the medical aspects of their needs, together with arrangements to prepare them for entry into employment; to consider the most effective use of resources for these purposes; and to make recommendations.'

Its report entitled *Special Educational Needs*, Cmnd 7212, was published in 1978.

52. DES, Circular 1/83, DHSS, Circular HC(83)3, *Assessments and Statements of Special Educational Needs*, 31st January 1983, para. 3.

53. DHSS, Circular HRC(74)17, *Arrangements for Vaccination and Immunisation Against Infectious Disease*, February 1974, para. 4.

54. Fit for the Future, op. cit., para. 9.15.

55. Ibid., p. 372.

56. See DHSS, Circular HC(77)20, *Health Service Development: Development of a Standard Computer Based Child Health System*, May 1977.

57. The rubella campaign was launched in November 1983. Its objective was to increase, over a three year period, the take-up of rubella vaccination amongst schoolgirls between the ages of

10 and 14 and adult women of childbearing age to 95% and 90% respectively. The DHSS's initiative on measles, which was announced in July 1984, aimed at a take-up rate of 90% by 1990. This was seen as the first step towards the elimination of the disease. DHAs were asked to take action on the recommendation that they should appoint a district immunisation co-ordinator and various other matters, such as the setting of target take-up rates for all the diseases covered by the childhood immunisation programme, consideration of the effectiveness of their action to promote rubella vaccination and the initiation of action locally to increase the take-up of whooping cough vaccination, in August 1985. See DHSS, Health Notice HN(85)19, *Health Services Management : Childhood Immunisation Programme*, August 1985, for further details.

58.   DHSS, DES, Scottish Office, and Welsh Office, *Prevention and Health*, Cmnd 7047 (London: HMSO, 1977), para. 26.

59.   Priorities for Health and Personal Social Services in England. A Consultative Paper, op. cit., para. 3.25.

60.   Royal Commission on the National Health Service, op. cit., para. 5.17.

61.   Ibid.. para. 5.17.

62.   DHSS, *Prevention and Health : Everybody's Business : A Reassessment of Public and Personal Health* (London: HMSO, 1976).

63.   Priorities for Health and Personal Social Services in England. A Consultative Paper, op. cit., para. 3.23.

64.   DHSS, Circular HC(76)10, *Health Services Development: Prevention and Health   Everbody's Business*, March 1976, para. 3.

65.   DHSS, *Prevention and Health, Reducing the Risk: Safer Pregnancy and Childbirth* (London: HMSO, 1977); DHSS, *Prevention and Health. Occupational Health Services: The Way Ahead* (London: HMSO, 1977); DHSS, *Prevention and Health. Eating for Health* (London: HMSO, 1978) and DHSS, Circular HC(77)3, *Non Smoking in Health Premises*.

66.   Preventive Medicine 1976/77, op. cit.,

67.   Royal Commission on the National Health Service, op. cit., para. 5.21.

68.   Care in Action, op. cit., para. 2.8.

69.   Ibid., para. 2.8.

70.   For further information on the state of health education in the first half of the 1980s see the series of articles in the following editions of the *Health and Social Services Journal*: 3rd February 1983, 'On the road to health', pp. 136-138; 10th February 1983, 'Getting across the facts of life', pp. 170-173; 17th February 1983, 'Keeping an eye on the figures', pp. 202-204; 24th February 1983, 'Pointing the way', pp. 241-242; 3rd March 1983, 'Aids for the educator', pp. 266-7 and 10th March 1983, 'Health in WHO's hands', pp. 294-5.

71.   DHSS, Circular HC(77)9, *Health Services Development : Organisation and Management of NHS Chiropody Services*, April 1977, para. 1.

72.   Ibid., para. 4.

73.   DHSS, Circular HC(79)9, *DHSS Planning Guidelines for 1979/80*, April 1979, para. 4.22.

74.   Royal Commission on the National Health Service, op. cit., para. 8.25.

75.   Priorities for Health and Personal Social Services in England, op. cit., para. 3.20. After a modest increase in spending up to 1979/80 it was assumed that expenditure would remain stable.

76.   Ibid. Since 1st August 1975 hospital doctors have also been able to participate in family planning procedures carried out for social as well as medical reasons.

77. DHSS, Consultative Paper attached to Health Notice HN(81)14, *Health Service Development: Cervical Cytology Recall Scheme*, April 1981, para. 5.

78. Ibid., para. 5.

79. Ibid., para. 5.

80. DHSS, Circular HC(81)14, *Health Services Development: Cervical Cytology Recall Scheme*, December 1981.

81. Ibid., paras. 10-12.

82. DHSS, Circular HC(84)17, *Health Services Development: Screening for Cervical Cancer*, July 1984, para. 3.

83. Ibid., para. 10.

84. DHSS, Dear Administrator Letter DA(85)8, *Cervical Cancer Screening*, April 1985.

85. House of Commons Paper No. 413 Session 1985/86, Forty Fourth Report from the Committee of Public Accounts, *Preventive Medicine*, para. 16.

86. DHSS, Circular HC(86)2, *Health Services Development: Resource Assumptions and Planning Guidelines*, January 1986, para. 6.

87. An inquiry held by Liverpool Health Authority in 1987 revealed that, between March 1983 and December 1985, a number of smear tests had been inaccurately processed and many women with abnormal smears had not been contacted. Similarly in Oxfordshire a woman died of cervical cancer because no one had followed up her abnormal smear.

88. Preventive Medicine 1976/77, op. cit., para. 277 and Royal Commission on the National Health Service, op. cit., para. 5.7. The members of the Royal Commission took the view that there was only a place for screening where high risk groups could 'be identified and treated effectively at acceptable cost'. On the issue of the practicality and desirability of mass screening they made two points; first that 'it would be quite impracticable to provide regular screening even for major diseases for the whole population ... (and) second there (was) no evidence that unselective screening of this kind would produce useful results'.

89. P. Townsend and N. Davidson, *Inequalities in Health, The Black Report* (London: Penguin Books Ltd, 1982), p. 163.

90. DHSS, Circular HC(78)14, *Community Dental Services: Extension of Scope to Include Handicapped Adult Patients*. Many health authorities were in fact providing a dental service for the handicapped prior to the issue of this circular.

91. DHSS, Circular HSC(IS)214, *Community Dental Staff: Introduction of New Clinical Structure and Terms and Conditions of Service*, November 1975, para. 11.

92. Circular HC(79)9, op. cit., para. 4.13.

93. Royal Commission on the National Health Service, op. cit., para. 9.51.

94. DHSS, Health Notice HN(83)16, *Health Services Development: Dental Health Surveys and Education Programmes*, May 1983.

95. Fit for the Future, op. cit., para. 14.56.

96. C. Partridge and M. Warren, *Physiotherapy in the Community. A descriptive study of fourteen schemes* (Canterbury: Health Services Research Unit University of Kent at Canterbury, 1977), p. 1.

97. Ibid., p. 1.

98. i.e. 328 physiotherapists out of a total of 4646 in 1974 and 635 out of 5586 in 1976.

99. DHSS, Circular HSC(IS)102, *Occupational Therapists: Joint Review by Area Health Authorities and Local Authorities*, December 1974, para. 1.

100. Ibid., para. 6.

101. Ibid., para. 4.

102. Ibid., para. 8.

103. Ibid., Summary.

104. DHSS, Note, *Occupational Therapy Service National Health Service and Local Authority Social Services*, December 1985, para. 1.

105. Ibid., para. 11.

106. Ibid., paras. 3 to 7.

107. Ibid., para. 13.

108. Ibid., paras. 14-15.

109. See the following articles in the *Health and Social Services Journal* (a) 19th October 1979, 'Sharing fifty-fifty all the way for Hastings', pp. 1352-1353 and (b) 2nd February 1984, 'Dual key health aids' pp. 140-142 for further details.

110. Ibid., (b) p. 140.

111. See G. Parker, 'Incontinence: A problem that won't go away', *Health and Social Services Journal*, 11th August 1983, p. 963.

112. DHSS, DS Letter 56/74, *NHS Reorganisation Dietitians*, 15 March 1974. Just prior to the 1974 reorganisation approximately 400 full-time dietitians were employed by hospital authorities and fewer than 20 by local health authorities.

113. See G. Sethi, 'Development of a district dietetic service', *Hospital and Health Services Review*, November 1979.

114. Royal Commission on the National Health Service, op. cit., para. 7.61.

115. See, for example, M. Pearson, 'Racist Notions of Ethnicity and Culture in Health Education', in S. Rodmell and A. Watt (eds.), *The Politics of Health Education. Raising the Issues* (London: Routledge and Kegan Paul, 1986), pp.38-56.

116. See *Primary Health Care in Inner London*, Report of a study group commissioned by the London Health Planning Consortium [Chair: E.D. Acheson], May 1981, Chapter 5.

117. See Royal College of Nursing, *Society of Primary Health Care Nursing, Primary Health Care Nursing A Team Approach*, Report of a working party (London: Royal College of Nursing, 1980).

118. DHSS, *The Primary Health Care Team*, Report of a joint working group of the Standing Medical Advisory Committee and the Standing Nursing and Midwifery Advisory Committee, [Chair: W. Harding] (London: DHSS, 1981)

119. DHSS, CNO(77)8, op. cit., Appendix para. 8.1.

120. Royal Commission on the National Health Service, op. cit., para. 10.75.

121. Ibid., para. 10.77.

122. Ibid., Appendix G, para. 3.1.

123. Ibid., Appendix G, summary sec. 3.

Chapter 8

The Structural Context of the Community Health Services

At the time of writing responsibility for the CHSs is more clearly defined and sharply focussed than at any time since 1974. This does not mean, however, that there is only one agency engaged in the management and delivery of CHSs. Even in health districts where there is a community unit, many other agencies both within the NHS and beyond contribute to their growth and development.

The main purpose of this chapter is to provide an overview of these agencies and to examine their contributions. The first part of the chapter is devoted to NHS agencies; the second to other agencies, both public and private, (i.e. local authorities, academic bodies, voluntary organisations, professional associations, private sector organisations, representative bodies, the media) and the last to what can be described as the network linking the various agencies at the local level.

In looking at the structural context of the CHSs in the late 1980s account also needs to be taken of how this might change. With the publication of the Griffiths Report, *Community Care: Agenda for Action,* in March 1988 and the white paper, *Working for Patients,* in February 1989, structural change is back on the political agenda. The implementation of the proposals in either, or both, of these documents will, almost certainly, have far-reaching consequences for many of the agencies engaged in the management and delivery of the CHSs.

The Griffiths Report was the product of a review of 'the way in which public funds are used to support community care policy' and contains 'advice on the options for action that would improve the use of these funds as a contribution to more effective community care.'[1] The review, which was commissioned by the Secretary of State for Social Services in December 1986, was his response to mounting concern over the cost of community care and the failure of the policies of successive governments to achieve the desired results, not least because of the multiplicity of agencies involved.

As Hunter and Judge point out, the thrust of the report's proposals was twofold. 'First, central government should take community care more seriously.'[2] According to Griffiths, in order to demonstrate its commitment to care in the community, 'central government should ensure that there is a Minister of State in the (Department of Health), seen by the public as being clearly responsible for community care.'[3] The Minister should be responsible for providing leadership and direction, setting policy objectives, monitoring local plans and reviewing and revising priorities in the light of changing circumstances.

Second, at local level the lead role should be taken by local personal social services authorities, operating within the framework of policies determined by the centre. This would mean that 'within the resources available' authorities should:

- 'assess the community care needs of their locality, set local priorities and develop local plans in consultation with health authorities in particular ... for delivering these objectives';

- 'identify and assess individuals' needs, taking full account of personal preferences..., and design packages of care best suited to enabling the consumer to live as normal a life as possible';

- 'arrange the delivery of packages of care to individuals...'; and

- 'act for these purposes as the designers, organisers and purchasers of non health care services, and not primarily as direct providers, making the maximum possible use of voluntary and private sector bodies to widen consumer choice, stimulate innovation and encourage efficiency'.[4]

Under these arrangements health authorities would continue to be responsible for 'medically required community health services, including making any necessary input into assessing needs and delivering packages of care'.[5] In other words, they would retain their responsibilities for the provision of health care, defined as the 'investigation, diagnosis, treatment and rehabilitation undertaken by a doctor or by other professional staff to whom a doctor ... has referred the patient ... health promotion and the prevention of ill health.'[6]

It is significant, however, that after acknowledging the important contribution which the community nursing services make to community care, Griffiths argued that his proposals allow for 'a great deal of ... flexibility over who does precisely what for whom.'[7] his seems to suggest that implementation of his proposals could lead to the privatisation of services like district nursing, since private nursing agencies, with their smaller overheads, might be in a better position than health authorities to compete successfully for the contracts to provide 'packages of care to individuals'.

Despite the government's acceptance, in part, of these recommendations (July 1989) the Griffiths Report has tended to be overshadowed by the Thatcher government's plans for the future of the NHS set out in *Working for Patients* and elaborated in a series of eight working papers.

These plans were the outcome of a twelve month review of the NHS, which was initiated by the Prime Minister in January 1988. The review was prompted by what the media and politicians had perceived as a 'crisis' in the NHS with over 3000 beds being closed due to inadequate resources (despite long waiting lists) and industrial action by various groups of health service staff in different parts of the country. During the course of the review it became increasingly clear that Ministers would use it as the basis for yet another major reform of the NHS. In the event the proposals outlined in *Working for Patients,* such as self-governing hospitals, budgets for GP practices and a far more business orientated approach to the management of the NHS, proved to be as radical as many had anticipated (although not as radical as others would have liked).

Although the plans put forward in *Working for Patients* relate primarily to the hospital and general practitioner services, because of their far-reaching nature, implementation inevitably would have profound implications for the CHSs. Furthermore, the few references to the CHSs in the white paper and working papers, despite being rather vague and ambiguous, lead one to a similar conclusion. For example, in the section dealing with self-governing hospitals, it is stated that 'the government is not proposing a rigid definition' of what constitutes a 'hospital' for the purposes of self government and that it would 'be sensible for a hospital to retain its existing obligations to run a range of community-based services.'[8] Unfortunately, it is not made clear which 'existing obligations' the authors of the white paper had in mind. However, elsewhere in the white paper, CHSs, such as district nursing and health visiting, were identified as one of the 'core' groups of services for which 'patients need guaranteed local access' and which DHAs would be expected to buy, as economically as possible, from their own hospitals, from other authorities' hospitals, from self-governing hospitals or from the private sector.[9]

Self-governing community units, to which passing reference is made in the first of the working papers,[10] could also supply these services. Despite this, however, in many of their comments on *Working for Patients,* Ministers have given the impression that they see the CHSs of the future as simply an extension of hospital based services rather than as a separate and distinctive component of health care in their own right and that the arrangements for managing them would be similar to those adopted by many districts for their community midwifery service.

Thus, the situation is far from clear and it is not possible to predict, with any degree of accuracy, the precise form which the structural context of the CHSs will take in the years ahead. Nevertheless, whatever happens, it is probable that many of the agencies which are at present active in the sphere of the CHSs will continue to contribute to their growth and development, even though the nature of this contribution may change.

The National Health Service

The position of the CHSs within the overall structure of the NHS is shown in Figure 8.1. Unlike the earlier diagrams of the structure of the NHS this shows the patients at the top (as opposed to the central government department) in order to symbolise the view expressed by Griffiths and the other members of the NHS Management Inquiry in 1983 (see Chapter 6) that 'the National Health Service is about delivering services to people.'[11] In other words, whatever the organisational structure of the NHS, the patient/client should come first.

As Figure 8.1 makes clear, one of the most significant characteristics of the NHS is its structural complexity. Instead of responsibility for the management of the NHS being concentrated within a single structure it is divided between a number of different types of agency (e.g. units of management, FPCs, RHAs), each of which has a range of functions to perform. In other words, the NHS has a composite rather than a unitary structure. This is hardly surprising given the complexity and magnitude of the task facing those with responsibility for the management and delivery of publically provided health care services, despite the changes brought about by the 1982 restructuring and the NHS Management Inquiry. Before looking more closely at these agencies and their roles and responsibilities with respect to the CHSs some additional points need to made about the structure of the NHS as a whole.

First, for the purpose of planning and organising the delivery of CHSs and HSs, England is divided into 190 districts and 14 regions and for administering the FPSs into 90 'localities'. Since there are considerable differences between districts and between 'localities' in terms of their populations, their extent, their socio economic composition and their range and scale of health care needs and facilities, each DHA and FPC faces a unique challenge as far as the management and delivery of services is concerned.[12] For example, the scale and mix of health care needs and problems in a compact, urbanised, working class district/'locality', where there is a high level of deprivation, are likely to be very different from those in a district/'locality' covering affluent, middle class, suburban/rural areas. Consequently, DHAs and FPCs need to be sensitive to demographic, social and economic factors when planning the provision of both primary and secondary health care services for their area.

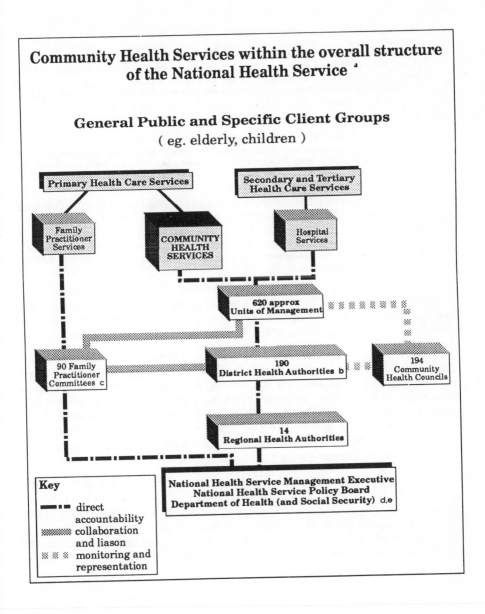

Community Health Services within the overall structure of the National Health Service [a]

General Public and Specific Client Groups (eg. elderly, children)

Primary Health Care Services

Secondary and Tertiary Health Care Services

Family Practitioner Services

COMMUNITY HEALTH SERVICES

Hospital Services

620 approx Units of Management

90 Family Practitioner Committees [c]

190 District Health Authorities [b]

194 Community Health Councils

14 Regional Health Authorities

National Health Service Management Executive
National Health Service Policy Board
Department of Health (and Social Security) [d,e]

Key

— · · — direct accountability
collaboration and liason
monitoring and representation

Figure 8.1

Notes

a.   This diagram does not include the 18 special health authorities, 7 of which exercise their responsibilities at national level (i.e. Prescription Pricing Authority; Central Blood Laboratories Authority; Rural Dispensing Authority; Mental Health Act Commission; National Health Service Training Authority; Health Education Authority and Disablement Services Authority) and 11 at local level (i.e. one for each of the 8 London post-graduate teaching hospitals plus Rampton Hospital Board; Broadmoor Hospital Board and Moss Side and Park Lane Hospitals Board).

b.   For a full list of DHAs see Appendix V.

c.   Until 31st March 1985 FPCs were formally committees of what were known as 'lead' DHAs on which they were dependent for their staff, equipment and accommodation. Since then they have been independent employing authorities in their own right and have been funded by and accountable to the Secretary of State for Social Services. This change was brought into effect by the provisions of the Health and Social Security Act 1984.

d.   The Department of Health and Social Security was split into two separate departments (i.e. the Department of Health and the Department of Social Security) in July 1988.

e.   Advice on health care matters continues to be provided by the Standing Dental Advisory Committee, Standing Medical Advisory Committee, Standing Nursing and Midwifery Advisory Committee, Standing Pharmaceutical Advisory Committee and Joint Committee on Vaccination and Immunisation.

A second feature of the NHS's structure is that it is essentially a hierarchy of agencies. This means, in effect, that each type of agency exercises its responsibilities at a clearly defined level or tier. At present there are four main levels. These are shown in Figure 8.2, together with the title of the agency(ies) operating at that level.

The NHS is also hierarchical in the sense that instructions, advice, planning guidelines and resources flow from the national level through the structure and each agency has to account for its actions, performance and stewardship of resources to a higher level, by means of annual plans, review meetings, appraisal procedures and other mechanisms. Nevertheless, despite these hierarchical features, agencies at unit and district level have some autonomy and exercise some choice in making decisions regarding aspects of service delivery. This is one of the legacies of the 1982 restructuring exercise (see Chapter 6).

Lastly, and most importantly, CHSs continue to be linked, for planning purposes, to the hospital based secondary and tertiary services rather than the community based FPSs (i.e. the other major component of primary health care).[13] Thus, at the operational levels of the organisational hierarchy, responsibility for the management of CHSs is shared between the 190 DHAs and their units of management, whilst FPSs are separately administered by the 90 FPCs.

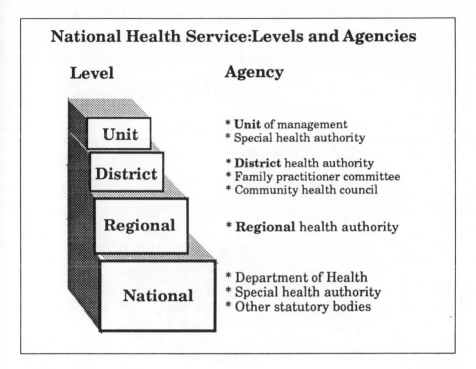

National Health Service:Levels and Agencies

Level   **Agency**

Unit
* **Unit** of management
* Special health authority

District
* **District** health authority
* Family practitioner committee
* Community health council

Regional
* **Regional** health authority

National
* Department of Health
* Special health authority
* Other statutory bodies

Figure 8.2

Units of Management

The principal task of staff working at unit level, including those responsible for the CHSs, is to secure the effective and efficient delivery of health care services, on a day-to-day basis, within a framework of policies laid down by the DHA. This involves not only providing services direct to clients but also designing and operating administrative systems to support the delivery of services (e.g. inviting parents to have their children vaccinated); sorting out problems associated with the malfunctioning of systems; organising rotas for clinical staff (e.g. clinical medical officers; health visitors); handling complaints from patients/clients and ensuring that premises (e.g. health centres; clinics) are adequately maintained and serviced.

In an average sized community unit (i.e. one responsible for a population of 250,000) there are likely to be about 300 service providers (e.g. nurses, dental officers, clinical medical officers, chiropodists); 70 administrative and clerical officers and a small number of ancillary staff (e.g. domestics, caretakers). However, some of the senior service providers spend a relatively large proportion of their time managing, as opposed to delivering, services. Further details of the various groups of staff employed in a community unit are provided in Figure 8.3.

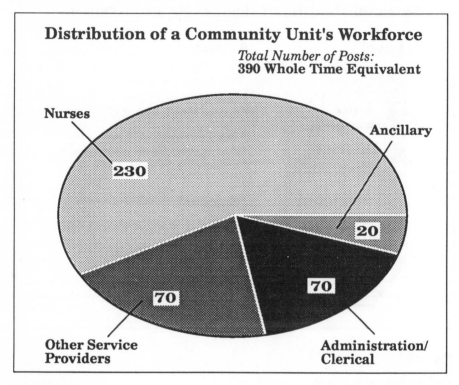

Distribution of a Community Unit's Workforce

Total Number of Posts:
390 Whole Time Equivalent

Nurses — **230**

Ancillary — **20**

Other Service Providers — **70**

Administration/ Clerical — **70**

Figure 8.3

Notes

a.   The principal groups of community nursing staff are district nurses, including a continence adviser, stoma care nurses, a diabetic adviser and an AIDS co-ordinator (approximately 115); health visitors (80) and school nurses (35).

b.   Other service providers include

*clinical medical officers (15);

*community dental service staff (i.e. dental officers, dental hygienists, dental therapists and dental attendants) (20);

*community physiotherapists (9);

*community occupational therapists (6);

*speech therapists (7);

*chiropodists and foot care assistants (9); and

*community orthoptists, dietitians etc (4).

c. Administrative and clerical staff include health education/promotion officers and their colleagues in the health education/promotion department (7).

d. Some community staff have not been included in this diagram (e.g. community midwives, CPNs) because they are usually on the establishment of another unit.

The cost of providing CHSs in an average sized district (late 1980s) is between £4m and £5m, compared with approximately £35m for other health care services (excluding FPSs). The precise amount depends upon a variety of factors including the skill of unit managers in pressing for additional resources during the budget negotiations; the population structure of the district and the range of services for which the unit has financial responsibility. Not surprisingly, a very large percentage of a community unit's budget (i.e. approximately 80%) goes on pay. Of the non-pay items, the most important are travelling expenses, linen services and printing and stationery. Figure 8.4 shows the distribution of a community unit's budget in terms of the services provided to clients/patients.

In addition to the direct provision of patient care services the staff of units of management carry out other important tasks. These include:

• gathering information, especially statistical data on levels of service provision (e.g. district nurses employed, chiropody patients treated), for transmission to higher levels of the NHS hierarchy (e.g. Department of Health);

• disseminating information to clients about the availability of services (e.g. times of child health clinic sessions; eligibility for chiropody treatment) and related matters (e.g. health education campaigns);

• controlling the use of resources (e.g. financial; human);

• quality assurance and personal service initiatives;

• contributing to the planning process; and

• liaising and co-operating with voluntary organisations and other bodies on matters of common interest (e.g. maternity services).

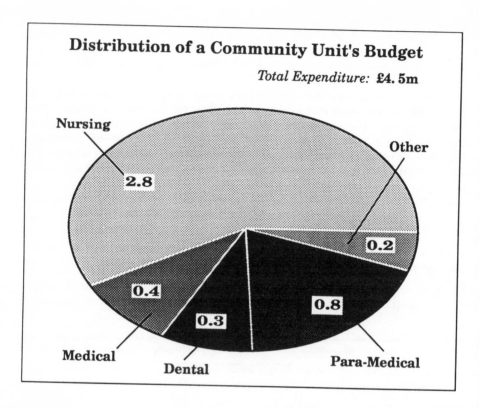

Distribution of a Community Unit's Budget

Total Expenditure: £4. 5m

Nursing — 2.8

Other — 0.2

Medical — 0.4

Dental — 0.3

Para-Medical — 0.8

Figure 8.4

Notes

a.   Approximately 50% of the expenditure on nursing services relates to district nursing; 35% to health visiting and 15% to school nursing.

b.   Medical services are mainly provided in pre-school, school health and family planning clinics.

c.   The paramedical services are physiotherapy; occupational therapy; speech therapy; chiropody; orthoptics and dietetics.

d.   Other services include home nursing aids and incontinence wear; health education/promotion and welfare foods.

e.   Expenditure on administration; training; surgical supplies; heating, lighting and cleaning; transport; maintenance of buidings etc has been apportioned over the patient care services shown in the piechart.

As noted in Chapter 6, the implementation of the recommendations of the NHS Management Inquiry at unit level means that ultimate responsibility for the management of each unit and the effective performance of these tasks now rests with a general manager, who is personally accountable to the district general manager. In exercising this responsibility general managers have had to give a considerable amount of thought and attention to the **management structure** of their unit not only at the time of their appointment but also on other occasions. Indeed, for many general managers, structural issues have been an ongoing preoccupation because it has proved extremely difficult to find acceptable ways of accommodating elements of both functional and general management. This is hardly surprising given the inherent contradictions between the traditional concept of functional management, with its stress on professional standards, autonomy and accountability and the concept of general management, espoused by Griffiths and his colleagues, with its stress on efficiency and effectiveness and managerial control and accountability.

In their search for a 'modus vivendi' between functional and general management, community unit general managers have experimented with a wide variety of arrangements and so far a standard approach has not emerged. As a result, the differences between the management structures of community units are in some respects greater than their similarities. Nevertheless, despite this diversity, for the purpose of analysis it is possible to identify two broad categories of unit, namely those where the influence of functional management and professionalism remains strong and those where there has been considerable movement towards the application of the principles of general management below the post of general manager.

An example of the first type of management structure is provided in Figure 8.5.

Notes to Figure 8.5

a.   The holders of these posts are members of the unit management group. In addition, there is often a GP representative on the unit management group (usually the chair of the local medical committee).

b.   The holders of these posts have district wide managerial responsibility for their services and in some districts they are members of the district's management structure as opposed to that of the community unit.

c.   During the late 1980s a relatively large number of health authorities appointed a consultant community paediatrician to provide, in many cases, clinical leadership for the medical officers working in the community. In the past this had usually been the responsibility of either a principal/senior clinical medical officer or a specialist in community medicine/district medical officer.

d.   The district dental officer usually has direct access to the DHA in respect of the exercise of professional/statutory responsibilities and the provision of advice on dental matters.

e.   Although a majority of health education departments are located within community units, a survey carried out in 1987 by the Department of Health and Community Studies, Leeds Polytechnic, showed that in a sizeable minority of authorities health education was still managed at district level. Furthermore, over 50% of the heads of health education departments remained managerially and/or professionally accountable to a community physician (e.g. district medical officer, specialist in community medicine).

f.   The other groups of community staff (shown in Figure 8.3) are usually professionally (and sometimes managerially) accountable to a district head of service, who is a member of the management structure of another unit (or more rarely the district). For example, community physiotherapists are accountable to the district physiotherapist (acute unit); community occupational therapists to the district occupational therapist (acute or psychiatric unit); community dietitians to the district dietitian (acute unit) and community orthoptists to the district orthoptist (acute unit). In addition community midwives are accountable to the director of midwifery services (acute unit) and CPNs to the senior nurse [psychiatry] (psychiatric unit).

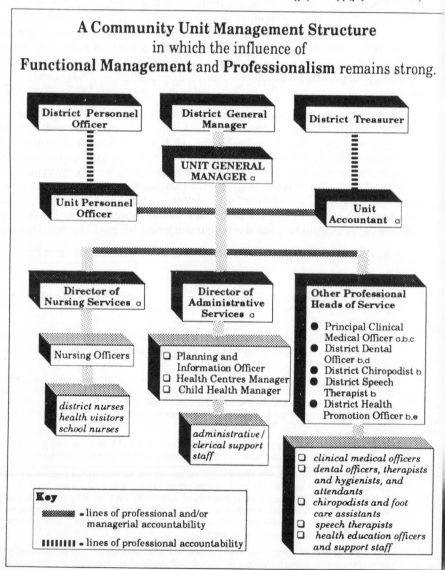

A Community Unit Management Structure
in which the influence of
Functional Management and **Professionalism** remains strong.

Figure 8.5

Where community unit general managers have applied successfully the principles of general management at sub-unit level (i.e. below the post of general manager) they have invariably adopted a form of **locality management**. This has involved dividing the district into a number of geographically based sub-districts or localities and decentralising responsibility for a range of functions, such as budgetary control, service delivery, planning and information and personnel, to locality managers (see Figure 8.6). Appointments to locality manager posts are made on the basis of the managerial skills and abilities of candidates as opposed to their professional backgrounds.

The main reasons for localising or decentralising the management of services has been to enable sub-unit managers to build up a more detailed picture of the particular health care needs of the communities for which they are responsible; to foster a more integrated approach to service delivery; to ensure that managers take more account of the views of clients; to provide a means of forging closer links with other decentralised services (e.g. general medical services; personal social services), and to play a larger role in the allocation of resources.[14] According to Dalley, the philosophy of decentralisation 'can be summed up in four words: accountability, responsiveness, participation and co-ordination.'[15] In other words locality management is seen as a way of revitalising attempts to deal with some the basic problems facing those responsible for managing and delivering CHSs.

Figure 8.6 provides an example of a community unit management structure based on the principles of locality management.

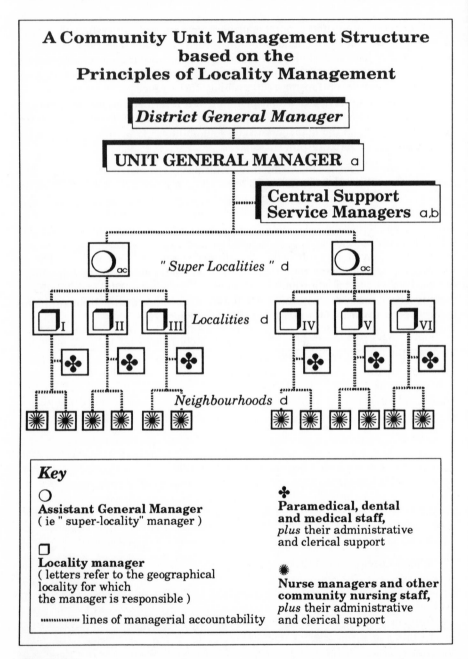

A Community Unit Management Structure based on the Principles of Locality Management

District General Manager

UNIT GENERAL MANAGER a

Central Support Service Managers a,b

" Super Localities " d

Localities d   I   II   III   IV   V   VI

Neighbourhoods d

Key

○
Assistant General Manager
(ie " super-locality" manager)

□
Locality manager
(letters refer to the geographical locality for which the manager is responsible)

.... lines of managerial accountability

♣
Paramedical, dental and medical staff,
plus their administrative and clerical support

✹
Nurse managers and other community nursing staff,
plus their administrative and clerical support

Figure 8.6

Notes

a. Holders of these posts, together with a GP representative, comprise the unit management group.

b. Unit Accountant; Unit Personnel Officer and Unit Planning and Information Manager.

c. Assistant general managers and locality managers are managerially responsible for all staff within their respective boundaries. Thus, medical, nursing and paramedical staff are managerially accountable to the locality manager, as opposed to a professional head of service. However, in most of the districts which have adopted a form of locality management clinical staff of this kind continue to be professionally accountable to a professional head of service, who is generally designated a district adviser.

d. Dalley suggests that in an average sized district with a population of 240,000, the 'super-localities' would have populations of approximately 120,000, localities 40,000 and community nursing neighbourhoods or patches 20,000 (see Chapter 9 for a detailed discussion of neighbourhood management).

Source: Based on diagram in G.Dalley, 'Decentralisation: A New Way of Organising Community Health Services', *Hospital and Health Services Review,* March 1987.

Significantly, a survey undertaken by the primary health care group of the King's Fund in late 1986 to find out how many authorities were thinking of decentralising their activities showed that decentralisation was becoming a central concern for most of them. Of the 161 districts who responded, 140 stated that they had plans to decentralise. However, there was a great deal of variation as to what this was likely to mean in practice. For example, only a third planned to decentralise all of the following functions: management, service delivery, budgets, planning and information; and of the 100 districts intending to appoint locality managers only half were expected to be Griffiths-type general managers, the remainder being traditional nurse managers. Thus, the adoption of some form of decentralisation does not necessarily mean a significant shift from functional to general management.

Subsequent surveys carried out by the King's Fund indicate that, even though some authorities have changed their minds regarding locality management, most of those who had stated that they planned to decentralise have now done so. However, despite the enthusiasm for decentralisation and locality management, it should be remembered that it is hardly a new idea. A number of local health authorities adopted a similar approach to the administration of their services in the 1940s and 1950s (see Chapter 3).

Whatever management structure they have adopted, community unit general managers have all felt the need to retain some kind of **senior management team** to provide them with support in their task of managing the affairs of the unit. Although there is considerable variation in the size and composition of these teams, the frequency with which they meet and their formal title (e.g. unit management group, unit management team, unit executive), their terms of reference all tend to be similar. Thus, they are usually responsible for keeping under review the needs of the district for community based health care services and the provision of services; considering, and planning the implementation of district and unit policies; determining the short-term programme of the unit, in consultation with other senior staff, and debating key management issues which affect the unit as a whole. These include: Korner implementation and performance indicators; consumerism; relations with other agencies; management development; financial management and income generation.

Although the **Korner recommendations** for the CHSs should have been implemented from the 1st April 1988, a number of units/districts encountered serious difficulties in setting up the systems to produce the required information and consequently missed the deadline. These difficulties were due, in part, to unrealistic expectations regarding the capabilities of computer software and, in part, to an underestimation of the amount of advance planning and preparation that was required. In particular, many districts failed to allow sufficient time for staff to participate in the design of data capture procedures and for staff training.

Implementation of the Korner recommendations is only the first step towards the development of a comprehensive information strategy and the production of a coherent set of **performance indicators** for the CHSs (see Chapter 6). In a consultation paper on the community services, (June 1987), the Performance Indicator Group drew attention to the fact that the exisiting performance indicators offered only 'a limited insight into services provided outside hospitals' and that with regard 'to indicators for prevention and community services, a great deal of work remained to be done.'[16] The paper went on to make a series of recommendations for indicators in respect of 'services to the community' and 'patient care in the community'. Some examples are given in Table 8.1.

TABLE 8.1 *Some Recommendations of the Performance Indicator Group for the Community Services*

Services to the Community

Children and Maternity Services

* For midwives and health visitors separately: The number of face to face contacts on ante-natal domiciliary visits in the district related to the number of births in the district.

* For speech therapists, physiotherapists and occupational therapists separately: Number of therapists' first contacts in the year with children aged under 5 years related to total district resident population of children under 5 years.

Family Planning Services

* Number of contacts with patients at family planning services related to the resident population.

Immunisation

* For diphtheria, tetanus, pertussis, polio and measles: Number of children, resident in the district, immunised before their 1st birthday related to the total number of children resident in the district reaching their 1st birthday during the previous 12 months.

* For rubella: Number of girls resident in the district, immunised against rubella before their 13th birthday, related to the total number of girls resident in the district reaching their 13th birthday during the previous 12 months.

Health Surveillance and Early Detection of Diseases

* Total cost of surveillance programmes related to 100 surveillance contacts.

Screening for Specific Conditions

* Adult screening programmes for cervical cytology: Number of women resident in the district, known to have had a smear in the last 5 years, related to the total population of women resident in the district.

Contact Tracing Programmes

* Number of cases of disease identified from contacts traced related to the total number of traced contacts.

Patient Care in the Community

Services for the Mentally Ill

* Number of first contacts in the year by the community psychiatric nursing staff related to the resident population.

Services for the Mentally Handicapped

* Percentage total of community health nursing staff employed in the community.

Services for the Elderly

* Number of district nursing staff related to resident population aged 75 years and over.

* Number of first contacts in the year of chiropodists/ physiotherapists/speech therapists/occupational therapists with persons aged 75 and over, related to resident population aged 75 and over.

Source: Performance Indicator Group, *Performance Indicators For the NHS : Community Services,* Consultation Paper No.6

Although the recommendations in this paper were reasonably well received, during the consultation process it became increasingly clear that more thought and attention needed to be given to this subject. As a result, a working group, consisting of managers, health care professionals (e.g. a midwife, a physiotherapist), information technologists and DHSS officials and chaired by a consultant physician and adviser on priority care services for Yorkshire Regional Health Authority, was set up to look in depth at performance indicators for the CHSs. Its first report was circulated to health authorities, professional associations and other interested parties for their comments in the Summer of 1988.

At the beginning of their report the members of the working group expressed their agreement with the following assertions, which had been made by the Performance Indicator Group and others:

• the purpose of indicators is to inform judgements and to stimulate inquiry about how well NHS services are being provided,

• the number of indicators should be restricted to achieve a manageable package,

• indicators of District level achievement are the most appropriate for a national system of comparability, and

• the definition of community health services includes services delivered to maintain the health of a population (e.g. immunisation) as well as those delivered to individual patients (e.g. by district nurses).[17]

However, in devising their indicators they did not adhere strictly to the Performance Indicator Group's requirement that they should draw only on data from the Korner minimum data sets and other quantitative data which were available. Thus, some of the key indicators recommended by the working group fell 'outside these constraints' and were accompanied by a recommendation that 'consideration should be given to modifying the minimum data set to allow such indicators to be developed.'

Moreover, in seeking 'measures of quality in community service provision' (to which the Performance Indicator Group had drawn particular attention) the members of the working group felt that far more needed to be done at national level before it was possible 'to offer a truly reliable estimate of quality in the community services' and that, in the short-term, considerable reliance would have to be placed 'on local ascertainment of access, choice, consumer satisfaction, comprehensiveness and appropriateness of provision.' Nevertheless, by devising indicators which reflected 'outcome and overall effectiveness of services, their accessibility and their variety' the working group believed that they had offered some "proxy' glimpses of quality.'[18]

Significantly, the working group also drew attention to the fact that since there was no readily available information about the work of GPs it had not been possible to reflect in their proposed indicators 'the importance of primary care teams in securing good (quality) community health provision.' In their view the collection and sharing of such data was another essential prerequisite for the future development of accurate measures of quality in the provision of community based health care services. Examples of the kind of performance indicator recommended by the working group can be found in Table 8.2.

TABLE 8.2 *Some Recommendations of the Working Group on Indicators for the Community Health Services*

Community Maternity Services

* First line indicators[a]: Perinatal mortality and maternal mortality (in collaboration with the maternity services indicator set).
* The percentage of all deliveries in the District where either the date of the first ante-natal assessment was in or after the twentieth week of gestation or there was no ante-natal assessment (indicates serious failure of ante-natal supervision).

Services for Children

* First line indicator: The number of children resident in the District reaching their first birthday in the year who had their hearing tested before they were aged one related to the District resident population reaching their first birthday in the year.
* Number of Health Visitor first contacts in the year with children aged one related to the total District population of children aged one (Contacts with those under one year are so universal as not to justify an indicator. There appears to be no way of identifying second and subsequent contacts by Health Visitors in the first year of life).

Family Planning Services

* First line indicator: The number of pregnancies (deliveries and terminations) of women under 16 related to the District resident female population aged 10 - 15.
* The total cost of Health Authority Family Planning Services related to the total number of all contacts with Family Planning Services (This serves as an indication of the direct commitment of Health Authorities to Family Planning Services).

Immunisation

* First line indicator: The notification rates of measles and pertussis.
* For combined measles, mumps, rubella vaccine the number of children immunised by age five and age six separately related to the District resident population reaching their fifth and sixth birthday respectively, in the year.

Health Surveillance and Screening

* Survival rates and standardised mortality rates for carcinoma of the cervix. (An indicator of health surveillance effectiveness.)
* The total cost of all screening programmes for specific conditions related to 100s of screening tests.

Contact Tracing

* First line indicator: The number of cases of Tuberculosis identified from contacts traced related to the total number of Tuberculosis contacts.

Health Promotion

* The total cost of health promotion and education programmes related to 1000s resident population.
* Standard mortality ratios for various conditions (e.g. alcohol related deaths, hypertensive disease, I H D[b] in persons under 60, deaths due to accidents)

Services for Mentally Handicapped People

* The number of first contacts by community mental handicap nurses in the year with persons aged 16 and over related to the District resident population aged 16 and over.

Services for Mentally Ill People

* The number of first contacts by community psychiatric nurses in the year with persons aged 15 and under related to the resident population aged 15 and under.
* The number of deaths by suicide of district residents related to the District resident population.

Services for Elderly People

* The total number of first contacts in the year by District Nurses with persons aged 75 and over related to the resident population of District aged 75 and over.
* The number of deaths from hypothermia in District residents aged 75 and over related to the District resident population aged 75 and over.

Terminal Care

* The number of deaths of District residents in NHS hospitals anywhere as a percentage of all deaths of District residents.

Key

a.   A 'first line' indicator is one 'which typifies the service being considered.'

b.   Ischaemic heart disease.

Source: *Health Service Indicators.* Report of the Working Group on Indicators for the Community Health Services

A consultation paper describing joint proposals from the Department of Health and Performance Indicator Group for district profiles was also circulated for comment in mid-1988. A district profile can be defined as 'a snapshot of (a) district covering such information as size and composition of population and socio-economic factors such as size of families, numbers of over 75s living alone, and numbers of ethnic minorities.'[19] Strong support for this concept came from the members of the working group on the grounds that 'comparability of community health services depends to a large extent on there being good 'matches' between Districts in respect of: socio-economic status, density of population, hospital provision, housing stock, and social services.'[20] Thus, once profiles are available it is intended to group districts with similar characteristics into 'clusters' to facilitate comparison.

As a result of these developments it is probable that information systems and performance indicators will continue to preoccupy those responsible for the management of the CHSs for many years to come.

Many of the initiatives taken by community units during the mid-1980s to secure a more **consumer-orientated approach** to the planning and delivery of services have become standard practice. Consequently a large percentage of community unit management groups are taking action to ensure that clients are provided with adequate information about the availability of services (and that, where necessary, this information is available in a variety of languages); to obtain the views of clients on aspects of service delivery and incorporate these in the policy-making process; to help 'front line' staff relate to clients in a more friendly, supportive and helpful manner and to raise the profile of the unit and project a more positive and favourable image of its activities.

By the very nature of their service responsibilities, community units are brought into **contact with a wide variety of agencies,** both public and private (see Figure 8.7). As a result, management groups often have to devote a considerable amount of time to dealing with inter-agency issues, such as demarcation disputes and the allocation of responsibility for particular services and clients; taking joint initiatives in the development of services; sharing information and the provision of financial support for services. Many of these issues are examined in more detail in the last part of this chapter.

In many community units increasing recognition is being given to the need for a more positive and systematic approach to **management development.** It is hoped that this will strengthen management skills at every level within the unit. Such an approach has often required a major change in the unit's culture. It has also meant that senior managers have had to find effective ways of increasing staff awareness of their management development needs and of responding to these needs. The application of individual performance review at second and third in line officer level has provided some units with a formal means of identifying training needs. In responding to these needs, units have made use of a variety of approaches, including secondments, externally organised courses and seminars, 'in-house' management development workshops, quality circles and project groups. Whether these initiatives will achieve the desired results, namely increased efficiency and effectiveness in the management and delivery of services, remains to be seen. There are signs, however, that they are helping managers cope with the many new challenges which they are having to face.

With respect to **financial management,** although CHSs have generally fared better in terms of resources than HSs, managers have still been faced with some extremely difficult budgetary decisions (see Chapter 6). The budgets for CHSs have been cash limited since the mid-1970s and therefore a decision to expand one service has invariably meant that another service has had to stand still or, in certain circumstances, contract. Moreover, a much higher priority is now being given to monitoring expenditure and the operation of budgetary control procedures. In addition, many unit management groups are devolving responsibility for the control of budgets to 'front line' managers (e.g. nursing officers) who are directly involved in the utilisation of resources.

One other development that is likely to be of long-term significance is the experimentation with management budgeting, which is taking place in number of of districts specially selected for this purpose. The first two districts chosen by the centre were Bromley and Worcester and District. The official reason for developing management budgeting (or resource management as it now called) is to enable the NHS 'to give a better service to its patients, by helping clinicians and other managers to make better informed judgements about how the resources they control can be used to the maximum effect.'[21] This requires the development of systems which will enable managers to know exactly how much it costs to carry out particular types of clinical activity.

Work on the pilot projects at Bromley and Worcester began in February 1985 and by late 1986 the DHSS was able to report that encouraging progress had been made. Moreover:

The picture (was) one of high commitment from community medical and nursing staff, the increasing involvement of GPs and, despite delays in making some of the sub-systems fully operational, the emergence of important bene-fits. In particular, the process of identifying activity down to the level of individual patient contacts (was) having direct operational value in planning the day-to-day work of services and the discipline of developing better infor-mation flows (had) led to (the agreement of) much clearer divisions of responsibility and accountability between the consultants, the GPs and the field teams of district nurses, midwives, health visitors and paramedical staff.[22]

Encouraged by the success of the pilot projects the DHSS announced that it was extending the experiment to a limited number of second generation community sites and expressed the hope that resource management systems would be estab-lished in every unit with responsibility for CHSs by 1991.

As the financial situation has become increasingly difficult, with budget incre-ments often being insufficient to meet even the cost of pay and price increases and with the demand for health care services constantly growing, some managers have sought to supplement their financial resources by raising money from the private sector or directly from clients. Methods used have included selling advertising space, securing sponsorships, catering enterprises, franchising, and the introduc-tion of charges for car parking on health authority property.

According to Sargent, two events are recognised as being instrumental in encouraging the development of what is now generally referred to as **income generation**. One of these was the commissioning of a report from management consultants by Central Manchester Health Authority on the possibility of raising additional income. The report (December 1984) received widespread coverage in the media when it was offered for sale at £100 per copy in order to recover the consultants fees! The second event was the production of a report for the Secretary of State on 'the maximisation of existing revenues and the generation of additional income to the NHS.' For reasons not disclosed by the government, this report, which was completed early in 1986, has never been published. However, it would appear that many of its recommendations have influenced what has happened subsequently in respect of income generation.[23]

Early in 1988 it was announced that the NHS Management Board would be setting up a unit 'to help authorities develop and implement income generation projects, to develop policy on income generation and to disseminate good practice'.[24] This was followed up, in April 1988, with a letter to all general managers from Ian Mills the NHS Management Board member responsible for income generation and the Income Generation Unit. The purpose of the letter was to outline the centre's initial thinking regarding the areas in which health authorities could generate income and to encourage them 'to identify and develop their own sources of additional income.'[25] According to the letter the areas which appeared to offer the most potential included:

• 'commercial concessions to retailers and other opportunities for leasing space';

• 'static advertisements for services and products on billboards or interior noticeboards ...' ;

• 'development of catering facilities of all descriptions for visitors, for staff and for local organisations';

• 'the sale of services such as health screening, child minding... computer programming, documentation, printing, photocopying, artwork ...';

• 'charges for rationalised and secure car parking facilities'; and

• 'sale of goods ...'[26]

In addition to these initiatives, many of the legal obstacles which had restricted the income generation potential of health authorities have been removed. Under the provisions of Section 7 of the Health and Medicines Act 1988 they now have delegated powers to raise funds from a far wider variety of sources than were previously available to them. These include the power to generate income through the acquisition, production, manufacture and supply of goods; the acquisition and management of land and property; the supply of accommodation and services; the provision of new services and instruction and the development and exploitation of ideas and 'intellectual property.'[27] Moreover, charges are to be calculated on what is considered to be 'the appropriate commercial basis.'

Although the scope for community units to generate income is relatively limited, managers are still expected to develop schemes for this purpose. Action taken in this respect include the provision of condom machines in health centres and clinics; selling toothbrushes at community dental clinics; letting advertising space in clinics and photographic sessions at baby clinics. It can be argued, however, that the time and effort devoted to these initiatives in relation to the amount of income generated does not represent 'value for money'.

It is, of course, difficult to predict what is likely to appear on the agenda of community unit management groups in the years to come. However, in the short-term, it is probable that the following issues relating to the management of resources (in particular human and financial resources and information) will have a high priority: the implementation of affirmative action and positive discrimination measures (e.g. the targetting of resources) needed to meet the health care needs of those living in areas where there is much deprivation and consequent ill-health; the provision of data for effective screening programmes and the development of new forms of health promotion activity.

In the longer term, a great deal will depend on what changes Ministers decide to make to the way in which CHSs are managed. For example, self- governing status for community units will undoubtedly result in management groups having to give a very high priority to their pricing policies, since the survival of the unit will depend upon it being able 'to sell' its services on a sufficient scale to generate the income it needs to pay staff and meet its other costs. Moreover, if community units merge with acute units, the interests of curative, hospital based services are likely to take precedence over preventive, community based services.

District Health Authorities

At district level the principle of 'dual management' applies. This means that, in formal terms, there are members charged with responsibility for policy-making and officers responsible for the implementation of policy headed by a district general manager. In practice, however, the distinction between making and implementing policy is not clear-cut and officers often play an important part in the determination of policy and members in its implementation.

Not surprisingly, given that most members can devote only a relatively small amount of time to their health authority duties, their involvement in both the making and implementation of policy tends to be very limited. Nevertheless, through attendance at health authority meetings and membership of visiting panels, they can make a valuable contribution to service development. Visits are of particular importance since they 'enable members to gain knowledge of services, meet staff and, most important of all, monitor the quality of care provided.'[28] Furthermore, some authorities have established visiting panels, with permanent memberships, for each unit of management or group of services, and thereby provide members with an opportunity to specialise. Thus, in authorities of this kind there is likely to be a group of members with particular responsibility for monitoring the CHSs.

Notwithstanding the formal distinction between health authority officers and members, at district level the general manager and chair are both responsible for ensuring that the functions of the DHA, in respect of CHSs (and other health care services), are carried out effectively and efficiently. The most important of these responsibilities are summarised below:

* employing the administrative and clinical staff (e.g. health centre managers, school nurses, health visitors, speech therapists);

* setting objectives and targets to meet needs and tackle problems, in the light of national and regional guidelines;

* determining priorities and planning the development of services;

* allocating resources to their units;

* monitoring the implementation of plans and the performance of units;

* making arrangements for the surveillance, prevention, treatment and control of communicable disease;

* providing advice and support for their units in specialist areas, such as financial control and audit, personnel and training, estate management, management services, and information technology;

* disseminating information down to units, up to the RHA and Department of Health, and out to the public at large and other organisations; and

* inspecting and registering private nursing homes (in some districts this function is performed at unit level).

As Acheson and his colleagues argued, in their report on the future development of the public health function, in exercising these responsibilities 'it is crucial that DHA Chairmen, members and officers recognise the need for their (actions) and decisions to be based on an assessment of the principal health problems of the population for whom they are responsible.'[29] In effect, this means ensuring that the community medicine/public health specialty is represented at the highest levels of the DHA's management structure and that adequate opportunities are provided for specialists in community medicine to contribute to the planning and policy-making processes.

Unfortunately, however, since general management was introduced at a time when 'the nature of the public health functions of health authorities was not clearly defined, and the credibility of the specialty of community medicine had in some places become compromised' (see Chapter 5), it has 'tended unintentionally to confuse' the image of community medicine and sometimes 'to weaken the position of community physicians.' For example, in 13 authorities community medicine was not represented on the district management group or its equivalent; many management group posts held by community physicians had 'unfamiliar titles', such as director of service evaluation and director of quality assurance, and the holders were expected to perform roles for which medical expertise was not an essential requirement; and in some authorities 'the need for the allocation to a community physician of responsibility and accountability for the overall balance of medical advice to the authority (was) not recognised.'[30]

In order to deal with this undesirable situation the members of the Acheson Committee of Inquiry recommended that every DHA 'should appoint a named leader of the public health function in their district who should be known as the Director of Public Health.' The main duties of the director of public health and his/her colleagues would be:

- To provide epidemiological advice to the DGM and the DHA on the setting of priorities, planning of services and evaluation of outcomes.

- To develop and evaluate policy on prevention, health promotion and health education involving all those working in this field.

- To undertake surveillance of non-communicable disease.

- To co-ordinate control of communicable disease.

- To act as chief medical adviser to the authority.

- To prepare an annual report on the health of the population (or, to quote the former MOH duty 'To inform himself as far as practicable respecting all matters affecting or likely to affect the public health in the [district] and be prepared to advise the [health authority] on any such matter').

- To act as spokesperson for the DHA on appropriate public health matters.

- To provide public health medical advice to, and link with, local authorities, FPCs and other sectors in public health activities.[31]

In late 1988 the Conservative government announced its acceptance of the principal recommendations of the Acheson Report and the Department of Health issued a circular in which it set out the action that DHAs (and RHAs) are required to take in order to improve the health of their populations.[32] This includes the appointment of a director of public health and arranging for him/her to issue an annual report on the health of the population; the regular review of the health of the population for which they are responsible and the identification of areas for improvement; the setting of 'quantified service objectives to deal with any problems in the light of national and regional guidelines and available resources'; the monitoring and evaluation of progress towards their stated objectives 'including the development of indicators of outcome'; and arranging for 'the surveillance, prevention, treatment and control of communicable diseases' within their boundaries.[33]

Although the recommendations of Acheson and his colleagues were not as radical as some public health advocates would have liked, their implementation could have major implications for community unit managers since in many districts they are at the forefront of efforts to secure a more proactive and interventionist approach to health care (e.g. they could affect the relationship between public health/community medicine and other community based professions, such as district nursing and health education).

In exercising their public health and related responsibilities DHAs are required to collaborate with other agencies. Section 22 of the 1977 Act states that DHAs must co-operate, and plan services jointly, with local authorities 'in order to secure and advance the health and welfare of the people of England...'. This principle now extends to collaboration with FPCs and voluntary organisations, as well as local authorities. Significantly, the circular referred to above states that, in order to discharge its responsibility for the health of the population, every health authority should 'maintain close collaboration with local authorities, FPCs, the (Health Education Authority) and other public and voluntary agencies in matters affecting the health of the public with particular reference to **the prevention of disease and the promotion of health** (emphasis added).'[34]

The most visible of the mechanisms designed to facilitate collaboration are the joint consultative committees, which date from the 1974 reorganisation of the NHS. Since 1985 FPCs and voluntary organisations, as well as DHAs and local authorities, have been represented on them.[35] In addition to the joint consultative committees, it is normal practice for the agencies involved to set up joint care planning teams and various kinds of working group to enable officers from each of the agencies to discuss matters of common concern and to find appropriate and cost-effective ways of responding to health care and related needs in the community.

Because the underlying objective of collaboration is to put into practice the principles of community care this particular function of DHAs has a special significance for the CHSs. Consequently some CHSs staff are actively involved in collaborative enterprises of the kind discussed later in the chapter.

DHAs are accountable for their performance to RHAs. They also depend on RHAs for their financial resources, and in exercising their planning responsibilities they are expected to adhere to the guidelines laid down by RHAs.

Family Practitioner Committees

Although the chair and members of FPCs, and their staff, play no direct part in the management of the CHSs, through membership of joint consultative committees and participation in other collaborative enterprises, such as the establishment of cervical cytology call and recall systems and working groups on contemporary health care problems (e.g. drug abuse), they have an input into the planning and development of certain services. Given that CHSs and FPSs are closely related, collaboration of this kind is clearly desirable and since the mid-1980s it has been officially encouraged. For example, in the report of the Joint Working Group on Collaboration between Family Practitioner Committees and District Health Authorities (1984), the case for collaboration was made in the following terms:

> We believe that the primary health care services, both the community services provided by the health authorities and those provided by family practitioners, are key components in the provision of health care. They are essential to the prevention of ill health, the promotion of good health and the early detection and treatment of illness and are the cornerstone of the high quality and cost effective health service which we all wish to see. The achievement of these goals in the future depends, to a considerable extent, on the ability and willingness of DHAs and (FPCs) to work together as partners.[36]

As well as identifying specific areas of service provision where collaboration was felt to be desirable, the members of the working group made a number of recommendations as to ways in which FPCs could be more involved in the planning of primary health care services. These included the need for:

- FPCs to 'broaden their experience and technical capacity' and for DHAs to ensure that their plans do, in fact, 'encompass health services as a whole and not just those under their immediate control';

- FPCs to prepare a profile and strategy statement every five years and an annual programme;

- an interchange of staff, particularly at middle management level, between FPCs, DHAs and the DHSS;

- FPC and DHA chairs to meet regularly;

- FPCs 'computer systems to be technically capable of exchanging information with DHA systems'; and

- the DHSS and Society of Family Practitioner Committees (see below) to 'investigate ways of publicising 'good practice' in organising family practitioner work so as to promote collaboration activities and that health authorities make their experience of internal reorganisation available to FPC colleagues.'[37]

Since 1985, when FPCs became employing authorities in their own right, various steps have been taken in different parts of the country to put these principles into practice. Often this has involved the establishment of formal and informal links between, on the one hand, FPCs and the local professional committees, which represent the interests of practitioners,[38] and, on the other, community units and DHAs. Formal links include GP representation on the community unit's management group and joint working parties and planning groups on a variety of subjects, such as health promotion, drug dependency, child health, diabetes, dental services, cervical cytology, the health care needs of ethnic minority communities and the care of the terminally ill. However, the most effective links are generally the informal ones and these involve the establishment and maintenance of good and open relations between staff of the FPC and of the DHA and the development of mutual trust and respect and a willingness to share information and ideas.

The DHSS/Department of Health has also taken a number of steps to facilitate collaboration. First, it has required FPCs, as part of their new planning responsibilities, to give priority to the establishment and maintenance of links with health authorities and other bodies and to indicate in their annual programmes what they have done in this respect.[39]

Second, it has sponsored a number of demonstration projects in respect of services where there is a degree of overlap between the activities of CHSs staff and family practitioners. The focus of one of these, which was set up in April 1986, was on dental services in East London. The steering group for the project consisted of senior community managers from three DHAs (i.e. City and Hackney, Tower Hamlets and Newham); the administrator of City and East London FPC; a researcher from the King's Fund, who was responsible for co-ordinating the project, and a lecturer from the dental institute of the London Hospital. Its role was to oversee the project, to support and advise a development worker, who had been appointed to carry out the detailed work, and to provide the necessary links between the project and the planning and policy-making procedures of the four authorities. Predictably, one of the main conclusions of this project was the need for mechanisms to ensure that community dental staff, general dental practitioners and other professionals working the community were much better informed about the availability of dental services and the respective roles and responsibilities of the community dental and general dental services.[40] Three similar projects have also been set up in Dorset, Durham and Manchester 'to identify solutions to problems which have arisen in the organisation and delivery of community child health services.'[41] The Department of Health hopes that it will be able to issue guidance to all DHAs and FPCs based on the findings of these projects.

Last, in the white paper *Promoting Better Health* (see Chapter 9) the centre stressed the importance of FPCs and other statutory agencies and voluntary bodies working 'together effectively to maximise their resources in the interests of patient care (and to) avoid wasteful gaps or overlaps in (service) provision', and indicated that it would take positive steps to encourage effective collaboration in FPC 'localities' where it remained weak.[42] According to the authors of the white paper effective collaboration had led to 'many valuable initiatives at both national and local levels', such as screening for cervical cancer, the establishment of a national breast cancer screening service and the alignment of the planning system for FPSs with that for CHSs and HSs. In the white paper reference was also made to two further studies which the Department of Health was sponsoring. The purpose of these studies was to examine the way in which primary care services were being planned, co-ordinated and delivered. One of the studies was carried out in Halton by Cheshire FPC in conjunction with Halton Health Authority, and the other in Loughborough by Leicestershire FPC and Leicestershire Health Authority.

In their reports, (Autumn 1988), both of the study teams were critical of the existing state of affairs, in particular the failure of most family practitioners to communicate with colleagues and to look for ways of crossing the FPS-CHS divide. In the words of the Halton report, 'the sense of isolation was a predominant characteristic in nearly all of the independent establishments we visited - with no evidence of any great effort or desire to rectify this.' As a result opportunities for collaboration between members of the same profession and between disciplines were not being fully exploited.

Thus, despite some movement towards closer relations, it remains to be seen whether substantial progress can ever be made towards securing a more integrated approach to the provision and development of CHSs and FPSs. Significantly, the Halton and Loughborough study teams both reached the conclusion that the only way to overcome the traditional divisions between the two groups of services and the isolation of many family practitioners was to convert FPCs into primary care authorities.[43] Since this would mean transferring responsibility for the CHSs from DHAs and units of management to FPCs, such a recommendation is likely to be strongly opposed by those engaged in managing and delivering the CHSs.

Community Health Councils

The principal role of CHCs is to represent the interests of patients in respect of all aspects of health care provision. More specifically CHCs:

- help individuals who are having difficulty in obtaining a service or wish to make a complaint;

- disseminate information on the availability of health care services in their area;

- carry out surveys to find out the views of members of the community on health care matters;[44]

- visit health care institutions, with a view to highlighting any deficiencies in the quality of services provided;

- identify health care needs in their community;

- promote the health care interests of minority groups and the weaker and less articulate members of the community;[45]

- respond to particular health care needs by setting up innovative projects; and

- represent the interests of the community in the planning process.

Thus CHCs are able to play a part, albeit a limited one, in helping to make community based health care services more accessible and acceptable to the population at large and in identifying and meeting some of the health care needs which are the particular concern of those responsible for them. In other words CHCs are in a position to make a positive contribution to the realisation of the objectives of the CHSs (see Chapter 1). As a result there is clearly a need for a close working relationship between CHSs staff and the members and officers of CHCs.

However, it is important to ensure that such a relationship does not undermine the independence of CHCs or 'blunt their cutting edge' when they are required to comment critically on the actions of community units and DHAs.

Regional Health Authorities

The principle of 'dual management' (see above) also operates at regional level, with political and managerial leadership being provided by the chair of the RHA and the regional general manager respectively. Although the 14 RHAs which they lead do not have any specific roles to play in respect of the provision of CHSs,[46] in exercising their general responsibilities they are in a position to influence the policies of their DHAs in respect of the CHSs if they choose to do so. These responsibilities include:

- appointing some of the members of their DHAs;

- allocating resources to their DHAs (e.g. a number of RHAs have earmarked funds for particular initiatives in the sphere of community based health care);

- preparing planning guidelines for their DHAs;

- monitoring and reviewing the implementation of plans at district level and holding their DHAs to account;

- managing the capital programme;

- providing advice and support to DHAs and units in respect of specialist areas (e.g. litigation, catering, public relations, supplies); and

- disseminating good practice by organising workshops and seminars and publicising successful innovations.

Significantly, although there are considerable differences of approach, all RHAs now include health promotion objectives in their strategic plans. Furthermore, over half have regional health promotion groups and some RHAs (e.g. North Western and Mersey) have appointed a senior officer with specific responsibility for health promotion.

Agencies at the Centre

The legacies of the NHS Management Inquiry at the national level were the Health Services Supervisory Board and the NHS Management Board (see Chapter 6). Although these bodies had different functions, their primary role was to provide the NHS with effective leadership from the centre. However, the Supervisory Board became progressivly less active and ultimately the Management Board was left with sole responsibility for the central direction of the NHS. It was then announced in the white paper *Working for Patients* that the NHS Management Board was to be replaced by an NHS Policy Board, with responsibility for determining the broad strategic framework for health care, and an NHS Management Executive, with responsibility for the provision of management support and operational skills. The initial membership of the Policy Board and the Management Executive is shown in Table 8.3.

TABLE 8.3: *The Composition of the NHS Policy Board and Management Executive (1989)*

NHS Policy Board

* Kenneth Clarke MP (Secretary of State for Health) - Chair
* Sir Roy Griffiths - Deputy Chair
* David Mellor MP (Minister of Health)
* Roger Freeman MP (Parliamentary Under Secretary of State at the Department of Health)
* Sir Christopher France (Permanent Secretary, Department of Health)
* Sir Donald Acheson (Chief Medical Officer)
* Duncan Nichol (NHS Chief Executive)
* Professor Cyril Chantler (Professor of Paediatric Nephrology at Guys Hospital)
* Julia Cumberlege (Chair, South West Thames Regional Health Authority)
* Sir James Ackers (Chair, West Midlands Regional Health Authority)
* Sir Graham Day (Chair, Rover Group and Cadbury Schweppes)
* Sir Robert Scholey (Chair, British Steel)
* Sir Kenneth Durham (Chair, Woolworths)

NHS Management Executive

* Chief Executive (Duncan Nichol)
* Director of Operations (Graham Hart)
* Director of Finance (Sheila Masters)
* Director of Family Practitioner Services (Bryan Rayner)
* Director of Information and Review (Mike Fairey)
* Director of Nursing (Patsy Wright-Warren)
* Director of Personnel (Peter Wormald)
* Director of Estates (Idris Pearce)
* Medical Director (Ron Oliver)

It is argued that these arrangements will provide for stronger leadership and for clearer decision-making at national level and will lead to 'fewer central priorities for health service managers and less involvement in local issues'.[47]

The Secretary of State for Health, as Chair of the NHS Policy Board and as the political head of the Department of Health, is expected to provide the NHS with political direction. In performing this role, which has as much significance for the CHSs as it does for other health care services, he is assisted by the Minister of Health and the Parliamentary Under Secretary of State, by the other members of the Policy Board and Management Executive and by civil servants. This role involves:

* determining the ideological framework within which the NHS operates;

- negotiating with the Treasury and other government departments for the NHS's share of public expenditure, through the Public Expenditure Survey process;

- stimulating debate and discussion on health care issues through the issue of green papers (e.g. on primary health care - see Chapter 9) and other types of consultative document (e.g. on DHA use of FPC patient registration data - see below);

- setting objectives, initiating policies and developing services (e.g. in respect of AIDS, 'Look After Your Heart Campaign');

- preparing and publishing white papers (which indicate the government's intentions with regard to areas of public policy), on aspects of health care (e.g. *Promoting Better Health : The Government's Programme for Improving Primary Health Care* - see Chapter 9);

- when necessary, sponsoring legislation to give effect to these policy proposals and piloting the legislation through Parliament (e.g. Health and Medicines Act 1988);

- allocating resources to regional and special health authorities[48] and ensuring that resources are used in an effective and efficient manner;

- issuing circulars and other circularised communications (e.g. health notices; executive letters) on aspects of health care policy;

- collecting and disseminating information;

- negotiating with professional associations, trade unions and other bodies on personnel matters in particular and health care policy in general;

- facilitating experimentation in service delivery and management by setting up demonstration projects; and

- liaising with other central government departments on issues and problems affecting the NHS and health care policy (e.g. Home Office, with regard to the problem of drug abuse; Department of Education, with regard to the school health service; Ministry of Agriculture, Fisheries and Food, in respect of food safety).

Most of the detailed work of the department is carried out by civil servants organised into divisions. There are in 1989 four groups of administrative divisions within the Department of Health and two groups providing common services for the Departments of Health and Social Security. These are:

- Health and Personal Social Services Group (Department of Health);

- Finance Group (Departments of Health and Social Security - Common Services);

- NHS Management Executive Operations Group (Department of Health);

- NHS Management Executive Personnel Group (Department of Health);

- Family Practitioners and Medicines Group (Department of Health); and
- Principal Establishments and Finance Group (Departments of Health and Social Security - Common Services).

Of these, the first four are of particular importance for the CHSs.

The Health and Personal Social Services Group

This group consists of four divisions: health services (HS); priority care (groups) (PC); community/childrens services (CS); and children, maternity and prevention (CMP). The principal function of these divisions is the development of national policies and priorities for the health and personal social services.

Each division comprises a number of branches. Examples of branches, and the policy areas (of particular concern to CHSs managers) with which they deal, are:

HS2 branch: terminal care, women's health;

HS3 branch: health services for ethnic minorities;

PC1 branch: care and services for elderly and physically disabled people, liaison with voluntary bodies;

CS4 branch: co-ordination of primary care and community care policies, joint funding and joint planning policies;

CMP1 branch: health education, prevention of ill-health, nutrition, maternity and child health services;

CMP2 branch: misuse of alcohol, services for drug users, prevention;

CMP3 branch: family planning, vaccination and immunisation;

AIDS UNIT: co-ordination of policy, public information campaign, guidance to health and social services professionals, research, statistics, international issues, National AIDS Trust.

Many aspects of policy become the subject of circulars issued by the branches[49] and it is this part of their work which is of most immediate significance for CHSs managers.

Finance Group

Included within this group are:

- the Directorate of Health Authority Finance, which is responsible for presenting the case for spending on the health and personal social services during the Public Expenditure Survey; handling the parliamentary estimates for expenditure; determining revenue and capital allocations to health authorities; liaison with parliamentary select committees (see below) and monitoring spending;

- the Directorate of Financial Management, which is responsible for ensuring that resources are used in an efficient and effective manner and that they are adequate financial control and information systems for this purpose and for auditing the accounts of health authorities;

- the Statistics and Research Division, which is responsible for compiling statistics of health service activities, and personnel and remuneration statistics of staff; handling the statistical aspects of the implementation of the Korner recommendations; producing performance indicators and developing computer applications for management information systems;

- the Economic Adviser's Office, which incoporates an operational research service; and

- the Research Management Division, which is primarily concerned with the provision of advice on the scientific aspects of the department's work and its research and development policies and programmes.

NHS Management Executive Operations Group

The principal functions of this group are:

- health authority liaison, including regional accountability reviews and monitoring policy; policy on health authority management and organisation; the appointment of health authority chairs and members and policy in respect of the quality of CHSs and HSs;

- monitoring health authority building programmes;

- guidance to health authorities on estate and property management; and

- policy relating to procurement and supplies.

NHS Management Executive Personnel Group

As its title suggests this group is concerned with issues relating to the pay and conditions of service of staff directly employed by the NHS and personnel policy in general. However, it also incorporates the NHS Information Technology and Planning Division, which is responsible, amongst other things, for the development of policies in respect of the funding of information technology for the CHSs and HSs; following up the recommendations of the Korner Steering Group on Health Services Information; and development work on performance indicators, NHS information policy and planning and review systems for the CHSs and HSs.

Alongside the administrative divisions there are a number of divisions staffed by civil servants with backgrounds in medicine, nursing, dentistry, and pharmacy. The medical divisions are headed by the government's Chief Medical Officer;[50] the nursing division by the Chief Nursing Officer; the dental division by the Chief Dental Officer and the pharmaceutical division by the Chief Pharmaceutical Officer. The principal role of these divisions is to provide professional input to the policy-making process.

Thus, within the Department of Health, responsibility for the CHSs is fragmented, rather than concentrated within a single division. As a result, relationships (professional, political and administrative) between the periphery (i.e. units of management and DHAs) and the centre on issues relating to the CHSs are more complex than might otherwise be the case.

As well as exercising leadership in the allocation of resources, initiation of policy and development of services, Ministers and civil servants at the Department of Health also play a key role in responding to requests from **MPs**, both individually and collectively, for information about aspects of health care. These requests are made to enable MPs to carry out one of their most important functions, namely that of scrutinising the making and implementation of public policy and, in the process, holding Ministers and civil servants to account. The methods used by MPs for this purpose include parliamentary questions,[51] adjournment debates and, most importantly, investigations by select committees of the House of Commons. In carrying out their investigations members of select committees obtain information not only from Ministers and civil servants but also from other interested parties (e.g. pressure group representatives, health authority members and officers).

In the case of policies relating to the CHSs two select committees are of particular significance. These are the **Social Services Committee** and the **Public Accounts Committee**.

Since it was set up in 1979, the **Social Services Committee** has undertaken a number of investigations into subjects of direct relevance to those responsible for the management and delivery of the CHSs. These include peri-natal and neo-natal mortality (1979/80, with a follow-up inquiry in 1983/84); the NHS Management Inquiry (1983/84); community care, with special reference to adult mentally ill and mentally handicapped people (1984/85); the misuse of drugs, with special reference to the treatment and rehabilitation of misusers of hard drugs (1984/85); primary health care (1986/87); problems associated with AIDS (1986/87); resourcing the NHS (1987/88) and the future of the NHS (1987/88). In addition, it has reviewed, on an annual basis, the spending plans and priorities of the DHSS, including those relating to the CHSs.[52]

As its title suggests, the **Public Accounts Committee**, is responsible for scrutinising the way in which public money has been spent. In exercising this responsibility the members are assisted by the staff of the National Audit Office, headed by the Comptroller and Auditor General, who audit the public accounts including those recording expenditure on the CHSs.[53] It is the reports made by the Comptroller and Auditor General to the House of Commons on the outcome of its audit investigations that usually provide the starting point for the enquiries undertaken by the Public Accounts Committee.

Since the Public Accounts Committee is concerned with spending on an extremely wide range of public services the amount of time it can devote to health care services in general, and CHSs in particular, is limited. Nevertheless, during the 1980s it investigated a number of relevant topics. For example, joint finance was subject to investigation during the 1982/83 session of Parliament; value for money developments in the NHS (1985/6); aspects of preventive medicine (1985/86); internal audit in the NHS (1987/88); developments in community care (1987/88) and the management of the FPSs (1987/88).[54]

The end product of a select committee investigation is usually a report containing a summary of the committee's findings and a set of recommendations. The report is designed to stimulate debate and thereby influence policy. However, although reports usually receive a certain amount of publicity, many commentators consider their influence on policy to be relatively limited. Nevertheless there are those like Ham, who argue that the high profile of the Public Accounts Committee and Social Services Committee in the 1980s, demonstrates the need to revise this somewhat negative view of their influence.[55]

Apart from these two there is one other select committee which from time to time addresses issues of concern to CHSs managers. This is the **Committee on the Parliamentary Commissioner for Administration** (the holder of the post of Parliamentary Commissioner for Administration also holds that of Health Service Commissioner, which was established in 1973).[56] Its principal functions of are to monitor the activities of the Parliamentary Commissioner for Administration/Health Service Commissioner and to consider his special and annual reports.

The **Health Service Commissioner** and his staff are responsible for investigating complaints from anyone who feels that s/he has suffered injustice or hardship as a result of a failure in a hospital or community based service provided by a health authority; a failure by a health authority to provide a service which it has a duty to provide and maladministration on the part of a health authority.[57] However, certain matters, such as the exercise of clinical judgement and contractual and commercial transactions, cannot be investigated by the Commissioner and his staff. Examples of matters relating to the CHSs which have been investigated by the Health Service Commissioner include the allocation of space within a health centre; a child's school health records; discharge arrangements made for domiciliary care and failures in speech therapy services.[58] Not surprisingly, however, the vast majority of complaints relate to HSs.[59]

During the past few years epitomes (i.e. summaries) of the reports of the Health Service Commissioner on selected cases have been circulated to general managers, with an exhortation to disseminate them as widely as possible and, where appropriate, to use them for training purposes. It is felt that this is the best method of ultimately reducing the incidence of complaints.

Three other types of agency at national level to which particular reference needs to be made are **advisory and related bodies; special health authorities** and **registration bodies**.

As their title suggests, the principal function of **advisory bodies** (which may be either temporary or permanent) is to provide Ministers and civil servants with advice on aspects of public policy and service delivery. In the words of Smith, they are an 'important medium of communication between the government and organised interests'[60] and thereby provide the government with a means of tapping outside sources of information and expertise. Despite various attempts by the Thatcher government to reduce the number of advisory bodies they still permeate virtually every sphere of public policy-making.

In the field of health care policy, the most important advisory bodies are the standing advisory committees (see Figure 8.1) and similar bodies, such as the Maternity Services Advisory Committee (to which reference was made in Chapter 7), and the Health Advisory Service and National Development Team for People with a Mental Handicap (formerly the Development Group for the Mentally Handicapped).

The members of the **standing advisory committees** are leading figures in the relevant fields, and their advice is often sought on matters of concern to those responsible for developing the CHSs. For example, in 1987 the Conservative government consulted the Standing Medical Advisory Committee, the Standing Nursing and Midwifery Advisory Committee and the Standing Pharmaceutical Advisory Committee about the professional and ethical issues of prescribing by nurses (as recommended by Cumberlege and her colleagues), with a view to producing appropriate guidance for health authorities. Similarly, in 1988 the Joint Committee on Vaccination and Immunisation produced a sustantially revised edition of its handbook, *Immunisation against Infectious Diseases*.

Other advisory bodies which can be said to make a contribution to the development of the CHSs include the: Committee on Medical Aspects of Food Policy;[61] Expert Advisory Group on AIDS; Independent Scientific Committee on Smoking and Health;[62] Working Group on Asian Health Care; and Working Group on Trials of Early Detection of Breast Cancer.

The **Health Advisory Service** 'exists to maintain and improve the standards of management and organisation of patient care services, mainly those for the elderly and mentally ill.'[63] It was founded in 1969, in response to public disquiet about conditions in a number of long-stay institutions (e.g. Ely Hospital, Cardiff) and until 1976 was known as the Hospital Advisory Service. Its name was changed to reflect the extension of its remit to include community based services for the elderly and mentally ill. At the same time responsibility for the mental handicap services was transferred to the newly created National Development Group for the Mentally Handicapped.

The Health Advisory Service is headed by a director who is appointed by, and reports directly to, the Secretary of State for Health. The director is assisted by teams of health service managers and health care professionals who are seconded from their regular duties within the NHS. Their main method of working is an investigatory visit to a DHA and its units of management followed by a report, in which the visiting team comments on its findings and makes recommendations. The purpose of each visit and report is:

● to look at existing services for the client group concerned,

● to provide an objective assessment of these services,

● to advise those concerned on how to build constructively on what they have by concentration on methods of management and patient care organisation, interdisciplinary collaboration, education and training of all grades of staff, co-operation between agencies, especially in planning and mobilisation of the necesssary resources.[64]

Furthermore, the Health Advisory Service also keeps central government informed about services for the elderly and mentally ill and highlights situations where changes in policy may be needed to overcome difficulties being experienced at the grass roots; collaborates with the Social Services Inspectorate of the Department of Health to promote effective co-operation between health and local authorities; and identifies and disseminates good practice. Some examples of good practice in the provision of community based health care services for these client groups, to which reference was made in *1985/86 and 1986/87 Annual Reports* of the Health Advisory Service, are listed in Table 8.4.

TABLE 8.4 *Community Based Health Care Services for the Elderly and Mentally Ill: Some Examples of Good Practice Taken from Annual Reports of the Health Advisory Service*

* The employment of a Nurse Consultant (Services for the Elderly) by Cambridge Health Authority to help hospital and community nurses develop a systematic approach to the management of elderly patients and to disseminate good practice. (85/86)
* Training for nurses, home helps and other carers provided by occupational therapists and physiotherapists in Portsmouth and South East Hants Health Authority. (85/86)
* The home incontinence laundry service ... and the 'hospital at home' intensive support scheme both provided by Peterborough Health Authority. (85/86)
* The community-based Drug Advice and Treatment Agency established by the Scunthorpe Council on Drug Misuse. (85/86)
* The planning document, *The Balanced Provision of Care,* produced by Richmond, Twickenham and Roehampton Health Authority, which provides an informed and creative review of good community mental health practice. (86/87)
* Collaboration between the district chiropodist of Basildon and Thurrock Health Authority and the Community Services Division of the Basildon Borough Council to enable volunteers to undertake a co-ordinated programme of simple toenail cutting for the elderly. (86/87)
* The community dental services for the elderly provided by West Dorset Health Authority and Solihull Health Authority. (86/87)

Source: Health Advisory Service, *Annual Reports.*

In response to the growing problem of drug abuse a **Drug Advisory Service** was set up in 1986, under the auspices of the Health Advisory Service. The principal function of this service is to visit selected health authorities in order to give advice on how best to establish or develop further services for problem drug users.

The Health Advisory Service, the National Development Team for People with a Mental Handicap and the Drug Advisory Service are required to operate, in the words of Merrison and his colleagues, 'by persuasion rather than coercion.'[65] Whether or not this is the most appropriate method of operation is open to question. Some commentators argue that, in view of the seriousness of the matters with which they deal, all these services need 'more teeth' in order to ensure improved standards. Others, however, take the view that the dissemination of good practice and exhortation is a more appropriate, and effective approach, given the decentralised nature of health care administration in this country. Interestingly, a recommendation by the Social Services Committee in its report on primary health care (1986/87), that the remit of the Health Advisory Service should be extended to cover all primary care services, was rejected by the Conservative government because it was doubted 'whether the HAS approach could be successfully translated to the much broader question of delivering primary health care through a quite different form which include(d) a large number of independent contractors.'[66]

Of the **special health authorities** the one which is of particular relevance for the CHSs is the **Health Education Authority**, which was set up in 1987 as a successor to the Health Education Council. Whilst the establishment of most special health authorities has generated very little public debate and controversy, this was not the case when the Thatcher government announced in 1986 that it intended to replace the relatively independent Health Education Council with a special health authority. This was because it was felt by critics of the move, like David Player (the last Director General of the Health Education Council) and Professor Peter Townsend, that the new authority would be insufficiently bold in promoting the cause of health education and promotion especially when this might embarrass the government of the day or upset powerful vested interests. Many of these fears were confirmed in March 1987 when Sir Brian Bailey (the last chair of the Health Education Council and first chair of the Health Education Authority) cancelled the official launch of the controversial report, *The Health Divide : Inequalities in Health in the 1980s*, which was mentioned in Chapter 1.[67]

The Secretary of State, however, argued that since the new agency would be an integral part of the NHS it was likely to 'be more responsive than an outside body (could) be to the needs of the service and in turn (would) have more influence in setting priorities for the service and ensuring that the needs of health education and promotion (were) properly recognised.'[68] Its functions are:

- advising the Secretary of State for Social Services on matters relating to health education;

- undertaking health education activity;

- for that purpose planning and carrying out national and regional or local programmes or other activities in co-operation with health authorities, Family Practitioner Committees, local authorities and local education authorities, voluntary organisations and other persons or bodies concerned with health education;

- sponsoring research and evaluation in relation to health education;

- assisting the provision of appropriate training in health education;

- preparing, publishing or distributing material relevant to health education;

- providing a national centre of information and advice on health education.

It also exercises the functions of the Secretary of State with regard to the provision of financial aid and facilities to other organisations engaged in health education.[69]

Despite the controversy surrounding its establishment, some observers consider that the Health Education Authority has demonstrated both its independence by its willingness to tackle politically sensitive issues such as alcohol abuse, occupational health and aspects of food policy, and its value by taking the lead in the Conservative government's ongoing campaign to increase public awareness of the dangers of AIDS and persuade those at risk of the need to change their behaviour. Nevertheless, in the words of a King's Fund Institute briefing paper, it 'must help give health promotion greater national prominence by becoming an active advocate for the public health' if it is to 'become a potent force for positive change' in health care policy.[70] Furthermore, many critics of the Conservative government's policy towards health promotion have argued that the Health Education Authority, like its predecessor, is primarily a tool of the establishment and does not have the necessary power to tackle the underlying causes of ill-health, such as poverty, bad housing and inequality.

Although the **registration bodies** are not formally part of the NHS, they undoubtedly influence the way health care services develop.[71] Their principal functions are to: regulate entry to their respective professions by deciding which forms of education and training and types of qualification are acceptable; maintain a register of those qualified to practise; promote the application of high ethical and professional standards within their professions; and discipline those practitioners whose conduct and behaviour is deemed to be unsatisfactory (i.e. by removing, either temporarily or permanently, their names from the register of those qualified to practise).

In the case of the CHSs the most important registration bodies are the United Kingdom Central Council and the National Boards for Nursing, Midwifery and Heath Visiting and the Council for the Professions Supplementary to Medicine (in particular the Chiropodists Board; Dietitians Board; Occupational Therapists Board; Orthoptists Board and Physiotherapists Board). Because of their responsibility for the content and standard of the education and training required for membership of their respective professions, registration bodies are inevitably concerned with any developments which may affect the roles of members and their relationship with other professions and need to keep abreast of what is happening at the grass roots level. For example, the Education Officer (District Nursing) of the English National Board visits health authorities to find out how factors such as local policies, the scarcity of resources at unit level and the changing demands and expectations of clients are influencing the practice of district nursing.

Significantly, the changing character and increasing importance of community nursing referred to elsewhere (see Chapters 7 and 9), is given full recognition in the report of the Project 2000 Group, which was set up by the United Kingdom Central Council in 1985 'to determine the education and training required in preparation for the professional practice of nursing, midwifery and health visiting in relation to the projected health care needs in the 1990s and beyond and to make recommendations.' In the words of the Project 2000 Group: 'The need for a reorientation of initial preparation (i.e. basic nurse training) was one theme which emerged strongly' from its review. Consequently, 'an emphasis on care in the community, on care in the home, a stress on assessing health needs, promoting self-care and independence' are key elements in its proposals for the future pattern of nurse training.[72] Clearly, the implications of proposals of this kind for those engaged in community nursing are considerable.

Beyond the National Health Service

By their very nature, many of the CHSs have more in common with services provided outside the NHS than within. Furthermore, during the 1980s, due to a growing awareness of the need for a more proactive and community based approach to health care, there has been a resurgence of interest in the CHSs from a wide range of sources. Thus, it is not really surprising that many non-NHS agencies are now actively involved in facilitating, and directly contributing to, their growth and development. The most important of these agencies are local authorities; academic, research and related organisations; voluntary organisations; professional associations; representative bodies; private sector organisations and the media.

Local Authorities

Although the loss of responsibility for the CHSs in 1974 represented a major diminution of the health care role of local authorities, they were still in a position to continue making a contribution to the health and well-being of their area. Through the provision of services for which they retained responsibility, such as environmental health,[73] housing, recreation, education and personal social services, they had the potential to play a major part in the health care arena. Furthermore, as Acheson and his colleagues pointed out in their report, *Public Health in*

England, 'increasingly, local authorities are becoming concerned about the need to ensure that policies on housing, education, leisure and recreation and transport support and encourage healthy lifestyles and access to appropriate services.' In their view, 'the role of local authorities in the area of health promotion and disease prevention is vital and expanding.'[74]

It was also anticipated at the time of the 1974 reorganisation that local authorities would maintain their involvement in the development of health care initiatives through the joint planning of services and other forms of collaboration with health authorities and, after 1985, with FPCs and voluntary organisations. However, collaboration has not lived up to expectations. One major difficulty is the fact that the NHS and local government operate on the basis of significantly different principles. The NHS is primarily a **national** service (as its title suggests) and, although it is administered at local level by appointed health authorities, the ultimate objective is to minimise differences between communities in respect of the quantity and quality of the services available (i.e. to secure a degree of 'territorial justice'). In contrast, local government involves the provision of a number of separate **local** services which may differ in their quantity and quality according to the political preferences of communities expressed through their democratically elected councils.

Other problems, which have hindered the development of collaboration between local and health authorities, have been:

- the feeling on the part of many local authorities that if they collaborated too closely with health authorities it would undermine their independent status and might lead ultimately to the loss of their responsibility for personal social services;

- differing priorities regarding collaboration, with local authorities considering it less important because of their responsibility for a much wider range of public services;

- the fact that since 1982, in many parts of the country, the boundaries of local and health authorities have not been coterminous;

- the greater likelihood of local authority members being influenced by the possible electoral consequences of unpopular measures (e.g. moving mentally handicapped people into a residential area which does not wish to have them); and

- the inadequacy of the resources available for funding joint projects and the continuing uncertainty surrounding local government finance.

Many of these problems were highlighted in 1986 with the publication of a report from the Audit Commission for Local Authorities in England and Wales entitled *Making a Reality of Community Care*.[75]

Nevertheless, there have been some notable examples of effective collaboration. In its report, the Acheson Committee of Inquiry made a complimentary reference to 'the collaboration between Bradford City Council and Bradford Health Authority in the preparation and delivery of their AIDS Health Education Campaign.'[76] Other examples of succesful collaboration include the development of a local health audit by Oxford City Council and Oxfordshire Health Authority;[77] the joint administration of a special intensive domiciliary care scheme for infirm elderly people (which offers an alternative to long-term hospital care) by Darlington Health Authority and Durham County Council Social Services Department; a study of the relationship between health and social deprivation in the City of Bristol carried out by Avon County Council Planning Department, the Bristol and Weston Health Authority and the Department of Social Administration, University of Bristol.[78]

Underpinning some of these initiatives has been a significant revival of interest in health care issues on the part of many urban local authorities, which has resulted in a number of them establishing a health committee and a health unit. Furthermore, during the mid-1980s the Association of Metropolitan Authorities (which represents the interests of urban authorities) took steps to co-ordinate the work of its members in the field of health and to encourage more of them to set up committees and units and, in 1986, the Association established its own health working group.

The main reason for these developments is a growing unease amongst local authority members and officers about the adverse effects of bad housing, education, and environment and poverty on health. Although it is not yet clear whether local authorities can make a major contribution to the resolution of these problems, in reasserting their interest in public health care they have demonstrated that the concept of collaboration associated with the 1974 reorganisations as far too narrow. They have also shown that they intend to play a key role in the 'new' public health movement which has emerged during the 1980s.

With the government's acceptance of the Griffiths' proposals for the reform of community care (see above), it is clear that local personal social services authorities will be in an even stronger position to take health care initiatives. Moreover, this development will be welcomed by those commentators and professionals who believe that community based health care services should again be subject to local democratic control.

Academic, Research and Related Organisations

Policy-making is not only an institutional and political process but also an 'intellectual activity'.[79] Ideas and academic analysis also play an important part in the implementation of policy and the delivery of public services, along with political considerations, organisational factors and professional judgement. In the case of the CHSs, various academic institutions have made important contributions to the evaluation of existing services; the identification and analysis of the needs of particular client groups; the development of new approaches to meeting needs and managing and delivering services and the education and training of staff (through the provision of courses, conferences and workshops).

First, there are the NHS Management Education and Training Centres. These are based in a number of universities (e.g. Birmingham, Manchester) and are able to draw upon local expertise and facilities. Although their research and teaching activities are usually oriented towards the HSs, some of their research output and courses are also of relevance to CHSs managers. For example, most of the pioneering work on performance indicators was carried out by John Yates at Birmingham and he has also played a part in their subsequent development.

Second, during the 1980s the Institute of Health Services Management has taken an increasing interest in the CHSs. In response to the recommendations of the Joint Working Group on Collaboration between Family Practitioner Committees and District Health Authorities (see above), it has introduced an option in primary care for those studying to become either diplomates or affiliates of the Institute. It has also given evidence to the Social Services Committee on a variety of matters relating to primary care in general and the CHSs in particular.

Third, since its establishment by the Royal College of Physicians in 1972, the Faculty of Community Medicine has played a leading role in promoting the cause of community medicine. Although the Faculty's principal responsibility is to set and maintain the standards of professional training in community medicine, it has encouraged the provision of courses in aspects of health care management by university departments of community medicine. For example, the Department of Community Medicine (now Community Health) at the University of Manchester has run workshops for community unit general managers.

Fourth, the research councils (i.e. Medical Research Council and Economic and Social Research Council) fund a wide variety of research projects in universities, polytechnics and other academic institutions, some of which relate to aspects of community based health care.[80] Similarly the Alcohol Education and Research Fund, which was set up in the early 1980s under the provisions of the Licensing (Alcohol Education and Research) Act 1981, is able to finance projects designed to find more effective ways of helping those with drink problems.

Fifth, an important role is played by the King's Fund Centre. This was set up in 1963 by the King Edward's Hospital Fund for London 'to provide a forum for discussion and study and to help accelerate the introduction of good new ideas and practice in the planning and management of health and social services.' It also seeks to bridge the gap between those who undertake research projects and those directly engaged in the management and delivery of services and to facilitate the exchange of information and ideas. It does this mainly through courses, conferences and workshops organised by the King's Fund College.[81]

One project of particular relevance to CHSs staff was started in 1986 by the primary health care group of the King's Fund Centre with funds provided by the DHSS. The object of the project, has been to look at different ways of organising the CHSs and to assess the feasibility of introducing locality or patch based management (see above). Also in 1986, the King's Fund established, as another separate entity, the King's Fund Institute for Health Policy Analysis 'to provide balanced and incisive analysis of important and persistent health policy issues.' The four issues initially selected for analysis: resource allocation; health promotion; technology assessment and priority services are all of direct relevance to the CHSs.

During the late 1980s, the growing concern of the King's Fund (along with many other organisations) for public health and class differences in health was demonstrated by the publication of a 300 page study of the latest evidence on these issues. Entitled *The Nation's Health, a strategy for the 1990s*, this study underlined the points made in the *Black Report* and *The Health Divide : Inequalities in health in the 1980s* (see above) and argued that epidemiologists have had to continue producing reports of this kind because central government had not simply failed to take strategic action to improve the health of the poorest members of society, but, by its actions, had made their situation worse.

Last, other 'think tanks', such as the Health Promotion Research Trust; the Centre for the Study of Primary Care and the Nuffield Centre for Health Services Studies contribute to the generation and diffusion of new ideas and sustain the spirit of intellectual inquiry which are essential if services are to develop.

Thus, it can be argued that without the involvement of academic organisations there would be far less innovation in the way that CHSs are managed and delivered.

The Voluntary Sector

In Section 128 of the 1977 Act voluntary organisations are formally defined as bodies which engage in activities that 'are not carried on for profit and are not provided by a local or public authority.' In practice, however, there is not always a clear-cut boundary between the voluntary and public sectors. As indicated in earlier chapters, voluntary organisations played a key part in the initial development of many of the CHSs and for long periods they shared responsibility with public authorities for the delivery of services.

Although the voluntary sector's involvement in service delivery is no longer as extensive as it was, voluntary organisations continue to make a significant and varied contribution to the provision and development of services. Furthermore, this contribution receives official recognition, since voluntary organisations are represented on joint consultative committees (see above) and other bodies (e.g. CHCs) and many of them receive some of their income from public funds.

Today the voluntary sector encompasses a very large number and many different types of organisation, in terms of their size, structure, scale of activity, role and finances, and this applies as much to those voluntary organisations which are active within the sphere of the CHSs as it does to the voluntary sector in general. To illustrate this point details of some of the organisations which contribute to the provision of CHSs are summarised in Table 8.5.

TABLE 8.5 *Some Examples of Voluntary Organisations Active in the Community Health Services*

Accept National Services: founded 1975.

The objects of Accept are 'to promote education, training, preventive measures, treatment and research connected with alcohol, tranquilliser and drug misuse.' It runs special centres at which multidisciplinary day clinic treatment (i.e. individual counselling and group therapies) is available. The aim of these clinics is 'to help people resolve underlying problems and function effectively in life without (the) false props of alcohol or drugs.'

Action on Smoking and Health (ASH): founded 1971.

ASH was set up by the Royal College of Physicians 'with the aim of alerting the public to the dangers of smoking; and preventing the disease, disability and premature death which it causes.' It pursues this aim by producing and disseminating literature to the media, health care professionals, teachers and others concerned about the problem of smoking. ASH is financed mainly by means of a grant from the Department of Health. (Membership 1400 individuals and 80 firms and other organisations).

Association for All Speech Impaired Children (AFASIC): founded 1968.

The aims of AFASIC are 'to promote the early assessment and diagnosis of speech and language disorders in children'; to sponsor research and to seek ways of improving the health, social, employment and educational services for speech impaired children. (Membership 1500).

British Association for Services to the Elderly (BASE): founded 1974.

The aims of BASE are to improve the quality of services for elderly people and to offer training programmes for those who care for the elderly. Its membership of 1100 is multidisciplinary and includes district nurses; social workers and volunteers as well as relatives of elderly people.

British Diabetic Association (BDA): founded 1934.

The BDA was the first self-help group for diabetics to be established in the UK. It is now recognised by the government as the 'official spokesman' for diabetics and plays a key role in helping diabetics to understand their condition and treatment. The BDA also raises money for research and provides a programme of activities for diabetic children and teenagers. (Membership 110000).

The Chest, Heart and Stroke Association (CHSA): founded 1899.

The CHSA provides financial support for research into chest disease and strokes; undertakes all forms of health education and helps chest, heart and stroke patients and their families. (Membership approximately 400).

College of Health: founded 1983.

The principal motivation behind the establishment of the College of Health was a desire 'to redress the imbalance of power between medical professionals and their patients.' Thus, its primary role is that of education and the provision of information on health matters to members of the public. More specifically the College aims 'to promote self-care and preventive health and to help people make the best of the NHS and alternative therapies when they are ill.'

Community Health Group for Ethnic Minorities

This group offers free, 24 hour, interpreter and translation services, in more than 20 languages, and an information service for community nurses, GPs and other health care professionals, who come into contact with members of ethnic minority communities during the course of their work. It also runs courses, conferences, and seminars on aspects of health and ethnicity.

Family Planning Association (FPA); founded 1930.

Since transferring its clinics to area health authorities in the mid-1970s the FPA has concentrated on disseminating information on family planning services, methods of contraception and related subjects and on running courses for health care professionals and others, who are involved in sex education and/or the provision of advice on personal relationships. (Membership 800).

The Marie Curie Memorial Foundation: founded 1948.

This foundation is primarily concerned with the welfare of cancer patients, through the provision of community nursing services for patients in their own homes, as well as residential nursing homes, and with the promotion of research into the causes of cancer and its prevention and alleviation. Many DHAs make use of the Marie Curie nursing services.

National Association for Maternal and Child Welfare (NAMCW): founded 1911.

The object of the NAMCW is 'the furtherance of education in matters connected with maternity and child welfare and the study of prevention of mortality and ill health among mothers and young children.' It pursues this object by organising conferences; disseminating information; giving advice when consulted by, and submitting evidence to, government departments and committees of inquiry, on aspects of maternity and child welfare policy and holding examinations in child care for senior school pupils.

National Society for Cancer Relief (NSCR): founded 1911.

Over the years the NSCR has developed Macmillan home care services throughout the country, 'to bring hospice care into patients' own homes.' In many districts specially trained Macmillan nurses work alongside district nurses and GPS. They offer help and advice on the relief of pain and comfort and support to members of the patient's family. Grants are also given to help families cope with the additional costs of caring for a cancer patient at home.

The Queen's Nursing Institute (QNI): founded 1887.

The QNI is no longer involved with the direct provision of district nursing services or the basic education and training of district nurses as it was in the past (see Chapters 2 and 4). Today its principal roles are the administration of a large number of trust funds from which it makes grants and pays annuities to serving and retired district nurses who are in need and the provision of an expanding post-basic educational programme for district nurses. Whenever necessary the Institute also makes representations to public bodies (e.g. government departments) with a view to safeguarding the interests of the profession.

Sources: Based on material from *The Hospital and Health Services Year Book*; CBD Research Publication, *Directory of British Associations Edition 9* and *The Voluntary Agencies Directory 1987* (London: Bedford Square Press/NCVO, 1987).

As the information in Table 8.5 indicates the contributions made by voluntary organisations to the CHSs are many and varied. They include:

- the provision of skilled help by trained personnel (e.g. Marie Curie Memorial Foundation's domiciliary nursing service for cancer patients);
- counselling services (e.g. Accept, Community Cancer Care);
- the provision of courses and seminars for carers (e.g. Age Concern, Community Health Group for Ethnic Minorities, Queen's Nursing Institute);
- enabling people to define their own health needs and begin to meet them by establishing self-help or mutual-help groups (e.g. Hyperactive Childrens' Support Group, Narcotics Anonymous);
- fund raising (e.g. Spastics Society);
- increasing public awareness of particular aspects of health care (e.g. National Rubella Campaign, Sickle Cell Society);
- collaborating with health authorities in respect of the provision of services (e.g. in Leicestershire the British Red Cross Society, together with the DHA and local personal social services authority, have negotiated a tripartite agency agreement to provide an effective distribution service for aids to daily living);
- the dissemination of information designed to help those in need (e.g. a booklet produced by British Diabetic Association which contains listings of the carbohydrates and calories in all the main types of fast foods);

- experimentation with and pioneering new forms of care (e.g. Help for Hospices)

- acting as advocates for change by putting pressure on public authorities with a view to influencing policy at every level (e.g. Age Concern, ASH);

- promoting and/or sponsoring research (e.g. Action for Research into Multiple Scelerosis, British Paediatric Association, National Diabetes Foundation, Nutrition Association); and

- working with sections of the community who might be intimidated or alienated by their perception of official agencies (e.g. family planning services provided by the Brook Advisory Service specifically for teenagers).

It can be argued therefore that, without the proliferation of voluntary organisations and their increasingly varied contributions to the development of services, the overall quality of what is available to clients/patients would be much poorer. Furthermore, as McNaught argues, CHSs managers 'should work in close liaison with voluntary groups and organisations' to help secure the 'more sensitive (and) people orientated approaches to service delivery' referred to in Chapter 1.[82]

Professional Associations

Bodies of this kind seek to promote and protect the interests not only of their members but also of those in receipt of the services their members provide. Thus, they can be said to be motivated by altruism, as well as self-interest. The most important of the professional associations with some, at least, of their members actively engaged in the provision of CHSs are listed in Table 8.6.

TABLE 8.6 *The Principal Professional Associations with Members Active in the Community Health Services*

Name	Year Founded	Branches	UK Membership late 1980s
British Association of Occupational Therapists	1974	20	7500
British Dietetic Association	1936	11	1800
British Orthoptic Society	1937	4	930
Chartered Society of Physiotherapy[a]	1894	78	21000
College of Speech Therapists	1953	-	3950
District Nursing Association	1971	-	3000
Health Visitors' Association	1896	120	16000
Institute of Health Education	1962	n.a.	n.a.
Society of Chiropodists	1945	50	5320
Society of Community Medicine[b]	1974	14	680

Key
n.a. = information not available.

Notes

a. Includes an Association of Community Physiotherapists.

b. Successor to the Society of Medical Officers of Health, founded 1856 (see Chapter 3 for a discussion of the role of the Society).

Sources: CBD Research Publication, *Directory of British Associations Edition 9*, and The Institute of Health Services Management, *The Hospital and Health Services Yearbook*, 1988 Edition.

Professional associations use a variety of methods to express their views on matters of concern. For example, in 1988 the Health Visitors' Association, which is one of the more radical and outspoken professional associations, used the pages of its journal to draw attention to the increasing number of 'cot deaths' and the opportunity provided by the Social Services Committee's investigation into primary care to urge caution in respect of the Conservative government's suggestion that GPs should be more involved in child health surveillance activities and to express its support for the principle of neighbourhood nursing (see Chapter 9).

Representative Bodies

Representative bodies are a special type of pressure group. They are usually established and funded by a group of agencies to provide them with a means of speaking collectively on issues in which they have an interest. There are two representative bodies which have a particular interest in the CHSs, as well as other health care services. These are the National Association of Health Authorities and the Society of Family Practitioner Committees.

Both of these organisations, like other representative bodies, use a variety of methods to articulate their views on contemporary issues. These include: holding conferences; submitting evidence (both written and oral) to parliamentary select committees and other bodies; conducting surveys; publishing written material of various kinds and press briefings. In addition, representative bodies may arrange for a particular issue or problem to be investigated by a specialist working group, comprising experts from their member organisations, with a view to identifying and disseminating good practice.

For example, in December 1985 the National Association of Health Authorities, together with the National Council for Voluntary Organisations, set up a joint working group 'to review the issues and processes involved in achieving effective relations at all levels between Health Authorities and Voluntary Organisations; and to identify good practice and make recommendations for the future.' The report of this working group, entitled *Partnerships for Health* (1987), contains some extremely useful advice on collaboration between health authorities and voluntary organisations, as well as some examples of good practice, and demonstrates the value of this kind of exercise. Other subjects of relevance to CHSs staff on which the National Association of Health Authorities published reports during the second half of the 1980s included cervical cancer screening, health services for black and minority ethnic groups (see Chapters 7 and 9) and the special educational needs' provisions of the Education Act 1981.

Private Sector Organisations

Although private sector organisations (i.e. sole traders, partnerships, companies, which are primarily concerned with the maximisation of profits) are not as involved with the provision of CHSs as they are with other types of health care service, they are still in a position to play a number of important roles.

First, they provide certain services direct to patients. For example, many people who need the services of a chiropodist or physiotherapist have private treatment because they prefer to do so or because they cannot secure treatment under the NHS. There are also many private nursing agencies offering domiciliary nursing and related services (e.g. home care assistance for bathing, toileting and companionship). Indeed in some health districts authorities are forced to make use of agencies of this kind to obtain cover for unfilled vacancies, sick leave and holidays. In addition, many of those who practice alternative clinical techniques, such as acupuncture, hypnotherapy and homeopathy, are to be found in the private sector. Second, many of the goods and items of equipment needed by community units (e.g. welfare foods, dressings) are supplied by private sector organisations. Third, contracts for various ancillary services (e.g. cleaning health centres, maintaining equipment) are often held by companies.

Last, businesses may collaborate with health authorities on joint ventures. Not surprisingly, many of the income generation initiatives referred to earlier have involved collaboration between health authorities and private sector organisations. For example, some firms have arranged, in conjunction with health authorities, screening sessions and health education programmes for their employees and paid for the services provided. Another form of collaboration is where the private sector organisation sponsors an initiative being taken by the health authority (e.g. in respect of staff training or health promotion).

Since the Thatcher government is seeking to increase the involvement of the private sector in the provision of health care, contact between community unit staff and the world of business will undoubtedly grow. Furthermore, as indicated above, it is possible that ultimately some of the CHSs, which are mainly or exclusively provided by health authority employees, such as district nursing, chiropody and community physiotherapy, will be privatised.

The Media

In the context of the CHSs the media, both local and national, act as a two-way channel of communication between those responsible for developing, managing and delivering services and the public. The media performs this role by:

- reporting what it considers to be 'newsworthy' about the CHSs to readers, listeners and viewers;

- providing educational information on health care matters to the public at large (e.g. heart disease; healthy eating habits);

- transmitting critical and supportive comments and statements made by individuals and groups about services to policy-makers, managers and service providers (e.g. by publishing letters and reporting the activities of pressure groups); and

- highlighting particular needs and generating demands for action through investigative articles and programmes and editorial comment.

The British Dietetic Association, has identified the use of the media as one of the key aspects of the work of the dietitian. This includes writing books and preparing articles for publication in magazines, journals and newpapers of a professional and lay nature and appearing in, advising on and writing for TV and radio programmes concerned with any aspect of nutrition and dietetics (e.g. phone-ins, current affairs and extended news programmes about topical items; documentaries on issues associated with the link between food and health).

The Network of Agencies at Local Level

Thus, the picture which emerges is one of considerable complexity, with both NHS and non-NHS agencies contributing in many different ways to the development of community based health care and related services. This means that at the 'grass roots' level, those units of management which carry much of the burden for organising the delivery of CHSs on a day-to-day basis, inevitably come into contact with most of the other agencies. Consequently, it is not unreasonable to conceive of these units as occupying the central position within a network of agencies. This point is illustrated by Figure 8.7.

Community units relate to the other agencies shown in Figure 8.7 in a number of different ways. Some of the most important relationships are discussed below.

The Network of Agencies engaged in the Provision and Development of Community Health Services

Voluntary Organisations/ Pressure Groups

Professional Associations

Private Sector

Media

Units of Management with Responsibility for Community Health Services

Representative Bodies

Academic/ Research Institutions

District Health Authorities and Other Units

Local Authorities

Family Practitioner Committees

Community Health Councils

Figure 8.7

The Exchange of Information

Since information is a vital resource for any organisation, and because knowledge is power, this relationship is often one of the most contentious. For example, since the mid-1980s there has been an ongoing debate on government proposals to make more widely available the information held by FPCs on persons registered for general medical services.[83] In the words of Acheson and his colleagues:

FPCs have access to a vital database, the patient register, which is not available in any other equivalent form. The register has a number of uses: it

is the basis on which call and recall systems operate for screening purposes: it provides a sample frame for designing local research studies; it permits assessments of population changes between censuses. Although in some places, FPCs have already agreed to give health authority staff access to the register, this is by no means the rule.[84]

Similarly, in a consultation paper on this subject, which was issued by the DHSS and Welsh Office in November 1987, the point was made that those who favour DHAs and their units of management having open access to patient registration data argue that it 'should form the basis for a comprehensive community index with which to plan the delivery of health services within a District.'[85]

On the other hand there are those who oppose DHA access to registration data on the grounds that such a development would amount to a breaching of the principle of confidentiality. In their view 'registration data is provided for the sole purpose of obtaining general medical services from a family doctor' and consequently if it were to be passed on to a DHA this could 'amount to a breach of trust which could undermine the doctor/patient relationship.'[86] Opponents also argue that for personal or family reasons many people do not wish their address or age to be more widely known than is absolutely necessary and would therefore feel uneasy if such information were to be held by more than one agency. This issue remains unresolved, but the government feels that with adequate safeguards, such as those provided by the Data Protection Act 1984, and by the introduction of a users' code,[87] it should be possible to allay fears and thereby secure the advantages, in terms of improved services, which the sharing of registration data would bring.

Joint Ventures

The participants in joint ventures believe that by pooling their resources the enterprise will be more successful than might otherwise be the case. Some examples of joint ventures, to supplement those referred to earlier in the chapter, are provided below.

During the late 1980s a relatively large number of community units/DHAs and FPCs have jointly appointed 'facilitators' to promote a more positive approach to preventive medicine on the part of GPs, by helping them 'to develop their organisation and services in ways conducive to health promotion.'[88]

From the mid-1980s staff from Aston University and Darlington Health Authority have worked together on an action research project prompted by the authority's need for an 'information system that would serve the needs of community health service professionals ..., provide management with information on the community health services; and collect the Korner minimum data set.'[89] A key element in this project has been the high level of participation by health care professionals in the design of the input and output media for the system.

Most DHAs now collaborate with the Marie Curie community nursing service in order to ensure that those caring for cancer patients at home receive some help and support. This usually involves the provision of a nurse to look after the patient so that the carer can have a good night's sleep, a short break or continue working. The service is managed locally by DHA staff and is funded on a 50/50 basis by the DHA and the Marie Curie Memorial Foundation.

In Nottingham the DHA used joint finance monies to set up (1982) and continue funding a self-help team, which is managed by the Nottingham Council for Voluntary Service. The principal function of the team is to support self-help groups for those whose quality of life is seriously affected by long-term illnesses or health care problems, such as AIDS, back pain, drug misuse, fertility problems, partial sight and solvent abuse.

Financial Assistance

One important aspect of this relationship is the provision of financial assistance to voluntary organisations out of unit/DHA budgets. Two health districts where policies for financial aid to the voluntary sector have been developed in a systematic and coherent manner and where the budgetary allocations for this purpose are over ten times the national average are North Warwickshire and Coventry.

In North Warwickshire, to qualify for a donation voluntary organisations must: perform functions which promote health by providing a service or by complementing a service that the authority also provides; and give 'good value for money' when compared with what the authority could do with the same funds. The DHA also gives preference to locally (as opposed to nationally) based organisations and to those 'which can demonstrate both a willingness and an ability to raise funds from other sources.' However, the DHA does not discriminate against organisations, which might experience difficulties in securing financial support from elsewhere, because they are concerned with 'unfashionable areas of care'.[90]

Coventry Health Authority's grants and donations policy incorporates two broad categories of financial support namely 'arms-length' support, and contractual agreements. In the case of 'arms-length' support, the authority makes a general grant to the organisation to enable it to pursue its objectives and does not lay down any specific conditions or operate any detailed controls. However, there has to be a clear understanding between the two parties regarding the organisation's objectives and an acceptance of the need for periodic reviews of the progress being made towards their realisation. In contrast, contractual agreements are used in situations where the voluntary organisation is providing a specific service for the authority on an agency basis (see below) and involve far more detailed monitoring and control.

Pressure Group Activity

This can be defined as the attempt by one or more organisations to influence the policy-making and policy-implementation processes of another, with a view to securing a particular outcome. The strategies adopted for this purpose are extremely varied and include writing letters; seeking allies (e.g. the media, sympathisers within the organisation concerned); providing a service in order to highlight gaps in the services available from official sources; distributing propaganda; organising petitions; lobbying and demonstrating. Units with responsibility for CHSs, are both subject to pressure from a wide variety of organisations and may themselves engage in pressure group activity, either alone or, more commonly, in collaboration with other bodies.

The kinds of organisations which might seek to exert pressure on community units and their staff include residents' associations campaigning for better clinic facilities; self-help groups seeking funds; feminist groups aiming to change male-orientated approaches to women and their health and groups lobbying for the introduction of new services or the expansion of existing services (e.g. 24 hour domiciliary nursing service; chiropody).

Although it is relatively rare for community units to campaign openly on a particular issue, they will often provide moral support for those who are doing so and staff may be encouraged to speak out formally on matters that concern the unit (e.g. fluoridation of the water supply, no-smoking policies). Furthermore, staff often share the values and views being expressed by particular groups. For example, many community unit staff would be in sympathy with the aims of the Public Health Alliance, which was launched in 1988 as an umbrella organisation for individuals and groups committed to the principles of the 'new' public health movement. Significantly, a number of these groups are seeking to secure far more radical changes to the approach of public agencies to health care than those which have traditionally campaigned within the health arena.

Delivery of Overlapping Services

Because the boundary between CHSs and other health care services is extremely blurred there are many situations where community units need to co-operate with other units and agencies in order to minimise wasteful duplication and/or to ensure that services are developed in a coherent manner. Examples of services where there is considerable overlap include: family planning and cervical cytology; dental services; vaccination and immunisation and other aspects of child health care; health promotion; and maternity services.

Although some progress has been made towards securing a more integrated approach to the delivery of services of this kind, much remains to be done. As the members of the Joint Working Group on Collaboration between Family Practitioner Committees and District Health Authorities (see above) observed in their report effective collaboration between agencies depends on:

- 'a mutual understanding and respect for each other's role and responsibilities';

- 'the identification of areas of common interest and concern and the establishment and pursuit of common goals, policies and programmes in these areas';
- 'agreements concerning the sharing of information'; and
- 'the creation of formal arrangements and informal links to secure co-operation ... by the simplest means and at levels appropriate to the functions concerned'.[91]

Although these precepts were propounded in respect of relationships between DHAs and FPCs they are of general application and demonstrate the magnitude of the task facing those seeking to secure a more co-ordinated approach to the delivery of overlapping services.

Because of the sensitive nature of many of these relationships and the fact that relations between agencies are notoriously difficult to manage in a constructive manner, senior managers of community units need to devote a considerable amount of attention to this particular aspect of their role. Thus, as indicated above, relationships with other agencies is one of the key issues facing community unit management groups. Astute managers recognise the need to give a higher priority to inter-agency relations in the interests of developing a more varied and integrated range of community based health care services for their district and a more dynamic and innovative approach to the management and delivery of services. In the present climate the achievement of these objectives depends more than ever before on the co-operation and support of other agencies.

A Pluralist View

Having examined the agencies which constitute the structural context of the CHSs and discussed some of the ways in which they relate to each other, one further question remains to be considered, namely which agencies have the greatest influence in making and implementing policies? In other words, how is power distributed between these agencies?

In order to address questions of this kind various academics have developed models designed to further understanding of the policy-making process and the manner in which power is distributed. The approach taken in this chapter would suggest that the policy-making/power distribution model which best fits the CHSs is that of pluralism. In the pluralist model of policy-making the resources which contribute to power (e.g. money, expertise, support) are evenly distributed between a wide variety of competing interests, and policies are the product of negotiation, compromise and mutual adjustment between the groups and/or agencies which represent these interests. As Burch and Wood indicate: 'Pluralists emphasise interests rather than formal institutions as the key element within the policy making system... These interests interact with one another and policy emerges after a process involving bargaining and conciliation.'[92] Thus, adapting Ham's remarks on health policy in general, pluralists would explain developments in the CHSs and policies relating to the CHSs, in terms of the interplay between 'official groups in governmental agencies and outside interests exerting pressure on these agencies.'[93]

In the case of the CHSs, the major interests to which pluralists would draw particular attention are summarised below:

- government ministers (e.g. ideological considerations);
- senior civil servants in the Department of Health (e.g. administrative and clinical considerations);
- health authority members (e.g. needs of their area);
- health authority officers (e.g. aspects of service delivery);
- community health councils (e.g. clients generally);
- professional bodies (e.g. status and security of staff);
- voluntary organisations (e.g. specific groups of clients);
- private sector organisations (e.g. profit maximisation);
- academic, research and related institutions (e.g. quality of services); and
- media (e.g. issues of public concern).

They would also emphasise the extent to which power is evenly spread between these interests and the way in which they compete with each other, both nationally and locally, to determine policy in respect of different aspects of the CHSs (e.g. service developments; management arrangements; resource allocation; staff training; health education initiatives).

Not surprisingly, such an approach to the analysis of policy-making has a large number of critics. For example, many would argue that it does not take sufficient account of the unequal distribution of power which characterises the real world. In their view, within the health care arena as a whole, medicine is the dominant interest and it is in a position to ensure that, in most instances, only policies of which it approves are made and implemented. In the words of Saks, 'it would be difficult at this stage to regard the medical profession as anything less than a very powerful interest group in the health field in the period since the nineteenth century in this country.'[94]

Nevertheless, despite the undoubted power of the medical profession a case can be made to support the view that traditionally it has been far more concerned about policies for specialist health care services in hospitals and general medical services than policies for the CHSs. Consequently, the situation in respect of policies for the CHSs has been more akin to pluralism than to a dominant interest model of policy-making/power distribution.[95]

Furthermore, although the structural context of the CHSs may well be subject to some significant changes during the next few years, it is likely that the CHSs will continue to be shaped by influences emanating from a wide variety of sources. In other words, pluralism will remain a feature of the way in which policies are made and services managed and delivered. Thus, the future development of the CHSs will be affected not only by the ideology of the party in power and the interests of the medical profession but also by pressures from sources as disparate as bodies representing the various professional groups with members practising in the community, health authority members and officers, the voluntary sector, the private sector and academic institutions.

Footnotes

1. *Community Care. Agenda for Action. A Report to the Secretary of State for Social Services by Sir Roy Griffiths* (London: HMSO, 1988), p. iii.

2. D. Hunter and K. Judge, *Griffiths and Community Care : Meeting the Challenge* (London: King's Fund Institute, 1988), p. 4.

3. Community Care : Agenda for Action, op. cit., para. 1.2.

4. Ibid., para. 1.3.

5. Ibid., para. 1.6.1.

6. Ibid., para. 6.12.

7. Ibid., para. 6.13.

8. *Working for Patients : The Health Service in the 1990s*, Cm 555 (London: HMSO, 1989), para. 3.16.

9. Ibid., paras. 4.13-4.15.

10. *National Health Service Review. Working Paper 1. Self-Governing Hospitals* (London: HMSO, 1989), para. 1.2.

11. *NHS Management Inquiry*, General Observations, para. 3.

12. As the information in Appendix V indicates, districts range in size from Leicestershire, with a population of 875000 (mid-1986 estimate), to Rugby, with a population of 84900. The largest 'locality' is Hampshire, with a population of 1,523,900, and the smallest the Isle of Wight, with a population of 122,900.

13. The situation in Wales is very similar to that in England, but in the other parts of the UK it is significantly different. In Scotland there are 15 health boards with responsibility for the management of health care services as a whole (i.e. FPSs as well as CHSs and HSs) and in Northern Ireland 4 health and social services boards, which, as their titles suggest, combine responsibility for health services with that for personal social services.

14. Adapted from the aims and objectives of Islington Health Authority. For further details of Islington's approach to locality management see G. Dalley and G. Shepherd, 'Going local' gathers speed', *The Health Service Journal*, 23 July 1987, pp. 850-851, and S. Malin and G. Shepherd, 'Hats off to going local', *The Health Service Journal*, 7 July 1988, pp. 762-763.

15. G. Dalley, 'Decentralisation; A New Way of Organising Community Health Services', *Hospital and Health Services Review*, March 1987, p. 72.

16. Performance Indicator Group, *Performance Indicators for the NHS : Community Services*, Consultation Paper No. 6, June 1987.

17. *Health Service Indicators*. Report of the Working Group on Indicators for the Community Health Services, July 1988, para. 4.

18. Ibid., para. 18.

19. *NHS Management Bulletin*, September 1988, Issue No. 15, p. 15. See also Performance Indicator Group, *District Profiles*, A Consultation Paper, July 1988.

20. Health Service Indicators. Report of the Working Group on Indicators for the Community Health Services, op. cit., para. 8.

21. DHSS, Health Notice HN(86)34, *Health Services Management: Resource Management (Management Budgeting) in Health Authorities*, November 1986, para. 3.

22. Ibid., para. 10.

23. See J. Sargent, 'Generating Income in the NHS', *Public Finance and Accountancy*, 6th January 1989, pp. 10-11, for further details. Sargent, who is currently the Director of Finance, Bury Health Authority, was the author of the report on income generation produced for the Secretary of State in the mid- 1980s.

24. NHS Management Board, Executive Letter EL(88)P/50, 5th April 1988, para. 3.

25. Ibid., para. 1.

26. Ibid., para. 4.

27. Health and Medicines Act 1988, Section 7(2)(f).

28. The National Association of Health Authorities, *NHS Handbook*, 3rd Edition (London: Macmillan Reference Books, 1987), p. 3.

29. *Public Health in England. The Report of the Committee of Inquiry into the Future Development of the Public Health Function* [Chair: Sir D. Acheson], Cmd 289 (London: HMSO, 1988), para. 4.26.

30. Ibid., para. 2.10.

31. Ibid., para. 5.2.

32. Department of Health, Circular HC(88)64, *Health Services Management. Health of the Population: Responsibilities of Health Authorities*, December 1988.

33. Ibid., para. 2.

34. Ibid., para. 3.

35. Under the provisions of SI No. 305 1985, The Joint Consultative Committees Order 1985, paras. 5-6, 'The number of members by which a health authority, Family Practitioner Committee or local authority shall be represented on a (JCC) shall be such as may be agreed between all the bodies to be represented on it and persons appointed to a (JCC) may be, but need not be, members of the body by which they are appointed....there shall (also) be included on each (JCC) three members appointed by voluntary organisations.'

36. *Report of the Joint Working Group on Collaboration between Family Practitioner Committees and District Health Authorities*, 1984, para. 65.

37. Ibid., pp. 20-21.

38. In every FPC 'locality' there are four local professional/representative committees (i.e. local medical committee, local dental committee, local pharmaceutical committee and local ophthalmic committee). These committees are recognised by law and members are elected by the practitioners. They also have the right to be consulted by the FPC on a variety of matters affecting their profession.

39. See DHSS, Circular HC(FP)(86)2, *Management Arrangements for Family Practitioner Committees, Operational Requirements and Guidelines 1986-87*, February 1986, paras. 9.1 and 9.2; DHSS, Circular HC(FP)(87)3, *Management Arrangements for Family Practitioner Committees,*

Operational Requirements and Guidelines 1987-88, April 1987, para. 7 and DHSS, Dear Administrator Letter FPCL 132/88, *Key Ministerial Aims for FPCs 1989-91*, 28th September 1988, Appendix I, para. ii.

40. For further details see P. McVeigh, 'Healthcare collaboration: Joint plans get some bite', *The Health Service Journal*, 16th October 1986, and P. McVeigh, 'Getting to know your dentist', *The Health Service Journal*, 5th November 1987.

41. *Promoting Better Health, The Government's Programme for Improving Primary Health Care*, Cm 249 (London: HMSO, 1987), p. 76.

42. Ibid., para 10.2.

43. See 'General practice gets a drastic prescription', *The Health Service Journal*, 3rd November 1988, p. 1290.

44. For example, in 1977/78 Worthing CHC carried out a survey of the health and social needs of the elderly; in 1984/85 Sheffield CHC conducted a survey of attitudes towards maternity services and in 1986/87 East Dorset CHC undertook a survey of health visiting services for the under-fives.

45. For example, in the late 1980s City and Hackney CHC campaigned for action to be taken in respect of the health care problems arising from the high level of deprivation amongst the ethnic minority communities.

46. In certain parts of the country (i.e. the metropolitan areas) RHAs manage the ambulance service.

47. For further details of the functions of the NHS Policy Board and NHS Management Executive see NHS Management Bulletin, May 1989, Issue No.21, pp. 1-3.

48. At the time of writing, resources continue to be allocated to RHAs on the basis of the Resource Allocation Working Party (RAWP) formula. As mentioned elsewhere (see Chapter 5), one element of the formula takes into account the fact that some age groups make greater use of the CHSs and that, in order to secure an equitable distribution of resources regional populations need to be weighted accordingly. Set out below are the patterns of usage based on data from the original RAWP Report, which relate to the early 1970s, and from the 1988/89 Cash Limits Exposition Booklet.

% of CHS Expenditure

Age Group	RAWP Report	1988/89 Booklet	Difference
0-4	50%	35%	-15%
5-14	24%	14%	-10%
15-64	2%	26%	+24%
65+	24%	25%	+1%

These figures reflect very clearly the relative decline in importance of CHSs for children (e.g. health visiting; school health service) and the relative increase in importance of CHSs for those aged between 15 and 64 (e.g. family planning, physiotherapy).

49. For example, in January 1988 Health Services Division 2 issued a circular on cervical cancer screening and in March 1988 Branch CS4B issued a circular on Sir Roy Griffiths' Report on Community Care.

50. See Chapter 3 for a fuller discussion of the role of the Chief Medical Officer. One of his principal tasks remains the publication of an annual report, *On the State of the Public Health*, in which the health of the nation is reviewed and attention is drawn to matters of particular concern. Not surprisingly, recent reports have highlighted the problems of AIDS and HIV infection and

coronary heart disease; the environmental health issues arising from the Chernobyl disaster and the need to develop health care indicators which will enable clinicians and managers to assess the results of treatment in terms of their actual benefit to patients.

51. Questions from MPs to Ministers can be about consitituency matters (e.g. On 8th February 1988, Andrew Hunter MP received written answers from Edwina Currie Parliamentary Under Secretary of State at the DHSS to a number of questions he had asked about health visiting services in Basingstoke and North Hampshire health district for further details see Hansard (Commons) Vol. 127 No. 89 Written Answers Section col. 105/6) or broader national issues (e.g. On 10th March 1988, Christopher Butler MP received a written answer from Anthony Newton Minister of Health to a question he had asked on the integration of community nurses into the primary health care team see Hansard (Commons) Vol. 129 No. 112 Written Answers Section col. 112; on 12th April 1988, Harriet Harman MP received written answers from Edwina Currie to a number of questions she had asked about cervical cancer screening see Hansard (Commons) Vol. 131 No. 128 Written Answers Section col. 109; and on 22nd April 1988, David Atkinson MP received a written answer from Edwina Currie to a written question he had asked about the chiropody service see Hansard (Commons) Vol. 131 No. 136 Written Answers col. 596).

52. For the report of the Social Services Committee, together with the proceedings, minutes of evidence and appendices, on peri-natal and neo-natal mortality see House of Commons (HC) Paper No. 663(I) to (IV), Session 1979/80; on NHS Management Inquiry, HC Paper No. 209 and 209(i) to (iv), Session 1983/84; on community care, with special reference to adult mentally ill and mentally handicapped people, HC Paper No. 13 i and ii Session 1984/85; on the misuse of drugs, HC Paper No. 208 and 208(i) to (vi), Session 1984/85; on primary health care, HC Paper No. 37(i) to (vi) and 37(I) and (II), Session 1986/87; on problems associated with AIDS, HC Paper No. 182(i) to (xv) and 182(I) to (III), Session 1986/87; resourcing the NHS, HC Paper No. 264, Session 1987/88; and on the future of the NHS, HC Paper No. 613, Session 1987/88. For the most recent report on public expenditure on the social services see HC Paper No. 687, Session 1987/88.

53. Under the provisions of Section 6 of the National Audit Act 1983: 'The Comptroller and Auditor General may carry out examinations into the economy, efficiency and effectiveness with which any department, authority or other body (including health authorities) ... has used its resources in discharging its functions.'

54. For the report of the Public Accounts Committee on joint finance see House of Commons (HC) Paper No. 160, Session 1982/83 (8th Report of Session); on the dispensing of drugs, HC Paper No. 551, Session 1983/84 (29th Report); on value for money in the NHS, HC Paper No. 335, Session 1985/86 (42nd Report); on aspects of preventive medicine, HC Paper No. 413, Session 1985/86 (44th Report); on internal audit in the NHS, HC Paper No. 156, Session 1987/88 (11th Report); on community care, HC Paper No. 300, Session 1987/88 (26th Report) and the management of the FPSs, HC Paper No. 553, Session 1987/88 (46th Report).

55. C. Ham, *Health Policy in Britain*, 2nd Edition (London: Macmillan, 1985), pp. 117-119.

56. The posts of Health Service Commissioner and Parliamentary Commissioner for Administration have always been held by the same person. From 1973 to 1976 this was Sir Alan Marre; from 1976 to 1979 Sir Idwal Pugh and from 1979 to 1985 Cecil Clothier. The current holder of these posts is Sir Anthony Barrowclough.

57. See Section 115 of the 1977 Act.

58. For further details of these cases see the appropriate reports of the Health Service Commissioner (i.e. allocation of space within a health centre and child's school health records *Health Service Commissioner First Report for Session 1985-86 Selected Investigations Completed April-September 1985*, House of Commons (HC) Paper No. 27 Session 1985/86; discharge arrangements for an elderly person *Health Service Commissioner Third Report for Session 1987-88 Selected Investigations Completed April-October 1987*, HC Paper No. 232 Session 1987/88;

failures in speech therapy service *Health Service Commissioner Fifth Report for Session 1987-88 Annual Report for 1987-88*, HC Paper No. 534 Session 1987/88.

59.   As data in the following table indicate the number of grievances investigated by the Health Service Commissioner and his staff which relate to of the CHSs is extremely small by comparison with the total number of grievances investigated.

Health Service Commissioner : Analysis of Categories of Investigated Grievances

Category			Year		
	1983/4	1984/5	1985/6	1986/7	1987/8
Administration: day-to-day (community health)	3 (2)	1 (1)	1 (0)	4 (3)	4 (3)
Failure in service: community	3 (3)	11 (5)	1 (0)	1 (1)	1 (1)
Subtotal	6 (5)	12 (6)	2 (0)	5 (4)	5 (4)
Other	344 (178)	431 (203)	524 (302)	478 (286)	520 (317)
Total	350 (183)	443 (209)	526 (302)	483 (290)	525 (321)

Notes

a. The figures in brackets indicate the number of grievances for which there was found to be some justification.

b. Some grievances relating to the CHSs may be included in other categories (e.g. attitudes of medical and nursing staff; handling of grievances by a health authority).

Source: *Health Service Commissioner Annual Reports 1983-84* (HC Paper No 537 Session 1983/84); *1984-85* (HC Paper No. 455 Session 1984/85); *1985-86* (HC Paper No. 481 Session 1985/86); *1986-87* (HC Paper No. 31 Session 1987/88) and *1987-88* (HC Paper No. 534 Session 1987/88).

60.   B. Smith, *Policy Making in British Government : An Analysis of Power and Rationality* (London: Martin Robertson, 1976), p. 69.

61.   The terms of reference of the Committee on Medical Aspects of Food Policy are as follows:

'To consider and advise on: (1) the medical and scientific aspects of policy in relation to nutrition; (2) at the request of, or in association with, the Food Standards Committee, the Advisory Committee on Pesticides, the Food Additives and Contaminants Committee, or any other committee, as appropriate, the medical and nutritional aspects of developments in the agricultural and food industries, including the fortification and extraction of food; (3) at the request of the Departments, any matters falling within these terms of reference.'

62.   The members Independent Scientific Committee on Smoking and Health are appointed by the Health Ministers to advise them and, where appropriate, the tobacco industry, on 'the scientific aspects of matters concerning smoking and health, in particular: (i) to receive in confidence full data about the constituents of cigarettes and other smoking materials and their smoke and changes in these; (ii) to release to bona fide research workers for approved subjects such of the above as is agreed by the suppliers of it.' The role of the Committee is also 'to review the research into less dangerous smoking and consider whether such further research, including clinical trials and epidemiological studies, needs to be carried out; and to advise on the validity of research results and of systems of testing the health effects of tobacco and tobacco substitutes and on their predictive value to human health.'

63.   Health Advisory Service, *Annual Report-June 1987*, p. 4.

64. Ibid., p. 4.

65. Royal Commission on the National Health Service [Chair: Sir A. Merrison], *Report*, Cmnd 7615 (London: HMSO, 1979), para. 19.38.

66. Promoting Better Health, op. cit., p. 69.

67. In this report it was shown that the disparities in health between different social classes, to which the Black Report had drawn attention, were as great as they had always been.

68 Statement to Parliament 21st November 1986, quoted in Public Health in England, op. cit., para. 4.23.

69. See SI No. 6 1987, *Health Education Authority (Establishment and Constitution) Order 1987*.

70. *Healthy Public Policy : a role for the HEA* (London: King's Fund Institute, 1987).

71. See N. Chaplin (edited for The Institute of Health Service Administrators) *Health Care in the United Kingdom* (London: Kluwer Medical, 1982), p. 99.

72. United Kingdom Central Council for Nursing, Midwifery and Health Visiting, Project 2000 ; A New Preparation for Practice, 1986, para. 2.35.

73. The environmental health responsibilities of local authorities include the control of noise, air and water pollution; securing the sufficiency and wholesomeness of water supplies; food inspection and food hygiene; refuse collection and disposal; health and safety at work; the abatement of statutory nuisances (e.g. an animal kept in such a place or manner as to be prejudicial to health or a nuisance; dust or effluvia caused by any trade, business, manufacturing or other process, which is prejudicial to the health of, or a nuisance to, those living in a particular area); pest control; aspects of animal health and port health.

74. Public Health in England, op. cit., para. 4.46.

75. Not surprisingly, the report draws particular attention to those problems which need to be tackled in order to secure a sound financial base for inter-authority collaboration. For example, the point is made that 'local authorities are often penalised through the grant system for building the very community services which government policy favours' and that the funds for joint projects are 'too limited'. For further details see, The Audit Commission for England and Wales, *Making a Reality of Community Care* (London: HMSO, 1986), especially Chapter 2.

76. Public Health in England, op. cit., para 4.47.

77. The aim of Oxford's local health audit is 'to optimise the health promoting aspects of city council services. This involves determining the health implications of council services and developing a managerial method of processing the audit, which relates overall council health targets to the activity of the council departments.' For further details see, D. Grice and P. Fryer, 'Giving Good Counsel on Health', *The Health Service Journal*, 28th April 1988, pp. 480-481.

78. See also C. Thunhurst (Department of Applied Statistics and Operational Research, Sheffield City Polytechnic), *Poverty and Health in the City of Sheffield : a report of a study conducted (for) the Environmental Health Department*, Sheffield (Sheffield City Council, 1985).

79. K. Banting, *Poverty, Politics and Policy* (London: Macmillan, 1979), p. 4.

80. Examples include: diet in infants; evaluation of early detection programmes for cancer; risk factors for low birth weight; identification of deafness in neo-nates; epidemiology of tuberculosis in immmigrants; nutritional requirements during weaning and early childhood; economic and health services consequences of smoking; value of using care attendants for elderly persons following their discharge from hospital and services and requirements for the terminally ill.

81. Topics covered by courses and workshops recently organised by the King's Fund College have included the planning of primary health care services; the development of local mental health services; the pursuit of quality in community services and locality management and planning.

82.   A. McNaught, 'Where are the Community Services Going?', Hospital and Health Services Review, January 1983, p. 16.

83.   Registration data comprise name, address, date of birth, sex, NHS number and name of GP, with whom the person is registered.

84.   Public Health in England, op. cit., para. 4.37.

85.   DHSS and Welsh Office, *District Health Authority Use of Family Practitioner Committee Patient Registration Data*, A Consultation Document, November 1987, para. 6.

86.   Ibid., para. 8.

87.   According to the consultation paper a user's code might include the following rules:

        ' the list only to be released to a bona fide (named) official of the DHA

        the list to be retained by the DHA under standing instructions which govern its use

        the data only to be used for 'proper' health purposes

        the list would not be made available to members of the public or unauthorised DHA staff.'

88.   Public Health in England, op. cit., para. 4.34.

89.   See D. Avison and P. Catchpole, 'Unconventional Korner', *The Health Service Journal*, 23 June 1988, pp. 704-705 for further details.

90.   *Partnerships for Health*, National Association of Health Authorities/ National Council for Voluntary Organisations, Report of a joint working party, 1987, p. 19.

91.   Report of the Joint Working Group on Collaboration between Family Practitioner Committees and District Health Authorities, op. cit., para. 12.

92.   M. Burch and B. Wood, *Public Policy in Britain* (Oxford: Martin Robertson, 1983), pp. 39-40.

93.   C. Ham, op. cit., p. 194.

94.   M. Saks, 'The Politics of Health Care' in L. Robins (ed.), *Politics and Policy Making in Britain* (London: Longman, 1987), p. 55.

95.   There are, of course, many other models of policymaking/power distribution. Unfortunately, due to shortage of space, it is not possible to consider them in this book. However, more attention will be given to them in the companion volume on contemporary issues in the CHSs. For a fuller a discussion of models of policy-making/power distribution in the context of health care generally see C. Ham, op. cit., and M. Saks, op. cit.

Chapter 9

Aspects of Service Delivery

Despite the problems faced by the NHS in the 1980s, those responsible for managing the CHSs have been able not only to expand existing services but also to develop new ones. As a result the range and variety of the CHSs are greater than they have ever been. Furthermore, the CHSs are at present attracting an unprecedented amount of attention from a wide variety of sources. Optimistically one might predict that future health service historians will view the final twenty years of the 20th Century as a watershed in the development of the CHSs. However, there are grounds for believing that the CHSs, as presently constituted and organised, will be subjected to 'drastic surgery' and thereby lose their distinctive identity.

The higher profile enjoyed by the CHSs in the late 1980s is due partly to the managerial and organisational changes arising from the 1982 restructuring exercise and the implementation of the recommendations of the NHS Management Inquiry, and partly to changing attitudes towards the provision of health care. Increasingly, the dominance of the curative hospital based services is being called into question. At the same time more emphasis is being placed on the contribution which the community based preventive and caring services can make to health care provision. These challenges to the traditional patterns of health care come from many quarters and are founded on profoundly different ideologies.

The Thatcher government has sought to reduce public spending, to minimise state involvement in the provision of welfare and to shift responsibility for health care away from statutory agencies. To this end, amongst other things, it has promoted the development of the private, profit-making, sector. However, it is aware that for the foreseeable future a totally private health care system is impracticable and, at the present time, politically unacceptable, and that for health care a mix of public and private provision will need to continue. Whilst the private sector operates across the whole range of health care services, traditionally it has been more involved and effective in the treatment of short-term, curable diseases. Since these have an apparently infinite capacity to absorb public resources, the Conservative government is happy to support private sector organisations in their bid to increase their share of this type of health care activity. Other health care functions, however, have attracted less attention from the private sector. These include: health promotion and illness prevention; the care of the long-term and chronically sick; and rehabilitation and after-care; to which the CHSs have always made a significant contribution. Moreover, it is likely that the need for these will increase if there is a major expansion of private sector involvement in the provision of acute hospital services.

In addition, for at least 30 years successive governments have been committed to a policy of care in the community. As a result large numbers of elderly, mentally ill, mentally handicapped and chronically sick patients, once cared for in NHS institutions, have become the responsibility of the community care services, of which the CHSs are a significant component. However, during the 1980s there has been increasing concern about the poor quality or non-existence of facilities for many of those patients who have been discharged into the community. The rapidly increasing cost of community care, in particular the large sums of money being paid by central government to private residential homes, has also been of concern. Furthermore, problems have arisen because of the multiplicity of agencies engaged in the provision of community care services. As mentioned in the previous chapter, this led to the review of community care undertaken by Sir Roy Griffiths. The changes proposed by the government in response to the Griffiths recommendations are likely to have significant consequences for the CHSs.

As well as looking for ways of rationalising the arrangements for community care, the Conservative government has also been seeking to develop a more coherent policy towards primary health care. To this end it published, in April 1986, a long-promised green paper on the subject entitled *Primary Health Care : An Agenda for Discussion*.

In the introduction to the green paper, primary care services were defined as 'the front line of the health service', encompassing 'all those services provided outside hospitals'[1] not only by family practitioners, but also by CHSs staff. The point was also made that these services had 'never before been comprehensively reviewed.'[2] The green paper, however, dealt only with the FPSs in a systematic and detailed manner. This was partly because the Cumberlege Report on community nursing (see below) was published on the same day as the green paper and it was felt that together the two documents provided 'the opportunity for a wide-ranging examination of the main elements of the primary care services.'[3] It can also be argued that the government's key objectives for primary care services were of as much significance for the future direction of CHSs, as for the FPSs. These were:

• to make services more responsive to the consumer;

• to raise standards of care;

• to promote health and prevent illness;

- to give patients the widest range of choice in obtaining high quality primary care services;
- to improve value for money; and
- to enable clearer priorities to be set for family practitioner services in relation to the rest of the health service.[4]

However, reading between the lines of the green paper it is not hard to reach the conclusion that part of the Conservative government's 'hidden agenda' for primary care is a significant expansion of the role of family practitioners at the expense of CHSs staff. For example, although recognition was given to the importance of co-operation and teamwork in primary care,[5] no mention was made of health centres, which had originally been seen as an essential prerequisite for effective teamwork. In their place the government appeared to favour the concept of the health care 'shop' run on business lines by family practitioners, but offering the full range of primary care services.[6] Given the change of policy towards health centres, which had occurred in 1980, and the Thatcher government's commitment to a larger role for the private sector in health care, this was hardly surprising. Nevertheless, developments of this kind have serious implications for the future of existing health centres. Indeed some health authorities, anticipating the compulsory privatisation of health centres, have sought to sell their premises to GPs and anyone else who might be interested in purchasing them. Thus, for the first time the number of DHA owned health centres is falling.

Moreover, with respect to other aspects of the CHSs, such as the pre-school child health services, the school health service, the community dental service, family planning and cervical cytology screening, services provided by community based paramedical staff and health education, the green paper could be seen as either an implicit or explicit threat. Consequently, it created a certain amount of anxiety on the part of those concerned about the future of the CHSs.

Nevertheless, most commentators considered it to be a fairly anodyne document and it is difficult not to agree with the conclusion of the editorial in *The Health Service Journal* that 'seldom, if ever before, (had) the gestation period of an elephant resulted in the production of a mouse.'[7] Despite this assessment of its contents, the green paper generated a wide ranging debate not only on the issues and questions it raised but also on primary care generally. It also prompted the Social Services Committee to undertake the investigation into primary care, which was referred to in the previous chapter. At the same time the health ministers took a variety of steps to consult with interested parties and to ensure that anyone who wished to comment on the proposals in the green paper was able to do so.[8]

According to the government, the consultation process demonstrated that there was 'wide support' for its objectives. In addition, from the comments received it identified the following themes as being of particular importance:

- concern about the extent of preventable disease;

- the value which consumers - whether individuals or families - place on accessible, effective, and sympathetic FPSs and CHSs;

- the need of consumers for better, more detailed, and more accessible factual information about practitioners and the range and pattern of services they provide;

- the need to meet the varied requirements of elderly people;

- a growing interest in the promotion of good health; and

- the need to improve services in deprived areas, particularly inner cities and isolated rural areas.[9]

The government acknowledged that it was necessary to address these themes and believed that the best way of doing so was to require 'practitioners to increase the range and quality of the services they provide(d).'[10]   In November 1987 the Conservative government published a white paper, *Promoting Better Health: The Government's Programme for Improving Primary Health Care*, in which it spelt out its conclusions on the comments it had received, both on the green paper and the Cumberlege Report, and the action it intended to take. At the same time it published the Health and Medicines Bill, which was needed to give legislative effect to some of the changes it wished to make.

Arguably, from the point of view of the CHSs, one of the most significant statements of intent in the white paper related to the primary health care team and the employment of ancillary staff by GPs. According to the white paper the government remained 'firmly committed to the continued development of primary health care teams'. However, it also believed 'that the restrictions on the types and numbers of staff whom the family doctor is encouraged to employ through the direct reimbursement scheme should ... be removed.'[11] This suggested that it saw the teams of the future as being composed of GPs and their employees (e.g. nurses, chiropodists, social workers). Whilst such an arrangement might be more convenient administratively, it is hardly in keeping with the orginal concept of a team of professionals from different backgrounds, but enjoying equal status. The implications of the white paper and the bill (which received the royal assent in November 1988) for specific CHSs are considered elsewhere in this chapter.

Subsequently, in January 1989, the Conservative government published its white paper, *Working for Patients*, and in late February, a series of working papers, which spelt out in more detail its proposals for the future of the NHS. As indicated in the previous chapter, under these proposals CHSs may become the responsibility of either the trusts set up to run self-governing hospitals (and their associated community based services) or self-governing community units or both. However, it is still possible, even under the white paper proposals, that some at least of the CHSs may become the responsibility of GPs. This is because, in keeping with one of the principles which underpinned the earlier white paper on primary health care - namely an extended role for GPs, the section of *Working for Patients* which deals with the practice budgets scheme states that 'the inclusion of staff costs within the budget will encourage practices to consider whether, for example, **to employ more nursing and other staff** (emphasis added).'[12] Although the CHSs are not explicitly mentioned, it seems likely that practices with their own budgets will be encouraged to offer services traditionally provided by CHSs staff.

Nevertheless, whilst the responsibility for the delivery of the CHSs may change, there can be little doubt that as a result of demographic and epidemiological trends the increasing demand for services of this kind will continue. The well documented growth of the elderly population during the present century and the increase in the number of people who are over the age of 75 is of immense significance for the CHSs, whoever is responsible for providing them. Justifiably the elderly make heavy demands on the health and social services. Moreover, in many cases, curative hospital based services are of peripheral value to the elderly, whilst the skills of community nurses, chiropodists, social workers and other community based carers can have a major impact on their health and well-being. With regard to epidemiological patterns, the main causes of death in the late 1980s are heart disease, cancer and cerebro-vascular disorders, and the most common health problems, colds, back pain and depression. Along with AIDS, these have proved resistent to curative approaches to health care. Thus, both the long-term care of those who cannot be cured and the maintenance of the health of those who have not yet succumbed represent a major challenge for the CHSs.

Significantly, since the 1970s the contribution which CHSs and other forms of primary health care can make to the health and well-being of individuals and of communities has received increasing international recognition. Of particular importance in this respect was the conference on primary health care held in Alma-Ata in 1978. Sponsored by the WHO (which a few months earlier had set the objective of 'an acceptable level of health for all by the year 2000'[13]) and the United Nations Children's Fund, the conference has played an important part 'in establishing what is meant by primary health care' and in encouraging governments to give it a higher priority when formulating their strategies for health. The immediate outcome of the conference was the *Declaration of Alma-Ata*. The ten articles of the declaration include a clear statement of principles on which primary care should be based and services developed. For example Article VII states that:

Primary health care ...

addresses the main health problems in the community, providing promotive, preventive, curative and rehabilitative services accordingly;

includes at least: education concerning prevailing health problems and the methods of preventing and controlling them; maternal and child health care, including family planning; immunisation against major diseases; prevention and control of local endemic diseases;...

requires and promotes maximum community and individual self-reliance and participation in the planning, organisation, operation and control of primary health care, making fullest use of local, national and other available resources; and to this end develops through appropriate education the ability of communities to participate; ...

relies, at local and referral levels, on health workers, including physicians, nurses, midwives, auxiliaries and community workers ... suitably trained socially and technically to work as a health team and to respond to the expressed health needs of the community.[14]

These principles have proved to be extremely influential and have helped to strengthen the position of those committed to the development and expansion of effective primary care services in their respective countries, whether developed or developing. Indeed, most of the major targets approved by the WHO Regional Committee for Europe in 1984, which were mentioned in Chapter 1, relate to primary care.[15]

It is therefore clear that, at the present time, the CHSs face not only threats and challenges to their traditional autonomy but also opportunities for future growth and development. Many of the pressures referred to above are all pushing in the same direction, that is towards an enlarged role for the CHSs in the health care of the population. However, whilst there may be broad agreement over the desirability of expanding the community care services there is considerable disagreement over the means of achieving this objective. This is apparent in some of the questions which have arisen in the debate surrounding the various official publications mentioned above. For example, what is the proper relationship, both professional and managerial, between the CHSs and GP services, between CHSs and HSs and between primary health care services and personal social services? What needs to be done to secure a team approach to the delivery of primary care? How should community carers be educated and trained? In what ways can more resources be secured to cope with the rapidly increasing demand for community based health care services? It is issues of this kind which preoccupy the professions whose members play the key role in the delivery of CHSs.

Professionals in the Community

Many professional groups are at the forefront of developments in the CHSs and they serve as the focus for the major part of this chapter. The groups in question are: community nurses (in particular health visitors, district nurses, community midwives, school nurses, and CPNs); paramedical staff (i.e. chiropodists, speech therapists, occupational therapists, physiotherapists, dietitians, and orthoptists); and others (i.e.) clinical medical officers; community dental officers; and health education officers. In the sections which follow, particular attention is given to the contribution of these professional groups to the CHSs; to their most pressing concerns and how these might be resolved; and to the future direction which they might take.

Community Nurses

As noted in Chapter 7, in 1985 the Thatcher government set up a small team, led by Julia Cumberlege, to review the community nursing services (i.e the Community Nursing Review Team). This action was prompted (according to the white paper, *Promoting Better Health*) by changes in the training, skills and knowledge of community nursing staff and the organisation of the services provided, which had taken place during the previous 10 years, and by 'the changing demographic structure of the population, in particular the increase in the number of elderly people'.[16] The commissioning of the review also demonstrated the significance attached by the government to community nursing and its interest in the future role of community nursing within primary care.

The report of the review team, entitled *Neighbourhood Nursing - A Focus for Care* (April 1986), has played an important part in setting the agenda for those seeking to advance the cause of community nursing. Furthermore, the review team's analysis of the existing state of affairs and its recommendations for the future have stimulated a lively debate.

Although the terms of reference of the review covered all the community nursing services, in the report an interesting distinction was made between 'core' and 'peripheral' groups of nurses. Cumberlege and her colleagues reserved the term 'community nursing' for the services provided by those groups which they regarded as being central to their investigation namely 'health visitors, district nurses, school nurses and their support staff of registered and enrolled nurses and nursing auxilliaries' (i.e. 'core' groups). Other groups of community nursing staff, that is community midwives, CPNs and community mental handicap nurses, other specialist nurses working in the community and practice nurses employed by GPs (i.e. 'peripheral' groups), were referred to specifically by name.[17]

The relative sizes of the 'core' and 'peripheral' groups of community nursing staff at the time of the review team's investigation are shown in Figure 9.1. It was estimated that, after making allowance for other qualified nurses and the fact that many nurses were employed on a part-time basis, there were over 50,000 nursing staff working in the community. Since then it is likely that this total will have increased to between 52000 and 53000 community nursing staff.

In making the distinction between the 'core' and 'peripheral' groups of community nursing staff it can be argued that the team was in danger of undermining one of its major objectives, namely securing greater cohesion amongst the professionals concerned. Moreover, the basis of the distinction can be questioned. For example, traditionally community midwives have been seen as a 'core' group, thus their exclusion is worthy of comment. According to Cumberlege and her

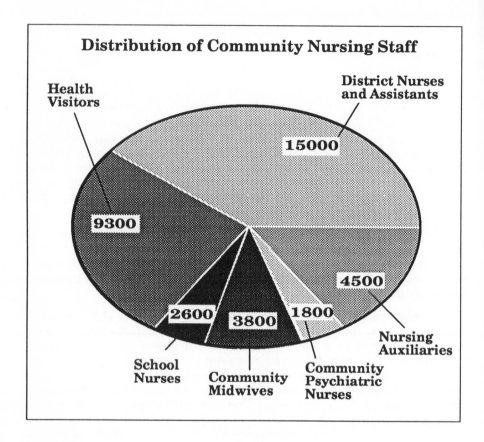

Figure 9.1

Source: *Neighbourhood Nursing-A Focus for Care*, p.10.

colleagues they were excluded 'principally because midwifery services (had) so recently been reviewed and integrated services (i.e. hospital and community) (were) developing well.' Given the importance of the contribution of midwives to community nursing it is unfortunate that the team took this view.

The review team went on to identify the shortcomings of the existing services. In this respect it made reference to a general lack of direction within community nursing and to the need for those responsible to sit back and take stock. 'At times nurses and their managers have not stopped to consider exactly what they are trying to achieve....If we had to summarise in a phrase what is wrong with community nursing services it is that they are in a rut.'[18]

To justify these general comments Cumberlege and her colleagues made a number of more specific criticisms which they referred to as a 'chain of weakness'. In their view:

- 'The needs of individuals and the communities in which they live are not being systematically identified.'

- 'Health visitors, district nurses and general practitioners, despite belonging to primary care teams, are not adequately or deliberately co-ordinating efforts to encourage and build on the informal networks of support which exist in neighbourhoods.'

- 'Community nurses spend much of their time routinely collecting data on their caseloads and workloads, but they and their managers have little use for the management information which may be produced from it.'

- 'Traditional working methods tend, as a result, to prevail, and health visitors and district nurses allow themselves to become set in roles which leave a great proportion of their professional skills not only under-used but very often unused...'.[19]

Lastly, they expressed concern about the overlap of the functions of the various professional groups involved. According to the review team, hospital and community nurses; GPs, community nurses and midwives; community nurses and social workers (in respect of the assessment of client needs) and even the community nurses themselves frequently duplicate one another's work. In short the team agreed 'with the Royal College of Nursing that the contribution of nursing to primary health care is 'far less than its potential'.[20]

The team also expressed the fear that, although there was a general commitment (on the part of the government and many of the professions involved) to switching health care resources from hospital based to community based services, 'the voices of health staff and vulnerable people scattered throughout the community may not be strong enough to prevail over those who demand unlimited resources for high technology medicine.'[21]

Nevertheless, despite the perceived problems and existing shortcomings of community nursing, the review team was optimistic about the future and put forward some constructive recommendations. During the previous few years there had been a substantial increase in the number of community nurses and significant improvement in their training, knowledge and skills. Furthermore, it believed that community nursing could 'become a major force for change and improvement in the community health services.'[22] In its view this would be achieved by breaking down traditional demarcation lines between health visitors, district nurses and school nurses, thereby fostering a more flexible approach to community nursing with, for example, health visitors making greater use of their nursing skills and district nurses their counselling skills. For this approach to work it would be necessary also for community nursing to be organised on a more local, or neighbourhood, basis. To this end, the review team recommended 'that in each District neighbourhood nursing services should be established' (for a population of 10,000 and 25,000 people). 'Health visitors, district nurses and school nurses, with their support staff would thus provide a strong, closely integrated, locally managed service near to the consumer.'[23]

In their detailed recommendations the members of the team developed this basic proposal and indicated how it might be implemented.

- 'Each neighbourhood nursing service should be headed by a manager chosen for her management skills and leadership qualities, and she should be based in the neighbourhood.'

- 'Community midwives, community psychiatric nurses and community mental handicap nurses should ensure through their respective managers and the neighbourhood nursing manager, that their specialist contributions are fully co-ordinated with the work of the neighbourhood nursing service.'

- 'All other specialist nurses who work outside hospital should be based in the community and managed as part of the neighbourhood nursing service. Each specialist nurse should be assigned to one or more neighbourhood services ...'

- 'The principle should be adopted of introducing the nurse practitioner into primary health care. Subject to the agreement of local general practitioners .... Her key tasks would be to interview patients and diagnose and treat specific diseases in accordance with the agreed medical protocols; refer to the general practitioner patients who have medical problems which lie outside the written protocols; be available for all patients who wish to consult the nurse practitioner; give counselling and nursing advice to patients consulting her direct or referred to her by a general practitioner; conduct screening programmes... ; maintain patient-care programmes ...; refer patients for further nursing care to the neighbourhood nursing service.'

- 'The DHSS should agree a limited list of items and simple agents which may be prescribed by nurses as part of a nursing care programme, and issue guidelines to enable nurses to control drug dosage in well-defined circumstances.'

- 'To establish and be recognised as a primary health care team, each general medical practice and the community nurses associated with it should come to an understanding of the team's objectives and individuals' roles within it.'

- 'That understanding should be incorporated into a written agreement signed jointly by the practice partners and by the manager of the neighbourhood nursing service on behalf of the relevant health authority.'

- 'The agreement should name the doctors and community nurses who together form the primary care team and should guarantee the right of team members to be consulted on any changes proposed in its composition...'
- 'The Government should invite the Health Advisory Service, ... to take on responsibility for identifying and promoting good practice in primary health care.'
- 'Subsidies to general practitioners enabling them to employ staff to perform nursing duties should be phased out.'
- 'Within two years the United Kingdom Central Council for Nursing, Midwifery and Health Visiting and the English National Board should introduce a common training course for all first-level nurses wishing to work outside hospital in what are now the fields of health visiting, district nursing and school nursing.'
- 'The provision of nursing services in the community should remain the responsibility of district health authorities. We would urge, however, that in due course the Government should give consideration to amalgamating family practitioner committees and district health authorities and so bring all health care services under the control of one body.'
- 'Health care associations should be formed, each covering one or more neighbourhoods'.[24]

This last recommendation was designed to secure the participation of consumers in the planning of health care services at neighbourhood level and it reflected the review team's firmly held belief that community health should be seen as a partnership in which the people themselves actively participate alongside health care professionals.[25]

In **response to Cumberlege** much of the comment came from those with an interest, particularly a professional interest, in the subject matter of the report. Consequently, the views expressed were often influenced by thinly disguised professional self-interest. This does not necessarily invalidate them, but it does mean that they need to be treated with caution. The groups, which were particularly active is this respect were: those defined as being central to the investigation (i.e. the 'core' groups); those seen as 'peripheral' to the investigation; social workers; CHSs managers; and GPs.

Predictably, the response of the **'core' community nursing professions** was favourable. In the words of an article in *'Patching In'*: 'The Cumberlege Report has been widely welcomed by nurses because it gives them a high profile and a central role in the provision of community health services.'[26] Typical of the comments from individual health visitors was that of Robertson, 'The proposals provide an exciting challenge and some very useful pointers for the next phase in the history of (health visiting).'[27] Similarly, Kratz writing in the *Nursing Times*, described the report as 'an impressive document which comes to grips with some of the thornier questions which have faced non institutional nursing care and emerges with some original solutions' and she considered the model agreement as 'possibly one of the most important aspects of the report.' In her view the report 'makes one hopeful for the future of nursing in general and for nursing in the community in particular.'[28] However, despite the positive views expressed by individuals, the collective response of the 'core' professions was somewhat low key. This suggested that whilst they welcomed the proposals they were sceptical about the likelihood of their implementation.

The response of the members of the **'peripheral' community nursing professions** can best be described as guarded approval. On the one hand, they recognise the potential for their profession, consequent upon the development of a more visible and prestigious community nursing service. On the other, they felt the need to draw attention to a variety of concerns, many of which arose from a belief that their particular interests were not adequately taken into account by Cumberlege and her colleagues.

For example, the official response of the community psychiatric nursing profession, which was prepared by Brooker, highlights many of these concerns:

- the report asks no specific questions regarding consumer awareness of community psychiatric nursing;

- the team did not consider the financial implications of twenty-four hour access to professional support, which for CPNs, would undoubtedly mean working a significant number of anti-social hours;

- much of the report is based on the assumption that people live in and are accepted by a community. For many of the clients of CPNs this is not the case;

- the relationship between the new neighbourhood nursing teams and existing district mental health services is not made clear;

- the training needs of CPNs were not addressed and the report actually overstated the number of trained CPNs in post;

- the role-blurring, favoured by the Cumberlege team could make CPNs redundant, especially where a neighbourhood nurse has pursued the mental health option during her training.[29]

Brooker concluded that CPNs would have liked to be recognised as members of neighbourhood nursing teams. Moreover, although the Community Psychiatric Nursing Association agreed with the concept of the neighbourhood nursing team, it was difficult for the profession 'to express much enthusiasm for the report of the review team', because it had not acknowledged 'the exciting work being undertaken by CPNs already in primary health care.'[30] It was also felt that the review team's recommendations were somewhat rigid and inexible, in that CPNs could have been included as 'core' members of neighbourhood nursing teams where they had considerable experience of primary care. For example, in Oxford CPNs had been attached to GP practices since 1972 and had built up a wealth of knowledge for which there appeared to be no use.

Not surprisingly, the virtual exclusion of **social work** from the Cumberlege Report caused disappointment amongst some social workers who felt that their contribution to community health care had not been given sufficient recognition. In addition, Smith (a former director of social services) expressed some concern regarding the whole concept of neighbourhood nursing teams. He felt that the neighbourhood concept would lead to 'a doubling of the number of nurse managers but (would) leave them still with spans of supervision that most textbooks would regard as overextended.'[31] Moreover, it would cut across existing organisational structures for child guidance, community psychiatry and personal social services. He also regarded Cumberlege and her colleagues as rather woolly and evasive when they sought to explain exactly how the 'peripheral' professions would relate to the neighbourhood nursing services. They suggested that these professions should keep their present management structures, but develop better lines of communication with the rest of the community nursing structure. However, they offered no clear guidelines as to how this could be achieved and conveniently ignored the fact that if their proposals were actually implemented there would be far more community nursing teams with which the 'peripheral' professions would have to communicate.

Smith went on to accuse the review team of missing the 'opportunity ... to define the primary care team in terms which would include teachers, social workers, residential workers in respite care, occupational therapists and other paramedical personnel as members rather than people from sister agencies with whom good relations need somehow to be built up.'[32] Furthermore, he argued that it apparently ignored the similarities between community nursing and social work and thus failed to learn valuable lessons from the recent experiences of those engaged in the provision of personal social services. As Smith argued: 'The problems of social work and nursing in relating to the community have great and usable similarities; indeed in organisational terms, (they) have often tackled the same issues ... Carving natural neighbourhoods out of modern urban sprawl is not at all as easy as the (review team) suggest; the long debate on patch working in social services departments is splendidly apt but is never referred to.'[33]

The failure to learn from the experiences of other professions is exemplified in the review team's approach to an issue which had been faced by the social work profession in the early 1970s, namely that of specialism versus generalism. To some extent the report was inconsistent on this issue. On the one hand, it recommended generic (i.e. generalist) community nursing, thus acknowledging the many imperatives which make the generic approach desirable. The logic of health care needs as they appear in the community; the importance of teamwork and inter-agency collaboration in meeting these needs and the necessity of using scarce resources as efficiently as possible all testify to the importance of breaking down professional barriers and blurring the demarcation lines which have emerged in recent years.

On the other hand, the members of the review team also recognised that there was a continuing need for specialist contributions from trained staff with the skills, knowledge and experience to deal with particular problems in greater depth. (e.g. diabetes; terminal care).

In principle there is no reason why a satisfactory division of labour between specialist and generalist cannot be secured in community nursing. In practice, however, such an outcome is unlikely. This is because, amongst groups who are unsure of their professional standing, there is a feeling (possibly fostered by the way in which the medical profession has developed during the 20th Century) that only through specialisation can the high level of expertise and technical competence, necessary for true 'professionalism', be realised. Moreover, the generic approach to social work training, which was introduced in response to the recommendations of the Seebohm Committee (1968), has proved to be both unacceptable to the profession and undesirable from the point of view of the client, as the comments on the role of social workers in cases of child abuse testify.

Although there are some references to management issues in the Cumberlege Report, these are confined to the role of the professional nurse manager in relation to the neighbourhood nursing team and the advocacy of a merger between FPCs and DHAs. This, however, has not inhibited **CHSs managers** from expressing their views on the review team's recommendations. Since many managers have been attracted by the principle of decentralisation or 'going local' they have tended to respond in a positive manner to the concept of neighbourhood nursing. They also recognise the need for personal services, like nursing, to be organised as close to the point of service delivery as possible and that relatively few economies of scale can be achieved in a community setting, where patients are dispersed and many have long-term problems which can be dealt with only on a domiciliary basis.

Nevertheless, a number of managers have had reservations and concerns. For example, Haggard (General Manager of South Derbyshire's Community Unit), writing in *Patching In*, wondered whether she was the only manager to feel nervous about 'plunging into patching'.[34] In her view, the Cumberlege proposals raised many questions which needed to be resolved if neighbourhood nursing was to work satisfactorily.

First, what is the most appropriate size for a neighbourhood? It has to be small enough for people to identify with it otherwise the whole point of neighbourhood nursing is lost. On the other hand if a neighbourhood is too small: it would be viable neither managerially (e.g. it could not cope with the absence of one member of staff for a period of maternity leave); nor professsionally (e.g. it would not allow for specialisation and the regular release of members for training courses and other activities necessary for the maintenance of clinical excellence).[35]

Second, consideration must be given to the nature of the relationship between the neighbourhood and unit of management, with responsibility for the CHSs. For example, how much autonomy should the neighbourhood nursing teams possess?

Should nurse managers be given budgets and how should resources be allocated between teams? Who should allocate staff to neighbourhoods (on the assumption that some neighbourhoods would be more desirable to work in than others)? Who should be responsible for the recruitment and selection of community nurses? Who should provide cover if one neighbourhood was short staffed? How should the performance of the team be evaluated?

Third, many managers foresaw problems arising from the division of responsibility between neighbourhood nursing teams and primary health care teams and between community nurses and GPs and they also anticipated particular difficulties in inner city and rural areas. To some extent these arose from the inherent contradictions between, 'zoning' on which the concept of the neighbourhood nursing team is based, and, 'attachment', which was introduced in order to facilitate the development of primary health care teams. As Cumberlege and her colleagues pointed out:

> *A primary health care team is normally formed by the 'attachment' of district nurses and health visitors to a general practice. It serves the patients registered with the practice. Most general practices are, however, not related to a defined geographical area. A district health authority and the community nursing services ... have responsibility for all the residents of a defined area. It is an anomalous situation ...*[36]

Furthermore, 'attachment' makes the provision of a comprehensive service less likely, since district nurses and health visitors are not in as good a position to build up a detailed and intimate knowledge of the residents of a particular geographical area as they are when they are 'zoned'.

It may also result in:

● time and money being wasted in excessive travelling by nursing staff;

● community support networks not being tapped;

● some people not receiving the community nursing services to which they are entitled 'because their needs go unseen';[37] and

● reciprocal arrangements having to be negotiated between neighbouring DHAs because GP practice areas cross their boundaries.

However, although the members of the review team were well aware of the problem, they were unsure as to how it could be resolved. Apart from expressing pleasure at the fact that some GPs were 'limiting their practices to a defined geographical area' and hoping, rather optimistically, that this kind of 'zoning' would spread, they had few suggestions to make regarding the reconciliation of the principles of 'attachment' and 'zoning'. They recognised that in the unlikely event of GPs agreeing to the transfer of patients between lists, to minimise the overlapping of practice areas, such a move, except on a voluntary basis, 'would probably cause more offence than efficiency.' Moreover, if such an objective were to be pursued by directing new patients to particular lists 'it would take years to complete the whole zoning exercise.'[38] Thus, the best that the review team could offer was a rather uneasy coexistence between the concepts of the primary care team and neighbourhood nursing.

Finally, there are likely to be conflicts between the concept of the generic manager and the development of locality management (see Chapter 8) and that of the nurse manager leading a team of community nurses. How can the professional accountability and expertise of nurses be safeguarded if they are managerially accountable to someone from a different professional background (e.g. administration; physiotherapy)?

Although Haggard and others were, on balance, in favour of the Cumberlege recommendations they felt that these questions must be addressed and satisfactory answers found before they could be implemented successfully . As both personal social services authorities and the NHS have discovered, there are no natural communities on which to base neighbourhood teams. Therefore, why should the Cumberlege proposals be any more successful than earlier attempts to adopt a more localised approach to service delivery?

Judging by the vehemence of their reactions to the recommendations of Cumberlege and her colleagues, there can be little doubt that **GPs** were the group which felt it had most to lose, in terms of autonomy and prestige, from their implementation. Dr John Chisholm, chair of a BMA working party which gave evidence to the review team, argued that if the Cumberlege proposals were implemented it would lead to the establishment of a community nursing structure operating in parallel to that for general medical services and a significant expansion in both the role and numbers of nurse managers. In his view developments of this kind would damage the relationship between GPs and nurses and undermine the primary health care team.[39]

At a conference on primary health care held in November 1986 GPs made it clear that in their opinion community nursing, far from developing along the lines of the Cumberlege proposals, should be made the administrative responsibility of FPCs and based on GP practices. Moreover, they were opposed to the expansion of nurse manager posts; nurse practitioners and formal agreements between members of the primary health care team.

At the same conference the chairman of the General Medical Services Committee of the BMA, Dr Michael Wilson, described the report as 'essentially political and provocative, prepared by a policy unit whose main contact appear(ed) to have been with philosophers, privateers and trendy professors.' According to another delegate it was 'shoddy, unconvincing, naive and ill- researched' and was 'an insult to everyone in primary care', since it sought 'to change the whole basis of the community nursing service with very little evidence collected in very little time.'[40]

The antipathy of GPs to the recommendations of the review team can best be explained by reference to the nature of the relationship between community nurses and GPs, which dates back to the inception of both professions in the 19th Century. At that time, a predictable and conventional pattern emerged in which the nurse was subservient to the doctor. This reflected gender relationships within society at large as well as nascent professional relationships within hospitals. Such a pattern has remained (if not unchallenged) and even the 'attachment schemes' designed to facilitate the development of multidisciplinary teamwork in the community have tended to reinforce the assistant or handmaiden status of the nurse.

This state of affairs and, in particular, the supremacy of the GP vis-a-vis community nurses, was overtly challenged by Cumberlege and her colleagues. They offered an alternative model for the relationship based on professional equality and a genuinely shared responsibility for community health. At the heart of this new relationship was the written agreement in which the rights of all members of the primary health care team were recognised. In Part Two of the Cumberlege Report - *Programme for Action* - it was suggested that the agreement might include provision for regular monthly meetings of team members; the sharing of records and consultation on any changes in working practices. Furthermore, in cases where GPs were not prepared to enter into an agreement of this kind they would receive only those nursing services which the neighbourhood nurse managers decided to provide and these would not carry any guarantees. As if to add insult to injury, the review team also recommended that the financial incentives for GPs to employ their own practice nurses should be phased out.[41]

In some respects these recommendations had something of the gauntlet about them since they struck at the heart of professional autonomy, and the supremacy, to which GPs had been accustomed and had jealously guarded for many decades. Thus, the negative response of GPs was both predictable and, in some respects, understandable. It seems likely, therefore, that the full **implementation of the Cumberlege proposals** will founder on the rock of medical opposition. Nevertheless, the fact that such radical ideas could be put forward in the report of a government appointed review team indicates that times are changing and that the mood, in many quarters, is sympathetic to the Cumberlege philosophy, insofar as it relates to a change in the relationship between nurses and GPs.

The Conservative government's response to the Cumberlege recommendations and the views expressed in the debate to which they gave rise was contained in *Promoting Better Health* and in a circular issued on the day the white paper was published.[42] In the white paper the government referred to the circular which it had issued 'inviting Health Authorities in England to review the way in which their community nursing services (were) managed' and announced its intention of looking further 'at the legal status, functions and qualifications for employment of nurse practitioners'; consulting with the professional standing advisory committees on the question of giving nurses more freedom to prescribe and supply certain drugs and appliances and supporting the provision of training courses for practice nurses.[43] It also agreed that the management and delivery of community nursing services needed to reflect the views of consumers and that teamwork in primary care was essential. However, on the contentious issue of whether or not there should be written agreements between members of primary care teams, Ministers expressed their support for the Social Services Committee's view that the 'emphasis should be on 'agreement' rather than on 'written'.[44] Furthermore, they did not accept that subsidies for practice nurses should be phased out. On the contrary they indicated their intention to extend the scheme whereby GPs are reimbursed some of the cost of employing their own staff.(See above.)

The circular also contained the DHSS's response to requests from health authorities for guidance as to how they should set about establishing neighbourhood nursing teams. It began by reaffirming the government's commitment to prevention and health promotion; the development and expansion of primary care; teamwork and improving the quality of services especially in inner cities and other deprived areas; and collaboration and consultation between statutory agencies and voluntary organisations.

However, the only changes and developments in the organisation of community nursing services which the government was prepared to consider were those which:

- contributed to the development of primary health care teams;
- recognised that general practice was based on practices with overlapping areas to ensure that patients had a choice of GP;
- ensured that community nurses were linked to GPs;
- allowed for local variations to meet local needs;
- involved no additional expenditure; and
- made effective use of scarce resources.

Moreover, although the circular gave general support to the principle of a more local organisation for community nursing services (i.e. based on neighbourhoods, localities or patches), it suggested that this was not always appropriate or practicable. For example, local organisation was likely to be more difficult in large urban areas which could not be easily subdivided into smaller units; in inner cities with a large number of single-handed GP practices and in areas where there were many GPs with small lists and/or operating from poor premises. In areas of this kind even 'attachment schemes' were difficult to operate on an economic basis and the geographic organisation of community nursing was probably a more practical proposition.

In planning the restructuring of their community nursing services on a neighbourhood basis health authorities were directed to take account of factors such as: demographic patterns; the physical environment; and the distribution of statutory and voluntary services.They were also instructed to consult with FPCs, professional advisory bodies, local authorities and CHCs.

Taken together, the white paper and the circular can be said to represent an attempt by the Conservative government to give its general support to the Cumberlege proposals without alienating GPs. Thus, although they contain a reasonably clear endorsement of the philosophy of neighbourhood nursing, the guidance to health authorities is more guarded and conditional than the members of the review team would have liked. Moreover, it is clear that Ministers have been keen to protect the interests and independence of GPs by watering down or failing to support some of the team's more radical proposals.

Given the Thatcher government's equivocal position on the Cumberlege Report it is worth considering how influential it has been at the 'grass roots' level. Significantly, data collected by the primary health care group of the King's Fund (see Chapter 8), as part of its study of the extent to which DHAs have adopted a decentralised approach to the management of their CHSs, show that a relatively large number of health authorities responded positively to the concept of neighbourhood nursing. The group's initial survey of DHAs in 1986 indicated that 63% (of the 159 DHAs which responded in the appropriate manner) had plans to introduce Cumberlege style neighbourhood nursing teams. A further survey in January 1988 showed that of the 128 DHAs (67%) which completed the team's questionnaire, 36 had already introduced neighbourhood nursing teams; 41 were planning to do so; 19 were undecided and were keeping the matter under review and 32 had decided against their introduction.

Where neighbourhood teams had been established there was considerable variation in their size, although the majority had between 15 and 25 members. Most neighbourhoods had a population of between 20,000 and 30,000. All but one district had health visitors, district nurses and school nurses in their teams. Interestingly, in 16 districts, teams also included other types of nurse (e.g. CPNs) and, in some cases, paramedics and administrative and clerical staff. Although 27 districts indicated that team managers had either a health visiting or district nursing background, professional accountability appeared to be the biggest single issue facing managers with regard to neighbourhood nursing. In other words they had to find ways of ensuring that field staff had adequate support in their professional practice when managed by someone from a different branch of nursing or from a non-nursing profession. From responses to the questionnaire it was clear that districts had sought to resolve this issue in a number of different ways, such as twinned teams, designated clinical support posts within teams and dual-qualified team managers.

Another issue thrown up by the survey was that of training and preparation for the changes. Other issues 'not revealed by the survey but known to be of concern (were) those of establishing good relationships with GPs; building and maintaining staff morale through changing times; and developing accurate means of evaluating the new ways of working.'[45] In spite of these unresolved issues and the ongoing debate surrounding the Cumberlege Report it is likely that, in some districts at least, neighbourhood nursing has a future and that as a result 'there is ... a greater sense of direction for community (nursing) services than for many years'.[46]

Alongside the more general issues arising from the introduction of neighbourhood nursing, **health visitors** continue to face a variety of dilemmas relating specifically to the nature and status of their profession. In essence, these have remained largely unchanged throughout this century. However, during the 1970s and 1980s the dilemmas have become far more salient and this has led some within the profession to speak in terms of a crisis in health visiting. For example, in 1988 Shirley Goodwin, the General Secretary of the Health Visitors' Association, used her keynote speech at the Association's annual study conference to address, 'health visiting's crisis of identity (and) ... fear for its survival (which are) currently generating much distress, pain and anger'. According to Goodwin, these have to be acknowleged and confronted if the profession is 'to move forward with confidence.'[47]

More specifically a number of concerns have been identified. First, many health visitors feel they are 'trapped in a narrow and restrictive straightjacket of health visiting practice' and are therefore unable to tackle problems in a more flexible and imaginative manner. As Goodwin observed, the sense of 'frustration and helplessness' to which this gives rise is due 'at times to the blinkered professional culture on the part of practitioners' and in some cases to the 'rigid policies' operated by a number of DHAs. Unfortunately, these authorities have perpetuated the 'health visiting by numbers' approach, in which 'the only measurable products' of the health visitors workload are head counts of the individuals visited or seen, and have thereby prevented 'health visitors from exercising fully their professional judgement as to when, where and how clients' health care needs can best be met.' For Goodwin, the way ahead in respect of this concern is to encourage DHAs and those responsible for managing their health visiting services to set objectives not in terms of activity levels (e.g. numbers of visits) but 'in terms of the measurable outcome of that activity, for example the percentage of a given target client group contacted by the health visiting service for a given purpose.'[48]

Second, the caseload pattern remains a problem both for individual health visitors determining their own priorities and for their managers concerned with the deployment of resources and with strategy. The percentage of time spent by health visitors in meeting the needs of the 0 to 4 year olds and their mothers has fallen steadily since the early 1970s. This has been compensated for by additional work with those aged 5 to 64, rather than the elderly.

Health visiting is traditionally associated with babies and young children (see Chapter 2). This focus remains an important one as the priorities document produced by the Health Visitors' Association in the early 1980s made clear (see Chapter 7). Children have always been seen as a suitable target for a variety of social policy measures. Not only are they deemed to be 'deserving', but action to secure the well-being of children is considered to be a good investment for the future

(N.B.Black Report). Moreover, during the second half of the 1980s the importance of work with families where there are small children has been highlighted by a number of factors.

Recent research into the phenomenon known as 'sudden infant death syndrome' (i.e. 'cot death') has shown that health visitors could make a greater contribution in this sphere. In addition child accidents are now the major cause of death in children aged over one year and 'health visiting has yet to respond effectively to this tragic statistic.'[49] Moreover the health visitor's role in cases of child abuse (previously referred to as non-accidental injury to children) has changed. Whilst legislation places primary responsibility for the care and protection of abused children and children at risk of abuse on local authorities (i.e. Children and Young Persons Act 1969; Child Care Act 1980), the findings of various committees of inquiry concerning particular cases of child abuse suggest that a major problem in dealing with such cases is the lack of effective inter-agency collaboration (e.g.the Report of the Inquiry into Child Abuse in Cleveland chaired by Lord Butler-Sloss[50]). Concerns of this kind prompted the DHSS and Welsh Office to issue 'a guide to arrangements for inter-agency co-operation for the protection of children from abuse', which was published under the title *Working Together* in 1988. From the point of view of health visiting the most significant points made in this document are that since all parents have contact with pre-school child health services the health visitor has an important preventive role and may well be the first to suspect that a child may be at risk; and 'inter-agency procedures should be brought into action at the earliest possible stage and in respect of every allegation.'[51]

Thus, although health visitors have always had responsibilities in this respect, these have become more explicit. It therefore seems likely that for the foreseeable future the health visitor must continue to play a key role in respect of the care of young children.

At the same time there is a growing need for the skills of the health visitor to be applied in respect of other client groups (e.g. elderly, disabled and chronically sick). Additionally, attempts to develop a more positive approach to health with a greater emphasis on the promotion of health, the prevention of disease and health maintenance mean that they should be made available to the population at large.

Clearly, without a substantial increase in resources it would not be possible for health visitors to meet adequately all these demands for their services. One possible solution to the resource issue would be for the profession to adopt a more selective approach. This would mean that only families who were deemed to be facing particular problems or who came within a high risk category would be visited. Furthermore, the point is made by Goodwin that there are 'large question marks over some of (the) traditional approaches to child health promotion, much of which is based upon a disease detection and medicalised model of child health screening and surveillance.'[52] Current practice is 'based upon the wrong premise that the detection of significant abnormality depends mainly upon the application of repeated checks and screening tests, whereas the true position is that the vast majority of abnormalities are identified at or soon after birth or are subsequently brought to the attention of health visitors and doctors by parents.'[53]

There has been little support for such an approach within the profession. At present the lay view of the health visitor is that of a family visitor who is non-threatening; has easy access to every home and gives good advice and practical help when it is needed. It is feared that if the universal nature of health visiting were to be abandoned s/he would be seen increasingly as someone whose intervention was unwelcome, founded, as it would be, on an unfavourable assessment of the family's ability to cope and therefore as someone who threatened the stability and unity of the family. The consequences for health visitors of such a change in their image could be dire. Access to homes might well be curtailed; the legitimacy of the health visitor's educative function could be called into question and her work with all groups could be impeded.

There is already an element of informal selectivity with 'competent' families being visited less frequently than those who, for one reason or another, are less able to cope without support. It seems likely that this will continue and that, at least in the short-term, the determination of priorities and caseload patterns will remain matters for the individual health visitor and his/her manager to resolve.

Third, Goodwin drew attention to the question mark which is hanging over the relative contributions to health of 'individual health teaching, advice and social support provided by health visitors and of other social and environmental factors such as housing, low income and access to responsive primary medical care.' In her view the efforts of health visitors will have only a limited impact if they mainly rely on 'telling people how to live more healthily', since public policies have a far greater influence on people's lifestyle than anything that can be done on a one-to-one basis. It is therefore essential for health visitors not to lose sight of the fact that one of the key principles on which their profession was founded was the 'acceptance of a ... responsibility to seek to challenge and influence public policy, rather than submissively assisting people to live with its consequences, taking all the blame themselves for their unhealthy lifestyles.' Indeed, this aspect of the profession's role has a higher priority than ever before and considerable attention is being given by the Health Visitors' Association to the promotion of 'more health-enhancing public policies.' Nevertheless, there remains an obvious tension between the overtly political activities of health visitors collectively and the essentially individualistic approach which they adopt when exercising their clinical responsibilities.'[54]

A fourth issue facing health visitors arises from the doubts which have been expressed by some as to the appropriateness of the professional approach in health visiting. Since its establishment in the 19th Century health visiting has taken the professional route and this strategy has yielded many rewards. Health visiting has secured a certain amount of prestige and health visitors are, in general, a respected, well understood and accessible group of community based health care workers. However, the story is not one of unmitigated success. Health visitors (along with other groups of community nurses) have not secured equality with GPs. Nor have they made a significant impact in the sphere of policy-making. Although health authorities are required to have at least one member with a nursing/health visiting background, their policies rarely reflect the health visiting viewpoint. Moreover, relatively few health visitors have risen to senior management positions and only a handful of general managers have a health visiting background.[55]

Amongst those who study the primary care professions there are some who argue that the professional approach is not necessarily the most constructive or the most appropriate. Here the need is less for someone who is highly trained, a specialist and a member of a professional association and more for someone with a wide range of less sophisticated skills. Most health visitors however, remain committed to a professional approach and seek to overcome its defects not by abandoning it, but by refining and enhancing it. For example, there have been moves (not supported by all members of the profession) to develop a health visiting process similar to that adopted for other branches of nursing some years ago. Amongst other things, a health visiting process would serve to make the health visitor's role more, rather than less, formal and explicitly professional. There is also continued emphasis within the profession on education, research and specialisation. Furthermore, in the present climate, it is clear that a non-professional approach would undermine the position of health visitors vis-a-vis GPs and reduce their influence within the policy -making arena.

One final concern is that of the relationship between health visiting and other health care professionals working in the community. The interdependence of community health care professionals was clearly an issue lying at the heart of the Cumberlege Report. However, as well as the more general aspects of this issue, health visitors regularly face the specific challenges and dilemmas of practising alongside a variety of other professionals. They have been seen as key members of not only neighbourhood nursing teams, but also primary health care teams. They are dependent on other professions for access to data about their caseloads and, to some extent, for their referrals. In addition, they often need to refer their clients to other services. Moreover, they have to collaborate on a regular basis with district nurses, nursery school teachers, social workers, occupational therapists, wardens of elderly persons homes and many other groups. Since the publication of *Working Together* (see above) they have a clear duty to collaborate with other professionals, particularly within the local authority, with respect to the care and protection of abused children. Thus, the establishment and maintenance of good relations with other professionals and the fostering of a team spirit is considered by many to be an essential ingredient of the work of the health visitor.

Since teamwork is regarded as being of such importance for effective health visiting (as well as many other aspects of health care) it seems almost sacrilegious to subject it to criticism. Nevertheless, as Noon bravely suggests, there are some drawbacks to the team approach. For example, services may be co-ordinated to such an extent that options are removed from clients and, to those who feel vulnerable, co-ordination may be perceived as a network closing in on them. Moreover, for the professionals the problems involved in working together harmoniously may be so monumental as to outweigh the advantages of teamwork.[56] However, 'it seems clear that teamwork is upon us ... (and) the concept of teamwork is likely to persist.'[57]

In the light of these issues and concerns and 'imperatives for change' Goodwin suggests that a 'positive programme for future health visiting practice' should be based on the certain premises. For example:

- 'Health visiting is and must continue to be a universal health promotion and prevention service, available to all on an unsolicited basis as well as on request, and requiring no test of need.'

- 'Within this universalist context, health visiting must be actively offered to certain target client groups, their selection based on an assessment of local need, and on local and national policies and priorities for care, in consultation with other agencies and representatives of the community...'

- 'Health visiting contact with target groups must involve the application of a range of interventions not restricted to routine home visiting or traditional child health clinics; and must place a major emphasis upon group and community interventions ...'

- 'Health visitors must work closely with members of the primary care team and other relevant agencies to ensure that effort is maximised and unnecessary duplication of care avoided.'[58]

Within this framework it would be up to local managers to determine and agree what kind and level of service should be offered to those living in their district. According to Goodwin it is vital that objectives and targets for the health visiting service should be specified in writing and reviewed at regular intervals.[59]

How far Goodwin's framework for the future development of health visiting practice will be implemented is clearly a matter for conjecture. If one takes a pessimistic view, it is possible that in a more entrepreneurially-orientated health care system there may be no place for health visiting at all. However with increasing concern about the welfare of children and the elderly and the growing interest in the promotion of health, the role of health visitors may acquire renewed kudos.

In many respects the role of the **district nurse** is less ambiguous than that of the health visitor. Moreover, in the 1970s and 1980s this role has expanded both in terms of the number of patients treated by district nurses and the intensity and sophistication of the nursing care which they are often having to provide. This is due to demographic trends, the development of 'hospital at home' schemes and the policy of community care for the priority groups.

However, despite this expansion, the years since 1981 (when post-basic training for district nurses was made mandatory - see Chapter 7) have been characterised by a growing concern, on the part of district nurses, to protect their professional interests. Such concern has been reflected in the tone of many of the articles on clinical and non-clinical issues published, since 1986, in *The Journal of District Nursing* and elsewhere.

For example, an article in June 1988 drew attention to the unsatisfactory nature of the balance between hospital- and community-orientated health care services in the following terms: 'The Medical Officer of Health has disappeared and been most inadequately replaced by someone on the DMT. 'Public Health' has largely been forgotten. There are advocates ... but I sometimes wonder if they can make themselves heard above the cacophony of the consultants and the waving of shrouds.'[60] As a result, district nursing (and other community based professional groups) have failed to secure the recognition, status and resources they deserve.

Various aspects of the education and training of district nurses have also been a cause for concern. Although the introduction of mandatory training for district nurses and the location of this training in institutions of further and higher education, as opposed to schools of nursing, was a significant advance and represented the climax of a long struggle, it has not proved to be a complete success. Initially the response from nurses to this change was encouraging and there was an increasing number of applicants for district nurse training. However, despite the recognition given to the need for, and value of, community based nurse training in Project 2000, since 1984 the situation has deteriorated. There has been a decline in the number of recruits to district nursing and some health authorities apparently have been willing to employ registered general nurses in the community without making explicit provision for their future training, whilst others have failed to meet the needs of practical work teachers. According to James, education and training are essential prerequisites for professional status and therefore need to be taken seriously by district nurses and their employers. In his view it has never been 'so vital for district nursing to establish its credibility as a specialist area within the community that requires specialist training of a breadth and depth hitherto ignored by almost everyone except the district nurses themselves and of course the patients.[61]

Concern regarding professional legitimacy is also reflected in articles dealing with the lack of public understanding and awareness of the distinctive role of the district nurse. The point is made in an editorial that, even though only a very small percentage of patients are cared for in hospitals, most of the public see the nurse as 'a bed-pan carrying young woman who is interested in a new uniform for her hospital work' because this is how she is portrayed by the media.[62] Even when recognition is given to the distinctive community role of district nurses, there is an emphasis on routine duties such as the dressing of varicose ulcers and the giving of bed baths.[63] Significantly, these tasks, although clearly vital, are not considered to be professionally respectable. Almost certainly this is because they are manual tasks which most people could carry out with a little training. Those concerned about the professional image and status of district nursing are therefore keen to play down duties of this kind and to stress the higher level responsibilities. It has even been suggested that district nurses should replace GPs as the sick patient's first point of contact with the formal health care system.[64]

District nurses have been caring for the sick at home for over a 100 years and there is no shortage of patients needing this type of care. Why therefore should district nurses be so concerned about the standing of their profession? The explanation is complex and will be approached from at least three angles.

First, partly as a consequence of the community care policies, other professions increasingly see their future in terms of community based service delivery. Thus, district nursing faces growing competition from professions previously located in the hospital sector (e.g. physiotherapy, occupational therapy, dietetics). In addition, there has always been a certain amount of tension between those professions based in the community. In a climate of change and uncertainty this tension could develop into open competition and conflict. So, whereas in the past district nurses and health visitors worked alongside each other with a reasonably clear understanding of the division of labour between them, in the fields of health education, health promotion, advice, counselling, assessment and monitoring, the demarcation lines are now less clear.

Second, there is a perceived threat to district nursing from the decision by some social services authorities to employ home care assistants. Their idea is to establish a relationship with elderly people while they are in hospital and then to visit them at home to offer practical help and facilitate their rehabilitation. One of the alleged advantages of employing staff of this kind is that it saves money. There is, however, concern about the relationship between home care assistants and district nurses and it might be more appropriate for them to be an adjunct to the district nursing service rather than an alternative.

Such fears have been increased by the Griffiths Report on community care. This envisages an expanded role for local authorities in that they would be made responsible for the planning of care packages for the elderly and other priority groups (see Chapter 8). The report also recommended the introduction of community aides, who would not have the qualifications and expertise of district nurses but would undertake some of their work. There are already areas where the referral of an elderly person leaving hospital goes to the social services department for a social worker, as opposed to a district nurse, to make the initial assessment of needs. If this arrangement is adopted in an area with a neighbourhood nursing team led by a manager without a background in district nursing then the position of the district nurse is likely to be even more at risk. 'It is in these areas where, unless district nurses let managers know about the vital nature of their expertise, they could see their role being eroded by social services.'[65]

Some commentators, such as Young, suggest that in the face of these threats district nurses should not adopt a solely defensive stance but should go on the offensive and argue the case for an expansion of their role. In his view district nurses should contribute to the making of community care policies; lead the community team (which would include Griffiths-style community aides); carry out all initial assessments of people leaving hospital; delegate responsibilities to members of the community team; monitor and evaluate the care given on a domiciliary basis; and play a leading role in the training of community carers.

Third, the emergence of an increasing number of specialist posts in district nursing, has led some observers to fear that the profession might fragment (see Chapter 7).

However, despite the importance of the issues and fears outlined above, many contributors to *The Journal of District Nursing* feel that they are being increasingly overshadowed by one further cause for concern, namely the unwillingness of district nurses (unlike health visitors - see above) to participate in what can de described as the political aspect of their professional role. For example, Young's concern about the adverse consequences for district nursing of the Griffiths Report on community care is compounded because district nurses remain silent on the subject. 'I do not think district nurses or their managers are voicing their fears and concern regarding this report enough ... District nurses are not particularly vocal or united in making their feelings heard.'[66] Similarly in 1987 the editor wrote 'as community nurses you could have the last word, but you really all need to stand up and shout together. Your combined voices could be deafening - and the public would be firmly on your side.'[67] Despite the logic of this message it appears to have had little effect since a year later she was moved to write: 'Alas you seem to have been very quiet.'[68]

Nevertheless, even if district nurses retain their separate identity, there are those who feel that in order to maximise the effectiveness and efficiency of the service major changes need to made to their training and working practices. These include: greater emphasis in training on the links between district nursing and other community services with a view to increasing the referral rate of patients to these other services; closer monitoring and review of caseloads and patterns of service delivery; the development of information systems which take account of the views of clients and the outcome of treatment; and initiatives to reduce the amount of gender and racial stereotyping in the interests of securing a more equitable distribution of scarce resources.[69] Concern has also been expressed at the hierarchical manner in which many district nursing services have been managed traditionally. Critics argue that this has prevented managers from making effective use of the wealth of expertise at the 'grass roots' level. In their view those exercising managerial responsibility should 'in part reverse the channels of communication'[70] so that there are more opportunities for those at the 'sharp end' to contribute to the management of the service. The concept of neighbourhood nursing, with its emphasis on more localised management units, would be a step in the right direction since it has at least 'the potential for facilitating dialogue between patients, nurses and managers.'[71]

Whilst it is not clear what the future holds for district nursing, there can be little doubt that there will be an increasing demand for the service, as the number of elderly people continues to rise, more attention is given to the needs of the disabled people, and hospital throughput rates continue to rise. The way the service is organised and managed will almost certainly be subject to some major changes.

Even though their responsibilities are more diverse than they have ever been, **community midwives**, like district nurses, continue to have reasonably well defined roles to perform at the ante-natal, confinement and post-natal stages.

At the ante-natal stage they assist at GP clinics (e.g. weighing expectant mothers, checking blood pressure); conduct clinics on their own; make home visits for various reasons (e.g. where further investigation is required because the results of tests were abnormal); follow up defaulters (i.e. women who miss their clinic appointments) and take parentcraft and relaxation classes.

With regard to care during confinement they attend and conduct over 80% of home deliveries. After falling for many years the percentage of births taking place at home started to rise again during the second half of the 1980s, although the number remains very small. It is common practice for two midwives to attend a home delivery to ensure that, if complications arise, there is someone on hand to go for medical help.[72] They also conduct a small percentage (approximately 4%) of hospital deliveries, usually in GP units. However, they may be in the maternity unit of the district general hospital if the authority operates a 'domino' delivery scheme (i.e. domiciliary in and out). This is where the midwife, who has provided a mother with ante-natal care, escorts her to hospital; conducts the delivery, with medical help on hand should the need arise; and accompanies the mother home again a few hours after the birth. Lastly, they assist with other hospital deliveries to maintain their expertise.

At the post-natal stage they liaise with hospital midwives and visit all mothers and babies at home to ensure that they are making satisfactory progress. Although this responsibility lasts until the baby is at least 28 days old, it is common practice for visits to cease after 10 days if there are no problems. As the data in Figure 9.2 indicate the amount of time mothers spend in hospital, following the birth of their child, is falling. For example, between 1975 and 1985 the percentage who left hospital within three days of the birth of their child increased from under 20% to over 30%. As a result of this trend the number of home visits which community midwives have to make is rapidly increasing.

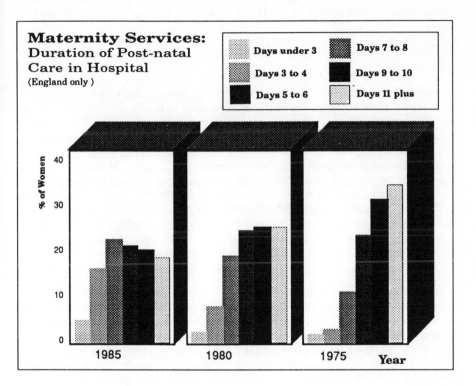

Figure 9.2

Source: DHSS, *Health and Personal Social Services Statistics for England*, 1988 edition, Table 8.2.

Community midwives also make a contribution to the provision of family planning services; to the health education of children, by giving talks in schools on aspects of pregnancy, confinement and post-natal care and to the training of GPs, nurses and other professional groups. In addition, they are often invited to attend child abuse case conferences and since the publication of *Working Together* (see above) they have a more clearly defined role in this respect.[73]

Information specially collected for the Community Nursing Review Team from the heads of midwifery services in 45 districts showed that 'their greatest concern was the duplication of effort between midwives and general practitioners, mainly during the antenatal period.' They felt that this was because of 'a lack of understanding by general practitioners of the midwife's role'.[74] Unfortunately, however, neither the heads of midwifery nor the review team appeared to have any suggestions as to how to make GPs more aware of the role of community midwives and their contribution to maternity care.

Given their commitment to 'consumerism', it is not surprising that the members of the review team accepted the principle, advanced by the heads of midwifery and many others from whom they received advice, that: 'all mothers should be able to make an informed choice about how and where to have their baby and about the sort of support they should be given before and after the birth.' Moreover, 'if this (meant) short-stay or 'domino' delivery schemes and post natal support from a midwife for up to 28 days, maternity services should be geared to provide it.'[75] Similarly, in their planning guidelines issued in July 1988 the DHSS made it clear that DHAs, in collaboration with FPCs, should seek to improve the maternity care provided within hospitals and community settings by 'finding out, and taking appropriate action ... on, the views, wishes and needs of women ... '[76] However, despite the apparent commitment, it remains to be seen whether 'consumerism' results in any significant changes being made to the existing pattern of maternity services.

With regard to the management of the community midwifery service, Cumberlege and her colleagues reached the conclusion that existing arrangements should not be disturbed. 'For continuity and consistency of care through pregnancy, childbirth and postnatally, we see value in that service still being integrated with the midwifery service provided in hospital, and in the two arms being managed as a whole.'[77] However, some community midwives are not happy with this arrangement and feel that it does not result in them receiving the recognition they deserve. Furthermore, it cuts them off from other groups of CHSs staff and often means that they are an afterthought when decisions about the allocation of accommodation in health centres and clinics are being taken.

Other issues on which some midwives, both community and hospital, feel strongly include: the extent to which childbirth has been wrested from midwives and women by male doctors; the fact that only between 20% and 30% of qualified midwives are actually in practice; the no-strike policy of the Royal College of Midwives; and the failure of a few managers to support those people campaigning against cuts in midwifery services. Many are also concerned that their skills are not being fully utilised. In their view midwives ought to be given full responsibility for the ante-natal care of the 85% to 90% of prospective mothers whose pregnancy is 'normal'.

Nevertheless, despite these concerns, the prospects for community midwifery appear to be fairly good. As the growth in the number of community midwives indicates (from under 3000 in the mid-1970s to over 4000 in the mid-1980s), the demand for their services is increasing. Furthermore, in the clinical regrading exercise, community midwives have usually secured higher grades than their hospital based colleagues, in recognition of their wider range of responsibilities.

Despite being one of their 'core' groups of community nurses, Cumberlege and her colleagues had little to say about **school nurses** in their report. Since school nurses have traditionally regarded themselves as the 'poor relations' vis-a-vis other groups of community nurses this was unfortunate. Moreover, it also means that those seeking to enhance the status of school nursing, through improved training (see Chapter 7), have not received the kind of support and encouragement that they might have expected.

Nevertheless, some DHAs have revised their policies for school nursing with a view to making the objectives and priorities of the service more explicit and providing school nurses with a range of higher level responsibilities. In many cases this has meant reducing the amount of time devoted to hygiene inspections and giving a higher priority to health surveillance; professional advice and support; the care of chidren with special needs and health promotion. This development was endorsed by the guide *Working Together* (see above), which stressed the importance of health surveillance programmes for the early identification of abused children. Of particular significance is the fact that the school nurse was recognised as being 'well placed to identify children who are being harmed or who may be at risk of harm.'[78]

At the same time the Health Visitors' Association supported these initiatives in a booklet containing guidance 'to assist school nurses and their managers in the efficient and appropriate deployment of school nurses in responding to the health needs of children in school and elsewhere.'[79] The Association felt that 'school nurses are the keyworkers in the school health service' and that as a result they 'must be trained, managed, remunerated and employed in sufficient numbers' to enable them to practise safely and effectively and to be confident of their role and function. It also recommends that:

- 'Every health authority should have a stated philosophy and a policy for (its) school nursing service ... .'

- 'Every school should have a named school nurse to whom reference can be made on all health matters relating to children at school, and to whom children themselves can have direct access.'

- 'All school nurses should undergo the appropriate ... education and training course either on, or as soon as possible after, taking up employment in school nursing.'

- 'School nurses should carry out surveillance programmes according to local policy.'[80]

- 'School nurses should take every opportunity to offer (children) the information necessary to enable them to make informed choices about their behaviour and lifestyle, the overall aim being to encourage each child gradually to assume responsibility for their own care.'

- 'In relation to children with special needs, school nurses should prepare all concerned for their admission to school, provide reports for the Statement of Special Educational Needs (see Chapter 7) and act as a resource for and support to the child, the family and school staff.'

- 'School nurses ... (should) bring to the attention of the responsible authority any elements within the school environment likely to endanger health or impede learning.'

- 'School nurses should act as the link between the child, home, doctor, school and the relevant statutory, professional and voluntary agencies.'[81]

According to the Association, school nurses should be managed by someone with a background in community nursing and the appropriate qualification(s) and experience in school nursing and/or health visiting. However, it is opposed to the arrangement, still found in some districts, by which health visitors are required to monitor and supervise the work of the school nurse. This would seem to imply that the Association hopes that eventually school nurses will acquire greater autonomy and a higher status within community nursing.

Whatever aspirations the Health Visitors' Association may have, the future of school nursing is bound up with that of the school health service as a whole. If, as seems possible, the government transfers responsibility for the health surveillance of children of school age from school nurses and doctors to GPs and their staff (see below), the repercussions for school nurses would be considerable. In these circumstances they would almost certainly face either redundancy or redeployment and erosion of their status.

Community Psychiatric Nurses (CPNs) differ from other groups of community nurses in that they originated in hospitals (as opposed to the community) and it is only since the early 1960s that psychiatric nurses have become involved in the care of patients in community settings. This development has been mainly in response to the requirements of the government's commitment to care in the community and the closure of long-stay psychiatric hospitals (see Chapter 4).

The future of community psychiatric nursing is uncertain. One possibility is for CPNs to become more involved in primary health care which would include important health education functions as well as the prevention of ill-health. Developments of this kind are already taking place in areas where CPNs are located in health centres and are accepting referrals from a wide range of health care professionals. An alternative is for them to concentrate on developing their more traditional role which implies making a major contribution to the setting up of community care facilities and services for patients discharged from long-stay institutions. This latter course of action has been advocated by the Director of the Health Advisory Service (see Chapter 8) and endorsed by the Social Services Committee.[82]

To some extent it will be necessary for CPNs to pursue both strategies. However, it is likely that one will receive more emphasis than the other and that this will affect the future orientation and image of the profession. Greater involvement in primary health care would require a far more proactive stance founded upon a belief in the validity of community health care in its own right. Whereas a more specific concern for the community care of patients discharged from hospital would involve a continuing reactive stance based upon the assumption (albeit implicit) that community health care is an adjunct to, or extension of, the hospital sector, from which it derives its legitimacy.

Another issue facing CPNs concerns the nature of their relationship with others working in the field of mental health, such as psychologists, psychiatrists, occupational therapists and social workers. In this respect they are in a similar position to health visitors and many other groups of community health professionals. On the one hand, there is a need for CPNs to work closely with other professionals so that they can acquire an understanding and appreciation of their roles and break down barriers in the interest of providing a more co-ordinated and effective service for clients. On the other hand, CPNs have (like other groups) faith in the value of greater professionalisation as a means of enhancing their prestige, visibility and command of resources. Again the ultimate aim is to ensure that their clients receive the best possible care that they are able to provide. On balance, teamwork and collaboration appear to be in the ascendency as far as community psychiatric nursing is concerned. For example, the voluntary organisation MIND has proposed the establishment of a new staff group called 'community mental health workers', which would incorporate CPNs, to facilitate this development. However, in some respects the aims of teamwork and greater professionalisation are in direct conflict with each other (this is discusssed more fully in Chapter 10).

With regard to community nursing as a whole, the prospects should be extremely bright and the prevailing mood one of opitimism. In quantitative terms, they are a force to be reckoned with. Moreover, since community nurses have 'specific skills in case finding, assessment, provision of direct care, and teaching individuals and families how to prevent disease, how to manage their own health and how to care for themselves and others when sick, injured of disabled',[83] they are in a position to make a significant contribution to the provision of primary health care. It is also clear that the need and demand for their services shows no sign of diminishing. On the contrary, all the socio-demographic indicators point to continued growth in the demand and need for community based nursing services.

In reality, however, many community nurses are profoundly pessimistic about the future and see the services for which they are responsible as being under threat. Factors giving rise to this state of affairs include the lack of resources, both financial and human; the negative attitudes of professional groups, with whom community nurses come into contact, in particular GPs; and, most importantly, the proposed changes in community care.

Most groups of community nurses have responded to the malaise within their profession by seeking to redefine roles and relationships and to redetermine priorities and, in certain cases, by engaging in political activity. Whether this will be sufficient to maintain the integrity of community nursing and, by implication the CHSs as a whole, will depend, to some extent, on the support which community nurses can secure from other groups of community based professional staff.

Paramedical Staff

One of the most significant developments of recent decades has been the increasing involvement of members of certain paramedical professions in community based health care namely: chiropody, speech therapy, physiotherapy, occupational therapy, dietetics and orthoptics. Of these, only chiropody and speech therapy, originated in the community. Until the 1970s, the other four professions were primarily based in the hospital sector. It is now recognised, however, that all these professions can make a valuable contribution to the care of patients in community settings and thereby relieve the pressure on hospitals. In a letter to *The Times* signed by the Secretaries of the Society of Chiropodists, the British Dietetic Association, the British Orthoptic Society, the Society of Radiographers, the British Association of Occupational Therapists and the Chartered Society of Physiotherapy, the point was made that members of these professions helped to minimise the use made of other health care resources by getting patients fit enough to leave hospital at the earliest possible opportunity and by keeping them fit enough to remain in their own homes for as long as possible.[84] Moreover, the role of community paramedical staff in this respect has influenced planning for HSs.

In many respects the role of **chiropodists** in the community is clear and unequivocal. Their concern with the care of feet distinguishes them from other professions. Moreover, adequate foot care is widely accepted as a crucial ingredient of community care since it enables people to remain mobile and independent and to continue living in their own homes. Without an effective chiropody service many more elderly people would require some form of institutionally based care. Thus, unlike a number of the professions examined in this chapter, chiropody is not faced with the problem of justifying its existence. However, it shares with other community based professions a preoccupation with professional status and security. Indeed, many articles about professional issues of this kind have been published in *The Chiropodist* (The Journal of the Society of Chiropodists).

Broadly these can be seen as issues of: expertise and exclusiveness, which may be regarded as the twin pillars of professional security. The profession is anxious to establish and maintain chiropody as a field of expertise for which a specific type and period of training is required and to ensure that only those who have been trained in this way have the exclusive right to practise as chiropodists. This dual focus was reflected in an editorial in *The Chiropodist* : 'To see B.Sc. degrees in chiropody, and to see surgical intervention now becoming an accepted part of professional practice, is a milestone of note in the profession's history ...'[85]

If chiropodial activities were generally accepted as requiring high levels of skill and training for their effective performance there would be little dissent from the view that only those with appropriate qualifications should be allowed to carry them out. However, this is not the case. Most people cut their own toenails and many consider other aspects of footcare as a normal part of personal hygiene. Thus, professional chiropodists are often seen as providing footcare of this kind for those who cannot provide it for themselves, due to age or disability, rather than performing tasks which are beyond the competence of the 'lay person'. Another editorial accused the government of damning chiropodists with faint praise in its white paper, *Promoting Better Health*, by suggesting that they could help the elderly to remain mobile.[86]

If the profession is to secure the recognition it desires, in terms of the expertise involved in the care of feet, then it has to pursue two key objectives. First, it has to persuade people - members of other professions and the public at large - that footcare is an essential prerequisite for good health and should not be viewed lightly. With this objective in mind articles have appeared in *The Chiropodist* on such matters as the appropriate shape of shoes; the importance of good footwear and the potential damage to feet caused by the use of baby walkers. Indeed one contributor was moved to write: 'A few years ago campaigners against artificial additives in foods were considered to be cranks ... but now 'additive-free' is a selling point blazoned on every packet. Foot faddists will soon, I am sure, inherit the shoe kingdom.'[87]

Second, chiropodists have to persuade members of other professions and the government that they possess skills of a sufficiently high level to warrant the attribution of professional status. To this end, the Society of Chiropodists published a booklet in 1988 that was unashamedly entitled *The Chiropodist: a specialist in the medical team*. Similarly, members of the profession were extremely proud of the fact that they were called upon to act as expert advisers in respect of requests made by parents to the DHSS for additional shoes for their children on the grounds that their children's foot ambulatory problems had led to excessive shoe wear.

The profession is also quick to defend itself when there is any suggestion that the work of chiropodists is not of a particularly high level. For example, a letter from a doctor which implied that there was a distinction between foot surgery and chiropody prompted several replies from chiropodists who were keen to rectify this misconception. One of those who replied concluded his letter by arguing that if chiropodists seriously wished 'to succeed in extending (their) professionality' then they should be more active 'in making others aware of (their) potential'.[88]

Not surprisingly, the Society of Chiropodists welcomed the recognition, given in the white paper, *Promoting Better Health*, to the need for chiropodists to be members of the primary health care team. However, it also expressed concern over the possibility, that this might mean employment by GPs (see above). In the view of the Society, since chiropodists were 'responsible for their own diagnoses and treatment of patients without medical referral' and were 'sometimes the first and often the only contact made with primary care services by many people, who (did) not necessarily see their general practitioners very frequently', they should be members of 'the primary health care team in (their) own right.' Moreover, 'as in the case of direct employment in the National Health Service, only state registered chiropodists should be eligible for any contractual arrangements for the provision of chiropody services as members of a primary health care team.'[89]

The reference to state registration brings out the issue of exclusiveness referred to above. In particular it highlights the division between the registered and unregistered arms of chiropody and the desire of the registered arm to protect its privileged position. Most state registered chiropodists adopt a somewhat elitist and, on occasions, hostile approach to unregistered practitioners, who are generally seen as a threat. They also fear that if they display an unwillingness to carry out basic footcare tasks and a clear preference for only higher level work they might find their 'position compromised by the complete opening up of employment within the NHS to all sections of the profession.'[90]

They acknowledge that whilst chiropody remains divided there is little chance of achieving the closure of the profession or, at least, a greater degree of central regulation, so that only recognised members of the profession could describe themselves as chiropodists. For this reason there have been many attempts to heal the rift between the two arms. For example, in 1987 the Council of the Society of Chiropodists took the lead in arranging discussions with the other bodies representing the interests of chiropodists to see if there was any possibility of establishing a federation of chiropodial representative bodies. The role of the federation would have been to find common ground on which to base a campaign for the closure of the profession. Unfortunately, relatively little progress was made during these discussions. A year later, in a letter to the Secretary of the Institute of Chiropodists, one of the Ministers at the DHSS stated that 'the Government would be prepared to reopen the question of closure of the chiropody profession only with the agreement of all the bodies representing practitioners, whether registered or unregistered, whose interests would be affected by restrictions on the use of the title chiropodist.'[91]

Chiropodists are not only discomforted by the existence of unregistered practitioners, but also fear encroachment from two other sources. First, they are suspicious of the potential growth of self-treatment in the field of footcare. A battle with Cuxson Gerrard and Co., the manufacturers of carnation footcare treatment, fought on the pages of *The Chiropodist*, highlights this concern. The dispute began with the publication of an article which suggested that harm might ensue from the use of one of these products. The company responded by pointing out that it had always acted responsibly. For example, if their customers were in any doubt about their condition it was recommended that they consult a chiropodist. In the view of the company, they and the chiropodists had 'a common cause in better footcare' and that more would be achieved 'by working together than by acting like adversaries.'[92] Whilst, at one level, this is irrefutable, at another level, acceptance of this view by the profession would seriously endanger its standing and security.

Second, chiropodists also see a direct threat from GPs. This threat was encapsulated in a deliberately naive question posed in *The Chiropodist*, namely: 'Why (do) patients with foot problems take them to GPs instead of to chiropodists?'[93] Since chiropodists are aware that most people will visit their family doctor with almost any physical ailment, at least in the first instance, the answer to this question is, in one respect, fairly obvious. It was asked, however, because like many other professional groups anxious to enhance their status, chiropodists must do more to persuade the public that (with some justification) they know more about particular aspects of health care than GPs.

The image of the fully qualified expert, with his/her own distinctive and esoteric contribution to make within primary health care is the one presently sought by the leading members of the chiropody profession. However, such a goal is not shared by all members of the profession nor is it one that will necessarily be achieved. Moreover, given the need for flexibility and adaptability in health care, it is not certain that an image of this kind is in the best interests of the profession or, for that matter, the clients.

Like the other professions, **speech therapy** has been experiencing problems which prompted the General Secretary and Administrator of the College of Speech Therapists to write to all district general managers. He was concerned about reports which suggested that the speech therapy service was 'not responding as effectively as it should to the needs of the communication handicapped.' In his view, speech therapy, as 'a young profession, with an input into so many areas, spanning both health and education and concerned with total communication' should have been one of 'the NHS's success stories.' Unfortunately, however, there seemed to be 'growing shortages of the more skilled and experienced staff, lowered morale, and increasing frustration.'[94] The main purpose of this letter was to find out how those at district level perceived the situation and thereby establish whether there was the basis for a common approach to the problems facing the profession and what might be done to solve them.

One indication of the growing recognition of the value of speech therapy and the inadequacy of the services, which are available, to cope with demand is the fact that there are around thirty charities concerned with speech disorder. Their primary roles and those of Vocal (an umbrella organisation for the charities) is to campaign for more and better speech therapy services and to help families obtain the services they need.

A particularly dramatic illustration of the lengths to which some parents have been prepared to go to secure the services of a speech therapist was provided by the mother of a nine year old boy with a congenital speech defect who took her local education authority (Lancashire County Council) to court for failing to meet her son's need for speech therapy. Significantly, the High Court decided in favour of the mother on the grounds that once it had been decided that a child's need for therapy was an educational one then under the provisions of the Education Act 1981 (see Chapter 7) the local education authority had a duty to provide it.[95]

Similarly in a report published by the National Association of Health Authorities in 1988 the point was made that the special educational need provisions of the Education Act 1981 generated so much paperwork that speech therapists were spending nearly half their time on administrative duties.

Thus, for speech therapy, the main problems have been those associated with the scarcity of resources. The value of the contribution made by speech therapists to meeting the needs of adults as well as children with speech disorders is generally recognised. For example, in 1985 the Health Advisory Service recommended that there should be a substantial increase in speech therapy for the elderly. Moreover, it is accepted that speech therapists possess distinctive skills which do not overlap, to any significant extent, with those applied by members of other professions. Unfortunately, however, these skills are in increasingly short supply as more and more potential clients are coming to realise how speech therapy can help them. As the National Association of Health Authorities report argued: 'It is a case of limited human resources being spread even more thinly than before'.[96]

However, on a more positive note, since January 1988 there has a full-time officer at the Department of Health with responsibility for advising civil servants and Ministers on the provision, planning and development of speech therapy and other rehabilitation services and the implications for in-service training of government policies. As a result it is to be hoped that, at central government level, speech therapy will receive the recognition it deserves.

Physiotherapy has been defined by the Chartered Society of Physiotherapy as 'the use of physical means to prevent injury, to treat both injury and disease, and to assist in the process of rehabilitation by developing and restoring the function of the body so that the patient may return to as active and independent life as possible.'[97] By using the techniques at their disposal, physiotherapists have a key role to play in the areas of pain relief, healing and rehabilitation.

The aims of a district physiotherapy service are:

*deliver effective and appropriate physiotherapy in an efficient and econ-
... ical way ... to reach all in need of (the) service in the most appropriate
... ation, at the right time, with courtesy, compassion and with clinical and
... er-personal skills of a consistently high standard ... to work with others to
... mote independence, good health ...(and) to prevent injury and disease.*[98]

... mid-1970s the 'appropriate location' for the delivery of physiotherapy to
... ing number of patients has been either a health centre, or the patient's
home, or a local authority home for the elderly or disabled. Although the latest
data on NHS staffing levels do not indicate how many of the 9000 plus WTE
physiotherapists are employed in the community, there has been a steady increase
in the number of community based physiotherapists since the 1970s and it is
probable that by the late 1980s approximately 40% of physiotherapy treatment
took place in non-hospital settings.

According to Burnard, community physiotherapy schemes have been established for many different reasons. These include the need to:

- provide treatment for patients who are 'isolated at home due to acute illness',
  such as strokes and chest complaints, or as a result of a progressive disability;

- provide 'immediate treatment for patients whose general practitioners have no
  direct access to hospital physiotherapy departments';

- ensure that where treatment is directly related to problems at home (e.g.
  children and elderly) it is provided in the most relevant setting;

- instruct carers in both the handling and management of disabled persons at
  home and the application of simple treatment procedures to complement
  those carried out by physiotherapists; and

- facilitate the earlier discharge of patients from hospital.

It is generally felt that these needs can best be met by physiotherapists working in
the community as members of a primary health care team, but retaining their
managerial and professional links with their institutionally based colleagues.[99] For
example, in its evidence to the Griffiths Review of community care the Chartered
Society of Physiotherapy recommended that 'the provision of care in the community should enable physiotherapists to maintain their professional links with
hospital colleagues while participating in patient care within the primary health
care team.'[100]

To some extent, community physiotherapists share with other community
based professionals the need to clarify the exact nature of their role and their
relationship with those who do not have a background in physiotherapy. However,
since physiotherapy is a reasonably well defined area of professional expertise, role
ambiguity is unlikely to present community physiotherapists with problems of the
same magnitude as those which confront some of the other professional groups.

Nevertheless, physiotherapists are concerned about a number of developments which they perceive as being threats to their professional status. Many of these relate to the recruitment and training of physiotherapists, which is a particular problem since they are in short supply. On this issue the Chartered Society of Physiotherapy expressed concern about the professional standards of those trained overseas. It also undertook an investigation into the feasibility of introducing training on a part-time basis for students in this country. Similarly, North Lincolnshire Health Authority carried out an investigation into whether the shortage of physiotherapists was being aggravated by the high entry standards laid down by the profession.

One possible solution to this is to make greater use of less well qualified helpers to perform routine tasks. However, many physiotherapists are extremely unhappy about any proposals which imply a dilution of professional standards. They argue that whilst low level jobs may be given to helpers, supervision is essential and that the vitally important assessment function, which can only be performed by a fully qualified professional, must not be jeopardised by developments of this kind.

Like other professional groups, physiotherapists are also concerned about the implications of GPs being able to employ a far wider range of staff under the ancillary staff scheme. Thus, whilst welcoming the fact that physiotherapists are acknowledged as members of the primary health care team in the white paper, *Promoting Better Health*, the Chartered Society of Physiotherapy has made it clear that it would be opposed to making any significant changes to the present organisational arrangements. In its view community physiotherapy should remain part of a district managed service, since in general these arrangements are working well. Moreover, it is not appropriate for physiotherapists to be the direct employees of GPs on the grounds that:

- the 'uncontrolled development of practice-employed physiotherapists would severely distort (the) ability of the NHS to deploy its manpower effectively;'

- 'the relationship between doctors and physiotherapists is now firmly based on mutual professional referral' and this principle would be undermined if GPs became the employers of physiotherapists, since they would 'acquire a very substantial measure of direction over a physiotherapist's professional practice'; and

- such a development would give rise to major questions about professional accountability; arrangements for the maintenance of professional standards; the right of physiotherapists to refer to other physiotherapists in specialist practice; provision of training facilities and access to the necessary equipment.

However, the Chartered Society of Physiotherapy is not opposed to 'attachment schemes' or to schemes whereby GPs purchase physiotherapy services from the district physiotherapist, since these enable physiotherapists working in the community to retain their links with hospital based colleagues and their independence.[101]

Another major problem facing district physiotherapists and their senior colleagues is that of managing the service at a time when resources are severely limited and demands are increasing from all sides. According to one district physiotherapist, it is much more difficult for professionals simply to maintain, rather than to develop and expand services.[102] Interestingly, in some districts the shortage of resources is more apparent in the sphere of equipment, than of staff. Thus, efforts have been directed at raising money from charitable sources for the purpose of purchasing essential equipment. Increasingly physiotherapists, are having to look for ways of supplementing their resources. This may well involve the selling of services, such as training in back care and the ergonomics of the workplace, for which there are frequent requests.

Hopefully, despite the scarcity of resources, the expansion of community physiotherapy services will continue. As the Chartered Society of Physiotherapy pointed out in its comments on the major theme of *Promoting Better Health* (i.e. the need to shift the emphasis in primary care from the treatment of illness to the promotion of health and the prevention of disease), 'physiotherapists are uniquely placed, as professionals, to take up this theme and as members of the primary health care team to be involved in screening programmes, back care and keep fit classes, cardiac rehabilitation and so on.'[103] They therefore have the potential to make a significant contribution to the future development of community based health care services.[104]

One important difference between **occupational therapy** and the other paramedical professions with members working in the community is the fact that a relatively large number of occupational therapists (approximately 20%) are employed by local personal social services authorities. Furthermore, some of the occupational therapists employed by health authorities are actually based in local personal social services departments. This is mainly because local authorities need to have the skills of the occupational therapist at their disposal in order to meet their obligations to the disabled under the provisions of the Chronically Sick and Disabled Persons Act 1970 (see Chapter 4) and subsequent legislation, such as the Housing Act 1974, the Rating (Disabled Persons) Act 1978 and, most significantly, the Disabled Persons (Services Consultation and Representation) Act 1986 (see below).

Whilst the employment of occupational therapists in local government is both necessary and understandable it does have a number of drawbacks for the profession and for clients. The Health Advisory Service drew attention to a number of these in its *Annual Report for 1984/85*:

> *The position of occupational therapists employed by local authority social services departments often seems to us to be anomalous. They are often working in relative isolation, perhaps one to a district or area office, and do*

not have managerial or support staff of their own profession. Their activities are frequently confined to the assessment for and provision of aids and adaptations, an important duty but one which does not use more than a fraction of their training. Most have no time to advise patients and families about rehabilitation and have no input to the residential homes for the elderly where staff would often benefit greatly from their skills. Local authority occupational therapists carry very high active case loads. Occupational therapy students rarely train in local authority departments. [105]

These drawbacks were exacerbated by the lower salaries of occupational therapists employed by local authorities and the failure to develop effective channels of communication between the two services. Official concern about this state of affairs prompted the DHSS to write to all local personal social services authorities and DHAs in December 1985, suggesting how the situation might be improved (see Chapter 7).

Fifteen months later this initiative was followed up with the distribution of a questionnaire to every local personal social services authority and DHA. The key findings were that:

- there was an increasing amount of collaboration between principal and district occupational therapists through joint planning; the joint funding of posts (by 1st April 1987 432 jointly funded posts had been established - 152 in personal social services and 280 in the NHS) and the operation of arrangements for the provision of aids and appliances to clients living at home (over 84% of authorities collaborated for this purpose and by 1st April 1987 there were approximately 32 joint equipment stores with a similar number being planned);

- there was 'an enormous variation in the number of occupational therapists per head of population' (for a population of 250,000 the range in the social services was from 6 to 25 + established posts and in the NHS from 6 to 117 posts);

- the number of disabled people waiting for assessment varied considerably and did 'not always reflect the numbers of occupational therapists in post';

- waiting lists were needed because the demand for occupational therapy was growing at a faster rate than the resources at the disposal of service managers (resource problems were due not only to insufficient numbers of posts but also to an overall shortage of qualified occupational therapists, which often made it difficult to fill vacant posts) and the information helped managers to determine service priorities;

- there was 'extreme concern' regarding the additional resources, which would be needed when the provisions of Section 3 of the Disabled Persons (Services Representation and Consultation) Act 1986 (relating to the assessment of the needs of disabled persons) came into force; [106] and

- decisions as to which authority was responsible for providing particular items of equipment to clients living in their own homes was 'a matter for local negotiation' and that once clients had been assessed they generally received the equipment they needed within 2 to 3 weeks.

In the light of these findings and the fact that the demand for the services of occupational therapists was growing and supply was limited it was argued that better use needed 'to be made of existing occupational therapy resources'. This meant having 'effectively managed and supervised services; appropriate use of occupational therapy helpers (and) proper clerical and administrative support to ensure procedures are followed and the service provided.' It was also necessary to rationalise 'the wide variety of staffing numbers in authorities across the country' and to review 'policies relating to the provision of equipment and the role of Joint Equipment Stores.'[107]

One suspects that, although well-intentioned, proposals of this kind do not impress most occupational therapy managers or the profession at large, since they fail to address the underlying problem, namely the grave shortage of qualified occupational therapists. Reference was made to this problem by the Comptroller and Auditor General in his report on manpower planning for the NHS professional and technical staff group (December 1986). Although the DHSS had progressively increased the number of bursaries awarded annually to occupational therapy students and had given authority for the establishment of a new school of occupational therapy (which was due to open in 1987), the latest available figures (March 1985) showed 'that 19.2 percent of posts for occupational therapists which DHAs in England were prepared to fund remained unfilled after three months.'[108] Whatever the causes of this situation, there has been relatively little improvement since 1985, as the evidence presented by the staff side to the Review Body for Nursing Staff, Midwives, Health Visitors and Professions Allied to Medicine indicates.[109] Efforts are being made to increase the numbers of occupational therapists by persuading those with appropriate qualifications who had taken a break in service to return and by establishing another new school of occupational therapy. In addition heavy reliance is being placed on local initiatives to minimise the inconvenience and hardship which clients suffer when resources are scarce.

According to a booklet published by the British Dietetic Association in 1986: '**Dietitians** apply the science of nutrition to the feeding of groups and individuals in health and disease. They are primarily advisors and teachers at all levels from fellow professionals in many spheres to the general public.'[110] Their specific responsibilities can be grouped into five main areas.

The first area is preventive work, which involves education and research in schools and other academic institutions, community based organisations and industry. Second, there are therapeutic activities, of which the most important is advising patients about their diet. The third area is work in industry, which includes the provision of dietary advice and information to food manufacturers. A fourth area is the education and training of student dietitians. Lastly, dietitians use the media to communicate information on aspects of diet and nutrition. This involves writing books and articles for professional and lay journals and magazines and appearing on radio and television.

Since 1974 dietitians have become, to some extent, more community-orientated and many health authorities now employ dietitians to work specifically in community settings. Of the 1000 or more WTE dietitians employed by the NHS it is likely that approximately 30% are designated community dietitians. According to the British Dietetic Association the primary aim of community dietitians is to promote health and prevent disease amongst the local population by improving dietary habits and increasing public awareness of the link between nutrition and health.

However, although in principle the aim is clear, in practice work in community settings is less well defined than it is in hospitals and, as with other professional groups, it is the process of clarifying and demarking the specific roles of community dietitians which gives rise to many of their problems and dilemmas. These can be illustrated by reference to the description of the work of the community dietitian contained in the British Dietetics Association's pamphlet entitled *Dietitians in the Community*.

Community dietitians work with many other agencies and engage in a wide variety of activities. They work with the primary health care team providing advice, information and training to members and with the health education service contributing to running and evaluating campaigns, courses, study days and teaching. They work with local organisations, such as mother and toddler groups, ethnic groups and old peoples groups, providing support and helping to establish and run slimming clubs, healthy eating clubs for children and similar activities. They work with social services, giving advice on aspects of nutrition to residential homes, luncheon clubs and meals on wheels, and contributing to the training of staff with responsibility for the feeding of clients. They work with the education service, advising on nutrition in schools and providing guidance to children, parents and teachers on good dietary practice. Lastly, as members of the district dietetic service they contribute to the provision of dietary advice and information to the health authority, the training of student dietitians, local research projects and the evaluation of the service. Increasingly, DHAs have a district-wide food policy, which applies to catering arrangements in their establishments.

Thus, there are potential areas of overlap between the work of the community dietitian and that of other community based professionals. For example, the work of dietitians in schools might well overlap with that of the school nurses, especially in the field of health education. Similarly an important part of the health visitor's role is the provision of advice and information about diet and the feeding of babies and young children. In principle the roles of the school nurse and the health visitor are distinct from the role of the dietitian and the intention here is not to advocate the blurring of professional boundaries. It is rather to draw attention to the fact that, in seeking to develop their profession through expansion into new areas in the community, dietitians will almost inevitably come into conflict with other professional groups. Ideally, the professions involved should negotiate an acceptable division of labour and thereby clarify the parameters of professional responsibility, but this will not be easy.

Orthoptists are concerned with the early diagnosis and treatment of squints in children and of eye disorders in the case of adults. The profession originated in the hospital sector, during the inter-war period.[111] Its professional body, the British Orthoptic Society, was established in 1937 and orthoptists were brought within the scope of the Council for Professions Supplementary to Medicine in 1966.[112] By the late 1980s there were about 1000 state registered orthoptists.

During the 1980s orthoptists, like other paramedical staff, gradually moved out of hospitals into the community. Baroness Trumpington, made specific reference to this development in her speech at the Golden Jubilee Dinner of the British Orthoptic Society (1987):

> *One of the greatest changes in the delivery of health care in the life time of your profession has been the development of community care, in which you have played a full part ... We see your work ... as a most important part of preventive medicine ... In caring for the elderly ... or helping to rehabilitate stroke patients suffering from double vision, you are also supporting the all-important thrust of NHS community care policies, which are to enable people to live as normal a life in the community as possible.*[113]

The move towards a more community based profession, however, has undermined the traditional pattern of working for orthoptists. This was based on an unambiguous and accepted hierarchy in which orthoptists received and dealt with referrals from ophthalmologists. In the community the situation is very different. Here orthoptists themselves generally have to take the initiative and their role is less clear-cut, especially in respect of their relationship with members of other professions. As a result there is a danger that in taking the lead and carving out a role in the fields of prevention, screening and health education, they will, like dietitians, come into conflict with other professional groups, especially health visitors. Nevertheless, they do have a distinctive role to play in surveillance

Like most of the community professions, orthoptists are concerned about aspects of the education and training of those seeking membership of their profession. For example, the British Orthoptic Society expressed concern about the large number of small schools of orthoptics within the NHS, which it would like to see rationalised with education and training being concentrated in a smaller number of academic centres. The British Orthoptic Society has also made recommendations to the Department of Health for improving the standard of education and these, together with the appropriate costings, are being considered by the Department in consultation with DHAs.

Other Professional Groups

Of all the community based professional staff, arguably it is the **clinical medical officers** who are under the greatest threat. They contribute to the CHSs in three main areas: pre-school child health clinics (e.g. vaccination and immunisation, health surveillance); school health clinics (e.g. medicals and screening tests); and family planning clinics (e.g. giving advice and supplying and fitting appliances; taking cervical smears). In these areas many people feel that clinical medical officers have played an important role and one which could not have been performed as effectively by any other group of professionals. Moreover, although vaccination and immunisation and family planning services are also available from GPs, many clients appreciate an element of choice because of the highly personal nature of the services concerned. However, it would appear from the green and white papers that the government's long-term objective is to shift all the responsibility for these services onto GPs. As the following quotation from the green paper implies the days of the clinical medical officer may well be numbered.

> *For some 70 years doctors have been employed by health or local authorities to provide and manage a range of preventive and caring services, mainly for young children. To provide these community medical services, District Health Authorities in England and Wales currently employ some 6,000 doctors, many part time (i.e clinical medical officers) ... About 70 per cent of the work of these doctors is spent on child health, and a large part of this time is given over to regular checking of children under school age to monitor progress and see what further help they may need. Yet these checks can most satisfactorily be carried out when the doctor has continuing responsibility for the child and is thus fully aware of his or her medical and family background.* **This means that family doctors may be best placed to provide this service.** *A number already do so, often working directly with health visitors.* **The Government wishes to increase the number of family doctors involved in this work** (emphasis added).[114]

Furthermore, in mid-1988 the DHSS made it clear that one of the policy aims of DHAs should be 'to collaborate with FPCs in developing the contribution of suitably trained family doctors to child health surveillance of the under-5s'.[115] Significantly, the contribution of clinical medical officers to screening pre-school children was not mentioned. Thus, although one of the government's declared objectives is 'to give patients the widest range of choice in obtaining high quality primary care services', it seems as though this principle is not going to apply in respect of the vaccination and immunisation and surveillance of pre-school children.

Since there have been few authoritative statements about the school health service, the situation regarding its future is less clear. DHAs have been encouraged by the DHSS 'to explore and exploit the potential for surveillance and prevention through school based services ... (and to) review the scope and effectiveness of their existing school health service programmes with (local education authorities) and other interested organisations'.[116] This suggests that, although the service may be subject to some modifications, clinical medical officers might continue to have an important role to play. However, such a view is likely to be unduly optimistic. There are grounds for believing that the government would like to increase the involvement of GPs in the surveillance of school children so that eventually the school health service can be dismantled. For example, if it becomes accepted practice for GPs to operate a screening system for pre-school children then it is probable that eventually they will also play a part in the screening of school age children.

The threat to DHA family planning services is even greater and more immediate than that to the child health surveillance work of clinical medical officers. In September 1988 it was reported that at least 30 DHAs had already closed family planning clinics as an economy measure.[117] In the view of the DHAs concerned and the Department of Health this was justified on the grounds that adequate contraceptive services were available from GPs, despite the fact that in its planning guidelines issued in July 1988 the Department had stated that DHAs 'should strike a balance between (family planning) services provided by specialist clinics and those provided by GPs, bearing in mind in particular: (i) the need to give choice to encourage full take-up; (ii) the need for separate, less formal, arrangements for young people; (and) (iii) their wider health role - for instance in cervical smear testing...'[118]

Predictably, the closure of DHA clinics has been strongly criticised on a number of grounds by the Family Planning Association and others. First, it is claimed that they provide a better service to the patient and are more economical than GP services. For example, according to Dr Christine Watson, senior clinical medical officer (family planning and 'well woman' services) at Lewisham and North Southwark Health Authority: 'All our family planning services are extremely cost effective and we are able to provide a comprehensive service, including well women care, psychosexual and vasectomy counselling, domciliary visiting and advice on IUD and Depo-Provera use. It is a Rolls Royce service which GPs cannot hope to match.'[119] Furthermore, research has shown that the staff of DHA clinics provide more thorough treatment, spend longer with patients, offer more choice of contraceptive method and represent better 'value for money' than GPs. Second, since 1023 DHA family planning clinics are registered for training purposes compared with only 28 GP premises, the clinics paid their way by providing the bulk of the family planning training for doctors and nurses. Lastly, many women, especially teenagers, prefer the anonymity of clinics.

Despite the force of these arguments, the statistical evidence would appear to suggest that the popularity of DHA family planning clinics has remained fairly constant whilst the contraceptive services provided by GPs have grown in popularity. As the data in Figure 9.3 show, between 1976 and 1986 there was relatively little change in the number of persons attending DHA family planning clinics.

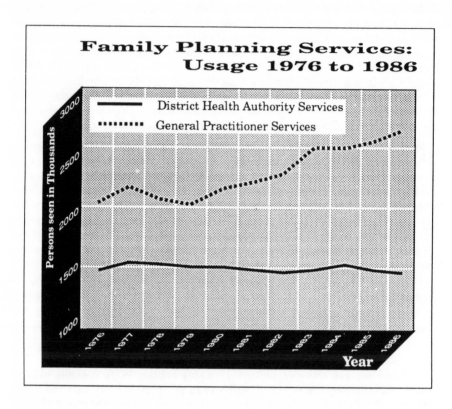

Figure 9.3

Source: DHSS, *Health and Personal Social Services Statistics for England,* various editions

In contrast, the number of persons seeing their GP for family planning purposes increased significantly.

However, what cannot be determined from these data is the value placed on the family planning services provided by clinical medical officers working for the DHA and the distress and frustration which would be caused were these services to disappear.

In seeking to resist any moves towards the transfer of their responsibilities to GPs, clinical medical officers face a number of major problems. First, in political terms they are without doubt the weakest group within the medical profession. This is partly because the school health and family planning services have always been regarded as fringe activities as far as the medical profession as a whole is concerned.

Furthermore, in the work of clinical medical officers there is a strong proactive element whereas the predominant orientation of medicine has traditionally been reactive. Second, a very large number of clinical medical officers are employed part-time and work for the DHA on a sessional basis. For example, in 1986, the total number of clinical medical officers was 5240 whereas there were only 2,186 WTE posts. Third, a majority of clinical medical officers are women (in 1986 just over 60% of the staff employed were women and 72% of the WTE posts were held by women).

Furthermore, in the second half of the 1980s, the health departments made it clear in their evidence to the Review Body on Doctors' and Dentists' Remuneration that they considered the levels of pay for clinical medical officers to be 'generous in comparison with pay for other non-consultant grades, notably specialists' and with that of GPs and that therefore 'a smaller increase ... (in pay) relative to other career grades was justified.' In support of this view they pointed out that clinical medical officers worked 'fixed hours and (had) a more limited range of responsibilities than other career grades; and that no special qualifications (were) needed to enter' the clinical medical officer grade or to be promoted to senior clinical medical officer.[120]

Although the staff of the **community dental service** are not under the same kind of threat as clinical medical officers, there are clear signs that the government would like to make significant changes to their responsibilities. At the time of the publication of the Health and Medicines Bill (November 1987) the government declared that it was going to replace the statutory requirement of the 1977 Act 'that the Secretary of State provide under the NHS for the dental inspection and treatment of school children with a power for him to provide such dental inspections and treatment and dental health education.' In other words the provision of dental care for school children would no longer be a mandatory requirement (see Chapter 7). Thus, if the proposal had been implemented, DHAs would have been able to choose whether or not to provide a service of this kind and, as was argued by Jerry Hayes (a Conservative backbencher) during the second reading debate on the bill, 'authorities that (were) hard-pressed for resources - in other words most of them - (would) say that they (had) an opportunity to cut out a non-acute service.'[121]

The government sought to justify the proposed change in the law by arguing that it would 'enable the community dental services to develop in such a way that they (could) offer an improved service to those groups who (had) difficulty in obtaining the services of a general dental practitioner.'[122] It was also felt that health authorities should have 'discretion to redirect ... resources away from the routine treatment of children - who (could) be, and for the most part (were), looked after in the general dental service - and towards providing health education for children in schools.'[123] In their evidence to the Review Body on Doctors' and Dentists' Remuneration, the health departments also expressed the belief that the proposed change 'indicated the need for a smaller, more specialised community dental service in the future entailing an orderly, phased rundown of manpower.'[124]

Predictably, these proposals for the community dental service were opposed by the British Dental Association and various other groups and, in the event, amendments made to the legislation by the House of Lords ensured that DHAs would be required to continue to provide a dental inspection and treatment service for school children. Thus, under the provisions of the Health and Medicines Act 1988, the Secretary of State still has a 'duty to provide ... for the dental inspection of pupils in attendance at schools maintained by local education authorities ... (and) for the the dental treatment of such pupils'. He also has to provide 'for the education of such pupils in dental health.' In the long-term, however, it may prove to be of significance that these duties are qualified by the words 'to such extent as he (i.e. Secretary of State) considers necessary to meet all reasonable requirements', which did not appear in the 1977 Act. Furthermore, it seems likely that at some time in the future, the government will try again to curtail the activities of the community dental service.

Nevertheless, for the time being, the community dental service has had a reprieve as far as its principal client group is concerned and community dental officers and their colleagues now have the opportunity, resources permitting, of developing further their educative role amongst school children and of exercising their other responsibilities to the full. These remain: the screening of school children; the provision of dental treatment to school children and other groups; dental health education; and epidemiological studies designed to monitor changes in the dental health of particular groups and the community at large.

In a circular on the future development of community dental services (February 1989), the responsibilities of DHAs and their dental officers were spelt out in the following terms:

• 'the monitoring of the dental health of all age groups in the population and the planning of local dental services jointly with FPCs';

• 'the provision of dental health education and preventive programmes';

• 'the provision of facilities for a full range of treatment to patients who have experienced difficulty in obtaining treatment in the general dental service ...'

• 'the screening of the teeth of children in state funded schools at least three times in each child's school life (this may need to be more frequently e.g. in areas (with) generally poor dental health).'[125]

Many district dental officers also see themselves as having a campaigning role in respect of issues such as the fluoridation of the water supply and the adverse effects of low income and poor diet on dental health.

One further point, unlike clinical medical officers, community dental officers have the advantage of being a fairly influential group within the dental profession.

This has not always been the case, but during the 1980s community dental officers have secured increasing respect from their peers for their contribution to the dental health of the population at large.

For a variety of reasons **health education** (or health promotion as it is now generally known)[126] can be regarded as the cinderella of the community based professions.

First, some commentators would argue that health education/promotion is not a fully fledged profession since practitioners lack many of the trappings of professional status, such as an offically approved programme of training and a formal system of registration. Moreover, health education officers do not possess a distinctive and coherent set of skills, based on a body of theoretical knowledge, which when applied, produces verifiable results. According to Watt, health education is 'a profession generally in constant search of a method of practice that will counter sustained and ingrained criticisms of ineffectiveness.'[127]

Second, as Moran observes, in institutional terms 'health education lacks a secure professional ... base.' Despite the transfer of responsibility for health education from local government to the NHS in 1974, 'it has always been part of a specifically medical hierarchy led successively by the Medical Officer of Health and more recently the District Medical Officer',[128] and this has left it marginal from the point of view of prestige and resources.

Third, health education is politically vulnerable. This is because it is mistakenly perceived by some politicians as 'a convenient and cheap solution' to moral and ethical health care 'problems', such as drug abuse and AIDS, which health education officers do not, in fact, have the power and resources to tackle effectively. As a result the justification for having separate health education departments might well be called into question. According to Moran, health education is also subject to two strands of attack from those on the right of the political spectrum: 'an ideological objection to interference from the 'nanny state', and post-Griffiths managerialism with its emphasis on easily-demonstrable 'cost-effectiveness'.'[129]

Fourth, by its very nature health education/promotion is an extremely broad activity and one in which all health service staff should play a part. Moreover, as has been mentioned on a number of occasions, the government is formally committed to shifting 'the emphasis in primary care from the treatment of illness to the promotion of health and the prevention of disease.'[130] This means, in effect, encouraging a more preventive and educative approach throughout the service. Should this objective be realised, it can be argued that any claims which health education officers may make regarding the distinctiveness of their function will be further undermined.

Last, health authorities are finding it increasingly difficult to recruit suitably qualified staff for their health education departments and a large number of posts are usually vacant. This is mainly due to the fact that the salaries of health education officers are unattractive and have kept pace not even with those in the two professions from which they have traditionally been recruited, namely teaching and nursing.

Moreover, the situation is exacerbated by the fact that, as a new profession, health education has been seeking to establish itself at a time when the climate has not been favourable to professionalisation. Consequently, there is now great pessimism amongst health education officers regarding the future. Nevertheless, they continue to perform useful roles. For example, they act as catalysts; provide support; give advice to, and train, other staff; and monitor and evaluate health education activities.

As catalysts they bring to the attention of the public and professionals, patterns of behaviour which are likely to damage health, and stimulate the taking of appropriate remedial action. Support, in the form of expertise, literature, and personnel, is provided within the NHS and to outside organisations, such as education authorities and private companies. Similarly, health education officers give advice to members of other health care professions (e.g. health visitors, physiotherapists) and to the staff of non-NHS organisations and, most importantly, play a key role in their training.

Despite the inherent difficulties involved in measuring the outcome of initiatives taken by health education officers, the need for some kind of monitoring and evaluation is generally accepted. This usually involves an assessment of the relative effectiveness of different types of health education strategy. Unfortunately, however, the extent to which health education officers can monitor and evaluate is often severely circumscribed by a lack of resources.

It is clear from the foregoing discussion that **the groups of professional staff responsible for the delivery of CHSs** are preoccupied with a wide variety of issues, such as education and training; the maintenance of standards of practice; registration; public image; relations with members of other professional groups; the use of 'assistants'; self-treatment; and their changing role in the community. Many of these issues could be said to spring from a lack of confidence and a common concern over professional status, which is more problematic in a community as opposed to a hospital setting.

In hospitals, professionals derive security from the fact that they work in close proximity to colleagues and members of other professional groups and that there is a clear division of responsibility. By contrast, in the community they are, more often than not, working alone and without close supervision and there is less contact with colleagues. As Cumberlege and her colleagues indicated, professional support is often in short supply for nurses (and by implication other professionals) based in the community. Moreover, professional boundaries are less clearly delineated. Thus, it can be argued that it is more important for professionals working in the community to campaign uncompromisingly for the raising of educational and professional standards than it is for their hospital based colleagues, who have more immediate access to help, advice and second opinions.

Furthermore, in the late 1980s, the situation has been exacerbated by the threat (real or perceived), from the policies of the Conservative government, to the NHS in general and the CHSs in particular. As a consequence, all the professionals working in the community face a dilemma. On the one hand, if they do not secure the standing and exclusivity they desire, it is possible that, to some extent, their role will be usurped by others and it will be difficult, if not impossible, to maintain standards of care. On the other hand, if they are successful in their efforts to raise educational and professional standards the end result might be very similar. This is because the costs of employing professionals would rise and the government might respond by looking for cheaper and more flexible alternatives.

Other Service Developments

In addition to the specific concerns of the various professions which play a leading role in the delivery of the CHSs, a number of other developments are worthy of consideration. Some of these relate to longstanding issues, such as vaccination and immunisation and cervical cancer screening, and others to relatively recent additions to the health care agenda, such as drug misuse and HIV infection and AIDS.

Vaccination and Immunisation

Despite the improvement in the take-up rates for vaccination and immunisation against diphtheria, whooping cough, poliomyelitis, tetanus, measles, tuberculosis and rubella during the first half of the 1980s (see Chapter 7), they remained poor by comparison with many other countries. Moreover, there were significant variations in take-up rates between different parts of country. This prompted the Public Health Laboratory Service Communicable Disease Surveillance Centre to carry out a survey of pre-school immunisation programmes, the results of which were published in April 1987.

The principal objective of the survey team was 'to discover the reasons for the variation in immunisation performance by health districts in England and Wales.'[131] Not surprisingly, the team found that variation reflected 'not only the populations served, but the enthusiasm of those providing the service, and the organisation of the programme.'[132]

In the light of its findings the survey team made the following recommendations:

- DHAs which had not appointed a district immunisation programme co-ordinator should do so immediately;

- immunisation co-ordinators should implement programmes in close consultation with representatives from all relevant disciplines (e.g. health visiting, general practice, health promotion);

- a formal training programme for service providers;

- 'all districts should maintain a computerised register of resident children';

- service providers should be given regular feedback on immunisation performance;

- the identification of children moving in and out of districts should be improved;

- in districts where the main burden of immunising children fell on DHA clinics, the feasibility of nurses giving immunisations should be explored; and

- 'specific strategies, for example domiciliary immunisation, should be developed for hard to reach groups, and areas within a district where uptake (was) low.'[133]

It was hoped that implementation of these recommendations would help DHAs improve their take-up rates and reach the target of 90% coverage by 1990, which had been set and endorsed by the European Office of WHO in the early 1980s.

During the second half of the 1980s, central government has also continued to give a high priority to improving the take-up rates for the main childhood vaccination and immunisation programmes (see Chapter 7). This commitment was clearly reflected in the circular on resource assumptions for 1989/90 and planning guidelines for the period 1989/90 to 1990/91 (July 1988). Significantly, the circular indicated that health authorities would shortly be provided with new guidance on childhood immunisation based on revised advice from the Joint Committee on Vaccination and Immunisation. Moreover, this guidance would include reference to: the need for authorities to make substantial progress towards achieving the take-up rate prescribed by WHO; the introduction of a combined measles, mumps and rubella vaccine later in the year; the key role of the district immunisation co-ordinator in maximising take-up rates; and the need to ensure the immunisation against hepatitis B of those at risk.[134]

The new guidance was duly issued and the first week in October 1988 was set as the date for the introduction of the combined measles, mumps, and rubella vaccine. The target group for the new vaccine was children of around 15 months old. Unfortunately, however, problems arose over the costings of the new programme and the availability of vaccine with the result that what was 'hailed as the biggest change in immunisation policy for 20 years' was marred by controversy.[135]

Cervical and Breast Cancer Screening

Continuing concern over various aspects of the revised arrangements for **cervical cancer screening,** which had been introduced during the first half of the 1980s (see Chapter 7), prompted the DHSS to issue yet another circular on the subject in

January 1988. The declared purpose of this circular was to consolidate the 'existing requirements for cervical cancer screening.'[136] These were that:

- by 31st March 1988 all DHAs should have implemented computerised call and recall systems;

- 'all women aged 20 to 64 should be invited for screening within five years of the implementation of the system, unless their general practitioner has indicated that they should be excluded';

- women within this age range should then be recalled at least every five years;

- the system should provide for GPs 'to be notified whenever a woman registered with them is due for call or recall';

- 'women should be given the choice of having a smear taken either by their GP or at a (DHA family planning) clinic';

- 'local health education programmes should aim to encourage women to respond to screening invitations' and everything possible should be done to follow up non-responders whilst 'recognising that women ultimately have the right to choose not to participate in screening programmes'; and

- DHAs should produce the information they need to monitor adequately the effectiveness of their screening programme.[137]

Since experience had shown that 'for some women, appropriate follow-up action (had) not been taken after the identification of abnormal cytology', the DHSS also provided DHAs with guidance, by means of an annex to the circular, on fail-safe mechanisms for the follow-up of cervical smears. This was based on the principal that the doctor taking a smear, which proved to be abnormal, should accept responsibility for taking all reasonable steps to ensure that the woman concerned received suitable treatment.

However, despite the Conservative government's desire to secure the development of an effective screening service and the fact that 94% of DHAs had their computerised call and recall systems operating by 31st March 1988, many problems remain. First, in early 1989 the Women's National Cancer Control Campaign produced survey results which indicated that between 40% and 60% of women were ignoring their screening appointments. The main reasons for women not coming forward were fear, lack of information and impersonal computer invitations.[138] Thus, the Campaign felt that far more should be done to educate women about cervical cancer and to personalise the process and set up its own helpline to provide counselling, support and information.

Second, a survey conducted by the National Association of Health Authorities in late 1988, showed that more than 50% of DHAs were suffering from backlogs in the checking of smears and 25% were unable to provide GPs with the results within a month of the smear being taken. The principal cause of these backlogs was a lack of resources, especially those of laboratory staff and time. As a result, a small number of DHAs were restricting their screening programmes to particular age groups within the range 21 to 64.[139]

Third, evidence suggests that some laboratories are not alerting GPs to the fact that they have taken their smears in an incorrect manner and that as a result it is not possible to test them accurately. Furthermore, in these cases the test results are shown as normal by the laboratories when, in fact, some of the women from whom the smears are taken might well be developing pre-cancerous cells. Thus, there is clearly a need for GPs to receive regular feedback on the quality of their smears (as recommended by the circular mentioned above) and for those whose performance is poor to be given further training in the taking of smears.

It would therefore seem that a great deal remains to be done before the public can have complete confidence in the arrangements for cervical cancer screening.

Notwithstanding the problems associated with cervical cancer screening, in early 1987 the government announced that it intended to establish a national **breast screening service**, based on the recommendations of the Forrest Report. The objective of the service is to ensure that all women between the ages of 50 and 64 are called for screening at 3-yearly intervals with optional screening for those aged 65 and over. As in the case of cervical cancer screening, the record maintained by FPCs of those registered for general medical services is to be used for the purpose of identifying the names and addresses of those due for screening and DHAs are to finance the running costs of the call/recall programme.

However, there are those who doubt whether screening will significantly reduce the number of deaths from the disease. They also claim that it may do more harm than good by causing unnecessary mastectomies and emotional distress.[140] In response to concerns of this kind (which had been considered by the Forrest Committee) the Department of Health issued, in March 1989, a circular and guidelines on the subject of quality assurance for the radiological aspects of mammography.[141] As the circular made clear, 'a high level of quality is essential to maximise the benefits and minimise the adverse effects of screening'. Thus health authorities were asked to 'nominate a quality assurance manager and establish a quality assurance reference centre in each Region ...; include the need to comply with the quality assurance system in the job descriptions of all staff participating in the breast screening programme; and ensure that staff are adequately trained.' In recognition of the importance of the quality assurance initiative, which was intended to cover consumer satisfaction (i.e. 'minimising anxiety and maximising acceptability'); mammography; pathology; treatment and information, the Department of Health has also made funds available to support its development.

Despite the attention being given to the issue of quality, it seems unlikely that those responsible for the development of breast cancer screening will avoid all the problems associated with cervical cancer screening. This is not only because it is always difficult to apply the lessons of earlier experience, but also because of the practical challenges and ethical dilemmas inherent in any form of screening (see Chapter 10).

Initiatives in Respect of HIV Infection and AIDS

Although the spread of human immunodeficiency virus (HIV) infection and AIDS is not exclusively a problem for health care professionals working in the community, in tackling this problem it is clearly necessary to mobilise community, as well as institutionally, based health care resources. Moreover, in the words of Ferlie and Pettigrew: 'In many ways AIDS has been the archetypal general management issue - involving complex and perhaps unexpected linkages across conventional units of management and making demands on hospital, community and preventive services.'[142] It is also increasingly recognised that many other publically provided services, such as housing, welfare rights and meals on wheels, have a contribution to make and that health care professionals therefore need to collaborate with colleagues in other fields in responding positively to the needs of the victims of the AIDS crisis.

The Conservative government's broad policy aims in respect of HIV infection and AIDS, which were initially set out in its response to the Social Services Committee's report on the problems associated with AIDS, are to prevent the spread of HIV infection and to provide 'diagnostic and treatment facilities and counselling and support services for those infected or at risk.'[143] Moreover, health authorities are expected to:

- 'encourage the development of community based prevention initiatives aimed at helping individuals in selected target groups (e.g. those attending genito urinary medicine clinics, drug misusers, prostitutes, homosexual men, male prisoners and their families) to change behaviour which puts them at risk of HIV infection';

- review, in collaboration with the Health Education Authority, the effectiveness of the material used in locally run health education programmes 'paying particular attention to (their) success in maintaining public awareness and reaching defined target groups';

- 'review within the Joint Consultative Committee arrangements made between ... (the relevant public agencies) for co-ordinating hospital and community care and for working with the voluntary sector; and make improvements where necessary';

- 'review systems for the local monitoring and surveillance of HIV infection, and for predicting future caseloads, in the light of the requirements of the AIDS (Control) Act 1987[144] and with due regard for confidentality safeguards'; and

- determine the additional staff resources required to meet the health care needs of AIDS sufferers and 'develop and implement appropriate training strategies to enhance available skills.'[145]

Although the government has stressed the importance of working with voluntary organisations, many critics feel that by comparison with the voluntary sector it has been sluggish and unimaginative in its approach.

In acting upon the DHSS's guidelines and their own assessment of the situation a relatively large number of DHAs have appointed AIDS co-ordinators. Significantly, most of these co-ordinators are based in community units and in a few cases the posts have been jointly funded. According to Wood, the principal functions of co-ordinators are to work with public and voluntary agencies 'raising awareness (and) providing support, training and counselling to all sectors of the community.'[146] Of these activities the development of counselling services for not only those suffering from AIDS but also for their families and friends and the counsellors themselves has a very high priority. Co-ordinators also play an important part in the recruitment of volunteers to work with AIDS sufferers and others affected by the epidemic; the establishment of resource centres and support networks and the implementation of outreach initiatives, such as setting up telephone helplines and making contact with those groups who, for whatever reason, are not prepared to use the services provided by the statutory agencies. Moreover, they contribute to the training of community staff who might come into contact with sufferers during the course of their work. It is to be hoped that appropriate safety precautions become a matter of routine for all health workers. Only time will tell what other kinds of action will need to be taken.

It is becoming increasingly clear, however, that more attention needs to be given to the educational strategies designed to limit the spread of AIDS and to monitoring both the short-term and long-term effects of these strategies.[147] One of the debates surrounding these strategies has been the question of whether they should be directed at the population at large or at target groups. For example, at an Institute of Geographers conference in January 1989, Andrew Lovatt of the University of Lancaster argued that further large, broad-based, national advertising campaigns were pointless since those so far undertaken had failed to change significantly the sexual habits of heterosexuals. In his view, the need was for locally based campaigns, specifically targeted at groups such as drug misusers, homosexual men, promiscuous heterosexuals and others whose behaviour puts them into a high risk category. In other words, he favoured campaigns of the kind advocated by the DHSS in its planning guidelines and being developed by many AIDS co-ordinators. Lovatt also recommended that DHAs should publish statistical data on the number of HIV positive and AIDS patients in their area to make people take notice. However, this might prove to be counterproductive since in some districts the numbers would be very small thereby encouraging complacency. Furthermore, since HIV infection and AIDS are not at present officially notifiable diseases the accuracy of the statistics would clearly be suspect.[148]

Nevertheless, everything possible needs to be done to communicate the message that AIDS is an 'equal opportunities virus' (i.e. everyone is at risk) and that preventive measures are the only effective safeguard against the disease, until an effective vaccine/cure is found. Thus, AIDS is clearly a major challenge for those who are committed to the development of a far more preventive and proactive approach to health care and this is likely to be the position for many years to come.

Services for Drug and Alcohol Misusers

The escalating problem of drug misuse, to which attention was drawn in Chapter 7, and the spread of HIV infection and AIDS amongst drug misusers has prompted the DHSS to provide health authorities with an increasing amount of guidance as to how they should respond to the problem and the kinds of service they should provide for drug misusers. The government's policy aims are to:

- 'provide a service for those who have, or are at risk of, health or social problems as a result of their use of illicit or prescribed drugs';

- 'provide advice and counselling services for those with or at risk from HIV infection, including advice on safer drug and sexual practices, and, where appropriate, ensuring the availability of sterile injecting equipment and condoms to enable misusers to put this advice into practice';

- 'ensure that these services are accessible, well-publicised and attractive to clients';

- 'ensure account is taken of the views of service users ... ';

- 'enable clients to be treated in their own homes where possible, and to maintain existing family links and responsibilities and employment where practicable and in the interests of both the client and the household'; and

- encourage DHAs to consult with other agencies about developing services to 'meet the needs of people with problems over the whole range of substance misuse (drugs, alcohol, polydrug misuse).'[149]

In this sphere of service provision, as in others, key concepts are 'accessibility' and 'informality', which generally means a more community-orientated approach. Studies of community based initiatives, such as that of Powell and Lovelock, have identified three main areas of concern. These are 'the notion of a broadly based service, the development of the multidisciplinary team, and how far the shift of the service to a community base has encouraged and promoted collaboration between the statutory and voluntary agencies.'[150] Not surprisingly, the evidence suggests that the success of these initiatives very much depends upon the ability of managers and, in particular, service providers to deal effectively with these concerns and thereby develop services which are comprehensive, flexible, sensitive to local needs, multidisciplinary and genuinely joint ventures between public and voluntary agencies. Thus, in this sphere of service provision a high priority needs to be given to the fostering of teamwork and inter-agency collaboration.

During the 1970s and 1980s there has been a growing recognition, on the part of public authorities, of the seriousness of the problem of alcohol abuse and of the need to develop services and facilities for alcohol misusers. In its guidelines for the planning period 1989-91 the DHSS indicated that it proposed to issue new guidance on services for alcohol misusers to health authorities 'within the next year or so' and that in the meantime health authorities should continue to develop their existing services in collaboration with local authorities and other public and voluntary agencies. Of particular importance in this respect was the need for measures to prevent alcohol misuse (e.g. health education materials for teenagers) and 'an adequate, accessible range of services (medical - including detoxification facilities - , nursing, social services, and voluntary advice and counselling) to meet the needs of problem drinkers.'[151]

The promised new guidance was published in February 1989. Some idea of the priority attached by central government to the problem of alcohol misuse can be guaged from the fact that the circular containing the guidance was issued by no fewer than six departments and was addressed not only to health authorities but also to a wide range of other agencies. The stated purpose of the circular was to provide 'advice about ways local organisations can work together to plan, manage and make more effective use of existing resources to tackle the problem ...' It recommended that in each geographical area one agency should 'take the lead in initiating local planning and act as a focal point for action on alcohol problems.' Moreover, in the event of difficulties arising over who should call the initial meeting of the agencies involved 'the General Manager of the District Health Authority should do so.'[152]

As well as dealing with a variety of practical issues, such as arrangements for pooling information and targeting existing resources, the circular also outlined the roles of agencies involved in dealing with the problem of alcohol misuse and the action which they might take and identified many sources of advice.

Incontinence Service

In many health districts managers have been finding it increasingly difficult to control the cost of supplying patients with incontinence products. This is primarily because the service has traditionally been both demand led and free at the point of delivery (i.e. anyone who has been assessed as needing products of this kind has been supplied with them), whereas for many years managers have had to operate within cash limited budgets. Very often this has meant overspendings on the incontinence wear budget have had to be offset against underspendings on other budget heads (i.e. virement).

It has also led to a number of DHAs introducing some form of rationing, with the result that in September 1987 the DHSS had to draw the attention of regional general managers to the fact that over the previous 18 months it had been receiving 'an increasing number of complaints that the supply of incontinence pads to people living in the community (had) either been severely restricted or stopped altogether.'[153] Although the response of the department to these complaints had been to point out that it was 'for health authorities to determine their own priorities in the light of local needs and circumstances', it was felt that the situation was sufficiently serious to warrant finding out more about the incontinence policy being pursued in every part of the country. Thus, regional general managers were requested to provide answers to the following questions for each DHA in their region.

- 'What is done to ensure that people who need these aids have an adequate supply (?). Who assesses what level of supply is appropriate and how is it controlled(?).'

- 'Are there any restrictions on the supply of pads to people ... living in their own homes ... living in residential homes (?). If so, do the restrictions apply both to adults and to children (?).'

- 'Approximately how much does the DHA spend on incontinence pads... (?)'

- 'What arrangements exist for collaboration with local authorities (?). Has the DHA's policy on the supply of incontinence aids been drawn up in co-operation with the Social Services Department (?).'

- 'Does the DHA have a written policy on continence ... (?)'[154]

Although most general managers have responded to this request, no formal guidance has yet been issued by the centre.

Cutting across all these service developments, and those considered elsewhere in the chapter, are a number of special initiatives designed to improve the community based health care facilities for particular client groups and those living in areas of deprivation. As mentioned in Chapter 7, since the late 1970s and early 1980s, increasing attention has been given to the distinctive health care needs and problems of ethnic minority communities and the inner city and to the development of strategies designed to meet these needs and tackle these problems.

Of the various national and local initiatives taken in response to the needs of **ethnic minorities**, McNaught has drawn a distinction between those of a 'service' nature and those aimed at 'management or training'. 'Service' initiatives are those where an attempt has been made 'to provide specific services for ethnic minority groups', such as the introduction of sickle cell anaemia and thalassaemia screening and the funding of voluntary organisations. The initiatives aimed at 'management or training' are designed 'to improve the capacity of the health system to understand' and therefore respond more effectively 'to the needs of ethnic minorities on an individual and corporate basis.'[155] Examples include DHSS funding of training in health and race and the appointment of ethnic advisers by a number of DHAs.

However, one of the most important initiatives, namely the 'Asian Mother and Baby Campaign', has both a 'service' and a 'management/training' element. The 'Campaign' was launched in 1984 with the aim of improving the access of Asian mothers to ante-natal care and bridging the cultural and linguistic gap between NHS staff and Asian mothers (see Chapter 7). It had been prompted by the recognition that Asian mothers were experiencing difficulties in using exisiting maternity and child care services and the fact that there was within the Asian community a relatively high peri-natal mortality rate. A key part in the 'Campaign' was played by 80 WTE linkworkers, who were funded by the DHSS and appointed to work in 16 health districts with substantial Asian populations. The linkworkers were Asian women, who spoke English and at least one Asian language, and it was their job to follow up mothers who missed their clinic appointments, assist health care workers in communicating with mothers and advise on the appropriateness, in cultural terms, of the advice given. In her report on the 'Campaign' (1987) the Director, Veena Bahl, concluded that for a campaign of this kind to be successful it was necessary 'to demonstrate that it has a clear, relevant and achievable aim;...win, by careful preparation, the support of the authority, the professions, other health staff and the community; (and) instil a sense of responsibility for ensuring health care delivery appropriate to a multi-racial, multi- cultural society'.[156] From the available evidence it would appear that in terms of these criteria the 'Campaign' has been relatively successful. Moreover, as McNaught points out, although there has been some criticism of the assumptions on which it was based, 'it has provided the starting point for discussion and further work in many authorities on racial inequality.'[157]

Nevertheless he argues that most initiatives have been based on the premise that access to existing services is the major problem and that far less attention has been given to 'the development of different approaches to service delivery and the eradication of racial discrimination'. Consequently, in his view, a great deal more needs to be done, particularly through community health initiatives, 'to improve the sensitivity and quality of health care to a group suffering disadvantage.'[158]

This view was also expressed at a management seminar on ethnic minority health, which the DHSS organised in November 1987,[159] and is reflected in a report (1988) of the National Association of Health Authorities' working party on health services for black and minority ethnic groups (see Chapter 8).[160] In preparing their report the members of the working party were guided by the following principles which they regarded as being of fundamental importance:

- 'access to NHS provision should be equally available to all';
- 'NHS provision should be sensitive to the needs of all groups in society';
- 'if service provision in the NHS is to become flexible and responsive to the needs of black and minority ethnic groups, positive action is needed at all levels particularly the participation of members from black and minority ethnic groups in management planning';
- 'a fundamental examination of recruitment training and racial awareness within the NHS is required at all levels';

- '...Britain is now a multi-racial and multi-cultural society and the NHS needs to adapt to its changing population'; and

- 'acknowledge that individual, cultural and institutional racial discrimination exists within the NHS and appropriate measures should be taken to remove it and prevent its occurrence.'[161]

Thus, in terms of both its analysis of the existing situation and its prescriptions for the future, the working party's report has helped to increase awareness of the ways in which the NHS discriminates against members of ethnic minority communities and the action which should be taken to eliminate these discriminatory practices.

The Conservative government's continuing concern about the poor quality of primary health care services in **inner cities** has been demonstrated by the fact that in both the green and white papers a whole chapter was devoted to this particular issue. However, whether the proposals put forward in these documents and the action central government has taken so far will prove to be an adequate response to the health needs of those living in inner city areas is an open question.

Although most of the ideas and proposals contained in the green and white papers related to general medical services,[162] recognition was given to the important contribution which effectively organised community nursing services can make to the provision of health care in inner city areas. For example, the green paper suggested that the introduction of neighbourhood nursing teams would help to improve standards of care in inner cities 'because these are areas where there is most scope for rationalisation of the ways in which members of the primary health care team operate.'[163] Similarly, in the white paper it was suggested that in areas of acute deprivation nurses, organised on a neighbourhood basis, would be in a position to 'identify gaps in service provision and help to mobilise any existing community support networks.'[164] Cumberlege and her colleagues, however, were more concerned about the problem of retaining staff in inner city areas and underlined the fact that in London the annual turnover rates for district nurses were between 13.5% and 40.0% and for health visitors between 14.7% and 28.0%. In their view, measures likely to ease the situation included 'the development of a career grade for community nurses, more flexibility over work sharing and the employment of part-time staff, the provision of better working conditions, and the availability of peer group support from other professionals.'[165]

Despite the good intentions of Cumberlege and the authors of the green and white papers, critics argue that they have failed to get to grips with the roots of the problem. In their view these are essentially socio-economic and include high levels of unemployment, low income levels, bad housing conditions, pollution and poor diet. Significantly, particular attention was drawn to factors of this kind at a three-day conference, 'UK Healthy Cities', held in Liverpool in 1988. Liverpool, which has a mortality rate 29% above the national average, is one of 25 official participants in the WHO's European Healthy Cities project[166] and the conference provided an opportunity for delegates from Europe and North America to discuss ways of tackling the health care needs of cities. The main conclusion of the conference was that far more emphasis needed to be placed on public health and preventive measures and that each city should draw up its own 'agenda for action'.

In Britain most of the action taken to deal with the health care needs of those living in the inner city has focused on the delivery of existing services and has not involved the more fundamental changes in orientation recommended by the Liverpool conference. Indeed, some would argue that the policies of the Thatcher government have not only failed to tackle the basic causes of the problem but have actually made the situation worse by creating more unemployment and poverty and by reducing the funds available for investment in public health.

Health for All by the Year 2000?

It can be argued that many of the health care needs and problems of the late 1980s, to which this chapter has drawn attention, are more likely to be satisfactorily met and resolved by strategies based on proaction and prevention rather than reaction and cure. Although some significant advances have been made, it is clear that a great deal remains to be done, particularly if the WHO's objective of 'an acceptable state of health for all by the year 2000' is to be realised. Furthermore, there can be little doubt that effective progress towards the realisation of this objective is dependent upon a higher level of commitment to primary care, on the part of government, and upon the provision of more opportunities for health care professionals based in the community to apply their distinctive skills and expertise. In other words, as the WHO and other bodies have emphasised, far greater recognition needs to be given to the contribution which the CHSs, community medicine and public health initiatives can make to the health and well-being of individuals and communities.

At the present time there are at least three fundamental challenges facing those who are committed to the realisation of the WHO's objective. First, the well publicised links between deprivation and ill-health and the gross inequalities in morbidity and mortality to which they give rise must be tackled in a more determined manner. For example, Liverpool Health Authority in its *Public Health Annual Report for 1988* called for a greater emphasis on preventive work and for a planned increase in the money available for health promotion to tackle the city's very serious health care problems. Similarly, a non-medical health promotion team employed by East Anglia Regional Health Authority looked at ways of raising the profile of health promotion in the 1990s and has been encouraging local communities and groups to articulate their health care needs.[167]

More attention also needs to be given to the refinement of health status indices, such as those produced by Jarman,[168] and to their utilisation in the allocation of resources. For the CHSs, indices of this kind, and the statistical data from which they are derived, are of particular importance since they can be used to identify which geographical areas are most in need of support and thereby serve as the basis for measures of positive discrimination which it is felt necessary to take. For example, a strong case could be made for taking account of the distribution of babies with a low birth weight when determining how many health visitors to allocate to a particular zone or GP practice. At district level the percentage of babies weighing under 2500 grammes at birth ranges from 4.5% in the Isle of Wight to 10.6% in Brent (see Appendix V for further details) and it is probable that within some districts the variations between different areas are even greater.

A second challenge arises from the newer health care needs, such as AIDS, drug misuse and alcoholism, to which community based responses are more likely to be effective than those based on hospitals. As suggested above, assertive health education and personal support counselling have a vital part to play in meeting needs of this kind. Moreover, in seeking to reach those most at risk and those who need help, health care professionals often have to adopt an approach which is less formal than is usual or possible in a hospital setting. Only in this way can they begin to overcome the suspicion, antipathy and fears of many of those who need their services. Responses to this challenge are frustrated, however, by the process of resource allocation. Because of the stigma attached to them, community based initiatives of this kind tend to be accorded a far lower priority than the more prestigious services provided in hospitals.

Third, there are signs that in certain areas of health care, which are of particular concern to CHSs staff, a number of the advances made during the past few decades may be at risk. In 1986 the infant death rate rose for the first time in 16 years. Although the rise was due solely to sudden infant death syndrome (which implies that it was caused by social factors) and did not continue into 1987, it does indicate that there is little room for complacency. Furthermore, it suggests that more needs to be done to improve the quality of maternity and child health services, especially since infant mortality rates in this country have been deteriorating in relation to those of most other developed countries. In 1986 there was also an increase in the number of notified cases of tuberculosis and there is evidence of a deterioration in the dental health of children.

Similarly, in 1987/8 the number of people who smoke started to rise for the first time in 10 years and many health promoters fear that this is the first sign of a reversal of the downward trend which began in the mid-1960s. One of the main reasons for this appears to be the fact that the price of cigarettes has fallen in real terms due to the decision of the Conservative government not to increase the tax on tobacco in the 1987 and 1988 budgets.[169] As Reid points out, in his comments on the *Declaration of Alma-Ata*, 'in both developed and developing countries, the rising tide of death and suffering caused by tobacco will be brought under control only if governments have clear strategies for dealing with the subject to complement individual decisions to abjure this lethal addiction.'[170] Thus, if the efforts of health educators are to be successful in reducing the level of smoking they need the active support of government, which in this country means a willingness to accept the political unpopularity of increasing duties on tobacco products. In the words of Dr

John Dawson, head of the BMA's scientific division, 'wingeing increases of 2 or 3 per cent are no use. There is a direct link (between) price and consumption. Smokers want to stop and we know a significant price increase is the trigger that many need to help them.'[171] It would appear therefore that if the situation is not to deteriorate further there needs to be renewed commitment to health promotion.

Taken together the geographical inequalities in health; the emergence of new health needs and the deteriorating situation in various spheres of health care, particularly in the community, are undoubtedly formidable barriers to the achievement of the objective of health for all by the year 2000. Moreover, without concerted action at both national and local level it seems unlikely that these barriers can be overcome.

However, despite a claim by the Chief Medical Officer at the Department of Health that prevention and health promotion has climbed higher up the government's agenda[172] and the positive statements about health promotion and illness prevention in *Promoting Better Health*, there are relatively few signs that the government is willing to take the lead in reversing the traditional bias against a preventive and proactive approach to health care and to make available the resources needed to create a healthier environment. On the contrary, the government's stance could be said to have exacerbated the situation. In the first place, as indicated earlier, it would appear that some of the existing mechanisms for health surveillance, such as the pre-school health service and the school health and dental services, are under threat. In the second place, the government has been somewhat lethargic in its response to mounting evidence of the nature and cause of certain kinds of preventable disease. According to a report from the National Audit Office 'the government has been slow to respond to the danger of heart disease and its policy is inadequate and lacking in planning.'[173] In the third place, government initiatives designed to increase personal and commercial freedoms, such as the relaxation of the licensing laws, have taken insufficient account of their implications for health. Moreover, the uncertainty surrounding the future of the NHS (which has been increased by the white paper, *Working for Patients*) has undermined still further the morale of many of those seeking to develop preventive strategies at the local level. Consequently, the prospects for achieving the objective of health for all by the year 2000 are poor.

Footnotes

1.   DHSS, *Primary Health Care: An Agenda for Discussion*, Cmnd 9771 (London: HMSO, 1986), p. 1.

2.   Ibid., p. 2.

3.   Ibid., p. 2.

4.   Ibid., p. 49.

5.   Ibid., p. 2.

6.   Ibid., p. 10.

7. *The Health Service Journal*, 24th April 1986, p. 537.

8. Over 6,000 copies of the green paper and Cumberlege Report were distributed to approximately 2,700 organisations and 180,000 copies of a summary leaflet to the public at large. 12 public consultation meetings were held in different parts of the country and evidence was taken for a total of 110 hours from 370 witnesses representing 73 organisations. Over 2,200 written comments were received. These included comments from 250 organisations representing the interests of consumers, volunteers and professionals.

9. DHSS, *Promoting Better Health. The Government's Programme for Improving Primary Health Care*, Cm 249 (London: HMSO, 1987), para. 1.7.

10. Ibid., para. 1.8.

11. Ibid., paras. 3.45 and 3.47.

12. *Working for Patients. The Health Service in the 1990s*, Cm 555 (London: HMSO, 1989), para. 6.5.

13. See J. Fry and J. Hasler (eds.), *Primary Health Care 2000* (London: Churchill Livingstone, 1986), for further details.

14. Ibid.

15. See Chapter 1, footnote 23.

16. Promoting Better Health, op. cit., para. 7.4.

17. DHSS, *Neighbourhood Nursing A Focus for Care*, [the Cumberlege Report] (London: HMSO, 1986), Definitions. The terms 'core' and 'peripheral' were not used in this way by the review team.

18. Ibid., Foreword and p. 2.

19. Ibid., p. 11.

20. Ibid., p. 9.

21. Ibid., Foreword.

22. Ibid., p. 19.

23. Ibid., Foreword.

24. Ibid., pp. 62-64, supplemented with material from pp. 32-33.

25. Ibid., pp. 59-61.

26. *Patching In*, No. 2, February 1987, p. 3.

27. C. Robertson, *Health Visiting in Practice* (London: Churchill Livingstone, 1988), p. 216.

28. C. Kratz, 'The Radical Solution or the Safe Option', *Nursing Times*, April 30th May 6th 1986, p. 18.

29. *Community Psychiatric Nursing Journal*, January/February, 1987, Vol.7, No. 1.

30. Ibid.

31. J. Smith, 'Oh Mrs Cumberlege!', *The Health Services Journal*, 22nd May 1986, p. 700.

32. Ibid.

33. Ibid.

34. E. Haggard, *Patching In*, No. 3, April 1987.

35. Ibid.

36. Neighbourhood Nursing A Focus for Care, op. cit., p. 14.

37.   Ibid.

38.   Ibid., p. 15.

39.   Reported in *The Health Service Journal*, 26th June 1986, p. 844.

40.   See *The Health Service Journal*, 20th November 1986, p. 1508.

41.   For further details see Neighbourhood Nursing A Focus for Care, op. cit., pp. 39-41.

42.   DHSS, Circular HC(87)29, *Health Services Development: Community Nursing Services and Primary Health Care Teams*, November 1987.

43.   Promoting Better Health, op. cit., paras. 7.12 and 7.14.

44.   Circular HC(87)29, op. cit.

45.   *Patching In*, no. 5, July 1988, p. 6.

46.   Ibid., p. 3.

47.   S. Goodwin, *Whither Health Visiting?*, Keynote Speech, Health Visitors' Association Annual Study Conference, Bournemouth 1988, p. 1.

48.   Ibid., pp. 2-3.

49.   Ibid., p. 3.

50.   *Report of the Inquiry into Child Abuse in Cleveland* [Chair: Lord Justice Butler-Sloss], Cm 412 (London: HMSO, 1988).

51.   DHSS and Welsh Office, *Working Together* (London: HMSO, 1988), para. 1.3.

52.   S. Goodwin, op. cit., p. 3.

53.   Ibid., p. 3.

54.   Ibid., p. 4.

55.   *The Health Service Journal*, 15th May 1986.

56.   M. Noon, 'Teams: The Best Option?', *The Health Service Journal*, 6th October 1988, pp. 1160-1.

57.   Ibid.

58.   S. Goodwin, op. cit., pp. 7-8.

59.   Ibid. See p. 9 for details.

60.   Editorial comment, *The Journal of District Nursing*, June 1988, p. 22.

61.   E. James, 'Moving On', *The Journal of District* Nursing, September 1988, p. 14.

62.   Editorial comment, *The Journal of District Nursing*, June 1988, p. 22.

63.   Editorial comment, *The Journal of District Nursing*, July 1987, p. 26.

64.   Ibid., p. 26.

65.   L. Young, 'Reaction to Agenda for Action', *The Journal of District Nursing*, October 1988, p. 12-14.

66.   Ibid.

67.   Editorial comment, *The Journal of District Nursing*, July 1987, p. 26.

68.   Editorial comment, *The Journal of District Nursing*, June 1988, p. 22.

69.   For further details, see series of five articles on management issues in district nursing by F. Badger, E. Cameron, H. Evers and R. Griffiths, *The Health Service Journal*, (i) 'Caseloads under

Review', 10th November 1988, pp. 1327-8; (ii) 'Nursing in Perspective', 17th November 1988, pp. 1362-3; (iii) 'Facing Care's Unequal Shares', 24th November 1988, pp. 1392-3; (iv) 'Put Race on the Agenda', 1st December 1988, pp. 1426-7 and (v) 'Care at a Crossroads', 8th December 1988, pp. 1454-5.

70. Ibid., (v).

71. Ibid., (v).

72. In 1987 a midwife was dismissed (on grounds of gross misconduct) by her employer, Croydon Health Authority, for conducting a home delivery without a second midwife being present. However, she won her appeal against her dismissal and was reinstated.

73. Working Together, op. cit., para. 3.2.

74. Neighbourhood Nursing A Focus for Care, op. cit., p. 26.

75. Ibid., pp. 26-27.

76. DHSS, Circular HC(88)43, *Health Services Development : Resource Assumptions and Planning Guidelines*, July 1988, Appendix 4, p. 12.

77. Neighbourhood Nursing A Focus for Care, op. cit., p. 27.

78. Working Together, op. cit., para. 3.3.

79. Health Visitors' Association, *Meeting Schoolchildren's Health Needs: The School Nurse's Role*, October 1988, Foreword.

80. Ibid., para. 2.7. In the absence of a formal national policy for the health surveillance of schoolchildren the Association recommends that it is good practice for the school nurse to ensure that, as a minimum: the health status of schoolchildren is monitored by the school nurse in the course of regular and planned contacts taking place at 2 yearly reviews conducted jointly by the school nurse and the child and continuing until at least the age of 13 years.Children with known health problems and deficits are reviewed on a regular basis by the school nurse, involving the doctor as necessary and in accord with locally agreed procedures .Where parents, teachers or the children themselves are concerned about any aspect of health, a review is undertaken by the school nurse and/or doctor as appropriate with referral for assessment made in accord with locally agreed procedures.Visual acuity, using a Snellen Chart, is checked at ages 8, 11 and 14 years, except those with 6/9 vision and with a family history of myopia, who should be checked annually .Colour vision is checked by the age of 11 years using Ishihara Plates for boys and girls. If height is below the third centile at school entry but appears to be growing parallel to it, a further measurement is made at 7 years. For all other children, measurement of height beyond school entry should be made only if there is doubt about the significance of measurements already obtained or where previous records are incomplete.

81. Ibid., see Section 6 for a summary of the major recommendations.

82. House of Commons Paper No. 13 Session 1984/85, Second Report from Social Services Committee, *Community Care with special reference to adult mentally ill and mentally handicapped people*, paras. 192-193.

83. Neighbourhood Nursing A Focus for Care, op. cit., p. 9, evidence from Royal College of Nursing.

84. *The Times*, 31st December 1987.

85. *The Chiropodist*, Vol. 43, No. 4, April 1988, p. 55.

86. *The Chiropodist*, Vol. 43, No. 3, March 1988, p. 37.

87. *Tne Chiropodist*, Vol. 43, No. 4, April 1988, p. 67.

88. Ibid., p. 68.

89. Ibid., p. 50.

90. *The Chiropodist*, Vol. 43, No. 6, June 1988, p. 101.

91. Quoted in *The Chiropodist*, Vol. 43, No. 3, March 1988, p. 37.

92. Ibid., p. 48.

93. *The Chiropodist, Vol. 43, No. 6, June 1988, p. 107.*

94. Letter from Mr D. Wiseman (General Secretary and Administrator of the College of Speech Therapists) to general managers, dated 8th June 1987.

95. R v Lancashire County Council, Ex p M; QBD; 7th November 1988.

96. National Association of Health Authorities, *Health Authorities Concerns for Children with Special Needs*, a Report of the Survey of Health Authorities on the Implementation of the Education Act 1981, 1988, p.6.

97. Quoted in C. Partridge and M. Warren, *Physiotherapy in the Community. A descriptive study of fourteen schemes* (Canterbury: Health Services Research Unit, University of Kent at Canterbury, 1977), p. 1.

98. Extract from document produced by Rotherham Health Authority's Physiotherapy Department.

99. S. Burnard, 'Development of a Community Physiotherapy Service', *Physiotherapy*, Vol.74, No. 1, January 1988, p. 5.

100. For further details of the Chartered Society of Physiotherapy evidence to the Griffiths review of community care see, *Physiotherapy*, Vol. 73, No. 11, November 1987, pp. 594-5

101. For further details of the Chartered Society of Physiotherapists' response to 'Promoting Better Health' see, *Physiotherapy*, Vol 74, No. 4, April 1988, p. 201

102. S. Clifton, District Physiotherapist, Rotherham Health Authority.

103. Physiotherapy, Vol. 74, No. 4, op. cit.

104. For further details of community physiotherapy, see A. Gibson (ed.), *Physiotherapy in the Community* (Cambridge: Woodhead-Faulkner, 1988), especially Chapter 1, in which the role of the physiotherapist in the community is examined in some detail, and Chapter 2, in which consideration is given to the setting up of a community physiotherapy service.

105. Health Advisory Service, *Annual Report June 1984- June 1985*, p. 10.

106. Section 3 of the Disabled Persons (Services Consultation and Representation) Act 1986 requires a local authority when making a statement of a disabled person's needs for social services to provide:an opportunity for him/her or his/her representative to make representations on the needs for social services as they perceive them; if requested to do so, a written statement either specifying the needs which it thinks call for the provision of services and outlining the services it intends to provide or stating that, in its view, no services are required; and, in both instances, explaining the basis on which the assessment has been made; an opportunity for him/her or his/her representative to make further representations; to consider these and to inform him/her of the outcome together with reasons.

107. DHSS, *April 1987 Survey of District & Principal Occupational Therapists Working in NHS and LASS Departments in England.*

108. National Audit Office, Report by the Comptroller and Auditor General, *National Health Service: Control over Professional and Technical Manpower*, House of Commons Paper No. 95 Session 1986/87, para. 3.13.

109. For example, in the *Fifth Report on Professions Allied to Medicine of the Review Body Nursing Staff, Midwives, Health Visitors and Professions Allied to Medicine*, Cm 361, April 1988, reference

is made to the fact that the highest vacancy rates were in occupational therapy (i.e. 13.4% compared with 12.8% in 1986).

110. The British Dietetic Association, *Dietitians in the Community*, May 1986.

111. The first training college for orthoptists, the Maddox School of Ocular Training, was founded in 1929. Students at the college gained their clinical experience at the Royal Westminster Ophthalmic Hospital. However, like many of the other new professional groups orthoptists had a long struggle before they received the recognition they deserved from doctors. In the early days doctors often saw the orthoptist's office as 'somewhere to send tiresome children and awkward mothers.'

112. Orthoptists were the first (and so far the only) new professional group to be admitted to the Council for Professions Supplementary to Medicine following its establishment in 1960. The professions admitted in 1960 were dietitians, medical laboratory scientific officers, radiographers, physiotherapists, remedial gymnasts and occupational therapists. Speech therapists, however, opted for exclusion.

113. British Orthoptic Society, Golden Jubilee Celebrations March 13th and 14th 1987, Brochure.

114. Primary Health Care, An Agenda for Discussion, op. cit., p. 19.

115. Circular HC(88)43, op. cit., Appendix 4, p. 13.

116. Ibid., p.13.

117. Reported in *The Health Service Journal*, 1st September 1988, p. 984.

118. Circular HC(88)43, op. cit., Appendix 4, p. 2.

119. 'NHS Family Planning will it fade away', *The Health Service Journal*, 24 September 1987, p. 1099.

120. Review Body on Doctors' and Dentists' Remuneration, *Eighteenth Report 1988*, Cm 358, para. 122.

121. Hansard (Commons), Vol. 124, No. 59, 7th December 1987, col. 64.

122. Hansard (Commons), Vol. 139, No. 208, 1st November 1988, col. 858.

123. Hansard (Commons), Vol. 124, No. 59, 7th December 1987, col. 37.

124. Review Body on Doctors' and Dentists' remuneration, op. cit., para. 126.

125. Department of Health, Circular HC(89)2, *Health Services Management : The Future Development of Community Dental Services*, February 1989, para. 2. The circular also makes it clear that in exercising these responsibilities those concerned 'will be required to monitor levels of dental health throughout the population, to identify special needs, to encourage the use of the general dental service, and to provide a safety net service of treatment for those whose needs cannot be met in the general dental service, or the provision of treatment which may not be generally available in the general dental service, such as general anaesthetics, orthodontics, or preventive therapies.' (para. 3)

126. 'Health promotion' is a much broader concept than 'health education' and incorporates action designed to improve the health status of individuals and communities. This includes education and attempts to persuade those in positions of authority (e.g. Ministers, councillors, managers) of the need to pursue policies which facilitate the adoption of healthier lifestyles (i.e. making healthier choices the easier ones). Thus, 'health education' can be seen as one component of 'health promotion'.

127. A. Watt, 'Community Health Education: A Time for Caution?', in S. Rodmell and A. Watt (eds.), *The Politics of Health Education. Raising the Issues*, (London: Routledge and Kegan Paul, 1986), p. 141.

128. G. Moran, 'Radical Health Promotion: A Role for Local Authorities', Ibid., p. 127.

129. Ibid., p. 123.

130. Promoting Better Health, op. cit., Foreword.

131. N. Begg and J. White, *A Survey of Pre-School Immunisation Programmes in England and Wales: Results of a study carried out in 1986 by the PHLS Communicable Disease Surveillance Centre*, April 1987, p. 1.

132. Ibid., p. 31.

133. Ibid., pp. 31-33.

134. Circular HC(88)43, op. cit., Appendix 4, p. 1.

135. The principal problems were a shortage of funds and an inadequate supply of vaccine. Although the Department of Health had promised DHAs extra funds to pay for the vaccine it was estimated that the amount available would only cover half the cost of the new programme. The Department of Health sought to justify this shortfall by pointing out that the vaccination programme would generate savings (i.e. as a result of fewer children catching measles and mumps) of 3.50 for every pound spent. However, DHAs argued that these were long-term savings (i.e. of up to 10 years) and it was therefore unfair to take them into account at the time of the programme's introduction.

136. DHSS, Circular HC(88)1, *Health Services Management Cervical Cancer Screening*, 12th January 1988.

137. Ibid.

138. A detailed typology of reasons for non-attendance for computer-managed cervical screening, developed by a research team at the Christie Hospital, Manchester, was published in the 20th Edition of the NHS Management Bulletin, April 1989. Details are given below:

      'Inaccessibility: Women who no longer live at the address on the register, or who have died.

      Ineligibility: Women who have been previously screened within the qualifying period determined by policy.

      Unsuitability: Women who are disqualified on other grounds, whether permanently, e.g. hysterectomy or temporarily, e.g.pregnancy.

      Failed communication: Women who live at the address recorded but who do not receive their invitation or who are subject to some other breakdown of communication, e.g. illiteracy.

      Incorrect: Women who did in fact attend but who have been.

      Classification: mistakenly identified as non- attenders.

      Refusal: Women who receive their invitation, have no valid reason to believe the test is inappropriate ..., but who decide not to attend. They may do this because of practical problems connected with the appointment or the venue; or their invalid belief that the test is inappropriate for them; attitudinal barriers i.e. dislike of being tested; fear and fatalism.'

139. National Association of Health Authorities, *Call and Recall*, 1988.

140. Two leading critics of mass screening are Dr P.Skrabanek, a lecturer in community health at Trinity College, Dublin, and Dr J.LeFanu, a medical author and London based GP.

141. Department of Health, Circular HC(89)6, *Health Services Management Breast Cancer Screening: Quality Assurance for Mammography*, March 1989.

142. E. Ferlie and A. Pettigrew, 'AIDS: Responding to Rapid Change', *The Health Service Journal*, 1st December 1988, pp. 1422-3.

143. Circular HC(88)43, op. cit., Appendix 4, p. 9.

144. Under the provisions of the AIDS (Control) Act, 1987, health authorities are required to produce periodical reports on matters relating to AIDS and HIV. These reports also have to be published.

145. Circular HC(88)43, op.cit., Appendix 4, pp. 9 10,

146. P. Wood, *Care and Management of Persons with AIDS and HIV Related Conditions : Evolving Role of an AIDS Co-ordinator*, ENBCC 934, 1988, p. 1.

147. Whilst returns from clinics for sexually transmitted diseases indicate that homosexual men have modified their sexual behaviour, it is essential to ensure that these changes are sustained.

148 For some of the problems involved in obtaining accurate figures of the numbers dying from AIDS see J. Bobby, P. Spencer, J. Wyatt and R. Farmer, 'AIDS Deaths in the UK How Complete are the Figures?', *Public Health*, 1988, Vol. 102, pp. 519-524.

149. Circular HC(88)43, op. cit., Appendix 4, p. 11.

150. J. Powell and R. Lovelock, 'Open Door for Drug Abusers', *The Health Service Journal*, 31st March 1988, p. 365.

151. Circular HC(88)43, op. cit., Appendix 4, p. 11.

152. The circular [HN(89)4 -*Alcohol Misuse*] was issued by the Department of Health, Home Office, Department of Education and Science, Department of Employment, Department of Transport and the Welsh Office. The other agencies to which it was addressed included the police and probation authorities; nonmetropolitan county and district councils; metropolitan district councils and London borough councils; voluntary organisations and professional associations.

153. DHSS, Dear RGM Letter D(87)45, 24 September 1987, *Provision of Incontinence* Pads, p. 1.

154. Ibid., pp. 1-2.

155. A. McNaught, *Health Action and Ethnic Minorities* (London: Bedford Square Press for National Community Resource Centre, 1988), p. 15.

156. Asian Mother and Baby Campaign, *A Report by the Director, Miss Veena Bahl* (London: DHSS, 1987), para. 71.

157. A. McNaught, op. cit., p. 16.

158. Ibid., p. 21.

159. DHSS, *Ethnic Minority Health. A Report of a Management Seminar*, 1988.

160. National Association of Health Authorities, *Action Not Words. A Strategy to Improve Health Services for Black and Minority Ethnic Groups*, 1988.

161. Ibid., p. 6.

162. For example, financial incentives for GPs in inner city partnership areas to form group practices and improve the quality of their practice premises and experimental schemes involving the employment of salaried family doctors to provide primary health care services 'to the homeless and rootless who might otherwise have difficulty in obtaining medical assistance.'

163. Primary Health Care: An Agenda for Discussion, op. cit., p. 44.

164. Promoting Better Health, op. cit., para. 9.15.

165. Neighbourhood Nursing - A Focus for Care, op. cit., p. 53.

166. For further details of the situation in Liverpool see J. Ashton and H. Seymour, *The New Public Health : the Liverpool experience* (Milton Keynes:Open University Press 1988).

167. *Promoting Health in East Anglia*, Conference Report 1988, Regional Health Promotion Team, East Anglia Regional Health Authority.

168.   The Jarman Index incorporates the following census variables: elderly living alone (weighting 6.62); aged under 5 (4.64); one parent families (3.01); unskilled (3.74); unemployed (3.34); overcrowding (2.88); changed address in last year (2.68) and ethnic minorities (2.50).

169.   The situation is likely to get worse after 1992 when tax regimes of the countries of the European Community are harmonised.

170.   Sir J. Reid, 'Alma-Ata and After - The Background', in J. Fry and J. Hasler (eds.), op. cit.,   p. 12.

171.   Reported in *The Independent*, 18th January 1989.

172.   Claim made at the 'UK Healthy Cities' Conference in Liverpool, 1988.

173.   *The Independent*, 22nd February 1989. For further details, see National Audit Office, Reported by the Comptroller and Auditor General, *National Health Service:Coronary Heart Disease*, House of Commons Paper No. 208, Session 1988/89, especially Part 2: 'Prevention of Coronary Heart Disease'.

Chapter 10

Conclusion: The Past in the Present

In reviewing the growth and development of the CHSs it has become clear that although the past is, in some respects at least, a 'foreign country', it is also surprisingly 'familiar territory'. This is because many of the issues which currently preoccupy those concerned with community health and other welfare services, are very similar to those which engaged their predecessors. Writing about the evolution of welfare provision in this country, Clarke and his colleagues make the point that 'the historical development of state welfare has, since the end of the nineteeth century, involved recurrent political and ideological conflict over the causes of social problems to which welfare is a response and over the 'proper' role of the state in welfare.'[1] In their view 'the contemporary arguments around the future of welfare in Britain draw on a legacy of well-established positions and arguments about welfare and the state.'[2]

The aim in this final chapter is to analyse some of the more important of the longstanding issues surrounding the CHSs and to make explicit the nature of the tensions inherent within them. These issues spring from the position of the CHSs within the health care system and from the distinctive contribution which they make to the health of the population. Of particular importance in this respect is the emphasis which the CHSs place upon the prevention of illness and promotion of health and the provision of care for vulnerable groups.

Prevention requires a proactive approach, in which service provision is initiated by the provider rather than the recipient. Such an approach to service delivery, however, gives rise to major administrative and ethical issues. These relate to the 'capture' and use of information, and to the rectitude of intervening in the lives of those who are healthy and have not sought professional help. In other words there exists an underlying tension between the benefits which preventive health measures confer and the rights of individuals to freedom of choice.

With regard to the provision of care, an important characteristic of vulnerable groups (such as children, the elderly and the handicapped) is that their needs typically arise in clusters, requiring inputs from a number of different professions. This raises important questions about the co-ordination and management of care, a particularly delicate problem because the professions concerned are protective of their autonomy and are generally answerable to different bodies.

Also, both prevention and care require CHSs to be accessible and acceptable to those they seek to serve, and adaptable to changing needs and circumstances (see Chapter 1). Such requirements have fostered a continuing debate as to the most appropriate arrangements for administering the CHSs and whether services should be available to the whole population or on a more selective basis.

Contemporary Issues in the Community Health Services

All of these issues have recurred throughout the history of the CHSs, from which it is reasonable to conclude that they are inherent in the nature of the services themselves. They generate genuine dilemmas to which there are no easy answers. It is more a question of achieving a balance between conflicting positions and inevitably this involves trade offs between the merits and drawbacks of each. Nevertheless, the rationale for this chapter is that a better understanding of the present and more effective planning for the future can be achieved through an examination of the past. To this end, the following areas have been selected for closer consideration: a proactive approach to service delivery; universality/selectivity; professionalisation; collaboration and teamwork; and decentralisation.

A Proactive Approach

The bias towards proaction within the CHSs has a long history and pre-dates by many decades the current enthusiasm for health promotion and prevention. The school health service, for example, which was established in 1907, is based on such an approach (see Chapter 2). However, proaction raises several important and, in some respects, intractable issues regarding both the administration of services of this kind and the ethical questions to which they give rise.

The most significant administrative issue has to do with the acquisition and utilisation of information about those for whom proactive services are intended. For example, those responsible for running a health surveillance and screening programme need accurate information about the population in order to identify the target group. They also need information about the target group in order to follow up those who do not respond to requests for screening and to ensure that everyone who is screened receives adequate feedback and, where necessary, treatment which may be costly. Moreover, detailed records need to be kept of the resource cost of each type of screening activity. Unless this is done it could be said that, since managers and service providers should be operating effective and efficient systems, they are failing both in their obligations to patients and in their responsibilities to taxpayers.

The collection of information for screening purposes is by no means a new issue. For example, in the second half of the 19th Century it soon became apparent that the embryonic health visiting service could not begin to exercise its responsibilities with regard to advising new mothers and monitoring the health of babies in the manner intended unless it was supplied with timely and accurate information about births. Then, as now, questions of both a logistic and ethical nature had to be dealt with before a reliable information system could be established.

From a practical point of view, perhaps the most important lesson to be learned since the establishment of the first surveillance programmes in the 19th Century is the fact that the acquisition of information is costly. Procedures have to be established and staff time devoted to the completion of forms time which cannot therefore be spent on direct patient care. This can cause frustration and resentment particularly if the significance and relevance of the information being gathered is not immediately apparent to the service providers, who are usually a major source of much of the information that is needed.

It follows, therefore, that those devising information systems should give considerable thought to the type of information required; the uses to which it will be put and the costs and benefits involved. Significantly, one of the criticisms of management made by the Community Nursing Review was that much of the information collected and recorded by community nurses was never used. Time and attention needs to be given not only to the systems themselves but also to those who will have to operate them since their co-operation is vital. Ideally they should be consulted at every stage about the nature of the activities on which information is being gathered, what is to be collected and the uses to which it will be put. Furthermore, once systems are operational there should be a continuous dialogue between managers and service providers so that problems can be identified and rectified, adaptations can be made to take account of changing circumstances and any assurances which have been given are honoured.

A related issue, which also has ethical connotations, is whether information collected for one purpose should be used for another. In the 19th Century there was a fear regarding the compulsory registration of births that the information would be used for purposes which were different from and more sinister than those officially given. Similarly, many GPs take the view that the information supplied by patients for registration purposes should not be used as the basis for a community index, although it would provide an extremely valuable source of data for screening purposes. As pointed out in Chapter 8, they argue that many patients could well feel disturbed if they discovered that personal information supplied to their GP was in the hands of another organisation and being used for a quite different purpose. However, if appropriate information already exists it is clearly a waste of resources to collect it again.

Amongst the other ethical questions to which a proactive approach to service delivery gives rise, the most important are those to do with personal freedom and choice. In order to undertake preventive measures, health care professionals have, by definition, to intervene in the lives of those who are and who view themselves as being healthy. Such intervention is regarded by some writers, such as Emile Zola, as unwarranted. Even those who accept that intervention may be justified in certain circumstances require convincing that the benefits clearly and undeniably outweigh the costs. In the case of some of the CHSs this may not be the case. For example, in Chapter 9 attention was draw to the fact that there are those who feel that the proposed national breast screening system will do more harm than good. A similar position has been adopted, at various times, in respect of vaccination.

On the other hand there is mounting evidence to suggest that intervention in the lives of those who are healthy can be justified in terms of the potential reduction in the incidence of disease and premature death. The eradication of smallpox and the decline in the occurrence of diseases such as poliomyelitis and measles testify to the success of vaccination programmes. Cervical and breast cancer can be diagnosed and treated successfully at the pre-symptomatic stage. Many people therefore argue that professionals have a responsibility to ensure that eveyone receives services of this kind, even if it involves an infringement of their personal freedom.

Given these concerns the question arises as to whether a proactive approach designed to prevent illness and promote health should involve compulsion and be based on mandatory legislation or allow for choice and rely on education. Whilst compulsion appears, on the face of it to be neater, cheaper and less equivocal, in practice it can give rise to many problems. If it is to be effective, provision has to be made for the enforcement and policing of the arrangements. Furthermore, allowance has to be made for any legitimate exemptions.

In this country the principles of compulsion and choice have both been applied in the spheres of health maintenance and promotion and the prevention of illness. For example, many public health measures, such as those relating to the purity of food and water, have been based on compulsion. The ongoing dispute over the fluoridation of the water supply, however, in the interests of securing improvements in dental health, demonstrates the strength of feeling to which compulsion can give rise, even in the field of public health.

In contrast, where measures (such as the introduction of screening programmes) are of a more personal kind there has generally been a marked reluctance to use the force of the law to secure compliance. In other words, those people for whom the measures are intended are permitted an element of choice. However, there are exceptions as the legislation on the compulsory wearing of seat belts and crash helmets and the restrictions on smoking in public places testify. Perhaps the crucial factor with measures of this kind is the degree of public support which they command. If there is a great deal of support then it can be said that the population is willing to be compelled for the benefit of its health and well-being.

Nevertheless, there remains an obvious tension between the principles of compulsion and choice and neither is without its drawbacks as the history of vaccination in this country demonstrates. As mentioned in Chapter 2, during the second half of the 19th Century the vaccination of children against smallpox was made compulsory. Although this resulted in a significant increase in vaccination rates, the costs of achieving this were considerable both in terms of the infringement of personal liberty and in respect of the administration of the scheme. Thus, in the 20th Century the principle of compulsion was gradually modified and long before it was formally abandoned in 1948 it had ceased to operate in any meaningful sense. Since 1948 the guiding principle, with regard to the vaccination of children, has been one of parental choice. This, however, has given rise to a variety of logistic problems and has meant that resources, especially money and staff time, have had to be devoted to persuading parents of the value of vaccination in order to maximise take-up rates. Moreover, even where considerable attention has been given to the education of parents, the efforts of those involved have sometimes been undermined, at least in the short-term, by adverse publicity in respect of particular types of vaccine. For example, in Chapter 7 it was noted that during the 1970s concern over whooping cough vaccine led to a significant drop in the take-up rate with the result that the incidence of the disease dramatically increased and it was only possible to reverse this trend with a series of costly campaigns.

Therefore, some would argue that the expense involved in maintaining the principle of parental choice and at the same time seeking to maximise take-up rates is too great and that the time has come to reintroduce compulsion. However, such a view is very much a minority one and the experience of compulsory vaccination in the 19th Century suggests that this approach is probably not the answer. A compromise would be to adopt the practice found in other countries of linking vaccination to access to other services. For example, eligibility for child benefit or entry to nursery school could be dependent on the production of an up-to-date vaccination record. Nevertheless, whilst this might salve the consciences of those who find compulsion distasteful it would probably raise practical problems of a similar magnitude to those encountered in respect of parental choice.

Thus, whilst vaccination, surveillance programmes and other proactive measures are undoubtedly laudable, before embarking on an initiative of this kind full account should be taken of the lessons of history. Proaction is usually very costly. Many forms of proaction require the establishment and maintenance of accurate databases and by exposing more of the 'iceberg' of disease they increase the demand on curative health care services. Moreover, proaction raises questions of an ethical kind which cannot be resolved easily. However, despite the importance of these lessons, many of them have not been learnt as the long running saga of cervical cancer screening clearly demonstrates (see Chapters 7 and 9).

Universality/Selectivity

The growing pressure on resources in the late 20th Century has led some of those concerned with the CHSs to reconsider the question of whether they should be available to the whole population (i.e. on a universal basis) or only to those on low incomes (i.e. on a selective basis). In the early years of the CHSs it was generally assumed that the wealthier sections of society either would not require these services or would make their own arrangements. Thus, in the 19th and first part of the 20th Century the CHSs were, to a significant extent, selective in their approach. In other words they were designed primarily to meet the needs of the less well-off, by making available to them some of the services to which the wealthy already had access.

Whilst the CHSs became more widely available during the 1920s and 1930s, it was not until the Beveridge Report of 1942 that universality was accepted as the legitimate basis for the delivery of welfare services. Consequently, the provisions of the 1946 Act, including those which related to the CHSs, were strongly influenced by the principle of universality. A number of arguments have been used to support the application of a universal approach to the delivery of community based health care services. First, universal services are not considered to be socially divisive and thus they avoid the problems of stigma associated with many selective services. For instance, since health visitors are responsible for **all** families with young children there is far less stigma attached to their visits than those of other welfare workers. Second, a universal approach maximises the chances of reaching those in greatest need. An example would be the school health service, which still plays an important part in detecting 'defects' in schoolchildren that would otherwise go unnoticed. Third, it affords services a high degree of public, and consequently political, support. Lastly, by comparison with selective services, the administration of universal services is relatively simple and therefore cheap.

Despite the persuasiveness of these arguments, the experience of the last forty years has shown that the universal approach is not without its drawbacks. First, although universal services are relatively cheap to administer, they are very expensive to provide. Those opposed to a universal approach argue that greater selectivity represents a more rational use of scarce resources because it allows them to be concentrated on those in greatest need. Second, even with universal services, clients tend not to use them equally. Generally speaking the better educated and more affluent members of society make greater use of universal services. This applies to most CHSs including district nursing and the paramedical services. Finally, by providing equal services to people in unequal positions, universality maintains rather than reduces existing inequalities.

Given the fact that neither approach has proved to be entirely satisfactory many attempts have been made to find a middle way which blends the best features of each. Since the mid-1960s these attempts have usually involved some form of positive discrimination. This means that services are targeted at groups, defined as being in greatest need, as opposed to being provided either for the population as a whole or for selected individuals.[3] The most commonly used criteria for identifying such groups are geography, category of need (e.g. physically disabled) and ethnic orgin. Not surprisingly, the CHSs have been influenced by these developments. Examples include the location of clinics in areas where clients are less likely to have their own transport; the use of 'at risk' registers in determining the distribution of health visiting resources and the designation of priority groups for the purpose of controlling access to NHS chiropody services.

In spite of the attractions of positive discrimination, this approach also has its disadvantages. In the first place it does not entirely avoid stigmatisation. Although the identification process is less personalised, nonetheless it involves the labelling of individuals in terms of the group to which they belong. In the second place, positive discrimination is likely to be successful only if adequate resources are made available for the groups identified as being in greatest need. Unfortunately, this has not always been the case and positive discrimination, like selectivity, has tended to be used as a way of coping with the growing pressure on resources.

The dilemmas posed by the universality/selectivity debate are as pertinent to the CHSs as they are to other parts of the welfare system. For those with responsibility for the CHSs the objective must be to effect an appropriate balance between the three approaches in terms of securing 'value for money' in the use of scarce resources and maximising access to services.

Professionalisation

There can be little doubt that the increasing professionalisation of the CHSs, to which attention was drawn in Chapter 9, poses many problems for those responsible for managing them. Whilst few would subscribe to the view expressed by George Bernard Shaw that 'all professions are conspiracies against the laity', attitudes towards professions and professionalisation are often ambivalent. On the one hand it is important that the public is assured that those providing personal services are adequately trained and educated and will behave in a way which is consistent with a professional code of ethics. Moreover, for the service providers, professionalisation can be seen as a rational response of an occupation to the need to promote and protect its own interests. On the other hand, professional exclusivity is seen as a barrier not only to effective teamwork (see below) but also to greater flexibility in the use of resources. Furthermore, in raising standards and enhancing their status professions have contributed to the recruitment and other problems which afflict many CHSs managers today.

At the root of these problems, however, is an unresolved (and possibly unresolvable) tension between, on the one hand, the professional culture and, on the other, the managerial culture. This tension arises from a number of inherent contradictions between the values of 'professionalism' and the values of 'managerialism'.

First, there is a contradiction between the value of **autonomy**, to which profes-sions attach particular importance, and that of **control**, which lies at the heart of 'managerialism'. As Laffin points out, 'the central and defining aim of a profession is the maximisation of its autonomy or freedom from control by others, both within the immediate work setting and in the institutionalised regulation of the relations between the professionals and the consumers of their services.'[4] In other words, members of a profession wish to distance themselves from other groups and to decide for themselves how best to respond to the needs and problems presented by their clients. Such a stance, however, inevitably brings them into conflict with managers. This is because management is 'the controlling activity in any organisa-tion' and managers are 'the people concerned in achieving the objectives of the organisation ... and the use of resources to those ends: manpower..., money, materials, equipment and time'.[5] Thus, if they are to realise organisational objec-tives, managers must exercise a degree of control over the resources at their disposal, of which professional expertise is usually the most valuable. Within the CHSs, as well as the NHS as a whole, the tension between professional autonomy and managerial control continues to preoccupy those in positions of authority.

Second, whereas professionals tend to stress the need for, and importance of, **specialisation**, because of the nature of their responsibilities managers often have to adopt a more **generalist** approach. All professions claim that their members possess special competences and that these distinguish them from non-members. Moreover, in order to acquire these competences it is necessary to undertake a rigorous programme of specialist training and 'apprenticeship'. Whilst clearly this is desirable, from the point of view of the quality of service which those who successfully complete the programme can then provide to their clients, it does have a number of adverse consequences. In particular, it tends to narrow the perspective of professionals and make it difficult for them to take a broader view of the issues which directly affect them and the context within which they work. It also distances them from managers for whom a broader view is essential. One facet of effective management is the ability to recognise and, where appropriate, respond to con-straints and opportunities present and foreseen within the environment. In order to acquire this facility aspiring managers must broaden their horizons and avoid the narrow specialisation associated with 'professionalism'. In other words mana-gers have to be generalists in the sense that, in directing the affairs of their section, department or organisation, they need a general understanding of both the services provided by their staff and the various external pressures and demands which may affect the delivery of these services.

Third, there is a contradiction between the professional's overriding concern with the needs of the **individual client** and that of the manager for the needs of **clients collectively**. In situations where professionals are engaged in the delivery of services direct to clients, the needs of the individual usually take precedence over all other considerations, such as the resource implications of their decisions. Rightly, professionals acknowledge that they must do all in their power to meet the needs of those who require their services. This is because it is in their dealings with clients that their credibility as a professional is most at stake. Managers, however, are usually faced with the task of determining how best to deal with the needs of clients collectively within the resources available. Given that resources are always limited whilst needs are usually unlimited, inevitably this means that managers have to adopt some kind of explicit or implicit rationing procedure in order to secure a balance between resources and needs. In so doing it is essential, from the point of view of equity, that managers take account of the needs of clients as a whole rather than give preferential treatment to individuals.

Lastly, within the professional culture there is a preoccupation with the **short-term** and within the managerial culture with the **longer-term**. In dealing with the needs of individual clients many professionals have to decide on an appropriate response within a very short time span. Although some professionals may be in a position to undertake a certain amount of planning for the future, the nature of their responsibilities is such that priority has to be given to meeting present needs.

For the manager, however, responsibility for setting objectives means that they must look ahead. As one of the most distinguished writers on management theory, Handy, has commented, 'the manager is, above all, responsible for the future ... Much of his time should be given to anticipating the future, making assessments of contingencies, and adjusting his plans and resources accordingly, setting the culture and climate, picking and developing his people. In general, the higher a man rises in an organisation, the longer needs to be his time-horizon and the more of his time he should spend thinking about it.'[6]

Whilst in principle the roles of 'professional' and 'manager' may be quite separate, in practice the distinction is frequently blurred by the fact that the management function is fulfilled by a professional person. Combining the roles, however, does little to reduce the tension between the two cultures. As the following quotation from Drucker makes clear, it creates its own set of problems:

> *But the best professional employee rarely makes a good (manager). It is not that he normally prefers to work alone, but that he is bored, if not annoyed, by administration (and management). The good professional employee also has little respect for the (manager). He respects the man who is better professionally than he is himself. To promote the good professional employee into a (management) position will only too often destroy a good professional without producing a good manager. To promote only the good (potential manager) who more often than not will not be the outstanding professional in the group will appear to the professional employee as irrational, as favouritism or as a reward for mediocrity.*[7]

Of course one way of resolving this dilemma would be to adopt the principle advocated by the NHS Management Inquiry Team, led by Griffiths, and appoint 'the best person for the job, **regardless of discipline** (emphasis added).'[8] However, in certain circumstances such a solution may well raise more problems than it solves since it goes against the goal of self-management which is a fundamental principle of 'professionalism'.

Within the CHSs the issue of professional self-management is by no means a new phenomenon. In some respects the whole history of the CHSs can be seen as the struggle by various groups of staff (initially midwives, health visitors and district nurses and more recently chiropodists, speech therapists and other paramedical staff) to promote the cause of 'professionalism' in their respective fields; to secure recognition for their distinctive contribution to health care; to establish the right to manage themselves; and to overcome some of the constraints associated with 'managerialism'.

For example, it is not without significance that in his book about the development of the district nursing service in Liverpool, which was published in 1899, Herbert Rathbone (William's nephew) was moved to comment favourably on the fact that 'the friendly and sympathetic interest of the lady superintendents ... (had helped to prevent) the work from becoming **too professional** (emphasis added) and ... (to keep) before the matrons and nurses the great social and moral reformation they (were) assisting.'[9] Thus, even at this early stage in the development of the CHSs, there were those who felt the application of specialist skills might militate against the realisation of broader goals. On the other hand, with the recognition of the need for district nurse training in the 1860s and the founding of the Queen Victoria Jubilee Institute for Nurses in the late 1880s, district nursing was beginning to acquire, albeit in embryonic form, some of the attributes of a profession.

Moreover, district nursing was not alone in this respect. Indeed, by the early years of the 20th Century the process of professionalisation had progressed further within health visiting and midwifery, than it had within district nursing. For midwives, the setting up of the Central Midwives Board in 1902 helped to create the conditions within which standards could be raised and greater autonomy could be secured. Even though opinions differ as to the exact significance of the provisions of the Midwives Act 1902 (see Chapter 2) application of the principle of a 'licence to practice' to midwifery was, at the very least, of symbolic value.

For health visitors, the most significant developments were those relating to the expanding role of local authorities in the field of maternity and child welfare. According to Dingwall, Rafferty and Webster, by 1914 health visiting was, unlike district nursing, 'fully accepted as part of the state social services ... (and) health visitors were a vital extension to the Medical Officers of Health in their surveillance of local populations.'[10] It was also 'firmly established as an organised occupation for educated women with its own representative association.'[11] In other words, health visiting had taken the first steps towards the acquisition of full professional recognition and status.

Subsequently superintendent health visitors were appointed, in some places, to organise and manage the service on a day-to-day basis and to advise the MOH on aspects of health visiting policy. Similarly, the implementation of the Midwives

Act 1936 led to the appointment by MOsH of non-medical supervisors of midwives, with responsibility for the supervision of all midwives in their area specifically in relation to matters of professional discipline. Those appointed to this post had to be practising midwives and, in the words of Lamb, they often 'combined 'supervision' with 'management'.'[12] Thus, by 1948, whilst MOsH retained overall responsibility for the services provided by their staff, limited recognition had been given to the principle of professional self-management in health visiting and midwifery.

In the case of district nursing the situation was rather different since the voluntary nursing associations continued to play a major part in the running of the service. Nevertheless, in certain parts of the country, county nursing superintendents were appointed as service managers and, according to Lamb, 'these appointments were much welcomed by the nurses since they provided professional support from experienced district nurses.'[13]

Given these developments, it is not really surprising that in 1947 the Ministry of Health recommended that local health authorities should appoint a superintendent or chief nursing officer to manage all three domiciliary nursing services (i.e. health visiting, midwifery, district nursing). Many authorities, however, did not adopt this recommendation, since it was felt that services of this kind should be the direct responsibility of the MOH. Moreover, in these authorities 'community nurses appeared to accept without question that they were subordinate to the medical officer of health'.[14] Consequently, it was not until the publication of the Mayston Report in 1969, that the principle of professional self-management (or functional management) finally gained general acceptance as the most appropriate basis for organising the community nursing services.

During the next few years this principle was adopted by the vast majority of local health authorities and was particularly influential as far as the post-reorganisation nurse management structures, outlined in Chapter 5, were concerned. Indeed, between the early 1970s and mid-1980s there were no serious challenges to the principle of professional self-management and it came to be applied to most of the professions with members engaged in the provision of community based health care services (e.g. chiropody, speech therapy).

Since the introduction of general management, however, increasingly the legitimacy of this principle has been called into question and the tension between the professional and managerial cultures has become more acute. This is because by the mid-1980s views concerning the running of the health services had changed. The traditional administrative style was considered less appropriate and a more proactive managerialist approach came to be favoured (see Chapter 6).

As a result of these developments, recognition is now being given to the education and training implications of 'managerialism' by the professions (e.g. Project 2000). Nevertheless, many professionals still fear that, as a result of the introduction of general management, their status and autonomy will be undermined and some of the gains made in the past will be lost. Thus, for them, general management is seen as a retrograde step and one which may ultimately result in a devaluation of their expertise and a deterioration in the quality of service that they are able to provide to their clients.

Collaboration and Teamwork

The clients of CHSs are likely to require not only those services provided by health authorities but also those provided by local authorities, voluntary organisations and family practitioners. Thus, in the interests of securing coherent care for clients and ensuring the most effective use of scarce resources, co-ordination of effort is vital.

The agencies which contribute to the provision of health care in the community are highly interdependent in that they share with one another certain goals (such as the prevention of ill-health and the care of vulnerable groups); they have clients in common (such as the elderly, children and the mentally disordered); and all have to operate within an increasingly difficult financial regime. Furthermore, changing epidemiological and demographic patterns during the 20th Century have further weakened the power of agencies to act independently. This interdependence is not, however, reflected in their administrative arrangements. Responsibility for the CHSs and for contiguous services is fragmented. Clearly, it is not possible for them all to be under the same administrative roof. Boundaries have to be drawn some-where. Moreover, history demonstrates that it is not necessarily self-evident how service responsibilities should be distributed between different agencies. Invariably decisions have been made through a process of negotiation and compromise and have tended to reflect what was politically possible rather than what was desirable from a rational point of view.

Arguably, the administrative boundary with the most far-reaching consequen-ces is that which separates the CHSs from the services provided by GPs and other family practitioners. This boundary has existed since at least 1911, when the administration of GP services was made the responsibility of newly created insur-ance committees, rather than local authorities which were by then playing an increasingly important role in the development of the CHSs. The main reasons for establishing insurance committees were the unwillingness of GPs to be subject to local authority control and their desire to retain their independent contractor status. Since then CHSs and general medical services have been administered by separate and distinctive organisations operating on different principles. Whilst this arrangement may have suited the GPs themselves, it has never been in the best interests of health care in general and primary care in particular. Moreover the increasing burden on those working in the primary care sector in the late 20th Century, has made the continuing isolation of GPs, in what Klein has called their 'autonomous enclave',[15] even more unacceptable. The failure of successive govern-ments to tackle this issue and bring general medical services into the mainstream of health care administration demonstrates how, in certain circumstances, the political and public interest can take second place to the professional interest.

More significantly, however, it has meant that it has been extremely difficult (if not impossible) to plan and develop the primary care sector in a coherent and comprehensive manner.

Less serious, but nonetheless important, difficulties have also been experienced in respect of relations between the CHSs and HSs and between the CHSs and other social care services. Again this has resulted in a situation where contiguous services are less compatible than they should be.

The need to minimise the deleterious effects of organisational fragmentation has long been recognised and has prompted the establishment of a variety of structures and procedures designed to bring together those bodies on opposite sides of the administrative divide. Invariably, however, these have been based on unrealistic expectations for the development of constructive relations amongst the organisations concerned. For example, the co-ordinating committees and other collaborative devices of the tripartite era failed to secure the integrated approach to health care anticipated by the founders of the NHS. Similarly, despite joint funding, the joint consultative committees and associated bodies introduced in 1974 for the purpose of fostering collaboration between health authorities and local personal social service authorities have not fully realised their potential. It is also likely that, notwithstanding the exhortations of central government, collaboration between DHAs and FPCs will fail to develop in the manner intended.

The reasons why effective collaboration between agencies has proved to be so difficult to achieve are not hard to find. Agencies, even those in the public sector, are in a competitive situation and tend to see other organisations, particularly those providing similar services, as rivals rather than as allies or partners. Thus, they will only collaborate spontaneously if it can be demonstrated that the benefits outweigh the costs and there is no threat to their interests, status and autonomy.

However, even if agencies were prepared to collaborate in the manner intended, an integrated approach to service delivery would not necessarily be guaranteed. For this to happen collaboration at the organisational and managerial levels has to be supplemented by teamwork at the 'grass roots' level. In other words, whilst collaboration in the spheres of service planning, determining priorities and resource allocation may be a necessary condition for the integration of services it is not a sufficient one. Unfortunately, however, there is little historical or contemporary evidence to suggest that collaboration between service providers is any easier to secure than it is between organisations and their managers. On the contrary in some respects it is an even more difficult objective to realise.

For more than 35 years (see Chapters 4 and 7), strenuous efforts have been made to facilitate teamworking in the primary care sector through the development of the primary health care team. At first sight, bringing together carers from different professional and organisational backgrounds into a shared work setting would seem to offer a way of ensuring the provision of a coherent, efficient and appropriate service for patients and of overcoming any problems arising from the fragmented nature of the community care services. However, although it is difficult to generalise because of the many different arrangements which exist in various parts of the country, it would appear that, despite the logic of teamworking, very little real progress has been made since the concept of the domiciliary team was first mooted in the 1950s.

This lack of progress has been due, in part, to a number of practical contraints. A team needs a physical base where formal and informal meetings can take place; patients can be seen and group sessions undertaken. The fact that only a very small number of health centres were opened during the first twenty years of the NHS did not help in this respect. Whilst the absence of a suitable physical base does not preclude the development of teamworking it certainly makes it less likely. Similarly, logistic problems created by the disharmony of geographical boundaries, work patterns, lines of accountability and administrative arrangements and the inherent contradictions between the principles of 'attachment' and 'zoning' (see Chapters 4 and 9) have severely restricted what can be done to bring carers together. For example, at the very simplest level, ensuring that extremely busy professionals, like district nurses, health visitors and GPs, are free to meet with each other on a regular basis can often place too great a strain on the organising abilities of overstretched managers.

Underlying these logistic factors, however, are some more fundamental reasons for the failure to secure effective teamwork at the 'grass roots' level. Like organisations, professions will not collaborate spontaneously. As implied above, their natural tendency is to do all in their power to protect their autonomy and that of their members and to resist any development, including inter-professional teamwork, which might impinge on their freedom to act independently.

Thus, there is an inherent tension between teamwork and 'professionalism'. The imperatives of teamwork are in direct conflict with those of 'professionalism'. The latter stresses the exclusive right and ability of members of particular professions to perform certain tasks. It seeks therefore to emphasise the distinctive nature of these tasks and the unique contribution which professionals bring to them. In contrast, teamwork involves the breaking down of barriers of this kind, the identification of shared objectives and the development of joint approaches to the resolution of common problems. As a result it is hardly surprising that, in the words of Barber and Kratz, 'many attempts at teamwork have failed because of professional isolationism, real or perceived threats to professional identity and a lack of understanding of the roles and responsibilities of others.'[16]

Within the primary care sector the situation is exacerbated by the fact that many of the professional groups engaged in service delivery are extremely anxious to preserve their separate identity and thereby protect the gains which they have secured only after a hard struggle. Thus, both the long established community professions (e.g. health visiting) and the professions which originated in the hospital sector, but since the 1970s have sought to establish a role for themselves in the community, (e.g. physiotherapy) have cause to be wary of developments like the team approach which might undermine their professional status. Moreover, for professionals any change in their working practices must be seen to offer clear and immediate benefits either to themselves or to their patients for it to be regarded as a profitable investment of time and effort. Very often, the benefits associated with a team approach are neither obvious nor immediate. As a result, teamwork has a low priority.

Thus, on the basis of past experience, it would be fair to conclude that the prospects for joint working are poor. Some commentators, however, argue that whilst the strategies adopted in the past have not been effective, there are alternatives which are likely to prove more successful. Hudson, for example, suggests that greater use should be made of financial and other incentives to facilitate collaboration and teamworking and that central government should be prepared to adopt a more directive approach when problems arise. Although suggestions of this kind have some merit, it is doubtful whether genuine collaboration and teamwork can ever be secured either by bribery or by coercion.

An alternative tactic is to try to foster attitudes and values conducive to teamwork during the process of professional education. Some progress has been made in this respect with joint teaching of various professional groups in departments of health studies, community health and primary health care. However, much more needs to be done and the results of such an approach will be apparent only in the longer-term.

For those with responsibility for the CHSs, the dilemmas posed by collaboration and teamwork remain as acute as they have always been. On the one hand, the effectiveness of community based health care services depends, to a significant extent, on the development of integrated approaches which cross administrative and professional boundaries. On the other, approaches of this kind threaten the separate identity of the CHSs and the distinctive contribution of some of the professions involved in their delivery. Indeed, some observers would go further and suggest that collaboration and teamwork with those organisations and professional groups that are neither committed to, nor sympathethic towards, the principles on which the CHSs are based might well do more harm than good.

Decentralisation

The concern to find a suitable administrative structure for the CHSs has given rise to an ongoing debate regarding the appropriate degree of local control. At first sight the moves towards a more decentralised approach to service management and delivery, through the introduction of locality management and the application of the concept of neighbourhood nursing recommended by Cumberlege and her colleagues (see Chapters 8 and 9) might appear to be a radical innovation. However, this is an illusion. Locality management and neighbourhood nursing are, in essence, attempts to restore some of the values inherent in the 'localism' and 'parochialism', which flourished in the past, but in recent decades have been the casualties of increasing centralisation.

When the foundations of the CHSs and other forms of welfare provision were being laid in the 19th Century the relationship between the centre and the localities was very different from that which prevails today. Central government had very little power to control and direct the activities of the localities. This was due to a variety of factors. First, the centre provided very few of the resources needed to establish and develop services. Most of the finance was raised locally and this ensured the autonomy of the agencies involved. Second, with less sophisticated means of communication, it was far more difficult, if not impossible, for the centre to impose its will and monitor performance. Lastly, at that time the prevailing political philosophy was that of 'laissez-faire'. It was widely believed that in both the social and economic spheres the state should intervene as little as possible. Furthermore, whenever action by the state was deemed necessary to deal with an urgent or intractable problem it was usually considered preferable for the initative to be taken at local level.

In their different ways the establishment of the health visiting, district nursing and pre-school child health services exemplify the importance of local rather than central initiatives in welfare provision during the second half of the 19th Century. They also demonstrate the extent to which a decentralised approach to service delivery can exploit local knowledge and commitment; give expression to the values of 'civic pride' and local autonomy; and grasp, what Laski has called, 'the genius of place'.[17] Significantly, those initiatives which were taken by the centre, such as the introduction of a system of compulsory vaccination in the 1870s and the development of procedures designed to ensure that births were notified to those who could provide some form of post-natal care, were not very successful.

In spite of the benefits to be derived from relying on those at local level to initiate, deliver and control their own services, by the early years of the 20th Century the drawbacks were becoming all too apparent. Of increasing concern were the considerable variations in the quantity and quality of services available in different parts of the country. The provision in some areas was exceptionally good (e.g. Liverpool in respect of district nursing; Huddersfield in respect of maternity and child welfare services), whilst in others it was either poor or non- existent. As the century progressed diversity on this scale became increasingly untenable. Many feel that, since community health and other welfare services were making an important contribution to well-being and productivity, they should be made available to everyone in the interest of maximising their beneficial effects. Moreover, attitudes towards the role of government changed, with increasing emphasis being placed on the value of collectivism and the need for the centre to promote the health, and ensure the well-being, of everyone regardless of where they lived. In order to do this it was necessary for the centre to increase its powers over the localities with a view to securing a greater degree of 'territorial justice'.

As noted in Chapter 3, in the case of the CHSs the centre took various steps, when the NHS was established, to ensure greater uniformity. Of particular importance were the provisions of Part III of the 1946 Act which greatly extended the statutory duties of local authorities with regard to the provision of CHSs. Furthermore, during the tripartite era, the centre used a variety of financial and other measures to influence the behaviour of local health authorities. Nevertheless, despite these centralising trends local health authorities retained a fair degree of autonomy with the result that services continued to be characterised as much by their diversity as their uniformity. In addition, the values of diversity and local control continued to receive recognition in the schemes of decentralised administration adopted by some local health authorities and the delegation arrangements operated under the provisions of the Local Government Act 1958.

These last vestiges of 'localism' were swept away in the 1974 reorganisation of the NHS and subsequent developments. First, the transfer of responsibility for the CHSs from elected and relatively autonomous local health authorities to appointed and hierachically organised RHAs and AHAs significantly reduced the democratic element in the running of services and the amount of autonomy at the local level. Second, as discussed in Chapter 5, in the mid-1970s, through the introduction of a planning system and review procedures designed to establish and monitor standards of performance, the government sought to secure greater equality in the availability of services throughout the country.

Nevertheless, in retrospect these developments can be seen as the high water mark of centralisation as far as the CHSs are concerned. During the 1980s there was a gradual retreat from the 'centralism' of the late 1970s. The 1982 restructuring exercise, based on the 'localist' principles set out in *Patients First*, and the subsequent establishment of community units; the appointment of unit general managers to provide effective leadership at the local level, as recommended by the NHS Management Inquiry and, during the second half of the 1980s, the introduction of locality management and neighbourhood nursing in various parts of the country all helped to restore a degree of legitimacy to the value of localism. However, it would be both wrong and naive to assume that the wheel has come full circle. Despite the 'localist' rhetoric (see Chapter 8), which emphasises the importance of local decision-making and flexibility in running services, it seems unlikely that the centre would ever allow the degree of diversity, seen in the past, to return. The dilemma posed by the 'centralist'/'localist' dichotomy remains. On the one hand, 'centralism' stifles local initiative and limits the extent to which those at the 'grass roots' can respond in a distinctive manner to locally perceived needs and problems and take full account of the knowledge and commitment which is available in each locality. Some would also argue that for services like the CHSs which have a strong personal element, values of this kind are of particular importance. On the other hand, if taken to extremes 'localism' can result in gross territorial inequalities and a failure to respect individual rights to services. History demonstrates that whatever the arrangements for the administration of CHSs an inevitable compromise always has to be reached between the claims of 'localism' and of 'centralism'.

Having examined a number of issues, it is reasonable to conclude that those responsible for the management and delivery of the CHSs face continuing dilemmas. Moreover, the situation has been exacerbated by developments, such as the Griffiths Report, *Community Care : Agenda for Action*, and the NHS white paper, *Working for Patients*, which have generated a climate of anxiety.

Whither the Community Health Services?

What then does the future hold? Notwithstanding the government's acceptance of the Griffiths recommendations for the future of community care (July 1989) there remains considerable uncetainty regarding the future of health care in general. Thus it is possible to identify a number of alternative scenarios for the future development of the CHSs,which are not necessarily mutually exclusive. The least radical of these is based on the assumption that the CHSs retain their separate identity and continue to evolve incrementally in much the same way as they have done since the 19th Century. In this scenario there would be little change in the distribution of responsibility for managing and delivering them with the key roles continuing to be played by NHS employees. Thus, managerial leadership would remain at local level and the well-being of the services, in terms of resources and profile, would continue to depend on the skill of the general manager of the community unit. Similarly, the professions would remain at the forefront of developments regarding the setting and monitoring of standards and the delineation and adaptation of services, in response to changing patterns of need. At the heart of this scenario there would continue to be an ongoing tension between the desire for professional exclusivity and distinctiveness and the need for greater openness, accountability and flexibility on the part of the professions in the interest of securing a more collaborative and dynamic approach to service delivery.

A variant of this scenario involves the introduction of the concept of the self-governing community unit. Although something of an afterthought, this idea was referred to explicitly in Working Paper 1[18] and its implications for the management and delivery of the CHSs are worthy of consideration. Its application would almost certainly intensify the tension between the professional service providers and the service managers to which attention has already been drawn. This is because it would throw into even sharper relief the clash between the two cultures, as managers sought to do everything possible to maximise the unit's resources by offering its services at the most competitive price (e.g. to local authorities under the Griffiths proposals). Although some account would need to be taken of the quality of the services on offer, it can be argued that considerations of quality would invariably be tempered by the disciplines of the market. For most professionals, such an approach to the provision of health care services is anathema.

The central feature of a second and more radical scenario is the transfer of responsibility for most CHSs to family practitioners. This would mean a significant change in the pattern of employment of CHSs staff, with family practitioners, particularly GPs, becoming major employers of community nurses and paramedical staff. It is also probable that another component of this scenario would be the conversion of FPCs into primary care authorities, which would have a key role in planning services and the payment of practitioners. Almost certainly a development of this kind would substantially reduce the power of the community nursing and paramedical professions within the primary care sector and would drive a wedge between nurses and paramedical staff working in hospitals and those employed by GPs. It would undermine the efforts being made to raise standards and to enhance the status of professions and would create serious problems with regard to the organisation and supervision of practical training. Moreover, it might also result in significant changes to the arrangements for pay determination. In short, it would be a disaster for those professional groups which are seeking to distance themselves from the medical profession. It is therefore not surprising that groups made clear their opposition to this scenario in their response to the white paper *Promoting Better Health* (see Chapter 9). There are many others who would regard the realisation of such a scenario as a backward step primarily because GPs have traditionally adopted a reactive, as opposed to a proactive, approach to health care. In addition, they feel that most GPs lack the necessary skills and aptitude to manage, in a sensitive and productive manner, those from non-medical backgrounds. Thus, in their view, there would need to be a major shift in the professional culture of GPs before they could effectively exercise responsibility for many of the CHSs.

A third scenario is one suggested in *Working for Patients*. Underlying this is the premise that the CHSs should be seen as extensions of the HSs and therefore they should be managed by the trusts set up to run hospitals should they become self-governing. From the point of view of the professions this would at least avoid the fragmentation implicit in the previous one. However, it would almost certainly undermine the position of those professions committed to a more preventive and proactive approach to health care. This is because hospital based staff have traditionally adopted a curative and reactive stance and, given their dominance within the health care system, their approach is the one which would undoubtedly prevail. Moreover, curative services are likely to have far more potential than preventive services for the generation of income. Thus, in terms of the allocation of resources, there is little doubt that curative services would have top priority.

The most radical scenario involves the wholesale privatisation of the CHSs and the complete dismantling of existing administrative structures. Whilst such a scenario reflects the Thatcher government's belief in the efficacy of market forces and the value of entrepreneurial drive and initiative, it represents the very antithesis of everything for which the professions have striven. Furthermore, although it might be possible to conceive of a situation in which the price mechanism determined the supply of certain services for which there is an obvious demand, such as domiciliary nursing and physiotherapy, it is very unlikely that it could operate effectively for the more preventive services like health visiting and health education.

Whatever the future holds for the CHSs, two things are certain. First, there will be no diminution in the need for services of this kind. Indeed, all the evidence suggests that the need will increase. Second, the issues raised earlier in this chapter will continue to preoccupy managers and service providers. Although they cannot be resolved in any definitive sense, it is important for those concerned about the future to have some understanding of the nature and the significance of these issues. In this book it has not been possible to do more than scratch the surface: hence the need for a companion volume in which these issues, and their implications for the management and delivery of the CHSs, are examined in greater detail.

Footnotes

1.   J. Clarke, A. Cochrane and C. Smart, *Ideologies of Welfare : From Dreams to Disillusion* (London: Hutchinson, 1987), p. 12.

2.   Ibid., p. 17.

3.   Examples of positive discrimination include educational priority areas, housing action areas and the reserving of certain occupations for those on the register of handicapped persons.

4.   M. Laffin, *Professionalism and Policy : The Role of the Professions in the Central-Local Government Relationship* (Aldershot: Gower, 1986), p. 21.

5.   R. Knowles, *Modern Management in Local Government*, 2nd Edition (Chichester: Barry Rose, 1970) p. 10.

6.   C. Handy, *Understanding Organisations*, 3rd Edition, (London: Penguin, 1985), p. 373.

7.   P. Drucker, *The Practice of Management* (London: Heinemann, 1955), p. 295.

8.   NHS Management Inquiry, General Observations, para. 21.

9.   H. Rathbone, *A Short History and Description of District Nursing in Liverpool* (Liverpool: D. Marples, 1899).

10.   R. Dingwall, A. Rafferty and C. Webster, *An Introduction to the Social History of Nursing* (London: Routledge, 1988), p. 190.

11.   Ibid.

12.   A Lamb, *Primary Care Nursing* (London: Bailliere Tindall, 1977), p. 133.

13.   Ibid., p. 132.

14.   Ibid., p. 134.

15.   R. Klein, *The Politics of the National Health Service* (London: Longman, 1983), p. 97.

16.   J. Barber and C. Kratz (eds.), *Towards Team Care* (London: Churchill Livingstone, 1980), Preface.

17.   H. Laski, *The Grammar of Politics*, 5th Edition (London: George Allen and Unwin, 1967), p. 412.

National Health Service Review. Working Paper 1 : Self-Governing Hospitals (London: HMSO, 1989), para. 1.2.

APPENDIX I LOCAL HEALTH AUTHORITIES (England and Wales)

Name	Estimated Residential Population		Relationship with Executive Council[1]	Committee/ Administrative Arrangements - March 1966[2]
	1951	**1971**		

County Boroughs (CB)

Created Prior to 1948

Name	1951	1971	Relationship	Committee
Barnsley	75120	76020	Coterminous	E
Barrow-in-Furness	66860	64365	ditto	A
Bath	79600	83390	ditto	A
Birkenhead	142000	138450	ditto	B
Birmingham	1112400	1015240	ditto	A
Blackburn	110500	102430	ditto	B
Blackpool	145700	151510	ditto	A
Bolton	167200	155765	ditto	A
Bootle	74810	74665	ditto	E
Bournemouth	138700	149760	ditto	A
Bradford	290900	294585	ditto	A
Brighton	155500	158635	ditto	A
Bristol	443700	424120	ditto	A
Burnley	84460	76785	ditto	E
Burton upon Trent	48930	50610	ditto	A
Bury	58460	68220	ditto	A
Canterbury	29600	31380	Kent AC (1948)and London South East (1965)	A
Cardiff	243800	277350	Coterminous	A
Carlisle	67400	71925	ditto	B
Chester	48500	62480	ditto	A
Coventry	258200	334215	ditto	A
Croydon	250100	n.a.[3]	ditto	n.a.
Darlington	84860	86165	ditto	A
Derby	140800	220200[4]	ditto	E
Dewsbury	53090	51525	ditto	A
Doncaster	81600	82670	ditto	A
Dudley	62470	185620[4]	ditto	B
Eastbourne	57340	66760	East Sussex AC and Hastings CB (1971)	B
East Ham	120600	n.a.[3]	Coterminous	n.a.
Exeter	76400	92820	Devon AC (1948) and Torbay CB (1968)	A
Gateshead	115000	95140	Coterminous	A
Gloucester	66900	90050	Gloucestershire AC (1948)	A
Great Yarmouth	51100	50020	Coterminous	A
Grimsby	93320	95830	ditto	A
Halifax	97870	91975	ditto	A
Hastings	64760	72165	East Sussex AC and Eastbourne CB (1971)	D
Huddersfield	128200	131765	Coterminous	A
Ipswich	104300	123355	ditto	A
Kingston upon Hull	299000	286470	ditto	A
Leeds	505800	492615	ditto	A
Leicester	284700	283155	ditto	A
Lincoln	69180	74095	ditto	E
Liverpool	786600	607110	ditto	A

Manchester	701500	540480	ditto	A
Merthyr Tydfil	60500	55520	ditto	B
Middlesborough	146700	n.a.[5]	ditto	A
Newcastle upon Tyne	292300	219755	ditto	B
Newport	105000	112710	Monmouthshire AC (1948)	A
Northampton	103300	126925	Coterminous	D
Norwich	120200	120785	ditto	E
Nottingham	306000	297560	Nottinghamshire AC (1948)	A
Oldham	120600	106550	Coterminous	A
Oxford	106700	100640	Oxfordshire AC (1948)	D
Plymouth	218700	240585	Coterminous	B
Portsmouth	245900	194605	ditto	A
Preston	118600	98335	ditto	D
Reading	115000	131115	ditto	D
Rochdale	88180	92305	ditto	B
Rotherham	81940	85365	ditto	A
St Helens	109600	104965	ditto	A
Salford	177600	130500	ditto	A
Sheffield	512300	518800	ditto	E
Smethwick	76510	n.a.[6]	ditto	n.a.
Southampton	177900	212725	ditto	B
Southend-on-Sea	151000	164080	ditto	D
Southport	83330	85030	ditto	A
South Shields	107000	101105	ditto	D
Stockport	141200	140605	ditto	A
Stoke-on-Trent	273600	266365	ditto	A
Sunderland	181000	217560	ditto	A
Swansea	160300	172475	ditto	D
Tynemouth	66200	69615	ditto	A
Wakefield	59180	59130	ditto	A
Wallasey	101300	98000	ditto	B
Walsall	114000	185210[4]	ditto	A
Warrington	80350	68570	ditto	B
West Bromwich	87360	167000[4]	ditto	B
West Ham	171000	n.a.[3]	ditto	n.a.
West Hartlepool	72340	n.a.[7]	ditto	B
Wigan	84150	81765	ditto	D
Wolverhampton	162300	270080[4]	ditto	A
Worcester	60130	72440	ditto	A
York	106200	104825	ditto	A

Created between 1948 and 1974

Hartlepool (1966)	n.a.[7]	97905	Coterminous	n.a.
Luton (1964)	n.a.[8]	161735	Bedfordshire AC (1964)	B
Solihull (1964)	n.a.[8]	108115	Warwickshire AC (1964)	n.k.
Teesside (1968)	n.a.[5]	398235	Coterminous	n.a.
Torbay (1968)	n.a.[8]	106085	Devon AC and Exeter CB (1968)	n.a.
Warley (1966)	n.a.[6]	164780	Coterminous	D

Administrative Counties (AC)

Anglesey	50650	59660	Coterminous	B
Bedfordshire	315900	303185	Luton CB (1964)	A
Berkshire	295700	503360	Coterminous	A
Brecknockshire	55900	52935	ditto	E
Buckinghamshire	389600	589445	ditto	D
Caernarvonshire	123100	118865	ditto	B
Cambridgeshire	175300	296290[9]	ditto	A
Cardiganshire	54120	52325	ditto	A
Carmarthenshire	170600	163160	ditto	A
Cheshire	822000	1,115390	ditto	A

Cornwall	338120	376500	ditto	D
Cumberland	217100	219710	ditto	D
Denbighshire	170000	183630	Flintshire AC (1948)	A
Derbyshire	683900	666805	Coterminous	A
Devon	506700	450145	Exeter CB (1948) and Torbay CB (1968)	D
Dorset	294100	358695	Coterminous	D
Durham	900300	816515	ditto	D
East Suffolk	217600	257245	ditto	D
East Sussex	339200	444140	Eastbourne CB and Hastings CB (1971)	A
Essex	1597400	1198005	Coterminous	A
Flintshire	144800	176745	Denbighshire AC (1948)	A
Glamorgan	731400	753945	Coterminous	A
Gloucestershire	430700	560545	Gloucester CB (1948)	A
Hampshire	646000	1002910	Coterminous	A
Herefordshire	126800	139015	ditto	A
Hertfordshire	614700	927150	ditto	D
Huntingdonshire	70100	203525[10]	ditto	A
Isle of Ely	88400	n.a.[9]	ditto	n.a.
Isle of Wight	93400	106835	ditto	D
Kent	1544400	1367650	Canterbury CB (1948) and London South East (1965)	D
Lancashire	2040900	2517495	Coterminous	
Leicestershire	346700	485900	Rutland AC (1948)	D
Lincs(Holland)	101300	106040	Coterminous	A
Lincs(Kesteven)	130600	158285	ditto	A
Lincs(Lindsey)	309200	377590	ditto	A
London	3353000	n.a.[11]	ditto	n.a.
Merioneth	40500	34600	ditto	A
Middlesex	2270000	n.a.[11]	ditto	n.a.
Monmouthshire	317500	351495	Newport CB (1948)	A
Montgomeryshire	45540	43395	Coterminous	A
Norfolk	369600	444955	ditto	E
Northamptonshire	255900	342855	ditto	A
Northumberland	437600	505275	ditto	D
Nottinghamshire	534600	677670	Nottingham CB (1948)	A
Oxfordshire	179000	272815	Oxford CB (1948)	D
Pembrokeshire	90390	98330	Coterminous	A
Radnorshire	19900	18230	ditto	B
Rutland	21570	27005	Leicestershire AC (1948)	E
Shropshire	292200	337550	Coterminous	A
Soke of Peterborough	63530	n.a.[10]	ditto	n.a.
Somerset	472500	595620	ditto	A
Staffordshire	854300	736735	ditto	A
Surrey	1352700	1003685	London South West (1965)	A
Warwickshire	490400	626470	Coterminous	A
Westmorland	66800	70700	ditto	A
West Suffolk	120600	165550	ditto	D
West Sussex	316600	491885	ditto	A
Wiltshire	390800	487630	ditto	A
Worcestershire	402400	456315	ditto	C
Yorks (East Riding)	212500	256150	ditto	A
Yorks (North Riding)	378400	328580	ditto	A
Yorks (West Riding)	1587300	801930	ditto	C
Isles of Scilly	1880	2005	ditto	C

London Boroughs (Created 1st April 1965)

Name	Estimated Residential Population 1971	Relationship with Executive Council[12]	Committee/ Administrative Arrangements[2]
Barking	161375	London, North East	A
Barnet	308980	Middlesex	D
Bexley	218970	London, South East and Kent	D
Brent	282140	Middlesex	C
Bromley	307590	London, South East and Kent	D
Camden*	203975	London, Inner	A
Croydon	336795	London, South West and Surrey	A
Ealing	303220	Middlesex	A
Enfield	269045	Middlesex	A
Greenwich*	218225	London, Inner	B
Hackney*	221065	London, Inner	A
Hammersmith*	187150	London, Inner	D
Haringey	241150	Middlesex	C
Harrow	205030	Middlesex	B
Havering	248565	London, North East	D
Hillingdon	235420	Middlesex	C
Hounslow	207560	Middlesex	A
Islington*	201545	London, Inner	A
Kensington and Chelsea*	188930	London, Inner	D
Kingston	140880	London, South West and Surrey	D
Lambeth*	307620	London, Inner	A
Lewisham*	269635	London, Inner	A
Merton	178885	London, South West and Surrey	A
Newham	238290	London, North East	A
Redbridge	240560	London, North East	D
Richmond	176065	London, South West and Surrey	A
Southwark*	262775	London, Inner	A
Sutton	169890	London, South West and Surrey	A
Tower Hamlets*	165375	London, Inner	A
Waltham Forest	235800	London, North East	C
Wandsworth*	302860	London, Inner	C
Westminster*	235980	London, Inner	A
City of London	4050	London, Inner	E

Key

* = Inner London Boroughs which, together with the City of London, comprise the area of the Inner London Education Authority. *n.a.* = not applicable. *n.k.* = not known

Notes

1. Either coterminous or combined with named authority(ies).
2. Details of the different types of arrangement are set out below:-
   A. Authorities with a health committee, to which the Medical Officer of Health was responsible, and a welfare committee, to which a Chief Welfare Officer or Director of Welfare Services was responsible.
   B. Authorities with separate health and welfare committees, to which the Medical Officer of Health was responsible for both groups of services.
   C. Authorities with a joint health and welfare committee or a health committee, with responsibility for welfare as well as health services, to which both the Medical Officer of Health and a Chief Welfare Officer or a Director of Welfare Services were reponsible.
   D. Authorities with a joint health and welfare committee or a health committee, with responsibility for welfare as well as health services, to which the Medical Officer of Health was responsible

for both groups of services.

E. Other arrangements:-

o   Authorities with a health committee, to which the Medical Officer of Health was responsible, and a social service or a social care committee or a welfare committee, reponsible for welfare services, to which a Chief Welfare Officer or a Social Service Officer was responsible (Bootle; Burnley; Sheffield and Norfolk).

o   Authority with a health committee, to which the Medical Officer of Health was responsible, and a joint housing and welfare committee, to which a Housing Manager and Welfare Director was responsible (Barnsley).

o   Authority with a health committee, to which the Medical Officer of Health was responsible, and a welfare services committee, to which a Chief Executive Officer of the Committee was responsible (Derby).

o   Authorities with a health committee, to which the Medical Officer of Health was reponsible, and a welfare committee, to which the Town Clerk was responsible (Lincoln and Norwich).

o   Authorities with a joint health and welfare committee or a welfare committee, to which the Clerk of the Council was responsible (Rutland and Breconshire).

o   Authority with a joint health and welfare committee, to which a Health and Welfare Officer was responsible (City of London).

3. On 1st April 1965 the County Boroughs of Croydon and of East Ham and West Ham were incorporated into Greater London and their areas formed the nucleii of the London Boroughs of Croydon and Newham respectively (see below).

4. Large increase in population due to major boundary extensions.

5. On 1st April 1968 the County Borough of Middlesborough was incorporated into the newly created County Borough of Teesside.

6. On 1st April 1966 the County Borough of Smethwick was incorporated into the newly created County Borough of Warley.

7. On 1st April 1966 the County Borough of West Hartlepool was incorporated into the newly created County Borough of Hartlepool.

8. The Boroughs of Luton and Solihull acquired county borough status on 1st April 1964. The County Borough of Torbay was created on 1st April 1968 and incorporated the former Borough of Torquay and the Urban Districts of Paignton and Brixham.

9. On 1st April 1965 Cambridgeshire AC was merged with the Isle of Ely AC. The 1971 population figure is for the new combined county.

10. On 1st April 1965 Huntingdonshire AC was merged with the Soke of Peterborough AC. The 1971 population figure is for the new combined county.

11. As a result of the reorganisation of local government in the greater London area during the 1960s, the Administrative Counties of London and Middlesex were abolished on 31st March 1965 and their functions were taken over by the Greater London Council and London borough councils (see below).

12. As a result of the reorganisation of local government in the greater London area the following changes were made to the executive councils:-

o   the London Executive Council was retained and retitled London, Inner;

o   the Middlesex Executive Council was retained and kept the same title;

o   a new executive council, titled London, North East, was created to cover those parts of Essex, which were incorporated in Greater London;

o   the Kent Executive Council was retitled London, South East and Kent; and

o   the Surrey Executive Council was retitled London South West and Surrey.

Source: Ministry of Health, *Annual Reports*, various years; *Census Reports for 1951 and 1971* and Home Office, Department of Education and Science, Ministry of Housing and Local Government and Ministry of Health, *Report of the Committee on Local Authority and Allied Personal Social Services* [Seebohm Report] Cmnd 3703 (London: HMSO, 1968), Appendix H.

APPENDIX II LOCAL HEALTH SERVICES : FINANCIAL DATA (England and Wales)
A) Gross Revenue Expenditure

Year	Expenditure				Income		
	Employee Costs[1]	Running Costs[2]	Debt Charges[3]	Total	Sales, Fees etc.[4]	Specific Govn't Grants[5]	Balance[6]
	£'000	£'000	£'000	£'000	£'000	£'000	£'000
1948/49	──24,307──		143	24,450	2,534	9,926	11,990
1949/50	──31,893──		227	32,120	2,383	14,873	14,864
1950/51	──35,607──		379	35,986	2,602	16,582	16,802
1951/52	21,700	16,942	513	38,455	2,932	17,683	17,840
1952/53	25,300	16,915	689	42,904	3,257	19,756	19,891
1553/54	25,400	16,808	808	43,016	3,338	19,723	19,955
1954/55	27,300	16,917	920	45,137	3,475	20,692	20,970
1955/56	30,300	17,802	1,018	49,120	3,730	22,559	22,831
1956/57	33,100	19,843	1,127	54,070	4,093	24,831	25,146
1957/58	35,400	21,226	1,217	57,843	4,376	26,576	26,891
1958/59	37,400	23,075	1,184	61,659	4,560	28,393	28,706
1959/60	42,100	24,785	1,239	68,084	5,028	191	62,865
1960/61	44,700	26,293	1,491	72,484	5,331	97	67,056
1961/62	49,700	29,864	1,726	81,290	5,817	88	75,385
1962/63	54,100	31,113	2,052	87,265	6,240	60	80,965
1963/64	58,326	34,872	2,529	95,727	6,896	52	88,779
1964/65	64,907	36,509	3,100	104,516	7,686	68	96,762
1965/66	80,459	33,730	3,779	117,968	8,419	84	109,465
1966/67	87,940	36,567	4,334	128,841	8,703	134	120,004
1967/68	97,569	38,076	4,980	140,625	9,065	212	131,348
1968/69	103,904	42,298	5,851	152,053	9,701	266	142,086
1969/70	108,259	49,421	9,175	166,855	12,442	368	154,045
1970/71	130,544	57,243	10,322	198,109	15,067	768	182,274
1971/72	91,962	42,756	5,797	140,515	7,820	350	132,345
1972/73	107,921	49,280	6,521	163,722	9,626	474	153,622
1973/74	126,808	56,507	8,692	192,007	10,625	507	180,875

Notes

1.Salaries, wages, superannuation etc.
2.Heating and lighting, supplies etc.
3.Principal and interest.
4.Welfare foods, domestic help, family planning appliances etc. (see Chapter 3 for details).
5.Grant aid towards the cost of local health services as a whole (to 1958/59) and individual services (see Chapter 3 for details).
6.i.e. net expenditure financed out of rate income.

B) *Revenue Expenditure on Individual Services*

i) Net Revenue Expenditure : Selected Services 1949/50 to 1967/68

Year	CM £'000	MD '£000	HV '£000	HN £'000	VI £'000	PR £'000	MH £'000
1949/50	7,454	4,322	2,022	3,401	325	1,076	1,292
1950/51	7,643	4,770	2,523	4,176	470	1,306	1,311
1951/52	7,660	4,494	2,560	4,426	456	1,578	1,553
1952/53	9,184	4,583	2,789	4,836	461	1,708	1,709
1953/54	7,602	4,540	2,906	5,250	544	1,818	1,874
1954/55	7,790	4,421	2,951	5,422	529	1,944	2,129
1955/56	8,114	4,647	3,254	5,913	566	2,122	2,450
1956/57	8,793	5,084	3,388	6,537	654	2,244	2,930
1957/58	9,271	5,419	3,686	6,825	1,050	2,387	3,336
1958/59	9,585	5,722	3,923	7,124	1,764	2,530	3,686
1959/60	9,232	6,224	4,222	7,668	2,103	2,321	3,962
1960/61	9,341	6,420	4,443	7,883	1,692	2,757	4,964
1961/62	10,120	6,927	4,722	8,254	2,757	2,931	6,203
1962/63	10,880	7,523	5,022	9,011	1,821	3,217	7,543
1963/64	11,606	8,348	5,722	9,939	1,259	3,725	9,277
1964/65	12,315	8,655	6,247	10,635	1,292	4,129	11,429
1965/66	13,143	9,430	7,003	11,965	1,272	4,510	13,863
1966/67	15,922	10,681	8,396	13,785	1,640	5,624	18,438
1967/68	16,946	10,609	8,671	14,424	1,457	6,226	21,929

Key

CM = care of mothers and young children.
MD = midwifery.
HV = health visiting.
HN = home nursing.
VI = vaccination and immunisation.
PR = prevention of illness, care and after-care.
MH = mental health.

Source: Ministry of Health, *Annual Reports,* various years.

ii) Gross Revenue Expenditure : All Services 1969/70 to 1973/74

Year	HC £'000	CM £'000	MD £'000	HV £'000	HN £'000	VI £'000
1969/70	1,580	22,755	11,268	10,428	16,874	2,102
1970/71	2,607	26,588	12,934	13,310	20,493	2,738
1971/72	4,018	18,542	14,464	15,420	24,466	3,497
1972/73	5,819	20,152	15,760	17,808	28,927	3,732
1973/74	8,946	22,197	17,753	20,622	34,716	4,090

Year	AM £'000	PR £'000	DH £'000	FP £'000	Other £'000	Total £'000
1969/70	34,618	40,577	25,213	582	858	166,855
1970/71	39,877	48,879	29,120	935	758	198,109
1971/72	46,486	11,114	na	1,716	792	140,515
1972/73	53,933	13,076	na	3,598	917	163,722
1973/74	61,779	15,135	na	5,552	1,217	192,007

Key

HC = health centres.
CM = care of mothers and young children.
MD = midwifery.
HV = health visiting.
HN = home nursing.
VI = vaccination and immunisation
AM = ambulance
PR = prevention of illness, care and after-care
DH = domestic help.
FP = family planning.

C) Expenditure Totals

Year	Price Index[1]	LHS Revenue		as % of LGE	LHS Capital		SHS Revenue	
		Actual £m	Constant £m		Actual £m	Constant £m	Actual £m	Constant £m
1948/49	100	24.45	24.45	2.8	0.96	0.96	6.59	6.59
1949/50	104	32.12	30.88	3.8	2.24	2.16	5.58	5.36
1950/51	107	35.99	33.63	4.1	2.05	1.92	5.80	5.42
1951/52	118	38.46	32.59	3.9	2.21	1.88	6.34	5.37
1952/53	128	42.90	33.52	4.0	1.88	1.47	6.92	5.40
1953/54	132	43.02	32.59	3.8	1.83	1.38	7.41	5.61
1954/55	133	45.14	33.94	3.7	1.96	1.47	7.92	5.95
1955/56	140	49.12	35.09	3.7	2.05	1.47	8.85	6.32
1956/57	147	54.07	36.78	3.6	1.91	1.30	9.77	6.65
1957/58	153	57.84	37.81	3.5	1.91	1.25	10.29	6.72
1958/59	158	61.66	39.02	3.6	2.26	1.43	10.92	6.91
1959/60	158	68.08	43.09	3.7	3.30	2.09	12.02	7.60
1960/61	160	72.48	45.30	3.6	4.46	2.79	12.73	7.96
1961/62	165	81.29	49.27	3.6	6.18	3.74	13.70	8.30
1962/63	172	87.27	50.74	3.6	8.12	4.72	14.77	8.58
1963/64	175	95.73	54.70	3.6	9.46	5.41	15.80	9.03
1964/65	181	104.52	57.74	3.6	10.63	5.87	16.49	9.11
1965/66	189	117.97	62.42	3.6	10.97	5.80	18.18	9.62
1966/67	196	128.84	65.74	3.6	10.50	5.36	19.33	9.86
1967/68	202	140.63	69.62	3.5	12.67	6.27	20.82	10.31
1968/69	212	152.05	71.72	3.5	13.53	6.38	22.83	10.77
1969/70	223	166.86	74.82	3.1	13.41	6.01	24.60	11.03
1970/71	237	198.11	83.59	3.2	18.71	7.90	28.60	12.07
1971/72	260	140.52	54.04	2.0	12.23	4.71	32.70	12.58
1972/73	279	163.72	58.68	2.0	15.78	5.66	38.42	13.77
1973/74	304	192.01	63.16	2.0	20.59	6.77	43.70	14.38

Key
LGE = local government expenditure
Note
In the absence of a more precise index the constant price figures have been calculated using the retail price index. Since this does not fully reflect the impact of inflation on the cost of providing the local health services and the school health service during the tripartite era they should be treated with a certain amount of caution.

Sources: Ministry of Health (1948/49); Ministry of Local Government and Planning (1949/50); Ministry of Housing and Local Government (1950/51 to 1964/65) and Welsh Office (1965/66 to 1967/68) and Department of the Environment and Welsh Office (1968/69 to 1973/74), *Local Government Financial Statistics;* Central Statistical Office, *Annual Abstract of Statistics,* and Department of Education and Science, *Statistics of Education Volume 5.*

APPENDIX III LOCAL HEALTH AUTHORITIES : PERFORMANCE INDICATORS
(England and Wales)
County Boroughs
(CB)

Name	1965 Pop	HVs[1] No	HVs[1] Per Pop	DNs[1] No	DNs[1] Per Pop	Health Centres[2] 70	71	72	73	74
Barnsley	75500	9.0	8389	12.0	6292	0	0	0	0	0
Barrow-in-Furness	64600	8.4	7690	12.5	5168	0	0	0	0	na
Bath	82760	9.0	9196	18.0	4598	0	0	0	0	na
Birkenhead	143660	15.0	9577	18.0	7981	0	0	1	1	na
Birmingham	1102660	143.0	7711	196.0	5626	4	6	7	12	14
Blackburn	103070	2.8	36811	21.0	4908	5	4	4	4	5
Blackpool	150440	17.0	8849	33.0	4559	0	0	0	0	0
Bolton	157990	17.0	9294	29.0	5448	2	2	4	4	4
Bootle	82750	14.2	5827	13.0	6365	0	0	0	0	na
Bournemouth	151050	21.0	7193	28.0	5395	0	0	0	0	na
Bradford	298090	40.0	7452	45.0	6624	0	0	1	1	3
Brighton	162520	27.0	6019	47.0	3458	0	0	0	0	0
Bristol	430900	50.0	8618	76.0	5670	3	5	8	8	8
Burton upon Trent	50380	3.6	13994	11.0	4580	0	0	0	0	0
Bury	62710	6.5	9648	11.0	5701	0	0	0	1	na
Canterbury	32560	4.5	7236	6.0	5427	0	0	0	0	na
Cardiff	260170	50.0	5203	45.0	5782	2	3	3	7	7
Carlisle	71240	12.0	5937	10.0	7124	0	0	0	0	0
Chester	59800	6.9	8667	9.0	6644	0	0	1	1	na
Coventry	330270	39.0	8468	53.0	6232	1	1	1	1	1
Darlington	84390	10.0	8439	11.0	7672	0	0	1	1	1
Derby	129190	19.0	6799	23.0	5617	0	0	0	0	0
Dewsbury	53320	11.0	4847	11.0	4847	0	0	0	0	na
Doncaster	86690	5.1	16998	13.0	6668	0	0	0	0	na
Dudley	64050	7.0	9150	11.0	5823	1	0	1	1	na
Eastbourne	64620	8.8	7343	20.0	3231	0	1	1	1	1
Exeter	82370	12.0	6864	20.0	4119	1	1	1	1	na
Gateshead	101560	16.0	6348	18.0	5642	0	0	0	0	0
Gloucester	72240	10.7	6751	15.0	4816	1	1	1	1	na
Great Yarmouth	52700	7.5	7027	10.0	5270	0	0	0	0	na
Grimsby	95150	11.8	8064	16.0	5947	0	0	0	0	0
Halifax	95090	5.0	19018	22.0	4322	1	0	1	1	1
Hastings	66660	9.5	7017	17.3	3853	0	0	0	0	na
Huddersfield	132330	14.0	9452	19.0	6965	0	0	0	0	na
Ipswich	120750	8.7	13879	25.0	4830	0	0	0	0	na

Kingston upon Hull	299570	37.0	8096	48.0	6241	1	0	1	1	1
Leeds	509290	66.0	7717	71.0	7173	0	1	1	1	2
Leicester	267030	38.0	7027	55.0	4855	2	2	2	4	7
Lincoln	76910	9.0	8546	14.0	5494	0	0	1	1	na
Liverpool	722010	114.0	6333	126.0	5730	1	1	1	1	1
Luton	150700	25.0	6028	26.0	5796	0	0	0	0	na
Manchester	638360	90.0	7093	110.0	5803	0	1	2	2	na
Merthyr Tydfil	58050	5.9	9839	12.0	4838	1	1	2	2	2
Middles' (Teesside)[3]	157180	21.0	7485	20.0	7859	2	2	3	3	na
Newcastle upon Tyne	257460	48.0	5364	48.0	5364	0	1	1	3	4
Newport	106600	21.6	4935	21.7	4912	0	0	1	1	na
Northampton	121410	7.0	17344	18.0	6745	0	0	0	1	na
Norwich	119170	15.0	7945	16.0	7448	0	0	0	0	1
Nottingham	310990	37.5	8293	62.0	5016	3	3	3	5	6
Oldham	111480	16.0	6968	22.0	5067	0	1	1	1	1
Oxford	109320	15.0	7288	23.0	4753	5	5	8	8	8
Plymouth	212550	23.0	9241	40.0	5314	0	1	1	1	na
Portsmouth	216280	33.0	6554	23.0	9403	0	0	0	0	2
Preston	109030	13.5	8076	20.0	5452	0	0	1	1	na
Reading	124470	16.0	7779	15.5	8030	0	0	0	0	0
Rochdale	86490	8.0	10881	21.0	4119	0	0	0	1	1
St Helens	104440	12.8	8159	18.5	5645	0	0	0	0	na
Salford	148260	25.0	5930	12.0	12355	0	0	0	1	na
Sheffield	488950	50.0	9779	90.0	5433	3	2	4	4	5
Smethwick(Warley)[4]	67370	7.3	9229	10.0	6737	0	0	0	0	1
Solihull	101210	12.0	8434	15.0	6747	0	0	0	0	0
Southampton	209020	20.0	10451	32.0	6532	0	0	1	1	na
Southend-on-Sea	166390	9.2	18086	29.0	5738	0	0	1	1	1
Southport	79980	12.0	6665	19.0	4209	0	0	1	1	1
South Shields	108540	13.0	8349	13.0	8349	0	0	0	1	1
Stockport	141770	16.0	8861	24.0	5907	0	0	1	2	2
Stoke-on-Trent	276630	26.0	10640	38.0	7280	4	5	5	5	5
Sunderland	188340	30.0	6278	35.0	5381	3	3	4	4	4
Swansea	170990	20.0	8550	27.0	6333	0	1	1	1	na
Torbay[5]	-	-	-	-	-	0	0	0	0	0
Tynemouth	72240	10.0	7228	10.0	7228	0	0	0	0	1
Wakefield	60100	4.6	13065	11.7	5137	0	0	0	0	0
Wallasey	103090	11.0	9372	17.0	6064	0	0	0	0	0
Walsall	120290	9.0	13366	12.0	10024	0	0	1	1	1
Warrington	74720	9.6	7783	15.0	4981	1	1	1	1	na
West Bromwich	98040	6.5	15083	13.0	7542	0	0	1	1	na
West Hartlepool[6]	78630	13.0	6048	12.0	6553	0	0	0	0	na
Wigan	77690	9.3	8354	14.0	5549	0	0	1	1	2
Wolverhampton	150210	23.0	6531	26.0	5777	0	0	0	0	0
Worcester	68240	10.0	6824	20.0	3412	0	1	1	1	1
York	105910	16.0	6619	18.0	5884	1	1	1	2	2

Administrative Counties (AC)

Name										
Anglesey	55460	7.0	7923	9.0	6162	1	1	1	1	1
Bedfordshire	269880	35.0	7711	51.0	5292	2	2	3	4	4
Berkshire	447950	92.0	4869	103.0	4349	1	1	3	3	3
Brecknockshire	54460	6.1	8928	17.5	3112	0	0	0	0	na
Buckinghamshire	532990	34.0	15676	77.0	6922	1	2	2	6	8
Caernarvonshire	120030	18.0	6668	35.0	3429	0	0	0	0	0
Cambridgeshire and Isle of Ely	291020	29.2	9966	51.0	5706	4	6	6	6	na
Cardiganshire	53330	8.0	6666	30.0	1778	0	0	0	1	na
Carmarthenshire	166320	14.4	11550	37.0	4495	1	1	1	3	3
Cheshire	1004730	102.0	9850	119.0	8443	5	5	10	11	16
Cornwall	347150	60.0	5786	79.0	4394	1	1	2	3	7
Cumberland	225570	35.0	6445	53.0	4256	0	0	0	0	na
Denbighshire	178480	19.5	9153	51.0	3500	0	0	0	0	1
Derbyshire	778030	57.0	13650	145.0	5366	0	1	2	4	6
Devon	563800	55.0	10251	118.0	4778	22	25	29	33	34
Dorset	330150	33.0	10005	54.0	6114	0	0	1	2	2
Durham	974860	107.0	9111	134.0	7275	3	6	9	10	11
East Suffolk	244830	19.3	12685	44.4	5514	0	0	0	1	1
East Sussex	408150	58.5	6977	74.0	5516	1	1	1	1	2
Essex	1054850	119.0	8864	160.0	6593	1	1	2	6	9
Flintshire	158240	13.0	12172	34.0	4654	0	0	1	1	1
Glamorgan	761260	113.0	6737	161.0	4728	5	8	11	14	20
Gloucestershire	542800	70.0	7754	100.0	5428	2	3	3	4	5
Hampshire	879500	90.0	9772	128.0	6871	3	5	7	7	12
Herefordshire	138250	21.0	6583	26.0	5317	1	1	1	1	na
Hertfordshire	860420	99.0	8691	121.0	7111	2	4	4	4	4
Huntingdon and Peterborough	179840	18.0	9991	19.0	9465	0	0	0	0	na
Isle of Wight	96270	11.0	8752	23.0	4186	0	0	1	2	2
Kent	1264030	143.0	8839	192.0	6583	0	1	1	2	3
Lancashire	2326890	306.0	7604	536.0	4341	5	6	10	13	27
Leicestershire	444580	36.0	12349	87.0	5110	0	1	2	3	10
Lincs (Holland)	104680	5.2	20131	15.5	6754	0	0	1	1	na
Lincs (Kesteven)	146390	12.0	12199	27.0	5422	0	1	1	1	na
Lincs (Lindsey)	352230	38.0	9269	54.0	6523	7	7	7	12	na
Merioneth	38270	4.6	8320	13.0	2944	0	0	0	1	1
Monmouthshire	353250	33.6	10513	68.0	5195	8	8	8	9	8
Montgomeryshire	43690	5.6	7802	15.3	2856	1	1	2	2	na
Norfolk	407710	38.0	10729	69.0	5909	0	0	0	1	1
Northamptonshire	301640	30.0	10055	66.0	4570	2	5	4	5	7
Northumberland	498430	82.0	6078	95.0	5247	0	4	6	8	10
Nottinghamshire	634320	60.0	10572	104.0	6099	4	7	11	13	17
Oxfordshire	229340	27.0	8494	37.0	6198	2	3	4	6	6
Pembrokeshire	95920	13.0	7378	26.0	3689	1	1	1	2	4
Radnorshire	18240	3.7	4930	7.2	2533	0	0	0	0	na
Rutland	27460	3.0	9153	3.5	7846	0	0	0	0	na
Shropshire	317270	35.0	9065	48.0	6610	0	0	1	1	3
Somerset	549320	69.0	7961	112.0	4905	3	4	6	6	11
Staffordshire	1072640	136.0	7887	129.0	8315	3	3	5	7	7
Surrey	967770	139.0	6962	153.0	6325	3	6	9	12	13
Warwickshire	545250	66.0	8261	109.0	5002	0	0	1	3	3
Westmorland	66950	12.1	5533	23.6	2837	0	0	0	1	1

West Suffolk	143340	19.0	7544	30.0	4778	0	0	0	0	1
West Sussex	444690	52.0	8552	97.0	4584	1	1	4	6	na
Wiltshire	464860	70.5	6594	65.0	7152	2	2	2	2	2
Worcestershire	472630	56.0	8440	81.0	5835	0	1	1	4	6
Yorks (East Riding)	241520	23.0	10501	46.0	5250	0	1	2	2	3
Yorks (North Riding)	423900	41.0	10339	69.0	6143	1	1	3	3	7
Yorks (West Riding)	1731100	191.0	9063	284.0	6095	16	15	21	26	na
London Boroughs										
Barking	172970	23.0	7520	30.0	5766	0	0	0	0	0
Barnet	316460	40.0	7912	39.0	8114	0	1	1	2	3
Bexley	215480	26.0	8288	33.0	6530	1	1	1	1	na
Brent	294850	34.0	8672	45.0	6552	0	1	2	2	2
Bromley	301450	26.7	11290	40.0	7536	0	0	0	0	0
Camden	240970	36.0	6694	41.0	5877	0	0	0	0	1
Croydon	328380	31.0	10593	61.0	5383	0	0	1	1	1
Ealing	303660	37.0	8207	45.0	6748	0	0	0	0	na
Enfield	268870	18.0	14937	41.0	6558	0	0	1	1	1
Greenwich	231770	47.0	4931	54.0	4292	2	2	0	0	0
Hackney	253810	39.0	6508	44.0	5768	2	2	3	4	4
Hammersmith	215240	35.0	6150	42.0	5125	1	1	1	1	1
Haringey	256750	32.0	8023	33.0	7780	1	1	1	1	1
Harrow	209600	28.0	7486	23.0	9113	0	0	0	0	0
Havering	250430	26.6	9415	28.0	8944	1	1	1	1	1
Hillingdon	233020	30.0	7767	27.0	8630	0	0	0	0	3
Hounslow	207550	21.8	9521	32.5	6386	0	5	5	5	5
Islington	256610	38.0	6753	43.0	5968	1	1	1	2	na
Kensington and Chelsea	216810	34.0	6377	37.0	5860	0	0	0	0	0
Kingston upon Thames	146470	18.0	8137	24.0	6103	0	0	1	2	2
Lambeth	339560	53.0	6407	53.0	6407	0	0	0	0	0
Lewisham	289560	45.0	6435	65.0	4455	1	0	1	2	2
Merton	185340	26.0	7120	36.0	5143	0	0	0	0	0
Newham	260070	46.0	5654	51.0	5099	0	0	0	0	0
Redbridge	247960	23.0	10781	35.0	7085	0	0	1	1	1
Richmond upon Thames	181130	31.2	5805	38.0	4767	0	0	0	0	0
Southwark	308460	46.0	6706	62.0	4975	2	2	2	3	3
Sutton	166790	18.0	9266	32.0	5212	1	1	1	1	1
Tower Hamlets	204560	35.0	5845	40.0	5114	0	0	0	0	0
Waltham Forest	241400	23.4	10316	50.0	4828	2	3	3	3	3
Wandsworth	331660	39.0	8504	50.0	6633	0	0	0	0	0
Westminster	266770	36.0	7410	42.0	6352	0	0	0	0	0
City of London	4660	0.8	5750	1.9	2421	0	0	0	0	0

Notes

1. Planned establishment for 1966/67.
2. Number open as at 31st March.
3. Middlesborough CB was incorporated into the newly created Teesside CB on 1st April 1968.
4. Smethwick CB was incorporated into the newly created Warley CB on 1st April 1966.
5. Torbay CB was created on 1st April 1968.
6. West Hartlepool CB was incorporated into the newly created Hartlepool CB on 1st April 1966.

Sources: Ministry of Health, *Health and Welfare : The Development of Community Care, Revision to 1975/76, Cmnd 3022*, and The Institute of Municipal Treasurers and Accountants and The Society of County Treasurers, *Local Health Services Statistics, 1969/70 and 1970/71*, and, *Local Health and Social Services Statistics, 1971/72*, and Chartered Institute of Public Finance and Accountancy and Society of County Treasurers, *Local Health and Social Services Statistics, 1972/73 and 1973/74*.

APPENDIX IV AREA HEALTH AUTHORITIES :
DEMOGRAPHIC DATA AND PERFORMANCE INDICATORS

	Est Pop	%-5	%+65	IMR	HV Pop	74	75	76	77	78	79	80	81
Northern Region													
Cleveland	567,900	7.4	11.0	16.0	7790	8	8	8	8	8	9	9	9
Cumbria	473,600	6.4	15.4	14.1	5286	2	2	3	5	5	7	7	7
Durham	610,400	6.6	13.5	16.4	6044	7	7	7	7	9	11	12	12
Northumberland	287,300	6.3	14.9	14.9	4962	6	7	9	10	12	12	13	18
Gateshead	222,000	6.6	13.4	14.0	6325	4	4	4	5	5	5	5	6
Newcastle upon Tyne	295,800	5.8	15.3	16.9	5127	4	5	5	5	5	5	5	5
North Tyneside	202,600	6.3	13.1	15.6	4929	5	5	5	6	7	8	8	9
South Tyneside	166,800	6.1	14.1	13.6	6043	4	4	4	4	4	5	5	5
Sunderland	295,700	7.2	12.5	12.5	5914	7	8	8	8	10	10	11	11
						47	50	53	58	65	72	75	82
Yorkshire Region													
Humberside	848,600	7.0	13.6	14.0	6105	11	12	12	12	13	13	13	13
North Yorkshire	653,000	6.3	16.4	13.6	5486	12	13	12	13	14	14	15	15
Bradford	458,900	7.0	14.6	16.1	5263	13	13	13	15	16	18	18	18
Calderdale	190,100	6.8	16.0	18.8	8525	2	2	2	3	3	6	6	7
Kirklees	372,500	7.1	14.5	17.8	6107	5	5	5	6	7	9	9	12
Leeds	744,500	6.5	14.4	15.2	6363	7	11	12	12	12	16	19	21
Wakefield	306,500	7.0	12.5	12.5	5783	2	6	10	12	16	18	19	19
						52	62	66	73	81	94	99	105
Trent Region													
Derbyshire	887,600	6.5	14.2	15.3	6631	6	6	8	10	10	10	12	14
Leicestershire	837,900	6.8	13.1	14.7	5972	11	11	11	14	17	19	20	20
Lincolnshire	524,500	6.8	14.7	16.1	7325	12	13	16	16	16	18	19	20
Nottinghamshire	977,500	6.8	13.3	14.5	6427	22	25	26	27	27	31	31	35
Barnsley	224,400	6.9	12.9	15.4	7101	2	4	5	5	5	6	7	10
Doncaster	286,500	7.1	11.8	15.0	6526	6	7	7	7	8	9	10	10
Rotherham	249,400	7.5	11.2	12.6	7025	3	6	6	6	7	7	7	8
Sheffield	558.000	6.0	15.3	13.2	6723	10	11	11	12	12	13	13	14
						72	83	90	97	102	113	119	131
East Anglia Region													
Cambridgeshire	563,000	7.3	12.8	12.1	6106	10	11	11	15	15	15	17	19
Norfolk	662,500	6.7	16.8	12.0	7059	0	0	0	4	4	8	9	14
Suffolk	577,600	7.1	15.3	10.8	6170	4	4	4	6	6	7	8	8
						14	15	15	25	25	30	34	41
North West Thames Region													
Bedfordshire	491,700	7.6	10.8	13.0	5476	6	6	8	9	10	10	10	10
Hertfordshire	937,300	6.5	11.4	13.0	5351	6	8	10	9	9	9	9	10
Barnet	305,200	6.1	15.5	13.2	8088	3	4	4	5	5	5	5	6
Brent and Harrow	456,700	6.2	14.6	13.2	5234	0	2	2	2	2	2	3	4
Ealing, Hammersmith and Hounslow	662,900	6.3	14.5	16.1	5401	6	6	6	7	9	10	10	10
Hillingdon	230,800	6.1	12.9	14.5	5431	3	4	4	4	4	4	4	5
Kensington,Chelsea and Westminster	377,500	3.8	15.2	14.6	5723	0	0	0	0	1	1	1	2
						24	30	34	36	40	41	42	47

North East Thames Region

Essex	1,426,200	7.0	13.5	11.5	6696	11	11	11	12	13	15	15	19
Barking and Havering	393,000	6.4	13.0	13.3	8543	1	1	1	1	1	1	1	1
Camden and Islington	357,400	4.9	15.1	17.8	6154	4	4	6	6	7	7	7	7
The City and East London	574,300	6.5	14.9	16.0	6283	7	8	8	8	9	9	9	9
Enfield/Haringey	489,100	6.3	15.1	12.0	7456	0	0	2	2	4	4	4	4
Redbridge and Waltham Forest	455,300	6.2	15.9	13.4	6504	4	7	7	7	7	8	8	9
						27	31	35	36	41	44	44	49

South East Thames Region

East Sussex	655,600	5.1	24.6	17.1	4789	2	2	2	2	2	4	4	5
Kent	1,448,100	6.9	15.3	13.9	6029	4	4	4	5	6	8	10	10
Greenwich and Bexley	420,700	6.3	13.5	13.7	5442	2	2	2	4	4	4	4	4
Bromley	299,100	5.9	14.1	14.4	5697	0	0	0	0	0	0	0	0
Lambeth, Southwark and Lewisham	752,500	5.9	15.0	15.7	5144	2	4	4	4	8	8	9	10
						10	12	12	15	20	24	27	29

South West Thames Region

Surrey	1,002,900	6.1	14.0	11.8	4425	20	22	23	24	22	22	23	24
West Sussex	623,400	5.9	20.6	12.9	6303	14	14	14	15	15	16	17	18
Croydon	330,600	6.4	13.2	14.7	7140	2	2	2	2	2	2	3	3
Kingston and Richmond	302,400	5.6	16.6	12.3	3910	2	2	2	2	2	2	2	2
Merton, Sutton and Wandsworth	620,700	5.9	15.6	13.0	4749	3	6	6	6	6	6	6	6
						42	46	47	49	47	48	51	53

Wessex Region

Dorset	575,800	5.6	20.7	12.4	5894	3	6	7	8	8	9	9	9
Hampshire	1,456,100	6.8	13.7	12.6	5627	15	15	15	17	19	19	24	24
Isle of Wight	111,300	5.6	21.7	13.7	5483	2	2	2	2	2	2	2	2
Wiltshire	512,800	7.4	13.0	13.0	5122	4	6	7	7	7	7	10	12
						24	29	31	34	36	37	45	47

Oxford Region

Berkshire	659,000	7.2	11.2	14.7	5020	3	5	6	7	9	9	9	9
Buckingham	512,000	7.4	11.4	13.5	3290	9	12	12	12	13	13	13	14
Northamptonshire	505,900	7.6	13.4	12.6	4541	8	8	8	9	11	11	12	12
Oxfordshire	541,800	6.5	12.1	10.1	4174	25	25	24	25	25	26	26	27
						45	50	50	53	58	59	60	62

South Western Region

Avon	920,200	6.4	15.0	12.7	5329	16	17	17	19	19	20	20	21
Cornwall and Isles of Scilly	407,100	6.4	18.0	14.4	5750	9	11	14	15	18	18	19	20
Devon	942,100	6.0	19.5	13.6	6547	37	39	41	43	43	44	44	45
Gloucestershire	491,500	6.6	14.4	11.3	5314	4	5	6	7	7	7	8	8
Somerset	404,400	6.3	16.6	12.4	5725	8	8	8	10	10	10	12	12
						74	80	86	94	97	99	103	106

West Midlands Region

	EstPop	%-5	%+65	IMR	HV Pop								
Hereford and Worcester	594,200	7.0	13.8	14.5	4642	7	9	9	12	13	15	15	15
Salop	359,000	7.2	13.2	15.4	5847	3	3	4	4	5	6	6	7
Staffordshire	997,600	6.9	11.8	15.6	6290	19[e]	20[e]	21	22	23	23	27	27
Warwickshire	471,000	7.2	11.6	15.0	5153	2	2	2	2	3	3	3	3
Birmingham	1,058,800	6.4	13.5	16.6	6560	16	19	19	19	20	21	22	23
Coventry	336,800	7.1	11.5	14.8	6025	1	1	2	2	2	3	3	3
Dudley	300,200	7.1	11.6	13.8	7234	1	2	2	4	4	5	5	6
Sandwell	312,900	6.6	13.5	15.9	6758	3	4	4	4	4	4	5	5
Solihull	199,600	7.3	9.7	13.5	6587	0	0	0	0	0	0	0	0
Walsall	268,600	7.5	10.6	15.8	6380	3	3	3	3	2	2	2	2
Wolverhampton	266,400	7.2	12.3	20.5	8273	1	1	2	2	2	2	2	5
						56[e]	64[e]	68	74	78	84	90	96

Mersey Region

	EstPop	%-5	%+65	IMR	HV Pop								
Cheshire	916,400	7.1	12.4	15.6	6238	11	14	14	15	17	17	17	16
Liverpool	539,700	5.9	14.8	14.0	4574	1	1	1	5	5	5	5	7
St Helens and Knowsley	384,100	7.7	10.7	13.7	6286	5	5	6	6	7	8	10	10
Sefton	306,000	6.6	15.1	13.8	7249	1	2	2	3	3	3	3	4
Wirral	348,200	6.6	13.9	12.0	6623	5	5	5	9	10	10	10	10
						23	27	28	38	42	43	45	47

North Western Region

	EstPop	%-5	%+65	IMR	HV Pop								
Lancashire	1,375,500	6.4	16.6	15.5	5746	15	17	20	28	31	34	36	37
Bolton	261,000	7.2	14.0	16.8	5241	4	6	7	8	8	9	9	10
Bury	181,200	7.3	13.2	10.6	5663	3	7	7	7	7	7	8	8
Manchester	490,000	5.9	14.9	17.1	5303	0	2	2	2	6	6	8	8
Oldham	227,500	7.3	13.9	14.9	5254	2	3	6	6	7	8	8	8
Rochdale	210,200	7.5	12.9	20.7	4204	2	3	3	3	4	4	4	4
Salford	261,100	6.5	14.0	17.9	5676	4	4	5	6	6	7	7	8
Stockport	292,900	6.8	13.3	15.4	4857	6	7	7	7	9	9	9	10
Tameside	222,100	6.9	13.7	13.5	6914	2	2	2	3	3	4	4	5
Trafford	227,400	6.5	13.8	15.2	4323	4	4	4	4	5	5	5	6
Wigan	310,700	7.6	12.6	13.8	5840	3	5	5	5	5	5	5	5
						45	60	68	79	91	98	103	109

KEY

EstPop = estimated home population as at 30 June 1986.

%-5 = percentage of population aged 0 to 4 (inclusive).

%+65 = percentage of population aged 65 and over.

IMR = infant mortality rate (i.e. deaths under 1 year per 1000 live births).

HV Pop = population per head of health visiting staff at 30 September 1976 (figure calculated by dividing population by the number of health visiting staff).

Sources: OPCS, *Local Authority Vital Statistics,* 1976 edition, Table 2 Series VS no.3 and Table 7 Series PP1 no. 2; DHSS and Child Poverty Action Group, *Reaching the Consumer in the Ante-Natal and Child Health Services : Report of Conference 4 April 1978,* pp. 47-53 and The Institute of Health Service Administrators, *The Hospital and Health Services Year Book,* various editions.

APPENDIX V DISTRICT HEALTH AUTHORITIES DEMOGRAPHIC DATA AND PERFORMANCE INDICATORS

		Population		LBW	IMR	HV	DN	Health Centres				
	Est Pop	%-5	%65+			Pop	Pop	83	84	85	86	87
Northern Region												
Darlington	123900	6.0	16.1	5.9	12.2*	4877	2331	2	2	2	2	2
Durham	235900	6.2	13.9	7.7	12.1	5181	2755	2	2	2	2	2
East Cumbria	177400	5.8	16.5	7.3	13.1	4918	2024	4	4	4	4	4
Gateshead	207300	6.0	15.6	7.1	13.5	3897	2711	7	7	7	7	7
Hartlepool	90700	7.0	13.8	7.5	7.4*	3908	2725	0	0	0	1	1
Newcastle	281400	6.3	16.5	7.2	9.1	3476	1780	6	6	6	6	6
North Tees	175800	7.2	11.7	7.0	8.9	5407	2452	4	4	4	4	4
North Tyneside	192300	6.1	16.5	7.2	10.5	4255	2468	10	10	10	10	10
Northumberland	301000	6.0	15.7	6.9	8.2*	3643	2530	17	19	19	19	19
North West Durham	86100	5.9	16.8	6.5	5.7*	4651	2604	1	1	1	1	1
South Cumbria	172600	5.6	18.0	6.9	8.4*	3998	2064	4	4	4	5	5
South Tees	291100	7.2	12.8	7.3	9.4	4910	2576	5	5	5	5	5
South Tyneside	156900	6.3	16.2	7.1	11.0	4834	2583	5	5	5	5	5
South West Durham	153600	6.4	14.9	7.7	9.3*	4517	2672	7	7	7	7	7
Sunderland	297700	7.0	13.3	6.6	8.3*	4181	3099	12	12	12	12	12
West Cumbria	136600	6.3	14.3	7.1	9.6*	4191	1859	2	2	2	2	2
								88	90	90	92	92
Yorkshire Region												
Airedale	173000	6.1	17.1	9.7	9.5	3770	2606	9	9	9	10	10
Bradford	338300	8.2	13.7	9.4	18.1	3399	2106	11	11	11	11	11
Calderdale	193100	6.6	16.3	7.6	12.7	2826	2423	8	8	8	9	9
Dewsbury	164100	7.3	13.6	8.9	8.9	4651	2863	5	5	5	5	5
East Yorkshire	188900	5.3	17.3	6.0	9.0*	4551	2813	4	4	4	4	4
Grimsby	159000	6.9	14.5	7.3	9.9	5900	3261	0	0	0	0	0
Harrogate	134600	5.3	17.3	6.7	4.6*	5631	2725	4	4	4	4	4
Huddersfield	212500	6.3	15.5	7.5	12.9	4664	1934	6	6	6	6	6
Hull	306700	6.8	15.2	7.2	9.6	5641	2966	5	5	5	6	6
Leeds Eastern	349300	6.3	15.2	8.3	10.5	4312	3251	7	7	7	8	8
Leeds Western	361600	6.2	16.1	6.8	9.5*	4625	2890	12	12	12	12	12
Northallerton	113200	5.8	14.2	6.0	5.5*	4327	3283	6	6	6	6	6
Pontefract	166700	6.5	14.3	7.9	7.8*	4552	3320	11	11	11	12	12
Scarborough	143300	5.3	20.8	5.4	12.4*	4644	2312	2	2	2	2	2
Scunthorpe	193900	6.5	14.0	8.1	9.4	4594	3746	8	8	8	8	8
Wakefield	142700	6.4	13.6	6.9	8.5*	5389	3405	9	9	11	12	12
York	260500	5.9	15.3	6.3	6.9	4794	2923	7	7	7	8	8
								114	114	116	123	123
Trent Region												
Barnsley	222200	6.3	14.8	8.1	11.3	3204	2518	12	12	12	12	12
Bassetlaw	104900	6.0	14.0	6.4	8.8*	5066	2790	3	3	3	3	3
Central Nottinghamshire	285100	6.4	14.5	8.0	11.4	4463	2592	13	13	13	14	14
Doncaster	289300	6.7	13.7	7.3	9.2	3475	2276	13	18	18	18	18
Leicestershire	875000	6.7	14.0	7.7	11.7	4637	2174	25	25	25	25	25
North Derbyshire	361600	5.8	15.8	6.8	9.1	4555	2992	9	9	9	9	9
North Lincolnshire	267700	6.0	15.6	6.9	5.8*	5008	1935	13	13	14	14	14
Nottingham	616400	6.2	14.8	8.9	8.8	4303	3938	23	23	23	22	22
Rotherham	252100	6.7	13.5	7.6	12.0	4808	2590	8	8	9	9	9
Sheffield	534300	5.5	17.2	7.8	9.2	5042	1953	14	14	14	14	14
Southern Derbyshire	525600	6.3	15.3	6.9	9.3	5617	2567	7	7	7	7	7
South Lincolnshire	299600	5.7	16.7	5.9	9.5	5035	2534	6	6	6	6	6
								146	151	153	153	153

East Anglia Region

Cambridge	273300	6.1	14.7	5.7	6.5	4586	2385	10	10	10	10	10
East Suffolk	318400	6.7	17.0	5.6	7.4	5536	3640	7	7	7	7	7
Great Yarmouth and Waveney	194900	6.0	18.8	5.8	6.7*	5406	2376	1	1	1	1	1
Huntingdon	129800	7.5	10.7	7.3	5.6*	5069	3396	2	2	2	2	2
Norwich	465600	5.5	18.5	6.1	8.0	5171	3018	13	13	14	14	14
Peterborough	201100	7.3	13.4	7.7	6.7*	4501	2458	8	8	8	9	9
West Norfolk and Wisbech	184100	5.9	17.7	5.6	10.9	5103	2445	3	3	3	3	3
West Suffolk	224500	7.2	14.3	7.5	12.7	4331	3299	4	4	4	4	4
								48	48	49	50	50

North West Thames Region

Barnet	304600	6.4	16.0	7.2	7.7	4110	2667	6	6	6	6	6
Brent	255700	7.1	13.3	10.6	9.7	3924	3117	3	3	3	3	3
Ealing	295500	6.9	13.6	7.8	5.5	3507	2404	1	2	2	3	3
East Hertfordshire	293800	6.0	13.3	6.2	7.3	5313	3504	4	4	4	4	4
Harrow	201900	6.4	15.8	7.7	11.6	3770	2894	1	1	1	1	1
Hillingdon	231800	6.5	15.0	7.4	7.0	4077	3028	5	5	5	4	4
Hounslow and Spelthorne	283700	6.5	14.5	7.7	9.6	4133	2156	10	10	10	10	10
North Bedfordshire	245600	6.8	12.5	5.8	9.4	3438	2353	8	8	8	8	8
North Hertfordshire	186100	6.7	13.1	6.8	7.6	4724	4537	4	4	4	4	4
North West Hertfordshire	261200	6.3	13.7	6.6	9.2	4856	2986	0	0	0	0	0
Paddington and North Kensington	120500	6.5	13.7	8.7	7.4*	1828	2006	1	3	3	3	3
Riverside1	287700	5.4	15.2	6.3	7.1	3247	2021	3	3	4	5	4
South Bedfordshire	275300	7.7	11.6	7.2	10.5	4182	2538	3	3	4	4	4
South West Hertfordshire	244700	6.0	15.4	6.4	10.0	4712	3946	1	1	1	1	1
								50	53	55	56	55

North East Thames Region

Barking, Havering and Brentwood	457000	6.0	15.5	6.1	10.6	6201	4060	2	2	2	2	2
Basildon and Thurrock	281000	7.0	11.7	7.1	8.1	5999	3882	8	9	9	9	9
Bloomsbury	130800	5.1	16.8	9.5	10.1*	2671	1802	2	2	2	3	3
The City and Hackney	191900	7.8	13.7	9.1	11.5	2806	3360	8	8	8	8	8
Enfield	265400	6.4	15.9	7.7	6.8	6161	3391	2	2	2	2	2
Hampstead	108700	5.5	15.5	7.3	9.0*	3204	1885	1	1	1	1	1
Haringey	196100	7.0	13.4	8.0	9.1	4338	3186	3	3	3	3	3
Islington	168000	6.7	14.2	8.1	8.8	3521	2767	5	6	6	7	7
Mid Essex	287100	6.6	13.0	6.5	7.6	5227	4311	1	1	1	1	1
Newham	205200	8.2	13.6	9.9	11.0	4582	3116	4	4	4	4	4
North East Essex	298700	5.7	19.5	6.0	10.8	5293	4666	2	2	2	2	2
Redbridge	227900	6.1	16.5	6.9	10.4	5262	3305	5	5	5	5	5
Southend	320700	6.1	17.6	6.5	9.2	6552	3498	6	6	6	6	6
Tower Hamlets	152800	8.5	14.1	9.2	8.7	2029	2573	4	5	5	6	6
Waltham Forest	215800	7.0	16.1	8.8	10.7*	4302	2432	4	4	4	4	4
West Essex	253800	6.2	14.0	6.0	5.0*	5097	4096	3	3	3	3	3
								60	63	63	66	66

South East Thames Region

Bexley	220100	6.3	14.5	6.4	3.8*	4470	2414	3	3	3	3	3
Brighton	297700	5.4	21.3	7.5	7.3	3660	1775	3	3	3	3	3
Bromley	297000	5.6	16.3	7.5	6.4	4301	3196	0	0	0	0	0
Camberwell	212300	7.6	14.3	8.9	11.6	3125	2320	3	4	4	4	4
Canterbury and Thanet	301000	5.7	21.2	6.1	8.2	5503	2771	5	5	5	5	5
Dartford and Gravesham	220500	6.4	13.1	6.2	8.7	3671	2320	2	2	2	2	2
Eastbourne	227800	5.0	25.0	6.7	8.8*	3749	2012	4	4	4	5	5
Greenwich	217800	7.1	14.8	7.5	10.0	3873	2418	3	3	3	3	3
Hastings	164200	5.3	26.0	6.6	5.7*	4660	1616	0	0	0	0	0
Lewisham and North Southwark	317200	6.7	16.4	8.3	9.5	3103	2450	7	7	17	17	16
Maidstone	195500	6.1	13.4	5.5	11.1	5091	2903	0	0	0	0	0
Medway	323800	7.3	12.6	6.4	7.9	4956	2560	5	5	5	5	5
South East Kent	264400	6.0	18.1	6.4	8.2	3995	2694	1	1	1	1	1
Tunbridge Wells	195700	5.4	16.8	6.1	6.0*	5446	2754	1	1	1	0	0
West Lambeth	163500	6.7	14.4	8.7	14.3	3369	2073	0	0	2	2	2
								37	38	50	50	49

South West Thames Region

Chichester	178700	5.0	23.1	5.8	10.8*	5284	2289	6	6	6	6	6
Croydon	319300	6.7	13.7	7.0	10.9	5014	2494	3	3	3	3	3
East Surrey	185300	5.7	16.4	6.0	8.4*	4529	2200	4	4	4	4	4
Kingston and Esher	178500	5.8	17.5	7.4	8.9	4415	1974	2	2	3	3	3
Merton and Sutton	333500	6.3	16.8	7.0	8.2	4546	3185	3	3	3	3	3
Mid Downs	274100	6.5	13.7	6.6	9.2	4009	3375	6	7	7	7	7
Mid Surrey	167000	5.3	17.9	7.2	7.6*	4333	2367	3	3	3	3	3
North West Surrey	207900	6.0	15.2	6.9	8.9	4594	2519	7	7	7	7	7
Richmond, Twickenham and Roehampton	230200	5.6	17.8	6.4	7.9	3536	2152	2	2	2	2	2
South West Surrey	183600	5.8	16.7	6.1	8.7*	4825	2439	3	3	3	3	3
Wandsworth	188900	6.7	14.5	7.7	7.9	3404	2683	3	3	3	3	3
West Surrey and North East Hampshire	275600	6.5	11.0	6.7	8.3	4117	3032	5	5	5	5	5
Worthing	241900	5.0	26.7	6.3	7.8*	5065	2024	6	6	6	6	6
								53	54	55	55	55

Wessex Region

Basingstoke and North Hampshire	215000	6.8	11.9	6.5	9.8	4244	2810	6	6	6	6	6
Bath	396400	5.8	16.5	6.2	6.7	5495	3400	4	4	4	4	4
East Dorset	441800	5.3	22.6	6.9	8.5	5552	2166	7	7	7	7	7
Isle of Wight	124600	5.3	22.3	4.5	9.6*	4346	2799	3	3	4	4	4
Portsmouth and South East Hampshire	525900	6.4	14.8	7.2	9.9	4787	3010	11	13	13	13	13
Salisbury	123000	5.9	17.3	7.3	12.3*	3437	2396	3	3	3	3	3
Southampton and South West Hampshire	417500	6.2	16.6	6.2	7.8	4900	2819	7	9	9	9	9
Swindon	227700	7.2	12.8	7.3	9.7	3978	3798	5	5	5	4	4
West Dorset	196400	5.3	20.0	6.9	10.7	5083	3163	4	4	4	5	4
Winchester	208200	6.0	14.4	6.1	10.2	3928	2928	4	4	4	4	4
								54	58	59	59	58

Oxford HA

Aylesbury Vale	142500	6.8	11.7	5.3	3.1*	3738	2922	4	4	4	4	4
East Berkshire	361300	6.8	12.6	6.5	7.8	4320	2397	4	4	4	4	4
Kettering	253200	6.5	14.7	7.5	12.5	4345	2532	7	7	7	7	7
Milton Keynes	161800	8.8	8.7	6.6	6.9*	3627	4298	9	9	9	9	9
Northampton	301300	6.8	13.7	7.5	11.2	4417	2698	6	6	6	7	7
Oxfordshire	539600	6.6	12.9	6.7	7.2	4709	3164	26	26	26	26	24
West Berkshire	445000	6.5	12.0	7.1	11.3	4540	2824	5	5	5	4	4
Wycombe	271600	6.0	13.4	6.9	9.1	3997	2841	2	2	2	2	2
								63	63	63	63	61

South Western Region

Bristol and Weston	364800	6.1	16.5	6.6	10.9	3430	2546	11	12	12	12	12
Cheltenham and District	209100	5.7	17.5	8.3	10.4	5078	4023	1	1	1	1	1
Cornwall and Isles of Scilly	448200	5.8	18.8	5.7	9.6	5094	2166	21	21	21	21	22
Exeter	302600	5.5	20.9	6.8	12.6	5458	2800	13	12	12	12	12
Frenchay	219700	6.3	14.9	6.5	10.8	4157	2900	5	6	6	6	6
Gloucester	308000	6.3	15.3	5.9	7.7	5014	2653	7	7	7	6	5
North Devon	131500	5.7	18.8	6.5	11.4*	5207	3446	11	11	11	11	11
Plymouth	327900	6.3	15.7	6.9	8.1	4610	3055	10	10	10	10	10
Somerset	396400	5.8	18.1	6.3	5.8	4221	3320	14	14	14	14	14
Southmead	232300	6.1	15.4	5.8	10.0	4119	3397	6	6	6	6	6
Torbay	237000	5.1	23.9	6.6	9.8	5532	2215	11	11	11	11	11
								110	111	111	110	110

West Midlands Region

Bromsgrove and Redditch	164000	7.0	11.4	6.5	8.3*	4485	2626	5	5	5	5	5
Central Birmingham	180700	7.4	14.8	8.8	11.3	3291	2095	3	3	3	3	3
Coventry	310400	6.9	14.6	8.5	12.8	4554	2347	5	5	5	5	5
Dudley	300900	6.1	14.0	8.7	11.3	3622	2671	6	6	6	6	6
East Birmingham	199900	7.5	15.7	8.7	9.1	4428	1829	4	4	4	4	4
Herefordshire	153300	5.9	17.3	6.7	8.5*	4998	2288	3	3	3	3	3
Kidderminster and District	100900	6.1	14.5	6.7	13.2*	3106	1715	2	2	2	2	2
Mid Staffordshire	308000	6.3	12.2	6.9	7.4	5030	4148	7	7	7	7	7
North Birmingham	163900	5.9	14.6	7.5	9.9	3998	2476	3	3	3	3	4
North Staffordshire	460700	6.2	15.4	7.5	9.3	4459	2850	16	16	16	16	16
North Warwickshire	172800	6.4	13.0	6.4	7.4	4349	2559	2	2	2	2	2
Rugby	84900	6.0	14.0	6.7	10.9*	3809	2279	0	0	0	0	0
Sandwell	301100	6.7	15.5	9.8	12.0	4702	2118	5	6	7	7	7
Shropshire	392700	6.2	14.5	6.3	9.1	4037	2866	10	10	10	10	10
Solihull	202200	5.9	12.9	6.4	7.1*	5103	2808	1	1	1	1	1
South Birmingham	248100	6.6	15.4	8.8	12.3	4585	2534	10	10	10	10	10
South East Staffordshire	252300	6.7	11.7	7.2	7.1	4783	2860	9	9	9	11	11
South Warwickshire	223000	5.6	14.8	7.5	9.2	5239	2893	0	0	0	0	0
Walsall	261800	6.5	13.4	7.9	12.6	3426	3268	3	3	3	3	3
West Birmingham	211500	8.7	13.5	10.1	10.0	4133	2377	6	7	7	8	8
Wolverhampton	251900	6.6	14.8	9.2	11.4	4229	2795	8	8	8	8	7
Worcester and District	236300	5.9	15.5	6.2	9.2	3257	2436	5	5	5	5	5
								113	115	116	119	119

Mersey Region

	EstPop	%-5	%+65	LBW	IMR	HV Pop	DN Pop					
Chester	177700	6.1	14.1	5.0	9.7	4712	2344	3	3	3	3	3
Crewe	246700	6.3	14.2	6.1	8.8	6645	3030	4	5	4	4	5
Halton	142500	7.4	12.1	6.3	6.9*	4839	2335	6	6	6	6	6
Liverpool	483000	6.7	16.1	7.6	11.5	4129	1898	9	9	9	10	11
Macclesfield	178900	5.6	15.0	7.3	9.5*	5164	2436	1	1	1	1	1
Southport and Formby	118200	5.2	19.2	7.2	13.5*	4214	1878	1	1	1	1	1
South Sefton	179900	6.6	14.6	7.2	6.9*	4513	2266	4	4	4	4	4
St Helens and Knowsley	351800	7.0	12.6	6.8	7.3	4543	3012	11	11	11	11	11
Warrington	181600	6.7	12.9	7.3	9.4	4469	1988	5	5	5	5	5
Wirral	353800	6.4	16.3	6.3	10.0	4275	2616	12	12	12	12	12
								56	57	56	57	59

North Western Region

	EstPop	%-5	%+65	LBW	IMR	HV Pop	DN Pop					
Blackburn, Hyndburn, Ribble Valley	271000	7.1	15.3	8.0	12.2	3079	2618	11	11	11	11	11
Blackpool, Wyre and Fylde	318300	5.2	21.3	6.6	8.9	3237	1707	7	7	9	9	9
Bolton	261600	7.0	14.5	7.0	12.2	2900	1895	12	12	14	14	14
Burnley, Pendle and Rossendale	229400	7.2	15.9	7.6	13.6	3295	2381	8	8	9	9	9
Bury	172600	6.5	15.0	6.6	11.3	3781	2164	8	8	8	8	8
Central Manchester	125800	7.2	13.5	9.6	14.5	3045	2561	8	8	8	8	8
Chorley and South Ribble	192800	6.6	12.7	7.0	7.5*	3487	2047	9	9	9	9	9
Lancaster	130000	5.7	19.5	7.2	10.2*	3542	2089	3	3	3	3	4
North Manchester	145000	7.2	16.1	9.5	7.0*	2620	1604	3	3	3	4	4
Oldham	220000	7.1	14.7	8.9	10.1	3128	1830	9	9	9	9	9
Preston	125000	7.0	15.9	8.8	13.3	2874	1933	3	3	3	3	3
Rochdale	214100	7.4	13.7	8.1	12.7	3518	2311	4	4	4	4	4
Salford	239300	6.4	16.3	7.6	11.7	2899	1685	8	8	8	8	8
South Manchester	180700	6.7	15.9	8.4	11.8	3581	2078	1	2	2	2	2
Stockport	289900	6.2	14.8	7.2	10.5	3210	2742	11	11	11	11	11
Tameside and Glossop	244800	6.7	14.7	7.0	9.2	4168	2221	5	5	5	5	5
Trafford	216300	6.2	15.3	8.0	10.2	2622	2036	6	6	6	6	6
West Lancashire	106800	6.5	12.0	7.0	10.9*	2994	2969	7	7	7	7	7
Wigan	306600	6.6	13.6	7.0	6.7	3125	1965	5	6	6	6	6
								128	130	135	136	137

KEY

EstPop = estimated resident population at 30 June 1986.
%-5 = percentage of population aged 0 to 4 (inclusive).
%+65 = percentage of population aged 65 and over.
LBW = low birth weight (i.e. percentage of all births under 2500 grams).
IMR = infant mortality rate (i.e. deaths under one year per 1000 live births).
HV Pop = population per head of health visiting staff at 30th September 1986 (figure calculated from performance indicator C45 - health visiting staff/1000 under 5s).
DN Pop = population per head of district nursing staff at 30th September 1986 (figure calculated from performance indicator E 14 - district nursing WTE/1000 Pop 65 +).
* = figure calculated from less than 20 events which may affect its reliability.

Sources: OPCS, *Key population and vital statistics : local and health authority areas. Series VS no.13 PP1 no.9,* 1986 edition, Tables 2.2 and 4.2; DHSS, *Performance Indicators* (reworked) and The Institute of Health Service Administrators/The Institute of Health Services Management, *The Hospitals and Health Services Yearbook,* various editions.

...e following books are also published by Business Education Publishers Limited and can ...obtained either from your local bookshop or direct from the Publisher by photocopying ...e order on the next page or by telephoning 091 567 4963.

THE BTEC SERIES FOR STUDENTS

...re Studies for BTEC
...nd Edition)
...ig 1989   £16.50
...perback 680pp A4 format

The first edition of this text was published in 1986 to cover the first and second year core areas of BTEC National Courses in Business, Finance and Public Administration. With its substantial coverage of the core areas, Organisation in its Environment, Finance and People in Organisations and its case study based assignments, it has proved to be the most popular book used on BTEC courses nationally. The new edition is an updated version of the first book retaining a large number of its most popular features.

...usiness Law for BTEC
...ov 1987   £14.95
...aperback 368pp A4 format

This book provides a comprehensive coverage of Business Law taught on BTEC courses at National and Higher levels. It incorporates a range of assignments for which a lecturer's manual is available to Educational Institutions free of charge from the publishers.

...larketing for BTEC
...uly 1989   £16.50
...aperback 340pp A4 format

This is a new text suitable for students studying marketing as an option module on BTEC National level courses or marketing as a full or part unit on BTEC Higher National level courses.

...nformation Processing for BTEC
2nd Edition)
March 1990   £13.50
Paperback 300pp A4 format

A new edition of a popular text which covers the BTEC Information Processing Option Modules One and Two. It incorporates a range of assignments for which a lecturer's manual is available free of charge from the publishers.

Transferable Personal Skills for BTEC
Feb 1989   £12.50
Paperback 311pp A4 format

A new text which covers the range of personal skills identified by BTEC in its statement of common skills. It is written in an easy to read style which students will find stimulating and informative. The text facilitates the development of a transferable personal skills training programme.

Computer Studies for BTEC
Oct 1987   £14.95
Paperback 432pp A4 format

The book was written specially for the first year core areas of the BTEC National Computing course. A lecturer's manual is available free of charge from the publishers to cover the range of assignments included in this book.

Small Business Computer Systems for BTEC
Aug 1989   £12.50
Paperback 256pp A4 format

A new book designed to cover the SBCS module on the second year of BTEC National Computing courses. The book contains a range of practical skills based assignments which can be used to form the basis of an assignment programme.

Travel and Tourism
Sept 1989   £16.50
Paperback 320pp A4 format

A major new textbook designed to cover the course content of Travel and Tourism modules at BTEC National and Higher National levels and to be used as an introductory text for undergraduates.

Getting Started with Information Technology
Oct 1988   £11.50
Paperback 302pp A4 format

Aimed at students who are new to information technology, this practical book takes a step by step approach to introducing word processing, data bases, spreadsheets, accounting and integrated packages.

THE BTEC SERIES FOR LECTURERS/TUTORS

OTHER PUBLICATIONS

Core Studies:
A Tutor's Guide
Aug 1989 £18.50
690pp A4 format

Transferable Personal Skills : A Tutor's Guide
Feb 1989 £16.95
500pp A4 format

Transferable Personal Skills :
A Student Guide
Jan 1989 £12.50
311pp A4 format

Community Health Services
March 1990 £16.95
560pp A5 format

Marketing :
A Tutor's Guide
Sept 1989 £17.95
400pp A4 format

Small Business Computer Systems : A Tutor's Guide
Sept 1989 £15.50
320pp A4 format

Law for Housing Managers £14.95
468pp A5 format

3INESS EDUCATION PUBLISHERS LIMITED

ton House 10 Grange Crescent Stockton Road Sunderland SR2 7BN **Tel 091 567 4963**

ORDER FORM

E BTEC SERIES FOR STUDENTS	Retail Price	Quantity Required
e Studies for BTEC (2nd Edition) 1989	£16.50	
ness Law for BTEC 1987	£14.95	
keting for BTEC 1989	£16.50	
rmation Processing for BTEC (2nd Edition) 1990	£13.50	
nsferable Personal Skills for BTEC 1989	£12.50	
nputer Studies for BTEC 1987	£14.95	
ll Business Computer Systems for BTEC 1989	£12.50	
vel and Tourism 1989	£16.50	
ting Started with Information Technology 1988	£11.50	

HE BTEC SERIES FOR LECTURERS/TEACHERS/TUTORS		
re Studies for BTEC - A Tutor's Guide 1989	£18.50	
ansferable Personal Skills - A Tutor's Guide 1989	£16.95	
arketing for BTEC - A Tutor's Guide 1989	£17.95	
he Abbotsfield File - A Business in Action 1984	£39.95	
mall Business Computer Systems - A Tutor's Guide 1989	£15.95	
eaching Business Education 1990	£12.50	

)THER PUBLICATIONS		
Community Health Services 1990	£16.95	
_aw for Housing Managers (2nd Edition) 1986	£14.95	
An Introduction to Marketing 1989	£16.50	
Transferable Personal Skills - A Student's Guide 1989	£12.50	

Surname

Initials   Mr /Mrs / Miss / Ms

Address/Organisation

Tick Box as appropriate

Please Invoice :

☐ Individual

☐ Organisation (Please quote order number or reference)

Post Code   Tel:

* *All books are available by placing an order directly with the publisher (B.E.P.) or through any bookshop.*
* *For orders received from any Educational Establishment for books in the BTEC series an additional book will be supplied free of charge for every ten books ordered.*
* *For all books supplied postage is paid by the publisher (B.E.P.).*
* *All invoices are payable within 30 days.*